W9-AUX-595

Wiley CPAexcel®

Financial Accounting and Reporting
Part 1

Craig Bain, Ph.D., CPA
Ervin L. Black, Ph.D.
Charles J. Davis, Ph.D., CPA
Donald Deis Jr., Ph.D., CPA, CFE
Pam Smith, Ph.D., CPA, MBA

Wiley Efficient Learning™

Copyright © 2015 John Wiley & Sons, Inc. All rights reserved.

Published by John Wiley & Sons, Inc., Hoboken, New Jersey.

No part of this publication may be reproduced, stored in a retrieval system, or transmitted in any form or by any means, electronic, mechanical, photocopying, recording, scanning, or otherwise, except as permitted under Section 107 or 108 of the 1976 United States Copyright Act, without either the prior written permission of the Publisher, or authorization through payment of the appropriate per-copy fee to the Copyright Clearance Center, Inc., 222 Rosewood Drive, Danvers, MA 01923, (978) 750-8400, fax (978) 646-8600, or on the Web at www.copyright.com. Requests to the Publisher for permission should be addressed to the Permissions Department, John Wiley & Sons, Inc., 111 River Street, Hoboken, NJ 07030, (201) 748-6011, fax (201) 748-6008, or online at http://www.wiley.com/go/permissions.

Limit of Liability/Disclaimer of Warranty: While the publisher and author have used their best efforts in preparing this book, they make no representations or warranties with respect to the accuracy or completeness of the contents of this book and specifically disclaim any implied warranties of merchantability or fitness for a particular purpose. No warranty may be created or extended by sales representatives or written sales materials. The advice and strategies contained herein may not be suitable for your situation. You should consult with a professional where appropriate. Neither the publisher nor author shall be liable for any loss of profit or any other commercial damages, including but not limited to special, incidental, consequential, or other damages.

For general information on our other products and services or for technical support, please contact our Customer Care Department within the United States at (800) 762-2974, outside the United States at (317) 572-3993 or fax (317) 572-4002.

Wiley publishes in a variety of print and electronic formats and by print-on-demand. Some material included with standard print versions of this book may not be included in e-books or in print-on-demand. If this book refers to media such as a CD or DVD that is not included in the version you purchased, you may download this material at http://booksupport.wiley.com. For more information about Wiley products, visit www.wiley.com.

Library of Congress Cataloging-in-Publication Data:
ISBN 978-1-11913585-2
Version 7.12

Printed in the United States of America

10   9   8   7   6   5   4   3   2   1

Table of Contents

Financial Accounting and Reporting 9

Welcome 10

Financial Accounting Professors 12

Framework, Overview and Statements 14

Role and Standard-Setting Process

FASB and Standard Setting 15

Accrual Accounting 20

Financial Statements 27

Financial Accounting Standards Codification 32

Conceptual Framework of Financial Reporting by Business Enterprises

Objectives and Qualitative Characteristics 36

Assumptions, Accounting Principles 39

Fair Value Framework

Constraints and Present Value 43

Fair Value Framework—Introduction and Definitions 47

Recognition and Measurement 51

Inputs and Hierarchy 54

Disclosure Requirements 56

U.S. Securities and Exchange Commission (SEC)

SEC—Role and Standard-Setting Process 60

SEC Reporting Requirements 63

General-Purpose Financial Statements

Balance Sheet/Statement of Financial Position 69

Income Statement 77

Statement of Comprehensive Income 83

Statement of Changes in Equity 87

Sources and Uses of Cash 91

Operating, Investing and Financing Activities 95

Operating Cash Flows—Indirect Method 99

Notes to Financial Statements 116

Ratios—Liquidity/Solvency and Operational 122

Ratios—Profitability and Equity 126

Special Purpose Frameworks

Cash, Modified Cash, Income Tax 129

Personal Financial Statements 133

Private Company Council 139

Liquidation Basis of Accounting 144

International Accounting Standards Board (IASB)

IASB and Structure 146

IASB Accounting Standards 150

IASB Framework 156

IFRS for SMEs 160

IFRS—General Purpose Financial Statements 163

Financial Statement Accounts **172**

Cash and Cash Equivalents

Cash 173

Bank Reconciliations 176

Receivables

Accounts Receivable—Accounting and Reporting 180

Uncollectible—Direct Write-Off and Allowance 183

Allowance—Income Statement and Balance Sheet Approach 185

Notes Receivable 189

Criteria for Sale of Receivables 193

Factoring, Assignment, and Pledging 197

Notes Receivable—Impairment 200

Inventory

Introduction to Inventory 202

Periodic Inventory System and Cost-Flow Assumption 206

Perpetual Inventory System and Cost-Flow Assumption 213

Evaluation of FIFO and LIFO 217

Dollar-Value LIFO 220

Lower of Cost or Market 224

Gross Margin and Relative Sales Value Method 228

Retail Inventory Method 231

Dollar Value LIFO Retail 235

Inventory Errors 237

Losses on Purchase Commitments 239

Inventory and IFRS 241

Property, Plant and Equipment

Categories and Presentation 243

Capitalized Costs 244

Valuation 246

Interest Capitalization 1 249

Interest Capitalization 2 252

Post-Acquisition Expenditures 255

Nonaccelerated Depreciation Methods 257

Accelerated Depreciation Methods 260

Natural Resources 264

Impairment—Assets for Use and Held-for-Sale 268

Impairment and IFRS 273

PPE and IFRS 275

Investments

Introduction—Equity and Debt Investments 278

No Significant Influence

No Significant Influence 285

Cost Method and Transfers Between Classifications 291

IFRS—Investments 294

Significant Influence—Equity Method

Equity Method 299

IFRS—Equity Method 306

Joint Ventures 308

Investor Stock Dividends, Splits, and Rights 311

IFRS—Investment Property 314

Impairment of Debt and Equity Securities 318

Intangible Assets—Goodwill and Other

Introduction to Intangible Assets 320

Goodwill 325

Intangibles and IFRS 332

Payables and Accrued Liabilities

Current Liabilities 334

Specific Current Liabilities 338

Deferred Revenue

Deferred Revenue Principles 341

Specific Deferred Revenues 346

Long-Term Debt (Financial Liabilities)

Notes Payable 350

Bonds Payable

Bond Accounting Principles 357

Bond Complications 362

Bond Fair Value Option, International 365

Debt with Conversion Features and Other Options

Convertible Bonds 369

Bonds with Detachable Warrants 372

Modification and Debt Retirement

Refinancing Short-Term Obligations 376

Debt Retirement 379

Troubled Debt 384

Debt Covenant Compliance 392

Equity

Owner's Equity Basics 394

Stock Issuance 404

Preferred Stock 409

Treasury Stock 413

Dividends 419

Stock Dividends and Splits 423

Dividend Allocation 426

Stock Rights, Retained Earnings 430

Book Value Per Share, Quasi-Reorganization 434

Revenue Recognition

General Revenue Recognition 437

Other Revenue Situations 443

Contract Accounting 447

Costs and Expenses

Costs and Expenses 454

Compensated Absences 459

Deferred Compensation Arrangements

Pension Principles, Reporting 461

Pension Expense 466

Settlements, Curtailments, International 477

Nonretirement Postemployment Benefits 480

Retirement Benefits 482

Stock Compensation (Share-Based Payments)

Stock Options 488

Stock Awards 494

Stock Appreciation Rights 497

Income Taxes

Interperiod Tax Allocation Basics 500

Permanent Differences 503

Temporary Differences 505

Tax Accrual Entry 510

Interperiod Tax Allocation Process 514

Classification of Deferred Tax Accounts 518

Valuation Allowance for Deferred Tax Assets 521

Uncertain Tax Positions 524

Net Operating Losses 527

Financial Accounting and Reporting

Welcome

I. Business Enterprise Accounting and Reporting

A. Business enterprise accounting and reporting relates to for-profit enterprises in the Financial Accounting and Reporting (FAR) section of the CPA exam. The CPA exam focuses on the accounting and reporting represented on the four major financial statements: balance sheet, income statement, statement of cash flows and the statement of changes in equity. A very large amount of information is presented in FAR, but it all basically boils down to three functions:

1. Recognition;

2. Measurement;

3. Disclosure.

B. One of the most important threads running through the CPA Exam is the framework of concepts from which the FASB develops GAAP. This framework provides the theoretical underpinnings for all GAAP. The framework concepts are:

1. Primary qualitative characteristics - relevance and faithful representation;

2. Enhancing qualitative characteristics - comparability, verification, timeliness and understandability;

3. Assumptions - entity, going concern, time period and unit of measure;

4. Principles - historical cost, revenue recognition, matching and full disclosure;

5. Constraints - materiality and cost benefit.

Each of these concepts is covered in the material.

C. If you really understand these concepts, you then have a basis for figuring out specific questions in areas you may not have studied completely. Trust your training and your gut instinct when answering the questions. Basing your response off of the framework will serve you well.

D. All of the areas and topics in the AICPA Content Specifications for FAR are covered in the Study Text. Generally, the topics are presented in the Study Text in the same sequence as they are presented in the Content Specification. However, in a few cases, the order of presentation for some items is different than in the specifications.

1. The Content Specifications provide a complete list of matters subject to being tested on the exam, but the topics are not intended to be presented in a logical sequence for learning purposes.

2. Therefore, a few topics have been rearranged in the Study Text to present them in a more logical sequence for learning purposes.

E. In covering the material, you should spend more time on the areas most difficult for you. These may come from the following list of topic which are common on the exam:

1. Financial Statements, including the statement of cash flows;

2. Revenue recognition;

3. Financial instruments, including Investments, Bonds and Derivatives;

4. Stock options and Earnings per Share (EPS);

5. Pensions;

6. Leases;

7. Income tax accounting;

8. Inventories;

9. Accounting changes.

10. Business combinations;

11. Consolidated financial statements.

F. For each topic, outline the main GAAP (what is recognized and when, how much, and are there additional important disclosures). Concentrate on journal entries. If you know how to record the relevant journal entries and understand how they affect the financial statements, you are 85% there.

G. Don't ignore topics you feel are really challenging. You learned it once, so you can refresh your mind more easily than you think. Remember Dollar Value LIFO for example - if you have covered this in your classes, you can "relearn" it quickly.

H. International Financial Reporting Standards (IFRS) are also covered throughout the study materials. Significant differences between U.S. GAAP and (IFRS) are tested. Review the significant differences that are presented at the end of all relevant lessons of the Study Text. Focus on differences related to recognition and measurement.

I. Finally, when you study and review, don't just read passively. Because there is so much to remember, as you study:

1. Continually assess whether you understand the material;

2. Take notes in your own words on aspects that you find difficult to remember;

3. For the more complex material, jot out the main procedures and reasons for the procedure;

4. Periodically go back over your notes and you will find that the amount of material that seems most challenging begins to dwindle.

J. We are confident that you will succeed if you spend sufficient quality time studying the material and practicing the questions. Please let U.S. know if you feel there are areas where the material needs improving. Thank you.

~ Professors Charles Davis, Pam Smith, Allen Bizzell, and Erv Black.

Financial Accounting Professors

Dr. Craig Bain received his Ph.D. at Texas A & M University in 1983 and has held faculty positions at Boise State University and Northern Arizona University. He has performed research in accounting, accounting information systems, and financial accounting. Professor Bain has taught accounting both on the undergraduate and continuing education levels. He is also an experienced Certified Public Accountant.

Dr. Allen Bizzell has been involved with the CPA Exam for almost 30 years as a researcher, developer of exam-related materials, and review course instructor. He has conducted numerous CPA Exam-related studies, including several analyses of CPA Exam Candidates' Characteristics and Performance for the Texas State Board of Public Accountancy. He has developed CPA review materials and taught review courses at both the national and local levels. Included in his innovative review materials is the use of simple network diagrams to depict the relationships between related accounting concepts/topics and the appropriate treatment for each. These diagrams are powerful tools for not only understanding accounting materials, but also for retaining the knowledge needed to pass the CPA Exam.

Several publishers have approached Dr. Bizzell to develop financial accounting textbooks incorporating his instructional methodology. According to Dr. Bizzell, he has not done so because the traditional textbook does not lend itself to using all the elements of the methodology. He believes, "The CPAexcel approach is the first to provide the capabilities to capture and deliver to the user the benefits of the methodology."

Dr. Ervin L. Black completed his Ph.D. at the University of Washington in 1995 and has held faculty positions at Brigham Young University, University of Washington, University of Wyoming, and University of Arkansas. Dr. Black teaches undergraduate and graduate courses in international accounting and financial accounting. He has also taught CPA review courses for the past 12 years. Professor Black's research is primarily in the financial accounting and international accounting areas, with emphasis on examining the usefulness of firm financial characteristics in different settings. His research has been published in academic and practitioner journals and cited in the Wall Street Journal, Fortune and The Financial Times. Professor Black is active in the International and Financial Reporting Sections of the American Accounting Association. He is also an associate editor of the Journal of International Accounting Research. Prior to his academic career he worked for seven years in private industry as a financial analyst and corporate treasurer.

Dr. Charles Davis is currently Professor of Accounting in the College of Business Administration, California State University, Sacramento. His main teaching interest is financial reporting. He has taught in several educational and professional development programs including calculus for MBA students, CPA review courses, seminars for international groups from Russia, Turkmenistan, Latvia, and technical lectures in financial reporting for accounting professionals.

Prof. Davis's work has been published in several domestic and international academic and professional journals in the area of accounting and health care finance. In addition, Dr. Davis is a co-author of Intermediate Accounting, published by McGraw-Hill (2002), a mainstream accounting text used by many universities in the U.S. and internationally. Prof. Davis also has written several online accounting educational packages and has reviewed twelve academic accounting texts.

Prof. Davis has been involved in many consulting engagements in the area of financial reporting, real estate feasibility, EDP auditing and accounting systems, and has "Big Eight" accounting experience (now the "Big Four"). He is the recipient of teaching awards at California State University, Sacramento and the University of Illinois.

Dr. Pam Smith is KPMG Professor of Accountancy at Northern Illinois University. She has won awards voted on by her students (Executive MBA Golden Apple) and by her peers (Illinois CPA Society's 2008 Educator of the Year). As faculty advisor, Pam sparked the creation of an honor pledge and code of conduct. She is co-author of NIU's Building Ethical Leaders handbook and a developer of the college's BELIEF initiative (Building Ethical Leaders using an Integrated Ethics Framework), both of which have been integrated across the college. Because of her research in accounting for derivatives and hedging, she was called as an expert witness in the Enron trial. Pam and her husband are licensed handlers of their certified therapy dog, Shelby, who provides emotional therapy to seniors and special needs children.

Framework, Overview and Statements

FASB and Standard Setting

This lesson presents an overview of the standard-setting process in the United States.

After studying this lesson, you should be able to:

1. *Describe the role of the Financial Accounting Standards Board.*

2. *Describe the primary purpose of financial reporting.*

3. *List the three aspects of financial reporting addressed by GAAP.*

4. *Identify the major organizations in U.S. accounting standards.*

I. Introduction

A. Financial accounting and reporting is concerned with providing relevant information to investors and creditors (and other parties) for the purpose of making informed resource allocation decisions. These decisions are, in the main, whether to invest in a firm or to lend money to it.

B. Financial information is disseminated in many forms including news releases, prospectuses for future securities offerings, filings with the Securities and Exchange Commission (SEC), and annual reports to shareholders. Financial statements are the culmination of the accounting process and represent the most comprehensive financial information disclosures made by firms. The footnotes and other textual and tabular information provide supplementary information and help to explain the amounts disclosed in those statements.

II. Generally Accepted Accounting Principles (GAAP)

> **Definition:**
> *Generally Accepted Accounting Principles (GAAP)*: The rules of financial reporting for business enterprises. GAAP are also called "accounting standards."

A. **What GAAP addresses --** To ensure that financial reporting meets these objectives, a set of reporting rules called GAAP has been created. GAAP primarily address three aspects of financial reporting:

1. **Recognition --** A recognized item is recorded in an account and ultimately affects the financial statements.

2. **Measurement --** Concerns the dollar amount assigned to an item.

3. **Disclosure --** Many unrecognized amounts are reported in the footnotes to complete the portrayal of the firm's financial position and performance.

B. GAAP affects what is disclosed in financial statements and in what amount. For example, GAAP requires that many assets be reported at their historical cost, rather than at current market value. Without a relatively uniform set of GAAP, business entities would be free to report whatever amounts they desired.

III. Organizations Involved in Developing Accounting Standards

A. **Financial Accounting Standards Board (FASB) --** The FASB is currently the standard-setting body in the United States.

B. The **Securities and Exchange Commission (SEC)** is the federal government agency that administers the securities laws of the U.S. These laws affect firms that issue debt and equity securities to the public. Such firms register with the SEC and are called "registrants." The financial statements of these firms must be filed with the SEC and must be audited by independent third parties (CPA firms).

C. Congress granted the SEC the authority to establish GAAP for the firms within its jurisdiction (publicly traded firms) but generally has ceded this authority to a private sector body (currently, the FASB). In a few instances, the SEC has exercised its right to reverse or modify an accounting standard adopted by the private sector body. The SEC also has pressured the FASB to establish certain principles more quickly.

D. The FASB considers the potential reaction of the SEC to its proposed standards. The SEC frequently responds to the FASB's initial "exposure" draft providing useful commentary for the final pronouncement.

E. The **American Institute of Certified Public Accountants (AICPA)** is the national professional organization for practicing CPAs and has had a great impact on accounting principles over the years. The mission of the AICPA is to provide its members with resources, information, and leadership so that they may in turn provide valuable services for the benefit of their clients, employers, and the general public.

F. In 1939, the AICPA appointed its Committee on Accounting Procedure (CAP), the first private sector body charged with the responsibility of promulgating GAAP. CAP issued 51 Accounting Research Bulletins (ARBs). To the extent that an ARB has not been rescinded or superseded, it constitutes GAAP.

G. In 1959, the AICPA created the Accounting Principles Board (APB), another committee, to take over the work of CAP. The APB is the second private sector group designated to formulate GAAP. Members were required to be CPAs. The APB issued 31 opinions, many of which remain as GAAP, in whole or in part.

H. In 1971, the AICPA appointed the Wheat Committee, which recommended the formation of yet another private sector body - the FASB - to take over the reins from the APB. In 1973, the FASB assumed the role of standard setter for the accounting profession. The FASB is not affiliated with the AICPA.

I. The **FASB** is one of three parts of the current accounting standard-setting mechanism in the U.S. The other two are the Financial Accounting Foundation (FAF) - the parent body, and the Financial Accounting Standards Advisory Council (FASAC):

1. FAF - appoints the members of the FASB and its advisory councils, ensures adequate funding for the FASB, and exercises oversight over the FASB. Funding sources include fees levied on publicly traded firms under the Sarbanes-Oxley Act, contributions, and publication sales. The trustees of the FAF are appointed from organizations with an interest in accounting standards.

2. FASB - establishes financial accounting standards for business entities. The FASB is an independent body, subject only to the FAF.

3. FASAC - provides guidance on major policy issues, project priorities, and the formation of task forces.

J. The FASB is the current private-sector body that establishes GAAP for business entities. **The mission of the FASB** (in brief) is to:

1. Improve the usefulness of financial reporting;

2. Maintain current accounting standards;

3. Promptly address deficiencies in accounting standards;

4. Promote international convergence of accounting standards;

5. Improve the common understanding of the nature and purposes of information in financial reports.

K. Facts in brief about the FASB

1. Seven full-time members with renewable (for one additional term) and staggered 5-year terms.

2. Subject to FAF policies and oversight.

3. Members cannot have employment or investment ties with other entities.

4. Members need not be CPAs although typically the public accounting profession is represented; also the preparer (reporting firm) and investor communities are represented.

L. In promulgating GAAP, the FASB **applies the following principles**:

1. Accounting standards should be unbiased and not favor any particular industry; standards are for the benefit of financial statement users;

2. The needs and views of the economic community should be considered; the views of the accounting profession should not take precedence;

3. The process of developing standards should be open to the public and allow due process to provide opportunity for interested parties to make their views known;

4. The benefits of accounting standards should exceed their cost.

> **Note:** The FASB operated with seven Board members from its inception 1973 until 2008 when the Board was reduced to five members. The Board membership increased back to seven in early 2011. The FAF Chairman, Jack Brennan, gave this rationale for the change: "Returning the Board to the seven-member structure will enhance the FASB's investment in the convergence agenda with the International Accounting Standards Board (IASB), while addressing the unprecedented challenges facing the American capital markets in the months and years ahead."

M. The FASB uses the following process when issuing an accounting standard -- The FASB:

1. Considers whether to add a project to its agenda, in consultation with the FAF - the FASB receives many requests from its constituencies including the SEC, auditing firms, investors, and reporting firms to address new financial reporting issues and clarify existing standards;

2. Conducts research on the topic and issues a Discussion Memorandum detailing the issues surrounding the topic; the FASB's conceptual framework plays a role in this process by providing a theoretical structure for guiding the development of a specific standard;

3. Holds public hearings on the topic;

4. Evaluates the research and comments from interested parties and issues an Exposure Draft - the initial accounting standard;

5. Solicits additional comments, modifies the Exposure Draft if needed;

6. Finalizes the new accounting guidance and approves with a majority vote (four of seven affirmative votes);

7. Issues an Accounting Standards Update (ASU). The section on FASB Codification discusses the nature of an ASU in greater detail.

N. FASB's Emerging Issues Task Force (EITF) -- This group was formed to consider emerging reporting issues and to accelerate the process of establishing rulings on such issues. In this sense, the EITF acts as a "filter" for the FASB, enabling the FASB to focus on more pervasive issues. When a consensus of the 15 members is reached on an issue, no further action by the FASB is required. EITF pronouncements are included in GAAP. If the EITF is unable to reach a consensus, the FASB may become involved, ultimately revising an existing standard or adopting a new one.

IV. The Political Nature of the Accounting Standard-Setting Process

A. Parties, preferences, and outcomes -- The parties interested in the outcome of the standard-setting process may have opposing preferences and interests. Firm managers (referred to as "preparers" or "preparer firms") often prefer standards with lower compliance costs and that tend to portray their firms in a more positive light (higher earnings and assets, lower liabilities).

B. Financial statement users, on the other hand, prefer unbiased, transparent reporting. They want the facts. Investors also want conservative reporting-disclosure of less positive results under conditions of uncertainty or where the firm has a choice of reporting alternatives under GAAP. The FASB has pledged to adopt unbiased accounting standards, and thus has the interests of financial statement users in mind when developing accounting standards.

C. The FASB considers its conceptual framework, the collection of Statements of Financial Accounting Concepts (SFACs), a "constitution" or underlying set of theoretical concepts in its deliberations. However, the FASB does not create GAAP in a vacuum. Historically, the Board has been very responsive to the views of affected parties through its due diligence process and actively solicits public comment before adopting a final accounting standard.

D. User groups (for example, industry associations, financial institutions) influence the outcome of FASB standards by:

1. Making their views public through the financial press;

2. Providing input during the due process procedure;

3. Putting pressure on the SEC directly to change a proposed standard, or through the U.S. Congress.

E. The Board is careful to pay attention to this type of input, particularly when it helps clarify the issues. However, although the FASB has pledged to be unbiased rather than promulgate standards favoring a particular reporting position or industry, it has admitted to responding to pressure from interested parties.

F. For example, negative "economic consequences" is often the argument of an interested party. Economic consequences refers to the effect of a proposed standard on a firm's financial statements. A common argument against a proposed standard is that it will cause earnings to decline, thus reducing the firm's ability to raise capital. Although some observers believe that the FASB should not be sensitive to the views of reporting firms, there have been some spectacular cases in which the FASB has delayed an accounting standard or even reversed itself in light of the concerns reporting firms have had about the "economic consequences" of a proposed standard.

V. Enforcement of GAAP

A. Methods of enforcement

1. Accounting standards are not laws - they are not determined by legislatures but rather by private sector bodies. They are "generally accepted." GAAP are a type of regulation, imposed on the economic system by its constituents. Without GAAP, the economy and capital markets as we know them would not work. Investors need to have confidence in the numbers they receive. Without some kind of common language, the system could not function. Corruption would become much more prevalent than it is today.

2. However, the private-sector bodies that contribute to the formulation of GAAP have no enforcement authority. Rather, there are economic sanctions for firms not complying with GAAP. These sanctions include increased difficulty in raising debt and equity capital.

3. The SEC, however, does have the authority to penalize firms and managers subject to its jurisdiction when financial statements do not comply with GAAP. Public companies are violating the securities laws if they publish financial statements that materially depart from GAAP.

4. The SEC sends a "deficiency" letter to a registrant when an accounting irregularity is found. If the firm disagrees, the SEC may issue a "stop order" preventing trading in the firm's securities until the disagreement is resolved. Outright violations of the securities laws may result in criminal sanctions against managers, or fines against the company.

5. The enactment of the Sarbanes-Oxley Act of 2002 significantly affects the enforcement procedures relating to audits of public companies, and penalties for noncompliance with GAAP. The Auditing section of CPAexcel covers the implications of this Act in depth.

Accrual Accounting

This lesson presents an overview of GAAP and the basic theory of accrual accounting.

After studying this lesson, you should be able to:

1. *List the components of an external financial report.*

2. *Define generally accepted accounting principles (GAAP).*

3. *Explain the basic theory of accrual accounting.*

4. *Define accruals and deferrals and give examples of each.*

I. Introduction

A. Financial accounting is, like most types of accounting, a service activity.

B. The provision of information is accomplished through the issuance of a General Purpose External Financial Report. That is, the financial report issued by business enterprises, is a general purpose one intended for all external users. External users of financial reports do not have access to the internal records of businesses and thus are dependent on the information in the report. The report is a "general purpose" report because it is designed to meet the information needs of a broad class of users (mainly investors and creditors), rather than a predefined specific use report.

C. **External financial report** -- The general-purpose external financial report (also called the annual report) is prepared by applying Generally Accepted Accounting Principles (GAAP). The general-purpose external financial report has the following key components.

1. Income Statement;

2. Statement of Comprehensive Income;

3. Balance Sheet;

4. Statement of Changes in Owners' Equity;

5. Statement of Cash Flows;

6. Footnote Disclosures and supplementary schedules;

7. Auditor's Opinion.

D. **GAAP** -- The composition of GAAP includes principles, methods, and procedures that are generally accepted by the accounting profession. The majority of GAAP includes the pronouncements issued by the Committee on Accounting Procedure (CAP), the Accounting Principles Board (APB), and the Financial Accounting Standards Board (FASB). The FASB Codification is the sole authoritative source for such GAAP and includes guidance from the above sources. For publicly traded entities, the SEC has additional reporting guidelines.

E. **Authoritative GAAP**

1. Codification

   a. The FASB Accounting Standards Codification is the sole source of authoritative U.S. GAAP for nongovernmental entities, except for SEC guidance. All guidance in the Codification carries the same level of authority (one level of GAAP). There is no longer a hierarchy of GAAP.

   b. Accounting and financial reporting practices not included in the Codification are nonauthoritative.

    c. The Codification does not change GAAP but rather provides accounting standards in a newly structured electronic form. The Codification is a compilation and reorganization of existing GAAP before the Codification, with updates being added as they are promulgated. The individual accounting-standard form of presentation is not used in the Codification. Rather, material is organized by major area and topic. Basis for conclusions, appendices and other ancillary content are included in the Codification only if the material is considered essential to the understanding and application of GAAP.

    d. Some accounting standards have allowed entities to apply the provisions of superseded standards for transactions that have an ongoing effect on an entity's statements. Such superseded guidance continues to be authoritative but is not included in the Codification. Examples include pooling of interests and pension transition obligations.

    e. The Codification does not include guidance for non-GAAP matters including:

        i. Other Comprehensive Basis of Accounting;

        ii. Cash Basis;

        iii. Income Tax Basis;

        iv. Regulatory Accounting Principles.

2. No specified GAAP

    a. If guidance for a transaction or event is not specified in the Codification, authoritative GAAP for similar transactions or events should be considered before considering nonauthoritative GAAP. Sources of nonauthoritative guidance include widely recognized and prevalent practices, FASB Concepts Statements, AICPA Issues Papers, IFRS, and others. There is no implied hierarchy for these sources.

        i. The guidance for similar transactions or events is not followed if that guidance either prohibits the application of the guidance to the particular transaction or event, or indicates that the accounting treatment not be applied by analogy.

3. SEC guidance

    a. Authoritative GAAP include relevant SEC rules and interpretative releases (applicable only to publicly traded firms). The Codification includes relevant portions of SEC content but does not contain the entire text of relevant SEC rules, regulations, interpretive releases and staff guidance. For example, the Codification does not include SEC content related to Management's Discussion and Analysis and other items appearing outside the financial statements. The Codification does not replace or affect guidance issued by the SEC and is provided on a convenience basis.

    b. An adjacent lesson provides additional details on the structure and use of the Codification.

II. Accrual Basis of Accounting

    A. GAAP, and therefore the financial statements, reflect the accrual basis of accounting rather than the cash basis of accounting. Both U.S. and international GAAP reflect the accrual basis of accounting.

    B. Under the accrual basis, revenues are recognized when earned, regardless of the period of cash collection.

    C. Expenses are recognized when incurred, regardless of the period of cash payment.

    D. The accrual basis of accounting is preferred over the cash basis of accounting because it reflects a better association of revenues and expenses with the appropriate accounting period. The accrual basis of accounting recognizes all resource changes when they occur. The cash basis of accounting limits the recognition of resource changes to cash flows.

Example:

A firm sells $40,000 worth of goods during the year, and collects $30,000 on the resulting accounts receivable. There is no uncertainty regarding the collection of the remaining $10,000. Under the accrual basis, $40,000 of revenues would be recognized for the year; under the cash basis, only $30,000 would be recognized. The next year, when the remaining $10,000 of cash is collected, the cash basis would recognize $10,000 of revenue. The accrual basis would recognize no additional revenue. The accrual basis provides a more comprehensive measurement of the change in value of the firm resulting from income producing activities for a period because it does not limit the recognition of resource changes to the cash flows for that period. Accrual accounting much more fully reflects the economic substance of transactions.

E. Accrual basis accounting recognizes and reports the **economic activities** of the firm in the period the activity was **incurred**, regardless of when the cash activity takes place. The table below depicts the possible scenarios and the terminology related to timing differences. In essence, cash can precede or follow an economic transaction. The economic transaction is one that generates revenue or expense.

See example below.

The table displays a common theme for **accruals** and **deferrals**:
- when the economic event occurs first you create an accrual account (you are accruing the cash owed or to be paid as an asset or liability)
- when the cash activity occurs first you create a **deferral** account (you are deferring the recognition of an expense or revenue as an asset or liability).

Transaction	Event	Account created	Examples
Revenue	Cash received before revenue earned	Deferred revenue - liability	Rent, subscriptions, gift certificates
	Revenue earned before cash received	Accrued asset - asset	Sales on account, interest, rent
Expense	Cash paid before expense incurred	Deferred expense - asset	Prepaid insurance, supplies, rent, PP&E
	Expense incurred before cash paid	Expense incurred before cash paid	Salaries, wages, interest, taxes

Using the payment and receipt of $100 for rent, the entries made by the renter and rentee are shown below.

	Landlord (Rentee)	Tenant (Renter)
CASH RECEIVED THEN RENT EARNED		
Dec. entries: Rent paid December 31	↑ Cash　100 ↑　　　　　100 Unearned Rent (Rent revenue is deferred)	↑ Prepaid　100 Rent ↓ Cash　　　　　100 (Rent expense is deferred)
Jan. entries: January rent earned	↓ Unearned 100 (deferred) Rent ↑ Rent　　　　100 revenue	↑ Rent　　100 expense ↓ Prepaid　　　　100 Rent
RENT EARNED THEN CASH RECEIVED		
Dec. entries: December rent paid on January 1	↑ Accrued　100 Rent Revenue ↑ Rent　　　　100 revenue (Rent revenue is accrued)	↑ Rent　　100 expense ↑ Accrued　　　　100 Rent Expense (Rent expense is accrued)
Jan. entries: December rent collected	↑ Cash　100 ↓ Accrued　　　　100 Rent Revenue	↓ Accrued　100 Rent Expense ↓ Cash　　　　100

Important points to note. The revenue and expense are recorded in the period the economic event occurred (e.g. using the space). The accrual and deferral accounts are simply holding the revenue or expense amounts on the balance sheet until they can be recognized on the income statement.

Example:
Assume Mayer Corporation had $28,000 of revenue in the first year of operations, $6,000 was on account and $22,000 was paid in cash. Mayer Corporation incurred operation expenses of $15,800, $12,000 was paid in cash and $3,800 was owed on account at year-end. In addition, Mayer Corporation prepaid $2,400 for insurance that will not be used until the next year.

Below are an Income Statement, Balance Sheet and Statement of Cash Flows under the cash basis and accrual basis of accounting. Note that the ending cash balance is exactly the same under both cash and accrual basis. The difference is the *timing* of the receipt and payment of cash.

Cash Basis

Income Statement		Balance Sheet	
Sales	$22,000	Cash	**$7,600**
Op Exp	(12,000)		
Ins Exp	(2,400)		
Total	$7,600		

Statement of Cash Flows – Direct Method

Operating Activities

Sales		$22,000
Operating expense	(12,000)	
Insurance expense	(2,400)	
		(14,400)
Total Cash flow from Operating Activities		**$7,600**

See the following example.

Example:
Continuation:

Below are an Income Statement, Balance Sheet and Statement of Cash Flows under the accrual basis of accounting.

Accrual Basis

Income Statement		Balance Sheet	
Sales	$28,000	Cash	$7,600
Op Exps	(15,800)	Acct Rec	6,000
		Prepaid	2,400
			$16,000
		Acct Pay	3,800
		Equity	12,200
Total	$12,200		$16,000

Statement of Cash Flows – Indirect Method

Operating Activities

Net Income		$12,200
ΔAccounts Receivable	(6,000)	
ΔPrepaid Expenses	(2,400)	
ΔAccounts Payable	3,800	
Total Cash flow from Operating Activities		**$7,600**

See the following example.

Example:

J&L Pecans maintain accounting records on an accrual basis. In 20x6 J&L decided to convert to cash basis accounting. During 20x5 J&L reported $95,178 of net income. On January 1, 20X5 and December 31, 20x5 J&L had the following amounts.

	January	December
Accounts receivable	9,250	15,927
Unearned revenue	2,840	4,111
Accrued expenses	3,435	2,108
Prepaid expense	1,917	3,232

Conversion of J&L's income from accrual basis to cash basis can be viewed various ways. The simplest way is to use the accounting equation. Starting with the accounting equation, we follow simple algebra to isolate the change in cash.

1) $A = L + E$

2) $\Delta A = \Delta L + \Delta E$

3) $\Delta cash + \Delta other\ assets = \Delta L + \Delta E$

4) $\Delta cash = \Delta L + \Delta E - \Delta other\ assets$

1) is the accounting equation; 2) is the change in all of the variables in the accounting equation (still an equality); 3) is separating the changes in cash from the changes in all other assets; and 4) is isolating cash on the left side of the equation. Using equation 4) we can convert J&L Pecans from accrual to cash:

Conversion of Accrual Basis to Cash Basis

For the Year 20x5

Net income on an accrual basis	$95,178
Subtract increase in accounts receivable ($9,250 − $15, 927)	(6,677)
Add increase in unearned service revenue ($2,840 − $4,111)	1,271
Subtract decrease in accrued expense ($3,435 − $2,108)	(1,327)
Subtract increase in prepaid expenses ($1,917 − $3,232)	(1,315)
Net income on an cash basis	$87,130

IF you are asked to change from cash to accrual, you can still use the accounting equation formula, but the signs would be opposite those used in the conversion from accrual to cash.

Conversion of Cash Basis to Accrual Basis

For the Year 20x5

Net income on a cash basis	$87,130
Add increase in accounts receivable ($9,250 − $15, 927)	6,677
Subtract increase in unearned service revenue ($2,840 − $4,111)	(1,271)
Add decrease in accrued expense ($3,435 − $2,108)	1,327
Add increase in prepaid expenses ($1,917 − $3,232)	1,315
Net income on an accrual basis	$95,178

Financial Statements

This lesson presents a summary of the three primary financial statements.

After studying this lesson, you should be able to:

1. *Describe the form and content of the income statement.*

2. *Describe the form and content of the balance sheet.*

3. *Describe the form and content of the statement of cash flows.*

I. **Summary of the Primary Financial Statements** -- Here we present an overall summary of the basic financial statements. Later lessons will cover each statement in more depth.

A. **Income statement – Statement of profit or loss**

1. The income statement measures the performance of the firm for the period. It is dated for the entire period (e.g., for the year ended December 31, 20xx).

2. The income statement is prepared by applying the all-inclusive approach. That is, almost all revenues, expenses, gains, and losses are shown on the income statement and are included in the calculation of net income. A major exception here is prior period adjustments, which are the effects of corrections of errors affecting prior year net income. Prior period adjustments are shown on the Statement of Retained Earnings as adjustments to the beginning balance of retained earnings in the year the error is discovered.

3. There are other items that would appear to be income items but are not reflected in net income. These include unrealized gains and losses on investments in securities available-for-sale, certain pension cost adjustments, and foreign currency translation adjustments. These items are included in *comprehensive income*, which now is a required disclosure. However, except for items included in *comprehensive income* but not also in net income, prior period adjustments, and a few other items, the reporting of net income in the income statement reflects an "all inclusive" approach.

B. **Statement of Comprehensive Income**

1. The statement of comprehensive income reports all non-owner changes in equity over a period of time—the same time period as the income statement. This statement is also dated for the year ended December 31, 20xx.

2. The statement of comprehensive income includes net income (or loss) and the items included in comprehensive income that are not part of net income. Those items include:

   a. Unrealized gains and losses on available-for-sale securities

   b. Adjustments in the calculation of the pension liability

   c. Foreign currency translation adjustments

   d. Deferrals of certain gains or losses on hedge accounting.

C. **Balance sheet – Statement of financial position**

1. The balance sheet discloses the resources of the firm at a point in time. It is dated as of a specific date (e.g., December 31, 20xx).

2. The balance sheet is formally referred to as the Statement of Financial Position, but "balance sheet" is the more commonly used term. A business enterprise discloses its economic resources (assets) and the manner of financing the acquisition of those

resources (creditors, owners' contributions, and prior year's earnings) in the balance sheet.

3. **Formats for presentation**

    a. The presentation format for a balance sheet is typically one of two formats: the account format or the report format:

> Account Form
>
> Assets Liabilities
>
>   Stockholders' Equity

    b. In the account form, the assets are shown on the left side of the page, and the liabilities and owners' equity are shown on the right side. This format emphasizes the balance sheet equation: A=L+OE.

> Report Form
>
>   Assets
>
>   Liabilities
>
>   Stockholders' Equity

    c. In the report form, which is the most popular form, the three categories of accounts are listed from top to bottom, as in a report, with assets always shown first.

4. **Classification of accounts**

    a. Regardless of balance sheet format, assets, liabilities, and equities are presented on the balance sheet in a prescribed order, which is summarized below.

        i. *Assets* are presented in order of decreasing liquidity. The most liquid assets (such as cash) are shown first, and less liquid assets are shown last (such as property, plant and equipment).

        ii. *Liabilities* are shown in order of maturity. Current liabilities are presented first, and then, long-term liabilities are presented.

        iii. *Owners' Equity* items are shown in order of permanence.

> **Example:**
> For a corporation, the contributed capital accounts are shown first and retained earnings is typically shown as the final item in Stockholders' Equity. Retained earnings are thought to be less permanent due to the fact that dividends are a distribution of earnings.

5. **Balance sheet presentation**

    a. Balance sheet presentation reflects the classification of assets and liabilities. The classification criteria used for each is indicated below and is affected by the firm's operating cycle. The operating cycle of a firm is the period of time required to purchase or produce inventory, sell the inventory, and collect cash from the resulting receivables. For most firms, the operating cycle is significantly less than one year. For firms in some industries, such as construction, the operating cycle is longer than one year.

b. **Current assets --** Assets that are in the form of cash, or will be converted into cash, or consumed within one year or the operating cycle of the business, whichever is longer.

>
> **Example:**
> Cash, accounts receivable, short-term investments, inventory, and prepaid assets are current assets.

c. **Current Liabilities --** Liabilities that are due in the upcoming year or in the operating cycle of the business, whichever is longer, and that will be met through the transfer of a current asset or the creation of another current liability. Both criteria must be met in order for a liability to be classified as current.

> **Example:**
> Accounts payable, wages payable, income tax payable, unearned revenues, and warranty liability are current liabilities (for the last two items, only the portion to be extinguished within one year of the balance sheet would be classified as current). Also, the current portion of long-term debt is classified as current; it is the amount of debt previously classified as long-term that is now due within one year of the balance sheet date.

d. **Long-Term Assets and Long-Term Liabilities --** These are defined by exclusion. All assets that do not meet the criteria necessary to be classified as current> are classified as long-term assets. Likewise, all liabilities that do not meet the criteria necessary to be classified as current are classified as long-term liabilities.

> **Example:**
> Long-term investments, plant assets, certain deferred charges, and intangible assets are non-current assets. Notes and bonds payable and mortgages payable are long-term liabilities.

6. **Valuation and Measurement**

a. Balance Sheet Valuation is summarized below, but will be emphasized more in the coverage of individual balance sheet items. The point here is that the meaning of the dollar amount of an item listed in the balance sheet depends on the account being measured.

b. Several different measurement bases are currently used in the balance sheet. For example, an account receivable listed at $10,000 does not necessarily mean the same thing as $10,000 listed for an intangible asset.

See the following example.

Note:
CPA Exam questions tend to emphasize sections of the balance sheet. For example, a question might focus on the property, plant, and equipment section of the balance sheet or on the long-term liability section of the balance sheet. As we cover the individual items presented on the balance sheet, these problems will be a primary focus.

Account Type	Measurement Basis
Property, Plant & Equipment, Intangibles	Historical Cost and Depreciated/Amortized Historical Cost
Receivables	Net Realizable Value
Inventory	Lower of Cost or Market
Investments in Marketable Securities	Market Value
Liabilities	Present Value
Owners' Equity	Historical Value of Cash Inflows and Residual Valuation

D. Statement of Stockholders' Equity -- The statement of stockholders' equity (sometimes referred to as shareholders' equity) presents the changes in the owners' equity over a period of time—the same time period as the income statement. Like the income statement, this statement is dates for the year ended (e.g., December 31, 20xx). This statement presents the changes in contributed capital, additional paid-in capital, and retained earnings. These changes arise from the purchase and sale of shares of the entities stock, the changes in comprehensive income, and the payment of dividends.

E. Statement of Cash Flows

1. The statement of cash flows is the third of the three major financial statements required to be reported. It describes the major changes in cash by meaningful category. Like the income statement, it is dated for the entire period (e.g., for the year ended December 31, 20xx).

2. The purpose of the Statement of Cash Flows is to explain the change in cash and cash equivalents that has occurred during the past accounting year. Cash equivalents are short-term investments that:

   a. Are convertible into a known and fixed amount of cash; and

   b. Have an original maturity to the purchaser of three months or less.

> **Example:**
> A U.S. treasury obligation purchased when there are three months or less remaining to maturity is a cash equivalent. Investments in stocks are not cash equivalents because they have no maturity value and are not convertible into a specific unchanging amount of cash.

3. In reviewing the Statement of Cash Flows, it is important to remember the articulation between the balance sheet and the statement of cash flows. If the statement of cash flows employs a pure cash definition of funds, the first asset listed on the balance sheet will be cash. If the statement of cash flows employs a broader definition of funds (cash and cash equivalents), the first asset listed on the balance sheet will be Cash and Cash Equivalents.

4. The presentation of cash flows in the statement of cash flows follows a classification system established by the FASB. Cash flows are classified into three categories: operating, investing, and financing.

   a. **Operating** -- Those cash flows related to transactions that flow through the income statement.

    Example:
   Operating cash inflows include receipts from customers and interest. Cash outflows include payments to suppliers, to employers, and to taxing authorities.

   b. **Investing** -- Cash flows related to the acquisition and disposal of long-term assets and investments (other than cash equivalents and trading securities - these are operating).

    Example:
   Investing cash outflows include purchases of plant assets and investments. Cash inflows include proceeds from the sale of these items.

   c. **Financing** -- Cash flows related to the liabilities and owners' equity sections of the balance sheet.

   Example:
   Financing cash inflows include issuing debt and equity securities. Cash outflows include retirement of debt and equity securities, and dividend payments.

Financial Accounting Standards Codification

This lesson presents the Financial Accounting Standards Codification.

After studying this lesson, you should be able to:

1. *Describe the goals and purpose of the Codification.*

2. *Identify the main areas of the Codification.*

3. *Describe how you would research using the Codification.*

I. Financial Accounting Standards Codification

> **Caution:** It is important that you practice using the Codification before the exam so that valuable time is not wasted struggling with the interface during the exam. The Codification website has several useful tutorials for first-time users.

A. **Goals of the Codification --** The FASB Codification Research System is the online, real-time database by which users access the Codification. The Codification system became effective on July 1, 2009. The online nature of the Codification and its internal structure were designed to achieve the following goals:

1. Simplify the structure and accessibility of authoritative GAAP;

2. Provide all authoritative literature in a single location;

3. Reduce the time and effort required to research an accounting issue;

4. Reduce the risk of noncompliance with GAAP;

5. Facilitate updating of accounting standards;

6. Assist the FASB with research and convergence (IFRS) efforts.

B. **Updating the Codification**

1. Changes to authoritative GAAP are accomplished through FASB Accounting Standards Updates (ASU), including amendments to SEC content. No longer will separate FASB Statements or other documents be separately published. ASUs are designated chronologically by year. For example, ASU 2014 refers to the twelfth ASU issued by the FASB in 2014.

2. An ASU is a separate document posted on the FASB website and incorporated in the Codification. The ASU will (1) summarize the key aspects of the update, (2) detail how the Codification will change, and (3) explain the basis for the update. ASUs are not authoritative – ASUs are a vehicle to update the codification and are not permanent in their own right, but a way to amend the codification. When changes to the codification happen, the FASB updates the Codification and issues the ASU simultaneously.

3. During the transition period for an ASU to become effective, the Codification shows the new guidance as "Pending Text." When the new guidance is effective, the previous guidance (if any) is deleted and the new guidance takes its place.

4. Although updates no longer use the old FASB numbering system, the Codification provides access to the original standards used in creating the Codification.

5. The Codification provides links enabling users to provide feedback which then is directly transmitted to the FASB.

C. Codification Structure

1. **Overall Structure** -- Accounting guidance within the Codification has the following structure:

> Areas – Topics – Subtopics – Sections – Subsections – Paragraphs

    a. Each area has at least one topic. Within a topic, there are subtopics. Within subtopics, there are sections, and so forth. The topic, subtopic, and section levels reflect the structure used by international accounting standards.

2. **Areas** -- The highest level in the Codification is the area, of which there are nine, each with a specific numeric identifier:

    a. General principles (100);

    b. Presentation (200) (does not address recognition or measurement);

    c. Assets (300);

    d. Liabilities (400);

    e. Equity (500);

    f. Revenue (600);

    g. Expenses (700);

    h. Broad transactions (800) (transactions involving more than one area such as interest, and subsequent events);

    i. Industry (900) (special industry accounting).

3. **Topics** -- There are approximately 90 topics across the nine areas. For example, all asset topics are within 300 - 399. The number of topics varies by area, depending on the content within each area. For example, 310 is the receivables topic, within the Asset area.

4. **Subtopics** -- There is at least one subtopic within each topic. The "overall" subtopic appears within each topic. The number of subtopics within a topic varies by area, again depending on content. Each carries a numeric identifier. The "overall" subtopic contains the "big picture" level guidance for a topic. The other subtopics provide additional specific guidance and exceptions. For example, 310-40 is the Troubled Debt Restructurings By Creditors subtopic within the Receivables topic, which is within the Asset area.

5. **Sections** -- Each subtopic has the following sixteen sections with the associated numeric identifier:

00	Status
05	Overview and Background
10	Objectives
15	Scope and Scope Exceptions
20	Glossary
25	Recognition
30	Initial Measurement
35	Subsequent Measurement
40	Derecognition
45	Other Presentation Matters
50	Disclosure
55	Implementation Guidance and Illustrations
60	Relationships
65	Transition and Open Effective Date Information
70	Grandfathered Guidance
75	XBRL Definitions

a. The listing of sections is uniform across all subtopics, unless no material exists for a section within a particular subtopic. For example, 310-40-35 is the Subsequent Measurement section within the Troubled Debt Restructurings By Creditors subtopic within the Receivables topic, which is within the Asset area.

b. The section level is the primary research level because the accounting guidance in the form of paragraphs resides within the sections.

c. For SEC guidance, the same section numbering system is used with the addition of the letter "S" preceding the section number.

6. **Subsections** -- In some cases, a section is divided into subsections to facilitate the exposition. These are not numbered.

7. **Paragraphs**

a. The actual accounting standard material is provided in paragraphs within sections or subsections. For example, 310-40-35-2 is paragraph 2, Troubled Debt Restructuring, within the General subsection within the Subsequent Measurement section within the Troubled Debt Restructurings By Creditors subtopic within the Receivables topic, which is within the Asset area.

b. Paragraphs follow a hierarchical structure allowing lower level paragraphs to be associated with higher-level paragraphs within a group, similar to threads in an online discussion group. Greater-than symbols (>, >>, >>>) are used for nesting paragraphs.

c. Paragraph numbers do not change over time. New paragraphs will use a letter extension.

d. Entities are encouraged to use purely verbal references to Topic levels within the Codification for the footnotes to their financial statements because FASB standard numbers are no longer used. For example, to refer to requirements concerning interest capitalization, the footnote would refer to "as required by the Interest Topic of the FASB Accounting Standards Codification."

    e. The Codification standardized certain terms. For example, the Codification uses the term "entity" rather than "firm" or "company" and thus uses the term "intra-entity" rather than "intercompany." Moreover, the word "shall" is used for required treatments, rather than "should," "must," or other terms.

8. Industry

    a. Area 900 holds industry topics and contains only the guidance that is not otherwise applicable in the other eight areas. For consistency, the topics within the industry area are structured the same way as in the other areas. Agriculture is industry topic 905 for example. Within that topic, the receivables subtopic is listed and numbered as Agriculture - Receivables: 905-310.

    b. The general area topics include relevant guidance referenced to specific industries. Thus, the Codification is cross-referenced.

D. Researching the Codification

    1. The Codification provides four different ways for researching an issue:

        a. Browse the structure (illustrated above) in the menu provided;

        b. Search by key word(s); this mode allows narrowing of a search both by related term and by major area within the Codification structure;

        c. Enter the specific Codification location (using the numerical system within the Codification); this is designed for users who know their topic and section of interest;

        d. Search by previous GAAP standard number (e.g., by FAS 13).

    2. In addition, the Codification allows users to aggregate findings by similar content. For example, all Status sections for a topic can be accessed and joined without separately accessing the Status section for each subtopic.

    3. Moreover, information can be combined. For example, all content in a subsection may be viewed in one document without having to separately access each individual section.

E. What is excluded from the Codification?

    1. The Codification does not include accounting guidance related to:

        a. Other Comprehensive basis of accounting

        b. Cash basis accounting

        c. Income tax basis accounting

        d. Regulatory accounting principles (e.g., insurance)

        e. Governmental accounting standards

Objectives and Qualitative Characteristics

This lesson presents an overview of the conceptual framework related to the objectives of financial reporting and the qualitative characteristics of accounting information.

After studying this lesson, you should be able to:

1. *Describe the objective of financial reporting.*

2. *Describe the qualitative characteristics of accounting information.*

3. *List the primary qualitative characteristics of accounting information.*

4. *List the enhancing qualitative characteristics of accounting information.*

I. Conceptual Framework Outline

A. The FASB's Statements of Financial Accounting Concepts, as amended, comprise the conceptual framework for financial accounting. The framework does not constitute GAAP but rather provides consistent direction for the development of specific GAAP. The conceptual framework is a "constitution" for developing specific GAAP.

B. A listing of the parts of the conceptual framework follows. This outline lists the major subsections of the framework in a progression leading from definitions and general concepts to specific accounting principles, the ultimate purpose of the framework.

1. Objective of financial reporting;

2. Qualitative characteristics of accounting information;

3. Accounting assumptions;

4. Basic accounting principles;

5. Cost constraint;

6. Elements of financial statements.

II. Objective of Financial Reporting

A. The objective of general purpose financial reporting is to provide information about the entity useful to current and future investors and creditors in making decisions as capital providers.

B. Useful information includes information about:

1. The amount, timing, and uncertainty of an entity's cash flows;

2. Ability of the entity to generate future net cash inflows;

3. An entity's economic resources (assets) and claims to those resources (liabilities) which provides insight into the entity's financial strengths and weaknesses, and its liquidity and solvency;

4. The effectiveness with which management has met its stewardship responsibilities;

5. The effect of transactions and other events that change an entity's economic resources and the claims to those resources.

III. Qualitative Characteristics of Accounting Information

A. For financial statement information to be useful, it should have several qualitative characteristics. There are two primary characteristics and four enhancing characteristics, each of which has subcomponents. The following diagram shows the primary and enhancing characteristics and their components, as contributing to the objective of financial reporting.

Objective of financial reporting: decision usefulness

Primary qualitative characteristics

1. Relevance   2. Faithful representation

   a. Predictive value   a. Completeness

   b. Confirmatory value   b. Neutrality

   c. Materiality   c. Free from error

Enhancing qualitative characteristics

1. Comparability

2. Verifiability

3. Timeliness

4. Understandability

B. Primary characteristics (relevance, faithful representation) -- For information to be useful for decision-making, it must be both relevant and a faithful representation of the economic phenomena that it represents.

1. **Relevance (primary characteristic) --** Information is relevant if it makes a difference to decision makers in their role as capital providers. Information is relevant when it has predictive value, confirmatory value, or both.

   a. **Predictive value --** Information has predictive value if it assists capital providers in forming expectations about future events.

   b. **Confirmatory value --** Information has confirmatory value if it confirms or changes past (or present) expectations based on previous evaluations. For example, if reported earnings for a period bear out market expectations, then it has confirmatory value.

   c. **Materiality --** information that is material will impact a user's decision. Materiality is somewhat pervasive throughout the objectives of financial reporting in the sense that the financial statements should present material information because it is decision useful. The FASB believes that materiality is an entity specific attribute and that material information is relevant to the decision maker. Therefore, materiality is an attribute of relevance.

2. **Faithful representation (primary characteristic) --** Information faithfully represents an economic condition or situation when the reported measure and the condition or situation are in agreement. Financial information that faithfully represents an economic phenomenon portrays the economic substance of the phenomenon. Information is representationally faithful when it is complete, neutral, and free from material error. Faithful representation replaces reliability as a primary qualitative characteristic.

Example:
If a firm reports gross plant assets of $100,000, the firm must actually have purchased that much in plant assets and be currently using them in operations.

a. Completeness: information is complete if it includes all data necessary to be faithfully representative.

b. Neutral: information is neutral when it is free from any bias intended to attain a prespecified result, or to encourage or discourage certain behavior.

Example:
Firms may be reluctant to report losses. Neutrality requires that losses, if they are probable and estimable, be reported regardless of any possible effect on the firm.

c. Free from error: information is free from error if there are no omissions or errors.

C. **Enhancing characteristics** -- These are complementary to the primary characteristics and enhance the decision usefulness of financial reporting information that is relevant and faithfully represented.

1. **Comparability** -- The quality of information that enables users to identify similarities and differences between sets of information. Consistency in application of recognition and measurement methods over time enhances comparability.

2. **Verifiability** -- Information is verifiable if different knowledgeable and independent observers could reach similar conclusions based on the information.

3. **Timeliness** -- Information is timely if it is received in time to make a difference to the decision maker. Timeliness can also enhance the faithful representation of information.

4. **Understandability** -- Information is understandable if the user comprehends it within the decision context at hand. Users are assumed to have a reasonable understanding of business and accounting and are willing to study the information with reasonable diligence.

D. **Relevance and faithful representation may conflict** -- In such cases, a trade-off is made favoring one or the other.

Example: 1. Relevance over faithful representation. The pervasive use of accounting estimates (depreciation, bad debt expense, pension estimates) is an example of emphasizing relevance over faithful representation. Firms are providing estimates, rather than certain amounts. Reasonable approximations, although they cannot be perfectly reliable, are preferred by financial statement users to either (1) perfect information issued too late to make a difference, or (2) no information at all.

2. Faithful representation over relevance. In the opinion of many, the use of historical cost as a valuation base is an example of emphasizing faithful representation over relevance. Historical cost is very reliable because it is based on objectively verifiable past information. However, historical cost is considered to be less current and therefore less relevant than market value.

Note: Candidates should be able to identify the components of relevance and faithful representation. It helps to remember that there are three components to both qualities.

Assumptions, Accounting Principles

This lesson presents an overview of accounting assumptions and principles in the related conceptual framework.

After studying this lesson, you should be able to:

1. *List and describe the principles in the conceptual framework.*

2. *List and describe the assumptions in the conceptual framework.*

I. Accounting Assumptions

A. Entity Assumption -- We assume there is a separate accounting entity for each business organization.

Example:
The owners and the corporation are separate. The owners own shares in the corporation; they do not own the assets of the firm. The corporation owns the assets. The financial statements represent the corporation, not the owners. A firm cannot own itself. Treasury shares are not assets to the firm - no one owns treasury shares. A firm can sue and be sued. If a firm is sued, the owners are not liable.

B. Going Concern Assumption

1. In the absence of information to the contrary, a business is assumed to have an indefinite life, that is, it will continue to be a going concern. Therefore, we do not show items at their liquidation or exit values.

2. This assumption, also called the continuity assumption, supports the historical cost principle for many assets. Income measurement is based on historical cost of assets because assets provide value through use, rather than disposal. Thus, net income is the difference between revenue and the historical cost of assets used in generating that revenue. Without the going concern principle, historical cost would not be an appropriate valuation basis.

Example:
Prepaid assets, such as prepaid rent, would not be assets without the assumption of continuity.

C. Unit-of-Measure Assumption -- Assets, liabilities, equities, revenues, expenses, gains, losses, and cash flows are measured in terms of the monetary unit of the country in which the business is operated. Price level changes cause the application of this assumption to weaken the relevance of certain disclosures.

Example:
The amounts of all assets are added together even though amounts recorded at different times represent different purchasing power levels.

1. Capital maintenance and departures from the unit of measure assumption

a. The concept of capital maintenance is related to the unit of measure assumption. Capital is said to be maintained when the firm has positive earnings for the year, assuming no changes in price levels. When a firm has income, it has recognized revenue sufficient to replace all the resources used in generating that revenue (return *of* capital), and has resources left over in addition (income, which is return *on* capital). That income could be distributed as dividends without eroding the net assets (capital) existing at the beginning of the year. GAAP is based on the concept of "financial" capital maintenance. As long as dividends do not exceed earnings, and earnings is not negative, financial capital has been maintained.

    b. An alternative concept of capital maintenance is "physical" capital maintenance. This concept holds that earnings cannot be recognized until the firm has provided for the physical capital used up during the period. To measure the capital used up, changes in price level must be considered.

> **Example:**
> A firm uses up $5,000 worth of supplies in providing its service during the year, but to replace those supplies for use next year, $5,500 will have to be paid (10% increase in specific price of supplies). The "financial" capital maintenance model uses the $5,000 cost of supplies as the measure of revenue needed to maintain capital. If revenue for the current period is $5,000 and the firm had no other expenses, earnings would be zero and capital would just be maintained. The "physical" capital model would require revenue of $5,500 for capital to be maintained.
>
> GAAP does not require adjustments for price level changes and thus applies the "financial" capital maintenance concept in financial reports.

    D. Time Period Assumption -- The indefinite life of a business is broken into smaller time frames, typically a year, for evaluation purposes and reporting purposes. For accounting information to be relevant, it must be timely. The reliability of the information often must be sacrificed to provide relevant disclosures. The use of estimates is required for timely reporting but also implies a possible loss of reliability.

II. Accounting Principles

    A. Measurement -- At the time of origination, assets and liabilities are recorded at the market value of the item on the date of acquisition, usually the cash equivalent . This origination value is referred to as historical cost. For many assets and liabilities, this value is not changed even though market value changes. Other assets, such as plant assets and intangibles, are disclosed at historical cost less accumulated depreciation or amortization. Given the going concern assumption, revaluation to market value is inappropriate for plant assets, because the value of these assets is derived through use, rather than from disposal.

    B. There are measurement attributes other than historical cost that are used to represent items reported on the financials statements. Below is a brief summary and example of each measurement attribute.

        1. **Net realizable value --** This value is used to approximate liquidation value or selling price. It is the net value to be received after the costs of sale are deducted from the current market value

            a. Example: Lower cost or market for inventory valuation uses NRV.

        2. **Current replacement cost --** This value represents how much you would have to pay to replace an asset. Current replacement cost would represent current market value from the buyer's perspective.

            a. Example: Replacement cost is also used in inventory valuation.

        3. **Fair value --** This value is also referred to as current market value. It is the price that would be received to sell an asset (or the price to settle a liability) in an orderly transaction from the perspective of a market participant at the measurement date (see the fair value lessons for further discussion of fair value).

    a. Example: Current market value (or fair value) is used to value trading and available-for-sale securities.

  4. **Amortized cost** -- This value is historical cost less the accumulated amortization or depreciation of the asset.

    a. Example: Buildings and equipment are reported at historical cost less accumulated depreciation.

  5. **Net present value** -- This is the value determined from discounting the expected future cash flows.

    a. Example: The discounted future cash flows are used in many capital budgeting decisions.

C. Revenue Recognition Principle -- This principle addresses three important issues related to revenues. Below is a general view of revenue—see the revenue recognition lessons for more details.

  1. **Revenue Defined** -- *What* revenue is: Revenue refers to increases in assets or the extinguishment of liabilities stemming from the delivery of goods or the provision of services - the main activities of the firm.

  2. **When to Recognize Revenue** -- Revenues are recognized when the entity completes its performance obligation to a customer and the revenue is earned and realized (or realizable) . The performance obligation is completed when the goods or services are delivered (revenue is earned) and cash or promise of cash is received (realized). In general, there are five steps to allocate the components of revenue.

    a. Identify the contract with the customer (promise to deliver a good or service);

    b. Identify if there is more than one performance obligation;

    c. Determine the transaction price;

    d. Allocate the transaction price to the separate performance obligations (if there is more than one performance obligation);

    e. Recognize revenue when each performance obligation is satisfied.

  3. **Measure Revenue** -- *How* to measure revenue: Revenues are measured at the cash equivalent amount of the good or service provided.

Example:
A contract is entered into with the customer to deliver an automobile and provide a warranty on the parts associated with the automobile.

There are two separate performance obligations: deliver the automobile and provide parts if needed.

Determine the price of the automobile without the warranty or the price that the warranty is sold for separate from the automobile.

Allocate the transaction price to the separate performance obligations.

Recognize revenue when each performance obligation is satisfied. With respect to the automobile, revenue would be recognized upon delivery, with respect to the warranty, the revenue would be recognized over the warranty period.

D. Expense Recognition Principle -- This principle addresses when to recognize expenses and is sometimes referred to as the matching principle.

1. The matching principle says: *recognize expenses only when expenditures help to produce revenues*. Revenues are recognized when earned and realized or realizable; the related expenses are recognized, and the revenues and expenses are "matched" to determine net income or loss.

2. Expenses that are directly related to revenues can be readily matched with revenues they help produce.

3. Cost of goods sold and sales commissions are expenses that are directly associated and therefore matched with revenue. Other expenses are allocated based on the time period of benefit provided. Depreciation and amortization are examples. Such expenses are not directly matched with revenues. Still other expenses are recognized in the period incurred when there is no determinable relationship between expenditures and revenues. Advertising costs are an example.

E. Full Disclosure Principle -- Financial statements should present all information needed by an informed reader to make an economic decision. This principle is sometimes referred to as the adequate disclosure principle.

> **Example:**
> An aircraft manufacturer enters into a contract to build 200 airplanes for an airline company. As of the balance sheet date, production has not begun. Thus, there is no recognition of this contract in the accounts. However, a footnote should explain the financial aspects of the contract. This information is potentially of greater interest than many items recognized in the accounts.

Constraints and Present Value

This lesson presents an overview of accounting assumptions and principles in the related conceptual framework.

After studying this lesson, you should be able to:

1. *List and describe the constraints in the conceptual framework.*

2. *Describe how cash flow and present value are used in accounting measurements.*

I. Cost Constraint

A. The cost constraint on GAAP limits recognition and disclosure if the cost of providing the information exceeds its benefit. Firms may not omit disclosures if they are material and mandated by GAAP.

 Example:
A firm would not report its entire inventory subsidiary ledger in the footnotes or financial statements. The reporting of total inventory cost is sufficient. Reporting more detailed information is not worth the cost of doing so.

B. Note: Conservatism -- Conservatism is no longer a constraint and is not a qualitative characteristic. Conservatism (also called prudence) is the reporting of less optimistic amounts (lower income, net assets) under conditions of uncertainty or when GAAP provides a choice from among recognition or measurement methods.

1. Conservatism is a guideline that is used to limit the reporting of aggressive accounting information. Conservatism is used to avoid misleading internal and external users of the financial statements.

2. If estimates of an outcome are not equally likely, the preferred approach is to report the most likely estimate, rather than the more conservative estimate, if the latter is less likely.

3. It should be noted that overly conservative estimates can be misleading and cause over reporting in subsequent periods.

Example:
1. Conservatism usually arises when there is uncertainty and management must make estimates. The allowance for uncollectible accounts receivable is an estimate, but an overly conservative accrual of the allowance in the current year will lead to lower net income and assets in the current period, but would over report income in subsequent years.

2. When estimating a contingent liability that arises from a lawsuit, often legal counsel provides a range of outcomes, for example $500,000—$1,000,000 loss. Accruing the most conservative loss in the current period, $1,000,000, will result in a gain in the subsequent period when the loss is settled for an amount less than $1,000,000, for example $800,000.

DR: Contingent Liability	$1,000,000	
CR: Cash		$800,000
CR: Gain on settlement of contingent liability		200,000

II. Financial Statements, Recognition Criteria, Elements

A. A full set of financial statements should include the following

1. Financial Position at year-end (balance sheet);

2. Earnings for the year (income statement);

3. Comprehensive Income for the year - total nonowner changes (statement of comprehensive income);

4. Cash Flows during the year (statement of cash flows);

5. Investments by and Distributions to Owners during the year (statement of owner's equity).

B. Recognition and measurement criteria -- In relation to measurement and recognition of items in a financial report, the following criteria must be met:

1. **Definition** -- The definition of a financial statement element is met;

2. **Measurability** -- There is an attribute to be measured, such as historical cost;

3. **Relevance** -- The information to be presented in the financial report is capable of influencing decisions. The information is timely, has predictive ability, provides feedback value, and is material;

4. **Faithful Representation** -- The information is complete, neutral and free from material error.

C. Elements of Financial Statements -- Ten elements that appear in a financial report.

1. **Assets** -- Resources that have probable future benefits to the firm, controlled by management, resulting from past transactions. Note the three aspects of this definition.

2. **Liabilities** -- Probable future sacrifices of economic benefits arising from present obligations of an entity to transfer assets or provide services to other entities as a result of past transactions or events.

3. **Equity** -- Residual interest in the firm's assets, also known as net assets. Equity is primarily comprised of past investor contributions and retained earnings.

4. **Investments by Owners** -- Increases in net assets of an entity from transfers to it by existing owners or parties seeking ownership interest.

5. **Distributions to Owners** -- Decreases in net assets of an entity from the transfer of assets, provision of services, or incurrence of liabilities by the enterprise to owners.

6. **Comprehensive Income** -- Accounting income (transaction based) plus certain holding gains and losses and other items. It includes all changes in equity other than investments by owners and distributions to owners.

7. **Revenues** -- Increases in assets or settlements of liabilities of an entity by providing goods or services.

8. **Expenses** -- Decreases in assets or incurrences of liabilities of an entity by providing goods or services. Expenses provide a benefit to the firm.

9. **Gains** -- Increases in equity or net assets from peripheral or incidental transactions.

10. **Losses** -- Decreases in equity or net assets from peripheral or incidental transactions. Losses provide no benefit to the firm.

III. Using Cash Flow Information and Present Value in Accounting Measurements -- The concept statement addresses the use of present-value measurements. Like all concepts statements, it does not constitute GAAP but is used in the development of GAAP.

A. Measurement Issues

1. This Statement addresses only measurement issues, not recognition. The statement applies to initial recognition, fresh-start measurements, and amortization techniques based on future cash flows. A fresh-start measurement establishes a new carrying value after an initial recognition and is unrelated to previous amounts (e.g., mark-to-market accounting and recognition of asset impairments).

2. If the fair value of an asset or liability is available, there is no need to use present-value measurement. If not, present value is often the best available technique to estimate what fair value would be if it existed in the situation.

B. Present Value Measure -- When a present-value measure is used:

1. The result should be as close as possible to fair value if such a value could be obtained;

2. The expected cash flow approach is preferred, because present-value measurements should reflect the uncertainties inherent in the estimated cash flows.

C. Capture Economic Differences -- A present value measurement that fully captures the economic differences between various estimates of future cash flows would include the following:

1. An estimate of future cash flows;

2. Expectations about variations in amount or timing of those cash flows;

3. Time value of money as measured by the risk-free rate of interest;

4. The price for bearing the uncertainty inherent in the asset or liability;

5. Any other relevant factors.

D. Two Approaches -- The statement contrasts two approaches to computing present value:

1. **The traditional approach** (referred to as discounted cash flows) incorporates factors 2–5 above in the discount rate and uses a single most-likely cash flow in the computation. The traditional approach uses the interest rate to capture all the uncertainties and risks inherent in a cash flow measure. This is the approach that continues to be applied in some present value applications in financial accounting.

2. **The expected cash flow approach** uses a risk-free rate as the discount rate. That is, factors 2 – 5 are incorporated into the risk-adjusted expected cash flow and the discount factor is the risk-free rate.

> **Note:**
> The risk and uncertainty is incorporated into either the discount rate or the cash flows—not both!.

E. Expected Cash Flow Approach -- The expected cash flow approach uses expectations about all possible cash flows instead of a single most-likely cash flow. Both uncertainty as to timing and amount can be incorporated into the calculation. The Board believes that the expected cash flow approach is likely to provide a better estimate of fair value than a single value because it directly incorporates the uncertainty in estimated future cash flows.

See the following example.

Example:

1. (Example of uncertain amount) The amount of a cash flow may vary as follows: $200, $400, or $600 with probabilities of 10%, 60%, and 30%, respectively. The expected cash flow is $440 = $200(.10) + $400(.60) + $600(.30). The expected cash flow approach uses a range of cash flows with probabilities attached. Thus, the uncertainties of the cash flows themselves are reflected in the distribution of cash flows. Calculation of the present value is determined by using the probability weight cash flows discounted using the risk-free rate.

2. (Example of uncertain timing) A $100 cash flow might be received in 1, 2, or 3 years with probabilities of 10%, 60%, and 30%, respectively. Assuming an interest rate of 5%, the expected present value = $100(pv1, .05, 1)(.10) + $100(pv1, .05, 2)(.60) + $100(pv1, .05, 3)(.30). [(pv1, .05, 1) is the symbol for the present-value of a single payment of $1, due in 1 year discounted at 5%.] Calculation of the present value is determined by using the probability weight cash flows discounted using the risk free rate.

1. Different rates of interest may also be used in each of the single present value terms to reflect different risk for the different timing of cash flow.

F. The expected cash flow approach has been incorporated into Accounting for Asset Retirement Obligations.

Fair Value Framework—Introduction and Definitions

This lesson introduces fair value framework for accounting. The framework includes the definition of fair value, the techniques for measuring fair value whenever it is used in accounting, and disclosures required when fair value is used. This lesson describes the need for a fair value framework and the application of the framework in practice. This lesson also defines fair value and describes the individual components of the definition. In addition, the special conditions that apply separately to assets, to liabilities and to shareholders' equity are presented.

After studying this lesson you should be able to:

1. *Describe the need for a single definition of fair value and a framework for its application.*

2. *identify the items that are not within the scope of the fair value framework.*

3. *Define fair value for accounting purposes.*

4. *Describe the individual components of the fair value definition and how they affect the application of the definition.*

5. *Describe the special factors related to the application of the fair value definition separately to assets, liabilities, and shareholders' equity, and to a net portfolio of assets and liabilities.*

I. **Introduction** -- The use of fair value to measure and report financial statement items is required or permitted by a number of GAAP pronouncements (ASCs). Some of those pronouncements, however, provide somewhat different definitions of "fair value" and provide only limited guidance in the determination of fair value for GAAP purposes. As a consequence, in the past, inconsistencies have occurred in how fair value is measured in practice. ASC 820 provides a framework for how to measure fair value to achieve increased consistency and comparability in fair value measurements and expanded disclosure when fair value measurements are used.

> **Note:**
> As a result of the joint efforts of the IASB and the FASB, there are no significant differences between U.S. GAAP and IFRS related to the meaning of fair value, its measurement or required disclosures. According to ASU 2011-04: "The Boards (FASB and IASB) worked together to ensure that fair value has the same meaning in U.S. GAAP and in IFRSs and that their respective fair value measurement and disclosure requirements are the same (except for minor differences in wording and style)."

   A. **Objectives** -- In order to accomplish the objectives of ASC 820, it provides the following:

   1. A definition of fair value for GAAP purposes;

   2. A framework for measuring (determining) fair value for accounting purposes;

   3. A set of required disclosures about fair value measurement when it is used.

II. **Fair Value Defined**

> **Definition:**
> *Fair Value*: The price that would be received to sell an asset or paid to transfer a liability in an orderly transaction between market participants at the measurement date.

   A. In order to fully understand and apply this definition, several components of the definition need to be described further:

1. Fair value is a market-based measurement, not an entity-specific measurement.

2. The determination of fair value is for a particular asset or liability (or equity item), which may be either a standalone asset or liability (e.g., a financial instrument or a nonfinancial operating asset) or a group of assets/liabilities (e.g., a reporting unit or business). Fair value determination should consider the attributes (e.g., condition, location, restriction on asset use or sale, etc.) of the specific asset or liability being measured.

> **Note:**
> The fair value definition focuses on **how** to measure fair value not **when** to measure fair value.

3. The transaction to sell the asset or transfer the liability is a hypothetical transaction at the measurement date that would occur under current market conditions; it is not a transaction that would occur in a forced liquidation or distress sale.

4. Even when there is no observable market to provide pricing information about the sale of an asset or the transfer of a liability at the measurement date, a fair value measurement assumes that a transaction takes place at that date.

5. The assumed transaction establishes a basis for estimating the price to sell the asset or transfer the liability.

6. The hypothetical transaction to sell the asset or transfer the liability is assumed to occur in the principal market or, alternatively, in the absence of a principal market, the most advantageous market for the asset or liability, to which the entity has access, after taking into account transaction costs and transportation costs.

   a. The principal market is the one with the greatest volume and level of activity for the asset or liability within which the reporting entity could sell the asset or transfer the liability.

   b. The most advantageous market is the one in which the reporting entity could sell the asset at a price that maximizes the amount that would be received for the asset or that minimizes the amount that would be paid to transfer the liability.

7. The price determined in the principal or most advantageous market should not be adjusted for transaction costs - incremental direct cost to sell the asset or transfer the liability - which do not measure a characteristic of the asset or liability. However, cost incurred to transport the asset or liability to its principal or most advantageous market (the location characteristic of an asset) would be used to adjust fair value for measurement purposes.

> **Note:**
> Notice that although transaction and transportation costs are taken into account in determining the most advantageous market, transaction costs are not used (i.e., not deducted from the asset market price or added to the liability transfer cost) in determining the fair value of an asset or liability in the most advantageous market.

8. Market participants, as used in the definition, are buyers and sellers of the asset or liability that are:

   a. Independent of the reporting entity;

   b. Acting in their economic best interest;

   c. Knowledgeable of the asset or liability and the transaction involved;

   d. Able and willing, but not compelled, to transact for the asset or liability.

III. Application of Definition to Assets, Liabilities, and Shareholders' Equity

A. Application to Assets

1. The determination of fair value of a nonfinancial asset assumes the highest and best use of the asset by market participants, even if the intended use of the asset by the reporting entity is different; the concept of "highest and best use" does not apply to measuring the fair value of financial assets (or liabilities).

2. The highest and best use must take into account what is physically possible, legally permissible and financially feasible at the measurement date.

3. The highest and best use of an asset may be:

   a. In-use: Maximum value to market participants would occur through its use in combination with other assets as a group;

   b. In-exchange: Maximum value to market participants would occur principally on a standalone basis, that is, the price that would be received in a current transaction to sell the (single) asset.

B. Application to Liabilities

1. The determination of fair value of a liability assumes that the liability is transferred to a market participant at the measurement date; it is not settled or canceled.

   a. The liability to the counterparty (i.e., the party to whom the obligation is due) is assumed to continue after the hypothetical transaction.

   b. Nonperformance risk relating to the liability is assumed to be the same after the hypothetical transaction as before the transaction.

2. The determination of fair value of a liability should consider the effects of the reporting entity's credit risk (or credit standing) on the fair value of the liability in each period for which the liability is measured at fair value; a third-party credit enhancement should not be considered.

3. A separate input or an adjustment to other inputs to account for a restriction that prevents the transfer of liabilities should not be made in measuring fair value.

4. When a quoted price for the transfer of an identical or similar liability is not available, and the identical liability is held by another party as an asset, the liability should be measured from the perspective of the party that holds the item as an asset.

C. Application to Shareholders' Equity

1. The requirements for the determination of fair value apply to instruments classified in shareholders' equity that are measured at fair value (e.g., equity interest issued as consideration in a business combination).

2. The measurement assumes the instrument is transferred to a market participant at the measurement date and is measured from the perspective of a market participant that holds the instrument as an asset.

3. A separate input or an adjustment to other inputs to account for a restriction that prevents the transfer of a shareholder equity instrument should not be made in measuring the fair value.

4. When a quoted price for the transfer of an identical or similar shareholders' equity instrument is not available, and the identical instrument is held by another party as an asset, the instrument should be measured from the perspective of the party that holds the item as an asset.

D. Application to Net Financial Assets and Financial Liabilities

1. An exception to the requirement that fair value of qualified financial assets and financial liabilities be measured separately is permitted when a reporting entity manages risk associated with a portfolio of financial instruments on a net exposure basis, rather than on a gross exposure basis.

2. An entity that holds financial assets and financial liabilities and manages those instruments on the basis of their net risk exposure may measure the fair value of those financial assets and financial liabilities at:

    a. The price that would be received to sell a NET asset position for a particular risk, or

    b. The price that would be paid to transfer a NET liability position for a particular risk.

IV. Applicability -- The content of ASC 820 is for items that uses fair value measurement either as required or as permitted by GAAP, except in very limited situations. Specifically, the guidance of ASC 820 does **not** apply to:

    A. Accounting principles that address share-based payment transactions;

    B. ASCs that require or permit measurements that are similar to fair value but that are not intended to measure fair value, including:

        1. Accounting principles that permit measurements that are determined using vendor-specific objective evidence of fair value;

        2. Accounting principles that address fair value measurement for purposes of inventory pricing;

    C. Accounting principles that address fair value measurements for purposes of lease classification or measurement;

    D. ASCs that permit practicability exceptions to fair value measurement.

    E. Pervasive Applicability -- Other than the exceptions noted above, the content of ASC 820 must be followed when fair value measurement is used, either as required or permitted by other pronouncements.

Recognition and Measurement

The measurement of fair value is based on an exit price - the amount that would be received to sell an asset or paid to transfer a liability. In some cases, that amount will be the same amount as an entry price, but not in all cases. This lesson discusses the relationship between an exit price and an entry price and identifies those situations where the prices may be different amounts.

After studying this lesson, you should be able to:

1. *Describe the nature of an entry price and an exit price and distinguish between the two.*

2. *Identify reasons why an entry price and an exit price may not be the same amount on the same recognition date.*

3. *Describe the appropriate accounting treatment for any difference between entry price and exit price at the time of initial recognition.*

4. *Identify and describe the techniques or approaches used to determine fair value.*

5. *Describe when a technique or set of techniques will be appropriate to use to determine fair value.*

6. *Describe when a change in techniques may be appropriate and the consequence of such a change.*

I. **Fair Value Determination --** When an asset is acquired or a liability is assumed in an actual transaction, the price paid to acquire the asset or the price received to assume the liability (the "transaction price") is an entry price - the price paid when an asset or liability is initially recognized, which may or may not be fair value. Fair value of an asset or a liability is the price that would be received to sell an asset or paid to transfer a liability - an exit price.

   A. Conceptually, an entry price and an exit price are different.

   B. In many cases, the entry price (transaction price) and the exit price (fair value) will be the same at the date of initial recognition of an asset or liability and, therefore, constitute the fair value of the asset or liability at that date.

   C. In some cases, however, the entry (transaction) price may not be the exit price and therefore not be fair value at the date of initial recognition of an asset or liability. For example, the transaction price might not be fair value (exit price) if:

      1. The transaction is between related parties;

      2. The transaction takes place when the seller is under duress (e.g., in a liquidation sale);

      3. The unit of account for the transaction price is different from the unit of account that would be used to measure the asset or liability at fair value. For example, if the asset or liability measured at fair value is part of a business in a business combination, there are unstated rights associated with an asset that are measured separately, or the quoted price includes transaction costs - such as with oil;

      4. The market in which the transaction price takes place is different from the principal market (or most advantageous market).

   D. If an entity is required or permitted to measure an asset or liability initially at fair value and the transaction price at initial recognition differs from fair value, a gain or loss is recognized in earnings at initial recognition of the asset or liability (unless otherwise required by GAAP for that item).

1. The asset or liability would be recorded at fair value;

2. The difference between the transaction (entry) price and the recorded fair value (exit price) would be recognized as a loss or gain in the period of initial recognition.

II. Measurement Techniques

A. **Valuation Techniques/Approaches** -- In the determination of fair value for GAAP purposes, three valuation techniques or approaches could be used:

1. **Market approach** -- This approach uses prices and other relevant information generated by market transactions involving assets or liabilities that are identical or comparable to those being valued.

2. **Income approach** -- This approach converts future amounts to a single present amount. Discounting future cash flows would be an income approach to determining fair value.

3. **Cost approach** -- This approach uses the amount that currently would be required to replace the service capacity of an asset (i.e., current replacement cost), adjusting for obsolescence.

B. **Valuation Technique/Approach Selection** -- Which approach (or approaches) is appropriate to measure fair value will depend on the circumstances, including the availability of sufficient data for the respective approaches, and will maximize the use of relevant observable inputs and minimize the use of unobservable inputs.

1. In some cases, a single valuation technique will be appropriate (e.g., using quoted prices in an active market for identical assets or liabilities).

2. In some cases, multiple valuation techniques will be appropriate (e.g., when valuing an entire business).

   a. When multiple valuation techniques are used, the different results should be evaluated and weighted.

   b. When multiple valuation techniques are used, professional judgment will be required to select the fair value from within the range of alternative values that is most representative in the circumstances.

3. Under all valuation techniques, the valuation must take into account appropriate risk adjustments, including a risk premium for uncertainty.

C. **Consistent Application of Approach/Technique**

1. Valuation techniques used to measure fair value should be consistently applied.

2. A change in valuation technique or its application is appropriate if the change will result in a more representative fair value.

   a. A change in valuation technique or application may be appropriate, for example, if new markets develop, new information becomes available, previous information is no longer available, or valuation techniques improve.

   b. Changes in fair value resulting from changes in valuation techniques or applications are treated as changes in accounting estimates.

III. Fair Value Option --

A. An entity can apply the fair value option to an eligible item only on the date when one of the following events occur (an election date):

1. When the item is first recognized;

2. When an eligible firm commitment is established;

3. Specialized accounting for an item ceases to exist

    4. An investment becomes subject to equity method accounting (but is not consolidated) or to a VIE that is no longer consolidated;

    5. An event that requires the item to be measured at fair value, such as a business combination or significant modifications to debt instruments.

B. Entities that elect to use the fair value measurement (referred to as the fair value option) for eligible financial assets and financial liabilities must adhere to certain requirements. Those requirements include:

    1. The fair value option may be applied on an instrument by instrument basis, with limited exceptions.

        a. The fair value option may be elected for a single eligible item without electing it for other identical items with the following exceptions:

            i. If multiple advances are made to one borrower as part of a single contract and the individual advances lose their identity, the fair value option must be applied to all advances under the contract;

            ii. If the fair value option is applied to an investment that would otherwise be accounted for under the equity method of accounting, it must be applied to all of the investor's financial interests, both equity and debt, in that entity;

            iii. If the fair value option is applied to an eligible insurance/reinsurance contract, it must be applied to all claims/obligations and features/coverages under the contract.

        b. The fair value option does not have to be applied to all instruments issued or acquired in a single transaction (except as noted in 1, above). The fair value option may be applied to some of the individual instruments issued or acquired (e.g., shares of stock or bonds) in a single transaction, but not to other individual instruments issued or acquired in that transaction.

    2. The fair value option is irrevocable unless and until a new election date for the specific item occurs.

    3. The fair value option is applied only to an entire instrument and not to only specific risks, specific cash flows, or portions of an instrument.

    4. If the fair value option is elected for held-to-maturity securities, those securities will be treated and reported as trading securities.

        a. Gains and losses resulting from change in fair value will not be reported in other comprehensive income.

        b. Gains and losses resulting from changes in fair value will be reported in current income.

IV. Instruments Not Eligible for Fair Value Option -- Entities may NOT use fair value to measure and report the following financial assets and financial liabilities:

A. An investment in a subsidiary that is to be consolidated;

B. An interest in a variable interest entity that is to be consolidated;

C. Employers' and plans' obligations (or assets) for pension benefits, other postretirement benefits, post-employment benefits, and other employee- oriented plans;

D. Financial assets and liabilities recognized under lease accounting;

E. Demand deposit liabilities of financial institutions;

F. Financial instruments that are classified by the issuer as a component of shareholders' equity.

Inputs and Hierarchy

When determining fair value, many assumptions and sources of data may be used. In some cases, only limited assumptions and data may be required; for example, when quoted prices in an active market are appropriate and available. In other cases, however, a number of assumptions and a variety of data may be needed to develop a fair value measure. This lesson identifies the kinds of inputs that may be used and the relative importance of each.

After studying this lesson, you should be able to:

1. *Describe the nature of observable and unobservable inputs in determining fair value.*

2. *Describe the three levels of the fair value hierarchy and give examples of each.*

I. **Inputs** -- Inputs refer to the various assumptions that market participants would use in determining fair value, including assumptions about the risk inherent in using a particular valuation technique, as well as the risk inherent in using various inputs (data, assumptions, etc.) with each valuation technique.

    A. **Inputs used may be**

        1. **Observable** -- Inputs used in pricing an asset, liability, or equity item that are developed based on market data obtained from sources independent of the reporting entity.

        2. **Unobservable** -- Inputs that reflect the reporting entity's own assumptions used in pricing the asset, liability, or equity item that are developed based on the best information available in the circumstances.

    B. Valuation techniques used to measure fair value should maximize the use of observable inputs and minimize the use of unobservable inputs.

II. **Fair Value Hierarchy** -- The fair value hierarchy (provided in ASC 820) prioritizes or ranks the inputs to valuation techniques used to measure fair value into three levels:

    A. **Level 1** -- Inputs in this, the highest level, are unadjusted quoted prices in active markets for assets or liabilities (or equity items) identical to those being valued that the entity can obtain at the measurement date.

        1. Quoted prices in an active market provide the most reliable evidence of fair value and, except in unusual circumstances, should be used to measure fair value when available.

        2. Quoted prices should not be adjusted because the entity holds a sizeable position in the asset or liability relative to the trading volume in the market (often referred to as the "blockage factor").

        3. Adjustments to quoted prices generally result in a fair value measurement categorized in a lower level of the fair value hierarchy (i.e., Level 2 or 3).

    B. **Level 2** -- Inputs in this level are observable for assets or liabilities (or equity items), either directly or indirectly, other than quoted prices described in Level 1, above.

        1. This level includes:

            a. Quoted prices for similar assets or liabilities in active markets.

            b. Quoted prices for identical or similar assets or liabilities in markets that are not active-markets in which there are few relevant transactions, prices are not current or vary substantially, or for which little information is publicly available.

    c. Inputs, other than quoted prices, that are observable for the assets or liabilities being valued, including, for example, interest rates, yield curves, implied volatilities and credit spreads.

    d. Inputs that are derived principally from, or corroborated by, observable market date by correlation or other means (referred to as "market-corroborated inputs").

  2. Depending on factors specific to the asset or liability being valued, these inputs may need to be adjusted when applied to the asset or liability for factors such as: condition, location, and the level of activity in the relevant market.

  3. When market participants would apply a premium or discount related to a characteristic of an asset or liability being valued (e.g., a control premium), an entity should apply the premium or discount in measuring fair value.

  4. If significant unobservable inputs are used to adjust observable inputs, the resulting measurement may be categorized in Level 3.

C. Level 3 -- Inputs in this, the lowest level, are unobservable for the assets or liabilities (or equity items) being valued and should be used to determine fair value only to the extent observable inputs are not available.

  1. Unobservable inputs should reflect the entity's assumptions about what market participants would assume and should be developed based on the best information available in the circumstances, which might include the entity's own data.

  2. The reporting entity should not ignore information available about market participants' assumptions and should adjust its own data if information indicated that market participants would use different assumptions.

  3. When market participants would apply a premium or discount related to a characteristic of the asset or liability being valued (e.g., a control premium), an entity should apply the premium or discount in measuring fair value.

  4. When a valuation technique uses unobservable inputs to determine fair value subsequent to initial recognition and fair value at initial recognition is the transaction price, the valuation technique should be calibrated (adjusted) at initial recognition so that the results of the valuation technique equals the transaction price.

Disclosure Requirements

Any time fair value measurement is used, whether as required by GAAP or as permitted by GAAP, specific disclosures are required when financial statements are issued. This lesson identifies the most important of those disclosures.

After studying this lesson, you should be able to:

1. *Describe significant disclosures required for assets, liabilities, and equity items measured at fair value on a **recurring** basis.*

2. *Describe significant disclosures required for assets, liabilities, and equity items measured at fair value on a **nonrecurring** basis.*

3. *Describe the significant disclosure requirements for the election of the fair value option applied to assets, liabilities, and equity items.*

I. **Disclosures Required** -- GAAP requires the following disclosures when fair value measurement is used, either as required or permitted by other accounting pronouncements.

II. **For Assets and Liabilities that are Measured at Fair Value on a Recurring Basis** -- In periods subsequent to initial recognition (e.g., investments in trading securities measured on a recurring basis) the reporting entity must disclose the following information in the statement of financial position (balance sheet) for each interim and annual period for each major category of asset and liability:

A. The fair value measurements at the reporting date.

B. Segregated into each of the three levels within the fair value hierarchy.

C. Transfers into each level and transfers out of each level disclosed and discussed separately, with the amounts of any transfers between Level 1 and Level 2, the reasons for such transfers, and the policy for determining when those transfers occur disclosed separately.

D. For Levels 2 and 3, a description of the valuation techniques and inputs used to measure fair value and a discussion of changes in valuation techniques during the period, if any.

E. For fair value measurements in Level 3, unobservable inputs, a reconciliation of the beginning and ending balances, separately presenting changes during the period attributable to the following:

1. Total gains or losses recognized, showing separately those included in earnings and those included in other comprehensive income, and the line item(s) in which they are recognized in the respective statements;

2. Purchases, sales, issuances, and settlements, disclosed separately;

3. Transfer in and/or out of Level 3 disclosed separately, the reasons for such transfers, and the policy for determining when those transfers occur.

F. For fair value measurements in Level 3:

1. A description of the valuation process used;

2. Quantitative information about the unobservable inputs used;

3. A narrative description of the sensitivity of the fair value measurement to changes in unobservable inputs.

G. The amount of total gains or losses for the period that are attributable to the change in unrealized gains or losses relating to assets and liabilities still held at the reporting date and a description of where those unrealized amounts are reported in the Income Statement.

H. For nonfinancial assets, disclose if highest and best use differs from current use and why.

III. For Assets and Liabilities that are Measured at Fair Value on a Nonrecurring Basis -- In periods subsequent to initial recognition (e.g., an asset impairment that is not measured on a recurring basis) the reporting entity must disclose the following information in the statement of financial position (balance sheet) for each major category of asset and liability:

    A. The fair value measurements at the reporting date and the reasons for the measurement.

    B. Segregated into each of the three levels of the fair value hierarchy.

    C. For Levels 2 and 3, a description of the valuation techniques and inputs used to measure fair value and a discussion of changes in valuation techniques during the period, if any.

    D. For fair value measurements in Level 3, unobservable inputs, a description of the valuation process used and quantitative information about the unobservable inputs used.

    E. For nonfinancial assets, disclose if highest and best use differs from current use and why.

IV. Other Disclosure Issues

    A. The quantitative disclosures required above must be presented using a tabular format (examples are provided in ASC 820-10-55-100 through 820-10-55-107.

    B. Reporting entities are encouraged, but not required, to combine the fair value information disclosures under this ACS with fair value information disclosures required by other accounting pronouncements.

V. Disclosure Related to the Fair Value Options

    A. Fair Value Option Disclosures Objectives -- Disclosures required when the fair value option is elected are intended to accomplish the following objectives:

        1. The disclosures are intended to facilitate comparisons:

            a. Between entities that choose different measurement methods for similar assets and liabilities, and

            b. Between assets and liabilities in the financial statements of a single entity that selects different measurement methods for similar assets and liabilities.

        2. The disclosure requirements are expected to result in the following:

            a. Information to enable users of financial statements to understand management's reasons for electing or partially electing the fair value option.

            b. Information to enable users to understand how changes in fair value affect earnings for a period.

            c. Provide the same kind/amount of information about certain items that would have been disclosed if the fair value option had not been elected for the items.

            d. Information to enable users to understand the differences between fair values and contractual cash flows for certain items.

        3. To achieve these objectives and outcomes, required disclosures must be provided in both interim and annual financial statements.

        4. The disclosures, as outlined below, do not replace disclosure requirements in other existing GAAP pronouncements, including other pronouncements that require fair value measurement use and disclosures.

    B. Required Disclosures for Interim and Annual Statements of Financial Position (Balance Sheet) -- As of each date for which a Statement of Financial Position (Balance Sheet) is presented, the following must be disclosed:

1. Management's reasons for electing a fair value option for each eligible item or group of similar eligible items.

2. If the fair value option is elected for some, but not all, eligible items within a group of similar eligible items:

    a. A description of those similar items and the reasons for partial election;

    b. Information to enable users to understand how the group of similar items relates to individual line items on the Statement of Financial Position.

3. For each line item in the Statement of Financial Position that includes an item or items for which the fair value option has been elected:

    a. Information to enable users to understand how each line item in the statement relates to major categories of assets and liabilities;

    b. The aggregate carrying amount of items included in each line item in the statement that are not eligible for the fair value option, if any.

4. The difference between the aggregate fair value and the aggregate unpaid principal balance of:

    a. Loans and long-term receivables that have contractual principal amounts and for which the fair value option is used;

    b. Long-term debt instruments that have contractual principal amounts and for which the fair value option has been elected.

5. For loans held as assets for which the fair value option has been elected:

    a. The aggregate fair value of loans that are 90 days or more past due;

    b. If the entity's policy is to recognize interest income separately from other changes in fair value, the aggregate fair value of loans in nonaccrual status (i.e., loans for which interest income is not accrued);

    c. The difference between the aggregate fair value and the aggregate unpaid principal balance for loans that are 90 days or more past due, are in nonaccrual status, or both.

6. For investments that would have been accounted for under the equity method if the entity had not chosen to apply the fair value option, the information required by ASC 323, "The Equity Method of Accounting for Investments," including:

    a. The name of each investee and the percentage ownership of its common stock;

    b. The accounting policies of the investor with respect to investments in common stock.

C. **Required Disclosures for Interim and Annual Income Statements** -- For each period for which an Income Statement is presented, the following must be disclosed about items for which the fair value option has been elected:

1. For each line item in the Statement of Financial Position (Balance Sheet), the amount of gains and losses from fair value changes included in earnings for the period and in which line in the Income Statement those gains/losses are reported.

2. A description of how interest and dividends are measured and where they are reported in the Income Statement.

3. For loans and other receivables held as assets:

    a. The estimated amount of gains and losses included in earnings for the period attributable to changes in instrument-specific credit risk, and

    b. How those gains and losses were determined.

4. For liabilities with fair values that have been significantly affected during the reporting period by changes in the instrument-specific credit risk:

   a. The estimated amount of gains and losses from fair value changes included in earnings that are attributable to changes in the instrument-specific credit risk;

   b. How the gains and losses were determined;

   c. Qualitative information about the reasons for those changes.

D. Other Disclosure Requirements

1. In annual reports only, the methods and significant assumptions used to estimate fair value (of items for which the fair value option has been elected) must be disclosed.

2. If an entity elects the fair value option at the time an investment becomes subject to the equity method of accounting or when it ceases to consolidate a subsidiary, it must disclose:

   a. Information about the nature of the event, and

   b. Where the effect on earnings shows in the Income Statement.

SEC—Role and Standard-Setting Process

After studying this lesson, you should be able to:

1. *Recognize that there are mandatory exemptions from first time adoption as well as voluntary exceptions.*

2. *Describe the components of SEC's organizational structure.*

3. *Describe the SEC's role in the standard setting process.*

4. *List the main pronouncements issued by the SEC.*

I. Introduction

A. The SEC is a federal agency created by Congress after the 1929 stock market crash. It administers the U.S. securities laws, most notably the Securities Act of 1933 and the Securities Exchange Act of 1934. The SEC requires registrants (those publicly held companies under its purview) to adhere to U.S. GAAP when reporting financial statements, except those non U.S.-domiciled companies who may report using IFRS without a reconciliation to U.S. GAAP (see discussion below).

B. Although the SEC has the legal authority to prescribe accounting standards for publicly traded corporations, it continues to believe that standard setting should remain in the private sector, subject to its oversight. The SEC often agrees with the FASB's accounting standards, while communicating its preferences in comments on FASB Exposure Drafts and other documents. In a few cases, the SEC has rejected a FASB standard and in others has applied pressure to have a standard or proposed standard modified, or to come to a decision more quickly.

II. The SEC's Main Purposes

A. "The mission of the U.S. Securities and Exchange Commission is to protect investors, maintain fair, orderly and efficient markets, and facilitate capital information" (http://www.sec.gov/about/whatwedo.shtml). An important component of the mission is ease and access to information that is relevant to the decision maker. (Remember that relevance is a primary characteristic in the FASB's conceptual framework!)

B. The SEC regulates the issuance of securities by publicly traded companies and regulation of the trading of those securities on secondary markets. The SEC's intent is to ensure that there is adequate information in the public domain before firms issue securities and before those securities are subsequently traded. Some of the most critical information used by the participants in the marketplace is the financial information provided by the registrant. This is why the SEC is so involved with financial reporting and accounting standards.

C. The SEC's IDEA (Interactive Data Electronic Applications) database replaced the SEC's EDGAR (Electronic Data Gathering, Analysis and Retrieval System) database to facilitate the reporting of financial statement information in XBRL (Extensible Business Reporting Language) format which tags accounting data according to a taxonomy allowing users to quickly prepare any type of report they wish. The purpose of IDEA is to increase the efficiency of the securities markets by providing timely and accessible data.

D. The global economy has called for the need for one high-level, comprehensive set of accounting standards. The SEC has been the champion and driver in the U.S. to converge GAAP and IFRS. In 2005, SEC and top European Union officials agreed to a roadmap toward convergence between U.S. GAAP and IFRS.

E. In 2008, the SEC began accepting the financial statements of foreign private issuers prepared in compliance with IFRS without reconciliation to U.S. GAAP. This is a significant step toward acknowledging the IFRSs as issued by IASB. The reconciliation (complete on

Form 20-F) was considered to be an unnecessary requirement if the goal was one set of high quality standards. In addition, the cost of completing the reconciliation was viewed as a deterrent for foreign issuers to access the U.S. capital markets. Eliminating the requirement will hopefully encourage more foreign businesses to list their securities in the U.S.

1. A foreign private issuer is any foreign issuer other than a foreign government, **except** an issuer that meets the following conditions (Rule 205, Securities Act 1933):

   a. More than 50% of the outstanding voting securities are directly or indirectly owned by residents of the U.S. and

   b. Any of the following:

      i. The majority of its executive officers or directors are U.S. citizens or residents;

      ii. More than 50% of the assets of the issuer are located in the U.S.;

      iii. The business of the issuer is administered principally in the U.S.

F. When the SEC determines that a firm has reported in such a way that GAAP has been violated, it sends a deficiency letter to the firm. If not resolved, the SEC can then stop the trading of the firm's securities. If warranted the Department of Justice becomes involved and criminal charges for violations of the securities laws are filed.

Note:
Although the SEC can prescribe accounting standards, it has delegated that task to the private sector (currently the FASB). However, the SEC maintains the enforcement power for all publicly traded companies to assure compliance with U.S. GAAP.

III. SEC Organizational Structure

A. The SEC is a member of the International Organization of Securities Commissions (IOSCO), which consists of more than 100 securities regulatory agencies or exchanges across the globe.

B. The SEC has five commissioners appointed by the President of the U.S. and four divisions (collectively referred to as "the commission").

1. **The Division of Corporation Finance --** This division oversees the compliance with the securities acts and examines all filings made by publicly held companies. All filings go to this division.

2. **The Division of Enforcement --** When there is a violation of a securities law (except the Public Utility Holding Company Act), this division completes the investigation and takes appropriate actions. This division makes recommendations to the Justice Department concerning any punishments or potential criminal prosecution.

3. **The Division of Trading and Markets --** This division oversees the secondary markets, exchanges, brokers, and dealers.

4. **The Division of Investment Management --** This division oversees the investment advisers and investment companies under the Investment Company Act of 1940 and the Investment Advisers Act of 1940.

C. The Office of the Chief Accountant of the SEC is the most important office for standard setting. This office houses the technical expertise on accounting principles, auditing standards and financial disclosure requirements. This office also issues position papers for the SEC to consider and is the link between the SEC and the accounting profession. The Office of the Chief Accountant has oversight of the FASB and AICPA and is the voice of the SEC regarding standard-setting issues.

D. Laws Administered by the SEC:

   1. The Securities Acts of 1933 and 1934

   2. The Public Utility Holding Company Act of 1935

   3. Trust Indenture Act of 1939

    4.   Investment Company Act of 1940

    5.   Investment Advisors' Act of 1940

    6.   Securities Investor Protection Act of 1970

    7.   Sarbanes-Oxley Act of 2002

IV. Participation in Standard Setting

A. Even though the SEC delegates the creation of accounting standards to the private sector, the SEC frequently comments on accounting and auditing issues. The SEC communicates through an array of venues. SEC pronouncements, along with the FASB Accounting Standards Codification, comprise authoritative U.S. GAAP. Public companies must adhere to SEC pronouncements as well as U.S. GAAP; private companies do not have to adhere to SEC pronouncements. The main pronouncements published by the SEC are listed below.

    1. **Financial Reporting Releases (FRR)** -- These are formal pronouncements and are the highest-ranking authoritative source of accounting for public companies.

    2. **Staff Accounting Bulletins (SAB)** -- These provide the SEC's current position on technical issues. While SABs are not formal pronouncements (in the sense that they have not gone through any due process), they still are of importance to financial statement preparers, because they reflect the staff's current thinking on various technical issues.

 Example: An example is SAB 104 on revenue recognition. This SAB was adopted in response to concerns about premature recognition of revenue.

This SAB was issued to reduce the degree to which management could decide the timing and amount of revenue recognition. It lays out very specific principles affecting revenue recognition. It primarily addresses abuses by start-up and growing firms involved in complex transactions. Key provisions are:

Revenue should not be recognized before both legal and economic ownership of goods has passed to the buyer. Fees charged at the beginning of a revenue-generating arrangement should be recognized over the term of the arrangement. An annual fee is not fully earned until the seller has provided its service for the year.

In terms of the earned criterion, on the sale of products, the SEC presumes that the sale is not earned unless title has passed and the customer assumes the risks and rewards of ownership. In addition, in some cases, acceptance by the firm after installation is a required part of the earned criterion.

In terms of the realizability criterion, the SEC requires that the price is fixed or determinable and there must be persuasive evidence that an arrangement exists. This means that if the ordinary practice of a provider is to obtain a signed contract, then a signed contract must be obtained or revenue cannot be recognized (even if the work is done and the client has verbally accepted the work and paid for the good or service.)

B. Accounting and Auditing Enforcement Releases (AAER) -- These report the enforcement actions that have been taken against accountants, brokers or others.

 Example:
AAER No. 1585 against WorldCom on their massive accounting fraud - this was the mechanism to publicly report that the SEC was taking action against WorldCom.

SEC Reporting Requirements

After studying this lesson, you should be able to:

1. *Identify the main reporting requirements for the 1933 and 1934 Securities Acts.*

2. *Identify the forms used for registration of securities and subsequent reporting.*

3. *Identify the content that should be contained in these forms.*

I. Introduction

A. The 1933 Securities Act requires publicly traded firms offering securities for sale to the public in primary and secondary markets to file a registration statement, and to provide each investor with a proxy statement before each shareholders' meeting.

B. The 1934 Securities Act regulates the trading of securities after they are issued and provides the requirements for periodic reporting and disclosures.

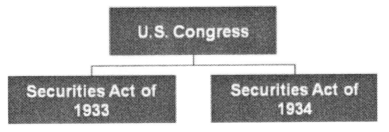

C. The formal SEC rules are found in the Code of Federal Regulations. All publicly traded companies (either public equity or public debt) must comply with the securities regulations. The governing regulations are Regulation S-X and Regulation S-K.

1. Regulations **S-X governs** the form and content of financial statements and **financial** statement disclosures. These include:

    a. Income statement;

    b. Balance sheet;

    c. Changes in shareholders equity;

    d. Cash flow statement;

    e. Footnotes to financial statements; and

    f. Qualification of accountants (independence rules).

2. Regulation **S-K governs** the form and content of **nonfinancial** statement disclosures. These disclosures are the content of the 10-K outside of the financial statements (remember that "S-K" governs the "10-K" nonfinancial statement content). The nonfinancial statement disclosures are

    a. Description of the business;

    b. Description of stockholder matters;

    c. Management's discussion and analysis (MD&A);

    d. Changes in and disagreements with accountants; and

    e. Information on directors and management.

> **Definition of a Security:** Section 2.1 of the 1933 Act defines a security as: Any note, stock, treasury stock, bond, debenture, evidence of indebtedness, certificate of interest or participation in any profit-sharing agreement, collateral trust certificate, reorganization certificate or subscription, transferable share, investment contract, voting trust certificate, certificate of deposit for a security, fractional undivided interest in oil, gas, or other mineral rights, or in general, any interest or instrument commonly known as a "security," or any certificate of interest or participation in, temporary or interim certificate for, receipt of, guarantee of, or warrant or right to subscribe to or to purchase any of the foregoing.

II. Initial Registration of Securities - The Securities Act of 1933

A. A company that wants to sell debt or stock in interstate offerings to the general public is required to register those securities with the SEC. Registration requires extensive disclosures about the company, management, and the intended use of the proceeds from the issue. The intent of the securities laws is, in part, to regulate the disclosure of financial information by firms issuing publicly traded securities.

B. Form S-1 is the basic registration form for new securities and it includes a list of required disclosures. The financial information includes a balance sheet dated within 90 days of the filing. Part 1 on Form S-1 is the prospectus that is supplied to each potential purchaser of the security.

    1. A prospectus describes the issuing company, the business operations and risks, the financial statements, and the expected use of the proceeds. The basic financial statements requirements are:

        a. Two years of balance sheets;

        b. Three years of income statements, statements of cash flow and statements of shareholders' equity;

        c. The financial statements must be audited;

        d. Prior statements are presented on a comparative basis;

        e. The SEC requires five years of selected financial information.

    2. Part 2 of Form S-1 includes information about the cost of issuing and distributing the security, more detailed information about the directors and officers and additional financial statement schedules.

C. Small registrations, under a certain monetary threshold or number of purchasers are considered to be private placements and are exempt from certain disclosures.

D. The offering process is diagrammed below:

> Issuer -> Underwriter -> Dealer -> Public

    1. The underwriter provides marking and distribution of the securities. The underwriter is often contractually obligated to sell the securities under one of the following arrangements:

        a. Firm commitment - the underwriter purchases the entire issue at a fixed price;

        b. Best efforts - the underwriter sells as many shares as possible;

      c. All or none - if the underwrite is unable to sell all (or a significant portion) then the issue may be canceled.

   2. Once the stock is issued, it may be traded over the counter by dealers or on an organized exchange.

III. Subsequent reporting of Securities - The Securities Exchange Act of 1934

  A. The 1934 Securities Exchange Act enacted reporting requirements for the purpose of fully disclosing relevant information about publicly traded firms. The SEC's reporting principles for information in the reports are found in Regulation S-X, Financial Reporting Releases (FRRs), and Staff Accounting Bulletins (SAB). Regulation S-X helps reduce redundancy in reporting by allowing for integrated disclosures whereby a company may satisfy certain Form 10-K disclosure requirements by referencing its shareholder annual report as long as that report includes the required disclosures. The following is a list of the most common required forms:

    1. Annual filing - Form 10-K;

    2. Quarterly filing - Form 10-Q;

    3. Report significant events affecting the company - Form 8-K;

    4. Proxy Statement. The report by which management requests the right to vote through proxy for shareholders at meetings.

  B. Filing deadlines. Filing deadlines depend on the size of the company. Company size is as follows:

    1. Large accelerated filer - a company with worldwide market value of outstanding voting and nonvoting common equity held by nonaffiliates of $700 million or more;

    2. Accelerated filer - a company with worldwide market value of outstanding voting and nonvoting common equity held by nonaffiliates that is $75 million or more but less than $700 million;

    3. Non-accelerated filer - a company with worldwide market value of outstanding voting and nonvoting common equity held by nonaffiliates less than $75 million.

Filing deadlines for filing after the reporting date are as follows		
Filer	10-K	10-Q
Large accelerated filer	60 days after fiscal year end	40 days after quarter end
Accelerated filer	75 days after fiscal year end	40 days after quarter end
Non-accelerated filer	90 days after fiscal year end	45 days after quarter end

  C. Form 10-K is the required vehicle for reporting annual financial information to the SEC. The 10-K is separated into four parts. The content of each part is outlined in the following chart:

Part I

1. Description of the business

   A. Risk factors

   B. Unresolved staff comments

2. Description of properties

3. Legal proceedings involving the company

4. Submission of matters to a vote of stockholders

Part II

5. Market price of common stock, dividends & stockholder matters

6. Selected financial data

7. Management's Discussion and Analysis (MD&A) of financial condition and results of operations

   A. Quantitative and qualitative disclosures about market risk

8. Financial statements and supplementary financial information

9. Change in disagreements with accountants on accounting and financial disclosure

   A. Controls and procedures

Part III

10. Directors and officers

11. Executive compensation and transactions with executives

12. Security ownership by certain beneficial owners and by management

13. Certain relationships and related-party transactions

14. Principal accountant fees and services

Part IV

15. Exhibits; Signatures; Certification

1. The SEC requires the Management's Discussion and Analysis (MD&A) to be included in its reporting and, as such, provides a discussion of important aspects of the firm from the viewpoint of management. This report covers the firm's financial condition, changes in financial condition, results of operations, liquidity, capital resources and operations, identifies trends and significant events and uncertainties. The discussion also includes information about the effects of inflation and changing prices in nonquantitative form, and explanation of significant or unusual events and uncertainties and their effect or expected effect on the firm's financial performance. Also, the firm's important accounting policies are discussed in the MD&A.

   a. Forward-looking or prospective information is included for the purpose of assessing future cash flows. Prospective information is useful to the financial statement user because it promotes understanding of events, circumstances, trends, and uncertainties when there are material trends and uncertainties. When material, prospective information is required to aid the analysis of long and short-term liquidity, capital resources, material changes in a line item on the financial statements, and any preliminary merger negotiations.

    b. Prospective information should be prepared in accordance with GAAP, using information that is consistent with the plans of the entity, and with due professional care so not to mislead the user of the financial statements. Prospective financial statements should disclose information as to the purpose of the statements, assumptions, and significant accounting policies.

  2. In general, SEC registrants must disclose more information to the SEC than in the annual reports to shareholders. For off-balance-sheet financing relationships, the SEC requires firms to disclose all contractual liabilities and contingent liabilities, whether or not they are recognized in the accounts.

D. Form 10-Q reports the quarterly information to the SEC within 45 days (nonaccelerated filer) of the end of the quarter. (Only the first three quarters are reported because the 10-K reports the annual information.) Large companies designated as accelerated filers must file within 40 days. Disclosures are less extensive than in the 10-K and include information for the specific quarter and year-to-date information.

  1. The quarterly report is intended to provide investors with an update since the last annual report. The 10-Q is not required to be audited, but must be reviewed by the independent auditor.

  2. The financial statements presented are:

    a. Balance sheet for the quarter and prior fiscal year end;

    b. Quarterly and year-to-date income statements for this quarter and the same period in the previous year;

    c. Cumulative year-to-date statements of cash flow for the current and prior fiscal years.

E. Form 8-K reports significant events affecting the company such as material impairment, bankruptcy, entry or termination of a definitive agreement, changes in the registrant's CPA, changes in control etc. These are all events that the public shareholder should be aware of, as the events are significant enough to influence decisions.

F. Proxy statements are materials sent to the shareholders for vote. Proxy materials can address things such as election of directors, changes in the corporate charter, issuance of new securities, plans for a major business combination etc. Frequently these items are voted on during the shareholders annual meeting, but sometimes these matters need to be addressed during interim periods, in which case the proxy materials regarding the issue must be circulated.

IV. Corporate Governance

A. The Foreign Corrupt Practices Act of 1977 prohibits bribes of foreign governmental or political officials for the purpose of securing contracts or business. It requires publicly held companies to maintain an adequate system of internal control.

B. The Sarbanes-Oxley Act of 2002 (SOX) contains provisions to enhance corporate governance and to mitigate financial accounting abuses. A few of the significant provisions related to financial reporting are presented below.

  1. The SEC requires registrants to have annual audits of their financial statements. The auditing firm must be registered with the Public Company Accounting Oversight Board (PCAOB), a private-sector organization created by the 2002 Sarbanes-Oxley Act (the SEC has oversight authority for the PCAOB). The PCAOB provides oversight of registered auditing firms.

  2. Auditors are prohibited from providing nonaudit services to audit clients.

3. Audit committees are required to be composed of nonmanagement members of the Board of Directors, and the chair has to have financial experience.

4. Annual filing must include a management's report on the internal controls. This report must attest to the existence and effectiveness of the company's internal controls over corporate reporting.

5. There are Increased penalties for fraud and white-collar crime. Willfully failing to maintain audit records for 5 years is a felony. Criminal charges can be brought against corporate officers who fail to certify financial reports or who willfully certify statements they know do not comply with SOX.

Balance Sheet/Statement of Financial Position

This lesson presents an overview of the balance sheet.

After studying this lesson you should be able to :

1. *Identify the measurement bases used to measure the items on the Balance Sheet.*

2. *Distinguish between a current and noncurrent asset or liability.*

3. *Identify the items reported on the Balance Sheet .*

I. **The Balance Sheet**

A. **Background on the Balance Sheet**

1. The statement of financial position is another name for the balance sheet;

2. It is the only statement dated as of a point in time. The title consists of three lines:

ABC Company

Balance Sheet

As of December 31, 20x4

---

3. Only asset, liability and owners' equity accounts are represented (and related contra (-) and adjunct (+) accounts) and as such the balance sheet reports the entity's financial position at a point in time;

4. Total assets = total liabilities + owners' equity;

5. Many different measurement (valuation) bases are represented - total assets of $10 million is not really $10 million of the types of same dollars. Most reported account balances do not represent current market value;

6. The balance sheet provides information useful in assessing the entity's financial strengths and weaknesses, especially risk (relative proportion of debt to equity, for example), and the allocation of assets;

7. A classified balance sheet distinguishes current and noncurrent assets and liabilities which helps users assess liquidity;

8. Account balances reflect only the transaction-based U.S. GAAP recognition and measurement system. A transaction or event is required for recognition of all items. The balance sheet does not report all assets of the firm - only the assets acquired through a transaction. For example, internally generated goodwill is not recorded (recognized), and the recorded value of other intangibles such as trademarks may be significantly less than their current value.

B. **Factors limiting the interpretation of balance sheet information**

1. Assets and liabilities are acquired at different times and are not affected in the same way by inflation and specific price-level changes. This causes the recorded value of these accounts to be different from their current or real value and makes comparisons difficult;

2. Several different measurement bases are used (historical cost, depreciated historical cost, market (fair) value, realizable value, present value) which compromises the comparability characteristic of accounting information;

3. Consolidation of subsidiaries compounds the difficulties with interpretation of account balances when the parent and subsidiaries use different accounting methods;

4. The value of many assets is derived primarily through use (exceptions are investments, receivables); this value may differ considerably from book value and market value. How does the user really interpret book value when book value and market value are different?

C. **Measurement Bases for Balance Sheet Valuation** -- Because so many different measurement bases are represented in the balance sheet, the totals for assets and liabilities are difficult to interpret and compare across firms.

> **Definition:**
> *A Measurement Base*: This is the attribute of an account being measured and reported.

1. **Historical Cost or Other Historical Value** -- Some accounts are measured and reported at a fixed, unchanging historical amount. Examples include land, some investments, cash, prepaids, many current liabilities, contributed capital accounts, and treasury stock.

2. **Depreciated, Amortized, or Depleted Historical Cost** -- Other accounts reflect the remaining portion of a fixed unchanging historical amount. In some cases, the original cost or other relevant amount is maintained in one account, with a contra or adjunct account being subtracted from or added to that account for the purpose of reporting net book value (carrying value). Examples include property, plant and equipment; intangibles; natural resources.

3. **Market Value, a Type of Current Value** -- Examples include investments in marketable securities (stocks and bonds) for which the holding firm does not have significant influence and does not intend to hold to maturity (in the case of bonds). "Fair value," often used synonymously with "market value," is the selling price for assets and amount currently required to retire a liability. These are "exit" values rather than "entry" values.

4. **Net Realizable Value** -- This is another type of current value but one that is less in amount than the historical value. Net realizable value is the amount the firm expects to receive from the sale or collection of the item. Examples include accounts receivable and inventories.

5. **Present Value** -- The present value of a future cash flow is its discounted value. This is the primary measurement basis for noncurrent debt (mainly bonds and long-term notes). The present value is the measure of current sacrifice when extinguishing the debt at the balance sheet date.

6. **Aggregate of More than One Valuation Basis** -- Retained earnings-net income reflects all measurement bases through revenue and expense recognition.

D. **Classification of Assets and Liabilities** -- Assets and liabilities are classified as current or noncurrent. US GAAP defines only current items; the noncurrent classification represents items that are not classified as current. The purpose of this classification is to distinguish items that will affect the firm's liquidity in the near term (one year) from those that will not. Classification helps financial statement users assess the ability of a firm to pay its debts in the near future. Owners' equity accounts are not classified because they do not represent resources or obligations.

1. **Current Asset (CA)**

   a. An asset expected to be realized in cash or to be consumed or sold during the normal operating cycle, or within one year of the balance sheet date, whichever is longer.

    b. The operating cycle is the period of time from purchasing inventory to paying for the payable incurred on inventory purchase to the sale of goods to the collection of receivable and then to purchasing inventory all over again.

    c. For most firms the operating cycle is less than one year, but some firms, such as construction and engineering companies, have operating cycles exceeding one year. Construction in process, an inventory account found in construction firms' balance sheets, is a current asset even though the constructed asset may require several years to complete.

2. **Current Liability (CL)**

    a. A liability expected to be extinguished through the use of current assets or by the incurrence of other current liabilities.

    b. The "incurrence of other CL" part of the definition means that CL that are continuously refinanced (rolled over) by replacing them with other CL due later (but within one year of the balance sheet date) must still be classified as CL, even though no CA will be used to extinguish them in the year after the balance sheet date.

> **Example:**
> A note payable due 3/1/x2 is expected to be refinanced continuously on a 4-month basis, each time substituting a new 4-month note for the old. This note should be classified as a CL in the 12/31/x1 balance sheet because there is no certainty that the firm will not use CA in the next year to pay off the debt. The debtor firm cannot control the creditor who may decide not to refinance. Interest rates may increase substantially changing the strategy of the debtor firm. However, if the new note is due later than 12/31/x2 then the original note is classified as NCL.
>
> Only if the firm refinances an otherwise current liability with a noncurrent liability before the balance sheet is issued (or is available to be issued) can the original liability be reclassified as noncurrent. "Refinance" here includes:
>
> - Actually replacing the liability with a new one due beyond one year from the balance sheet.
>
> - Entering into an irrevocable agreement to do so with a capable creditor.
>
> - Issuing stock to extinguish the debt.

3. **Noncurrent Assets (NCA) and Noncurrent Liabilities (NCL)** -- Defined by default as assets and liabilities that are not current. The current/noncurrent distinction is important because firms would rather report more CA and less CL to appear more liquid and less risky in the short run. There is great incentive to move CLs into the NCL category, for example.

4. **Ratios for Liquidity**

    a. Current ratio = CA/CL. This ratio is frequently used as a measure of liquidity. Many analysts use a minimum value of 2 when evaluating firms because the extra CA provides a buffer for uncertainty, and CA includes inventories and prepaids that are not considered very liquid.

> **Study Tip:**
> The exam may ask the effect of certain transactions on ratios. Analyze the effect by determining whether the numerator or denominator has experienced the greater percentage change.

    b. Quick or acid-test ratio = (cash +- short term investments +- AR)/CL - this should be at least 1.00. This ratio provides a more rigorous test of liquidity.

    c. Effect of transactions on ratios.

> **Example:**
> Assume the current ratio exceeds 1. What is the effect on the current ratio of paying an account payable? Answer: both CA (cash) and CL (accts pay) decrease by the same amount. The ratio increases because the denominator falls by a greater percentage.

E. Balance Sheet Account Types by Category

1. For balance sheet reporting, assets and liabilities are typically reported in order from most liquid to least liquid. For example, current assets begin with cash and cash equivalents, then short-term investments, receivables, inventories and finally prepaids.

2. **Current Assets**

   a. Cash, cash equivalents, short-term investments, accounts receivable, other receivables, inventories, prepaids.

   b. Cash is the only account for which the following are the same:

      i. Nominal value;

      ii. Market value;

      iii. Realizable value;

      iv. Present value;

      v. Future value.

3. **Noncurrent Assets**

   a. Long-term investments, property, plant and equipment, intangibles, "other" assets (including long-term prepaids);

   b. Goodwill is by far the largest intangible in terms of dollar amount for many firms and equals the excess of the purchase price paid for another business over the market value of its net assets. Only when a firm is purchased by another is goodwill recognized in the balance sheet of the purchaser. Internally, generated goodwill is expensed.

4. **Current Liabilities** -- Accounts payable, accrued liabilities, unearned revenue, income tax payable, notes payable, current portion of long-term debt (the portion due within one year of the balance sheet date).

5. **Noncurrent Liabilities** -- Notes payable, bonds payable, lease liabilities, pension liabilities, postretirement health care liabilities, deferred taxes. (Although this item can appear in all four possible classifications (i.e., CA, NCA, CL, and NCL), the NCL category is by far the largest.)

6. **Owners' Equity - Two Main Types**

   a. Contributed capital (common stock, preferred stock, contributed capital in excess of par), treasury stock (a contra account);

   b. Retained earnings (total net income to date less total dividends to date).

F. Reporting Within the Balance Sheet -- the use of contra accounts (-) and "adjunct" accounts (+); valuation accounts.

1. **Contra and Adjunct Accounts**

   a. Accounts can be accompanied by contra and adjunct accounts;

b. A contra account has a balance opposite that of the associated account in terms of debit and credit. Contras can be debit or credit balances, and can be considered valuation accounts or merely accumulations of items such as depreciation and amortization over time;

c. An adjunct account has a balance that is the same as that of the associated account in terms of debit and credit. An adjunct can have either a debit or a credit balance. An adjunct account is added whereas a contra is subtracted.

2. **Valuation Accounts**

    a. A valuation account is one used to increase or decrease the book value of an item to a measure of current value.

    b. Not all contra or adjunct accounts are valuation accounts, but all valuation accounts are contras or adjuncts.

3. **Examples**

Example:

1. Accumulated depreciation is a contra account to property, plant, and equipment but is not a valuation account because net book value in this case is not equal to market value.

Property, plant and equipment	$40,000	(cost)
Accumulated depreciation	(5,000)	
Net book value	$35,000	(undepreciated cost)

2. Allowance for uncollectible accounts is a contra account to accounts receivable and is a valuation account because net accounts receivable is an approximation to net realizable value, a measure of current value.

Accounts receivable	$60,000	(sales value)
Allowance for doubtful accounts	(8,000)	
Net book value	$52,000	(net realizable value)

3. Valuation allowance for investments in marketable securities can be a contra or adjunct account and is a valuation account because it decreases or increases the net book value of the investment to current market value. The account is a contra if the market value is less than original cost, and is an adjunct if the market value exceeds original cost.

Investments in marketable securities	$30,000	(cost)
Valuation allowance	4,000	
Market value	$34,000	(market value)

4. Bond premium and discount are adjunct and contra accounts respectively but are not valuation accounts because the net bond liability is generally not equal to market value.

Bonds payable	$100,000	(face value)
Bond premium	3,000	
Net bond liability	$103,000	

G. The Balance Sheet and Firm Valuation

1. The total owners' equity of most publicly traded firms (also known as net assets or A - L) is significantly less than the market value of the firm because investors place a higher value on firms that include the investors' expectation of future earnings. Firms are usually worth much more than the sum of their individual net assets, even at market value.

2. There are three important valuations for a firm:

   a. **Total OE or net assets** -- This is the amount determined by current US GAAP and is found in the balance sheet;

   b. **Market value of net identifiable assets** -- The amount of cash that would remain after selling all identifiable assets (including identifiable intangibles) and paying off all liabilities. This amount is also called the firm's "split up" or liquidation value. To determine this amount, the firm must have its assets appraised;

   c. **Total value of the firm** -- Its "market capitalization" - the total value of the firm's outstanding stock. For publicly traded firms, this value can be found on Internet financial sites.

3. The difference between total OE and the market value of net identifiable assets is caused by identifiable assets and liabilities with market values different from their book values. Examples include investments and natural resources.

4. The difference between a firm's market capitalization and the market value of net identifiable assets is goodwill - an amount that cannot be identified with any individual recorded asset. However, goodwill is recorded for accounting purposes only when one firm purchases all or a controlling interest of another firm.

H. Market capitalization -- The market capitalization is generally many times recorded OE in amount. The purpose of the balance sheet is not to provide a firm's market value, but rather to provide information that is a starting point for valuing a firm and assessing its riskiness. The relative investment in plant assets, natural resources, investments, and in affiliated companies, along with the ratio of debt to equity provides investors with valuable information about the financial structure and direction of the firm. The trend in balance sheet values over time also provides useful information.

1. In addition, the balance sheet is largely historical, and is limited to transactions that have already taken place. It is not the responsibility of financial statements to provide current value. Rather, current value is a constantly changing amount based on investors' perceptions in the market at the time. In sum, the information in the balance sheet and other financial statement information is an input to market valuation, not the other way around. Stock prices react to changes in financial statement information and other information.

I. Debt disclosures -- These are perhaps the most important items found in the balance sheet, dollar for dollar. They indicate a quantifiable financial risk faced by the firm in the future.

J. Control and Subsidiary Accounts

1. The accounts reside in the ledger. The general ledger contains all accounts to be used in preparing the balance sheet. Some of these accounts are called **control** accounts because they report the aggregate balance of several subsidiary accounts.

> **Example:**
> The accounts receivable (AR) control account balance (in the general ledger) is the sum of the subsidiary AR account balances. For example, a firm has 100 subsidiary AR accounts, each one for a different customer. The sum of the 100 subsidiary AR balances equals the balance in the control AR account balance, which is reported on the balance sheet.

2. Control and subsidiary accounts are used for any account that consists of many individual accounts. Inventory, plant assets (property, plant ,and equipment) and accounts payable are examples.

3. A chart of accounts typically assigns account numbers to accounts for use in computerized information systems. For example, assets may be assigned numbers 100-199, liabilities 200-250 and so forth. Cash might be assigned the number 100, with AR control assigned number 104. Each account in the AR subsidiary ledger then could be numbered 104-1, 104-2 etc.

K. Accounting Cycle Review

1. The periodic accounting process leading to the preparation of financial statements is called the accounting cycle. The cycle steps used by a firm are specific to the information technology applied. The following is a representative list, in chronological order.

   a. Analyze relevant source documents (e.g., sales invoices) and record journal entries in a journal, a temporary listing of accounts affected and the amount by which they are to be changed by transaction, event, or adjustment.

   b. Post (distribute) the information from the journal to the accounts in the ledger, on a periodic basis. Only after posting, the account balances are updated.

   c. Record adjusting journal entries at the end of the accounting period. These journal entries record changes in resources and obligations not signaled by a new transaction or event. Examples include accrual of wages expense from the last payday to the end of the fiscal period, expiration of prepaids, and recognition of estimated expenses such as depreciation and warranty expense. These journal entries are also posted to the accounts.

   d. Prepare trial balances. Some firms prepare a trial balance, which is a test of the equality of the sum of debit account balances and credit account balances, before and after adjusting journal entries. A trial balance is a quick test for the presence of an error in recording or posting.

   e. Prepare the income statement, balance sheet, and statement of cash flows (often in that order). The first two are prepared directly from the ledger accounts or trial balance; the cash flow statement requires additional analysis.

   f. Close the temporary account balances (revenues, expenses, gains, losses) setting them to zero, and transfer the net income amount to retained earnings.

2. Throughout the accounting cycle, U.S. GAAP is applied primarily at the two journal entry steps (1 and 3), and in preparing the financial statements and note disclosures. Otherwise, the cycle is largely mechanical and usually not performed manually.

L. Special Journals

1. Similar to the control-subsidiary account distinction for ledger accounts, firms may use special journals, and a general journal. High volume similar transactions are recorded in special journals (for example, the sales journal) with very infrequent transactions being recorded in the general journal. Special journals facilitate the review and control of similar transactions (all sales, all cash receipts etc.).

2. **Advantages of Special Journals**

   a. Special journals simplify the recording of journal entries because each recording affects the same accounts each time. Your check register is an example - it is a cash receipts/payments journal. Each entry you make always affects cash, and you need only write into the register the other item affected (utility bill for example).

   b. The number of postings also is reduced because only the sum of the changes in the special journal accounts for the period need to be posted to the respective accounts.

    c. Separation of duties for improved internal control is fostered with the use of special journals. Only particular individuals may be authorized to access the sales journal for example, but not the cash receipts journal, or the general journal.

3. **Sales Journal as an Example of a Special Journal** -- A sales journal for a firm might record all cash and credit sales and have the following six columns:

Date	Customer	Invoice #	Dr. Cash	Dr. AR	Cr. Sales

Each line entered into the journal is a complete journal entry. Cash sales use all columns except for the Dr. AR column, and credit sales use all columns except for the Dr. Cash column. Special journals dispense with the "flush left" formatting for debits and "indenting right" for credits.

4. Periodic posting is as follows:

    a. Sum of the Dr. Cash column for a period is posted to the cash account;

    b. Sum of the Dr. AR column for a period is posted to the AR control account while each individual amount in that column is posted to the appropriate AR subsidiary account;

    c. Sum of the Cr. Sales account is posted to the sales account.

5. Posting is usually performed within the computerized system and is mechanical from the user's point of view. Posting references enables cross-referencing between journal and ledger. For example, the posting to the AR control account from the special journal might indicate the location of the total from the sales journal within the information system.

Income Statement

This lesson presents an overview of the balance sheet.

After studying this lesson, you should be able to:

1. *List and define the components of the Income Statement .*

2. *Identify the difference between economic income and accounting income.*

3. *Present the structure and components of the Income Statement .*

I. Background

A. Definition of Revenues, Expenses, Gains, and Losses

Definitions:
Revenues: Revenues represent increases in net assets or settlements of liabilities by providing goods and services. Revenues are related to the company's primary business operations.

Expenses: Expenses represent decreases in net assets or incurred liabilities through the provision of goods or services. Expenses are related to the company's primary business operations. Expenses provide benefit to the firm. Losses do not.

Gains: Gains represent increases in equity or net assets from peripheral or incidental transactions.

Losses: Losses represent decreases in equity or net assets from peripheral or incidental transactions. Losses do not provide value or benefit to the firm.

B. All-Inclusive vs. Current Operating Performance Views of the Income Statement

1. **All-Inclusive Income Statement --** The current income statement under GAAP is mostly an all-inclusive one in which essentially all revenues, expenses, gains, and losses are shown on the income statement and included in the net income calculation.

    a. **Exceptions --** There are exceptions to all-inclusive income statements.

        i. **Prior Period Adjustments --** Prior period adjustments are shown on the Statement of Retained Earnings and are the correction of accounting errors affecting income of prior years.

        ii. **Other Comprehensive Income Items (OCI)**

            1. Foreign currency translation adjustments;

            2. Unrealized holding gains and losses on securities available for sale;

            3. Pension and other postretirement benefit plan cost adjustments;

            4. Certain deferred derivative gains and losses.

        iii. The OCI items above are disclosed in the statement of comprehensive income discussed in a later lesson. The different income amounts for a period are related as follows:

Net income + Other comprehensive income = Comprehensive income

iv. Retrospective changes in accounting principle affecting income. These are treated as direct adjustments to retained earnings.

2. Current Operating Performance Income Statement

a. At the other end of the spectrum is the current operating performance approach to income statement preparation which would limit the income statement to normal, recurring items.

b. Many other items would be run through owners' equity and thus escape the attention of financial statement users who rely more heavily on the income statement.

c. Due to enhanced opportunities to manipulate net income, the all-inclusive approach was selected over the current operating approach for income statement presentation purposes.

C. Concepts of Income -- The accountant and economist have different ways to measure income. There are many different ways to approach the problem. GAAP takes an objective, arm's-length transaction approach to measurement and recognition.

1. Definition

> **Definition:**
> *Accounting income*: Revenues less expenses plus gains less losses.

a. That is, accounting income reflects recorded transactions, events and adjustments.

b. For many assets and liabilities, changes in market value are not recognized until substantiated by a transaction between willing parties.

c. Investments with readily determinable market values are an exception. These investments (trading securities, securities available for sale) are reported at market value. Moreover, inventories are written down to lower of cost or market.

2. Definition

> **Definition:**
> *Economic income*: The change in the net worth of a business enterprise during an accounting period.

a. The net worth of a business enterprise is described as the fair market value (FMV) of net assets (rather than total owners' equity per GAAP).

b. Thus, the FMV of a business on December 31 of a given year is compared with the FMV of the business on January 1 of that year to determine economic income.

c. Net income for the period would include all changes in FMV of assets and liabilities during the period.

d. Any investments by owners would be added and any dividends paid or treasury stock purchased would be subtracted, when making this calculation.

Market Value of Net Assets at Jan. 1	+	Net Income for the Period (including increases in FMV)	+	Owner Investments	−	Dividends and Stock Repurchases	=	Market Value at Dec. 31

e. The use of market values and other price level changes takes into account the changes in the value of the firm's assets and liabilities and goes beyond the recording of transactions. However, because GAAP is concerned with reliability of information, transaction-based reporting is the current model used.

II. Structure of the Statement

A. Continuing Operations and Other Items of Income -- The income statement is divided roughly into two portions.

1. **Top Portion --** The top portion includes routinely occurring items and other items that are appropriately included in income from continuing operations.

   a. The subtotal income from continuing operations is used by investors as a broad measure of operating income.

   b. GAAP is very loose in the top portion of the statement with regard to presentation.

   c. Income from continuing operations includes all income items other than those in the bottom portion of the income statement.

2. **Bottom Portion --** The bottom portion includes items that are specifically defined by GAAP as being unrelated to continuing operations.

   a. These items are not representative of the firm's ability to generate income and are unique items that will not be repeated. They are, however, components of total income.

   b. GAAP is very specific about the measurement and presentation of items in the bottom portion.

   c. Discontinued operations are presented at the bottom portion of the income statement. Discontinued operations are major components of an entity that are either sold or planned to be sold and thus are no longer part of continuing operations. A later lesson will discuss this item in detail.

B. Sample Income Statement -- A generalized income statement appears below.

	ABX Company
	Income Statement
	For the Year Ended December 31, 20x0
−	Net sales
	Cost of goods sold
=	Gross margin
−	Operating expenses
+	Miscellaneous revenues and gains
−	Miscellaneous expenses and losses
±	Unusual or infrequent items
=	Income from continuing operations before tax
−	Less income tax expense
=	Income from Continuing Operations
±	Income from Discontinued Operations (net of tax)
=	Net income

C. Presentation Requirements -- There is no prescribed way of displaying the items above income from continuing operations. For example, some firms provide a subtotal called "operating income" which would appear before miscellaneous items, but such disclosure is not mandated by GAAP.

D. Presentation Order -- Below income from continuing operations, the prescribed presentation is the order as shown above.

E. Income Tax Expense -- Income tax expense is attributable only to income from continuing operations. The tax effects of items below continuing operations are shown along with the item itself in a process called *intraperiod tax allocation.*

F. Multiple Disclosures

1. The total income tax effect for a given year is accomplished through multiple disclosures. The items for which intraperiod tax allocation is applied include:

   a. Discontinued operations;

   b. Other comprehensive income items;

   c. Adjustment for retroactive accounting principle changes;

   d. Prior period adjustments.

2. The first item is reported in the income statement; the third is reported in a special OE account called accumulated other comprehensive income, and the last two are reported in the retained earnings statement.

> **Example:**
> Intraperiod tax allocation and discontinued operations disclosure. An loss on discontinued operations before tax is $12,000, and the associated tax rate is 30%. The disclosure in the income statement below continuing operations would appear as:
>
> Less discontinued operations, net of $3,600 tax savings........$8,400

G. Intraperiod Tax Allocation -- Pertains to the tax effects for only one year. It is the allocation of the total tax consequence for that year among income from continuing operations, and the four items listed above. This process contrasts with *interperiod* tax allocation, which records a period's total tax consequence in current taxes payable and deferred tax accounts. Interperiod tax allocation is a much more extensive process and is covered in another lesson.

III. Unusual or Infrequent Income Items

A. GAAP requires that unusual or infrequent items be separately reported if material, as a component of income from continuing operations. Note that there is no longer a category for "extraordinary items" at the bottom of the income statement. Any unusual or infrequent items (such as an impairment loss) is show as a component of income from continuing operations.

IV. Formats Leading to Income from Continuing Operations -- Income from continuing operations includes the revenues, expenses, gains, and losses that are normal and recurring. In addition to including those items that are specifically related to primary business operations, income from continuing operations also includes those revenues, expenses, gains, and losses that are the result of incidental or peripheral activities. The presentation of income from continuing operations follows one of two formats, the single-step format or the multiple-step format. Note the required per share disclosures shown at the bottom of the income statements. Earnings per share are discussed in detail in later lessons.

A. Formats in Practice

1. Two formats have become accepted in practice: single-step and multiple step statements. There are many variants of each.

   a. Both provide the same information although the multiple-step format provides more subtotals and organization.

   b. Income from continuing operations and net income are the same amounts regardless of the format used.

   c. The format differences affect only the ordering in calculating income from continuing operations.

2. The presentation below income from continuing operations is mandated by U.S. GAAP and is the same regardless of how the top portion is presented.

B. Single Step Format -- The single-step format involves a presentation of income from continuing operations that is largely based on a single comparison. Total revenues and gains are compared with total expenses and losses in the single-step format. Below is a single-step illustration for the Wolf Company.

Wolf Company Income Statement For the Year Ended December 31, 20xx		
Revenues and Gains:		
Net Sales	$1,000,000	
Rent Revenue	10,000	
Investment Revenue	20,000	
Gain on Sale of Operational Assets	30,000	1,060,000
Expenses and Losses:		
Cost of Goods Sold	400,000	
Distribution Expenses	10,000	
General and Administrative Expenses	20,000	
Depreciation Expense	30,000	
Interest Expense	10,000	
Loss on Sale of Investments	20,000	(490,000)
Unusual or Infrequent Gains and Losses:		
Casualty Loss	(100,000)	
Gain on Sale of Real Estate	200,000	100,000
Pretax Income from Continuing Operations		670,000
Income Tax Expense		(201,000)
Income from Continuing Operations		469,000
Income from Discontinued Operations		
Results of Operations (less income tax expense of $30,000)	70,000	
Loss on Disposal of Business Segment (less income tax savings of 60,000)	(140,000)	(70,000)
Net Income		399,000
Earnings per Share:		
Income from Continuing Operations		4.69
Income from Discontinued Operations		(.70)
Net Income		$3.99

C. Multiple Step Format -- The multiple-step format involves a presentation of income from continuing operations that includes multiple comparisons of revenues, expenses, gains, and losses. In doing so, the reader is provided with the operating margin of the company, which is

the excess of operating revenues over operating expenses. In other words, these revenues and expenses are directly tied to the company's primary business operations. Beyond the operating margin, the incidental or peripheral gains and losses are shown in the presentation of income from continuing operations. Below is a multiple-step illustration for the Wolf Company.

Wolf Company Income Statement For the Year Ended December 31, 20xx		
Sales Revenue	$1,100,000	
Less Sales Returns and Allowances	(100,000)	
Net Sales		1,000,000
Cost of Goods Sold		(400,000)
Gross Margin		600,000
Operating Expenses:		
Distribution Expenses	10,000	
General and Administrative Expenses	20,000	
Depreciation Expense	30,000	(60,000)
Operating Margin		540,000
Other Revenues and Gains:		
Rent Revenue	10,000	
Investment Revenue	20,000	
Gain on Sale of Operational Assets	30,000	60,000
Other Expenses and Losses:		
Interest Expense	10,000	
Loss on Sale of Investments	20,000	(30,000)
Unusual or Infrequent Gains and Losses:		
Casualty Loss	(100,000)	
Gain on Sale of Real Estate	200,000	100,000
Pretax Income from Continuing Operations		670,000
Income Tax Expense		(201,000)
Income from Continuing Operations		469,000
Income from Discontinued Operations:		
Results of Operations (less income tax expense of $30,000)	70,000	
Loss on Disposal of Business Segment (less income tax savings of $60,000)	(140,000)	(70,000)
Net Income		6399,000
Earnings Per Share:		
Income from Continuing Operations		4.69
Income from Discontinued Operations		(.70)
Net Income		$3.99

Statement of Comprehensive Income

This lesson presents a discussion of the Statement of Comprehensive Income.

After studying this lesson you should be able to:

1. *Define comprehensive income.*

2. *List the components of other comprehensive income.*

3. *Identify the reporting alternatives for comprehensive income.*

I. **Background** -- In June 2011, the FASB issued ASU Topic 220 that changed the presentation of Comprehensive Income effective for fiscal years beginning after December 15, 2011.

> **Definition:**
> *Comprehensive income*: Is the sum of (1) net income, and (2) other comprehensive income. CI = NI + OCI

A. The new standard, ASU Topic 220, has aligned the U.S. GAAP presentation of Comprehensive Income with IFRS. That is, the significant change in the new standard is to permit only two ways to present comprehensive income—which is consistent with what is required by IFRS.

B. The requirement to disclose comprehensive income does not affect the computation of net income.

C. U.S. GAAP requires the disclosure of comprehensive income in a financial report. This disclosure can be accomplished in one of two ways:

  1. **Single statement of comprehensive income** -- This alternative presents the components of profit or loss (net income) within this single statement leading to net income as a subtotal. Displaying the other comprehensive income items leads to total comprehensive income.

  2. **Two statements** -- A separate income statement is presented (and as such it becomes part of a complete set of financial statements) immediately before the statement of comprehensive income. The net income amount resulting from the first statement is used as the beginning amount for the second statement, which then reports the other comprehensive income items leading to comprehensive income.

D. The companies choosing the two-statement approach have the option to begin the second statement with or without net income.

E. **Comprehensive income** -- Net income is not replaced by comprehensive income. The purpose of requiring the reporting of comprehensive income is to report the net change in equity (other than from transactions with owners) in a single amount and to provide a more complete picture of the total earnings of the firm for a period. This reporting contributes to the objective of reporting an "all inclusive" income amount.

II. **Comprehensive Income Defined**

A. Comprehensive income was designed to report the change in net assets during the period from all sources other than from transactions with owners acting as owners. There are two components of comprehensive income:

  1. Net Income;

2. "Other" Comprehensive Income.

3. It is the second category that causes comprehensive income to differ from net income. "Other" comprehensive income items are not currently recognized in net income. They are recorded directly as increases or decreases in owners' equity.

III. "Other" Comprehensive Income Items (OCI)

A. The following items are items included in the second category above, that is, they are included in comprehensive income but not in income:

1. Unrealized gains and losses on securities available for sale (AFS);

2. Unrecognized pension and postretirement benefit cost and gains. Currently, GAAP does not recognize all changes in these liabilities and assets immediately in income. Rather, some are recognized in other comprehensive income;

3. Foreign currency translation adjustments are changes in the value of foreign currency and accounts measured in foreign currency;

4. Certain deferred gains and losses from derivatives.

B. OCI items are typically reported net of tax. Alternatively, firms may report each item on a pretax basis with the net aggregate income tax effect reported as a separate item.

C. Comprehensive income does not include the following:

1. Retrospective effects of changes in accounting principle;

2. Prior period adjustments.

D. The above two items are both reported as adjustments to retained earnings. Therefore, comprehensive income accounts for most but not all non-owner changes in owners' equity.

IV. Reporting Comprehensive Income -- The following two examples of formats for reporting comprehensive income use assumed values.

Example: Separate statement of comprehensive income:

ABX Inc.

Statement of Comprehensive Income

For the Year Ended December 31, 20x7

Net income	$24,000
Other comprehensive income, net of tax	
Net unrealized holding loss on AFS	($7,000)
Unrealized pension cost adjustment	(2,000)
Other comprehensive income	(9,000)
Comprehensive income	$15,000

Comprehensive income is the sum of net income and other comprehensive income.

See the following example.

Example: Combined statement of income and comprehensive income: For this illustration, only the lower half of the income statement is shown.

ABX Inc.

Statement of Income and Comprehensive Income

For the Year Ended December 31, 20x7

Income from continuing operations	$14,000
Discontinued Operations, net of tax	10,000
Net income	$24,000
Other comprehensive income, net of tax	
Net unrealized holding loss on AFS	($7,000)
Unrealized pension cost adjustment	(2,000)
Other comprehensive income	(9,000)
Comprehensive income	$15,000

Comprehensive income is the sum of net income and other comprehensive income.

V. Accumulated Other Comprehensive Income (AOCI)

A. Accumulated other comprehensive income (AOCI) is the amount carried over from the previous period, and then either increased or decreased during the current period. This total is the running total of other comprehensive income items through the balance sheet date. Irrespective of the reporting option chosen for comprehensive income, U.S. GAAP requires that the total of other comprehensive income be separately displayed in the owners'-equity section of the balance sheet in an account with a title such as AOCI. AOCI is an owners'-equity (OE) account.

B. In addition, the accumulated balances of each individual component of other comprehensive income (OCI) must be reported. This information can appear in the balance sheet, statement of owners' equity, or footnotes. This disclosure allows the user to understand the changes in individual components of other comprehensive income.

C. Both net income and other comprehensive income items (OCI) occur each year and together yield comprehensive income. Net income is closed to retained earnings and OCI is closed to AOCI each year. Both retained earnings and AOCI are OE accounts.

D. Think of OCI as a separate but parallel "income" track, along with net income. "Net income is to retained earnings as OCI is to AOCI."

E. An item recognized in OCI one year may be recognized in net income in a later year. To avoid double counting in OE, the OCI item from the previous year is removed from AOCI. This is called a reclassification adjustment. The entity must disclose the reclassification adjustments and the effect of the reclassification adjustment on NI and OCI.

See the following example.

Example:
A firm recognizes a $5,000 unrealized gain on an AFS investment in year 1 OCI. In year 2, the AFS investment is sold for a $5,000 gain (recognized in net income causing retained earnings to increase by $5,000). At the end of year 2, the $5,000 unrealized gain from year 1 in AOCI is removed by reducing AOCI by $5,000 (the reclassification adjustment). The gain in OCI is "reclassified" as a gain recognized in net income. Without the reclassification adjustment, total OE would count the $5,000 twice. Reclassification adjustments are reported in the footnotes.

Statement of Changes in Equity

This lesson presents an overview of the Statement of Changes in Equity.

After studying this lesson, you should be able to:

1. *Identify the components included in the statement of owners' equity.*

2. *Construct a statement of owners' equity.*

I. **Background**

    A. Firms are required to report the changes in their owners'-equity (OE) accounts for the period. Supplementary schedules or footnotes may be used but often large firms report the Statement of Changes in Equity to meet this requirement.

        1. Other titles for this statement include Statement of Changes in Owners' Equity, Owners' Equity Statement, Statement of Shareholders' Equity, and Statement of Owners' Equity. Some firms prefer to only report a separate statement of retained earnings and report the other changes in the notes.

        2. In addition to the changes in OE accounts for the period, firms must also report the changes in the number of shares of equity securities. This information is the counterpart to some of the account changes in the statement of changes in equity, but measured in shares. Some firms report the share information in a column adjacent to the changes in the relevant accounts measured in dollars.

    B. The Statement of Changes in Equity effectively expands the OE section of the balance sheet by listing all the changes in those accounts, explaining how the beginning balance increased or decreased in deriving the ending balance. Reporting investments by owners and distributions to owners are important aspects of this disclosure. The statement is dated like the Income Statement and Statement of Cash Flows - for a period.

    C. The format of the statement varies.

II. **Format of the Statement --** The most common formats encountered are the vertical and horizontal formats.

III. **Vertical format --** In this format, each OE account is reported in a separate column of a spreadsheet-type document. The following is an example of this format for a single period.

    See the following example.

Business Enterprises, Inc.

Statement of Changes in Equity

For the Year Ended December 31, 20x2

	Common Stock	Contributed Capital in Excess of Par	Accumulated Other Comprehensive Income	Retained Earnings	Treasury Stock	Total OE
Balance, 1/1/x2	$40,000	$180,000	$20,000	$230,000	($30,000)	$440,000
Issued stock	5,000	30,000				35,000
Issued stock dividend	2,000	11,000		(13,000)		
Purchased treasury stock					(20,000)	(20,000)
Declared cash dividend				(25,000)		(25,000)
Net income				90,000		90,000
Other comprehensive income			(6,000)			(6,000)
Balance, 12/31/x2	$47,000	$221,000	$14,000	$282,000	($50,000)	$514,000

A. Each column reconciles the beginning and ending account balance for one account by disclosing all the changes in the account during the period. Total OE is also shown as a column. This format allows a check of accuracy by comparing total OE computed as (1) the sum of each transaction affecting OE, and (2) the sum of individual OE account balances.

B. In most cases, each event causing a change in OE requires at least two entries per row (more than one column affected). The total OE column is usually but not always affected. The stock dividend, for example, has no effect on total OE. Later lessons review the underlying accounting leading to the line items in this statement. Both net income (from the income statement) and cash dividends declared are entered into the retained-earnings column and total-OE column and have opposite effects. Treasury stock is a contra-OE account, a direct reduction to owners' equity.

C. The statement of comprehensive income is presented either in a separate statement or in a combined statement with net income. The firm is not required to report the components of other comprehensive income in this statement. However, accumulated other comprehensive income totals are reported.

D. Nonetheless, accumulated other comprehensive income (AOCI) has its own column. Recall that AOCI is the running total of all other comprehensive income (OCI) items. Any firm with AOCI will report it in the statement of changes in equity, regardless of its policy concerning reporting the statement of comprehensive income.

IV. **Horizontal format** -- Alternatively, the statement can be presented in horizontal format. Each account is explained from beginning balance to ending balance in one set of rows, one account schedule on top of another. The first two accounts for this format are shown as follows:

Common stock, 1/1/x2	$40,000	
Issued stock	5,000	
Issued stock dividend	2,000	
Common stock, 12/31/x2		47,000
Contributed capital in excess of par, 1/1/x2	180,000	
Issued stock	30,000	
Issued stock dividend	11,000	
Contributed capital in excess of par, 1/1/x2		$221,000

    A. After all the remaining accounts are entered, the totals of each account (to the left of each account schedule) add to total OE.

V. Comparative statements -- SEC registrants report three years of OE statements, as is the case with the income statement and statement of cash flows. The current year statement is shown comparatively with the statement for the previous two years. Again, either the vertical or the horizontal format is used for presentation.

    A. The comparative multi-year display for the vertical format for single year statements results in the statements of three years stacked one on top of the other. This type of display, thus, is vertical within each year and horizontal across years.

    B. The comparative multi-year display for the horizontal format for single year statements adds two more sets of columns, one for each year shown comparatively. This type of display, thus, is horizontal within each year and vertical across years.

VI. Other columns -- Other columns found in the statement of changes in equity include:

> Preferred stock;
>
> Contributed capital in excess of par, preferred;
>
> Contributed capital from treasury stock;
>
> Equity attributable to noncontrolling interests (minority interest);
>
> Equity attributable to the shareholders of the parent (the reporting company). The sum of this total and for minority interest yields the total OE of the reporting company.

VII. Other events -- Other events reported in the statement of changes in equity (and columns affected) include:

> Retrospective change in accounting principle affecting prior earnings (retained earnings and total OE);
>
> Restatement of income statement for an error affecting prior earnings - prior period adjustment (retained earnings and total OE);
>
> Contributed capital from conversion of bonds (contributed capital and total OE);
>
> Contributed capital from stock options and stock award plans (contributed capital and total OE).

A. The first two items above explain how the beginning retained earnings balance is affected by retroactive application of an accounting policy or error correction.

Sources and Uses of Cash

This section describes the requirement for providing a Statement of Cash Flows and identifies the primary purposes of such a statement. Those purposes indicate the kinds of information needs that the Statement of Cash Flows is intended to satisfy. This section also provides an overview of the content and format of the Statement of Cash Flows. Because the concept of cash may include other highly liquid items called "cash equivalents," such equivalents are defined and examples given. Next, the major sections of the Statement are identified. A graphic model summarizes the relationship between cash as it appears on Balance Sheets and the Statement of Cash Flows. This model facilitates an understanding of the general purpose and format of the Statement of Cash Flows.

After studying this lesson, you should be able to:

1. *Describe the purpose of a Statement of Cash Flows.*

2. *Define cash and cash equivalents.*

3. *List the categories included in a Statement of Cash Flows.*

I. **Statement of Cash Flows – Requirements and Purpose**

A. **Statement Requirement --** A Statement of Cash Flows is required for all business enterprises that report both financial position (Balance Sheet) and results of operations (Income Statement) for a period.

1. The Statement of Cash Flows (SCF) is a basic financial statement like the Income Statement and Balance Sheet.

2. A SCF is not required for certain investment-type entities (e.g., employee benefit plan entities).

B. **Statement Purposes**

1. The basic purpose of the Statement of Cash Flows (SCF) is to provide information about the cash receipts and cash payments for an entity to help investors, creditors, and others assess:

a. Past ability to generate and control cash inflows and cash outflows;

b. Probable future ability to generate cash inflows sufficient to meet future obligations and pay dividends;

c. The likely need for external borrowing.

2. The SCF also provides information about investing and financing activities that do not involve cash inflows (receipts) or outflows (payment) (e.g., acquiring a major long-term asset by incurring a liability).

C. The SCF must exactly explain the change in cash (and cash equivalents) between the beginning and end of the reporting period on the Balance Sheet.

1. **Cash equivalents are**

a. Short-term, highly liquid investments;

b. Readily convertible to known amounts of cash; and

c. Sufficiently close to maturity so that the risk of changes in value due to changes in interest rate is insignificant.

2. Investments are usually considered cash equivalents only when their original maturity is three months or less (e.g., treasury bills, money market funds). Investments in equity securities could not be cash equivalents because they are not convertible to a known amount of cash.

> **Example:**
> A T-bill purchased when there are only three months left in its term is a cash equivalent. But a T-bill purchased when there are four months left it its term does not become a cash equivalent after holding it one month.

3. The entity should disclose its policy for designating cash equivalents. A change in policy for designating cash equivalents is a change in accounting principle.

D. Information Reported

1. The SCF must report information in the following categories:

   a. Net Cash inflow or outflow from **Operating Activities**.

   b. Net Cash inflow or outflow from **Investing Activities**.

   c. Net Cash inflow or outflow from **Financing Activities**.

   d. Effects of **Foreign Currency Translation**.

   e. **Reconciliation** of net cash inflows/outflows (sum of the items listed above) with the reported change in cash and cash equivalents on the Balance Sheet.

   f. **Non-cash Investing and Financing Activities**.

E. SCF Graphic Presentation – See the following illustration.

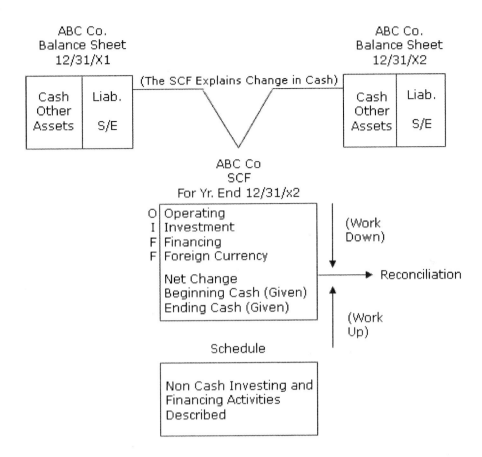

F. Comments on SCF Presentation

1. The categories used to explain the net change in cash and equivalents (operating, investing, financing, and foreign currency) should be presented in the order shown and can be remembered as OIFF ("Oh If' - I could only remember").

2. The categories used to explain the net change in cash (and equivalents) include items of both inflow (receipts) and outflow (payments).

3. The beginning and ending cash (and cash equivalents) are given on the balance sheets for the ends of the prior and current periods.

4. The change in cash (and equivalents) is a known amount, the difference between the beginning and ending cash (and equivalents), and can be "plugged" into the statement.

5. The OIFF elements must exactly explain the known amount of change in cash (and equivalents).

6. The new cash flow derived from the OIFF elements (working down) equals the derived change in cash (and equivalents) (working up).

G. The disclosure of noncash investing and financing activities must be on a separate schedule or other presentation, not on the face of the SCF.

II. Two Formats Allowed By GAAP

A. As discussed in detail later, the Statement of Cash Flows can be presented using either the direct or the indirect format.

B. The only difference between the two is in the operating activity section of the statement. The direct method reports the actual operating cash flows in the operating section. The indirect method reports the reconciliation of net income and net operating cash flow in the operating section. Both lead to the same subtotal: net operating cash flow. The following diagram shows the differences and similarities between the approaches.

	Direct Method	**Indirect Method**
Operating Activities:	Operating Cash Flows	Reconciliation
Investing Activities:	Investing Cash Flows	Investing Cash Flows
Financing Activities:	Financing Cash Flows	Financing Cash Flows

C. The direct method reports the reconciliation in a separate schedule.

D. Only the operating-activities section is different between the formats. Most firms use the indirect method.

Operating, Investing and Financing Activities

This section presents in detail the elements that make up the five major sections of the Statement of Cash Flows (SCF) and the requirements for disclosure of investing and financing activities that do not involve cash inflow or outflow. For the first three major sections - cash from operations, investing, and financing - the possible sources of cash inflows and outflows are identified. Next, the implications of foreign currency conversion on the dollar amount of cash are described and illustrated. The last major section of the Statement, the reconciliation, serves to prove that the net cash inflows and outflows and effects of foreign currency translation fully explain the change in cash between the beginning and the end of the period.

After studying this lesson, you should be able to:

> 1. *Identify the items included in the category financing activities on the Statement of Cash Flows.*

I. **Cash Flows from Operating Activities --** This category reports cash inflows and cash outflows that relate to items that enter into the determination of net income.

   A. The major cash flow items in this category are the following:

Inflows (Cash Received)	Outflows (Cash Paid)
From Customers	To Suppliers (Goods/Services)
Dividends (from Investment)	To Employees (Payroll)
Interest	Interest
	Income taxes

   B. Any cash inflow or cash outflow not properly classified as from investing or financing would be included as from operating activities (e.g., collection of a lawsuit settlement).

   C. The net of the above items constitutes "Net Cash Flow from Operating Activities," and can be positive or negative.

   D. The items that make up the "Cash Flow from Operating Activities" may be presented in the SCF using one of two possible approaches:

   1. Direct Approach - presents operating cash flow by classes of sources and uses.

   2. Indirect Approach - presents operating cash flow by adjusting accrual net income to operating cash flow (called the reconciliation of net income and net operating cash flow).

   E. The association of cash flows with income is one of the hallmarks of operating cash flows. Notice that interest paid and received and dividends received are all operating cash flows, but dividends paid is a financing cash flow. The first three flows are associated with income statement items (interest expense and revenue, dividend revenue), but dividends paid is not an income item; rather, it is a direct reduction in retained earnings. Dividends paid are a distribution of income.

   F. These alternative approaches to presenting cash flows from operation are covered later. Firms use either the direct method or the indirect method. The direct method shows both

   1. The operating cash flows by classes of sources and uses and

2. The reconciliation of net income and net operating cash flow. The indirect method shows only the reconciliation of net income and net operating cash flow. The indirect method therefore does not report the actual operating cash flows.

II. **Cash Flows from Investing Activities** -- This category reports cash inflows and cash outflows that relate to "investment in" and disposal of noncash assets.

A. The major cash flow items in this category are the following:

Inflows (Cash Received)	Outflows (Cash Paid)
Sale of Long-term Assets	Purchase of Long-term Assets
Collection of Loan Principal	Lending (to others)
Disposal of Debt and Equity Securities (of others) (Held-to-Maturity and Available-for-Sale Classifications)	Investment in Debt and Equity Securities (of others) (Held-to-Maturity and Available-for-Sale Classifications)
Sale of Other Productive Assets (e.g., Patent; but not Inventory)	Purchase of Other Productive Assets (e.g., Patent; but not Inventory)

B. Investment in and disposal of debt and equity securities of other entities includes those classified as Held-to-Maturity and Available-for-Sale.

C. Firms classify cash flows from purchases, sales, and maturities of investments in trading securities based on the intended purpose of the investment. If the firm plans to hold the securities only for a short time, then the related cash flows are classified as operating. If the intent of holding is other than for short-term speculation, then the related cash flows are classified as investing.

D. The net of above items constitutes "Net Cash Flow from Investing Activities," and can be positive or negative.

E. The items that make up the "Cash Flow from Investing Activities" are presented in the same manner, regardless of whether the direct or indirect approach is used to present "Cash Flow from Operating Activities."

III. **Cash Flows from Financing Activities** -- This category reports cash inflows and cash outflows that relate to how the entity is financed.

A. The major cash flow items in this category are the following:

Inflows (Cash Received)	Outflows (Cash Paid)
Sale of (Own) Stock	Repurchase Own (Treasury) Stock
Proceeds from Borrowing (Bonds, Notes, etc.)	Paying Back Lenders (Principal Only)
	Payment of Dividends

B. The net of above items constitutes "Net Cash Flow from Financing Activities," and can be positive or negative.

C. The items that make up the "Cash Flow from Financing Activities" are presented in the same manner, regardless of whether the direct or indirect approach is used to present "Cash Flow from Operating Activities."

IV. Effects on Cash of Foreign Currency Translation -- This category reports the effect on the change in cash (between the beginning and the end of the period) that results from changes in currency exchange rates.

    A. Companies that have transactions in foreign currencies or convert financial statements expressed in a foreign currency to statements expressed in dollars may incur a change in the dollar value of cash simply as a result of exchange rate changes.

Example:
A foreign subsidiary has a (nondollar) cash balance that does not change during 20X2 of 100,000 French francs (FF). The (spot) exchange rates were:

12/31/X1: 1 FF = $ .10

12/31/X2: 1 FF = $ .11

The dollar value of cash for U.S. reporting would be:

12/31/X1 (100,000 FF X .10)	$10,000
12/31/X2 (100,000 FF X .11)	$11,000
Net Increase in Cash	$ 1,000

    B. Changes in cash caused by changes in exchange rates must be shown "as part of the reconciliation of the change in cash and cash equivalents during the period."

> **Note:**
> See unit on Foreign Currency Accounting for a complete description of foreign currency transactions and translation.

        1. Foreign currency transactions that occur during the period and affect cash flow should be converted to their dollar equivalent using (1) the exchange rate in effect at the date of each transaction or (2) an average exchange rate for the period, if not materially different from the specific rates in effect on the dates of the transactions.

        2. Cash balances held in foreign currency at period end should be converted to dollars using the spot (current) exchange rate at the date of the Balance Sheet.

    C. The net of the above items constitutes "Net Effect (on Cash) of Foreign Currency Translation."

    D. The items that make up the "Net Effect of Foreign Currency Translation" are presented in the same manner, regardless of whether the direct or indirect approach is used to present "Cash Flow from Operating Activities."

V. Reconciliation of Change in Cash -- This category reconciles the net effect of operating, investing, financing cash flows and the net effect of foreign currency translation with the difference between cash (and equivalents) at the beginning and end of the period.

    A. The items in this category are

Net Increase (or Decrease) in Cash and Equivalents (during X2)

  + Beginning Cash and Equivalents (1/1/X2)

  = Ending Cash and Equivalents (12/31/X2)

    B. The beginning and ending Cash and Equivalents are given on the respective (1/1/X2 and 12/31/X2) Balance Sheets.

C. The difference between beginning and ending Cash and Equivalents = the net change (increase or decrease) in Cash and Equivalents (working up).

D. The net change in Cash and Equivalents is the amount that must be exactly explained by the Operating, Investing, Financing, and Foreign Currency categories (working down).

VI. Noncash Investing and Financing Activities -- This category reports significant investing and financing activities that occur, at least in part, without affecting (going through) cash.

A. Noncash activities must be presented in related disclosures (e.g., schedule or footnote).

B. If an Investing or Financing Activity involves part cash and part noncash, the cash portion should be a part of (on the face of) the SCF; the noncash portion should be disclosed in Noncash Investing and Financing Activities.

Example:
A $100,000 note payable is settled by a cash payment of $60,000 and issuing stock with a fair market value of $40,000.

The cash portion ($60,000) would be a Financing Cash Outflow.

The noncash portion ($40,000) would be disclosed as a noncash financing activity in the Schedule of Noncash Investing and Financing Activities.

Operating Cash Flows—Indirect Method

This section is concerned with the two alternative methods of presenting the first major section, "Net Cash Flow from Operating Activities." Regardless of which method is used for the first section: (1) the subtotal "Net Cash Flow from Operating Activities" will be the same and (2) the remainder of the body of the Statement will be the same in all respects. For each alternative, the appropriate components are identified, and the methodology for determining the amount of each component is presented. Virtually all possible components for each method are covered. The section includes a summary comparison of the alternative methods. The nature and content of the Statement of Cash Flows is summarized in a hypothetical statement, which includes the alternative presentations of cash flow from operating activities. The various sources and uses of cash shown in each section are assumed but are representative of a typical statement.

After studying this lesson, you should be able to:

1. *Describe the components of the operating activities on the Statement of Cash Flows using the direct method.*

2. *Complete the operating section on the Statement of Cash Flows using the direct method.*

3. *Describe the components of the operating activities on the Statement of Cash Flows using the indirect method.*

I. **Methods**

   A. The "Net Cash Flow from Operating Activities" section of the SCF may be presented using either:

   1. The Direct Method (approach);

   2. The Indirect Method (approach).

II. **Similarities in Methods --** The other major sections, ("Net Cash Flow from Investing Activities," "Net Cash Flow from Financing Activities," and the reconciliation with net change in cash) will be the same, regardless of whether the Direct or Indirect method is used. However, the additional disclosures will be different for the two methods, as described below.

III. **Graphic Representation of Presentation Alternatives** – See the following illustration.

Direct Method		**Indirect Method**
Statement		
Components of Cash Flows from Operating Activities (subtotal is same)	<--Different-->	Components of Cash Flows from Operating Activities (subtotal is same)
Cash Flows from Investing Activities	<--Same-->	Cash Flows from Investing Activities
Cash Flows from Financing Activities	<--Same-->	Cash Flows from Financing Activities
Effect of Foreign Currency Translation	<--Same-->	Effect of Foreign Currency Translation
Reconciliation with Cash Change	<--Same-->	Reconciliation with Cash Change
Additional Disclosures		
Non-Cash Investing and Financing	<--Same-->	Non-Cash Investing and Financing
Reconcile Cash Flows from Operating Activities with Net Income - in supporting schedule	<--(N/A)-->	(In Body of Statement)
(N/A - In Body of Statement)	<--(N/A)-->	Payments for Interest
(N/A - In Body of Statement)	<--(N/A)-->	Payments for Income Tax

IV. Body of the SCF -- As between the two methods (Direct and Indirect), in the body of the SCF only the presentation of "Cash Flows from Operating Activities" is different.

V. Direct Method (of presenting Cash Flow from Operating Activities) -- The Direct Method reports the components of Cash Flow from Operating Activities as individual items of gross receipts of cash (from revenue activities) and gross payments of cash (from expenses incurred).

    A. Operating Activities -- To derive net cash provided by operating activities using the direct method each item in the income statement is adjusted from an accrual basis to cash basis.

        1.   Under GAAP, the income statement is prepared on the accrual basis which recognizes accruals and deferrals. Therefore, the items of revenue and expense do not necessarily reflect cash received and cash paid. Income Statement items affected by accrual accounting must be adjusted to reflect the actual cash generated or used.

        2.   Graphic Representation of Cash to Accrual and back to Cash

        3.   Cash to Accrual (GAAP)

            See the following example.

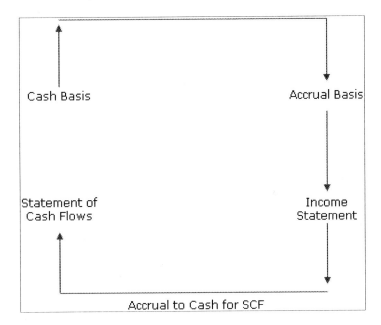

4. Key Point: The effects of accrual accounting (e.g., Receivables, Payables) used to measure net income have to be reversed out to get cash flows.

B. Direct Method Disclosure of Operating Cash Flows

1. Under the Direct Method of presenting "Cash Flows from Operating Activities," the section should separate cash flows for the following elements of operations:

   a. Collections from customers;

   b. Collections for interest and dividends (on loans made and investments);

   c. Collections from other operating sources;

   d. Payments to employees;

   e. Payments to suppliers;

   f. Payments for operating expenses;

   g. Payments for interest (on debt);

   h. Payments for income taxes;

   i. Payments for other operating uses.

2. The difference between these collections and payments is "Cash Flow from Operating Activities."

C. Procedures for Converting from Accrual Basis to Cash Basis -- In order to convert revenue and expense items on the accrual based income statement to the amount of cash they generated or used, the effects of accruals and deferrals must be taken out. The following subsections describe and illustrate the conversion process for the major types of items including cash collected from customers, cash payments to suppliers, and cash payments for (any) operating expense:

1. **Collection from Customers --** Revenues on an income statement may include accruals (revenue earned but not collected) and exclude deferrals (cash collected but revenue not earned). To derive cash actually collected from customers these accruals/deferrals must be reversed.

Example:
Assume the following information is from the Income Statement (20X2) and Balance Sheets (20X1 and 20X2) of ABC Co.:

Revenue (sales - 20X2)	$900,000
Accounts Receivable 12/31/X1	60,000
Accounts Receivable 12/31/X2	75,000
Net Increase - 20X2	$15,000
Unearned Revenue 12/31/X1	-0-
Unearned Revenue 12/31/X2	25,000
Net Increase - 20X2	$25,000

Schedule Calculation of Cash Collected from Customers - 20X2:

Revenues	900,000
Deduct: Increase in Receivables	-15,000*
Add: Increase in Unearned Revenue	25,000**
Cash Collected from Customers	$910,000

* Since Receivables increased by $15,000, that amount was recognized as revenue (Debit A/R; Credit. Revenue), but was not collected yet. (A decrease in Receivables would increase cash collected).

** Since Unearned Revenues increased by $25,000, that amount was collected (Debit Cash; Credit Unearned Revenue), but was not reported in revenues yet. (A decrease in Unearned Revenue would decrease cash collected).

Entry Calculation of Cash Collected from Customer - 20X2:

DR: Increase in Receivables (given)	$ 15,000	
Cash (Amount to Balance)	910,000	
CR: Increase in Unearned Revenue (given)		$ 25,000
Revenues (given)		900,000

2. **Cash Payments to Suppliers --** Cost of Goods Sold on an income statement may include changes in inventory and/or changes in accounts payable. To determine cash actually paid to suppliers for purchases these changes must be taken into account.

   See the following example.

Example:
The following information is from the Income Statement (20X2) and the Balance Sheets (20X1 and 20X2) of ABC Co.:

Cost of Goods Sold	$ 400,000
Inventory (12/31/X1)	100,000
Inventory (12/31/X2)	120,000
Net Increase - 20X2	20,000
Accounts Payable 12/31/X1	80,000
Accounts Payable 12/31/X2	90,000
Net Increase - 20X2	$10,000

Schedule Calculation of Cash Paid to Suppliers - 20X2:

Cost of Goods Sold - 20X2	$ 400,000
Add: Increase in Inventory	20,000
Total Purchases	420,000
Deduct: Increase in Accts. Payable	10,000 **
Cash Payments to Suppliers	$410,000

* Since Inventory increased, more goods were purchased than were in Cost of Goods Sold. (A decrease in Inventory would reduce purchases).

** Since Accounts Payable increased by $10,000, that amount of purchases (DR. purchases; CR. Accounts Payable) was not paid for yet. (A decrease in Accounts Payable would increase cash paid).

Entry Calculation of Cash Paid to Suppliers

DR: Cost of Goods Sold (given)	$400,000	
Increase in Inventory (given)	20,000	
CR: Increase in Accts. Payable (given)		$ 10,000
Cash paid to Suppliers (amt. to bal.)		410,000

3. **Cash Payments for Operating Expenses --** Expenses on an income statement may include accruals (expenses incurred but not paid) and/or deferrals (cash paid but expense not incurred). To derive cash actually paid for operating expenses these accruals/deferrals must be reversed.

   a. The required adjustments, as described above, and the example that follows apply to all types of expenses, even though the example uses General Operating Expense (I/S) and Prepaid Expense (B/S) items. The same analysis would apply to Selling, General and Administrative Expenses, Interest Expense, or Income Tax Expense.

   See the following example.

Example:

Assume the following information is from the Income Statement (20X2) and Balance Sheets (20X1 and 20X2) of ABC Co.

Operating Expenses - 200X	$ 150,000
Prepaid Expenses 12/31/X1	10,000
Prepaid Expenses 12/31/X2	5,000
Net Decrease - 200X	5,000
Operating Expense Payable 12/31/X1	20,000
Operating Expense Payable 12/31/X2	35,000
Net Increase - 200X	$15,000

Schedule Calculation of Cash Paid for Operating Expenses - 200X:

Operating Expense - 200X	150,000
Deduct: Decrease in Prepaid Expense	5,000
Subtotal	145,000
Deduct: Increase in Expenses Payable	15,000
Cash Payments for Operating Expenses	$130,000

* Since Prepaid Expense decreased, Operating Expenses included $5,000 paid for (prepaid) in a prior period, not paid for in the current period. (An increase in Prepaid Expense would increase cash paid).

** Since Operating Expenses Payable increased by $15,000, that amount of expenses (Debit - Operating Expenses; Credit - Expense Payable) was not paid for yet. (A decrease in Expense Payable would increase cash paid).

Entry Calculation of Cash Paid for Operating Expenses - X2:

DR: Operating Expenses (given)	$150,000	
CR: Decrease in Prepaid Expense (given)		$ 5,000
Increase in Expense Payable (given)		$15,000
Cash Paid for Operating Expenses (amount to balance)		130,000

4. **Cash Payments for Other Types of Expenses** -- The calculation methodology used to derive cash flow from operating expenses (in the examples above) can be used for other types of expenses (e.g., interest, income taxes, etc.)

D. **Presentation of "Cash Flow from Operating Activities" Direct Method** -- Using the cash flow values developed in the prior examples and assuming cash outflows for payments to employees, interest expense, and income tax expense, the "Cash Flow from Operating Activities" under the Direct Method would be presented as follows:

Cash Flow from Operating Activities		
Cash Collected from Customers (per above)		$910,000
Cash Payments:		
To Suppliers (per above)	$410,000	
To Employees (assumed)	50,000	
For Operating Expense (per above)	130,000	
For Interest (assumed)	20,000	
For Income Taxes (assumed)	40,000	
Total Cash Payments		650,000
Net Cash Provided by Operating Activities		$260,000

E. **Reconciliation of "Net Cash Flow from Operating Activities" with Net Income** -- If the Direct Method is used to present "Net Cash Flow from Operating Activities," a separate schedule must be provided which reconciles cash flow with Net Income.

1. The reconciliation shows the adjustments to Net Income necessary to arrive at Cash Flow from Operating Activities.

2. The schedule that presents the reconciliation is identical to the "Cash Flow from Operating Activities" section in the Statement of Cash Flows presented using the Indirect Method.

3. Reconciliation Presentation: Using values developed above and assuming other adjustments that will be covered in the Indirect Method, the reconciliation would be presented as follows:

Net Income		$110,000
Adjustment to Reconcile Net Income to Net Cash provided by Operating Activities:		
Depreciation Expense (assumed)*	$150,000	
Loss on Equipment Sale (assumed)*	5,000	
Undistributed Equity Revenue (assumed)*	(28,000)	
Amortization of Premium on Bond Investment (assumed)*	3,000	
Increase in Accounts Receivable (above)	(15,000)	
Increase in Inventory (above)	(20,000)	
Decrease in Prepaid Expense (above)	5,000	
Increase in Accounts Payable (above)	10,000	
Increase in Expense Payable (above)	15,000	
Increase in Unearned Revenues (above)*	25,000	
Total Adjustments		150,000
Net Cash Provided by Operating Activities		$260,000

(*Note: Items market with * are assumed at this point to illustrate a complete reconciliation of net income and cash flow from operating activities. The analysis of each of these items and the calculation of each amount is shown in the following section covering the Indirect method of deriving Net Cash Provided by Operating Activities).

VI. **Indirect Method (of presenting Cash Flow from Operating Activities)** -- The indirect method of presenting "Cash Flow from Operating Activities" begins with Net Income (accrual basis) and adjusts for items that entered into computing Net Income, but did not affect cash by the same amount.

    A. **Accruals and Deferrals** -- As previously discussed, under GAAP, net income is based on using accrual accounting which recognizes accruals and deferrals. In addition, certain items used in determining net income do not reflect the correct related cash flow (e.g., losses and gains). Therefore, net income does not reflect net cash flow from operations. Using the indirect method, net income is adjusted to derive net cash flow from operating activities by:

        1. Adding back non-cash charges (reductions) included in deriving Net Income; and

        2. Subtracting out non-cash credits (increases) included in deriving Net Income.

    B. **Indirect Method Disclosure of Operating Cash Flow** -- Under the Indirect Method, the Net Income must be adjusted by the following types of "Add Backs" and "Subtract Outs" to get Cash Flow from Operating Activities:

        1. **Add Back (to Net Income):** These items were deducted in getting net income, but did not cause cash to be used:

            a. Depreciation Expense;

            b. Amortization Expense;

            c. Depletion Expense;

            d. Losses (from sale of assets, etc.);

            e. Loss under equity method of accounting for Investments;

            f. Amortization of Premium on Bond Investment;

            g. Amortization of Discount on Bonds Payable;

            h. Decreases in current assets (accounts receivable, inventory, prepaid assets, etc.);

            i. Increases in Current Liabilities (accounts payable, deferred taxes, etc.);

            j. Increase in Unearned Revenue.

        2. **Subtract Out (of Net Income):** These items were added in getting net income, but did not cause cash to be received:

            a. Gains (from sale of assets, etc.);

            b. Amortization of Discount on Bond Investment;

            c. Amortization of Premium on Bond Payable;

            d. Undistributed income under equity method of accounting for Investments;

            e. Increases in Current Assets (accounts receivable, inventory, prepaid assets, etc.);

            f. Decreases in Current Liabilities (accounts payable, deferred taxes, etc.);

            g. Decrease in Unearned Revenue.

        3. Net Income adjusted by the foregoing items is "Cash Flow from Operating Activities".

C. Procedures for Adjusting Net Income for Non-Cash Debits and Credits -- In order to convert Net Income to the net amount of cash generated or used by operations, the non-cash debits must be added back and the non-cash credits subtracted. The following subsections describe and illustrate the adjustment process for the major types of add backs and subtract outs.

1. **Depreciation/Amortization/Depletion Expenses --** These are non-cash expenses that must be added back to Net Income (by the amount recognized as an expense).

   Note:
   Look for items with an income effect different from their effect on operating cash flow. These are the reconciling items.

   a. If the amount of expense is not provided, it can be derived from the balance sheet and related information, if given.

   b. Calculation of the unknown expense can be done using a Schedule or a T-Account approach.

Example:
Assume the following information is from the Balance Sheets (20X1 and 20X2) and additional disclosures of ABC Co.:

Accumulated Depreciation (A/D) 12/31/X1	$400,000
Accumulated Depreciation (A/D) 12/31/X2	500,000
Net Increase - 20X2	$100,000

Additional Information: Equipment with a book value of $25,000 (cost = $75,000 and accumulated depreciation = $50,000) was sold for $30,000.

Schedule Calculation of Expense:

Beginning A/D	400,000	
Add: Depreciation Expense	?	150,000
Subtotal	?	$550,000
Deduct: A/D on Equipment Sold	50,000	
Ending A/D	$500,000	

T-Account Calculation of Expense:

Accumulated Depreciation

	400,000
50,000	150,000 (forced)
	500,000

$150,000 should be added back to Net Income.

---

2. **Losses/Gains**

   a. These are non-cash deductions or additions in computing net income that must be added back to or subtracted from Net Income (by the amount recognized as a loss or gain).

b. If the amount of a loss or gain is not provided, it can be derived from the balance sheet and related information, if given.

 Example:
(assumes a loss) Assume the following information is from the additional disclosures of ABC Co.:

Additional Disclosure: During 20X2, Equipment with a cost of $75,000 and accumulated depreciation of $50,000 was sold for $20,000.

Schedule Calculation of Loss:

Sale Price		$20,000
Less: Cost	$75,000	
A/D	50,000	
Book Value		25,000
Loss on Sale		$ 5,000

$5,000 should be added back to Net Income.

---

3. **Equity Method Adjustments**

   a. An investor that uses the equity method to account for an investment must recognize its share of the investee's net income or net loss in the period it is reported by the investee, whether or not any dividends are paid by the investee. Therefore, the investor would make the following entries:

   i. Investee reports Net Income, Investor entry:

   > DR: Investment in Investee (asset)
   >
   >   CR: Investment (Equity) Revenue

   ii. Investee reports Net Loss, Investor entry:

   > DR: Investment (Equity) Loss
   >
   >   CR: Investment in Investee (asset)

   b. In either case, the investor has increased (with revenue) or decreased (with loss) its Net Income without any related cash flow.

   c. If the investee paid a cash dividend during the period, the Investor entry would be:

   > DR: Cash
   >
   >   CR: Investment in Investee (asset)

   d. Therefore, under the equity method only cash dividends received from the investee cause a cash flow. The adjustments to net income to get cash flow would be:

   i. If a loss, add back the amount of the loss.

   ii. If an income (revenue), subtract out the amount recognized as revenue that was not received as cash dividends.

Example:
Assume ABC Company owns 40% of XYZ Company and appropriately accounts for its investment using the equity method. During 19X2, XYZ had net income of $100,000 and paid cash dividends of $30,000.

Schedule Calculation of Amount to Subtract:

	XYZ Co.	ABC Co.
Net Income $100,000 X .40 =		$40,000
Less: Cash Dividend 30,000 X .40 =		12,000
ABC Revenue NOT Received as Cash		$28,000

$28,000 should be subtracted from Net Income.

4. **Amortization of Bond Premiums/Discounts** -- Bond Premiums and Discounts, whether related to an investment in bonds or the issuing of bonds, originate at the time the bonds are bought or sold. The subsequent amortization of a premium or discount will enter into net income (through interest income or interest expense), but will not generate or use cash. Therefore, the effects of premium or discount amortization must be added back to or subtracted from net income. Two illustrations are given:

   a. **Amortization of Premium on Bond Investment** -- When bonds are purchased for more than maturity value, a premium results.

      i. The related entry would be:

      DR: Investment in Bonds (at face value)

      DR: Premium on Bond Investment

         CR: Cash

      ii. The cash outflow would be recognized in the period the investment is made as a component of "Cash Flow from Investing Activities."

      iii. The subsequent amortization of the premium would be recorded by a periodic entry:

      DR: Interest Income

         CR: Premium on Bond Investment

         1. The debit to Interest Income reduces the amount of net income, but does not use cash.

      iv. The amount of amortization should be added back to Net Income.

      v. If the bonds had been acquired at less than maturity value, the resulting amortization of the discount would have to be subtracted from Net Income.

   b. **Amortization of Discount on Bonds Payable** -- When bonds are issued for less than maturity value, a discount results.

i. The related entry would be:

> DR: Cash
>
> DR: Discount on Bonds Payable
>
> > CR: Bonds Payable

ii. The cash inflow would be recognized in the period the bonds were sold as a component of "Cash Flow from Financing Activities."

iii. The subsequent amortization of the discount would be recorded by a periodic entry:

> DR: Interest Expense
>
> > CR: Discount on Bonds Payable

1. The debit to Interest Expense reduces the amount of net income, but does not use cash.

iv. The amount of amortization should be added back to Net Income.

v. If the bonds had been issued (sold) at more than maturity value, the resulting amortization of the premium would have to be subtracted from Net Income.

5. **Increases and Decreases in Current Assets and Current Liabilities --** Increases and decreases in current assets and current liabilities reflect differences between the amount of revenue or expense recognized for net income and the amount of cash received or paid. Two examples illustrate the relevant points:

a. **Increase in Accounts Receivable**

i. When sales are made on account, the related entry would be:

> DR: Assets Receivable
>
> > CR: Sales

ii. The sales amount (credit) enters into Net Income, but unless the account receivable is collected within the same period there is no increase in cash. Therefore, net income would have to be decreased by the amount of the uncollected account receivable.

iii. The aggregate change in accounts receivable will have the same effect on net income as shown above. Therefore, the amount of the aggregate change in receivables (and other current assets) must be used to adjust net income to get the related cash flows.

iv. Illustration Facts: Assume ABC Company's Accounts Receivable balances for 20X1 and 20X2 were:

Accounts Receivable 12/31/X1	$60,000
Accounts Receivable 12/31/X2	75,000
Net Increase - 20X2	$15,000

v. Because Accounts Receivable increased by $15,000, sales of that amount are included in Net Income, but the cash has not been collected. Therefore, $15,000 should be subtracted from Net Income.

vi. If Accounts Receivable had decreased, more cash would have been collected than sales recognized for the period. Therefore, the amount of decrease would have been added to Net Income to get the related cash flow.

vii. Increases and decreases in other current assets would be treated in the same manner.

b. Increase in Accounts Payable

i. When purchases are made on account, the related entry would be:

DR: Purchases (or other asset)
CR: Account Payable

ii. The purchase account (debit) enters into net income, but unless the accounts payable is paid within the same period there is no decrease in cash. Therefore, net income would have to be increased by the amount of the unpaid account payable.

iii. The aggregate change in accounts payable will have the same effect on net income as shown above. Therefore, the amount of the aggregate change in payables (and other current liabilities) must be used to adjust net income to get the related cash flows.

iv. Illustration Facts: Assume ABC Company's Accounts Payable balances for 20X1 and 20X2 were:

Accounts Payable 12/31/X1	$80,000
Accounts Payable 12/31/X2	90,000
Increase - 20X2	$10,000

v. Because Accounts Payable increased by $10,000, an expense (including possibly COGS) is included in net income, but the cash has not been paid. Therefore, $10,000 would be added to Net Income.

vi. If Accounts Payable had decreased, more cash would have been paid than expenses recognized for the period. Therefore, the amount of decrease would have to be deducted from net income to determine the related cash flow.

vii. Increases and decreases in other current liabilities would be treated in the same manner.

6. **Increases and Decreases in Unearned Revenues --** Increases and decreases in unearned revenues reflect differences between the amount of revenue recognized for net income and the amount of cash received. Therefore, the amount of these increases or decreases must be added back to or subtracted from net income to get the related cash flow. The following example illustrates the required adjustment:

a. Illustration Facts: Assume the following information is from the Balance Sheets (X1 and X2) of ABC Co.:

Unearned Revenue 12/31/X1	$ - 0 -
Unearned Revenue 12/31/X2	25,000
Increase - X2	$25,000

b. The increase occurred as a result of ABC making one or more of the following entries:

> DR: Cash
>
>   CR: Unearned Revenues

c. The debit to cash increased cash flow, but the credit to unearned revenue did not enter into net income. Therefore, net income understates cash flow for the period.

d. The amount of increases in unearned revenues must be added back to net income to determine cash flow.

e. If unearned revenue had decreased, it would have caused an increase in net income (DR: Unearned Revenue; CR: Revenues) without generating a related cash flow. Therefore, the amount of a decrease in Unearned Revenue must be subtracted from net income to determine the related cash flow.

D. Presentation of "Cash Flow from Operating Activities" - Indirect Method -- Using the cash flow values developed in prior illustrations, including those developed under the Direct Method, the "Cash Flow from Operating Activities" under the Indirect Method would be presented as follows:

Cash Flow From Operating Activities

Net Income (given)		$110,000
Adjustments to Reconcile Net Income to Net Cash provided by Operating Activities:		
Depreciation Expense (above)	$150,000	
Loss on Equipment Sale (above)	5,000	
Undistributed Equity Revenue (above)	(28,000)	
Amortization of Premium on Bond Investment (assumed)	3,000	
Increase in Accounts Receivable (above)	(15,000)	
Increase in Inventory (direct method) *	(20,000)	
Decrease in Prepaid Expenses (direct method) *	5,000	
Increase in Accounts Payable (above)	10,000	
Increase in Expenses Payable (direct method) *	15,000	
Increase in Unearned Revenues (above)	25,000	
Total Adjustments		$150,000
Net Cash Provided by Operating Activities		$260,000

(*Note: Items marked with * were developed in the illustration of the Direct Method. Under the Indirect Method, the adjustment for Inventory and Prepaid expenses would have been developed the same way the change in accounts receivable was developed. The adjustment for Expenses Payable would have been developed the same way the change in Accounts Payable was developed.)

VII. Direct/Indirect Comparison -- The Direct Method and the Indirect Method are alternative ways of developing and presenting "Cash Flow from Operating Activities." The most significant aspects of the two methods are:

A. The Direct Method presents cash flows in terms of the specific sources from which cash was received (inflows) and to which cash was paid (outflows).

B. The Indirect Method develops cash flows by adjusting net income, and does not (necessarily) identify the specific sources of cash inflows or outflows.

C. Under either method, the "Cash Flow from Operating Activities" will be the same amount.

D. Under either method, the other major sections of the Statement of Cash Flows -- Investing, Financing, Foreign Currency effects, and the Reconciliation of the Change in Cash -- **will be the same**.

E. The Direct Method is preferred (by the FASB).

F. Both methods require disclosure of the "Noncash Investing and Financing."

G. The Direct method requires an additional schedule to reconcile Net Income to Cash Flow from Operating Activities.

H. The Indirect Method requires an additional disclosure of the amount (of cash) paid for interest and dividends.

VIII. Summary Illustration of a Statement of Cash Flows -- A complete "Statement of Cash Flows" would take the following form:

ABC Company

Statement of Cash Flows

For the Year Ended December 31, 20X2

Cash Flows from Operating Activities:

Direct Method	Indirect Method
Cash Collected From:	**Net Income**
Customers	Add: Noncash Expenses
Dividends	Losses
Etc.	Decreases in Current Assets
Cash Payments To:	Etc.
Suppliers	Deduct: Noncash Revenues
Employees	Gains
Interest	Increase in Current Assets
Increase in Current Assets	Increase in Current Assets

--->Net Cash Provided By Operating Activities<---

|
|
V

Cash Flows from Investing Activities

Cash Received from:

Sale of Equipment

Collection of Loan

Etc.

Cash Paid to:

Purchase Equipment

Loan to (other)

Investment in (other)

Etc.

Net Cash Provided by Investing Activities

Cash Flows from Financing Activities

Cash Received from:

Sale of Own Stock

Proceeds from Borrowing

Etc.

Cash Paid to:

Repaying Debt

Paying Dividends

Etc.

Net Cash Provided by Financing Activities

Cash Effects of Foreign Currency Translation:

Add: Increase in Cash Due to Foreign Currency Translation

Deduct: Decrease in Cash Due to Foreign Currency Translation

Net Effect of Foreign Currency Translation

Net Change in Cash (and Cash Equivalents)

Beginning Cash (and Cash Equivalents) 1/1/X2

Ending Cash (and Cash Equivalents) 12/31/X2

Additional Disclosures:

Non-Cash Investing and Financing Activities

Direct Method	*Indirect Method*
Reconcile Cash Flows from Operating	Cash Paid for Interest
Activities to Net Income	Cash Paid for Income Taxes

Notes to Financial Statements

This lesson presents a discussion of the notes to the financial statements.

After studying this lesson, you should be able to:

1. *Describe the reason for footnote disclosures.*

2. *List the disclosures required in the footnotes.*

3. *Identify the significant differences in footnote disclosures under U.S. and International.*

I. **Notes to the Financial Statements**

A. **Financial Report Disclosures** -- To achieve the objectives of the full disclosure principle, the three primary financial statements are supplemented by footnote disclosures and disclosures that appear in related schedules. Summaries of the major required financial report disclosures follow.

> **Note:**
> Our recommendation is to have a familiarity with the terms and general disclosures. We do not recommend memorizing all the disclosure requirements because disclosure is not a major emphasis of the exam. Try to find similarities across different disclosure areas.

   1. **Summary of Significant Accounting Policies** -- The first footnote is typically a summary of significant accounting policies - the principles and methods chosen by management where GAAP allows a choice. Such disclosure is required. Users' understanding of financial statement amounts is greatly facilitated by knowing the methods used in preparing the statements. This footnote usually includes information about the following:

      a. The chosen depreciation method;

      b. The chosen method of valuing inventory;

      c. The securities classified as cash and cash equivalents;

      d. The basis for consolidation:

         i. Amortization policies;

         ii. Revenue recognition policies.

   2. This summary must include information about all significant accounting policies but is not required in interim statements if the policies have not changed.

   3. **Related Party Transactions** -- Companies must disclose the following information:

      a. The nature of the relationship between the related entities; (Related parties include a parent and its subsidiaries, a firm and its principal owners and management and members of their immediate families, a firm and its equity-method investees, and others.)

      b. A description of all related party transactions for the accounting years in which an income statement is presented in the financial report;

      c. The dollar amounts of the related party transactions for the accounting years in which an income statement is presented in the financial report;

      d. In relation to related parties, any receivables or payables from or to related parties as of the date of each balance sheet presented in the financial report.

B. **Noncurrent Liability Disclosures** -- Companies are required to disclose the following information about liabilities:

1. Combined aggregate amount of maturities on borrowings for each of the five years following the balance sheet;

2. Sinking fund requirements;

3. The aggregate amount of payments for unconditional obligations to purchase fixed or minimum amounts of goods or services;

4. The fair value of each financial debt instrument in the financial statements or in the notes;

5. The nature of the firm's liabilities, interest rates, maturity dates, conversion options, assets pledged as collateral, and restrictions.

C. **Capital Structure Disclosures** -- Companies are required to provide the following information related to capital structure:

1. **Rights and Privileges** of outstanding securities;

2. The **number of shares issued** during the annual fiscal period and any subsequent interim period presented;

3. **Liquidation preference** of preferred stock;

4. If the liquidation value of preferred stock is considerably in excess of par value or stated value of preferred stock, this information should be disclosed in the equity section of the balance sheet;

5. **Other Preferred Stock Disclosures** -- The following information can be disclosed in the footnotes or in the equity section of the balance sheet:

    a. Aggregate or per-share amounts at which preferred stock can be called or is subject to redemption through sinking fund operations;

    b. Aggregate or per-share amounts of arrearages for cumulative preferred stock.

6. **Redeemable Preferred Stock** -- For each of the five years following the balance sheet date, the amount of redemption requirements for all types of redeemable capital stock must be disclosed in the notes to the financial statements.

D. **Errors and Irregularities** -- A later lesson discusses the accounting for these items.

1. Errors are unintentional.

2. Irregularities are intentional.

3. Both require footnote disclosure. If prior year income is affected, a prior period adjustment is recorded which corrects the beginning balance of retained earnings and any other accounts affected in the year of discovery.

E. **Illegal Acts** -- Examples include illegal contributions and bribes. The Foreign Corrupt Practices Act was passed by the U.S. Congress to discourage such acts. The nature and impact of illegal acts on the financial statements should be disclosed fully in the notes.

II. **Management's Discussion and Analysis (MD&A)** -- This is a narrative written by management and, although not considered part of the footnotes, is nonetheless an important disclosure supplementing the financial statements.

A. Publicly held firms are required to include the MD&A in the annual report. It provides management's discussion about the operations of the firm, its liquidity, and capital resources.

B. Additional discussion involves management's view of the firm's financial condition, changes in financial condition, and results of operations through analysis of the financial statements. Explanations of the reasons for major changes in financial performance and financial position are examples. Discussion of the effects of significant and unusual events provides further insight.

C. Forward-looking information is provided that is not reflected in the financial statements. This includes management's general prognosis about future sales, effects of competition, and expected effects of general macroeconomic conditions. An example is a discussion of the effect of inflation or specific price-level changes on future sales and earnings. Another is a discussion of the possible effects of uncertainties on the firm's financial statements.

III. Disclosures for the Effects of Changing Prices

A. Background

1. During times of price instability, financial reporting can be distorted, especially for items measured using historical cost. Both the balance sheet and income statement items (e.g., depreciation expense) are affected. Both inflation (general price- levels) and specific price changes affect the interpretation of reported amounts.

2. In the past, large firms were required to provide extensive footnote disclosure about the effects of price changes on the financial statements. Because inflation has subsided, there currently is no such requirement although disclosure of information on the effects of changing prices continues to be encouraged.

> **Note:**
> It is expected that the remaining material in this subtopic will have a lower probability of being tested than other material in this lesson.

3. The remaining material in this subtopic provides a summary of price level changes.

B. General Price-Level Changes

> **Definitions:**
> *Inflation*: The increase in general prices for a period of time; deflation is the decrease in general prices. When inflation is 4%, there has been a 4% increase in the general price level index.
>
> *General Prices*: A market basket of items that the typical consumer purchases.

1. The Bureau of Labor Statistics publishes the CPI-U (Consumer Price Index for All Urban Consumers) which is an index reflecting the aggregate increase in the price of many goods and services used by individuals. It is one measure of inflation commonly quoted in the financial press. If inflation is 2% for an annual period, then the CPI-U has increased 2% for the year.

> **Definition:**
> *Nominal Dollars*: Measurements in the price level in effect at a transaction date. These measurements are not adjusted for inflation.

2. Financial statement amounts are measured in nominal dollars. If a firm purchased equipment and paid $10,000, that transaction is measured and reported in nominal dollars at $10,000. Price level changes are ignored.

> **Definition:**
> *Constant Dollars*: Measurements in the general price level as of a specific date. Constant dollar measurements reflect an adjustment for inflation and allow comparisons using dollars with the same purchasing power.

3. If equipment is purchased for $10,000 when the general price level index is 100, the constant dollar measurement for that equipment when the general price level index is 120 at a later date is $12,000 ($10,000 x 120/100). If the price of equipment had kept pace with inflation, the firm would have to spend $12,000 now to obtain the equipment it purchased for $10,000 on a previous date.

Note: In the adjustment ratio above (120/100), the numerator is the price level for the date on which the constant dollar measurement is desired. The denominator is the price level in effect on the date the transaction occurred.

a. Constant dollar adjustments allow comparisons of dollar amounts for transactions occurring on different dates. The effect of inflation is stripped away leaving "real" dollar measurements.

C. Specific Price Changes

Definition:
Specific Price Change: The change in the price of a specific good or service over a period of time.

1. If the price of crude oil increased from $17 to $18 per barrel, then the specific price level of oil increased 5.9% ($18 - $17)/$17.

2. **Restrictions --** Specific price changes refer only to specific goods and services and are not necessarily correlated with inflation (general price level increase) although frequently they are.

 Example:
1. The price of potato chips increased 3% during a period in which inflation was 2%. The specific price of potato chips moved in the same direction as inflation but the rate of increase was higher.

2. The price of computer chips has steadily declined over the last several years even though there has been moderate inflation. The specific price of computer chips has moved in a direction opposite that of inflation.

D. Effects of General Changes

Definition:
Purchasing Power: The purchasing power of an asset is the amount of goods and services that can be obtained by transferring the asset to another party.

1. During inflation, the purchasing power of an asset having a fixed unchangeable value decreases.

 Example:
The purchasing power of a $10 bill decreases during periods of inflation because the amount of goods and services that the bill can purchase declines. (There was a time that going to a movie cost $1.00. Now it costs as much as $8.00 for a movie. A dollar does not go as far as it used to.)

E. Monetary and Nonmonetary Items -- Assets and liabilities are categorized as (1) monetary or (2) nonmonetary, depending on whether the item has a fixed unchangeable value.

1. **Monetary Items** -- The specific price of monetary items cannot change. A $50 bill is always "worth" $50. An account receivable recorded at $3,000 is a monetary item because the claim the creditor has on the debtor is fixed at $3,000.

   a. **Examples of monetary items** -- Cash, most receivables, accounts payable, all liabilities payable in fixed dollar amounts, and certain investments in debt securities.

2. **Nonmonetary Items** -- The specific price of nonmonetary items can change. The value of an item of inventory purchased for $300 can change before it is sold. The item of inventory does not command a fixed value.

   a. **Examples of nonmonetary items** -- Inventory, plant assets, investments in equity securities, unearned rent, and other liabilities payable in goods and services.

F. Purchasing Power Gains and Losses -- The change in the purchasing power of an item due to a change in the general price level is measured only for monetary items because the specific price of nonmonetary items can change. During inflation, the amount of goods a $10 bill can purchase definitely decreases but the same cannot necessarily be said for an item of inventory originally costing $10. The value of the inventory item may increase with inflation but the value of the $10 bill cannot increase.

1. **Purchasing Power Gain** -- A purchasing power gain results from holding monetary assets during deflationary times or having monetary liabilities during inflationary times.

Example: A firm owes $4,000 on a note due in one year. If inflation is 10% during that year (beginning price level of 100, ending price level of 110), the purchasing power of the dollars paid at the end of the year is 10% less than the dollars borrowed. Thus, the firm has a purchasing power gain because the firm is paying 10% less in purchasing power to extinguish the debt than it received from the creditor. (This is why interest rates increase with inflation, to compensate the creditor for the loss in purchasing power during the term of the borrowing.)

Amount of debt required at 12/31, for the firm to be in the same purchasing power position it was in at 1/1:

$4,000(110/100) =	$ 4,400
Amount of debt actually owed at 12/31:	$(4,000)
Purchasing power gain	$ 400

If the debt increased to $4,400 by year-end, the firm would be in the same purchasing power situation as it was at the beginning of the year.

But it actually owes only $4,000. Therefore, the firm is $400 ahead in purchasing power at 12/31.

---

2. **Purchasing Power Loss** -- A purchasing power loss results from holding monetary assets during inflationary times or having monetary liabilities during deflationary times.

See the following example.

Example: A firm has a cash balance of $4,000 at the beginning of the year. If inflation is 10% during the year (beginning price level of 100, ending price level of 110), and the firm has had no change in its cash balance, the value of the dollars held at year-end is 10% less in terms of purchasing power. Thus, the firm has a purchasing power loss because the firm has 10% less in purchasing power than it had at the beginning of the year.

Amount of cash required at 12/31 to be in the same purchasing power position it was in at 1/1:
$4,000(110/100) = \hspace{3em} $ 4,400

Amount of cash actually held at 12/31: $(4,000)

Purchasing power loss \hspace{3em} $ 400

The firm's $4,000 cash will buy $400 less in goods and services at year-end compared with the amount it could buy at the beginning of the year.

3. **Computation** of purchasing power gain or loss with both monetary assets and liabilities.

Example:

	1/1/x8	12/31/x8
General price level indices	120	140
Monetary assets held	$2,000	$3,800
Monetary liabilities owed	1,500	2,500
Net monetary assets	$ 500	$1,300

Assume the price level index rose evenly throughout the year; therefore, the average price level in 19x8 was 130.

	Nominal dollars	Adjustment ratio	Constant dollars
Net monetary assets, 1/1/x8	$500	140/120	$ 583
Increase in net monetary assets	800	140/130	862
Net monetary assets at 12/31 needed to keep pace with inflation			$1,445
Net monetary assets actually held at 12/31			1,300
Purchasing power loss, 19x8			$145
			========

Summary

Purchasing Power Gain or Loss

Holding net monetary	Period of	
	Inflation	Deflation
Assets -	Loss	Gain
Liabilities -	Gain	Loss

Ratios—Liquidity/Solvency and Operational

This lesson presents financial statement ratios for liquidity/solvency and operational analysis.

After studying this lesson, you should be able to:

1. *Calculate and interpret liquidity and solvency ratios.*

2. *Calculate and interpret operational ratios.*

I. Background

> **Definition:**
> *Financial Statement Ratio Analysis*: The development of quantitative relationships between various elements of a firm's financial statements.

A. Ratio analysis enables comparisons across firms, especially within the same industry, and facilitates identifying operating and financial strengths and weaknesses of a firm.

B. The names given to ratios frequently indicate the nature of the quantitative analysis needed to develop the ratios.

> **Example:**
> Debt to Equity ratio = Total **Debt** (Liabilities) / Owner's **Equity**

C. Ratios can be grouped according to the major purpose or type of measure being analyzed. The major purposes or types of measures being analyzed are:

1. Liquidity/Solvency;

2. Operational Activity;

3. Profitability;

4. Equity/Investment Leverage.

D. Below is a diagram of the "big picture" of all ratios. This overview helps put the dozens of individual ratios into perspective and helps "see" how the balance sheet / income statement relationships tie together. This diagram also makes it easy to see the difference between ROA and ROE. **Return on Assets** (ROA) – measures operating performance *independent* of financing. **Return on Equity** (ROE) – explicitly *includes* the amount and cost of financing.

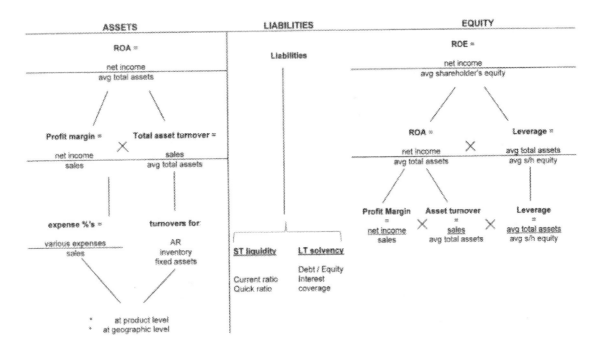

II. Liquidity/Solvency Ratios

A. Major liquidity measures

> **Definition:**
> *Liquidity Ratios (also known as Solvency Ratios):* Measure the ability of the firm to pay its obligations as they become due.

1. Working Capital: Measures the extent to which current assets exceed current liabilities and, thus, are uncommitted in the short term. It is expressed as:

> Working Capital = Current Assets - Current Liability
>
> Working Capital Ratio = Current Assets / Current Liabilities

2. Measures the quantitative relationship between current assets and current liabilities in terms of the "number of times" current assets can cover current liabilities.

   a. Is a widely used measure of the firm's ability to pay its current liabilities.

   b. Changes in Current Assets and/or Current Liabilities have determinable effects on the Working Capital Ratio (WCR):

WCR = Current Assets / Current Liabilities

An increase in current assets (alone) increases the WCR.

A decrease in current assets (alone) decreases the WCR.

An increase in current liabilities (alone) decreases the WCR.

A decrease in current liabilities (alone) increases the WCR.

If the WCR equals 1.00, equal increases or equal decreases in current assets and liabilities will not change the WCR; it will remain 1.00.

c. If the WCR **exceeds** 1.00:

   i. Equal increases in current assets and liabilities decrease the WCR.

WCR = CA 20,000 / CL 10,000 = 2

WCR = (CA 20,000 + 10,000) / (CL 10,000 + 10,000) = 30,000 / 20,000 = 1.5

   ii. Equal decreases in current assets and liabilities increase the WCR.

WCR = CA 30,000 / CL 20,000 = 1.5

WCR = CA 20,000 / CL 10,000 = 2

d. If the WCR is **less than** 1.00:

   i. equal increases in current assets and liabilities increase the WCR.

WCR = CA 10,000 / CA 20,000 = .50

WCR = (CA 10,000 + 10,000) / (CA 20,000 + 10,000) = 20,000 / 30,000 = .66

   ii. Equal decreases in current assets and liabilities decreases the WCR.

WCR = 20,000 / 30,000 = .66

WCR = 10,000 / 20,000 = .50

Acid-Test Ratio (also known as Quick Ratio) = (Cash + (Net) Receivables + Marketable Securities) / Current Liabilities

3. Measures the quantitative relationship between highly liquid assets and current liabilities in terms of the "number of times" that cash and assets that can be converted quickly to cash cover current liabilities.

Securities Defensive-Interval Ratios = (Cash + (Net) Receivables + Marketable Securities) / Average Daily Cash Expenditures

4. Measures the quantitative relationship between highly liquid assets and the average daily use of cash in terms of the number of days that cash and assets can be quickly converted to support operating costs.

Times Interest Earned Ratios = (Net Income + Interest Expense + Income Tax) / Interest Expense

5. Measures the ability of current earnings to cover interest payments for a period.

Times Preferred Dividend Earned Ratio = Net Income / Annual Preferred Dividend Obligation

6. Measures the ability of current earnings to cover preferred dividends for a period.

III. **Operational Activity Ratios** -- These measure the efficiency with which a firm carries out its operating activities.

Accounts Receivable Turnover = (Net) Credit Sales / Average (Net) Accounts Receivable (e.g., Beginning + Ending/2)

A. Measures the number of times that accounts receivable turnover (are incurred and collected) during a period. Indicates the quality of credit policies (and the resulting receivables) and the efficiency of collection procedures.

Number of Days' Sales in Average Receivables = (300 or 360 or 365 (or other measure of business days in a year)) / Accounts Receivable Turnover (computed above)

B. Measures the average number of days required to collect receivables; it is a measure of the average age or receivables.

Inventory Turnover = Cost of Goods Sold / Average Inventory (e.g. Beginning + Ending/2)

C. Measures the number of times that inventory turnover (is acquired and sold or used) during a period. Indicates over or under stocking of inventory or obsolete inventory.

Number of Days' Supply in Inventory = (300 or 360 or 365 (or other measure of business days in a year)) / Inventory Turnover (computed above)

D. Measures the number of days inventory is held before it is sold or used. Indicates the efficiency of general inventory management.

Operating Number of Cycle = Days in Operating = Number of Days' Sale in A/R + Length Cycle Number of Days' Supply in Inventory

E. Measures the average length of time to invest cash in inventory, convert the inventory to receivables, and collect the receivables; it measures the time to go from cash back to cash.

Ratios—Profitability and Equity

This lesson presents financial statement ratios for profitability and equity analysis.

After studying this lesson, you should be able to:

1. *Calculate and interpret profitability ratios.*

2. *Calculate and interpret equity ratios.*

I. Background

> **Definition:**
> *Financial Statement Ratio Analysis*: The development of quantitative relationships between various elements of a firm's financial statements.

A. Ratio analysis enables comparisons across firms, especially within the same industry, and facilitates identifying operating and financial strengths and weaknesses of a firm.

B. The names given to ratios frequently indicate the nature of the quantitative analysis needed to develop the ratios.

 Example:
Debt to Equity ratio = Total **Debt** (Liabilities) / Owner's **Equity**

C. Ratios can be grouped according to the major purpose or type of measure being analyzed. The major purposes or types of measures being analyzed are:

1. Liquidity/Solvency;

2. Operational Activity;

3. Profitability;

4. Equity/Investment Leverage.

II. Profitability Ratios -- These measure aspects of a firm's operating (income/loss) results on a relative basis.

> Profit Margin (on Sales) = Net Income / (Net) Sales

A. Measures the net profitability on sales (revenue).

> Return on Total Assets = (Net Income + (add back) Interest Expense (net of tax effect)) / Average Total Assets

B. Measures the rate of return on total assets and indicates the efficiency with which invested resources (assets) are used.

> Return on Common Stockholders' Equity = (Net Income - Preferred Dividend (obligation for the period only)) / Average Common Stockholders' Equity (e.g. (Beginning + Ending)/2)

C. Measures the rate of return (earnings) on common stockholders' investment.

> Return on Owners' (all Stockholders') Equity = Net Income / Average Stockholders' Equity (e.g. (Beginning + Ending)/2)

D. Measures the rate of return (earnings) on all stockholders' investment.

> Earnings Per Share (EPS -- Basic Formula) = (Net Income - Preferred Dividends (obligation for the period only)) / Weighted Average Number of Shares Outstanding

E. Measures the income earned per (average) share of common stock. Indicates ability to pay dividends to common shareholders.

> Price-Earnings Ratio (P/E Ratio) = Market Price for a Common Share / Earnings per (Common) Share (EPS)

F. Measures the price of a share of common stock relative to its latest earnings per share. Indicates a measure of how the market values the stock, especially when compared with other stocks.

G. Common Stock Dividends Pay Out Ratio =

> Total Basis = Cash Dividends to Common Shareholders / Net Income to Common Shareholder

> Per Share Basis = Cash Dividends per Common Share / Earnings per Common Share

H. Measures the extent (percent) of earnings distributed to common shareholders.

> Common Stock Yield = Dividend per Common Share / Market Price per Common Share

I. Measures the rate of return (yield) per share of common stock.

III. Equity/Investment Leverage Ratios -- These provide measures of relative sources of equity and equity value.

> Debt to Equity Ratio = Total Liabilities / Total Shareholders' Equity

A. Measures relative amounts of assets provided by creditors and shareholders.

> Owners' Equity Ratio = Shareholders' Equity / Total Assets

B. Measures the proportion of assets provided by shareholders.

Debt Ratio = Total Liabilities / Total Assets

C. Measures the proportion of assets provided by creditors. Indicates the extent of leverage in funding the entity.

Book Value per Common Stock = Common Shareholders' Equity / Number of Outstanding Common Shares

D. Measures the per share amount of common shareholders' claim to assets. (See the section on this ratio in the owner's equity module for more details.)

Book Value per Preferred Share = Preferred Shareholders' Equity (including dividends in arrears) / Number of Outstanding Preferred Stocks

E. Measures the per share amount of preferred shareholders' claim to assets.

Cash, Modified Cash, Income Tax

In addition to the GAAP-based general purpose financial statements described in prior lessons, there are other comprehensive basis of accounting that may be used by non-public business entities, specialized entities, and individuals to prepare financial statements. This lesson covers the major non-GAAP comprehensive basis of accounting used by non-public business entities. These bases of accounting are referred to as Other Comprehensive Basis of Accounting (OCBOA) or Special Purpose Frameworks.

This lesson covers accounting for the major non-GAAP comprehensive basis of accounting used by nonpublic business entities. A separate lesson covers the auditing of financial statements prepared using a "comprehensive basis other than GAAP" as set forth in SAS 800, Special Considerations—Audits of Financial Statements Prepared in Accordance with Special Purpose Frameworks. It should be noted that the cash, tax, and regulatory bases of accounting are commonly referred to as other comprehensive bases of accounting (OCBOA). The term OCBOA was replaced with the term "Special Purpose Framework" for auditors under SAS 800. OCBOA is no longer used in Generally Accepted Auditing Standards (GAAS). However, OCBOA is still commonly used in practice. A separate lesson is presented by Professor Don Tidrick, author of the Auditing and Attestation section of CPAexcel.

After studying this lesson you should be able to:

1. *Identify each separate basis of accounting:*

   -- Cash Basis

   -- Modified Cash Basis

   -- Income Tax Basis

   -- Other

2. *Describe the characteristics of each separate accounting basis.*

3. *Know how each separate accounting basis differs from GAAP.*

I. **Special Purpose Framework or Other Comprehensive Basis of Accounting --** General-purpose financial statements, as described in prior lessons, are based on generally accepted accounting principles (GAAP) for public business enterprises. There are circumstances, however, when financial statements not based on GAAP are used by non-public business entities to avoid the time-consuming and costly application of GAAP. For example, another comprehensive basis of accounting (other than GAAP) may be used by sole proprietorships, partnerships or small, closely held corporations when the entity does not have loan covenants or other requirements that mandate the preparation of GAAP-based financial statements. There are over 2.8 million partnerships and over 20 million sole proprietorships in the United States. Many of these nonpublic businesses use another comprehensive basis of accounting. The primary acceptable other comprehensive basis of accounting widely used by non-public businesses entities, including cash basis, modified cash basis and income tax basis, are covered in the following subsections. There are several categories of Special Purpose Framework or OCBOA financial statements:

Cash Basis;

Modified Cash Basis;

Income Tax Basis;

Regulatory Basis;

Other Basis with Substantial Support.

A. Cash Basis Financial Statements

1. Cash basis financial statements are based solely on cash receipts and cash disbursements. In a pure cash basis of accounting, revenues are recognized only when cash is received and expenses are recognized only when cash is disbursed. The principles of accrual accounting are ignored. In cash basis accounting, there is no attempt to recognize revenues when they are earned and no attempt to recognize expenses when they are incurred, nor is there a matching of related expenses to revenues or to the time period in which they would be recognized in accrual basis accounting.

2. Because, in a pure cash basis of accounting, cash received is recognized as revenue (DR. Cash/CR. Revenue) and cash paid is recognized as expense (DR. Expense/CR. Cash), a balance sheet-like statement would show only the asset Cash and Equity; there would be no other assets or liabilities shown. For example, a payment for capital assets (e.g., property, plant, or equipment) would be recognized as an expense, not as a long-term asset. Similarly, a collection of cash would be recognized as revenue, whether or not the good or service had been provided.

3. Example Journal Entries for Equipment Purchase of $10,000:

Cash Basis		Accrual Basis	
Equipment Expense 10,000		Equipment (asset) 10,000	
Cash	10,000	Cash	10,000

4. A pure cash basis accounting and resulting financial statements may be appropriate for small, very closely held businesses (e.g., sole proprietorships, small partnerships, etc.) where the owners/managers whose primary interest and even survival depends on cash flows.

B. Modified Cash Basis Financial Statements

1. Modified cash basis financial statements result from using a combination of elements of cash basis accounting and accrual basis accounting. Conceptually, modified cash basis accounting would be any point on a continuum between pure cash basis at one end and full accrual basis at the other; the greater the number of accrual basis elements adopted, the greater the modification of the cash basis.

2. A modified cash basis of accounting is acceptable as another comprehensive basis of accounting if the modification(s) has substantial support in practice. Substantial support likely would be established if:

   a. The modification is equivalent to an element of accrual basis accounting, and

   b. The modification is logical and consistent with GAAP.

3. The most common and acceptable modifications to cash basis accounting include:

   a. Recognizing the acquisition of property, plant, equipment and inventory as assets (rather than as expenses), and depreciating, amortizing or otherwise writing-off the assets in a regular manner, or

   b. Recognizing accounts receivable when revenues are earned and accounts payable when obligations are incurred, rather than deferring recognition until collections are received or payments are made, or

   c. Recognizing income taxes (and, perhaps, other significant taxes) when they become payable, rather than when paid.

4. When modifications to cash basis accounting are made, all related accounts must be reported using the same basis of accounting. For example, if long-term assets are recognized, then the related depreciation expense and accumulated depreciation must be recognized. Similarly, if debt is recognized, then the related interest expense (accrued and paid) must be recognized.

C. Income Tax Basis Financial Statements

1. Income tax basis financial statements result from using the federal income tax rules and regulations that a firm uses, or expects to use, in filing its income tax return. In income-tax basis accounting, the effects of events on a business are recognized when taxable income or deductible expense would be recognized on the tax return. Income is recognized on the financial statements in the period it is taxable and expenses are recognized on the financial statements in the period they are deductible. The specific requirements of federal income tax accounting specify different income and expense recognition rules depending on the nature of the item and the type of taxpayer. Therefore, financial statements based on the income tax basis of accounting will include items based on various recognition principles, from pure cash to full accrual accounting, depending on that tax codes treatment of these items.

2. Some items of economic and accounting consequence to an entity are never recognized for tax purposes. These are commonly called permanent differences. For example, proceeds from life insurance on officers or portions of intercompany dividends are not taxable income to an entity but provide cash to the entity. Similarly, the premium on life insurance on officers and certain fines are not deductible for income tax purposes but require the payment of cash. Under the income tax basis of accounting, nontaxable receipts (revenue) and nondeductible payments (expenses) related to these permanent differences generally would be recognized in a statement of revenues and expenses. That recognition may be made in one of three ways:

   a. As separate line items in the revenue and/or expense sections of the statement of revenues and expenses; this is the most common treatment;

   b. As separate line items shown as additions to or deductions from the net revenues and expenses;

   c. The nature and amounts disclosed in the notes to the financial statements.

3. Because items and amounts reported for tax purposes are subject to adjustment by the Internal Revenue Service (IRS), the corresponding amounts reported in tax-based financial statements are subject to change as the tax code is changed by U.S. Congress. Therefore, the notes to the financial statements should clearly indicate not only the basis on which the statements were prepared, but also that they are subject to change as a result of IRS determinations. When such adjustments do occur, the treatment in the financial statements will depend on the nature of the item adjusted.

   a. If the adjustment relates to an error in the tax return of a prior year, then a prior period adjustment is appropriate;

    b. If the adjustment relates to an item that is not an error and is not balance sheet related, then the adjustment would be treated as a current period expense (or income);

    c. If the adjustment relates to an item that is not an error and is balance sheet related, then the adjustment would be treated as a prior period adjustment.

D. **Other Acceptable Non-GAAP Basis of Accounting** -- In addition to the cash basis, the modified cash basis, and the income tax basis of accounting, two additional categories of other comprehensive basis of accounting exist. These additional categories of OCBOA are:

1. A basis of accounting used to comply with a regulatory agency that has jurisdiction over the reporting entity. Regulatory financial statements do fall under the category of a Special Purpose Framework for audit purposes.

    a. Examples would include financial statements filed with state insurance or public utility regulatory agencies.

    b. Regulatory-based financial statements should be restricted to use by the entity and the regulatory agency.

2. There also may be financial statements that we have not covered. These financial statements are prepared using a basis with a definite set of accounting and reporting criteria that has substantial support and which is applied to all material financial statement items. One example of these might be financial statements that had price level or inflation adjusted financial statements.

Personal Financial Statements

This lesson introduces personal financial statements, valuation and presentation of assets, liabilities, and net worth in personal financial statements. This lesson also describes the appropriate valuation of assets, liabilities, and net worth for personal financial statements. It concludes with the correct disclosure and presentation of those values in a personal Statement of Financial Condition (Balance Sheet), and the determination of the net worth element in that statement.

After studying this lesson, you should be able to:

1. *Describe the purpose of personal financial statements.*

2. *Identify the kinds of statements used to provide personal financial information.*

3. *Describe the appropriate basis for preparing those statements, and identifying the primary disclosures required with personal financial statements.*

4. *Identify the appropriate valuation of assets, liabilities, and net worth for personal financial statements Identify the appropriate valuation of assets for personal financial statements.*

5. *Describe the correct disclosure and presentation of those values in a personal Statement of Financial Condition (Balance Sheet).*

6. *Describe the determination and presentation of the net worth element in the personal Statement of Financial Condition.*

I. Purpose of Personal Financial Statements

A. Who uses and Why do they use Personal Financial Statements? The "entity" for which personal financial statements are prepared is an individual or a group of related individuals, including a husband and wife, or a family unit; they are not prepared for a business enterprise.

B. Personal financial statements typically are prepared in conjunction with personal borrowing, personal financial planning, contract requirements, or legal requirements.

C. Examples:

1. As part of an application for a major loan to be backed by personal assets.

2. As required by law for elected and other public officials.

II. Types of Personal Financial Statements

A. The following financial statements are typically appropriate for personal financial statements:

1. A Statement of Financial Condition (Balance Sheet) - required;

2. A Statement of Changes in Net Worth - optional, but is usually provided.

B. Comparative Statements of Financial Condition or Changes in Net Worth, which present information about the current and one or more prior periods, are optional.

C. The following financial statements are NOT appropriate as personal financial statements:

1. An Income Statement - not provided (although the changes in net worth would have much of this information);

2. A Statement of Cash Flows - not provided.

III. Basis for Preparing Personal Financial Statements

    A. Statement of Financial Condition (Balance Sheet)

        1. A personal Statement of Financial Condition is based on accrual accounting using fair value - known as current value. Current value represents the amount at which a buyer and seller would be willing to exchange the item. It is not a forced sale.

        2. The personal Statement of Financial Condition should report:

            a. Assets at estimated current values;

            b. Liabilities at estimated current amounts;

            c. Personal Net Worth as the difference between (1) and (2), above.

            d. Estimated income taxes are calculated as if assets had been realized and liabilities had been liquidated.

        3. The valuation and presentation of assets, liabilities and net worth are described in detail in subsequent lessons.

    B. Statement of Changes in Net Worth

        1. A personal Statement of Changes in Net Worth shows the amounts and causes of the changes in net worth for an individual, a husband and wife, or a family unit during a period. Assets and liabilities are recognized on an accrual bases.

        2. A personal Statement of Changes in Net Worth is presented in a standard change format. Example:

Allen Family
Statement of Changes in Net Worth
For the Year Beginning 1/1/X1
+ Increases in Estimated Values of Assets
- Decreases in Estimated Values of Assets
- Increases in Estimated Amounts of Liabilities
<u>+ Decreases in Estimated Amounts of Liabilities</u>
= Net Worth 12/31/X1

        3. Noncancelable commitments to pay future sums are presented at discounted amounts as liabilities if they are for fixed/determinable amounts, are not contingent, and do not require future service or performance.

IV. Asset Valuation

    A. Assets should be reported at estimated current values (fair value)based on an assumed arms-length transaction, net of disposal costs, if any.

    B. Asset Valuation Guidelines:

Assets Value	Possible Basis for Current Value
Receivables	Discounted cash flow
Marketable Securities/Options	Market quote (with adjustment for blockage factor if sale of the securities/options would influence market price)
Retirement Plans (Vested only)	Discounted cash flow; Present value
Life Insurance	Cash surrender value, less any loan outstanding against the policy
Closely Held Business	Appraisal; Discounted cash flow; Capitalized earnings; Liquidation value, net of disposal costs; Multiple of earnings
Real Estate	Value of recent comparable sales; Appraisal
Income Generating Property	Discounted cash flow
Intangible Assets	Discounted cash flow
Future Interests/Rights	Discounted cash flow

V. Asset Disclosure and Presentation Matters

A. The face value of life insurance policies also should be disclosed.

B. Significant interest in separate businesses should be shown as a single line item and amount for each business interest, measured at the estimated current value of the net assets, separate from other assets. See the following examples.

   1. A **significant** interest in an S Corporation should be shown at a single value separate from investments in marketable securities.

   2. A **significant** real estate activity that operates as a separate business entity should be reported as a separate line item at a single amount, the property value net of any mortgage(s).

C. Interest in a business activity that **does not function as a separate business** should be shown as the **separate** assets (at estimated current value) and **separate** liabilities (at estimated current amount) that comprise the business activity.

   1. Example: A real estate activity that does not operate as a separate business entity would be reported as both an asset (the property) and a liability (the mortgage).

D. Future interests and rights should be recognized as assets only if the interests or rights:

   1. Are fixed or determinable in amounts;

   2. Are not contingent on the holder's life expectancy or the occurrence of a specific event, including death or disability;

   3. Do not require future performances by the holder.

E. Assets should be listed in the Statement of Financial Condition in the order of liquidity, not separated into current/non-current categories.

VI. Liability and Net Worth Valuation and Presentation

A. Liability Valuation

1. Liabilities should be reported in a Statement of Financial Condition at estimated current amounts based on the lower of:

   a. The amount at which the liability could be settled currently (liquidation value), or

   b. The present value of cash to be paid in future settlement.

2. Liability Valuation Guidelines:

Liabilities	Possible Basis for Current Amount
Trade Payables	Lower of amount for current settlement or discounted (present value) of cash flow to pay in future
Noncancelable Commitments	Discounted (present value) of cash flow to pay in future
Income Tax Payable (prior and current periods)	Known and estimated amounts payable less withholding and estimated tax payments made
Income Tax Provision (for estimated net taxable gains reported on personal Statement of Financial Condition	Difference between (estimated current value of assets - estimated amount of liabilities) and their aggregate tax basis, multiplied by the current tax rate

VII. Liability and Net Worth Disclosure and Presentation Matters

A. Commitments or other liabilities should be recognized as a personal liability only if the obligations:

1. Are to pay a fixed or determinable amount;

2. Are not contingent on others life expectancy or the occurrence of a specific event, including death or disability;

3. Do not require future performances by others.

B. The income tax provision is computed as if the assets and liabilities were disposed/settled at fair value and the resulting excess over their tax basis were taxed under the currently applicable laws and rates.

See the following example.

Example:
The Allen family has the following personal items at the values shown:

Assets at current values	$535,000
Liabilities at current amounts	- 218,000
Net assets at Fair Value	$317,000
Tax Basis of Assets and Liabilities	- 117,000
Taxable Net Fair Value	$200,000
Current effective tax rate	x 25%
Provision for Income Tax	$ 50,000

The Provision for Income Tax should be shown in the Statement of Financial Condition as a separate line item between (other) Liabilities and Net Worth.

C. Liabilities (except Provision for Income Tax) should be listed in the Statement of Financial Condition in the order of maturity, not separated into current/non-current categories.

D. Net Worth Valuation and Presentation

1. The difference between assets (at current estimated value) less liabilities (at current estimated amount), and a provision for income tax on the estimated taxable gain is personal Net Worth.

2. Personal Net Worth should be shown in the Statement of Financial Condition after liabilities in a manner similar to Capital. See the following statement using information from the Allen Family example above.

Allen Family

Statement of Financial Position

Assets

Cash in Bank	$ 3,000
Investment	185,000
Automobiles	22,000
Home	325,000
Total Assets	**$535,000**

Liabilities

Credit Cards	$ 18,000
Car Notes	22,000
Home Mortgage	178,000
Total Liabilities	$218,000
Income Tax Provisions	50,000
Total Liabilities and Inc. Tax	**$268,000**
Allen Family Net Worth	**$267,000**

Private Company Council

The purpose of this lesson is to provide a description of the Private Company Council (PCC), its purpose, and the process for setting standards applicable to private companies. This lesson presents the definition of a Public Business Entity and the significant Accounting Standard Updates (ASUs) that relate to private companies.

After studying this lesson, you should be able to:

1. *Describe the purpose of the PCC and its role in the standard setting process.*

2. *Describe the definition of a public business entity.*

3. *Identify the significant accounting differences for private companies.*

I. **PCC Purpose** -- I. In May 2012, the Financial Accounting Foundation (FAF) approved the establishment of the Private Company Council (PCC), an organization that will assist in setting accounting standards for private companies. The PCC has two principal responsibilities:

   A. To work with the Financial Accounting Standards Board (FASB) to identify places within existing Generally Accepted Accounting Principles (GAAP) where there are opportunities for alternative accounting for private companies.

   B. To serve in an advisory capacity to the FASB on the appropriate treatment of items under consideration for new GAAP and how those items may impact private companies.

II. **PCC Process**

   A. PCC will review of existing U.S. GAAP and identify standards that require reconsideration. Any proposed alternative GAAP requires a two-thirds vote of all PCC members.

   B. Proposed modifications to U.S. GAAP approved by the PCC are submitted to the FASB for endorsement. If endorsed by a simple majority of FASB members, the proposed modifications will be exposed for public comment. Following receipt of public comment, the PCC will determine if any changes are warranted and take a final vote. If approved, the final decision then will be submitted to the FASB for final approval.

   C. If the FASB does not endorse the initial proposal or final modification, the FASB will provide to the PCC documentation describing the reason(s) for the nonendorsement and possible changes for the PCC to consider.

III. **The PCC Framework**

   A. The PCC Framework is used to determine whether and in what circumstances should the private companies have guidance for alternative recognition, measurement, disclosure, display, effective date, and transition reporting under U.S. GAAP. The differences between private companies and public companies are a driving force in determining whether alternative GAAP is warranted.

   B. The framework provides direction to evaluate the tradeoff between user-relevance and cost-benefit for private companies. To help identify information needs of users of public company financial statements versus users of private company financial statements the framework outlines five factors that differentiate the needs of the financial statement users. These factors can help identify opportunities to reduce the complexity and costs of preparing financial statements for private companies.

   1. Number of primary users and their access to management;

   2. Investment strategies of the primary users;

   3. Ownership and capital structure;

4. Accounting resources available to generate reporting and disclosure information;

5. Resources available for learning about new financial reporting guidance on a timely basis.

C. The framework discusses the five areas in which financial accounting and reporting guidance might differ for private companies and public companies:

1. Recognition and measurement;

2. Disclosures;

3. Display (or presentation);

4. Effective date;

5. Transition method.

IV. What is a Public Business Entity?

A. The PCC provides a definition for a public business entity because any entity that is not public is a private entity. It may seem kind of backward to not give a definition of a private entity but to give a definition of a public entity, but it is easier to define the characteristics of a public entity and therefore identify what entities cannot apply the standards set by the PCC.

B. The definition excludes not-for-profit companies and employee benefit plans. A public entity is one that (ASC 2013-12 para 2):

1. Is required by the SEC to file or furnish financial statements;

2. Is required by the Securities Act of 1934 to file or furnish financial statements with a regulatory agency other than the SEC (for example debt securities);

3. Is required to file or furnish financial statements with foreign or domestic regulatory agencies in order to sell or issue securities;

4. Has issued securities that are traded, listed, or quoted on an exchange or over-the-counter market;

5. Has securities that are not subject to contractual restrictions and is required by law, contract, or regulation to prepare U.S.GAAP financial statements and make them publicly available on a periodic basis.

C. The standalone financial statements of a subsidiary consolidated with a public company is not considered a public business entity for purposes of its standalone financial statements. However, the subsidiary is considered a public business for purposes of the financial statements that are included in an SEC filing.

> **Note:** Before electing any PCC accounting alternatives, the private entity should consider the likelihood that it may become a public business entity either through initial public offering or acquisition by another public entity. If the private entity becomes a public entity, retrospective reversal of all the accounting applied under PCC guidance is required.

V. Accounting for Goodwill (ASU 2014-02)

A. This ASU allows a private entity to amortize goodwill on a straight-line basis over 10 years, or less than 10 years if it is more appropriate. This means that the entity does not have to complete annual impairment testing. At the time of adoption of this standard, the entity must make an election to test goodwill impairment at the entity level or the reporting unit level.

B. The private entity must complete impairment testing when a triggering event occurs. When that event occurs the private entity must apply the impairment test following the guidance for a public entity. That is, the private entity has the option to apply the prestep qualitative assessment prior to the quantitative assessment. The measurements under the quantitative two steps are applied in the same manner as required under ASC 350.

C. This standard should be applied prospectively to goodwill existing as of the beginning of the period of adoption and new goodwill recognized in annual periods beginning after December 15, 2014, and interim periods within annual periods beginning after December 15, 2015. Early application is permitted, including application to any period for which the entity's annual or interim financial statements have not yet been made available for issuance.

VI. Simplified Accounting for Interest Rate Swaps (ASU 2014-03)

A. This simplified hedge accounting applies only to interest rate swaps for variable rate debt to fixed rate debt (cash flow hedge). Many private companies have difficulty obtaining fixed rate debt at a competitive interest rate. Therefore these companies frequently enter into an interest rate swap to convert the variable rate debt to fixed rates.

B. When certain criteria are met, the private entity can assume the swap is 100% effective. This assumption significantly reduces the testing needed for assessing and measuring ineffectiveness. The criteria are (815-20-25-131D):

1. Both the variable rate on the swap and the borrowing are based on the same index and reset period.

2. The terms of the swap are typical (a "plain-vanilla" swap), and there is no floor or cap on the variable interest rate of the swap unless the borrowing has a comparable floor or cap.

3. The repricing and settlement dates for the swap and the borrowing match or differ by no more than a few days.

4. The swap's fair value at inception (that is, at the time the derivative was executed to hedge the interest rate risk of the borrowing) is at or near zero.

5. The notional amount of the swap matches the principal amount of the borrowing. In complying with this condition, the amount of the borrowing being hedged may be less than the total principal amount of the borrowing.

6. All interest payments occurring on the borrowing during the term of the swap are designated as hedged whether in total or in proportion to the principal amount of the borrowing being hedged.

C. When these criteria are met the private entity can use the practical expedient of settlement value to measure the value of the swap versus measuring the swap at fair market value. Settlement value excludes the adjustment for performance risk and is generally viewed to be a simpler valuation.

D. The private entity must complete documentation requirements related to cash flow hedge accounting and must comply with the disclosure requirements for hedge accounting (Topic 815) and fair value (Topic 820).

E. This standard is effective for annual periods beginning after December 15, 2014, and interim periods within annual periods beginning after December 15, 2015, with early adoption permitted.

VII. Applying Variable Interest Entity (VIE) Criteria to Common Control Leasing Arrangements (ASU 2014-07)

A. Private companies are not required to apply the criteria for determining whether there is a variable interest in certain leasing arrangements. This exemption applies when:

1. The private company lessee and lessor are under common control;

2. The private company lessee has a leasing arrangement with the lessor;

3. Substantially all of the activity between the private company lessee and the lessor is related to the leasing activities; and

4. The private company lessee explicitly guarantees any obligation of the lessor related to the leased asset.

B. If this exemption is elected it should be applied to all of the leasing arrangements that meet the above conditions.

C. The private company does not need to provide the disclosures associated with a VIE, but rather would disclose the information related to the lease arrangement. The disclosure should include a description of the lease arrangements that exposes the private company lessee to provide financial support to the lessor.

VIII. Simplified Accounting for Intangible Assets Acquired in a Business Combination (ASU 2014-18)

A. Private companies have the option to not recognize certain intangible assets associated with a business combination. Specifically, private companies can elect to not recognize customer-related intangibles that cannot be sold or licensed independent of the business (customer contracts and relationships) and noncompete agreements separately from goodwill. These intangible assets are costly and complex to value.

B. In general, the acquirer in a business combination must recognize all intangible assets that are 1) separable or 2) arise from contractual or other legal rights.

C. Private companies will be excluded from this requirement with respect to customer contracts, customer relationships, and non-compete agreements. Customer contracts that are nontransferable would not need to be separately valued and recognized. Customer relationships are often nontransferable because the relationship is unique with the private company. Noncompete agreements are also often nontransferable because the agreement is with an employee (or former employee) and the private entity. A noncompete agreement is a legal arrangement to prohibit another party from competing with the entity in a certain market for a certain period of time.

D. Private companies must recognize other identifiable intangibles such as copyrights, trademarks, and patents, separately from goodwill. In addition, customer-related intangibles that can be sold or licensed independent of other assets of the businesses must be recognized. For example, customer lists and other customer information that can be sold or licensed independently of the business would meet the separability criterion and would be valued and recognized as part of the business combination.

E. An entity can early adopt and apply (or opt out of) this PCC option can be early adopted and applied (or opt out) to a qualifying transaction that occurs in 2014 but prior to the issuance of its financial statements. Private companies that do not choose early adoption can elect (or opt out of) of this guidance for the first qualifying transaction that occurs in 2015 or later. If the private company elected (or opted out of) of this guidance and subsequently changed the election (or opted out of), it would be considered a change in accounting policy and applied retrospectively.

F. If the private company elects the PCC guidance on intangibles, it must also adopt the goodwill accounting alternative described above (ASU 2014-02), which requires goodwill to be amortized over a

> **Note:**
> In other words, once the entity has elected to adopt (or opt out of) the alternative accounting for customer contracts, customer relationships, and noncompete agreements, any subsequent accounting should be consistently applied, or it is a change in accounting principle.

period of up to 10 years. The tandem requirement ensures that the customer-related and non-compete-related intangible assets embedded in goodwill are essentially amortized. The opposite is not required—if the private company elects to amortize goodwill, it does not have to elect this guidance on the intangible assets.

Liquidation Basis of Accounting

The purpose of this lesson is to provide a description of Liquidation Basis of Accounting. This standard provides guidance about when a company should report financial information using liquidation basis, the basic criteria for recognition and measurement, as well as disclosure requirements.

After studying this lesson you should be able to :

1. *Identify the disclosures required for an entity that is preparing statements under a liquidation basis.*

2. *Describe the principles for recognition and measurement of assets and liabilities that are presented under liquidation basis of accounting.*

3. *Describe when an entity should adopt liquidation basis of accounting.*

I. **Liquidation --** Liquidation is the process in which a company converts its assets to cash and settles its liabilities. An entity in liquidation is not a going concern, but rather an entity that has a plan for liquidation. Liquidation basis of accounting is required when liquidation is imminent. Liquidation is imminent when (ASU 2013-07):

   A. A plan for liquidation approved by the person (s) who have the authority to make the plan effective and the likelihood is remote that the execution of the plan would be blocked by other parties, or

   B. A plan for liquidation is being imposed on the entity by other forces (i.e., forced bankruptcy).

II. **Principles for Recognition and Measurement under Liquidation Basis of Accounting (ASU 2013-07):**

   A. Assets are presented at the amount of cash expected from the liquidation process. The entity should recognize the cash proceeds expected from the liquidation of assets not previously recognized under U.S. GAAP such as the proceeds associated with the sale of a previously unrecognized trademark. The asset values may not equal fair value because the assets are being sold through a process of liquidation which may deflate the assets value.

   B. Liabilities are recognized and measured in accordance with U.S. GAAP as required for those liabilities. The entity cannot assume that it will be legally released from the liabilities. The entity must not anticipate either judicial or creditor abatement of the obligations. Liabilities can be reduced only if legally forgiven. The entity cannot write down a liability in anticipation of forgiveness.

   C. The entity must accrue and separately present the expected costs associated with the liquidation. This would include any costs associated with the settlement of the entities assets and liabilities.

   D. The entity must present a statement of net assets in liquidation and a statement of changes in net assets in liquidation.

III. **Disclosures Required under Liquidation Basis of Accounting**

   A. Because the entity is no longer a going concern, disclosures are required that will aid the understanding of the entity's statement of net assets in liquidation and statement of changes in net assets in liquidation. The disclosures will help understand the amount of cash the entity expects to collect and the amount of cash the entity is obligated to pay during the course of liquidation. These disclosures included:

   B. A statement that the financial statements are presented using the liquidation basis of accounting

C. Description of the liquidation plan

D. Methods and significant assumptions used to measure assets and liabilities

E. Type and amount of costs and income accrued associated with the liquidation plan.

IASB and Structure

This lesson presents an overview of International Accounting Standards Board (IASB) and the structure surrounding its operations.

After studying this lesson, you should be able to:

1. *Identify the objectives of the IFRS Foundation.*

2. *Identify the roles of the various components of the IFRS Foundation and the IASB and the structure in which they interact.*

I. International Accounting Standards Board (IASB)

A. The IASB is a London (UK)-based organization formed to develop a single set of financial accounting standards worldwide. The board evolved from the International Accounting Standards Committee (IASC), which was established in 1973 for the same purpose by accounting organizations from ten countries including the UK and US. In March 2001, the IASC Foundation (IASCF), the parent of the IASB, was founded as a non-profit corporation (a Delaware 501-c3 corporation). Beginning April 2001, the IASB began its responsibility for standard setting, taking over from the IASC. As a result of a Constitution Review concluded in 2010, the IASCF was renamed the IFRS Foundation.

B. Objectives of the IASCF from its constitution

1. To develop, in the public interest, a single set of high-quality, understandable, enforceable, and globally accepted financial reporting standards based upon clearly articulated principles. These standards should require high quality, transparent and comparable information in financial statements and other financial reporting to help investors, other participants in the world's capital markets and other users of financial information make economic decisions.

2. To promote the use and rigorous application of those standards.

3. To take account of, as appropriate, the needs of a range of sizes and types of entities in diverse economic settings.

4. To promote and facilitate adoption of International Financial Reporting Standards (IFRSs) being the standards and interpretations issued by the IASB, through the convergence of national accounting standards and IFRSs.

C. International Financial Reporting Standards (IFRSs) are designed to be a single set of high quality financial reporting standards used by entities worldwide. In addition to IFRSs and Interpretations, the IASB has issued its Framework, which, like that of the FASB, is not GAAP but rather provides the theoretical underpinnings for IFRSs. The IASB Framework is discussed in a later section.

D. Like the FASB, the IASB has no enforcement powers. Compliance with international financial reporting standards is voluntary. The enforcement for publicly traded companies in national jurisdictions is the responsibility of securities regulators (for example, the SEC in the US). The International Organization of Securities Commissions (IOSCO) has pledged to support the process of coordinating national securities regulators to promote cooperation and high standards of regulation to maintain efficient capital markets on a global basis.

1. IOSCO, formed in 1983, is comprised of securities regulators from many countries, representing most of the world's capital markets. It is the international standard setter for securities markets. Its objectives include promoting high standards of regulation to ensure transparent and efficient capital markets, and promoting the integrity of markets by rigorous application and enforcement of standards.

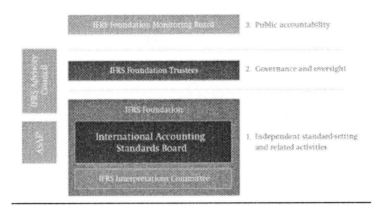

Source: www.ifrs.org

E. **Monitoring Board** -- The Monitoring Board is composed of public capital market authorities, such as the Chair of the SEC and IOSCO. The Trustees of the IFRS Foundation are accountable to the Monitoring Board. The responsibilities of the Monitoring Board include participating in the process for appointing Trustees and approving the appointment of Trustees. Thus, the activities including appointments made by the IFRS Foundation are transparent and accountable.

   1. The Monitoring Board includes the following members:

      a. Member from the European Commission;

      b. Chair of the IOSCO Emerging Markets Committee;

      c. Chair of the IOSCO Technical Committee;

      d. Commissioner of the Japan Financial Services Agency;

      e. Chair of the U.S. Securities and Exchange Commission;

      f. Chair of the Basel Committee on Banking Supervision as an observer.

   2. The Monitoring Board provides a formal link between the Trustees and public authorities. Through the Monitoring Board, securities regulators of countries using IFRS may be more effective in improving investor protection, market integrity, and capital formation.

F. **IFRS Foundation** -- The IFRS Foundation is governed by its trustees who represent global accounting standard-setters. The 22 trustees are from North America (6), Europe (6), Asia/Oceania (6), Africa (1), South America (1) and two from any region subject to maintaining overall geographical balance. Trustees are remunerated.

   1. The trustees appoint the members of IASB, IFRS Advisory Council, and IFRS Interpretations Committee. The IFRS Foundation is responsible for overseeing, reviewing effectiveness, and financing the IASB and appointing its members. The IASB informs the IFRS Foundation of its activities. The IFRS Advisory Council (formerly called Standards Advisory Council) provides strategic advice to IASB and informs the IFRS Foundation of its activities while the IFRS Interpretations Committee (formerly called IFRIC) reports to the IASB. As such, similar to the FAF and FASB, the organizational structure separates the governance body (IFRS Foundation) from the standard-setting body (IASB and IFRS Interpretations Committee). Note that the overall structure of the international standard-setting organization is designed using the FAF and FASB model.

2. Trustees serve terms of three years (renewable once) and are required to be financially knowledgeable and exhibit a strong commitment to the setting of high quality global financial reporting standards. Membership includes auditors, preparers, users, academics, and others. Typically, two of the trustees are senior partners of prominent international accounting firms.

G. **IASB** -- The Board is responsible for promulgating the IFRSs, including those for SMEs (small and medium-sized entities), and for approving Interpretations of IFRSs developed by the IFRIC. The 14 IASB members (increasing to 16 by July 1, 2012), two of whom are part-time, represent many different countries: Europe (4 members), Asia/Oceania (4), North America (4), Africa (1), South America (1), any area (2) to achieve a geographic balance.

1. Professional competence and practical experience are the main qualifications for Board members. Many are CPAs (or equivalent) with auditing experience, but also represented are securities analysts, individuals with corporate accounting experience, and academics. IASB members are paid employees of the IASCF but cannot also be trustees.

2. Board members serve terms of up to five years (renewable once). To avoid calling into question the independence of the Board, the full-time Board members must sever all employment relationships with current employers including rights to return.

H. **IFRS Interpretations Committee** -- The IFRS Interpretations Committee serves a similar role to the FASB's Emerging Issues Task Force, except that the IFRS Interpretations Committee's pronouncements (Interpretations) are reviewed by the IASB before they are issued. The Committee was called the Standing Interpretations Committee (SIC) before 2002 and International Financial Reporting Interpretations Committee (IFRIC) before July 1, 2010. The IFRS Interpretations Committee reviews issues arising in the context of IFRSs and issues Interpretations of those issues. The IFRS Interpretations Committee has 14 voting members and a nonvoting chair, all appointed by the IFRS Foundation trustees. Members are chosen based on their ability to maintain an awareness of current issues as they arise and their technical ability to resolve the issues. Members serve renewable terms of three years. Members are not remunerated for their services although their travel expenses are met by the IFRS Foundation.

I. **IFRS Advisory Council** -- The IFRS Advisory Council (formerly the Standards Advisory Council or SAC) advises the IASB on priorities and the views of interested organizations on major projects, as well as the benefits and costs of proposed standards. Its 30 or more members are appointed by the Trustees. The Advisory Council provides a forum for participation by organizations and individuals, with an interest in international financial reporting, having diverse geographical and functional backgrounds. Currently, the IFRS Advisory Council is comprised of representatives of over 40 organizations, including such organizations as the CFA Institute, Deloitte, Ernst & Young, Financial Executives International, IFAC, the International Monetary Fund, and the World Bank. In addition, the European Commission, Japan Financial Services Agency, and the U.S. Securities and Exchange Commission are observer organizations. When the IASB takes a position in conflict with the IFRS Advisory Council's opinion, the IASB provides a rationale for its position.

J. **Public accountability** -- The process of setting accounting standards is transparent and open to the public. To further increase its public accountability to the public, the IFRS Foundation Trustees are publicly accountable to a Monitoring Board of public capital market authorities. The Monitoring Board's responsibilities include providing assurance that the Trustees are discharging their duties as defined by the IFRS Foundation Constitution, and participating in and approving the appointment or reappointment of Trustees.

1. The Monitoring Board includes members from IOSCO, the European Commission, the Financial Services Agency of Japan (JFSA), and the U.S. Securities and Exchange Commission (US SEC). Through the Monitoring Board, securities regulators of countries using IFRS may be more effective in improving investor protection, market integrity, and capital formation.

K. Funding -- Financing the IFRS Foundation and the IASB is the responsibility of the trustees. Funding must be sufficient to ensure fulfillment of the standard-setting objectives without compromising the independence and objectivity of the standard-setting process.

1. As a private sector entity, the IFRS Foundation has no authority to impose funding requirements. However, the IFRS Foundation has worked closely with the governments of many countries to create national funding sources resulting in levy systems and national contributions through regulatory and standard-setting authorities and stock exchanges. Listed companies (and in some cases, nonlisted companies) pay mandatory government levies in those countries. Other sources include voluntary contributions by companies, accounting firms, financial institutions and others. In addition, income from the sale of IFRS subscriptions, educational materials, and other products provides an additional source of funds.

2. In the long-term, the IFRS Foundation will be working to develop a broadly based sustainable set of diverse sources of long-term funding involving the world's capital markets while discouraging free riders. The IFRS Foundation will strive to base the funding burden on ability to pay using GDP as the determining measure.

IASB Accounting Standards

This lesson presents an overview of International Accounting Standards Board (IASB) accounting standards.

After studying this lesson, you should be able to:

1. *Identify the IFRS Hierarchy.*

2. *Explain the overall objective of IFRS for Small and Medium Entities (SMEs).*

3. *Describe the due process for establishing IFRSs.*

I. International Accounting Pronouncements

A. Before 2001, the IASC issued International Accounting Standards (IASs) and SIC Interpretations. Standards issued after the IASB assumed standard-setting responsibility are called International Financial Reporting Standards (IFRSs), and the IFRS Interpretations Committee now develops Interpretations. The IASC issued 41 International Accounting Standards (IASs), which were adopted by the IASB. The IASB has revised many of those IASs as well as issued IFRSs. In practice, or where the distinction does not matter, IAS, IFRS, SIC, and IFRS interpretations are all referred to as IFRSs. The term "international GAAP" or "iGAAP" also is a frequently encountered description of the pronouncements of the IASB in the United States.

B. IFRS Hierarchy -- The following list provides the level of authority for IFRSs, from most to least authoritative. This hierarchy is included in IAS 8, *Accounting Policies, Changes in Accounting Estimates, and Errors (para 10 - 12).*

1. Requirements in IFRSs dealing with similar and related issues;

2. The definitions, recognition criteria, and measurement concepts for assets, liabilities, income, and expenses in the Framework;

3. If no such guidance exists, pronouncements of other standard-setting bodies using a similar conceptual framework, other accounting literature, and accepted industry practices provided there is no conflict with the first two levels above.

C. Principles-based Standards -- IFRSs are considered more principle-based (objectives-oriented) and less detailed compared with U.S. standards which are considered more rule-based and detailed. IFRSs allow for more professional judgment to be applied and are typically shorter and written more simply with fewer rules. IFRSs derive more directly from the Framework and accommodate fewer exceptions. U.S. standards generally are more detailed and often attempt to cover every conceivable situation but still require professional judgment in the application of the standards.

 Example:
Lease capitalization

Both US GAAP and IFRS require capitalization of leases when the lease is in substance the purchase of an asset. The lessee records an asset and noncurrent liability for the present value of lease payments.

If any one of four U.S. criteria is met, then the lease is capitalized under U.S. GAAP. Two of the criteria are quantitative. If the lease term is at least 75% of the useful life of the asset, or if the present value of lease payments is at least 90% of the fair value of the asset, the lease is capitalized. The 75% and 90% criteria are called "bright-line" thresholds.

> IFRSs are broader in the sense that basic principles are stated and few "bright-lines" exist. For the same leased asset, if the lease transfers "substantially all" the risks and rewards incidental of ownership, then the lease is capitalized.

D. IFRS for Small and Medium-sized Entities (SMEs)

1. This single IFRS is intended to be the basis for financial reporting by SMEs, estimated to represent approximately 95% of all companies - those that are not publicly traded (not listed). The standard, built upon the foundation of the entire set of IFRS for publicly traded entities, covers all reporting areas and is designed to simplify the financial reporting process for SMEs - it is the only accounting standard needed for SMEs.

2. This stand-alone IFRS was developed in response to strong international demand for a common set of simplified accounting standards enabling SMEs to report at less cost without compromising the results. The IFRS for SMEs is separate from the other IFRSs. It is not intended to be used by entities aspiring to be traded in capital markets, currently or in the future. The length of this multiple-topic complete but simplified standard was approximately 8% of the total length of all IFRSs at the time of its adoption in 2009.

3. **The IFRS for SMEs simplifies financial reporting in the following ways**

   a. Some topics and requirements are completely eliminated, if not relevant to private entities;

   b. Several recognition and measurement aspects are simplified;

   c. Where IFRS allows reporting options, the IFRS for SMEs requires only the simpler option;

   d. Disclosures have been reduced to approximately 10% of those required by the full set of IFRSs;

   e. Revisions to the SME standard will be limited to once every three years at most.

      i. Examples of omitted topics:

         1. Earnings per share;

         2. Interim financial reporting;

         3. Segment reporting.

      ii. Examples of simplified recognition and measurement:

         1. Goodwill is amortized ;

         2. All borrowing and R&D costs are expensed;

         3. Categories of investments in financial assets are reduced in number;

         4. Less prior data is required for first-time adoption.

      iii. Examples of simpler reporting options:

         1. No option to revalue plant assets and intangibles;

         2. Corridor amortization for defined benefit pension plans is eliminated;

         3. Proportionate consolidation is prohibited.

II. How IFRSs are Developed

A. The IASB employs a due process procedure similar to the FASB's when developing and adopting IFRSs. The IASB issues a discussion paper on the topic, followed by an exposure draft of a standard. Both documents are circulated to the public for comments, including discussions at round tables. After the comment period, all comments are reviewed and addressed, and the IASB then modifies the draft if necessary, and issues a final standard. Specific steps toward adoption of an IFRS are:

1. Add an item to the agenda based on factors including requests from constituents, consultations with the IFRS Advisory Committee, changes in previous standards and interpretations and the Framework, and the possibility of increasing convergence.

2. Discuss the issue and prepare a discussion paper outlining the main issues for a topic or issue.

3. Publish the discussion paper. Even though it is not a mandatory step, the IASB normally publishes one when it is a major new topic in order to solicit early comments. The paper may be reissued depending on comments. A simple majority of the Board is required to publish a discussion paper.

4. Prepare an Exposure Draft (ED) that has the tentative decisions of the Board. Several iterations may be required as the issues are tentatively decided. The Board votes on each version of the ED (9 votes minimum for passing if there are fewer than 16 members, and 10 votes if there are 16 members).

5. Issue the ED. The ED takes the form of the proposed standard, is a mandatory step, and is the primary way of obtaining the public's input.

6. Analyze comments to the ED. Another ED may be published if significant changes are required based on public comment.

7. Debate and issue the final IFRS with application guidance and basis for conclusions including the reasons for rejecting other solutions. There should be no significant aspect in the final standard not previously exposed in the ED. Minimum vote for adoption is nine if there are fewer than 16 members and 10 votes if there are 16 members.

8. Except for the voting on the ED and IFRS, the process is open to the public.

B. In addition to this process, the IASB may carry out field trials of a proposed standard whereby volunteer firms apply it to their financial statements.

C. IFRS Interpretations. The IFRS Interpretation Committee employs a similar process, open to the public, when developing its Interpretations.

1. The IFRS Interpretation Committee initiates its agenda items, based on its own analysis and the input of its constituents when it believes that practices divergent from existing guidance have emerged, or when there is a belief that a standard should be changed. There must be a significant and widespread divergence for an item to be added to the agenda.

2. For issues leading to an Interpretation, the IFRS Interpretation Committee, supported by the IASB staff, develops a draft Interpretation based on available information. Relevant authoritative literature and the conceptual framework are consulted. The draft identifies relevant IASB pronouncements and recommends appropriate accounting treatment. A consensus is reached when no more than four members vote against the draft. If the IFRS Interpretation Committee is unable to reach a consensus on an issue, it will discontinue its work and may recommend that the issue be considered by the IASB.

3. The draft Interpretation is made public and the IFRS Interpretation Committee considers the comments from interested parties. If the comments are significant, the modified draft is re-exposed.

4. The final Interpretation includes a summary of the relevant accounting issues, the consensus position reached on the appropriate accounting, references to relevant IFRS and conceptual framework sections, and the effective date.

5. The IASB must ratify the Interpretation with a minimum of nine IASB members in favor if there are fewer than 16 members and 10 if there are 16 members, in a public meeting.

The ratified Interpretation is issued by the IASB. If not approved, the IASB provides its reasons and decides whether it should refer it back to the IFRS Interpretation Committee, add it to its own agenda, or take no further action.

III. Accounting Standard Convergence

A. In 2002, the FASB and IASB signed the Norwalk Agreement, which formalized their commitment to the convergence of their accounting standards. The two boards pledged to remove existing differences between their standards so that they would be compatible, and to coordinate their future standard-setting agendas enabling concurrent work on the same issues.

B. The cooperation led to convergence on several issues including inventory costs, nonmonetary exchanges, share-based payments and accounting changes. The boards continue to work on more involved projects with the goal of convergence including business combinations, revenue recognition, the conceptual framework, and financial statement presentation.

C. Foreign firms listing their securities on U.S. markets were previously required to include a reconciliation of earnings and equity to U.S. GAAP (Form 20-F) in their financial statements. The SEC eliminated this requirement in 2007.

D. In 2008, the SEC issued a Roadmap for U.S. firms' use of IFRS. If all of the required milestones are met, U.S. publicly traded companies may be able to report under IFRS beginning December 2014. The milestones include the boards' coming to agreement on several major joint projects further aligning the two sets of standards, new funding and accountability models for the IFRS Foundation, more use of interactive databases, and increased education and training for IFRS in the U.S.

E. In 2010, the SEC developed a Work Plan to further study the convergence question. The SEC stated that by 2011, assuming completion of the joint convergence projects and the SEC's Work Plan, it will decide whether to incorporate IFRS into the U.S. reporting system, and if so, when and how. Based on comments to the Roadmap, if the SEC decides to incorporate IFRS in the U.S. reporting system, the first time U.S. firms would use the new system would be in 2015.

F. Whether and how the U.S. will incorporate IFRS into its financial reporting process remains to be seen. Throughout the portion of the FAR outline devoted to profit-oriented entities, specific differences between U.S. and IFRSs are discussed.

IV. First-Time Adoption of IFRS

A. The first-time adoption of International Financial Reporting Standards (IFRS) is governed by IFRS 1. The first time adopter must apply all standards effective at the reporting date of the entity's first IFRS-compliant financial statements and this application is retrospective. The International Accounting Standards Board (IASB) recognized that full retrospective application may not be practical or cost-beneficial. Therefore, there are some mandatory exceptions and elective exemptions to the initial adoption.

B. When does IFRS 1 Apply?

1. The guidance for first-time adoption applies when the most recent financial statements were prepared:

In compliance with U.S. GAAP;

In conformity with IFRS in all respects, except that an explicit and unreserved statement of compliance was not presented;

In compliance with U.S. GAAP with reconciliation to IFRS;

In conformity with IFRS but for internal use only;

In conformity with IFRS for consolidation purposes, but without a complete set of financial states or without presenting financial statements of previous periods.

C. Key Dates and Financial Statements

1. There are two key dates under IFRS 1. The "first reporting date" is the year-end date for the period for which IFRS is first applied. The "transition date" is the opening date of the earliest period for which full comparative financial statements under IFRS are presented.

Example:
If the first time adoption is December 31, 20X1, then that is the first reporting date for the entity. The transition date is the earliest period for which full comparative financial statements under IFRS are presented. If three years of balance sheets are required, January 1, 2008 is the transition date.

1. Upon adoption of IFRS the first set of statements must include three statements of financial position, two statements of comprehensive income, two separate income statements (if presented), two statements of cash flows and two statements of changes in equity. If filing with the SEC, three years of flow statements are required.

2. The entity must also apply IFRS 1 to any interim period report that is prepared in the first IFRS reporting year. That is, once IFRS is adopted interim restatement is also required.

Example:
Continue the assumption that the first IFRS reporting date is December 31, 20X1, and interim financial statements are required. The interim statements must be in compliance with IFRS along with comparatives. Therefore, the March 31, 20X1 interim reporting on Form 10-Q must be IFRS compliant as well as the comparative for March 31, 20X0.

1. Upon adoption of IFRS, the entity must present reconciliations of U.S. GAAP to IFRS to explain the impact of the adoption on equity and comprehensive income.

   a. A reconciliation of U.S. GAAP equity to IFRS equity as of the transition date;

   b. A reconciliation of the latest published U.S. GAAP equity to IFRS equity as of the most recent U.S. GAAP statement date;

   c. A reconciliation of U.S. GAAP total comprehensive income to IFRS comprehensive income for the same period.

2. **Mandatory Exceptions --** There are mandatory exceptions to the retrospective application of IFRS. IFRS 1 specifically prohibits restatement for certain transactions upon the initial adoption of IFRS because the application of the IFRS guidance in these areas would require judgments about past transactions that are not feasible on a post-hoc basis. The mandatory exceptions are:

   a. Derecognition of financial assets and liabilities;

   b. Hedge accounting;

   c. Assets held for sale and discontinued operations;

   d. Certain aspects of accounting for non-controlling interest;

   e. Use of certain estimates;

3. **Voluntary Exceptions --** There are voluntary exceptions to the retrospective application of IFRS. IFRS 1 permits exclusion of the application of the following accounting standards if there entity believes that the cost of application exceeds the benefits to the financial statement user. The main voluntary exceptions relate to the following topics:

   a. Business combinations;

   b. Share-based payments;

   c. Insurance contracts;

   d. PPE;

   e. Leases;

   f. Employee benefits;

   g. Effects of foreign exchange rates;

   h. Compound financial instruments;

   a. Assets and Liabilities of subsidiaries and joint ventures.

IASB Framework

This lesson presents an overview of the International Accounting Standards Board (IASB) conceptual framework.

After studying this lesson, you should be able to:

1. *Identify the purpose of the conceptual framework.*

2. *Identify the IASB framework objectives, qualitative characteristics and constraints.*

I. Background

A. The IASB's *Framework for the Preparation and Presentation of Financial Statements* (Framework) is similar to the FASB's Concepts Statements although much shorter in length. Like the FASB's, the IASB Framework does not constitute GAAP (exception, see below) but rather provides the basis for development of specific GAAP on a consistent basis. The IASB Framework is intended to apply to the financial statements of all entities, public or private.

   1. In rare cases where the IASB Framework is in conflict with an accounting standard for compelling practical reasons, the standard is used as the guidance.

   2. In cases where no applicable accounting exists, the IASB Framework may be considered as guidance for GAAP (see International GAAP hierarchy in the preceding lesson).

B. Purposes of the IASB Framework

   1. To assist the Board in developing new IASs and reviewing existing IASs; (The Framework was written when the IASC was the body promulgating standards. "IASs" here may be more loosely interpreted to include IASs, IFRSs, SICs, and IFRICs.)

   2. To assist the Board in promoting harmonization of standards by providing a basis for reducing the number of alternative accounting treatments permitted by IASs;

   3. To assist national standard-setting bodies in developing standards;

   4. To assist preparers in applying IASs and dealing with topics not yet covered by IASs;

   5. To assist auditors in forming an opinion as to whether financial statements conform with IASs;

   6. To assist users in interpreting financial statements prepared in conformity with IASs;

   7. To provide information for parties interested in the work of the IASC (now IASB).

C. General purpose financial statements. The Framework is concerned with general-purpose financial statements (similar to the FASB Concepts Statements), directed to provide financial information to a wide variety of users. "Financial statements" include (1) balance sheet, (2) income statement, (3) statement of changes in financial position (note that a later IAS requires a statement of cash flows), (4) notes and supplementary material. Excluded from the purview are directors' and management reports and the like.

D. One of the more involved joint convergence projects is the development of a common conceptual framework. This project's purpose is to develop a framework that will be the underlying conceptual support for future principles-based internally consistent accounting standards for the most useful financial reporting.

   1. The joint framework project is divided into eight phases or chapters with the goal of providing the framework in a single document:

      a. Objective and qualitative characteristics;

      b. Elements and recognition;

      c. Measurement;

      d. Reporting entity;

      e. Presentation and disclosure;

      f. Framework for a GAAP hierarchy;

      g. Applicability to the not-for-profit sector;

      h. Remaining issues.

2. In September 2010 the first phase of the joint convergence project was completed . As such, the **objectives, qualitative characteristics** and **constraints** sections discussed in previous FASB Conceptual Framework lessons apply to the IASB framework as well. The two constraints (materiality and cost effectiveness) also are included in Phase (a). The material from Phase (a) is not repeated here. Please refer back to the FASB Conceptual Framework lessons.

3. The portions of the original IASB Framework not yet modified by the joint IASB-FASB project are provided in this lesson. You will notice considerable similarity with the FASB framework.

4. The objective of financial reporting under the IASB Framework is similar to the FASB - to aid in the decision-making of the financial statement user. The Framework states (para 12): The objective of financial statements is to provide information about the financial position, performance and changes in financial position of an entity that is useful to a wide range of users in making economic decisions.

II. Elements of Financial Statements

A. The definitions of elements are at the center of the standard setting-process for the IASB. The Framework defines income and expenses in terms of assets and liabilities.

B. The five elements in the IASB Framework are:

    1. Assets;

    2. Liabilities;

    3. Equity;

    4. Income;

    5. Expenses.

      a. Difference -- The IASB Framework lists only half the elements found in the FASB Framework (which lists 10 elements). The IASB Framework does not include as elements the following items appearing in the FASB Framework's list of elements: investments by owners, distributions to owners, comprehensive income, gains, and losses. However, specific IFRSs address these elements within the context of the specific standard.

C. An item is recognized as an element if it meets one of the element definitions below, AND also meets the following two recognition criteria: (1) it is probable that a future economic benefit associated with the item will flow to or from the entity, and (2) the item has a cost or value that can be measured with reliability. In addition, the "substance over form" principle must be considered (for example, accounting for income taxes and for capital leases).

    1. Where only one or no criterion is met, note disclosure may be required.

    2. The Framework does not provide specific guidance on how to measure whether future benefits are "probable" although several international accounting standards include specific guidance pertaining to the relevant standard.

3. Similarly, there is no concrete guidance on reliable measurement, which often requires making a reasonable estimate. The framework contains little guidance on specific measurement bases noting that several are available with historical cost the most common, often being combined with other bases.

4. Failure to recognize in the financial statements an item satisfying the recognition criteria and one of the element definitions is not cured by disclosure in the notes.

5. Offsetting in financial statements is not allowed unless the procedure reflects the underlying substance of related events or transactions, or where permitted by an accounting standard.

D. Assets -- Currently, the IASB Framework definition is as follows (para 49 a): An asset is a resource controlled by the entity as a result of past events and from which future economic benefits are expected to flow to the entity.

E. Liabilities -- Currently, the IASB Framework definition is as follows (para 49 b): A liability is a present obligation of the entity arising from past events, the settlement of which is expected to result in an outflow from the entity of resources embodying future benefits.

F. Equity -- Currently, the IASB Framework definition is as follows (para 49 c): Equity is the residual interest in the asset after subtracting liabilities. Several sub-categories of equity are mentioned including funds contributed by shareholders, retained earnings, and reserves representing appropriations or capital maintenance adjustments.

G. Income -- Income represents increases in economic benefits deriving from increases in assets or decreases in liabilities that result in increases in equity (other than those related to contributions from shareholders).

1. Income may be realized or unrealized. Income includes both revenues (arising from ordinary activities) and gains. Gains are not treated as separate elements because they also may be due to ordinary activities, as well as from activities not in the ordinary course of business. Gains are usually reported separately from revenues.

   a. **Difference** -- The IASB Framework element is "income" which includes both revenues and gains, whereas the FASB Framework treats "revenue" and "gains" as separate elements.

H. Expenses -- Expenses represent decreases in economic benefits deriving from decreases in assets or increases in liabilities that result in decreases in equity (other than those related to distributions to shareholders).

1. Expenses may be realized or unrealized. An expense is recognized immediately for expenditures producing no future economic benefit qualifying as an asset.

2. Expenses result from ordinary activities. Losses also may result from ordinary activities and thus are not treated as separate elements. Losses may also arise from activities not in the ordinary course of business. Losses are usually reported separately from expenses.

   a. **Difference** -- The IASB Framework "expense" element includes losses whereas the FASB Framework treats "expenses" and "losses" as separate elements.

3. The Framework defines income and expenses in terms of assets and liabilities. As such, the Framework cautions that applying the matching principle should not result in recognizing items that do not meet the definition of assets and liabilities.

   a. **Difference** -- The FASB Framework has no such prohibition.

III. Assumptions

A. In the IASB Framework, there are only two underlying assumptions: (1) that the financial statements are prepared on the accrual basis, and (2) that the entity is a going concern. Their meaning is the same as in the FASB Framework.

1. **Difference --** Accrual accounting considers an assumption in the IASB Framework, but not in the FASB Framework.

B. Neither assumption needs to be stated as such in the notes. When material uncertainties exist as to the continuation of the entity, or when it is clear that the going concern assumption does not apply resulting in a different basis of reporting, the entity should disclose this information.

C. The framework does discuss economic entity, monetary unit, and periodicity as underlying concepts for the preparation of financial statements, but not as formal assumptions. Along with going concern, these three assumptions comprise the four FASB Framework assumptions.

IFRS for SMEs

Unlike U.S. GAAP, International Financial Reporting Standards (IFRS) include a set of accounting and reporting standards specifically intended for use by small and medium-sized entities. These standards, known as "IFRS for SMEs," are intended for use primarily by private entities and are a modification and simplification of the complete set of IFRS. For U.S. entities that qualify, IFRS for SMEs can be used as a U.S. GAAP-basis for the preparation of general-purpose financial statements. This lesson provides an overview of IFRS for SMEs, including which entities may use those standards and the major differences between those standards and other, more extensive, reporting standards.

After studying this lesson, you should be able to:

1. *Describe the major differences between the requirements of IFRS for SMEs and the requirements of standard U.S. GAAP and the complete IFRS.*

2. *Identify entities that are eligible to use IFRS for SMEs as the basis for preparing financial statements.*

I. **International Financial Reporting Standards (IFRS)** -- Issued by the International Accounting Standards Board (IASB), do not contain a concept comparable to "other comprehensive basis of accounting" (OCBOA), nor do they address the issue of personal financial statements. Therefore, there are no international standards for preparing financial statements under either of these bases of accounting.

A. **IFRS small and medium-sized entities**

1. Millions of companies worldwide can, and are, using "IFRS for Small and Medium Sized Enterprises" (IFRS for SMEs). In many of these countries (but not the U.S.) incorporated companies are required to have audited financial statements regardless of whether they are a public company with publicly traded equity or debt.

2. The IASB issued IFRS for SMEs in 2009. The IFRS for SMEs pronouncement is a modification and simplification of the full IFRS and is designed to be used primarily by private companies. Although simplified, it is still based on the IFRS conceptual framework. As set forth in IFRS for SMEs, the objectives of financial statements of small or medium sized entities are:

   a. To provide information about the financial position, performance and cash flows of an entity that is useful for economic decision-making by a broad range of users who are not in a position to demand reports tailored to meet their particular information needs (i.e., general-purpose financial statements for external users), and

   b. To show the results of the stewardship of management - the accountability of management for the resources entrusted to it.

3. IFRS for SMEs are not an "other comprehensive basis of account" as that concept is used in the U.S., but rather are a form of generally accepted accounting principles (GAAP) for U.S. entities and can be used by qualified U.S. companies as the basis for preparing financial statements. Thus, an entity that does not have to follow either standard U.S. GAAP or the full IFRS, may elect to prepare general purpose financial statements under the requirements of either an OCBOA or IFRS for SMEs.

B. **Eligibility for and Election of IFRS for SMEs**

1. IFRS for SMEs may be used by entities that **do not have** "public accountability." Under the standard, the following kinds of entities would have public accountability and, therefore, **would be precluded from** using IFRS for SMEs:

a. Entities that are required to file financial statements with a securities commission or other regulatory body for the purpose of issuing instruments in a public market, such as equity or debt securities;

b. Entities that hold assets in a fiduciary capacity for a broad group of outsiders, including:

   i. Banks;

   ii. Insurance companies;

   iii. Brokers and dealers in securities;

   iv. Pension funds;

   v. Mutual funds.

c. In addition, IFRS for SMEs are not intended for use by not-for-profit or governmental entities.

C. Characteristics of Financial Statements under IFRS for SMEs

1. Unlike OCBOA, IFRS for SMEs is based on the accrual basis of accounting, just as is standard U.S. GAAP. However, IFRS for SMEs is both less complicated and less voluminous than U.S. GAAP. Some of that simplification is reflected in the following key areas where IFRS for SMEs differs from U.S. GAAP:

   a. Accounting for financial assets and financial liabilities makes greater use of cost.

   b. The use of the cost method to account for investments over which the investor has significant influence is permitted; the equity method also is permitted, but not required.

   c. Inventories must be valued using FIFO or weighted-average cost; LIFO inventory valuation is prohibited.

   d. Capitalization of interest incurred during construction of an asset is not required.

   e. When the major components of an item of property, plant, or equipment have different patterns of consumption, depreciation must be based on a components approach.

   f. Goodwill and other intangible assets are amortized and assumed to have a limited life and, if the life cannot be estimated, a 10-year period must be used for amortization purposes.

   g. Impairment of goodwill is assessed using a one-step process, rather than a two-step process.

   h. A simplified approach to temporary differences is used for income tax accounting.

   i. If certain criteria are met, reversal of impairment charges is allowed, including for financial assets.

   j. Only certain hedge types are allowed and conditions for the use of hedge accounting for those types are less restrictive.

   k. There is no requirement for earnings per share or segment disclosures.

   l. Disclosure requirements are simplified in several areas, including:

      i. Financial instruments;

      ii. Leases;

      iii. Pensions.

2. The attractiveness of IFRS for SMEs is further enhanced by the fact that the IASB has limited the revision of the standards to once every three years, rather than the more or less continuous revisions made to U.S. GAAP and full IFRS.

D. Summary

1. A U.S. entity that is not **required** to follow either U.S. GAAP or full IFRS in the preparation of its financial statements may use one of four basis of accounting:

   a. Use, on an elective basis, U.S. GAAP;

   b. Use, on an elective basis, full IFRS;

   c. Use an Other Comprehensive Basis of Accounting;

   d. Use IFRS for SMEs.

2. Each of these bases would be considered the application of "generally accepted accounting principles" and the resulting statements could be audited by a U.S. CPA. An audit report of financial statements based on IFRS for SMEs might say something like the following:

   > "These statements fairly present the financial position, results of operations, and cash flows in conformity with the International Financial Reporting Standards for Small and Medium Sized Enterprises."

IFRS—General Purpose Financial Statements

This lesson presents the major differences in the reporting of the general purpose financial statements under IFRS: balance sheet (statement of financial position), income statement, statement of comprehensive income, statement of shareholders' equity, and the statement of cash flows.

After studying this lesson you should be able to :

1. *Identify major differences in the reporting of the general purpose financial statements under IFRS.*

I. **IFRS: Balance Sheet – Statement of Financial Position**

A. **IFRS Financial Statements**

1. The objective of financial statements is to provide information about the financial position, financial performance and cash flows of an entity that is useful to a wide range of users in making economic decisions. The financial information included in the financial statements along with the note disclosures assist users of financial statements in predicting the entity's future cash flows and, in particular, their timing and certainty.

2. Financial statements should *present fairly* the financial position, financial performance and cash flows of an entity.

3. A complete set of financial statements includes

   a. Statement of financial position (balance sheet);

   b. Statement of comprehensive income;

   c. Statement of changes in equity;

   d. Statement of cash flows;

   e. Notes; and,

   f. Statement of financial position at the beginning of the earliest comparative period for which an entity applies an accounting policy retrospectively or makes a retrospective restatement of items in its financial statements, or when it reclassifies items in its financial statements.

4. The financial statements and notes must be clearly identified, including the following information:

   a. Name of the reporting entity;

   b. Whether the statements are consolidated or of an individual entity;

   c. The date of the end of the reporting period or period covered;

   d. The presentation currency;

   e. The level of rounding (for example, amounts in millions).

5. Frequency of reporting - at a minimum, a complete set of financial reports at least annually, including comparative information.

B. **General Considerations for the Statement of Financial Position**

1. Both IFRS and U.S. accounting standards, require a classified statement of financial position (commonly called a balance sheet in the U.S.) to be reported. Each IFRS statement of financial position must present two classifications: current and non-current.

(The definitions of these terms are presented later in this lesson.) IFRS specifies a minimum listing of accounts that must be presented whereas U.S. GAAP does not have such specification, although SEC registrants must follow SEC guidelines that require specific line items.

2. IFRS requires more detailed note disclosures for various statements of financial position items, compared with U.S. GAAP. Under IFRS, the financial statements themselves are quite clean, meaning typical U.S. GAAP parenthetical disclosures such as wording "net of depreciation," "net of allowance for uncollectibles," and "at lower of cost or market" do not appear on IFRS financial statements but are disclosed in the notes to the financial statements.

3. IFRS does not require specific formatting of statement of financial position information. For example, both horizontal and vertical formats are acceptable. Firms may change the order of accounts, the title of the statements (for example, Balance Sheet is acceptable instead of the formal name, Statement of Financial Position) and the level of detail to provide the most useful information.

4. Typically, the ordering of the statement of financial position items for U.S. GAAP balance sheets starts with current items. Since IFRS does not have any recommended format, many countries use their customary formats, including presenting the items in reverse order, reporting noncurrent items before current items. In addition, within categories, the ordering may be the opposite of U.S. GAAP ordering, that is, from less liquid to more liquid, but this is simply a local format and not one required by IFRS.

C. IFRS Statement of Financial Position Format

1. A typical layout for an IFRS Statement of Financial Position is as follows: (Note: this order is commonly found in British or former British countries)

Assets

Noncurrent assets

  Property, plant and equipment

  Intangible assets

  Investments

    Total noncurrent assets

Current assets

  Inventories

  Trade receivables

  Cash and cash equivalents

    Total current assets

    Total assets

Equity

Equity attributable to owners of the parent

  Share capital

  Retained earnings

  Noncontrolling interest

    Total equity

Noncurrent liabilities

    Long-term borrowings

    Deferred income taxes

       Total noncurrent liabilities

Current Liabilities

    Trade payables

    Short-term borrowings

    Current tax payable

       Total current liabilities

       Total liabilities

       Total equity and liabilities

2. The above presentation of the statement of financial position emphasizes the long-run perspective. Within assets and liabilities, first displayed are the infrastructure assets that provide the long-term physical structure of operating capacity, and the means of obtaining the long-term financing of those assets.

3. Other variations include (a) reporting net assets (total assets less total liabilities), (b) reporting current assets and liabilities in one section labeling the difference as working capital or net current assets, and (c) ordering by liquidity where the entire statement of financial position is listed in order of liquidity, within assets and liabilities.

D. Required Statement of Financial Position Items (where present for an entity)

See the following example.

Property, plant and equipment

Investment property

Intangible assets

Financial assets

Investments accounted for using the equity method

Biological assets

Inventories

Trade and other receivables

Cash and cash equivalents

Noncurrent assets held for sale

Trade and other payables

Provisions - liabilities of uncertain timing or amount

Financial liabilities

Liabilities and assets for current tax

Deferred tax liabilities and deferred tax assets (can be classified noncurrent only)

Liabilities included in the disposal groups classified as held for sale

Non-controlling interests presented within equity

Issued capital and reserves attributable to the owners of the parent

1. The requirements may not apply to interim financial statements, if the entity reports interim financial reports according to IAS 34, *Interim Financial Reporting*. Those interim reports are more condensed.

2. U.S. GAAP discourages the use of the term "reserve" which is a category found within equity and liabilities under IFRS. IFRS permits this term. Examples include reserves arising from revaluation of plant assets, foreign currency translation, and recognition of expenses before they are legally due. Note that wherever the term reserve is used, it represents a specific purpose, and not simply "general" reserves that might be used to smooth earnings.

E. Definition of Current Assets and Current Liabilities

1. The definitions of current assets and liabilities for IFRS are worded slightly differently than those definitions under U.S. GAAP, but the result of their application will generally yield the same results.

2. An asset is classified *current* if it meets one of the following criteria:

    a. It is expected to be realized in, or is intended for sale or consumption in, the entity's normal operating cycle;

    b. It is primarily held for the purpose of being traded;

    c. It is expected to be realized within 12 months after the reporting period;

    d. It is cash or a cash equivalent unless it is restricted from being exchanged or used to settle a liability for at least 12 months after the reporting period.

    e. All assets not meeting any one of the above criteria are classified as noncurrent, being the default classification.

  3. A liability is classified current if it meets one of the following criteria:

    a. It is expected to be settled in the entity's normal operating cycle;

    b. It is held primarily for the purpose of being traded;

    c. It is due to be settled within 12 months after the reporting period;

    d. The entity does not have an unconditional right to defer settlement of the liability for at least 12 months after the reporting period.

    e. All liabilities not meeting any one of the above criteria are classified as noncurrent, being the default classification.

II. IFRS – Income Statement

A. General Considerations for the Income Statement

1. As with the statement of financial position, IFRS requires certain line items to be disclosed on the face of the income statement (see B. below). Other than certain earnings per share disclosures, U.S. GAAP standards have no such requirement.

2. In the U.S., it is generally accepted that either a single-step or a multiple-step format be used and the bottom portion of the income statement is prescribed by U.S. GAAP. However, specific IFRS standards do mandate that additional line items, headings, or subtotals depending on whether a firm is reporting a pertinent item be disclosed separately.

3. IFRS does **not** allow the reporting of income statement items as extraordinary (effective in 2015 U.S. GAAP also does **not** allow reporting of extraordinary items). The IASB concluded that such items arise from normal business risks faced by an entity. The nature or function of an item, rather than its frequency, should be the basis for its presentation.

4. Some of the IFRS terminology is also different from the U.S. GAAP counterpart. U.S. statements refer to the bottom line as "net income" or "net loss." For IFRS statements, that net amount is called "profit or loss for the period." It appears as a subtotal in the single statement option above or as the bottom line in the income statement under the two statement option. As another example, the term "turnover" is used for "sales" by some firms in their IFRS income statements, even though IFRS uses the term "Revenue." This is usually a cultural difference, as British companies refer to "Revenue" as "Turnover."

5. U.S. GAAP allows alternative measures of performance to be reported on the face of the income statement. Examples include earnings before interest, taxes, depreciation and amortization. Such reporting in the income statement is not included in the illustrative examples that are part of IAS 1, *Presentation of Financial Statements.*

B. Specific Items to be Reported in the IFRS Income Statement -- The following items are required to be reported on the face of the statement of comprehensive income (under either option above), subject to materiality constraints and the nature of the business. Material items should be presented separately either on the face of the income statement or in the footnotes.

Revenue

Finance costs

Share of the profit or loss of associates under the equity method

Tax expense

A single amount comprising the total of (1) after-tax profit or loss on discontinued operations, and (2) after-tax gain or loss on disposal of discontinued operations

Profit or loss

Each component of other comprehensive income (discussed in a later lesson)

Share of other comprehensive income of associates under the equity method

Total comprehensive income

C. Expense Classifications

1. IFRS requires firms to analyze expenses either by (a) function, or (b) nature of the expense. If a firm uses the functional system, the firm must disclose the additional information on the nature of expenses. This disclosure is usually in the notes. In the U.S. GAAP there is no such requirement although SEC registrants must report expenses by function.

   a. The *function* of expense reporting focuses on the activity to which the expense relates. Examples include cost of sales, distribution costs, and administrative expenses.

   b. The *nature* of expense reporting focuses on the type of expense. Examples include changes in inventories of finished goods and work in progress, raw materials and consumables used, employee benefit expense, depreciation and amortization expense.

2. The expense classification and disclosure may be presented either on the face of the income statement or in the notes.

3. Example of function of expense presentation in an income statement:

Revenue

Cost of sales

Gross profit

Other income

Less:

   Distribution costs

   Administrative expenses

   Other expenses

Profit before tax

4. Example of nature of expense presentation in an income statement:

> Revenue
>
> Other income
>
> Less:
>
> Change in inventories of finished goods and work in progress
>
> Raw materials and consumables used
>
> Employee benefits expense
>
> Depreciation and amortization expense
>
> Other expenses
>
> Total expenses
>
> Profit before tax

5. Reporting by expense function is more prevalent in IFRS financial reports.

III. IFRS – Statement of Comprehensive Income

A. Per Share Measures -- Comprehensive income per share is not prohibited under IFRS but is prohibited under U.S. GAAP.

B. A Fifth Other Comprehensive Income (OCI) Item

1. International accounting standards allow firms to revalue plant assets and intangibles to fair value (details in a later lesson). U.S. standards prohibit this practice. Under international standards, if the revaluation results in an increase in the value of the asset, the increase is called a revaluation surplus and is reported in other comprehensive income. This surplus is a fifth OCI item, in addition to the four under U.S. standards. The revaluation surplus can never be reclassified to affect net income. Once a firm has chosen to revalue assets - those revaluations cannot affect net income. See the lesson on fixed assets for more discussion of IFRS revaluation of fixed assets.

IV. IFRS – Statement of Shareholders' Equity

A. The IFRS and U.S. GAAP statements are quite similar. Under U.S. GAAP the statement of shareholders' equity can be presented in the footnotes, under IFRS it must be presented as a separate statement.

V. IFRS – Statement of Cash Flows

A. The differences between IFRS and U.S. GAAP relate to the classification of items as operating, investing or financing activities. The table below presents the major classification differences.

See the following example.

Item	IFRS	U.S.
Interest paid	Operating or financing	Operating only
Interest received	Operating or investing	Operating only
Taxes paid	Operating—In financing or investing if specifically identified with an item	Operating only
Dividends received	Operating or investing	Operating only
Dividends paid	Operating or financing	Financing only
Cash and cash equivalents	May include bank overdrafts	Bank overdrafts not allowed

VI. IFRS – Footnotes

A. **Footnotes** -- Footnotes, including the summary of significant accounting policies, are considered an integral part of a complete set of financial statements and thus are required for all entities reporting under international accounting standards.

B. International standards suggest the following order of footnote presentation:

1. Statement of compliance with IFRS;

2. Summary of significant accounting policies;

3. Supporting information for financial statement items.

C. The summary of significant accounting policies should include:

1. Judgments and key assumptions made in applying those policies;

2. Measurement bases used for recognition (e.g., historical cost, fair value);

3. Information enabling an assessment of the estimation uncertainty that could result in a material adjustment to the balances of assets and liabilities, which are point estimates in many cases.

D. Footnotes concerning financial statement items should be disclosed in the order of those financial statement items, which, in turn, should be cross-referenced to any related footnote.

E. Also to be included in the notes

1. The amount of dividends proposed or declared before the statements were authorized for issue (U.S. standards do not require disclosure of proposed dividends);

2. Additional information enabling an assessment of the firm's objectives, policies and processes for managing capital.

VII. Disclosures for the Effect of Changing Prices

A. The international accounting experience with reporting the effects of changing prices is similar to that of the U.S. Initially, entities were required to disclose the impact of changing prices on their results of operations and financial position. Firms could apply either general price level adjustments (inflation), or current replacement cost (specific prices). These requirements were withdrawn as inflation became less of a problem, although they are encouraged.

B. **Hyperinflationary economies** -- However, a significant difference between U.S. and international standards is the latter's requirement that firms operating in economies with very substantial inflation are required to provide disclosure of the impact of inflation.

C. This requirement specifically requires financial statements to be restated to reflect the current general price level. The restated statements are to be presented as the primary statements. International standards discourage reporting of the pre-restated financial statements. At present, there are very few such economies experiencing hyperinflation (defined roughly as 100% or more over three years) and as such this requirement does not affect many firms.

Financial Statement Accounts

Cash

This lesson presents a summary of the accounting for cash.

After studying this lesson, you should be able to:

1. *Define cash and cash equivalents.*

2. *Define compensating balances.*

3. *List the two main internal controls over cash.*

4. *Identify the main difference in reporting cash under IFRS.*

I. Articulation

A. The balance sheet and the statement of cash flows.

1. If a business enterprise uses the term **cash** on the statement of cash flows, the term used on the balance sheet will likewise be **cash**;

2. If a business enterprise uses the term **cash and cash equivalents** on the statement of cash Flows, the term on the balance sheet will be **cash and cash equivalents**.

B. A cash equivalent is a security with a fixed maturity amount and an original maturity to the purchaser of three months or less.

II. Accounting for Cash -- The main reporting issue for cash is what to include in this category of assets. Several items are included in the cash account for balance sheet reporting purposes, and there are others that at first appear to be cash but are excluded.

A. Cash -- The current asset, represents unrestricted cash. This is cash that is available to meet current operating expenses and obligations as they arise.

1. **Included in cash --** The components of cash include coin and currency, petty cash, cash in bank, and negotiable instruments such as ordinary checks, cashier's checks, certified checks, and money orders.

2. **Current liability --** An overdraft of a bank account occurs when checks honored by the bank exceed the balance in the account. An overdraft may be offset against other cash accounts with the same bank, but not against cash accounts with other banks. In the latter case, the overdraft is listed as a current liability.

3. **Excluded from cash --** Cash does not include certificates of deposit, legally restricted compensating balances, or restricted cash funds (such as a bond sinking fund). These amounts are either:

   a. not available for the immediate payment of debts; or

   b. management's intent is to use these resources for specific purposes. In addition, cash excludes post-dated checks received from customers (include these in accounts receivable), advances to employees (a receivable), and postage stamps (a prepaid expense).

B. Cash equivalents -- Although not cash, cash equivalents are so near cash that they are often combined with cash for financial statement reporting.

 Example: Cash equivalents include: U.S. Treasury obligations (bills, notes, and bonds), commercial paper (very short-term corporate notes), and money market funds.

C. Compensating balance -- This is a minimum balance that must be maintained by the firm in relation to a borrowing. Such a balance increases the effective rate of interest on the borrowing and reduces the risk to the lender.

1. With respect to compensating balances, if the balance is related to a short-term liability, the compensating balance is shown as a current asset (as in the example below), but is not considered a part of the unrestricted cash balance. If the compensating balance is related to a long-term liability, the compensating balance is a non-current asset.

> **Example:**
> A firm borrows $10,000 for one year at 6% but must maintain a $700 compensating balance in an account with the lender financial institution. The $700 is not included in the cash account but is rather reported in restricted cash, a current asset. The annual effective interest rate is 6.45% [($10,000 x (.06)/$9,300]. The net loan is only $9,300 ($10,000 - $700).

D. Cash is a monetary asset -- A monetary asset is an asset with fixed nominal (stated) value. The nominal value of a monetary asset does not change with inflation. Cash is the most "monetary" of all assets. There is no uncertainty as to the stated or nominal value of cash at present or in the future. A $100 bill is always worth exactly $100. However, the purchasing power of cash declines with inflation. The amount of real goods and services a fixed amount of cash can buy decreases as the general price level increases. The effect is the opposite during times of deflation.

III. Cash - The Importance of Internal Control Measures

A. Because cash is easily concealed and has universal value, companies go to great lengths to safeguard their cash. A variety of internal control measures are used to safeguard cash.

B. The auditing section of this course considers these measures in detail. For cash, the most popular ones are:

1. separation of duties;

2. bank reconciliations.

C. Separation of duties -- Makes it more difficult for employees to perpetrate fraud and gain access to the firm's cash.

1. Separation of Duties, in effect, forces employees to collude if they attempt to fraudulently remove any of the company's cash resources. At a minimum, the duties related to cash that should be separated are:

   a. custody of cash;

   b. recording of cash;

   c. reconciliation of bank accounts.

2. The reason for this minimum separation is to prevent an employee from pilfering cash and concealing the action by altering the records.

D. Bank reconciliations -- Bank reconciliations provide a check mechanism for both the company and the financial institution. In most cases, any errors detected in a bank reconciliation are the result of **honest** mistakes on the part of the company's employees or on the part of the bank's employees.

1. Bank reconciliations are necessary because cash transactions that occur near the end of a month or an accounting year may be recorded by the company but have not been

recorded by the financial institution. Likewise, there may be some cash transactions that have been recorded by the financial institution but have not been recorded by the company.

IV. U.S. GAAP - IFRS Differences -- The main difference between U.S. GAAP and IFRS is that bank overdrafts can be subtracted from cash, rather than classified as liabilities.

Bank Reconciliations

The purpose of this lesson is to provide guidance on bank reconciliations.

After studying this lesson, you should be able to:

1. *Identify the reconciling items in a book-to-bank and bank-to-book bank reconciliation.*

2. *Complete a simple bank reconciliation to the true cash balance.*

I. **Benefits** -- Bank reconciliations provide the following benefits:

   A. Enable a periodic comparison of the bank account balance and cash balance.

   B. Help identify errors in the firm's records or bank records.

   C. Establish the correct ending cash balance.

   D. Provide information for adjusting entries.

   E. Help reduce cash theft by employees if the reconciler does not have access to cash records or does not have access to cash (authorization to make disbursements, or cash custody).

II. **Simple Bank Reconciliation** -- This type of reconciliation explains the difference between the balance per books and the balance per bank at the end of the month. For example, the November 20x7 bank reconciliation would reconcile the balance per books on November 30, 20x7 with the balance per bank on November 30, 20x7.

   A. There are three formats for the simple bank reconciliation:

      1. **Bank to book** -- The starting point is the balance per bank. All adjustments are made to this balance to arrive at the balance per book.

      2. **Book to bank** -- The starting point is the balance per book. All adjustments are made to this balance to arrive at the balance per bank.

      3. **Bank and book to true balance** -- In this format, the bank balance and the book balance are separately reconciled to the **true** cash balance, which is reported in the balance sheet. The adjustments to the two starting points (bank balance and book balance) are those changes in cash that have not been recorded in the bank or the books at the end of the period.

      > **Note:**
      > The third format is the format that is typically emphasized on the CPA Exam and will be the focus of our coverage.

      See the following example.

Example:
Balance Per Bank, November 30, 20x7 XX

+ Deposits in Transit	+ X
+ Cash on Hand	+ X
− Outstanding Checks	− X
± Errors made by Bank	± X
True Cash	XX

Balance Per Book, November 30, 20x7 XX

+ Interest Earned	+ X
+ Note Collected	+ X
− Service Charges	− X
− NSF Check	− X
± Errors in **Firm's** Records	± X
True Cash	XX

4. **Explanations of adjustments to the bank balance**

   a. **Deposit in transit** -- These deposits have been made by the company but have not cleared the bank as of November 30, 20x7. This situation is typically related to a bank policy. For example, some banks have a policy that all deposits made after 2 p.m. of a given day will be reflected by the bank on the next business day.

   b. **Cash on hand** -- This amount reflects petty cash and undeposited cash receipts. You might think of cash on hand as being one step removed from being a deposit in transit. For example purposes, let's say a company makes a deposit at 3 p.m. on November 30, 20x7. Per bank policy, this deposit will be reflected by the bank on the next business day. This 3 p.m. deposit will be a deposit in transit. During the last two business hours of November 30, 20x7, the company collected additional cash of $200. This $200 of undeposited cash receipts will be considered cash on hand. This amount could not have been known by the bank as of November 30, 20x7.

   c. **Outstanding checks** -- This amount represents checks written and mailed by the company which have not cleared the bank by November 30, 20x7.

   d. **Errors made by the bank** -- This amount represents errors made by the bank. For CPA Exam purposes, it might be presented as a situation in which checks written by the ABC Company are subtracted from the balance of the ABZ Company. Alternatively, a deposit made by the ABZ Company may be added to the balance of the ABC Company. There are many types of errors that can be tested. The key is to determine which balance (book or bank) is in error, and by how much. The amount of the error is the adjustment to appear in the reconciliation.

5. **Adjustments to the book balance**

   a. **Interest earned** -- This amount represents interest earned on the checking account. This amount was added to the company's checking balance by the bank on November 30, 20x7. The company will record this amount upon receipt of the November bank statement.

   b. **Note collected** -- This amount represents principle and interest added to the company's checking balance by the bank upon collection of a note receivable. To fully understand the transaction, it must be remembered that the company secured the services of the bank to collect a note receivable. When the bank collected the note, the amount was added to the company's checking balance by the bank. The company will record the transaction when it receives the November bank statement or receives separate correspondence related to the note collection.

c. **Service charges** -- This amount represents service charges that the bank deducted from the company's checking balance on November 30, 20x7. The company will record the transaction upon receipt of the November 30, 20x7 bank statement.

d. **NSF checks** -- This represents "non-sufficient funds" checks received from customers. For example, a customer wrote a $500 check to the company, but the customer's checking balance was not large enough to cover the check payment. Upon determining the "NSF" check, the bank will reduce the company's checking balance. The company will record the "NSF" check upon receipt of the November 30, 20x7 bank statement or upon receipt of separate correspondence related to the "NSF" check.

e. **Errors in "firm's" records** -- This represents errors made in the company's records. For CPA Exam purposes, this situation might include some discussion of incorrect recording of cash receipts and disbursements. For example, a payment of $96 might have been recorded as a payment of $69. Alternatively, a cash receipt of $11,000 might have been recorded as a cash receipt of $1,100.

Example: The firm received a $320 check on account (correctly written by the customer) in November but recorded the amount as $230. The check cleared the bank in November. The firm's cash account is understated. The adjustment in the reconciliation would increase the cash account by $90 ($320 - $230).

Adjusting journal entries: Upon completion of the bank reconciliation, the company will prepare adjusting entries for each of the adjustments to the balance per books. Entries are required only for the adjustments to the book balance. These entries are illustrated below.

Interest earned on checking account:

Cash	XX	
Interest Revenue		XX

Note receivable collected by the bank:

Cash	XX	
Note Receivable		XX
Interest Revenue		XX

Services charges:

Service Charge Expense	XX	
Cash		XX

NSF check received from customer:

Accounts Receivable	XX	
Cash		XX

Note: The entry for the example error above which understated the cash account by $90 is:

Cash	90	
Accounts Receivable		90

III. U.S. GAAP - IFRS Differences -- There are no differences between U.S. GAAP and IFRS in the preparation of bank reconciliations.

Accounts Receivable—Accounting and Reporting

The purpose of this lesson is to understand the recording and valuation of accounts receivable.

After studying this lesson, you should be able to:

1. *Complete the journal entries for recording AR using the gross method and the net method for discounts and allowances.*

2. *Identify the U.S. GAAP and IFRS differences in valuing AR.*

I. **Receivables** -- This subsection provides an explanation of four different types of receivables.

A. **Accounts receivable** -- Typically related to customer transactions. That is, an account receivable is usually related to the sale of goods to customers or the provision of services to customers. The length of time related to this claim is very short, 30 to 90 days for most business enterprises. Due to this short time frame, an account receivable typically does not have an interest element.

B. **Notes receivable** -- Often related to non-customer transactions although many larger consumer items and transactions between businesses require a promissory note. Examples of transactions that relate to a note receivable include the sale of non-cash assets, lending transactions, and the conversion of other receivables. A note receivable is usually related to a longer time frame than an account receivable, and due to that fact, all notes have an interest element. Notes provide increased security for the seller firm, are often negotiable, and usually can be converted to cash with a third party more easily than accounts receivable.

C. **Trade receivable** -- Another name for customer accounts receivable.

D. **Non-trade receivables** -- Those receivables created in non-customer transactions.

II. **Balance Sheet Valuation of Receivable**

A. Receivables are valued on the balance sheet at net realizable value, the amount of cash that the entity expects to collect at due date or at maturity. Depending on the type of receivable, there are several factors that cause the valuation of a receivable to be less than its face or nominal value.

B. **Factors affecting receivable valuation** -- Several items affect the net valuation of receivables (and net sales). Accounts receivable typically reflects more adjustments than notes receivable. Accounts receivable is shown at its net collectible amount. The adjustments to accounts receivable include:

1. trade (quantity) discounts;

2. cash (sales) discounts;

3. sales returns and allowances;

4. non-collectible accounts.

C. **Recording methods**

1. In addition, two different methods of accounting for receivables may be used:

a. the *gross method,* which records receivables at gross invoice price (before cash discount); and

b. the *net method,* which records receivables at net invoice price (after cash discount).

2. **Using gross and net --** The following example illustrates the journal entries for the first three mentioned previously above using both the gross and net methods. Non-collectible accounts are described in the next section.

 Example:
Trade discount and initial recording

Sell $2,000 (list price) of goods, terms 3/10, n30. The sale is subject to a 5% trade discount.

	Gross	Net
Accounts Receivable	1,900	1,843
Sales	1,900*	1,843#

*{.95($2,000)}

#{$1,900(.97)}

The 3/10, n30 terminology indicates that a cash discount of 3% is available to the buyer if payment is remitted within 10 days after the sale. Otherwise, the gross price net of any returns and allowances is due 30 days after the sale. The **gross** invoice price is $1,900, the amount after the trade discount but before the cash discount. The net method records the sale at the gross amount less the 3% cash discount, or 97% of the gross invoice price.

---

3. **Cash discount**

 Example: Payment
is received within the 10-day discount period.

	Gross	Net
Cash	1,843	1,843
Sales Discounts	57	
Accounts Receivable	1,900	1,843

Sales discounts is contra to sales. It reduces gross sales to sales at its net amount. The net method records sales net of cash discount and does not require an adjustment for cash discounts taken by customers. The gross method separately records cash discounts taken by customers. Payment is received after the 10-day discount period.

	Gross	Net
Cash	1,900	1,900
Sales Discounts Forfeited		57
Accounts Receivable	1,900	1,843

Sales discounts forfeited is a miscellaneous revenue account. The net method separately records cash discounts not taken by customers.

---

4. **Returns and allowances**

Example:
A $200 allowance is made for a defect in the merchandise on the fifth day after sale

	Gross	Net
Sales Returns and Allowances	200	194*
Accounts Receivable	200	194

*{($200).97}

Sales returns and allowances is contra to sales. An allowance is a price reduction for merchandise kept by the customer. A $200 return would be accounted for in the same manner.

D. Adjusting entries -- At the end of the year, material probable and estimable cash discounts (under the gross method) and sales returns and allowances must be recorded in the year of sale for correct reporting of net sales and accounts receivable.

Example:
At the end of 20x8, a firm estimates that $30,000 of cash discounts will be taken by customers in 20x9, on 20x8 sales. The following adjusting entry is made at the end of 20x8:

| Sales Discounts | 30,000 | |
| Allowance for Sales Discounts | | 30,000 |

Allowance for sales discounts is contra to accounts receivable. The entry thus reduces both net sales and net accounts receivable. In 20x9, assuming $25,000 of discounts are actually taken on 20x8 sales, the allowance for sales discounts account is debited rather than sales discounts (which were recognized in the previous entry). The remaining $5,000 is treated as an estimate change, reducing the amount of estimated sales discounts to be recognized in the 20x9 year-end adjusting entry.

A similar journal entry is required for estimated sales returns and allowances.

III. U.S. GAAP - IFRS Differences

A. The main difference in the recognition criteria between U.S. GAAP and IFRS is that IFRS defines revenue from a balance sheet point of view and is based on the inflow of economic benefits during the ordinary course of business. This means that accounts receivable (and revenue) can be recognized if there is a firm sales commitment and the recognition criteria have been met. The revenue and asset are recognized when:

1. There are probably future economic benefits.

2. Revenue can be measured reliably.

3. Costs can be measured reliably.

4. Significant risk and rewards of ownership are transferred.

5. Managerial involvement is not retained as to ownership or control.

6. Therefore, a firm sales commitment may meet the IFRS criteria for recognition, but in the U.S. the revenue and asset from a firm sales commitment would not be recognized.

B. The measurement criteria for reporting receivables is very similar - the future economic benefit of the accounts receivable is analogous to the net realizable value. Therefore the valuation of AR is similar.

Uncollectible—Direct Write-Off and Allowance

This lesson presents the accounting and reporting of uncollectible accounts receivable.

After studying this lesson, you should be able to:

1. *Complete the entries for the direct write-off method for uncollectibles.*

2. *Complete the entries for the allowance method for uncollectibles.*

I. Introduction

A. The fourth factor affecting accounts receivable valuation is uncollectible accounts (the first three were trade discounts, cash discounts, and sales returns and allowances). This is the major issue affecting receivable valuation and income determination in the area of receivables. Bad debt expense (also called uncollectible accounts expense on the CPA Exam) is the account that records the effect of uncollectible accounts. Bad debt expense is on the income statement. The allowance for uncollectible accounts is a balance sheet account contra to accounts receivable. Bad debt expense traditionally has been considered a cost of doing business rather than a sales adjustment.

B. Most companies will use one of two methods to account for bad debt expense. The direct write-off method is the first method presented, followed by the allowance method.

II. Direct Write-Off Method -- This method records bad debt expense only when a specific account receivable is considered uncollectible and is written off. It can be used only when the firm is unable to estimate uncollectible accounts receivable reliably. Most large firms do **not** use this method.

A. **Negative** -- aspects of the direct write-off method - First, if the direct write-off method is employed, accounts receivable are over-valued on the balance sheet. Second, for companies employing the direct write-off method, the company usually recognizes the revenue from a credit sale in one year and typically recognizes the bad debt expense in a subsequent year. So, due to poor balance-sheet valuation and poor matching of revenues and expenses, the direct write-off method is **not** considered in accordance with GAAP unless there is no basis for estimating bad debts.

B. **Positive** -- aspects of the direct write-off method - Companies that use the direct write-off method justify its use for two reasons. First, the use of the direct write-off method may not be materially different in its effect on the company's financial statements relative to the allowance method. Second, the direct write-off method is simple and practical to use.

C. **Typical entries** -- Bad Debt Expense and Bad Debts Recovered are both income statement accounts. The first is an expense account, while the second account is a miscellaneous revenue account.

An account is deemed uncollectible:		
Bad Debt Expense	XX	
Accounts Receivable		XX
An account previously written off is collected:		
Cash	XX	
Bad Debts Recovered		XX

III. The Allowance Method -- The allowance method is the method of choice for most large firms and is required under GAAP if uncollectible accounts are probable and estimable. This method records an estimate of bad debt expense at the end of each year in an adjusting entry. An allowance (contra accounts receivable) is created at that time and reduces net accounts receivable. Thus, both income and net accounts receivable are reduced in the year of sale by the estimate of uncollectible accounts on the year's sales.

A. Positive -- Aspects of the Allowance Method -The positive aspects of employing the allowance method are twofold. First, the allowance method allows companies to value accounts receivables at net realizable value on the balance sheet. Second, the use of the allowance method allows companies to recognize the revenues and expenses from credit sales in the same accounting year. So, due to appropriate balance sheet valuation of receivables and much better matching of revenues and expenses, the allowance method is in accordance with GAAP when uncollectible accounts are estimable.

B. Typical entries

1. **End-of-period adjusting entry** -- This is the important entry. The allowance for doubtful accounts is recorded at year-end because the identity of the specific accounts that will be uncollectible and written off in a later period is unknown. The account is contra to accounts receivable.

Bad Debt Expense	XX	
Allowance for Doubtful Accounts		XX

C. Write-off of uncollectible accounts -- This entry has no effect on income or net assets or even net accounts receivable because the income effect of uncollectibles has already been recognized in the previous adjusting entry. The debit to the allowance decreases the allowance and thus increases net accounts receivable. The credit to accounts receivable decreases net accounts receivable.

Allowance for Doubtful Accounts	XX	
Accounts Receivable		XX

D. Recovery of accounts previously written-off -- These two entries reinstate the allowance account and record cash received.

Accounts Receivable	XX	
Allowance for Doubtful Accounts		XX
Cash	XX	
Accounts Receivable		XX

Allowance—Income Statement and Balance Sheet Approach

This lesson presents the income statement and balance sheet approach for determining the allowance for doubtful accounts.

After studying this lesson, you should be able to:

1. *Calculate the allowance and bad debt expense under the income statement approach and complete the necessary adjusting entry.*

2. *Calculate the allowance and bad debt expense under the balance sheet approach and complete the necessary adjusting entry.*

I. **Estimating Bad Debt Expense --** This section takes a closer look at the estimation of bad debt expense. The amount of bad debt expense in the first entry above, the year-end adjusting entry, may be estimated using two different approaches: the income statement approach or the balance sheet approach. As per a later discussion, it is possible to combine the two approaches. Regardless of the chosen approach, a business entity generally will choose one approach and apply it consistently from year to year.

A. **Income statement approach**

1. Based on observations of prior years, under this approach a company may estimate bad debt expense as a percentage of credit sales.

    > **Note:**
    > Remember that if you use the income statement approach, you are calculating an income statement number (bad debt expense).

2. If the income statement approach is chosen, the bad debt expense is equal to a percentage of the credit sales during a given accounting period. That is, if this approach is chosen, no consideration is given to the existing balance in the allowance account.

3. If the income statement approach is chosen, the matching objective related to the allowance method is the objective that is receiving the primary emphasis.

Example:
Credit sales for 20x7: $500,000

In the past five years, approximately 5% of credit sales have been uncollectible. The bad debt expense for 20x7 is $25,000 (.05 x $500,000). Please note the bad debt expense is $25,000 regardless of the balance in the allowance account prior to the adjusting entry.

B. **Balance sheet approach**

1. Based on observations of prior years, under this approach, the company estimates bad debt expense by analyzing the ending accounts receivable. This analysis may result in the application of a percentage to the ending accounts receivable. Alternatively, the company may analyze the ending accounts receivable by **aging** the ending accounts receivable. This aging process involves grouping receivables by the amount of time they have been outstanding. Once the aging schedule is completed, the company then applies the various estimates of inconvertibility to each group of receivables.

> **Note:** Remember that if you use the balance sheet approach, you are calculating a balance sheet number (allowance for doubtful accounts).

2. The analysis of ending accounts receivable has one simple objective: the determination of the **needed** or desired balance in the allowance account. By **needed** balance, we mean the balance needed to properly value accounts receivable on the balance sheet. The desired allowance balance equals the expected amount of write-offs to occur in the future based on the receivables at the balance sheet date.

3. Once the **needed** balance in the allowance account has been determined, the **needed** balance is compared to the existing balance in the allowance account. The difference in these two balances is the amount of bad debt expense to be recorded for the accounting period.

4. If a company elects to use the balance sheet approach, the company is more concerned with the balance sheet valuation objective related to the allowance method.

 Example:
Balance sheet

Accounts receivable on December 31, 20x7 - $200,000

Based on past experience, the company estimates that 6% of ending receivables will be uncollectible.

Prior to the end-of-period adjustment, the allowance for doubtful accounts had an existing $3,000 debit balance due to greater than expected write-offs.

Desired balance in the allowance account:

$200,000 X 6% = $12,000

As the existing balance in the allowance account is a $3,000 debit balance, the amount recorded in the end-of-period adjusting entry is $15,000.

C. **Combination of the income statement and balance sheet approaches** -- Some business entities prefer to combine the income statement and balance sheet approaches. For example, the entity might elect to use the income statement approach for the monthly adjusting entries for each month January through November. For the December entry, the balance sheet approach might be employed. The following examples illustrate both approaches.

Example: The allowance method and the two estimation methods.

The beginning balances of the current year pertaining to accounts receivable are taken from the current asset section of the balance sheet:

January 1 Balances:

Accounts Receivable	$250,000
Less Allowance for Doubtful Accounts	(6,000)
Equals Net Accounts Receivable	$244,000

The $6,000 remaining in the allowance account at the beginning of the year represents previous years' expected uncollectible accounts that have yet to be written off.

Events for the current year:

Write off a $4,000 account:

Allowance for Doubtful Accounts	4,000	
Accounts Receivable		4,000

Collect a $1,000 account written off last year:

Accounts Receivable	1,000	
Allowance for Doubtful Accounts		1,000
Cash	1,000	
Accounts Receivable		1,000

Credit sales for the year amount to $400,000; cash of $290,000 is collected on account:

Accounts Receivable	400,000	
Sales		400,000
Cash	290,000	
Accounts Receivable		290,000

Ending balances before adjustment:

Accounts Receivable	$356,000*
Allowance for Doubtful Accounts	3,000#

* $250,000 - $4,000 + $400,000 - $290,000

\# $6,000 - $4,000 + $1,000

The next two parts are independent (the firm would use only one of the two)

1. December 31 adjusting entry for bad debt estimate: assume the income statement approach and bad debts are estimated to be 3% of credit sales.

Bad Debt Expense .03($400,000)	12,000	
Allowance for Doubtful Accounts		12,000

Note that the $3,000 pre-adjustment allowance balance is not considered when recognizing bad debt expense. However, actual experience is used periodically to re-estimate the bad debt percentage of sales.

Resulting December 31 balance sheet disclosure:

Accounts Receivable	$356,000
Less Allowance for Doubtful Accounts	(15,000)#
Equals Net Accounts Receivable	$341,000

$3,000 + $12,000

2. Now assume the firm uses the balance sheet approach rather than the income statement approach at year end; in particular, it uses the aging approach to estimating bad debt expense. Total accounts receivable is partitioned into age categories. The older the category, the greater the probability of uncollectible accounts. The uncollectible percentage is based on past experience.

Age Category	Amount of Receivables	Uncollectible Percentage	Expected Uncollectibles
Current	$200,000	.01	$2,000
31-60 days	100,000	.05	5,000
Over 60 days	56,000	.10	5,600
	$356,000		$12,600

Total expected uncollectible accounts -- the desired ending allowance balance of $12,600 -- is the sum of uncollectible accounts across the age categories.

The sum of the total amounts in the age categories equals total gross accounts receivable.

December 31 adjusting entry:

Bad Debt Expense ($12,600 - $3,000)	9,600	
Allowance for Doubtful Accounts		9,600

The desired or needed ending allowance balance is $12,600. With $3,000 already in the allowance account, only $9,600 is required to be reported as bad debt expense. This approach automatically updates for changes in estimates.

Resulting December 31 balance sheet disclosure:

Accounts Receivable	$356,000
Less Allowance for Doubtful Accounts	(12,600)#
Equals Net Accounts Receivable	$343,400

Note: If given a problem similar to this example, the candidate may be required to compute the right-most column above. These amounts are the product of the amount of receivables in the age category and the uncollectible percentage.

II. **U.S. GAAP - IFRS Differences** -- There are no differences between U.S. GAAP and IFRS for estimating the allowance for uncollectible receivables.

Notes Receivable

This lesson presents the accounting for notes receivable.

After studying this lesson, you should be able to:

1. *Calculate the interest component of an interest-bearing note receivable.*

2. *Complete the journal entries for an interest-bearing note receivable.*

3. *Calculate the implicit interest on a non-interest-bearing note receivable.*

4. *Complete the journal entries for a non-interest-bearing note receivable.*

I. Introduction

A. A note is a more formal financial instrument than an accounts receivable. The key reporting issues are valuation of the note (at present value).

B. The maker of a note is the buyer or borrower (the debtor firm or individual). This party is making an unconditional promise to pay principal and interest over the note term. The holder of the note (seller or lender) is the creditor and is the firm recording the note receivable on its books.

C. All notes have an interest element. In an interest-bearing note, the interest element is explicitly stated, while in a non-interest-bearing note, the interest element is not explicitly stated but rather is included in the face value of the note.

D. Notes typically result from the sale of property, conversion of accounts receivable, and lending transactions.

II. Types of Notes

A. Interest-bearing notes receivable -- The interest element is explicitly stated. For example, the note might be identified as a three-year, 9% note receivable. The amount of cash to be collected from an interest-bearing note is the face amount of the note (principal) plus interest.

B. Non-interest bearing note receivable -- The interest element is not explicitly stated. For example, the note might be identified as a two-year, $13,000 non-interest-bearing note. The amount of cash to be collected from a non-interest-bearing note is the face amount of the note. That is, the face amount of the note includes principal and interest that will be collected at maturity date.

III. Recording a Note Receivable

A. Present value -- In accordance with U.S. GAAP, all notes are recorded at the present value of future cash flows (notes of less than one-year term need not be recorded at present value). The discount rate used in this calculation is the market rate of interest on the date of note creation (this rate may be different from the note's stated rate— the rate that appears on the note). Furthermore, any discounts related to notes will be amortized by applying the effective interest method.

B. Market value -- If the stated interest rate is equal to the market rate of interest, the present value of future cash flows will be equal to the face amount of the note. In this situation, no discounts will exist.

C. Interest/market rate -- If the stated interest rate is not equal to the market rate of interest, the present value of future cash flows will not be equal to the face amount of the note. In this situation, a discount related to the note will exist.

D. For a **non-interest-bearing note**, the present value of future cash flows will not be equal to the face amount of the note. In this situation, a discount related to the note will exist.

IV. Determination of Present Value of Future Cash Flows

A. Cash transaction -- If the transaction is a cash transaction, such as a lending transaction, the present value of future cash flows will equal the amount of cash that exchanged hands on the date of note creation.

B. Non-cash transaction -- If the transaction is a non-cash transaction, such as the sale of a non-cash asset and the receipt of a note receivable, the transaction will be recorded at the fair market value of the non-cash asset or the fair market value of the note receivable (present value of future cash flows), whichever one can be more clearly determined.

Example:
Simple interest note, stated rate equals market rate. A calendar-year fiscal-year firm receives a three-year, 6%, $10,000 note on March 1 of the current year from a sale. The note pays interest each September 1 and March 1. The first four entries are shown:

March 1

Note Receivable	10,000	
Sales		10,000

September 1

Cash (.06(1/2)$10,000)	300	
Interest Revenue		300

December 31

Interest Receivable (.06(4/12)$10,000)	200	
Interest Revenue		200

March 1 (following year)

Cash	300	
Interest Receivable		200
Interest Revenue (.06(2/12)$10,000)		100

Example:
Simple interest note, principal and interest are due in annual installments. A calendar-year fiscal-year firm receives a 12%, $300,000 note on May 1, 20x7. Beginning 20x8, the note calls for $100,000 of principal, along with interest on the outstanding note balance at the beginning of the period, to be paid each April 30.

Interest revenue recognized:

In 20x7: $300,000(.12)(8/12) =		$24,000
In 20x8: $300,000(.12)(4/12) +	$200,000(.12)(8/12) =	28,000
In 20x9: $200,000(.12)(4/12) +	$100,000(.12)(8/12) =	16,000
In 2010: $100,000(.12)(4/12) =		4,000

Example:
Each note payment includes principal and interest. A firm receives a 7%, two-year, $20,000 note from a sale, on January 1, 20x7. The note calls for two equal annual payments to be made beginning December 31, 20x7. The present value of an annuity of $1 for two periods at 7% is 1.80802. Let P = annual payment.

$20,000 = P(1.80802)

P = $11,062

January 1, 20x7	Note Receivable	20,000	
	Sales		20,000
December 31, 20x7	Cash	11,062	
	Interest Revenue		1,400*
	Note Receivable		9,662

*$20,000(.07)

This is the interest portion of the first payment.

The $9,662 is return of principal.

December 31, 20x8	Cash	11,062	
	Interest Revenue		724**
	Note Receivable		10,338

**($20,000 - $9,662)(.07)

This entry closes the note receivable account ($20,000 - $9,662 - $10,338 = $0).

Example:
Simple interest note, stated rate and market rates are unequal. A firm, which is not an equipment dealer, sells used equipment (cost, $40,000; accumulated depreciation, $16,000) and receives a two-year, 4%, $25,000 note on January 1, 20x8. The note calls for annual interest to be paid each December 31 beginning 20x8 with the principal due December 31, 20x9. The equipment has no known market value but the prevailing (market) interest rate at the date of sale is 8%. Relevant present values of $1 at 8% for two years: single payment, .85734; annuity, 1.78326.

The note is recorded at present value: $25,000(.85734) + .04($25,000)(1.78326) = $23,217. Thus, the note is recorded at a discount of $1,783 ($25,000 - $23,217). The true value of the note on receipt is $23,217 because this amount reflects the current market interest rate. This amount is also used as the fair value of the equipment in computing the gain or loss on disposal.

January 1, 20x8	Note Receivable	23,217	
	Accumulated Depreciation	16,000	
	Loss on Disposal	783	
	Equipment		40,000

(This entry records the note using the net method. The gross method would record the note at $25,000 and credit Discount on Notes for $1,783. Either approach is acceptable and both report the net notes receivable balance at present value.)

December 31, 20x8	Cash .04($25,000)	1,000	
	Note Receivable	857	
	Interest Revenue		1,857*

* .08($23,217)

The $857 amount is the increase in the value of the note for 20x8 because the cash interest was less than the growth in the note's present value over time. Had the gross method been used, the discount account would have been debited for $857 rather than the note receivable account. Under either reporting approach, the net note balance is now $24,074 ($23,217 + $857). This amount is the present value of the remaining payments at December 31, 20x8, which can also be computed as ($25,000 + $1,000)/1.08.

December 31, 20x9	Cash .04($25,000)	1,000	
	Note Receivable	926	
	Interest Revenue		1,926*
	Cash	25,000	
	Note Receivable		25,000

* .08($23,217 + $857)

Example:
Non-interest-bearing note. A non-interest-bearing note has a zero stated rate. The term **non-interest-bearing** is a misnomer, however, because the interest is included in the note's face value. Assume the same information as in the previous example except that there is no stated rate. Now the present value of the note is $21,434 [$25,000(.85734)]. The note is recorded at this amount. The entries are similar except that no cash interest is received. The first interest entry is shown:

| December 31, 20x8 | Note Receivable | 1,715 | |
| | Interest Revenue | | 1,715* |

* .08($21,434)

Criteria for Sale of Receivables

This lesson presents the criteria for when the transfer of receivables is a sale versus security for a loan.

After studying this lesson, you should be able to:

    1. List the three criteria for the transfer of AR to qualify as a sale.

    2. Complete the journal entries when the transfer of AR is a sale.

    3. Define what is meant by selling AR with recourse and without recourse.

    4. Identify the major differences between U.S. GAAP and IFRS accounting for transfer of AR.

I. **Using Accounts Receivable and Notes Receivable as Sources of Cash** -- Frequently, business entities use receivables as immediate sources of cash. The firm uses the receivables as collateral for a loan or sells the receivables to a third party rather than wait for the maker of the note to make all the required payments on the note. The reasons for the transactions that will be described are varied. In some cases, a company may elect to forgo the establishment of a collection department. That is, the company could decide that the establishment of a collection department is not economically feasible. In other cases, companies may need the cash related to a note receivable or accounts receivable to meet current operating expenses or to take advantage of a unique opportunity.

II. **The Parties Involved in a Transfer of Receivables are**

    A. The **maker**, which is the debtor that has borrowed funds or purchased an asset and provided a note to the original creditor.

    B. The **original creditor** (transferor), which is the firm that has loaned funds or sold an asset to the maker.

    C. The **third-party financial institution** (transferee), which provides the funds to the original creditor.

III. **Type of Transaction** -- When a company transfers receivables to a third party or uses the receivables as collateral for a loan, a determination must be made as to the substance of the transaction: Is it a sale or is it a loan? Codification 860-40 identifies the key characteristics of a sales transaction.

IV. **Criteria for Sale** -- Criteria for determining if the transfer of receivables is a sale:

    A. The transaction is a sale of the receivable if three conditions are met. If the three conditions are met, then control has effectively passed to the third party (transferee) and a sale is implied. The three conditions are:

        1. The transferred assets have been isolated from the transferor, even in bankruptcy.

        2. The transferee is free to pledge or exchange the assets.

        3. The transferor does not maintain effective control over the transferred assets either through an agreement that allows and requires the transferor to repurchase the assets or one that requires the transferor to return specific assets.

    B. **Conditions are met** -- If the above-listed conditions are met, the transaction is accounted for as a sale. The receivable is removed from the books of the transferor and a gain or loss on the sale of the receivable will be recorded.

    C. **Conditions are not met** -- If the listed conditions are **not** met, the transaction is actually a situation in which the transferor is borrowing funds and using the receivables as collateral for a loan. In this case, the receivable remains on the books of the transferor, and the transferor records a liability related to the borrowing transaction. In this case, the transferor will not record any gain or loss on sale of the receivable. Rather, the transferor will record interest expense related to the borrowing transaction.

V. Terms of Transaction

A. With recourse or without recourse

1. The transaction can be completed with recourse or without recourse. If the transaction is completed with recourse, the transferor is responsible for nonpayment on the part of the original maker of the receivable. This means that if the maker (original debtor) defaults, the original creditor must assume all the payments on the receivable.

> **Example:**
> Grotex Inc. sells merchandise to Swemby on account. Grotex is the original creditor. Grotex then transfers the receivable to a financial institution and receives 94% of the value of the receivable. Grotex is the transferor and the financial institution is the transferee. If the transfer is with recourse and Swemby fails to pay the receivable, then Grotex must pay the financial institution the full amount of the receivable. During the term of the receivable, Grotex has a contingent liability that can be noted in a footnote, or a contra asset account can be recorded, such as note receivable discounted, or the liability may need to be accrued in the accounts, depending on the probability that Grotex will be required to pay.

2. If the transaction is completed **without recourse**, the transferor is not responsible for nonpayment on the part of the maker of the receivable. Typically, nonrecourse transfers are accounted for as sales because control has passed to the transferee (financial institution).

B. Notification or non-notification basis -- The transaction can be completed on a notification basis or on a non-notification basis. If the transaction is completed on a notification basis, the maker of the receivable is informed of the transaction and typically is instructed to make payments to the third party. If the transaction is completed on a non-notification basis, the maker of the receivable is not informed of the transaction and continues to make payments to the original creditor.

See the following example.

Example:

The discounting of a note receivable is a common transaction involving the transfer of a receivable. The original creditor (transferor) discounts the note to a financial institution that charges a fee on the maturity value of the note. The maturity value is the face value plus interest, at the note's original rate, over the entire term of the note. The transferor receives proceeds equal to the maturity value less the fee. The Tiger Company has a $4,000, 90-day, 8% note receivable, which was received from a customer in settlement of an account receivable. The Tiger Company held the note for 30 days and decided to discount the note at Auburn National Bank. Auburn National Bank charges a 10% discount fee on the maturity value of the note (which includes the interest for the complete term of the note) for the two months it will hold the note. The proceeds to Tiger equal the maturity value less the fee.

Accrued interest for the 30 days the note was held by Tiger: $4,000(.08)(1/12) = $26.67

Cash Proceeds from the Discounting Transaction: Maturity Value of the Note:

$4,000 +($4,000)(.08)(3/12) =	$4,080
Less Discount Fee: $4,080(.10)(2/12) =	(68)
Equals Cash Proceeds	$4,012

Interest expense (if transaction is a borrowing) or loss (if transaction is a sale):

Carrying Value of Note at Date of Discounting: $4,000 + $26.67	$4,026.67
Less Cash Proceeds	($4,012.00)
Equals Interest Expense or Loss	$14.67

If the transaction is a sale (that is, if all three criteria of SFAS 140 are met), a loss of $14.67 will be recorded. If the transaction is a borrowing transaction, interest expense of $14.67 will be recorded.

Entries assuming a borrowing (all three criteria are not met):

Interest Receivable	26.67	
Interest Revenue		26.67
Cash	4,012.00	
Interest Expense	14.67	
Liability on Note		4,000.00
Interest Receivable		26.67

Entries assuming a sale (all three criteria are met)

Interest Receivable	26.67	
Interest Revenue		26.67
Cash	4,012.00	
Loss on Sale	14.67	
Note Receivable		4,000.00
Interest Receivable		26.67

For the sale transaction, if the note is discounted with recourse, Tiger has a contingent liability for the remaining two months of the note term. If the maker does not pay the note, then Tiger must. Tiger may report the liability in its footnotes or credit Notes Receivable Discounted rather than Notes Receivable in the journal entry immediately above, for $4,000. The Notes Receivable Discounted account is contra to Notes Receivable. This approach more prominently discloses the contingent liability.

VI. Transfers of Receivables Under IFRS

A. Both U.S. GAAP and IFRS seek to determine if the arrangement is a sale of the receivables or a secured borrowing. U.S. GAAP focuses on whether control has shifted from the transferor to the transferee. IFRS focuses on whether the transferor has transferred the rights to receive the cash flows from the receivable and whether substantially all the risk and rewards of ownership were transferred. Application of these criteria are quite complex. However, it is often noted that under IFRS criteria the transfer is less likely to be treated as a sale.

B. Criteria for transfer under IFRS 39

1. If the entity transfers substantially all of the risks and rewards of ownership, the transfer is treated as a sale.

2. If the entity retains substantially all of the risks and rewards of ownership, the transfer is treated as a secured borrowing.

3. If neither conditions 1 or 2 hold, the entity accounts for the transaction as a sale if it has transferred control and as a secured borrowing if it has retained control.

Factoring, Assignment, and Pledging

This lesson presents the accounting for factoring receivables and describes the assignment and pledging of AR.

After studying this lesson, you should be able to:

1. *Describe the difference between factoring with and without recourse.*

2. *Describe the difference between assigning and pledging AR.*

3. *Complete the journal entries when AR is factored with and without recourse.*

I. Other Types of Transactions Involving Transfers of Receivables

A. Factoring

1. **Transferor to factor** -- In a factoring, the transferor (original creditor) transfers the receivables to a factor (transferee, a financial institution) immediately as a normal part of business. The transferor prefers to pay the factor a fee in return for the factor's administration of the receivables. The factor often performs credit checks and collects the payments.

2. **Factoring without recourse** -- This type of factoring is usually accounted for as a sale because the factor has no recourse against the transferor if there is a default on the receivables. The factor (transferee) bears the cost of uncollectible accounts, but the seller (transferor) bears the cost of sales adjustments such as sales discounts and returns and allowances because they are considered preconditions.

Example:
A firm factors $20,000 of accounts receivable without recourse. The factor charges 5% and holds back an additional 3% for sales returns. Assume that actual sales returns equal the estimated amount. The transferor records the following entries:

Cash $20,000(1.00 - .05 - .03)	18,400	
Receivable from Factor $20,000(.03)	600	
Loss on Sale of Receivables $20,000(.05)	1,000	
Accounts Receivable		20,000
Sales Returns and Allowances	600	
Receivable from Factor		600

If the actual and estimated returns are not equal, the factoring agreement will specify which party receives the savings or bears the cost.

Note: In the example above, the transfer qualified as a sale - therefore the cost of the factoring is a LOSS ON THE SALE OF RECEIVABLES.

---

3. **Factoring with recourse** -- When receivables are factored with recourse, the three criteria of Codification 860-40 must be used to determine if the transaction is accounted for as a sale or a loan. The seller (transferor) bears the cost of bad debts as well as the cost of sales adjustments.

a. If accounted for as a sale, the entries are similar to factoring without recourse except that the transferor must estimate and record a recourse liability.

Example: A firm factors $20,000 of accounts receivable with recourse. The factor charges 2%. The firm estimates that its liability for bad debts (the recourse liability) is $1,000. The three criteria of Codification 860-40 are met. The holdback for sales adjustments is not illustrated in this example but is handled the same way as for factoring without recourse. The transferor records the following entries:

Cash $20,000(1.00 - .02)	19,600	
Loss on Sale of Receivables $20,000(.02) + $1,000	1,400	
Accounts Receivable		20,000
Recourse Liability		1,000

When accounts are deemed uncollectible, the transferor remits the necessary cash to the factor:

Recourse Liability	1,000	
Cash		1,000

Note: In the example above, the transfer qualified as a sale - therefore the cost of the factoring is a LOSS ON THE SALE OF RECEIVABLES.

b. If accounted for as a loan, the transferor maintains the receivables on its books, and records a loan and interest expense over the term of the agreement.

Example: A firm factors $20,000 of accounts receivable with recourse. The factor charges 2%. The firm estimates that its liability for bad debts (the recourse liability) is $1,000. The three criteria of Codification 860-40 are not met. The transferor records the following entries:

Cash $20,000(1.00 - .02)	19,600	
Discount on Factor Liability $20,000(.02)	400	
Factor Liability		20,000
Allowance for Doubtful Accounts	1,000	
Accounts Receivable		1,000

As payments on the receivables are made to the factor, the factor liability is extinguished and interest expense is recognized. The summary entry is:

Factor Liability	20,000	
Accounts Receivable		19,000
Cash (to pay for uncollectible accounts)		1,000
Interest Expense	400	
Discount on Factor Liability		400

Interest expense is recognized in proportion to collections on the receivables. If 75% of the receivables were collected by year-end, then $300 of interest would be recognized as of the balance sheet date.

> Note: In the example above, the transfer DID NOT qualify as a sale - therefore the cost of the factoring is INTEREST EXPENSE, and the accounts receivable are not removed from the books of the transferor until the receivables are collected.

II. **Assignment of Accounts Receivable** -- When accounts receivable are assigned, the borrower assigns rights to specific accounts receivable as collateral for a loan. The lender has the right to seek payment from these receivables should the borrower (original creditor for the accounts receivable) default on the loan. The borrower reclassifies the receivables as accounts receivable assigned, a subcategory of total accounts receivable. The borrower maintains the receivable records, and as cash is received, it is remitted to the lender in payment of the loan. The loan and the receivables are not offset on the borrower's balance sheet. When the loan is repaid, any remaining accounts receivable assigned are returned to ordinary accounts receivable status.

III. **Pledging of Accounts Receivable** -- Pledging of accounts receivable is less formal than assignment. Rights to specific receivables are not noted as collateral, and accounts receivable are not reclassified. Neither the accounting for the receivables nor the loan is affected by the pledge. Receivables in bulk are transferred to a trustee and can be used for payment of the loan in the event of default by the borrower (original creditor for the accounts receivable). The cash flows from the receivables are used to pay the loan. Footnote disclosure of the pledge is required.

Notes Receivable—Impairment

This lesson presents the definition of when a loan is impaired and presents the entries for impairment.

After studying this lesson, you should be able to:

1. *Define when a note receivable is impaired.*

2. *Complete the journal entries for the note impairment.*

I. **Impaired Loans Receivables are Written Down to**

A. The present value of the future cash flows expected to be collected using the original effective interest rate for the loan, or

B. Market value if this value is more determinable.

II. **The Write-Down (Loss)** -- This is accomplished with a debit to bad debt expense and a credit to a contra-receivable account. After the write-down, interest revenue is recognized under any of several methods found in practice, including the interest method and cost recovery methods (Codifications 310-10-35).

> **Example:**
> A firm holds a 7%, $10,000 note due December 31, 20x6. Annual interest is due each December 31. The note originated on January 1 several years ago. The 20x5 interest payment was not received and the firm believes, as of December 31, 20x5, that no more interest will be received. In addition, only $7,000 of the principal is expected to be received, and that amount will be delayed one year, to December 31, 20x7.
>
> The carrying value of the note on December 31, 20x5 is $10,700, which includes the $700 annual interest that was not paid by the debtor firm. The interest receivable is closed to note receivable. The resulting $10,700 note receivable balance remains on the books. A valuation account is used to write the note down to present value and the loss (bad debt expense) is recognized on this date. The present value of a single payment of $1 at 7% for two years is .87344. Two years is the remaining term of the note.
>
> December 31, 20x5
>
> | | | |
> |---|---|---|
> | Bad Debt Expense | 4,586* | |
> | Allowance for Decline in Note Value | | 4,586 |
>
> | | |
> |---|---|
> | *Carrying Value: | $10,700.00 |
> | Less Present Value:$7,000(.87344) | (6,114) |
> | Equals Impairment Loss | $ 4,586 |
>
> The allowance for decline in note value account is contra to notes receivable. The above entry reduces the net carrying value of the note to $6,114, the present value of remaining cash flows. For the remaining two years of the note term, the firm may choose from a variety of methods to recognize interest revenue. Two are illustrated here:
>
> | | Interest Method | Cost-Recovery Method |
> |---|---|---|
> | December 31, 20x6 | | |
> | Allowance for Decline in Note Value | 428 | No entry as the new carrying value has not been recovered |
> | Interest Revenue .07($6,114) | 428 | |

December 31, 20x7

Allowance for Decline in Note Value	458		No entry as the new carrying value has not been recovered
Interest Revenue		458	

.07($6,114 + $428)

Cash	7,000		7,000
Allowance for Decline in Note Value	3,700		4,586
Note Receivable		10,700	10,700
Interest Revenue			886

The interest method is applied as it is in any other note or bond situation. Interest revenue for a period is based on the net note balance at the beginning of the period. The cost recovery method delays recognition of interest revenue until the entire new carrying value ($6,114) is received. The only cash inflow in this situation occurred at the end of 20x7. Thus all the interest revenue is recognized in that year. The total interest revenue over the two years is the same for both methods.

III. Loan Impairment and IFRS

A. Impairments under IFRS have some general guidelines that will apply to loan impairment and other impairments we will discuss throughout the specific financial accounts. IAS 36 governs impairment of assets and in general the purpose of the standard is to make sure that assets are not carried at more than the recoverable amount. If the assets carrying value is greater than the amount that could be recovered through the assets use or by selling the asset, then it is impaired.

B. IFRS is more flexible in allowing reversal of impairment losses than U.S. GAAP. In each topical area where impairment is discussed, CPAexcel will let you know when the impairment can be reversed. The following discusses some terminology:

    1. Recoverable amount: the higher of the fair value less cost to sell or value in use:

        a. Fair value less cost to sell is the amount obtainable from the sale in an arms-length transaction between knowledgeable, willing and able parties.

        b. Value in use is the discounted present value of the futures cash flows expected from the asset.

    2. Cash-generating unit (CGU) is the smallest group of assets that can be identified that generates cash flows independently of the cash flows from other assets. Impairment tests are all applied to the individual asset level. If the cash flows for the individual asset are not identifiable, then you measure the cash flows from the cash-generating unit.

C. If there is any indication that the loan value has declined, an impairment loss would be taken as the difference between the carrying value and the recoverable amount. If the loan value subsequently increases, IFRS permits recovery of the impairment loss.

Introduction to Inventory

This lesson presents the basics for accounting for inventory including: components of inventory, FOB shipping point, FOB destination, consigned goods ,and costs capitalized to inventory.

After studying this lesson, you should be able to:

1. *List the three basic components of manufacturing inventory.*

2. *Define FOB shipping point and FOB destination.*

3. *Identify what is included in year-end inventory costs (goods in transit, consigned goods and capitalized costs).*

I. Inventory Definition and Description

A. This section address (1) the items, and (2) costs that should be included in the inventory account.

> **Definition:**
> *Inventory:* For a typical business entity inventory includes property held for resale, property in the process of production, and property consumed in the process of production.

B. A manufacturing company has all three types of inventory items. That is, a manufacturing company has:

1. finished goods inventory;

2. work-in-process inventory; and

3. raw materials inventory.

C. A merchandising company typically holds the inventory item that is best described as property held for resale. That is, a merchandising company has a single type of inventory item, usually referred to as merchandise inventory.

D. Inventories also include land (if the firm is a real-estate development company), and partially completed buildings and bridges (if the firm is a construction company). Inventories are always current assets to the seller even though they may be noncurrent assets to the buyer.

II. Ending Inventory

A. What items are included in ending inventory?

1. To address this question, you simply apply the ownership criteria. If the merchandise is owned by a business enterprise on the last day of the accounting year, regardless of location, the merchandise should be included in ending inventory.

2. Most of the merchandise owned by a business enterprise on the last day of the accounting year is typically located on the premises/property of that business enterprise. However, goods awaiting shipment to customers are not included in the firm's inventory if the customer has paid for the goods.

3. Merchandise owned and located off-site

a. Goods in transit

i. Ownership of goods in transit is determined by the test of title: FOB (free-on-board). FOB destination means that title to the goods transfers to the buyer when the goods reach the destination. Therefore, shipping terms of FOB destination Chicago means that the buyer owns the goods when they reach Chicago. FOB shipping point means title passes at the shipping point (the selling company's warehouse), therefore the goods belong to the purchaser as soon as it is loaded on a common carrier. In general, FOB shipping point means title passes at the shipping point and FOB destination means title passes at the destination. The test of title is important for the year-end cut-off because goods in transit can be included in only one firm's inventory: the buyer or seller.

> **Example:**
> **1.** A business entity is located in Auburn, Alabama and has a major supplier located in Seattle, Washington. On December 31, 20x7, some merchandise was placed on a train or a truck and was en route to Auburn, Alabama on that date.
>
> If the goods were shipped FOB shipping point, the purchased goods in transit should be included in the Auburn company's ending inventory.
>
> If the goods were shipped FOB destination, the purchased goods in transit should not be included in the Auburn company's ending inventory.
>
> **2.** Goods in transit to a customer - A business entity is located in Auburn, Alabama and has a major customer located in Chicago, Illinois. On December 31, 20x7, some merchandise was placed on a train or truck and was en route to Chicago on that date.
>
> If the goods were shipped FOB destination, the sold goods in transit should be included in the Auburn company's ending inventory.
>
> If the goods were shipped FOB shipping point, the sold goods in transit should not be included in the Auburn company's ending inventory.

b. **Goods on consignment**

   i. A business entity is located in Austin, Texas, and has signed an agreement with a manufacturer to be the sole retailer of the manufacturer's merchandise in the state of Texas. The Austin-based entity sells the merchandise in its Austin-area stores and reaches a consignment agreement with retail establishments in Houston, Dallas, San Antonio, Lubbock, and El Paso. The agreement is the typical consignment agreement. The retail stores outside of Austin will receive the merchandise and attempt to market the merchandise in their selected markets. If the merchandise is sold, the retailer will retain a sales commission and remit the remainder to the Austin-based business entity. If the merchandise is not sold, the retailer will return the merchandise to the Austin-based business entity. In this example, the Austin-based entity is the consignor, and the business establishments located in Houston, Dallas, San Antonio, Lubbock, and El Paso are all consignees.

   ii. In consignment arrangements, the merchandise is owned by the consignor. The merchandise is always included in the consignor's ending inventory even though the inventory typically is never on the consignor's premises.

> **Example:**
> Trend Inc. has $40,000 worth of its inventory held by a consignee at year-end. Trend also serves as a consignee and holds $30,000 of inventory on consignment for another firm. Only the $40,000 of inventory is included in Trend's ending inventory.

III. **Valuation of Inventory** -- The acquisition cost of inventory includes all costs incurred in getting the merchandise to the seller's premises and ready for sale. A good general rule is:

   A. **Capitalize in inventory all costs necessary to bring the item of inventory to salable condition.**

   1. These costs include freight and insurance in transit paid to the seller firm, any taxes paid on acquisition of inventory, material handling costs, and packaging costs. Interest on the purchase or construction of inventory is never included in inventory. Purchases discounts, and returns and allowances reduce the total cost allocated to inventory. Promotional costs such as advertising are not included in inventory because these costs do not help prepare the inventory for sale.

   2. Also not included are interest costs.

> **Example:**
> A firm incurred the following costs related to the acquisition and sale of inventory:
>
> | | |
> |---|---|
> | Direct Purchase Cost | $50,000 |
> | Purchases Returns | 4,000 |
> | Freight-In | 9,000 |
> | Freight-Out | 2,000 |
> | Interest on Purchase | 1,000 |
> | Sales and Other Taxes on Acquisition | 3,000 |
> | Packaging Costs (for sale) | 4,000 |
> | Insurance in Transit from Supplier | 500 |
> | Promotional Expenses | 2,500 |
>
> The inventory should be recorded at the following amount:
>
> | | |
> |---|---|
> | Direct Purchase Cost | $50,000 |
> | Purchases Returns | (4,000) |
> | Freight-In | 9,000 |
> | Sales and Other Taxes on Acquisition | 3,000 |
> | Packaging Costs (for sale) | 4,000 |
> | Insurance in Transit from Supplier | 500 |
> | Total Inventory Cost | $62,500 |
>
> The excluded costs are period expenses.

B. Inventory costs

1. Intermediate accounting considers the general issue of costing inventory but limits its consideration to merchandise inventory-inventory purchased for resale. The Management Accounting section of CPAexcel addresses a related issued issue - how to determine the cost of manufactured inventories. Manufactured inventory ultimately should reflect the actual cost of manufacturing.

2. **Fixed overhead is one of the four manufacturing input costs** -- The others are direct material, direct labor, and variable overhead. Fixed overhead does not vary with small changes in production volume and therefore is often allocated to production based on a predetermined overhead rate. For example, if direct labor hours is used for allocation purposes, and the fixed overhead allocation rate is $4 per direct labor hour, then a production run using 1,000 direct labor hours would receive an allocation of $4,000 of fixed overhead cost. The $4 rate is the ratio: (budgeted fixed overhead)/(budgeted direct labor hours).

3. **Fixed overhead rates** -- These are subject to estimation errors and are affected by the choice of denominator measure and the budgeting horizon reflected in the denominator. Assuming no numerator (fixed overhead cost) variation, if actual production is less than the production budgeted for the denominator, less fixed overhead will be applied to product than is actually incurred. Under-applied fixed overhead resulting from low production volume must be expensed rather than allocated back to product. Low production volume does not imply that the inventory produced should carry a higher cost or is in any way more valuable.

4. To ensure that unallocated fixed overheads are expensed, Codification 330-10-30 requires for external financial reporting purposes, that **"normal" activity** be used for the denominator level. Normal activity is a measure of the average production volume (as measured in units, direct labor cost or hours, machine hours, or other predicted amount) expected for a budget horizon typically extending beyond one year and takes into account lost production due to planned maintenance. The range in production volume over more than one period establishes the normal capacity amount. Shorter-range budgeted volumes should not be used as the denominator. During periods of abnormally low production, the use of actual production volume would result in higher overhead rates, causing more overhead to be allocated to product. By requiring normal capacity, higher amounts of fixed overhead will not be allocated to the product during low production periods. Fixed overhead that has not benefited production is not an asset and should be expensed as incurred.

5. The standard also requires that costs **including idle facility expense**, excessive spoilage, double freight, wasted materials, and rehandling costs be treated as current period costs rather than allocated to inventory and carried over to future periods. This is an example of invoking the conceptual framework definition of an asset rather than the matching principle.

6. The FASB also reaffirmed the concept that selling, general, and administrative expenditures not be treated as manufacturing costs but rather as period costs. Selling costs are not production costs.

Periodic Inventory System and Cost-Flow Assumption

This lesson presents the accounting for inventory under a periodic inventory system.

After studying this lesson, you should be able to:

1. *Describe the determination and presentation of the net worth element of such a statement.*

2. *Calculate cost of goods sold.*

3. *Calculate ending inventory under a periodic system using specific identification, weighted average, FIFO, and LIFO cost flow assumptions.*

I. Introduction

A. In accounting for inventories, business entities may elect to employ a periodic inventory system. If so, the beginning inventory balance is reflected in the merchandise inventory account throughout the year. That is, the merchandise inventory account will have an unchanging balance throughout the accounting year. The firm uses other means to obtain current inventory information for internal purposes. The periodic system is much less expensive to administer than is the perpetual system.

B. Recording acquisitions -- For companies employing the periodic inventory system, acquisitions of merchandise during the year will be recorded in the *purchases and related accounts*. The purchases account is used rather than the inventory account because a continuous record of the cost of inventory on hand at any time is not maintained under the periodic system.

C. Typical entries

1. Beginning inventory

Merchandise inventory: January 1, 20X7
Purchase of merchandise on account:
   Purchases   XX

      Accounts Payable   XX

  a. Purchases is a holding account for inventory charges and credits and is closed to ending inventory and cost of goods sold at the end of the period. The inventory account is not used to record purchases in a periodic system.

  See the following example.

Paid delivery charges on purchased merchandise		
Transportation In	XX	
Cash		XX
Returned damaged or defective merchandise		
Accounts Payable	XX	
Purchase Returns and Allowances		XX
Paid for merchandise and received cash discount		
Accounts Payable	XX	
Purchase Discounts		XX
Cash		XX
Sold merchandise on account		
Accounts Receivable	XX	
Sales		XX

2. Ending inventory

a. End of the period - Under the periodic inventory system, a physical count of ending inventory is required. Once the number of units in ending inventory has been counted, a value is assigned to the ending inventory, and the following year-end adjusting entry is prepared.

Merchandise Inventory (Ending)	XX	
Purchase Returns and Allowances	XX	
Purchase Discounts	XX	
Cost of Goods Sold	XX	
Merchandise Inventory (Beginning)		XX
Purchases		XX
Transportation In		XX

See the following note.

Note: The entry shown above allows a business entity to achieve multiple objectives. First, the ending balance of inventory is formally entered into the accounting system. Second, the beginning balance of inventory is closed. Also, the purchases and related accounts are closed. Finally, the cost of goods sold for the year is formally entered into the accounting system. Before this entry, cost of goods sold did not exist in the accounting records. Cost of goods sold is not directly observable in a periodic system. Rather, the value recorded for cost of goods sold is derived from the other amounts in the above entry. Another common way of computing cost of goods sold is by the basic inventory equations:

Net purchases = Gross Purchases + Transportation In (Freight In)

- Purchases Returns and Allowances

- Purchases Discounts

Beginning Inventory + Net Purchases = Ending Inventory + Cost of Goods Sold

3. Cost of goods sold is the last amount computed. In other words, it is a derived amount based on the other three values in the above equation. Also, "cost of goods available for sale" equals the value of either side of the above equation, although in published reports, cost of goods available for sale is shown as the subtotal of beginning inventory and net purchases.

4. The challenge is to determine the allocation of the left side total to the two components of the right side of the equation. Cost of goods sold, a major expense, is not recognized until goods are sold. Costs remain in inventory until sale.

Note: Transportation out (also called delivery expense and freight-out) is not included in inventory. Transportation out is a distribution or selling expense and is not an inventoriable cost.

 Example:
Data for a firm's inventory and related transactions follows:

Beginning Inventory	$20,000	Ending Inventory	$32,000
Purchases	100,000	Purchases Returns	4,000
Purchases Discounts	8,000	Transportation In	9,000
Transportation Out	6,000		

The firm's cost of goods sold is determined as follows:

Net Purchases = $100,000 + $9,000 - $8,000 - $4,000

= $97,000

Cost of Goods Sold = Beginning Inventory + Net Purchases - Ending Inventory

= $20,000 + $97,000 - $32,000

= $85,000

II. Cost-Flow Assumption

A. Beginning inventory + net purchases = ending inventory + cost of goods sold

B. To assign a value to ending inventory and cost of goods sold, we apply one of four cost-flow assumptions. These cost-flow assumptions are identified below. Although the merits of each flow assumption are discussed below, remember that firms are free to decide which assumption to choose.

C. Specific identification

1. If the business entity has somewhat large, distinguishable products, it might be appropriate to use specific identification. For example, an automobile dealer might find this cost flow assumption appropriate. To continue the example, the dealer counted a total of 49 automobiles in inventory at year-end. The dealer can identify each automobile by vehicle number and match the invoice cost by vehicle number as well. To value its ending inventory, the dealership is able to *specifically identify* the cost of each of the inventory items and then total the individual cost of all the inventory items. Likewise, the dealership can specifically identify the cost of each item sold and total these amounts to determine cost of goods sold for the period.

2. The specific identification assumption is not cost effective for most firms and allows firms to manipulate earnings.

Example:
If a firm has many identical items in inventory and desires to maximize net income, it can sell the least expensive items rather than the more expensive items. This example assumes a gradual increase in the specific price level of the inventory. The resulting lower cost of goods sold may erroneously imply to users of the financial statements that the firm can continue the reported level of gross margin (sales less cost of goods sold). However, the firm must eventually begin selling the more expensive items.

D. Weighted average cost-flow assumption

1. The term *weighted average* always implies the periodic inventory system. If the business entity selects this cost flow assumption, the weighted average cost per unit must be calculated. This calculation is shown below.

Weighted average cost per unit = cost of goods available for sale / number of units available for sale

2. The ending inventory valuation is equal to the number of units in ending inventory multiplied by the weighted average cost per unit. Likewise, the cost of goods sold for the period is equal to the number of units sold multiplied by the weighted average cost per unit.

3. The weighted average method treats each unit available for sale (beginning inventory and purchases) as if it were costed at the average cost during the period. It produces cost of goods sold and ending inventory results between those of FIFO and LIFO when prices change during the period.

E. FIFO

1. This cost-flow assumption is based on a *first-in, first-out* philosophy. At the end of the accounting period, it is assumed the ending inventory is composed of units of inventory most recently acquired. Conversely, the cost of goods sold is made up of the *oldest* merchandise. The FIFO cost-flow assumption reflects the way most firms actually move their inventory. *However, GAAP does not require that firms choose the inventory cost-flow assumption that reflects the actual movement of goods.*

2. During periods of rising specific inventory prices, FIFO produces the highest net income because cost of goods sold is costed with the lowest-cost (earliest) purchases in the period. Ending inventory reflects the highest (latest) costs. Sometimes FIFO ending inventory is used as an approximation to the current cost of ending inventory.

F. LIFO

1. This cost flow assumption is based on a *last-in, first-out* philosophy. At the end of the accounting period, it is assumed the ending inventory is composed of the *oldest* inventory layers, while the cost of goods sold is composed of the units of inventory most recently acquired.

2. During periods of rising specific inventory prices, LIFO produces the lowest net income because cost of goods sold is costed with the highest-cost (latest) purchases in the period. This feature of LIFO is considered an advantage because reported gross margin reflects the latest purchase costs and therefore is more indicative of future gross margin.

3. However, the ending inventory reflects the lowest (earliest) costs. Whenever the firm purchases (or produces) more units than it sells, a layer is added. This layer is costed with the earliest costs of the period in which the layer is added, under the periodic system. After several years of adding layers, ending inventory may reflect very old costs. Ending inventory under LIFO is a less reliable amount compared with FIFO ending inventory.

III. Calculating Cost of Goods Sold in a Periodic System

A. The ending inventory cost is typically found by counting the items in inventory at the end of the year and applying the appropriate costs, depending on the cost-flow assumption, to the items on hand. Cost of goods sold is computed last.

B. To calculate cost of goods sold for a company employing the periodic inventory system, the calculation shown below is used. This approach is the equation approach illustrated previously, placed into a schedule format.

Cost-of-goods-sold Calculation:

Beginning Inventory
+ Net Cost of Purchases
= Goods Available for Sale
- Ending Inventory
= Cost of Goods Sold

See the following example.

Example: The four cost-flow assumptions in a periodic system are illustrated in this example. The purchases and sales of the firm's one product are given in chronological order for the period. Assume the firm always actually sells the oldest units on hand first.

Beginning Inventory:	400 Units @ $10 per Unit
Purchase 1:	100 Units @ $11 per Unit
Sale 1:	200 Units

(Note: No unit cost is given. The cost assigned to

each sale depends on the cost-flow assumption chosen.)

Purchase 2:	200 Units @ $12 per Unit
Sale 2:	400 Units
Purchase 3:	200 Units @ $13 per Unit

The basic equation in units helps to identify the right hand side of the equation for costing purposes:

Beginning Inventory   + Purchases   = Ending Inventory   + Sales

400 Units   + 500 Units   = 300 Units   + 600 Units

Cost of Goods Available for Sale

    = Cost in Beginning Inventory + Total Purchases Cost

    = 400($10) + 100($11) + 200($12) + 200($13) = $10,100

The sum of ending inventory and cost of goods sold for all four methods must sum to $10,100. This amount is the cost of goods available for sale. During the period, there were 900 units available for sale.

C. Specific identification and FIFO

1. These two assumptions yield the same results in this case (although they need not in a given situation), because the firm always sells its oldest goods first.

Cost of Goods Sold= the Cost of the 600 Oldest Units Available During the Period		
= 400($10) + 100($11) + 100($12)		= $ 6,300
Ending Inventory = the Cost of the 300 Most Recently Added Units		
= 100($12) + 200($13)		= <u>3,800</u>
Sum of Ending Inventory and Cost of Goods Sold		$10,100

D. Weighted average

1. The average cost per unit for the period = $10,100/900 = $11.22

2. Both cost of goods sold and ending inventory reflect the average cost during the period.

Cost of Goods Sold	= $11.22(600)	= $6,732
Ending Inventory	= $11.22(300)	= 3,366
Sum of Ending Inventory and Cost of Goods Sold		$10,098*

(*off by $2 due to rounding of the average cost per unit)

E. LIFO

Cost of Goods Sold = the Cost of the 600 Most Recently Acquired Units Available

During the Period

= 200($13) + 200($12) + 100($11) + 100($10)   = $7,100

Ending Inventory   = the Cost of the 300 Oldest Available Units

= 300($10)   = 3,000

Sum of Ending Inventory and Cost of Goods Sold $10,100

F. Comparison

1. The cost of the inventory item sold by this firm steadily increased during the period. The ranking, highest to lowest in terms of dollar amount, of cost of goods sold and ending inventory:

Cost of Goods Sold		**Ending Inventory**	
LIFO	$7,100	FIFO	$3,800
W. Ave.	6,732	W.Ave.	3,366
FIFO	6,300	LIFO	3,000

NOTE: *Calculation of cost of goods sold:* This example calculated cost of goods sold directly. Although this may be possible for firms with low unit volume, for most firms using a periodic system, the ending inventory cost is measured first through an inventory count and application of unit costs, and then cost of goods sold is computed by subtracting the ending inventory cost from cost of goods available for sale.

NOTE: *Goods to be considered in the calculation of cost of goods sold:* A periodic system assumes all goods purchased anytime during the year are available for sale. The time period assumption of accounting supports this view. In this example, the last purchase occurred *after* the last sale. Thus, the last purchase could not possibly have been sold. However, LIFO included the last purchase as the very first purchase assumed sold, and the weighted average method also included the purchase in the computation of cost per unit. Given the time period assumption of accounting, the inclusion of the last purchase in the computations is appropriate.

Perpetual Inventory System and Cost-Flow Assumption

This lesson presents the accounting for inventory under a perpetual inventory system.

After studying this lesson, you should be able to:

1. *Complete the entries to record inventory under the perpetual system.*

2. *Calculate ending inventory under the perpetual inventory system using specific identification, weighted average, FIFO and LIFO cost flow assumptions.*

I. Typical Entries

A. In illustrating the typical entries for the perpetual inventory system, assume the merchandise inventory account balance on January 1, 20x7 is $100,000.

Purchases of inventory on account
Merchandise Inventory	XX	
Accounts Payable		XX

Paid delivery charges on purchased merchandise

Merchandise Inventory	XX	
Cash		XX

Returned damaged or defective merchandise
Accounts Payable	XX	
Merchandise Inventory		XX

Paid for merchandise and received a cash discount

Accounts Payable	XX	
Merchandise Inventory		XX
Cash		XX

Sold merchandise on account
Accounts Receivable	XX	
Sales		XX
Cost of Goods Sold	XX	
Merchandise Inventory		XX

B. The main differences between these entries and those for the periodic system are:

1. the use of the inventory account rather than purchases for the acquisition of inventory and adjustments such as returns and discounts; and

2. the recording of cost of goods sold at sale rather than at the end of the period.

C. **End of the period** -- A physical count of ending inventory should be completed to confirm inventory records. If inventory shrinkage has occurred (loss, theft, breakage), or if recording errors have been made, an appropriate adjusting entry would be prepared to reduce inventory to the amount per the physical count. The entry would reduce the inventory account and record a shrinkage loss.

D. **Cost-flow assumption** -- A perpetual system considers only goods on hand when computing cost of goods sold for a specific sale. As opposed to the periodic system, which considers all goods on hand during the period when computing cost of goods sold, a perpetual system computes cost of goods sold only for the goods that have actually been purchased through the date of sale.

E. **Specific identification** -- The results (values placed on cost of goods sold and ending inventory) for this cost flow assumption are the same for both the periodic and perpetual systems. The specific cost of each item sold is used to compute the cost of goods sold.

F. **Moving average** -- The term *moving average* always implies the perpetual inventory system. Rather than having a single weighted average cost per unit for the accounting period, the company computes a new weighted average cost per unit after each purchase of inventory. That moving average is used for costing all subsequent sales until another purchase takes place, at which time the moving average is modified by the new purchase. When merchandise is sold, the current weighted average cost per unit is multiplied by the number of units sold to determine the amount of the cost-of-goods-sold entry.

1. In a period of steadily rising prices, the moving average method (perpetual) results in lower cost of goods sold than the weighted average method (periodic). The moving average method applies earlier (and therefore lower) costs to sales during the year relative to the overall higher weighted average cost for the entire period.

G. **FIFO** -- The results (values placed on cost of goods sold and ending inventory) for this cost flow assumption are the same for both the periodic and perpetual systems. The cost of the beginning inventory and earliest units purchased are assigned to cost of goods sold leaving the most recent purchase costs to be assigned to ending inventory.

H. **LIFO** -- The results for LIFO-perpetual differ from those of LIFO-periodic. In the perpetual system, each sale is costed with the most recent purchase available preceding that sale. The periodic system uses the latest purchases for the entire period. Thus in a year of steadily rising prices, perpetual LIFO yields a lower cost-of-goods-sold figure because it uses earlier purchases. Periodic LIFO would assume the sale of the very latest purchases in the period irrespective of the sequencing of sales and purchases.

Example:

The data for the previous example of the four cost flow assumptions is now applied in a perpetual system in this example. The purchases and sales of the firm's one product are given in chronological order for the period. The firm sells the oldest units on hand first.

Beginning inventory:	400 Units @ $10 per Unit
Purchase 1:	100 Units @ $11 per Unit
Sale 1:	200 Units
Purchase 2:	200 Units @ $12 per Unit
Sale 2:	400 Units
Purchase 3:	200 Units @ $13 per Unit

Beginning Inventory	+ Purchases =	Ending Inventory	+ Sales
400 Units	+ 500 Units =	300 Units	+ 600 Units

Cost of Goods Available for Sale =   Cost in Beginning Inventory

+ Purchases Cost

= 400($10) + 100($11) + 200($12) + 200($13) = $10,100

The sum of ending inventory and cost of goods sold for all four methods must sum to $10,100. This amount is the cost of goods available for sale. During the period, there were 900 units available for sale.

I. **Specific identification and FIFO --** The results for both of these assumptions are the same for both the periodic and perpetual systems and are not repeated here.

A **moving average** is not needed until there is a sale to cost. The first sale occurs after the first purchase. The average unit cost of beginning inventory and the first purchase = ($4,000 + $1,100)/500 = $10.20. The following table illustrates the application of the moving averages.

Event	Units	Cost	Moving Average	Computation
Beginning inventory	400	$4,000		
+ Purchase 1	100	1,100		
=	500	5,100	$10.20	= $5,100/500
– Sale 1	(200)	(2,040)		= $10.20(200)
=	300	3,060		
+ Purchase 2	200	2,400		
=	500	5,460	$10.92	= $5,460/500
– Sale 2	(400)	(4,368)		= $10.92(400)
=	100	1,092		
+ Purchase 3	200	2,600		
=	300	3,692	$12.31	= $3,692/300

For example, Sale 1 is costed at $10.20, the moving average of goods on hand just before the sale. Removing those units leaves 300 units in inventory and $3,060 in cost. Purchase 2, at $12 per unit, is added into both the units and cost columns. $12 exceeds the previous moving average; therefore the moving average after Purchase 2 increases. That average is applied to Sale 2 and so forth. The final moving average of $12.31 reflects the higher purchase cost of Purchase 3 and will be used to cost sales the next period until the first purchase in that period is made.

Ending Inventory =	$3,692
Cost of Goods Sold = $2,040 + $4,368	6,408
Total = Cost of Goods Available for Sale	$10,100

J. **LIFO --** To cost sales, the latest purchases available at time of sale are used.

Cost of Goods Sold:

Sale 1 (200 units):100($11) (Purchase 1) + 100($10)(Beg. Inv.)=	$2,100
Sale 2 (400 units):200($12) (Purchase 2) + 200($10)(beg. Inv.)=	4,400
Total Cost of Goods Sold	$6,500

Ending Inventory:

From Purchase 3 (all remaining): 200($13) =	$2,600
From Beginning Inventory (100 Units Remaining): 100($10) =	1,000
Total Ending Inventory	$3,600

Check:

Cost of Goods Sold	$6,500
+ Ending Inventory	3,600
= Cost of Goods Available	$10,100

Evaluation of FIFO and LIFO

This lesson emphasizes the differences in FIFO and LIFO cost-flow assumptions.

After studying this lesson, you should be able to:

1. *Describe the income statement and balance sheet effect of using FIFO or LIFO valuation.*

2. *Describe what is meant by "LIFO liquidation" and the effect on the income statement.*

I. Evaluation of FIFO and LIFO

A. Regardless of price changes, the following effects hold and form the basis for comparing the two methods:

	Ending Inventory	Cost of goods sold
FIFO	Reflects latest costs	Reflects earliest costs
LIFO	Reflects earliest costs	Reflects latest costs

B. Thus, if inventory costs have been rising, LIFO shows lower ending inventory, higher cost of goods sold, and lower income. The opposite is true if costs have been declining.

C. FIFO

1. In assessing the relative attributes of FIFO, it is important to remember three important points of emphasis.

   a. If FIFO is employed by a business entity, the flow of costs is the same as the physical flow of goods for most firms.

   b. If FIFO is employed by a business entity, the balance sheet valuation of inventory is an approximation to current cost, which is considered more relevant than historical cost.

   c. If FIFO is employed by a business entity however, the matching of revenues and expenses on the income statement is not considered ideal. Frequently, a company will be matching the revenues of the current year with the cost of merchandise acquired in a prior accounting period.

2. Thus, if FIFO is chosen, the inventory value in the balance sheet is a current and relevant amount, but cost of goods sold (and therefore gross margin and income) are considered to be less current or relevant. FIFO favors the balance sheet. These effects hold regardless of the direction of price level changes (increase or decrease) during the period.

D. LIFO

1. In assessing the relative attributes of LIFO, it is important to remember three important points of emphasis.

   a. If LIFO is employed by a business entity, the matching of revenues and expenses on the income statement is significantly improved over FIFO . That is, the income statement involves the matching of revenues of the current year with the cost of merchandise acquired in the current year.

b. If LIFO is employed by a business entity, there are usually income tax advantages associated with that choice. In periods of rising prices, LIFO will result in a higher cost of goods sold and a lower tax burden for the business enterprise. However, due to the LIFO conformity rule, if LIFO is chosen for tax purposes, the firm must also use it for the books. Thus, the firm cannot reduce its taxes with LIFO and at the same time use FIFO for financial reporting purposes in the quest to maximize reported income.

c. If LIFO is employed by a business entity, the balance sheet presentation of inventory is less than ideal. For the company employing LIFO, inventory on the balance sheet typically reflects the cost of the "oldest" merchandise included in the company's inventory records. This means the balance sheet does not reflect the current cost of inventory and often times, means the inventory is undervalued on the balance sheet.

2. Thus, if LIFO is chosen, the inventory value in the balance sheet can be a very noncurrent and irrelevant amount, but cost of goods sold (and therefore gross margin and income) are considered to be much more current or relevant. LIFO favors the income statement. These effects hold regardless of the direction of price level changes (increase or decrease) during the period.

3. In addition, LIFO tends to minimize "inventory" profits (also called "phantom" or "illusory" profits).

> **Example:**
> Inventory costs have been rising. Sales for the year are $100,000 and cost of goods sold is $70,000 under LIFO and $60,000 under FIFO. The $70,000 of cost of goods sold under LIFO is an approximation to the cost of replacing the inventory sold during the period because it represents later purchases in the year. If the firm chooses FIFO, it reports $10,000 more in pretax earnings but that amount really is not disposable income because it must be used to replace higher cost inventory in the next accounting period. The $10,000 is thus illusory income.

E. Cost-Flow Assumptions

1. In choosing the appropriate cost-flow assumption, a business entity should select the cost flow assumption that allows the company to do the best job of determining periodic net income.

2. However, firms often choose FIFO to maximize their reported income. This in turn improves certain financial ratios and may be helpful in meeting requirements placed on the firm by its creditors. In addition, management compensation, if tied to income, will be maximized.

3. On the other hand, the main reason for choosing LIFO is to minimize income tax. The main advantage of choosing LIFO is tax minimization. The reporting benefit of providing the most current cost of goods sold figure is an unintended consequence for most LIFO firms. A negative consequence to LIFO that sometimes occurs is the tax effect of a LIFO liquidation.

II. LIFO Liquidation

A. What happens when the number of units purchased or produced is less than the number of units sold? Under LIFO, the computation of cost of goods sold for the current period first uses all the purchases for the period. Then it works backward in time and liquidates layers that were added in previous periods (latest layer added first), until the total number of units sold for the period is costed. A LIFO liquidation is that part of current period cost of goods sold represented by the cost of goods acquired in prior years.

B. LIFO liquidations occur either from (1) poor planning, or (2) lack of supply.

 Example:
Assume the following for the current year for a LIFO firm. The beginning inventory is composed of a single layer added in a previous year.

	Units	Unit Cost
Beginning Inventory	100,000	$35.00
Purchases	500,000	$55.00

Merchandise Sold During the Year: 505,000 Units

Cost of goods sold for the year under LIFO = $27,675,000 = 500,000($55) + 5,000($35). Under LIFO, the current year purchases are used first, and only then are the earlier layers used. (Note: the older inventory items are not actually present; rather, only the cost of those items is included in inventory. Remember that LIFO is a cost-flow assumption, not a description of the actual movement of goods.)

The amount of the LIFO liquidation, thus, is $175,000 ($35 x 5,000). 5,000 more goods were sold than acquired in the year. The $175,000 amount is that part of cost of goods sold represented by the cost of goods acquired in earlier years.

C. LIFO liquidations are to be avoided for two reasons

1. The main purpose for using LIFO is tax minimization. In the above example, assuming the firm will replenish the 5,000 units liquidated anyway, the firm increases its taxable income by $20 per unit unnecessarily. The $20 amount is the difference between the current period cost of $55 and the $35 cost in the older layer. Thus, taxable income will increase by $100,000 ($20 x 5,000). If the firm had been able to purchase 505,000 units in the period, this extra tax liability would have been avoided because the entire cost of goods sold would be based on the $55 unit cost.

2. For financial statement reporting, the main advantage of LIFO is in matching current period costs with current revenues. The liquidation distorts the relationship between current sales and current cost of goods sold. The larger the liquidation, the worse the distortion.

Dollar-Value LIFO

This lesson presents the calculation to determine ending inventory value using dollar-value LIFO.

After studying this lesson, you should be able to:

1. *Explain why a company would want to use dollar value LIFO.*

2. *Calculate ending inventory using dollar value LIFO. This calculation includes: a) converting ending inventory to base year costs; b) determine the increase in inventory at base year cost; c) convert the current year layer to current year costs; d) add current layer to beginning of year dollar value LIFO to derive end of year dollar value LIFO.*

I. Introduction

A. Remember that in this entire discussion, for external purposes the firm is using LIFO, applied through the DV LIFO method. The firm may use another cost flow assumption (typically FIFO) internally.

B. Reduces the Effect of the Liquidation Problem -- The Dollar-Value LIFO conversion technique takes a company's ending inventory in FIFO dollars (usually) and converts them to LIFO dollars. In doing so, the impact of the liquidation problem is reduced.

C. Allows Companies to Use FIFO Internally -- Most companies prefer to use FIFO for internal management reports and internal operating decisions. Dollar-Value LIFO allows companies an opportunity to do so.

Note:
For CPA Exam candidates, a discussion question is frequently included in Dollar-Value LIFO problems. That discussion question involves a discussion of the advantages of Dollar-Value LIFO over the quantity of goods LIFO approach (shown previously). These advantages are listed below.

D. Reduces Clerical Costs -- As mentioned earlier, most LIFO companies prefer LIFO for external reporting purposes and prefer FIFO for internal purposes. Through the use of Dollar-Value LIFO, a company can maintain a FIFO system for internal purposes, and then convert those results to LIFO for external purposes. Please note that through the use of Dollar-Value LIFO, a company must maintain only a single inventory system (FIFO) during the accounting period, thus reducing clerical costs.

II. Steps in Implementing Dollar-Value LIFO

A. The establishment of inventory pools simply means the company needs to group similar products into inventory groups. For example, a department store might have one inventory pool that includes appliances.

B. The conversion index can be calculated internally or obtained from an external source. Regardless of the method of acquisition, the conversion index represents the calculation shown below.

> Conversion Index = Ending Inventory in Current-Year Dollars / Ending Inventory in Base-Year Dollars

C. "Base-year" dollars refers to the specific price level for the pool in effect at the beginning of the year in which the firm adopted LIFO. When this index is multiplied by the increase in inventory for the year as measured in base-year dollars, the result is the increase in inventory in current costs - the layer added to DV LIFO ending inventory.

Example:

1. A firm using FIFO for many years decides to change to LIFO and use DV LIFO as the specific method of applying LIFO. The beginning inventory in that year is $40,000. That value, if not reduced to market via the LCM valuation process, is the beginning inventory in base year dollars for DV LIFO. If it represents market, then the value must be increased back to cost before applying LIFO.

2. If an external index is unavailable, the conversion index at the end of a year for a pool equals:

(current cost of ending inventory) / (base-year cost of ending inventory)

When FIFO is used internally, the ending inventory under FIFO is used as the current cost.

D. Conversion of the FIFO Ending Inventory to LIFO Ending Inventory for financial statement reporting purposes -- This is the objective of the DV LIFO method.

Example: A numerical example illustrates the steps. A firm adopts LIFO (DV LIFO) at the beginning of the current year (Year 1). The beginning inventory under FIFO is $2,000 at cost. That amount is the beginning inventory in base-year dollars (base-year cost). The base-year price index is defined as 1.00. All price changes are measured in relation to the base-year index of 1.00 for simplicity.

The FIFO ending inventory for the current year (Year 1) is $3,200. The ending inventory in base-year dollars is determined to be $2,909. Prices of this type of inventory have increased 10% for the year. An external price index at year-end is 1.10 for this type of inventory. (Note: this agrees with the internal price index, computed as $3,200/$2,909, which also equals 1.10).

1. Convert FIFO ending inventory to ending inventory at base-year cost

Ending inventory = FIFO ending inventory(1.00/1.10)

In base-year dollars : $2,909 = $3,200(1.00/1.10)

2. Compute the change in inventory in base-year cost.

Change in inventory in Base-year cost	=	Ending inventory in base-year dollars	–	Beginning inventory in base-year dollars
$909	=	$2,909	–	$2,000

This result is important because it shows that there has been a *physical* increase in inventory for the year. With the measurement of the dollar fixed at the base year, the increase could not have been caused by increases in the price level. The $909 amount is the layer added in the current year at base-year cost. But LIFO must measure layers at current cost. The next step accomplishes this objective.

3. Compute the current-year layer at current-year costs.

Current-year layer at Current-year cost	=	Current-year layer at base-year cost	×	conversion index
$1,000	=	$909		(1.10/1.00)

4. Compute ending inventory under DV LIFO (reported in the balance sheet).

Ending DV LIFO inventory	=	Beginning DV LIFO inventory	+	Current-year layer at Current-year cost
$3,000	=	$2,000	+	$1,000

1. This process illustrates that DV LIFO uses price-level indices to measure the inventory increase first in base-year cost, and then expresses each year's layer at current cost through the conversion index. The result is a DV LIFO ending inventory that is the sum of layers measured in current dollars for the period the layers were added. This method is called the *double-extension* method because the ending inventory is extended at both base-year cost and ending current-year cost.

2. The balance sheet for Year 1 reports $3,000 of inventory. This amount consists of two layers: beginning inventory of $2,000 and the Year 1 layer of $1,000. The two layers reflect different price-level indices (1.00 and 1.10 respectively).

3. Cost of goods sold is computed as in any periodic inventory context. Ending inventory as computed for DV LIFO is subtracted from cost of goods available for sale. The result is cost of goods sold.

Example: This example extends the previous DV LIFO example two more years to show how layers are accumulated, and how to handle a LIFO liquidation in DV LIFO.

Current (FIFO)	FIFO Cost of Ending Inventory	Ending Price Level Index
Year 2	$4,025	1.15
Year 3	4,100	1.20

Beginning DV LIFO inventory (from Year 1) $3,000

Ending inv. at base-yr cost = $4,025(1.00/1.15) = $3,500

Increase in inv. at base-yr cost = $3,500 - $2,909*= $591

Increase in inv. at Year 2 prices = $591(1.15/1.00) 680

Ending inventory, DV LIFO $3,680

*This amount is from step 1 of Year 1, the ending inventory at base-year cost for Year 1.

The $3,680 amount is really the sum of three layers reflecting different prices. This schedule helps to understand the result of DV LIFO:

Layer	In Base-Year Cost	Conversion Index	DV LIFO
Base	$2,000	1.00	$2,000
Year 1	909	1.10	1,000
Year 2	591	1.15	680
Ending Year 2 DV LIFO inventory			$3,680

Beginning DV LIFO inventory (from Year 2) $3,680

Ending inventory at base-year cost = $4,100(1.00/1.20) =$3,417

Decrease in inventory at base-year cost = $3,500* − $3,417 =$83

Decrease Year 2 layer by $83 at base-year cost

Decrease in Year 2 layer at DV LIFO cost = $83(1.15/1.00) = (95)

Ending DV LIFO $3,585

At current cost, inventory for Year 3 appeared to increase. However, after converting to base-year dollars (removing the effect of the price level increase), the inventory decrease, in physical quantity, was apparent. No layer was added in Year 3. The most recent layer added is reduced under "last-in, first-out."

*From year 2 base-year cost.

Again, the breakdown of layers at the end of Year 3:

Layer	In Base-Year Cost	Conversion Index	DV LIFO
Base	$2,000	1.00	$2,000
Year 1	909	1.10	1,000
Year 2	508*	1.15	584
Ending Year 3 DV LIFO inventory			(#) $3,584

* $591 − $83 decrease in base-year dollars
(#) $1 difference due to rounding

Lower of Cost or Market

This lesson presents the calculation for lower of cost or market (LCM) for inventory valuation.

After studying this lesson, you should be able to:

1. *Define cost, market, the floor and the ceiling used in the LCM calculations.*

2. *Complete a LCM calculation and determine what value should be shown on the balance sheet.*

I. Loss on Inventory

A. In addition to the normal valuation of inventory at cost and choice of inventory cost flow assumption (FIFO, LIFO), GAAP requires that firms recognize an end-of-period loss on inventory if its utility has declined. If market is below cost, then inventory must be written down to market. The loss cannot be postponed until the period of sale.

1. If cost < market, there is no loss recognition and the inventory is reported at cost.

2. If cost > market, a loss is recognized and the inventory is written down to market.

B. The result is that inventory is reported at the lower of cost or market (LCM). The total expense or loss is limited to the historical cost of the inventory. But the LCM valuation requirement shifts a portion of the cost as a loss or expense to the period in which the inventory has declined in value.

C. Balance Sheet Valuation of Inventory -- Lower of Cost or Market

> **Example:**
> An item of inventory costing $100 has a market value of $90 at the end of the current year. The holding loss of $10 is recognized in the current year. When the item is sold the following year, cost of goods sold reflects only $90. In this way, $10 of the total original cost of $100 is shifted to the year before sale, because that is the year the loss occurred.

1. **What is Cost?** The cost of ending inventory is determined by applying one of the four cost flow assumptions, and the general rule for including cost in inventory.

2. **What is Market?**

   a. Market is generally *replacement cost*, subject to a range of values defined by an established *ceiling value* and an established *floor value*.

   b. The ceiling value is net realizable value. That is, the ceiling value is calculated by reducing the sales price by the estimated cost to complete and sell the inventory.

   c. The floor value is net realizable value reduced by the normal profit margin.

3. **Calculating Market Value**

   a. If the replacement cost value is within the range established by the ceiling value and the floor value, market is equal to replacement cost.

   b. If the replacement cost value is greater than the ceiling value, market is equal to the ceiling value.

   c. If the replacement cost value is less than the floor value, market is equal to the floor value.

4. Market is also simply the middle amount (in dollar terms) of the three amounts: replacement cost, net realizable value, and net realizable value less normal profit margin. Market cannot exceed the ceiling or be less than the floor.

Example:
At year-end, the following values pertain to an item of inventory:

Cost	$100
Replacement cost	80
Selling price	120
Estimated cost of completion and selling	30
Normal profit margin	20

The three values to determine market value:

Replacement cost	80
Net realizable value = $120 − $30	= 90 (ceiling)
Net realizable value less normal profit margin =	$90 − $20
	= 70 (floor)

Market value = $80, which is replacement cost because it is between the ceiling and floor amounts. It is also the middle of the three figures in dollar terms. The final LCM valuation thus is $80 because market is lower than original cost ($100). The inventory would be reported at $80 and a holding loss of $20 would be recorded (cost of $100 less market of $80). If market had exceeded cost, then the inventory would be reported at cost.

1. If replacement cost were instead $95, then market value would be $90, the middle of the three figures determining market value.

2. If replacement cost were instead $65, then market value would be $70, the middle of the three figures determining market value.

Note: Market value cannot exceed the ceiling or be less than the floor.

D. **Summary** -- The LCM valuation process has two steps:

1. Compute market value (the middle of the three amounts);

2. Value inventory at the lower of original cost or market value (LCM).

Note: Candidates often become so involved with the first step that they forget to apply the second. Once you have found market, don't forget to compare it to cost (step 2) for the final valuation under LCM.

II. **Lower of Cost or Market Comparison**

A. GAAP allows flexibility in application of LCM, but the lower of cost or market comparison must be completed on a consistent basis from year to year. In making the comparison, a company can employ one of three approaches.

1. **Individual Item Basis** -- If a company has 1,000 inventory items and chooses the individual item approach, a total of 1,000 comparisons will be made to determine the lower of cost or market for ending inventory.

2. **Category Basis** -- If a company has 1,000 inventory items grouped into ten categories, a total of ten comparisons will be made to determine the lower of cost or market for ending inventory.

3. **Total Basis** -- If a company wishes, it can make a single comparison to determine the lower of cost or market for ending inventory.

B. The individual item basis yields the most conservative (lowest) inventory value (and largest holding loss) because for each item the lower of cost or market is chosen. There is no chance for items with market exceeding cost to cancel against items with cost exceeding market, as there is with the other two approaches.

Example:

LCM Application Level

Inventory	Cost	Market	Item	Type	Total
Category A.					
Item 1	$10	$7	$7		
Item 2	5	9	5		
Total	$15	$16		$15	
Category B.					
Item 3	$19	$24	$19		
Item 4	27	20	20		
Total	$46	$44		44	
Total	**$61**	**$60**	**$51**	**$59**	**$60**

The firm may choose from among $51, $59, and $60 as its LCM valuation for inventory. All three are lower than cost of $61. The higher the level of applying the LCM valuation procedure, the higher the resulting valuation.

III. **Lower of Cost or Market - Journal Entry** -- Once the lower of cost or market comparison is completed and the ending valuation is found (the lower of cost or market), the formal entry of this information can be achieved by employing the *direct method* or the *allowance method*. Under the direct method, any holding loss (difference between a higher cost and a lower market value) related to inventory is simply included in cost of goods sold. It is *directly* included in cost of goods sold. Under the allowance method, any holding loss related to inventory is separately identified in a contra inventory account with separate disclosure of the holding loss. Cost of goods sold does not include the holding loss under this method.

See the following example.

> **Example:** A firm uses the category level comparison to determine market value. Total cost of inventory is $30,000, and the total market value is $27,000 at the end of the year. To record the holding loss of $3,000, either of the two approaches can be used. The adjusting entry to record the loss under these approaches is:
>
> Direct method:
>
> | | | |
> |---|---|---|
> | Cost of goods sold | 3,000 | |
> | Inventory | | 3,000 |
>
> Allowance method:
>
> | | | |
> |---|---|---|
> | Holding loss | 3,000 | |
> | Allowance to reduce inventory to LCM | | 3,000 |
>
> The allowance method reports $3,000 less of cost of goods sold in the income statement but compensates by reporting a separate holding loss of $3,000. The allowance account, a contra inventory account, reduces net inventory in the balance sheet to $27,000 (LCM). Both methods yield the same net inventory valuation and income. However, the components of income are different under the two methods.

IV. **Replacement or Net Realizable --** When dealing with used inventory, damaged inventory, or repossessed inventory, it is appropriate to value inventory at replacement cost or at net realizable value. If an established used market exists, the business entity would typically use replacement cost to value this type of inventory. If no such market exists, the inventory will be valued at net realizable value.

V. **Valuation at Sales Price --** In situations in which it is difficult to determine costs and products are marketable at quoted market prices, it is appropriate to value inventory at sales price. Precious metals and agriculture products are two examples of inventory items that are typically valued at sales price.

Gross Margin and Relative Sales Value Method

This lesson presents the gross margin method for estimating ending inventory and allocation of inventory cost based on relative sales values.

After studying this lesson, you should be able to:

1. *Explain margin on sales versus margin on cost and be able to determine cost to sales.*

2. *Apply the Gross Margin Method to value ending inventory.*

3. *Apply the Relative Sales Value Method to value ending inventory.*

I. **Estimating Ending Inventory**

   A. For a variety of reasons, companies may need to estimate ending inventory using the gross margin method. A company may use an estimate of ending inventory for internal purposes during interim periods when a physical count is prohibitively expensive or when inventory is destroyed as the result of a casualty. The gross margin method can be used **only** for estimation purposes. It may not be used for financial reporting of inventory.

II. **Gross Margin Method**

   A. The gross margin method estimates cost of goods sold from sales using a percentage based on historical data. Then, ending inventory can be inferred from beginning inventory, purchases, and cost of goods sold.

   B. To use the gross margin method, a company must have a consistent gross margin percentage (margin as a percentage of sales or margin based on cost). If inventory is heterogeneous, the method should be applied to pools of inventory with relatively homogeneous gross margin percentages.

III. **Margin on Sales - Margin on Cost**

   A. Formulas:

   1. The margin on sales is gross margin divided by sales, or sales less cost of goods sold divided by sales.

   Gross margin percentage = margin on sales = (sales − cost of goods sold)/sales

   2. The margin on cost is sales less cost of goods sold divided by cost of goods sold.

   Margin on cost = (sales − cost of goods sold) / cost of goods sold

   B. The use of the gross margin method depends on how the margin on sales is expressed.

   C. Margin on cost is always greater than margin on sales because sales exceed cost. The two ways of expressing the margin are related. The following two examples show how each may be converted to the other.

   D. The goal is to use one of the two formulas to determine cost/sales. It is the cost/sales ratio that is used to determine cost of goods sold.

   See the following example.

Example:

1. Assume gross margin (also referred to as margin on sales) is 40%. Set sales to 1.00, and margin to .40. This implies that cost is .60 times sales:

    Sales   1.00
    − Cost   .60
    = Margin   .40

Therefore, margin / cost = .40 / .60 = .67. Thus, a gross margin percentage of 40% is equivalent to a margin on cost of 67%.

2. Assume margin on cost is 45%. Set cost to 1.00, and margin to .45. This implies that sales are 1.45 times cost.

    Sales   1.45
    − Cost   1.00
    = Margin   .45

Therefore, margin on sales = .45 / 1.45 = .31. Thus, a gross margin percentage of 31% is equivalent to a margin on cost of 45%.

Formulas can also be used to convert one margin expression to the other:

(margin on sales) / (1 − margin on sales) = margin on cost

(margin on cost) / (1 + margin on cost) = margin on sales

IV. Using the Gross Margin Method

A. The purpose of the previous short section was to describe how each of the two different expressions of margin can be converted into the other. If you are comfortable with this method, the use of the gross margin method is straightforward.

Beg. inventory + net purchases = end. inventory + cost of goods sold

Beg. inventory + net purchases = end. inventory + sales (cost/sales)

B. The second equation shows that cost of goods sold is estimated by sales multiplied by the cost-to-sales ratio. This ratio equals 1 − gross margin %, which can easily be computed using the conversion methods shown above. The unknown in the equation is ending inventory. The gross margin method allows an estimate of ending inventory.

See the following example.

Example:
A firm's inventory is destroyed by fire on April 4. Beginning inventory is $20,000, net purchases through April 4 are $250,000, and sales through April 4 amount to $320,000.

First, Assume the gross margin is 40%. Then the cost/sales ratio is 60%.

Beg. inventory	+ net purchases	=	end. inventory	+	sales(cost/sales)
$20,000	+ $250,000	=	?	+	$320,000(.60)
			ending inventory	=	$78,000

This is an estimate of the cost of inventory destroyed, i.e. the ending inventory at April 4.

Now assume the margin on cost is 45%. From the above examples of converting margins, the gross margin percentage is 31%, and therefore the cost/sales ratio is 69%.

Beg. inventory	+ net purchases	=	end. inventory	+	sales(cost/sales)
$20,000	+ $250,000	=	?	+	$320,000(.69)
			ending inventory	=	$49,200

In this example, the firm could not have counted the inventory destroyed but is able to estimate its cost for insurance purposes by applying the gross margin method. The method is also useful for budgetary and other internal reporting purposes when an exact calculation is not needed.

V. Relative Sales Value Method

A. Firms may be able to obtain significant discounts by purchasing different types of inventory from the same supplier. This may occur, for example, in a liquidation or distress sale. U.S. GAAP requires that the total price be allocated based on the market values or selling prices of the individual inventory items.

Example:
Three items of inventory were purchased for $45. The unit selling prices (for the buyer upon resale) are given below.

Inventory item	Unit sales price
A	$20
B	25
C	40
Total	$85

The cost of the inventory ($45) would be allocated to each item based on the relative sales value as demonstrated in the following calculation.

Item A is recorded at $10.59 = (($20 / $85) $45).

Item B is recorded at $13.23 = (($25 / $85) $45).

Item C is recorded at $21.18 = (($40 / $85) $45).

Retail Inventory Method

This lesson presents the retail inventory method for estimating ending inventory.

After studying this lesson, you should be able to:

1. *Calculate the cost to retail percentage for the Retail Inventory Method.*

2. *Calculate ending inventory using the Retail Inventory Method.*

I. **The Retail Inventory Method** -- This method is used by retailers to estimate ending inventory at cost. Most retailers know the markup on the inventory items and are able to count ending inventory at retail prices (ever see the store employees counting items on a shelf?). This method is used both for internal decision purposes and for financial reporting of cost of goods sold and ending inventory.

II. **The Basic Method**

A. The retail inventory method, which is really a family of related methods, is based on three basic calculations.

B. *First*, ending inventory at retail is calculated or counted at year-end. *Second*, the cost-to-retail ratio is calculated. *Third*, the ending inventory at retail is multiplied by the cost-to-retail ratio to arrive at estimated inventory at cost.

C. Cost of goods sold is an implied amount, rather than a directly calculated amount under this method.

D. The method can be shown in equation form: EI(cost) = EI(retail) x C/R, where EI is ending inventory and C/R is the cost-to-retail ratio for the period. The retail inventory method can be used with FIFO, LIFO, and average cost-flow assumptions. Also, an approximation to LCM valuation is possible with this general method. Cost of goods sold is found by subtracting ending inventory at cost from cost of goods available for sale.

E. Basic Structure of the Retail Inventory Method:

	Cost	Retail
Beginning Inventory	$200	$300
Purchases	2,000	3,000
Goods Available for Sale	2,200	3,300
Sales		(2,600)
Ending Inventory at Retail		700

Cost to Retail Ratio:
2,200/3,300 = 66 2/3%

Ending Inventory at Retail X Cost Ratio=Ending Inventory at Cost
$700 x 66 2/3% = $467
Cost of goods sold, then, is reported at the implied amount of $1,733 = $200 beginning inventory at cost + $2,000 purchases less $467 ending inventory.

F. This illustrates the "average" retail inventory method. It is one of five variations of the retail inventory method.

III. Terminology and Guidance in Applying the Retail Inventory Method

A. **Original Selling Price** -- Cost plus initial markup.

B. **Net Additional Markups** -- A net increase in the original selling price. This amount is the net sum of additional markups above the original selling price less additional markup cancellations. This amount is added only in the retail column and before computing the cost-to-retail ratio.

C. **Net Markdowns** -- A net decrease in the original selling price. This amount is the net difference between markdowns, which are reductions in the original selling price, and markdown cancellations. This amount is subtracted only from the retail column and before computing the cost-to-retail ratio.

Example:

1.

Cost:		$20
Initial markup		+ 10
Additional markup	$4	
Additional markup cancellation	(1)	
Net additional markup		+ 3
Final selling price		$33

2.

Cost:		$20
Initial markup		+ 10
Markdown	($4)	
Markdown cancellation	1	
Net markdown		(3)
Final selling price		$27

D. **Transportation In** -- Added in the cost column only, before computing the cost-to-retail ratio.

E. **Purchase Discounts** -- Subtracted in the cost column only, before computing the cost-to-retail ratio.

F. **Purchase Returns and Allowances** -- The amount of merchandise available for sale has declined. This amount is subtracted in both the cost and retail columns before computing the cost-to-retail ratio.

G. **Employee Discounts** -- The difference between the normal retail value of merchandise sold to employees and the amount actually paid by employees. This amount is subtracted along with sales from Goods Available for Sale at Retail to arrive at Ending Inventory at Retail, after computing the cost-to-retail ratio.

H. **Normal Spoilage** -- Shown at retail value, subtracted along with sales from Goods Available for Sale at Retail to arrive at Ending Inventory at Retail, after computing the cost-to-retail ratio.

I. **Abnormal Casualty Losses** -- Shown at both cost and retail, the amount of merchandise available for sale has declined. Reduce the cost and retail value of goods available for sale before computing the cost-to-retail ratio. This loss is usually recoverable through insurance.

IV. Variations -- The variations of the Retail Inventory Method are directly related to the calculation of the cost ratio. There are five variations, four of which are summarized below. The fifth is covered in the section titled "Dollar Value LIFO Retail."

    A. FIFO -- The C/R excludes the cost of beginning inventory from the numerator and the retail value of beginning inventory from the denominator. Thus, C/R measures the cost-to-retail ratio only for the current-period purchases on the assumption that all beginning inventory will be sold (**first-in, first-out**). If ending inventory consists entirely of current-period purchases, the C/R should not include beginning inventory.

    B. FIFO, LCM -- The cost ratio excludes the cost of beginning inventory from the numerator and the retail value of beginning inventory from the denominator. Then, in an effort to arrive at a more conservative cost ratio, the calculation also excludes net markdowns from the cost ratio. This causes the denominator of C/R to be larger, because net markdowns are not subtracted, and thus the ratio itself is smaller. When C/R is multiplied by EI(retail), the resulting EI(cost) is smaller, approximating the effect of LCM.

    C. Average -- The cost ratio includes beginning inventory, along with current period purchases in both the numerator and the denominator of C/R.

    D. Average, LCM -- The cost ratio includes beginning inventory, along with current period purchases, in both the numerator and the denominator, but excludes net markdowns from the cost ratio calculation.

> **Note:** On the CPA Exam, Average LCM is frequently referred to as the conventional retail inventory method. This method is the one most emphasized on the exam. The variations are presented here for completeness; however, the probability of questions on these variations is relatively low.

See the following example.

Example:
Four variations of the retail inventory method.

	Cost	Retail
Beginning inventory	$ 100	$ 145
Net purchases	600	900
Net additional markups		70
Net markdowns		− 30
Goods available for sale	$ 700	$ 1,085
Less sales		− 800
Equals ending inventory at retail		$ 285

EI(cost) is not computed above because computing that amount is the objective of the retail method and the amount depends on the variation chosen by the firm. Also, if the *count* of ending inventory at retail is less than $285, a shrinkage loss is indicated. The actual count of ending inventory is the value to use for computing EI(cost) in that case. The $285 amount is the ending inventory *that should be present*, at retail.

FIFO: C/R = $600/($900 + $70 - $30) = .6383

EI(cost) = .6383($285) = $181.92

(Beginning inventory is excluded from the ratio.)

FIFO, LCM: C/R = $600/($900 + $70) = .6186

EI(cost) = .6186($285) = $176.30

(Beginning inventory is excluded from the ratio and net markdowns are not subtracted in the denominator.)

Average: C/R = $700/$1,085 = .6452

EI(cost) = .6452($285) = $183.88

(Beginning inventory is included in the ratio.)

Average, LCM : C/R = $700/($1,085 + $30) = .6278

EI(cost) = .6278($285) = $178.92

(Beginning inventory is included in the ratio and net markdowns are not subtracted in the denominator.)

Dollar Value LIFO Retail

This lesson presents the Dollar-Value LIFO Retail method for estimating ending inventory.

After studying this lesson, you should be able to:

1. *Recognize that retail companies that use LIFO cost flow assumption must use DV LIFO.*

2. *Identify the order of the DV LIFO Retail calculation.*

I. **Introduction**

   A. This is the method used by companies that use the LIFO cost flow assumption when they apply the retail inventory method. The companies must use the dollar value approach in order to determine the LIFO layers. There are two independent steps:

      1. DV LIFO is first applied to inventory at retail only - and in the same way it was illustrated before. This results in the measurement of the current-period layer measured in current retail dollars. So, DV LIFO is restricted to retail dollar application.

      2. Then, the FIFO retail method (not LCM i.e., subtract markdowns when computing C/R) cost-to-retail ratio is applied to this retail layer yielding the increase in cost at current prices. Finally, this cost layer is added to beginning inventory at DV LIFO cost to yield ending inventory at DV LIFO cost.

II. **How to remember which step comes first?**

   A. Because inventory is counted at retail and the method is called "DV LIFO - Retail," apply DV LIFO first, then apply the retail method that deflates the amounts back to cost.

   See the following example.

Example: Assume the same information that was presented in the for the current year as in the previous example in the Retail Inventory Method lesson :

	Cost	Retail
Beginning inventory	$ 100	$ 145
Net purchases	600	900
Net additional markups		70
Net markdowns		− 30
Goods available for sale	$ 700	$ 1,085
Less sales		− 800
Equals ending inventory at retail		**$ 285**

Assume, the firm adopted DV LIFO at the beginning of the current year. Therefore, the beginning inventory at retail in terms of base year dollars is $145. The price index is set at 1.00 at the beginning of the year and has climbed to 1.08 by the end of the year. The DV LIFO retail method is applied to the current year:

BI DV LIFO		$ 100.00
EI(retail, FIFO) =	$285.00	
EI(retail, base-year dollars) = $285(1.00/1.08) =	$263.89	
Increase in EI(retail, base-year dollars) = $263.89 − $145 =	$118.89	
Increase in EI(retail, FIFO) = $118.89(1.08/1.00) =	$128.40	
Increase in EI(cost, FIFO) = $128.40(.6383)*		81.96
EI DV LIFO		**$181.96**

*Cost ratio for FIFO (not LCM) from previous example.

Later years are treated the same way. The DV LIFO method is applied as before, to subsequent year's retail dollars. Then, the FIFO cost-to-retail ratio for that year is applied to the retail layer measured in current retail dollars.

Inventory Errors

This lesson addresses how to correct for inventory errors.

After studying this lesson, you should be able to:

1. *Determine the impact of an inventory error on any component of the balance sheet or income statement.*

2. *Complete the journal entry necessary to correct an inventory error.*

I. Introduction

A. Inventory effects are analyzed with the basic inventory equation:

> Beginning inventory + net purchases = ending inventory + cost of goods sold

B. If beginning inventory is understated, then cost of goods sold is also understated, everything else being the same, because the equation must balance. If ending inventory is understated, cost of goods sold must be overstated, again because the equation must balance.

C. The journal entry and reporting for error corrections depend on both the error and the period of discovery.

 Example: The ending inventory for Year 1 is understated $4,000 because the items in one wing of the warehouse were not counted. The effects of this error, ignoring tax effects, are:

	Year 1	Year 2
Beginning inventory:	not affected	understated $4,000
Ending inventory:	understated $4,000	not affected
Cost of goods sold:	overstated $4,000	understated $4,000
Net income:	understated $4,000	overstated $4,000
Retained earnings:	understated $4,000	is now correct *

*This is what is meant by a counterbalancing error. If it is never discovered, retained earnings automatically corrects itself, and with the new count of inventory at the end of the second year, the error disappears. However, the errors in the two years' financial statements do not automatically correct and would be present in the comparative statements.

If the error is discovered in Year 2, the following entry is made to correct the beginning balance of retained earnings:

Inventory	4,000	
Prior period adjustment (to retained earnings)		4,000

A prior-period adjustment is to the account in which the correction of an error in prior year earnings is recorded. The income statement impact of the prior-period error is closed to retained earnings. The prior-period adjustment increases the year 2 beginning balance of retained earnings to its correct amount as if year 1 income were correct. In the comparative statements for years 1 and 2, income for year 1 would be increased to its correct amount. All other affected accounts for year 1 also would be corrected.

> If discovery occurs in Year 3, no entry is needed because counterbalancing has taken place. All year 2 ending account balances are correct. However, both year 1 and year 2 statements should be corrected if shown comparatively with year 3. All accounts for those years affected by the error would be restated to their correct amounts.

II. Error in Recording Purchases -- What if a purchase at year-end was not recorded in the year of purchase (year 1), but rather was recorded in the next year (year 2), the year of payment? Assume the goods were counted in EI in year of purchase.

A. If the error is never discovered

1. 1st year: purchases are understated, CGS understated, net income overstated, ending retained earnings overstated.

2. 2nd year: purchases are overstated, CGS overstated, net income understated, ending retained earnings is correct (error has counterbalanced).

3. But the errors remain in both years' statements shown comparatively with later statements.

B. If the error is discovered in year 2

Prior period adjustment (to retained earnings) XX	
Purchases	XX

1. Retained earnings at the beginning of year 2 is corrected by this entry, and year 1's income (and any other accounts affected) would be corrected in the year 1 statement reported comparatively with year 2.

C. If the error is discovered in year 3

1. No entry is needed because retained earnings is correct - the error has counterbalanced. The statements for years 1 and 2 would be corrected if shown comparatively with year 3.

Losses on Purchase Commitments

This lesson addresses what to do with losses on purchase commitments.

After studying this lesson, you should be able to:

1. *Explain what to do with losses when the commitment contract can be modified.*

2. *Explain what to do with losses when the commitment contract cannot be modified.*

I. **Introduction** -- Companies often commit (in a contract) to the purchase of materials to lock in the unit price of an item needed for production or resale in order to aid in cash flow budgeting and to protect against price increases. Sometime the market price of the item declines below the contract price. The accounting for this price decline depends on whether the contract can be revised in light of the changing market conditions.

II. **The Contract Can be Modified** -- In this case, the loss is required to be footnoted as a contingent liability, but is not accrued in the accounts because the loss is not probable given that the contract can be revised.

III. **The Contract Cannot be Modified** -- In this case, the loss must be accrued because the loss is probable and estimable. The inventory, when acquired, is recorded at market value and a loss is recognized for the difference between the market value and the contract price. If the contract has not been executed as of the balance sheet date, the following adjusting entry is made:

Loss on purchase commitment	xx
Liability on purchase commitment	xx

The amount equals the difference between the unit contract price and market price at year-end, multiplied by the number of units required to be purchased.

A. If the market price drops further in the second year, an additional loss is recognized when the contract is executed. Recoveries result in a gain but only to the extent of the previously recognized loss.

See the following example.

Example: In December, a firm contracted to purchase 200 units of prefabricated housing walls at $4,000 per wall. The contract is neither cancelable nor subject to revision. By December 31, the market price per wall had dropped to $3,900.

The adjusting entry at December 31 is:

Loss on purchase commitment	20,000	
Liability on purchase commitment		20,000*

* 200($4,000 − $3,900)

In January, at payment date, if the market price had decreased to $3,850, the following entry would be made:

Liability on purchase commitment	20,000	
Loss on purchase commitment	10,000*	
Inventory $3,850(200)	770,000	
Cash $4,000(200)		$800,000

* ($3,900 − $3,850)200

If the market price had been $3,950 at payment date, a gain of $10,000 would be recorded and the inventory would be recorded at $3,950 per unit. If the market price exceeded $4,000 at payment date, a gain of $20,000 would be recorded and the inventory would be recorded at $800,000, the original contract price. The contract price is the ceiling for recording the inventory. There is no floor.

Inventory and IFRS

This lesson presents the significant differences in the accounting for inventory under IFRS versus U.S. GAAP.

After studying this lesson, you should be able to:

1. *Identify the major differences in the accounting for inventory under IFRS versus U.S. GAAP.*

I. Inventory and IFRS

A. There are a few significant differences between the accounting for inventory under IAS 2 and that under U.S. GAAP. The table below summarizes these differences.

IFRS	U.S. GAAP
Lower of cost or net realizable value	Lower of cost or market
Same cost formulas must be used for inventory with a similar nature and use	May use more than one cost formula for similar inventories with similar use
Reversal of write down to net realizable value permitted	Reversal of the write down is prohibited
LIFO prohibited	LIFO permitted
Cost flow assumption mirrors physical flow	Cost flow assumption does not mirror physical flow

B. Under IFRS, inventory is reported at the lower of cost or net realizable value (NRV). Net realizable value is defined by IAS 2 as "the estimated selling price in the ordinary course of business less the estimated costs of completion and the estimate costs necessary to make the sale." This definition is consistent with the IASB philosophy that an asset should not be reported on the balance sheet at more than the net cash that is expected from the sale or use of that asset. Under U.S. GAAP inventory is reported and lower of cost or market (LCM) where market is defined as replacement cost with a ceiling (NRV) and a floor (NRV less normal profit margin). U.S. GAAP defines NRV the same as IFRS. However, U.S. GAAP uses NRV to determine a floor and ceiling when determining market value.

1. The adjustment to net realizable value is applied on an item-by-item basis; however inventory with similar characteristics can be grouped together. The process of applying lower of cost or NRV, and the entry made for the write-down, is similar to the process and entry used under U.S. GAAP. Under U.S. GAAP, inventory is reported and lower of cost or market (LCM) where market is defined as replacement cost with a ceiling (NRV) and a floor (NRV less normal profit margin). U.S. GAAP defines NRV the same as IFRS. However, U.S. GAAP uses NRV to determine a floor and ceiling when determining market value.

2. The same cost formulas (i.e., valuation method FIFO) must be applied to inventory that is similar in nature and use. In the U.S., there is no restriction and different cost formulas can be applied to inventory that is similar or with similar use.

3. Inventory is reassessed at each financial reporting date, and if there are further reductions the inventory is written down again. However, if the NRV of the inventory has increased, the previous write-down can be reversed (only to the extent of the previous write-down).

C. IFRS specifically prohibits the use of LIFO as a cost-flow assumption. In the U.S. approximately 30% of publicly traded companies use LIFO. The main motivation for LIFO in the U.S. is that it lowers net income and therefore lowers taxes. This difference in accounting is viewed as a significant barrier to convergence, as U.S. companies would be forced to recognize significant gains if they had to abandon LIFO.

D. The three methods of assigning value to inventory under IFRS are: FIFO, specific identification, and weighted average. IAS 2 presumes that the inventory valuation method will follow the physical flow of goods to the extent possible.

Categories and Presentation

This lesson presents the categories and presentation of plant asset account.

After studying this lesson, you should be able to:

1. *Define what is included in the categories of plant assets.*

2. *Describe the presentation and disclosures of plant assets.*

I. **Requirements for Inclusion in Plant Assets**

    A. To be included in plant assets, an asset must:

        1. Be currently used in operations;

        2. Have a useful life extending more than one year beyond the balance sheet date; and

        3. Have physical substance. Intangible assets are different from plant assets in that they have no physical substance.

    B. If land is held for investment purposes or for future development, it is excluded from plant assets because it currently is not a productive asset.

II. **Categories Within Plant Assets**

    A. Plant and Equipment -- This category of fixed assets is composed of buildings, machinery, and equipment. These assets have a finite useful life and can also be referred to as depreciable assets.

    B. Land improvements -- This asset differs from land in that it has a finite useful life and is depreciated. Examples of land improvements include parking lots, fencing, external lighting, and some landscaping.

    C. Land -- This category includes the site of a manufacturing facility, the site of administrative offices, and the site of any storage warehouses. Any plot of land in which a company has constructed facilities specifically related to primary business operations is included in this category. This category does not include real estate held for investment purposes. Land has an indefinite life and is, therefore, not depreciated. *It is the only asset in the plant asset category that is not depreciated or amortized.*

    D. Natural Resources -- Include such items as a gravel pit, a coal mine, a tract of timber land, and an oil well. This category of assets will produce income until all the natural resources are extracted and sold. These assets are frequently referred to as depletable assets.

Capitalized Costs

This lesson presents what is included in the plant asset account.

After studying this lesson, you should be able to:

1. *Determine what costs should be capitalized (versus expensed) upon acquisition of a plant assets.*

2. *Determine what costs should be capitalized (versus expensed) during the life of a plant asset.*

I. Costs that are Capitalized to Plant Assets

A. If the estimated time of benefit is related to the current accounting period only, the expenditure is recorded as an expense. Such expenditures are called revenue expenditures or period costs.

B. If the estimated time of benefit is related to the current and future accounting periods, the expenditure is capitalized. The term "capitalized" means included in an asset account.

C. If the expenditure is immaterial, the company will account for the expenditure in the most expedient way possible. This usually means the expenditure is recorded as an expense in the period of acquisition.

D. If the expenditure is material in amount, the accounting treatment of the expenditure will be determined by examining the estimated time of benefit related to the expenditure.

II. General Rule

A. Costs to capitalize on acquisition of plant assets.

B. The acquisition cost of property, plant, and equipment includes two components, the cash equivalent price or negotiated acquisition cost and the so-called **get ready costs**.

C. The **get ready costs** include all costs incurred to get the asset on the company's premises and ready for use. For example, the setting up and testing of new machinery is a **get ready** cost.

D. The general rule for capitalizing expenditures related to the acquisition of plant assets is similar to the rule for capitalizing costs to inventory.

E. *Capitalize all expenditures necessary to bring the plant asset to its intended condition and location.*

See the following example.

Example: The following list of expenditures shows a variety of costs related to plant assets and how to account for them.

Expenditure	Accounting treatment
Sales tax on equipment purchase	Capitalize to equipment
Cost to set up and test equipment	Capitalize to equipment
Cost to train employees to use equipment	Expense
Title fee on land purchase	Capitalize to land
Attorney fee for land purchase	Capitalize to land
Cost to raze an old building on land purchased	Capitalize to land
Proceeds on salvage material from razing	Reduce recorded land cost
Cost of landscaping	Capitalize to land improvements
Cost to excavate foundation for a building	Capitalize to building
Interest on purchase of plant assets	Expense
Interest during construction of building	Capitalize to building
Back property taxes on land just purchased	Capitalize to land
Annual property taxes on land	Expense
Cost of permits for construction	Capitalize to building

Note: Applying the general rule helps in classifying expenditures. For example, the cost to train employees to use equipment benefits the employees, not the equipment. Razing an old building on land just purchased is part of the process of preparing the land for its use. However, the cost to raze a building already owned by the firm increases the loss on disposal of the building.

Valuation

This lesson presents the valuation of plant assets when the exchange involves something other than cash.

After studying this lesson, you should be able to:

1. *Determine how to value plant assets in situations where the exchange involved something other than cash (i.e., credit purchase, securities, donation, group purchase or self constructed asset.)*

Note: In general, plant assets should be valued at the market value of consideration given in exchange, or at the market value (cash equivalent price) of the asset acquired, whichever is more readily determinable and reliable.

I. **Cash Equivalent Price or Negotiated Acquisition Cost**

A. **Methods of Acquiring Plant Assets**

1. **Cash Purchase** -- The cash equivalent price is simply the amount of cash paid for the asset on acquisition date.

2. **Deferred Payment Plan (credit purchase)** -- The cash equivalent price for an asset acquired through a deferred payment plan is the present value of future cash payments using the market rate of interest for similar debt instruments.

Example:
The list price of a plant asset is $30,000. The purchaser makes a $10,000 down payment and issues a 2-year non-interest bearing note for the remainder. The note calls for a single lump-sum payment of $20,000 to be made at the maturity of the note. The market rate of interest on such notes is 10%. The present value of a single payment of $1 received two years in the future at 10% is .82645. The entry to record the plant asset is:

Plant asset	26,529	
Cash		10,000
Note payable $20,000(.82645)		16,529

The note is recorded at present value. The list price of plant assets should not be used for valuation of assets. The list price is mainly a starting point for negotiations between the buyer and seller. Subsequent to acquisition, interest expense is recognized as the note approaches maturity. The interest is expensed. It is not added to the building account.

---

3. **Issuance of Securities** -- The acquisition cost of an asset acquired through the issuance of stocks or bonds is the fair market value of the security or the fair market value of the asset acquired, whichever can be most clearly determined. When a significant number of shares is issued, care must be taken to ensure that the issuance did not affect the share price.

4. **Donated Assets** -- Assets received in donation are recorded at their fair market value. A revenue or gain is also recorded.

5. **Group Purchases** -- If a group of fixed assets is acquired in a single transaction, the total negotiated price is allocated to the individual assets acquired. This allocation is based on the respective fair market values of the individual assets acquired.

Example:
For a lump sum price, a firm acquired three plant assets at a bargain price of $50,000. The individual market values of each asset are:

Market or appraised value

Building	$10,000
Land	30,000
Equipment	15,000
Total	$55,000

The recorded cost of each asset is based on its relative market value. The entry to record the purchase:

Building	($10,000/$55,000)$50,000	9,091
Land	($30,000/$55,000)$50,000	27,273
Equipment	($15,000/$55,000)$50,000	13,636
Cash		50,000

II. Self-Constructed Assets

A. **Components of Capitalized Cost** -- The capitalized cost of a self-constructed asset includes four components

1. **Labor** -- The direct labor charges related to the construction of the asset will be capitalized. Usually, labor charges are expensed in the period incurred, but in this instance, the labor charges are capitalized. This component of the cost of the asset includes any fringe benefits related to the basic labor cost.

2. **Material** -- The direct materials related to the construction of the asset will be capitalized.

3. **Overhead** -- The overhead charges related to the construction of the asset will be capitalized. Usually, the capitalization of overhead charges is accomplished by one of two approaches.

   a. **Incremental Overhead Approach** -- One approach is to capitalize *only* the incremental overhead. For example, if a company typically has $5,000,000 of overhead, but during the period of construction, overhead increased to $5,500,000, the incremental overhead related to the project is $500,000.

   b. **Pro Rata Overhead Allocation Approach** -- Another approach is to capitalize the overhead on a pro rata basis. For example, if the project represents 15% of the total direct labor hours for the period, 15% of the total overhead will be allocated to the project.

4. **Interest Cost Incurred During the Construction Period** -- (This topic is separately discussed in detail in a later lesson.) Capitalization of interest is allowed only when assets are constructed. When assets are purchased outright, any interest on debt incurred to purchase the asset cannot be capitalized.

B. Limitation on Recorded Value -- Market value at completion

1. In general, GAAP prohibits the recording of assets in excess of their market values. Recording a constructed asset at an amount exceeding its market value carries forward losses due to inefficient construction to later periods, which violates conservatism. Also, the future benefit of the asset is measured at its market value.

2. If the total cost of construction exceeds market value, a loss is recognized for the difference and the asset is recorded at market value.

Example:
The costs incurred to self-construct equipment are:

Labor	$20,000
Material	30,000
Incremental overhead	10,000
Applied overhead	5,000
Capitalized interest	8,000
Total	$73,000

During the construction phase, costs are accumulated in Equipment under Construction. The $73,000 amount is the final recorded amount if the market value equals or exceeds $73,000. If the market value were $80,000, the recorded value remains at $73,000 because gains cannot be recognized until realized through lower production costs. The Equipment under Construction account would be closed to Equipment.

Assume, however, that the market value is only $60,000:

Equipment	60,000
Loss on Construction	13,000
Equipment under Construction	73,000

Interest Capitalization 1

This lesson is the first on interest capitalization during construction. This lesson presents when it is appropriate to capitalize interest, calculation of average accumulated expenditures and calculation of interest eligible for capitalization.

After studying this lesson, you should be able to:

1. *Identify when interest capitalization is allowed.*

2. *Calculate the average accumulated expenditures during construction.*

3. *Calculate the weighted average or specific interest rate.*

4. *Calculate the amount of interest to be capitalized during the period.*

5. *Complete the journal entry for interest capitalization.*

I. **Introduction --** Capitalization of Interest

A. Interest cost is typically expensed in the period incurred. However, when a company constructs a fixed asset, the interest cost incurred during the construction period is considered a **get ready** cost and is, therefore, capitalized. Interest capitalization increases both plant assets and income. Assuming that all interest is first recorded in interest expense, the following adjusting entry capitalizes some or all of that interest:

Plant Asset Under Construction	xx	
Interest Expense		xx

B. Interest cost is capitalized only during the construction period. Prior to the construction period, interest cost was expensed. Any interest cost incurred subsequent to the construction period will likewise be expensed.

C. The *justification* for interest capitalization is that had the construction not taken place, the funds used in construction could have been used to reduce interest bearing debt. This **avoidable** interest is the amount of interest that would have been avoided had the construction not taken place. In a sense, the construction then **caused** that amount of interest, which therefore should be included in the cost of the asset constructed.

D. **Matching Principle --** Interest capitalization exemplifies the matching principle. Until the asset is in service, it cannot produce revenue. The asset is also not yet in its intended condition and location. Thus, expensing of the interest is deferred until the asset can provide revenues against which to match the interest expense.

> **Note:**
> The definition of an asset is not the underlying justification for interest capitalization. Interest does not increase the probable future value of an asset.

E. Capitalization of interest applies only to the construction of qualifying assets, such as assets constructed for an enterprise's own use or assets intended for sale or lease that are constructed as discrete projects (ships, real estate developments, etc.).

F. Qualifying assets require a significant time period for construction and are not routinely produced. Rather, the assets must be discrete projects individually constructed. Interest is not capitalized on the construction or manufacture of inventory items, even if the inventory requires significant time for completion (e.g., interest on the production of wine and tobacco products is not capitalized).

II. **Interest is Capitalized During Periods in Which All Three of the Following Conditions are Met**

A. Qualifying expenditures have been made. Cash payments, transfers of other assets, or the incurrence of interest-bearing debt all qualify. The incurrence of short-term noninterest-bearing debt (accounts payable for example) does not qualify because the firm has no opportunity cost on such debt.

> **Note:**
> If any of the three conditions are not met, interest capitalization ceases. The capitalization period concludes when the asset is substantially complete and ready for its intended use.

B. Activities that are necessary to get the asset ready for its intended use are in progress. (Construction is proceeding.)

C. Interest cost is being incurred. Only actual interest cost is capitalized. Imputed interest is not capitalized. The total amount of interest to be capitalized for a period is limited to actual interest incurred in the period.

III. **A Two-step Process is Involved in Computing Capitalized Interest** -- The two steps are: (1) compute average accumulated expenditures, and (2) apply the appropriate interest rate(s).

A. **Compute Average Accumulated Expenditures** -- A key concept in determining the amount of interest to be capitalized is avoidable interest. This is the interest on debt that could have been retired had the construction not taken place. To quantify that amount of debt, average accumulated expenditures (AAE) must be computed. AAE is the measure of the amount of debt, on an annual basis, that could have been avoided.

B. AAE = average cash (or other qualifying expenditures) investment in the project during the period. This is the amount of debt that could have been retired during the period.

> **Example:**
> **1.** A firm begins construction on January 1 by making a $40,000 construction payment to a contractor. On July 1, another $40,000 payment is made. AAE = $40,000 + $40,000(6/12) = $60,000. The July 1 payment was invested in the project only half of a year. The $60,000 represents the amount of debt, outstanding the entire year, which could have been retired.
>
> **2.** The previous example involved a small number of discrete cash payments. This example assumes that cash payments are made continuously throughout the period. The firm starts construction on January 1. By December 31 it has spent $120,000 in qualifying expenditures on the projects. Payments were made evenly throughout the year. AAE = $120,000/2 = ($0 + $120,000)/2 = $60,000. Although $120,000 was expended during the year, on average the firm had $60,000 invested in the project during the year. (This is the same logic as with a bank account. If you deposited equal amounts into your account each day for a year and ended with a $120,000 balance, your average balance would be $60,000 for the year assuming interest is paid at year-end.)

IV. **Apply the Appropriate Interest Rate** -- If AAE is the amount of debt that could have been retired for the year, then an interest rate multiplied by AAE is the amount of interest that could have been avoided. This is the amount of interest to be capitalized, subject to the limitation that capitalized interest cannot exceed actual interest cost for the period.

> **Example:**
> Using the previous examples of AAE ($60,000), if the interest rate were 10%, then $6,000 of interest would be capitalized ($60,000 × .10) assuming at least that much interest cost was actually incurred. If total interest expense for the period before capitalizing interest amounted to $11,000, then $6,000 of interest would be debited to the asset under construction, and only $5,000 of interest expense would be reported in the income statement.

V. But What Interest Rate Should be Used? U.S. GAAP does not limit capitalized interest to specific construction loan interest. Rather, the more general concept of **avoidable** interest is used. Two ways of computing total interest to be capitalized are allowed:

A. **Weighted Average Method** -- Capitalizes interest using the weighted average rate on all interest bearing debt.

B. **Specific Method** -- Capitalizes the interest on specific construction loans first. Then, if needed, capitalize interest on all other debt based on the average interest rate for that debt.

Example:
A firm began construction in January and spent $100,000 in qualifying expenditures by year-end. Expenditures were made evenly throughout the period. Debt outstanding the entire year:

	Principal	Annual interest
10% construction loan	$30,000	$3,000
Other debt (average interest rate, 8%)	60,000	4,800
Total	$90,000	$7,800

AAE = $100,000/2 = $50,000

VI. Computation of Capitalized Interest

A. **Weighted Average Method**

Weighted average interest rate = ($7,800)/$90,000 = 8.67%

Capitalized interest = 8.67%($50,000) = $4,335. This amount is less than total interest of $7,800 for the period. Therefore the capitalized interest is $4,335 and the interest expense is $3,465 ($7,800 − $4,335).

B. **Specific Method**

Capitalized interest = .10($30,000) + .08($50,000 − $30,000) = $4,600

1. This amount is less than total interest of $7,800 for the period. Therefore the capitalized interest is $4,600 and the interest expense is $3,200 ($7,800 − $4,600).

2. The specific method first uses the construction loan. The principal amount of that loan is only $30,000. But $50,000 (AAE) of debt could have been retired. The additional $20,000 of debt (to sum to the $50,000 AAE) is the portion of the nonspecific debt that could have been retired.

Note: Interest capitalized compounds over several periods. The interest capitalized in year 1 is included in AAE for year 2, thus increasing the amount of interest capitalized in year 2. Interest is therefore compounded and included in the asset account.
AAE is used only to compute capitalized interest. The ending balance in construction in progress is typically much larger than AAE for the period. Using the specific method in the above example, the ending balance in construction in progress after capitalizing interest is $104,600 ($100,000 construction payments + $4,600 interest capitalized).

Interest Capitalization 2

This is the second lesson on interest capitalization. This lesson presents a more detailed discussion of the limits on how much interest can be capitalized. It also offers more detailed examples of the interest eligible for capitalization.

After studying this lesson, you should be able to:

1. *Determine the limit on interest that is eligible for capitalization.*

2. *Calculate the weighted average or specific interest rate.*

3. *Calculate the amount of interest to be capitalized during the period.*

4. *Complete the journal entry for interest capitalization.*

I. **Limit on Interest Capitalization**

   A. Capitalized interest is limited to actual interest incurred because avoidable debt is the lower of (1) AAE (average accumulated expenditures) and (2) total interest-bearing debt. The actual amount of interest incurred sets the ceiling on interest to be capitalized.

       1. When AAE < total interest-bearing debt, reported interest expense for the period is the difference between total interest cost and the amount of interest capitalized. In this case, because AAE is less than total debt, not all debt could have been avoided.

       2. When AAE > total interest-bearing debt, all interest cost is capitalized and there is no reported interest expense for the period. In this case, all debt could have been avoided had construction activities not taken place.

   B. These points are illustrated in the next example.

       1. **Example with more than one nonspecific construction loan --** This example shows how to compute two different weighted averages. Construction on a project began January 1, 20x6 with a construction payment of $100,000 to the contractor. One additional payment of $120,000 was made July 1, 20x6.

       2. Debt outstanding during 20x6 (entire year):

> 5%, $120,000 construction loan
>
> 6%, 20,000 note payable unrelated to construction
>
> 4%, 30,000 note payable unrelated to construction
>
> AAE = $100,000(12/12) + $120,000(6/12) = $160,000

   3. **Specific method**

> Average interest rate on nonconstruction loans =
>
> $((.06)\$20,000 + (.04)\$30,000) / (\$20,000 + \$30,000) = .048$
>
> Interest capitalized = $.05(\$120,000) + .048(\$160,000 - \$120,000) = \$7,920$

a. **Interest on the specific loan** for the construction is used first, and then interest at the average rate for all other debt is applied to the excess of AAE over the construction loan. Interest is capitalized only up to avoidable debt - on the AAE.

b. **If AAE had been less** than the amount of the construction loan (for example, $100,000), then only the construction loan interest would be capitalized (interest capitalized in that case would be .05 × $100,000 = $5,000).

c. If AAE had been $200,000 (**more than total debt**), then all the interest for the period would be capitalized because total debt is less than $200,000. All the debt could have been avoided. Interest capitalized = .05($120,000) + .048($50,000) = $8,400

4. **Average Method**

> Average interest rate on all loans =
>
> (.05($120,000) + (.06)$20,000 + (.04)$30,000) / ($120,000 + $20,000 + $30,000) = .0494
>
> Interest capitalized = .0494($160,000) = $7,904
>
> Again, if AAE had been $200,000, then all the interest for the period would be capitalized because total debt is less than $200,000. Interest capitalized = .05($120,000) + (.06)$20,000 + (.04)$30,000 = $8,400

5. **Compounding of Capitalized Interest and Construction Balance**

a. Interest capitalized in one period becomes part of AAE for the next period. Using the example above (average method), the balance in the construction-in- process account at the end of the first period is $227,904 ($100,000 construction payment + $120,000 construction payment + $7,904 capitalized interest).

b. The next year, the calculation of AAE will begin with $227,904(12/12), with the payments during the second year receiving the appropriate rate for the period of time in the project. Thus, the $7,904 of interest capitalized the previous period will be part of the base on which interest is capitalized the next period - interest is compounded.

> **Note:**
> Interest may be capitalized on a quarterly or annual basis.

II. **Construction Payables** -- Unpaid construction input costs are not included in AAE until paid in cash. Until cash is paid, debt can be considered avoidable. Payables include wages payable, accounts payable for material, and utilities payable.

> **Example:**
> If the firm incorporated $20,000 of materials into a project as of the end of the period, but paid only $15,000 for them ($5,000 in accounts payable), qualifying expenditures include only $15,000 for purposes of computing AAE.

III. **Land and Capitalized Interest** -- The effect on interest capitalization of expenditures made for land depends on the purpose for acquiring the land.

A. For land used as a building site, the cost of the land is included in AAE for the building, and interest is capitalized to the building; (The land is not being constructed.)

B. For land developed for sale, interest is capitalized to the land;

C. For land held for speculation, no interest is capitalized because the land is in its condition of intended use, and there is no asset under construction.

IV. Interest on Borrowed Funds -- In some cases, the proceeds from a specific construction loan are not fully used for financing the construction until well into the construction phase. Part of the proceeds may be invested in a bank account or a debt security may be purchased. Interest revenue on unused proceeds temporarily invested is not offset against interest to be capitalized. The interest revenue is reported separately and has no effect on interest capitalized.

    A. Exception -- If the funds are externally restricted tax-exempt borrowings, then a right of offset exists because the funds are restricted to use in construction.

V. Partial Year Computations -- Construction projects may begin or end during a reporting period. Also, new debt may be incurred and other liabilities may be retired during a reporting period.

    A. Guidelines

        1. **Interest rate** -- adjust the interest rate for the fraction of the year the debt is outstanding. If new interest-bearing debt is incurred during an interest capitalization period, the interest rate reflects the period the debt was outstanding. Assume a firm capitalizes interest quarterly. If $100,000 of 12% debt is incurred May 1, then for quarter 2, $2,000 of interest is included in the numerator of the rate (2 month's interest), and $100,000 is included in the denominator.

        2. **Expenditures** -- weight by the percent of the period invested in the project. An expenditure occurring at the beginning of the second month of a quarter receives a weight of 2/3.

VI. Disclosure -- The amount of interest capitalized and expensed must be disclosed during a period in which interest is capitalized. Note that the amount of interest paid for the period to be disclosed as part of the Statement of Cash Flows—either as part of the statement, as a supplemental schedule or in a footnote.

Post-Acquisition Expenditures

This lesson presents a discussion how to treat post-acquisition expenditures.

After studying this lesson, you should be able to:

1. *Determine if an expenditure should be capitalized or expensed.*

2. *Complete the entries for the capitalization of a post-acquisition expenditure.*

I. **Introduction**

A. A post-acquisition cost is capitalized if, as a result of the expenditure, the asset is:

1. More productive (provides more benefits); *or*

2. Has a longer useful life.

B. Otherwise, the expenditure is expensed. Although an argument can be made that ordinary maintenance and repairs prolongs the useful life of an asset, the estimated useful life of an asset assumes a minimum level of periodic service.

C. Repairs keep the asset in an ordinarily efficient operating condition. Repairs do not typically extend the life of the asset or increase its value. Repairs are typically expensed in the period incurred.

II. **Accounting Treatment for Capitalized Expenditures**

A. **Additions** -- Extensions or enlargements of existing assets.

1. If an integral part of the larger asset, depreciate the addition over the shorter of its useful life or the remaining useful life of the larger asset.

2. If not, depreciate the addition over its useful life.

B. **Modifications** -- Improvements (betterments), replacements, and extraordinary repairs all involve a modification of an existing component or part of the larger asset.

C. **Accounting approaches**

1. Substitution: remove the accumulated depreciation and original cost of the old component, recognize the loss, and capitalize the post-acquisition expenditure to the larger asset. This alternative is available only if the accounting system maintained records of the old component cost and accumulated depreciation.

2. Increase the larger asset account by the post-acquisition cost. This approach is used when the productivity rather than the useful life of the larger asset is enhanced, and when the accounting system does not maintain records of the old component cost and accumulated depreciation.

3. Debit accumulated depreciation. This approach is used when the expenditure increases the useful life of the larger asset. The debit to accumulated depreciation **turns back the clock** on the life of the larger asset. This approach is suited especially to extraordinary repairs.

D. For each of these three approaches, the post-acquisition cost is depreciated over the shorter of its useful life or remaining useful life of the larger asset.

See the following example.

Example:
The boiler of a large office building is replaced with a more efficient boiler at a cost of $65,000. The useful life of the building is unaffected but the new boiler will reduce energy costs significantly. The cost of the old boiler was $40,000, and its accumulated depreciation subsidiary ledger account reflects a balance of $35,000. To record the replacement:

Accumulated Depreciation	35,000	
Loss on Replacement	5,000	
Boiler		40,000
Boiler	65,000	
Cash		65,000

Nonaccelerated Depreciation Methods

This is the first of two lessons on depreciation. This lesson presents the concepts for depreciation and certain depreciation methods.

After studying this lesson, you should be able to:

1. *Explain the concepts for depreciation.*

2. *Calculate depreciation under the following methods: straight-line, service hours and units of production.*

I. Nature of Depreciation

A. Depreciation is a *systematic and rational* allocation of capitalized plant asset cost to time periods. The term *systematic* implies that the allocation is not random but rather is made on an orderly basis. The term *rational* means that the process can be supported by appealing to how the asset is used. The process of depreciation matches the cost of the plant asset to periods in which the asset is used to generate revenue.

B. Depreciation is *not* a process of valuation. The amount of depreciation recognized in a period is not necessarily the decline in the market value of the asset, nor is it a measure of the amount of the asset **used up**. If depreciation expense is $10,000, this does not mean that $10,000 of the cost of the asset was used in generating revenue. The $10,000 amount is simply the amount allocated to the period based on the method chosen by the firm. The book value of a depreciable plant asset (original cost less accumulated depreciation to date), is the amount of original cost yet to be depreciated. Only coincidentally does book value equal market value.

C. Justifications -- There are two *justifications* for depreciation:

1. Assets wear out over time;

2. Assets become obsolete.

 Example:
Land is not depreciated because it does not wear out and does not become obsolete.

D. The acquisition cost of plant assets is a cost of doing business. Because plant assets have a useful life exceeding one year, their cost is allocated to the periods they benefit. Although the amount of asset decline is not observable, depreciation expense provides at least some measure of the cost of the asset to be included in total expenses on an annual basis.

E. Depreciation is not a source of funds. Although it provides a tax deduction, the same can be said for any deductible expense. Note that most firms use straight line (SL) depreciation for financial reporting, and MACRS (modified accelerated cost recovery system) for income tax reporting. MACRS is the same as the double-declining balance (DDB) method with a half-year convention applied.

F. Definitions

Definitions:
Book Value: Original cost less accumulated depreciation to date.

Depreciable Cost: Total depreciation to be recognized over the life of the asset. This amount equals original cost less salvage value.

Minimum Book Value: Salvage value. In no case is salvage value depreciated. Thus, book value always includes salvage value. An asset cannot be depreciated such that its book value is less than salvage value.

1. There are three kinds of **noncurrent assets** subject to depreciation or similar process. Different terms are used for each, but all involve a systematic and rational allocation of historical cost to time periods of use:

   a. Plant assets are *depreciated;*

   b. Natural resources are *depleted;*

   c. Intangible assets are *amortized.*

Definitions:

Adjusting Journal Entry: The adjusting journal entry for depreciation on nonmanufacturing assets is: DR: Depreciation expense; CR: Accumulated depreciation

Contra Account: Many firms include depreciation expense in Selling, General, and Administrative Expense and report the components in a footnote. Accumulated depreciation is a contra-plant asset account. The use of a contra account preserves the original cost information in the plant asset account.

Manufacturing Assets: For manufacturing assets, depreciation is included in overhead and allocated to production based on machine hours or direct labors. The result is that Work in Process is debited for depreciation cost. When the products are sold, Cost of Goods Sold includes depreciation. A separate expense for depreciation is not recorded for manufacturing assets.

II. Factors in Calculating

A. The amount of depreciation recognized each period is affected by the following four factors. Only the first factor, capitalized cost, is a definite amount. Two estimates are used, and the firm has a free choice among the available methods.

   1. Capitalized Cost;

   2. Estimated Useful Life;

   3. Estimated Salvage Value (the cost of the asset not subject to depreciation – the portion of initial cost expected to be returned at the end of the useful life);

   4. Method chosen.

B. Several methods of depreciation are acceptable under GAAP. They can be categorized into two basic types: (1) straight-line methods and (2) accelerated methods.

   1. Straight-Line Methods (a constant rate of depreciation)

   a. **Straight-Line Method** -- Annual depreciation is calculated by the formula shown below

   Cost – Salvage Value / Useful Life

   i. Annual depreciation is the same each year.

   ii. **Justification** -- The asset will provide essentially the same benefits per year. Buildings are appropriately depreciated on an SL basis.

Example:
An asset costing $22,000 with a salvage value of $2,000 and a useful life of 5 years is depreciated $4,000 each year using the SL method ($22,000 − $2,000)/5.

b. Service Hours Method

i. The life of the asset is defined in terms of service hours, and the depreciation rate per service hour is calculated by using the formula shown below. The number of total service hours the asset will provide must be estimated and used as the denominator.

Depreciation rate = (Cost − Salvage Value) / (Useful Life in Service Hours)

ii. Depreciation for any given year is calculated by multiplying the service hours for the year by this constant depreciation rate per service hour. Annual depreciation varies with the number of service hours provided in the year. There is no expectation that depreciation will be the same amount each year.

iii. **Justification** -- The asset will provide essentially the same benefits per service hour. A delivery vehicle is an example of an asset appropriately depreciated on the service hours method.

Example:
An asset costing $22,000 with a salvage value of $2,000 and a useful life of 5 years is depreciated on the service hours method. The asset is expected to provide 10,000 hours of service. In a given year, 2,500 hours of service are provided. The constant rate is $2 per service hour ($22,000 − $2,000)/10,000. Depreciation for the given year is $5,000 (2,500 × $2).

c. Units of Output Method

i. The life of the asset is defined in terms of units of output, and the depreciation rate per unit of output is calculated using the formula shown below. The number of total units the asset will produce must be estimated and used as the denominator.

Depreciation rate = (Cost − Salvage Value) / (Useful Life in Units of Production)

ii. Depreciation for any given year is calculated by multiplying the units of output for the year by this constant depreciation rate per unit of output. Annual depreciation varies depending on the number of units produced in the year. There is no expectation that depreciation will be the same amount each year.

iii. **Justification** -- The asset will provide essentially the same benefits per unit produced. Oil drilling equipment is an example of an asset appropriately depreciated on the units of production method.

Example:
An asset costing $22,000 with a salvage value of $2,000 and a useful life of 5 years is depreciated on the units of production method. The asset is expected to produce 1,000 units. In a given year, 300 units are produced. The constant rate is $20 per unit ($22,000 − $2,000)/1,000. Depreciation for the given year is $6,000 (300 × $20).

Accelerated Depreciation Methods

This is the second of two lessons on depreciation. This lesson presents accelerated depreciation methods.

After studying this lesson, you should be able to:

1. *Calculate depreciation under the following methods: sum-of-years digits and double-declining balance.*

I. **Accelerated Methods** -- Accelerated methods of depreciation recognize depreciation at a faster rate early in the life of the asset. Later in the life of the asset, the amount of depreciation per period declines. This pattern of depreciation holds regardless of how the asset is used in any given period.

A. **Justification**

1. The theoretical justification for using an accelerated method is related to the matching principle. It is assumed the asset will be more productive in the earlier years. Therefore, more depreciation expense is recorded during those earlier, more productive years. More expense is matched against revenue in the periods of greater benefit; less expense is matched when the asset provides less benefit.

2. Another justification is obsolescence. Assets subject to obsolescence (high-tech equipment for example) will provide most of their benefits early in their life. Therefore, more depreciation is recognized in those years.

B. **Effect** -- One effect of using accelerated methods is a stable annual total amount of expense related to plant assets. Early in the asset's life, more depreciation is recognized and less maintenance is required. Later in the asset's life just the opposite occurs. But the total annual expense is fairly stable.

C. **Methods**

1. **Sum-of-the-Years' Digits Method**

a. First, the sum of the years' digits must be calculated by using the formula shown below.

N = useful life in years.

$SYD = (N(N+1))/2 = 1 + 2 + ... + N$

SYD is the denominator of the fraction used each year to compute depreciation. The numerator is the number of years remaining at the beginning of the year.

Year 1 Depreciation: $(N/SYD)(Cost - Salvage\ Value)$

Year 2 Depreciation: $((N-1)/SYD)(Cost - Salvage\ Value))$

Year N Depreciation: $(1/(SYD))(Cost - Salvage\ Value))$

---

b. This method is accelerated because the highest annual amount of depreciation is recognized in year 1, the next highest in year 2, and so forth.

Example:
An asset costing $22,000 with a salvage value of $2,000 and a useful life of 5 years is depreciated on the sum-of-the-years' digits method.

SYD = 1 + 2 + 3 + 4 + 5 = 15 = 5(5 + 1)/2

Depreciation, year 1 = (5/15)($22,000 − $2,000) = $6,667

Depreciation, year 2 = (4/15)($22,000 − $2,000) = $5,333

.

.

Depreciation, year 5 = (1/15)($22,000 − $2,000) = $1,333

2. **Declining Balance Method**

   a. This method differs from those discussed previously in three ways:

   b. Salvage value is not used in the computation of depreciation

   c. Annual depreciation is based on the beginning book value of the asset. This book value declines over time, hence the name of this group of methods. This also is why salvage value is not subtracted. Book value always includes salvage value because salvage value is never depreciated.

   d. Each year, accumulated depreciation must be checked to ensure that book value does not fall below salvage value.

   e. The method allows rates between 100% and 200% of the straight-line rate.

Double declining balance method

Depreciation in year 1 = Cost(2/N)

Depreciation in year 2 = (Cost − depreciation in year 1)(2/N)

                    = (book value at beginning of year 2)(2/N)

Depreciation in year 3 = (Cost − depreciation in years 1 and 2)(2/N)

The rate (2/N) is twice the straight-line rate. N=useful life in years.
150% of declining-balance method
The calculations are the same as for double-declining balance except that (1.5/N) is the rate used.

Example: An asset costing $22,000 with a salvage value of $2,000 and a useful life of 5 years is depreciated on the double-declining balance method.
Depreciation, year 1 = $22,000(2/5) = $8,800 Depreciation,

    year 2   = ($22,000 − $8,800)(2/5) = $5,280

In some cases, strict use of the declining balance method results in recognizing more depreciation than depreciable cost. In the year that total depreciation exceeds depreciable cost, firms will change to the straight-line method and depreciate the remaining depreciable cost over the remaining useful life beginning in that year.

3. **Partial or Fractional Year Depreciation**

   a. Assets not purchased at the beginning of a fiscal year must be depreciated on a fractional year basis. Firms often use a simplifying convention such as: depreciate all assets a full year in the year of acquisition, and recognize no depreciation in the year of disposal. Over large groups of assets, these conventions are acceptable if applied consistently.

   b. However, a more exact approach is required on the CPA exam.

Example: A calendar or fiscal year firm purchased an asset costing $22,000 with a salvage value of $2,000 and a useful life of 5 years on April 1, 20x7. Let:
W1 = the first whole year of depreciation (April 1, 20x7 to March 31, 20x8),
W2 = the second whole year of depreciation (April 1, 20x8 to March 31, 20x9),
and so forth.
Regardless of the depreciation method used, depreciation for reporting years is found as:

20x7 depreciation $= (9/12)W1$ (asset held 9 months in 20x7)

20x8 depreciation $= (3/12)W1 + (9/12)W2$ (20x8 contains the last 3 months

of the asset's first year,

and the first 9 months

of the asset's second year)

The remaining years are treated the same way.
If the method chosen is double declining balance (DDB), then from the previous example:
W1 = $22,000(2/5) = $8,800
W2 = ($22,000 - $8,800)(2/5) = $5,280

20x7 depreciation $= (9/12)W1 = (9/12)($8,800)$ $= $6,600$

20x8 depreciation $= (3/12)W1 + (9/12)W2$

$= (3/12)($8,800) + (9/12)($5,280)$ $= $6,160$

For DDB, a short-cut approach is available:

20x8 depreciation $= (2/5)($22,000 - $6,600) = $6,160$

---

4. **Appraisal Methods** -- These methods are used when it is impractical to depreciate assets on an individual basis. Accumulated depreciation records are not maintained on individual assets, and no gain or loss is recorded on disposal.

   a. **Inventory (Appraisal) Method** -- This method is applied to groups of smaller homogenous assets. At the end of each year, the assets are appraised and recorded at market value. The appraisal is for the entire group which saves accounting costs. The decline in market value from the previous year is depreciation expense for the year. If assets were sold during the year, the proceeds from sale reduce depreciation expense.

Example:

January 1 appraisal value of group:	$20,000
Proceeds from disposal of some assets in the group:	$3,000
December 31 appraisal value of group:	$12,000

Depreciation expense for the year

$= ($20,000 - $12,000) - $3,000 = $5,000$

---

b. Group / Composite Methods

    i.   This system applies the straight-line method to groups of assets rather than to assets individually. Accumulated depreciation records are not maintained by asset; rather, only a control account is used to accumulate depreciation. Gains and losses are not recorded. The entry to dispose of an asset plugs the accumulated depreciation account.

> The composite depreciation rate = (annual group SL depreciation) / (total original cost of group)

    ii.   Depreciation for a year is the product of the rate and the original cost of assets remaining at the beginning of the year. Asset additions increase the total original cost on which depreciation is computed; asset disposals reduce the total original cost.

Example:
A firm purchased the following group of assets:

Asset	Number	Original unit cost	Salvage value	Useful life
A	10	$500	$100	4 years
B	5	600	300	3 years

The composite rate of depreciation =(10($500 − $100)/4 + 5($600 - $300)/3) / (10($500) + 5($600)) = .1875

The .1875 rate means that $.1875 of depreciation is recognized each year for each $1 of acquisition cost in the group. After a few years in which assets have been added and removed, if the original cost of the group of assets remaining on January 1 is $5,000, depreciation for that year is $937.50 ($5,000 × .1875).

Natural Resources

This lesson provides information on the accounting for natural resources.

After studying this lesson, you should be able to:

1. *Identify acquisition, exploration and development costs.*

2. *Determine the costs that are capitalized as part of the natural resource asset.*

3. *Calculate depletion of the natural resource asset.*

I. Natural Resources

> **Definition:**
> *Natural Resource*: A noncurrent asset that contains the cost of acquiring, exploring, and developing a natural resource deposit (e.g., timber, oil and minerals). It does not include the cost of extracting the resource.

A. The amount capitalized as natural resources is the sum of three different types of costs:

1. **Acquisition costs --** The amount paid to acquire the rights to explore for undiscovered natural resources or to extract proven natural resources.

2. **Exploration costs --** The amount paid to drill or excavate or any other costs of searching for natural resources.

3. **Development costs --** The amount paid after the resource has been discovered but before production begins.

B. Methods of accounting for exploration costs.

1. **Successful efforts method --** Only the cost of successful exploration efforts is capitalized to the natural resources account; unsuccessful efforts are expensed.

2. **Full costing method --** All costs of exploring for the resource are capitalized to the natural resources account. (The total amount capitalized cannot exceed the expected value of resources to be removed.)

3. The choice between successful-efforts and full-costing method is among the most important a firm has to make. The choice can have a large effect on net income and total assets. The successful efforts method best reflects the definition of an asset because only those efforts that located the resource are capitalized to the natural resource account. The full costing method reflects matching - capitalize all costs until the natural resource deposit produces revenue through sale of the inventory. Another justification for full costing is that all exploration efforts contributed to finding the resource.

C. After resources are discovered on the property, the cost to develop the property to enable extraction of the resource is capitalized to the natural resources account. Development costs pertain to facilities that will not be removed when the project is finished.

D. Removable assets such as drilling equipment, vehicles, and the like are recorded in their own separate accounts as plant assets.

II. Depletion

A. After all costs are capitalized to the natural resources account, the resource begins to be removed and depletion is recorded. Depletion is the term used to refer to the allocation of the cost of the natural resource to inventory. Depletion is taken on the natural resource asset (sum of the three costs above less the residual value).

B. Depletion is not an expense but an allocation of the natural resource from noncurrent assets to inventory. When units of the natural resource are depleted, inventory is debited and the natural resource account is credited. Because the useful life is directly associated with the amount of resources extracted, the activity or units of production base method is widely used.

> Depletion for a period = (depletion rate) x (number of units removed in period)
>
> Depletion rate = (Natural resources account balance - residual value) / (total estimated units)

C. The successful-efforts method results in a lower depletion rate but a higher exploration expense in periods of significant exploration.

III. Other Costs Involved in Natural Resource Extraction

> **Definition:**
> *Extraction costs:* Depreciation on removable assets, wages, and material costs pertaining to the extraction effort - these costs are debited to the inventory of resource, not to the natural resources account.
>
> *Production costs:* Additional processing costs after extraction - this cost also is debited to the inventory of resource, not to the natural resources account.

A. When the inventory of resource is sold, the costs that have been debited to it (depletion, extraction, production) are recognized as expense through cost of goods sold.

1. Depreciation on Assets Used in Extraction -- Depreciation on equipment used in the extraction effort is a component of total extraction costs. It does not contribute to depletion. The entry for extraction costs generally includes a debit to extraction costs and a credit to accumulated depreciation for depreciation on the cost of assets used in extraction. How the equipment is depreciated depends on whether it can be moved from one site to another.

   a. Equipment that can be used at more than one natural resource site - depreciate as usual over its useful life.

   b. Equipment dedicated to one site (often not movable or removable) - depreciate over the shorter of useful life or life of natural resource site. The most efficient method in this case is to use the units-of-production method with the same denominator as the depletion base.

IV. Financial Statement Presentation of Natural Resources

A. The natural resource account is presented as a noncurrent asset. The property associated with the natural resource is not classified as land because the land is not held as a building site, but rather to utilize the natural resource on the land.

B. Some firms classify the natural resource as an intangible asset because they have purchased the rights to utilize the land and do not own the land itself. These mineral rights are an intangible asset.

C. Once extracted, the natural resource noncurrent asset is transferred to resource inventory a current asset.

Example:
This illustrates the flow of the various cost types, the calculation of depletion, and recognition of cost of goods sold.

Acquisition cost of mine	$400,000
Exploration costs, year 1	
Successful	$50,000
Unsuccessful	$150,000
Development costs	$500,000
Extraction and production costs	$200,000
Total estimated tons of ore	100,000
Estimated residual value	$ 20,000
Tons removed in year 1	40,000
Tons sold in year 1	30,000

Entries:

	Successful Efforts		Full costing	
Natural resources	950,000*		1,100,000#	
Exploration expense	150,000			
Cash		1,100,000		1,100,000

* $400,000 + $50,000 + $500,000

$400,000 + $50,000 + $500,000 + $150,000

Note that full costing capitalizes all exploration costs whereas the successful efforts method capitalizes only the successful efforts and expenses the rest.

Inventory of ore	372,000*		432,000#	
Accumulated depletion		372,000		432,000

* (($950,000 − $20,000)/100,000 total tons)(40,000 tons removed)

(($1,100,000 − $20,000)/100,000 total tons)(40,000 tons removed)

Accumulated depletion is contra to the natural resources account. The amounts in this entry for the two methods are the reductions in the book value of the natural resources account allocated to the inventory account. The depletion base is depleted, with the resources flowing to the inventory account. There is no change in net assets or income at this point.

Inventory of ore	200,000		200,000	
Cash, materials, wages payable		200,000		200,000

The extraction and production costs also increase the inventory account. There is no income effect at this point because no inventory has been sold. Inventory cost has three components: depletion, extraction, and production.

Cost of goods sold	429,000*		474,000#	
Inventory of ore		429,000		474,000

* ($372,000 + $200,000)(30,000/40,000)

\# ($432,000 + $200,000)(30,000/40,000)

Of the 40,000 tons removed in the period, 30,000 were sold. Therefore, three-fourths of the inventory cost is expensed. One-fourth of the inventory cost will appear in the ending balance sheet of the firm. The entry to record the sale is not shown. It would be the same for both methods: dr. Accounts receivable, cr. Sales.

Impairment—Assets for Use and Held-for-Sale

This lesson presents the accounting and reporting for impairment of long-lived assets.

After studying this lesson you should be able to :

1. *Describe the two steps in the test for impairment of assets held in use.*

2. *Describe the impairment test for assets held for disposal.*

I. Introduction - Asset Categories

A. Assets subject to impairment fall into one of three categories:

1. Assets in use;

2. Assets held for disposal (sale); and

3. Assets to be disposed of other than by sale (by spin-off to shareholders, by exchange for other assets, or by abandonment).

B. Indicators of Impairment

1. Significant decrease in market value

2. Change in way asset used or physical change in asset

3. Legal factors / change in business climate or adverse action / assessment by regulator

4. Asset costs incurred greater than planned

5. Operating or CF flow losses from the asset.

C. Below is a diagram that presents an overview of the decisions that need to be made with respect to asset impairment.

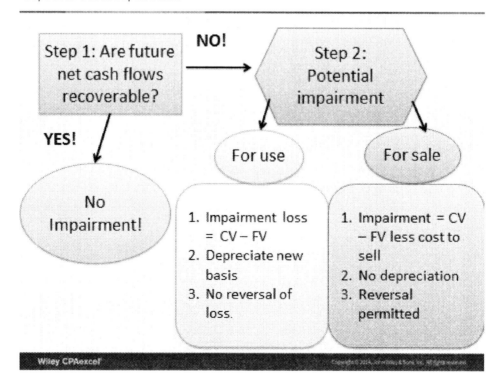

II. Assets in Use

A. **Assets in use** -- Are written down to fair value if their recoverable cost is less than book value. The amount of the impairment loss recognized is the difference between book value and fair value. Note that the determination of impairment is a step separate from the measurement of the loss; both use different values.

   1. **Fair Value (FV)** -- The price that would be acceptable to the firm and another party for the transfer of the asset. **Present value** is used when no active market exists for the asset.

   2. **Recoverable Cost (RC)** -- Is the sum of expected future net cash inflows from use and ultimate disposal. Costs of maintaining the asset are included in the computation of RC, reducing it. RC is a nominal sum, not a present value. RC is based on how the firm currently uses the asset; the expected remaining useful life is used in computing RC. RC is the net increase in cash expected from using and disposing of the asset over its remaining life. RC always exceeds FV because RC is not a discounted amount.

B. **Test for Impairment**

   1. If book value (BV) > RC then the asset is impaired because book value will not be recovered. If BV is $100 and RC is $70, then there is no accounting justification for reporting the asset of $100.

   2. If BV <= RC, then the asset is not impaired and no impairment loss is recognized. In this case, the book value is recoverable.

   3. Assets should be evaluated for impairment when certain indications are present, rather than on a regular basis. Significant declines in FV, changes in legal climate or physical nature of the asset are examples of signals that suggest an impairment may have occurred.

C. **Measurement of Impairment Loss**

   1. An impaired asset is written down to FV. The loss equals: BV - FV

   2. Note that the *test* for impairment uses BV and RC, while the *measurement* of the loss uses BV and FV.

D. **Examples**

Example:
1. An asset with a book value of $100 has a recoverable cost of $120 and a fair value of $75.

Test for Impairment: BV of $100 < RC of $120. The asset is not impaired because the book value is recoverable. There is no loss computation; there is no impairment loss.

2. An asset with a book value of $100 has a recoverable cost of $90 and a fair value of $75.

Test for Impairment: BV of $100 > RC of $90. The asset is impaired because the book value is not fully recoverable.

Loss Measurement: Loss = BV of $100 - FV of $75 = $25. The asset is written down to $75. The loss is a component of income from continuing operations.

The entry to record the loss of $25:

Impairment loss	25	
Asset or Accumulated depreciation		25

Accounting after recognizing the $25 loss.

a. The new BV of the asset is the FV of 75 and is used as the cost for future depreciation. The new depreciable cost is $75 less any residual value.

b. An impairment loss on an asset in use cannot be recovered; there are no upward revaluation or gains recognized if FV increases.

c. Additional impairments are possible.

E. Asset Groups -- Many, if not most, assets do not function independently, but are rather part of a working group. For purposes of the **test for impairment**, assets are grouped at the *lowest* possible organizational level at which cash flows can be identified. The 3 amounts (BV, FV, RC) are measured at this level. One intended effect of this rule on grouping at the LOWEST level rather than a higher one is to decrease the incidence of merging assets with impairment losses with those for which FV > BV in which case there would be fewer or no impairment losses recognized.

III. Assets Held-for-Sale (Disposal) -- Recoverable cost is not used for assets held for disposal. Rather, the test for impairment and the loss computation both use the same values (BV, and FV less cost to sell).

A. Decision to Dispose

1. If the decision to dispose of an asset and the ultimate disposal occur in the **same period**, the actual gain or loss on disposal is recognized in income from continuing operations. The disposal loss or gain equals the difference between FV and BV (if BV > FV, then a loss occurs; if BV < FV, then a gain occurs). Depreciation should be recognized to the date of the disposal unless the firm uses a convention for fractional year depreciation. The accumulated depreciation account is removed along with the asset's original cost.

2. If the decision to dispose **precedes** the period of disposal, an estimated loss is recorded if it is probable and estimable. Estimated gains are not recognized.

B. Held For Sale Criteria

1. There are six criteria for determining when an asset is considered held for sale. All six must be met for the accounting provisions to apply. Otherwise, the asset is considered in use.

   a. Management commits to a plan to sell the asset or group of assets;

   b. The asset must be available for immediate sale in its present condition subject only to terms that are usual and customary for such sales. This criterion does not preclude a firm from using the asset while it is held for sale nor does it require a binding agreement for future sale;

   c. An active program to locate a buyer has been initiated;

   d. The sale is expected to take place within one year. In limited cases, the one-year rule is waived for circumstances beyond the firm's control (for example, due to a new regulation or law, environmental remediation, or deteriorating market);

   e. The asset is being actively marketed for sale at a price that is reasonable in relation to its current value;

   f. Sale of the asset must be probable.

2. If the six criteria are not met at the balance sheet date but are met before issuance, treat the asset as held for use in those statements. If an asset held for sale fails to meet all six criteria at a later date, it is reclassified as held for use.

3. An asset held for sale is impaired if its BV exceeds its fair value less cost to sell at the end of the reporting period.

C. Held For Sale Accounting

1. The asset is written down to (fair value - cost to sell) - here the test for impairment and the measurement of the loss are the same. The term 'recoverable cost' is not used for assets for sale. If sale is expected beyond one year, the cost to sell is discounted.

2. Only direct incremental costs are used in the computation of cost to sell.

3. The impairment loss recorded equals the difference between the asset's BV and its (FV - cost to sell). The estimated cost to sell increases the loss.

4. The asset is removed from plant assets because it is no longer in use.

5. Depreciation is no longer recognized on the asset.

6. The results of operating the asset during the holding period are recognized in period of occurrence - estimated future operating losses or gains are not recognized until they actually occur. Note that although these assets are held for disposal, they may require maintenance and other cash expenditures. These are expensed as incurred.

7. The asset can be written up or down if held for another period - gains are limited to the amount of the initial impairment loss (BV cannot exceed the amount immediately before recording the initial impairment loss).

Example: A plant asset (cost $100,000; accumulated depreciation $40,000) has a current fair value of $30,000 at the end of Year 4. Management has decided to sell the asset as soon as possible during the next reporting period. The estimated direct cost to sell is $5,000. The six criteria of FAS 144 are met.

End of Year 4

Asset held for disposal	25,000*
Accumulated depreciation	40,000
Loss on asset held for disposal	35,000**
Plant asset	100,000

* $30,000 fair value − $5,000

** $60,000 old book value − $25,000 new book value. The loss of $35,000 is the impairment loss.

At the end of Year 5, the asset remains unsold. Fair value is now $20,000 and the estimated cost to sell is $12,000.

End of Year 5

New book value = $8,000 = ($20,000 − $12,000).

Loss on asset held for disposal 17,000 *

Asset held for disposal 12,000

* $25,000 book value at end of 20x4 − $8,000 new book value

Limit on Gains: Assume instead that at the end of 20x5 the fair value had risen to $70,000 and estimated cost to sell remained at $5,000. The difference between fair value and estimated cost to sell has increased from $25,000 to $65,000, an increase of $40,000. This amount exceeds the previous loss of $35,000. The maximum gain allowed is $35,000, the amount of the previous loss. Therefore, the asset would be written back up to $60,000 (the book value immediately before the initial impairment), and a gain of $35,000 would be recognized.

IV. Assets To Be Disposed Of Other Than By Sale

A. This category includes disposal by abandonment, by exchange for a similar asset, and by distribution to shareholders as a spin-off. Note that dissimilar asset exchange is not included in this category because that transaction is considered a sale - the culmination of an earnings process.

B. Accounting -- Continue to classify the asset as held for use until disposal occurs, and continue to depreciate the asset. Apply the impairment standards for assets in use. Compute recoverable cost as for assets in use. These assets are treated as such because even though the plan is to dispose of the asset, the firm will derive the remaining utility of the asset (if any) from operations rather than via disposal. For exchanges and spin-offs, an additional impairment is recorded at disposal if BV > FV.

C. These assets are not treated as assets for sale because there is no accounting income generated from a similar asset exchange, spin-off, or abandonment.

Impairment and IFRS

This lesson presents the significant differences in the accounting for impairment under IFRS versus U.S. GAAP.

After studying this lesson you should be able to :

1. *Identify the major differences in the accounting for impairment under IFRS versus U.S. GAAP.*

I. Impairment and IFRS

A. Under IFRS a financial asset is impaired when its carrying value exceeds the present value of the future cash flows discounted at the financial asset's original effective interest rate. Impairment applies only to those assets carried at cost or amortized cost. Assets carried at fair value with the unrealized gains and losses recording in income do not create an impairment loss because the impairment is already captured in the fair value. If the asset is carried at fair value through other comprehensive income, then any impairment would require reclassification of the impairment loss from OCI to earnings.

B. An entity must complete a review of its assets at each balance sheet date to determine if there is evidence that impairment may exist. IAS 39 provides a list of factors to consider in this review. Examples of these observable factors are:

- Significant financial difficulty of the issuer;

- Breach of contract such as default or delinquency in payments;

- Concessions granted to the borrower because of legal or financial reasons that otherwise would not have been considered;

- Bankruptcy of the borrower becomes a probability.

C. If there is objective evidence that impairment may exist, the entity should measure and record the impairment loss.

> The impairment loss exists when the recoverable amount is less than the carrying amount.

Major Differences

IFRS	U.S. GAAP
One-step process	Two-step process
Recoverable amount is the higher of – Fair value less cost to sell or – Value in use	Undiscounted cash flows from use establish recoverability (step one) Fair value is used for the impairment calculation (step two)
Discounting required in evaluation stage	No discounting of cash flows in step one
Impairment losses can be reversed if circumstances change (except for Goodwill)	No reversals permitted

Example:
1. Shelby Company is assessing Asset A for impairment and has determined the following:

Carrying amount:	$42,000
Future undiscounted cash flows:	$45,000
Discounted cash flows:	$40,000
Fair value:	$37,000
Fair value less cost to sell:	$35,000

U.S. GAAP (ASC 360)

Future cash flows $45,000 > Carrying amount $42,000 --> therefore NO impairment

IFRS (IAS 36)

Recoverable amount the great of FV less cost to sell or value in use --> $35,000 or **$40,000**

Recoverable amount $40,000 < Carrying amount $42,000 --> there IS impairment

Impairment loss: write down to the recoverable amount. $42,000 − $40,000 = $2,000

2. Shelby Company is assessing Asset A for impairment and has determined the following:

Carrying amount:	$50,000
Future undiscounted cash flows:	$45,000
Discounted cash flows:	$40,000
Fair value:	$37,000
Fair value less cost to sell:	$35,000

U.S. GAAP (ASC 360)

Future cash flows $45,000 < Carrying amount $50,000 --> there IS impairment

Impairment loss = write down to fair value. $50,000 − $37,000 = $13,000

IFRS (IAS 36)

Recoverable amount the great of FV less cost to sell or value in use --> $35,000 or **$40,000**

Recoverable amount $40,000 < Carrying amount $50,000 --> there IS impairment

Impairment loss = write down to the recoverable amount. $50,000 − $40,000 = $10,000

PPE and IFRS

This lesson presents the significant differences in the accounting for property, plant and equipment under IFRS versus U.S. GAAP.

After studying this lesson, you should be able to:

1. *Identify the major differences in the accounting for property, plant and equipment under IFRS versus U.S. GAAP.*

I. PPE and IFRS

A. There are a few significant differences in the accounting for PPE under IFRS than according to U.S. GAAP. The table below summarizes these differences.

IFRS	U.S. GAAP
Estimated useful life and depreciation method reviewed annually	Estimated useful life and depreciation method reviewed when events or circumstances change
Component depreciation required in some cases	No requirement for component depreciation
PPE can be revalued to fair value	Revaluation to fair value is not permitted
Interest earned on construction funds can offset the interest costs	Interest earned on construction funds are not allowed to offset the interest costs

B. Estimated useful life and depreciation method -- Under IFRS the company must review the remaining useful life, residual value, and depreciation method on an annual basis. Any changes in the estimated useful life, residual value, or depreciation method are accounted for prospectively.

C. Component depreciation -- When an item of PPE comprises of individual components for which different depreciation methods or rates are appropriate, each component is depreciated separately. For example, a building can be broken down into components: roofing, electrical system, plumbing system, structural, etc. Component depreciation is based on the premise that each component of the asset has its own useful life and fair value.

D. Fair value remeasurement -- Under IFRS, PPE can be remeasured to fair value if fair value can be reliably measured. If remeasurement is used, it must be applied to the entire class or components of PPE, such as land, buildings, or equipment. Increases in an assets fair value above original cost are recorded in a revaluation surplus account. Any decreases in an assets fair value below the original cost are recorded as losses to the income statement. When revaluation results in an increase in the asset, a debit is made to increase the assets value and a credit is made to an equity account (part of OCI) called revaluation surplus. If the asset is subsequently decreased during revaluation, then the previously established revaluation surplus is reduced to zero and a loss is recognized for any excess. If the fair value of the asset declines below its original cost a loss is recognized. If the fair value subsequently increases, a gain can be recognized to the extent of the loss and any additional gain is recognized in revaluation surplus.

See the following example.

Example: Assume Taylor Company revalued its building to fair value. The building had a net book value of $100,000 and a fair value of $120,000. The entry would be:

Building	$20,000	
Revaluation surplus, building		$20,000

Subsequent decreases in the building's fair value will first decrease the Revaluation surplus account and the excess recognized as a loss. Assume two years later the fair value of the building is $90,000

Revaluation surplus, building	$20,000	
Revaluation loss, building	10,000	
Building		$30,000

E. The above example is simplified by ignoring accumulated depreciation. There are two methods used to adjust accumulated depreciation: the proportional method and the reset method.

   1. In the proportional method accumulated depreciation is restate proportionately so the asset's carrying value after revaluation equals the revalued amount.

Example: Assume the cost of Taylor's building is $125,000 and the accumulated depreciation is $25,000 resulting in a net book value of $100,000. Both the building and accumulated depreciation are reset using the proportionate ratio of net book value to original cost (($125,000/ $100,000) = 1.20%). The 120% ratio will increase the asset and the accumulated depreciation proportionately as displayed in the following entry.

Building	$25,000[1]	
Accumulated depreciation, building		5,000[2]
Revaluation surplus, building		20000

[1]((125,000x1.2) = 150,000 − 125,000 = 25,000)
[2]((25,000x1.2) = 30,000 − 25,000 = 5,000)
After this entry the balances will be as follows:
New cost = $150,000 (125,000 × 1.2)
New accumulated depreciation = 30,000 (25,000 × 1.2)
New book value = 120,000 (150,000 − 30,000)

   2. In the reset method, accumulated depreciation is "reset" to zero by closing it to the building account, and then the building is adjusted for the revaluation.

Example: In the entries below, Taylor resets the accumulated depreciation to zero and records the revaluation surplus.

Accumulated depreciation, Building	$25,000	
Building		$25,000
Building	$20,000	
Revaluation surplus		$20,000

F. Depreciation will be computed on the newly revalued building carrying value. The balance in revaluation surplus is also "depreciated" over the remaining life of the asset. The "depreciation" on the revaluation surplus is taken directly to retained earnings.

G. The revaluation surplus is reported in equity until the property is sold. When the revalued property is sold the balance in revaluation surplus is closed directly to retained earnings.

H. Capitalized interest -- Under IFRS, the interest earned on the funds received for a construction loan can reduce interest cost. U.S. GAAP does not allow reduction of interest cost for the interest earned on the construction loans.

I. Investment Property -- Under IFRS, investment property is specifically defined as property held to earn rental income, or for capital appreciation, or both. Under U.S. GAAP, there is not a specific definition of investment property; such property is accounted for as PPE unless it meets the criteria to be classified as "held for sale."

1. Under IFRS investment property is initially recognized at cost, but subsequently can be measured using either the cost model or the fair value model. If the fair value model is used, changes in the fair value are recognized in profit and loss. U.S. GAAP allows only the cost model. Disclosure of the fair value of investment property is required, regardless of the measurement model used under IFRS, but investment property is not a **required disclosure for U.S. GAAP.**

Introduction—Equity and Debt Investments

When one entity acquires the debt or equity securities issued by another entity, it has made an investment in the securities of the issuing entity. How the acquiring entity accounts for and reports its investment depends on the nature, extent, and purpose of the investment, and, in some cases, whether or not the investing entity elects the fair value option. This lesson provides a frame of reference for the details of accounting for investments when the investor does not elect the fair value option. The details of accounting when the investing entity does not elect the fair value option are covered in the following lessons. The use of the fair value option is covered in a subsequent lesson.

After studying this lesson, you should be able to:

1. *Define certain investment terminology.*

2. *Identify the major classifications of investments for accounting purposes.*

3. *Provide a model that shows the accounting treatment for each classification.*

4. *Identify the levels of influence for accounting purposes derived from investments in debt and equity securities.*

5. *Describe the criteria for classifying investments in debt or equity securities into the correct level of influence.*

6. *Define and give examples of debt and equity securities.*

I. Investments held by companies

A. Terminology

> **Definition:**
> *Equity Securities*: Securities representing ownership interest or right to acquire or dispose of ownership interest.

1. Includes - common stock, preferred stock (except redeemable), stock warrants, call options/rights, put options.

2. Excludes - debt securities (even convertible debt), redeemable preferred stock, and treasury stock.

> **Definition:**
> *Debt Securities*: Securities representing the right of buyer/holder (Creditor) to receive from the issuer (Debtor) a principal amount at a specified future date and (generally) to receive interest as payment for providing use of funds.

3. Includes - bonds, notes, convertible bonds/notes, redeemable preferred stock.

4. Excludes - common/preferred stock, stock warrants/options/rights, futures/forward contracts.

II. Concepts

A. Recognized vs. Realized

1. A recognized gain/loss occurs when a gain or loss related to an investment (or other item) is recorded (recognized) in the financial statements, whether or not the investment

has been sold. For example, a gain or loss would be recognized if the change in market value of investment securities is reported in the financial statements before the securities are sold.

> **Note:**
> Recognition is an accounting concept - it means that we have recognized the item on the financial statements.

2. A realized gain/loss occurs when an investment (or other item) is sold (or otherwise disposed of). The difference between the cash or other consideration received and the carrying value of the investment is a realized gain or loss.

III. Investment in Equity Securities

A. The accounting and reporting of an investment in equity securities depends on:

> **Note:**
> Realization is an economic concept - it means that there is a culmination of the earnings process and cash or other consideration is given or received.

1. How much is owned;

2. How long it is held;

3. Whether the equity security is private or public.

B. The following table depicts the accounting and reporting of equity securities. Since equity ownership provides voting rights, the level of economic influence is determined by the level of stock ownership. This level of influence is a guide line because there may be other factors that contribute to the investor's ability to exercise significant influence or control. Subsequent lessons will discuss these other factors in more detail. The purpose of this lesson is to provide an overview of the investment categories and valuation basis.

Percentage Equity Ownership	0 - 20%	21 - 50%	> 51%
Level of Economic Influence (influence over operating, investing and financing activities)	Nominal	Significant	Control
Valuation Basis	Cost or fair value	Equity method or fair value	Equity method or cost method
Reporting Classification	Trading available-for-Sale	Equity Investment	Subsidiary
Balance Sheet Presentation	Investment - current or noncurrent	Investment - noncurrent	Consolidated financial statements

C. If the investor has **< 20% ownership**, there is **nominal influence** over the operating, investing and financing activities of the investee.

1. If the investee is publicly traded, where there is a readily determinable market value for the investee, then the investment is classified as **trading or available-for-sale**. (These investments are discussed in the lesson "No Significant Influence.")

2. If the investee is not publicly traded, and there is not a readily determinable market value, then the investment is classified as a **cost method** investment. (The accounting for this type of investment is included in the lessons on "Equity Method.")

3. The balance sheet presentation of **current or noncurrent** depends on management's intent for holding the security for the short term (typically the trading securities) or long term. AFS securities could be short or long-term.

D. If the investor has between **20% and 50% ownership**, then the investor can **significantly influence** the operating, investing and financing activities of the investee. Therefore, the investment is accounted for using the Equity Method of accounting.

   1. The default accounting for an investment with significant influences is **equity method**. A detailed discussion of equity method accounting is presented in subsequent lessons.

   2. If the investee is publicly traded and there is a readily determinable market value, then the investor has the option to value this investment at **fair value**. If this option is chosen then the investment is marked-to-market value with the unrealized gains and losses recorded in earnings. Once the investor chooses the fair value option it is irrevocable and the investment continues to be recorded at fair value.

   3. Investments with significant influence are usually reported as a **noncurrent** asset because buying and selling equity shares of this magnitude is relatively difficult to do. For example, if you owned 40% of a publicly traded company, it would be very difficult for you to sell that much stock in one block without severely diluting the selling price.

E. If the investor has >50% ownership of an investment, then the investor controls the investee. An investment of this magnitude creates a Parent / Subsidiary relationship.

   1. The default accounting for an investment with >50% ownership is equity method. The Parent company will record its equity investment in the Subsidiary on the Parent company's books. Equity method accounting is discussed more fully in the lessons "Equity Method."

   2. In some instances the Parent company can choose to use the cost method to account for its subsidiary. Cost method accounting is discussed more fully in the "Equity Method" lesson. The cost method can be used by the Parent company because the Parent's stand alone financial statements are (typically) not issued on a standalone basis. The Parent must consolidate, and therefore eliminate the investment in the Subsidiary.

   3. For financial statement presentation, the Parent must consolidate the Subsidiary and report consolidated financial statements of Parent + Subsidiary. Whether the Parent uses the equity method or the cost method to account for its subsidiary, the consolidated financial statements will be the same. The only difference is what is reported on the Parent's stand alone statements. Not that the Parent's stand alone statements are not in compliance with GAAP - GAAP requires that the Parent present consolidated statements. Consolidation is discussed more fully in the series of lessons on "Consolidations."

IV. Investment in Debt Securities

A. The accounting and reporting of an investment in debt securities depends on:

   1. How long it is held;

   2. Whether the debt security is private or public.

B. The following table depicts the accounting and reporting of debt securities. Debt ownership does not provide any voting rights; therefore, there is no economic influence from debt ownership. The critical criteria for accounting for debt investments are whether the company has the positive ability and intent to hold the debt security to maturity.

See the following illustration.

Debt Ownership	Publicly Traded		Private issue	
Positive ability and intent to hold to maturity	Held-to-maturity		Held-to-maturity	
No ability and/or intent to hold to maturity		Trading or available-for-sale		Trading or available-for-sale
Valuation Basis	Amortized cost	Fair value	Amortized cost	Fair value
Balance Sheet Presentation	Investment - noncurrent	Investment - current or noncurrent	Investment - noncurrent	Investment - current or noncurrent

C. The first criterion for a debt security to be classified as held-to-maturity (HTM) is that the investor must have the **positive ability and intent** to hold the security to maturity. By definition, only debt securities can be classified as HTM because equity securities do not mature.

1. The **ability to hold** debt to maturity may be evident in prior investments in debt securities and the investor has demonstrated that he/she holds the security for its entire life.

2. The **intent to hold** the debt to maturity may be evident by demonstrating that the investor does not need the cash associated with this investment. In other words, the investor has sufficient operating cash flows so there is no need to liquidate the investment in order to have enough cash flow for operating activities.

D. If the debt security is **publicly traded**, the investor has the option to account for the debt security at amortized cost or fair value.

1. If the investor intends to hold the debt security to maturity and wants to classify the security as held-to-maturity, the debt security must be valued at amortized cost.

2. If the debt is classified as HTM, it will be classified as a noncurrent investment until the year the security matures. At that time, the investment will be classified as current.

3. If the investor selects the fair value option and records the security at fair market value, the security will be classified as trading or available-for-sale and presented as current or noncurrent, depending on how long management intends to hold the debt.

E. If the debt security is **privately issued**, the investor will usually account for the debt security at amortized cost.

1. If the investor intends to hold the debt security to maturity and wants to classify the security as held-to-maturity, the debt security must be valued at amortized cost.

2. If the debt is classified as HTM, it will be classified as a noncurrent investment until the year the security matures. At that time, the investment will be classified as current.

3. If the investor classifies the debt investment as trading or available-for-sale, the debt should be valued at fair value. This classification will be unlikely because it will be difficult

to get a quoted price representing the fair value of private debt (Level 1 valuation). However, it is possible to use this classification; the investor would have to value the private debt using a valuation model and, depending on the extent that the inputs are observable, the debt valuation would be Level 2 or 3.

F. Below are examples for the accounting for investment in bonds. The accounting for a bond investment that is purchased and carried as an asset is the mirror image of the accounting for a bond that is issued and carried as a liability. Recall that a bond is a contract to repay borrowing at specified maturity date; interest is to be paid at specified intervals until maturity. When the entity invests in a bond, the interest received is interest income. The stated rate on the bond is the nominal rate and the effective rate of the bond is the market rate or yield.

1. When the bond is purchased for less than face value, effective rate is greater than stated rate and the bond is purchased at a discount.

2. When the bond is purchased for more than face value, effective rate is less than stated rate and the bond is purchased at a premium.

3. The discount or premium is amortized to interest income over the life of the bond

   a. Discounts or premiums should be amortized using the effective interest method. The straight-line amortization method can be used if it yields a similar result.

G. Bond investment is classified as held to maturity when there is positive ability and intent to hold the bond until maturity. Below are examples of the accounting for a bond classified as held to maturity:

 Example:
1. Bond purchased at par

Assume the entity purchases a 2-year, $100 bond, with 10% stated rate, pays semi-annually is purchased at 10%.

Purchase price:	PV of principle ($100, 4 periods, 5%) = .82270 =	$82.27
	PV of interest ($5, 4 periods, 5%) = 3.546 =	17.73
		$100.00

Entries at purchase date:

Bonds Investment	100	
Cash		100

Interest income—recorded every six months:

Cash	5.00	
Interest Income		5.00

2. Bond Purchased at a Discount

Assume a 2-year, $100 bond, with 10% stated rate, pays semi-annually is purchased at 12%.

Purchase price:	PV of principle ($100, 4 periods, 6%) = .79209 =	$79.21
	PV of interest ($5, 4 periods, 6%) = 3.46511 =	17.33
		$96.54

Beg PV	Discount	Interest Income	Cash Received	Amortization	Carrying Amount of Bond Investment
96.54	3.46	5.79	5.00	.79	97.33
97.33	2.68	5.84	5.00	.84	98.17
98.16	1.84	5.89	5.00	.89	99.06
99.05	0.95	5.94	5.00	.94	100.00
Totals		23.46	20.00	3.46	

Entries at purchase date:

Bond Investment   96.54

Cash   96.54

Interest income (effective interest method) for first 6-month period:

Cash   5.00

Bond Investment   .79

Interest Income   5.79

3. Bond Purchased at a Premium

Assume a 2-year, $100 bond, with 10% stated rate, pays semi-annually is purchased at 8%.

Purchase price: PV of principal ($100, 4 periods, 4%) = .8548 = $ 85.48

PV of interest ($5, 4 periods, 4%) = 3.6299 =   18.15

$103.63

Beg PV	Premium	Interest Income	Cash Received	Amortization	Carrying Value of Bond Investment
103.63	3.63	4.15	5.00	.85	102.78
102.78	2.78	4.11	5.00	.89	101.89
101.89	1.89	4.07	5.00	.93	100.96
100.96	0.96	4.04	5.00	.96	100.00
Totals	16.37		20.00	3.63	

Entries at purchase date:
Bond Investment   103.63

Cash   103.63

Interest income (effective interest method) for first 6-month period:
Cash   5.00

Bond Investment   .85

Interest Income   4.15

H. If there is no evidence of positive ability and intent to hold the bond investment to maturity, the bond investment must be classified as available for sale (AFS) or trading. These classifications require the bond investment to be carried at fair value.

1. A bond investment classified as AFS is reported at fair value with the unrealized gains and losses associated with the changes in fair value recorded as an unrealized holding gain or loss in comprehensive income. The interest income on the bond investment would still be accounted for as described above, but there would be an additional entry to adjust the bond investment to fair value.

2. Using the example above where the bond was purchased at a discount for $96.54, assume that at the end of the first 6-month period the fair value of the bond is $96.00. The interest income entry would be exactly the same as described above, but there would also be an entry to mark the bond investment to fair value using a valuation account for $1.33 ($97.33 − 96.00). The fair value adjustment account is used as a contra or adjunct account to adjust the unamortized value of the bond to fair value.

Fair value adjustment:		
Unrealized holding gain or loss—Equity	1.33	
Fair value adjustment (AFS bond investment)		1.33

3. If the entity intends to sell the bond in the short term, the bond investment would be classified as trading. A bond investment classified as trading is reported at fair value with the unrealized gains and losses associated with the changes in fair value recorded in earnings. The fair value adjustment would be:

Fair value adjustment:		
Unrealized holding gain or loss—Income	1.33	
Fair value adjustment (AFS bond investment)		1.33

No Significant Influence

This lesson covers investments where the investor does not hold significant influence over the investee. How the investor accounts for such an investment depends on the investor's intent with respect to the investment. For accounting purposes, three categories of investments are: (1) held-to-maturity, (2) trading, and (3) available-for-sale.

After studying this lesson you should be able to:

1. *Describe the criteria, accounting, and reporting for investments in debt securities classified as held-to-maturity.*

2. *Describe the accounting for the disposal of held-to-maturity investments at maturity or before maturity.*

3. *Describe the criteria, accounting, and reporting for investments in securities classified as trading.*

4. *Describe the accounting for the disposal of a trading investment.*

5. *Describe the criteria, accounting, and reporting for investments in securities classified as available-for-sale.*

6. *Describe the accounting for the disposal of an available-for-sale investment.*

I. **Overview**

A. The following table presents an overview of the definition, accounting, balance sheet reporting, and treatment of realized and unrealized gains and losses. This lesson discussions the first three investments listed on the table: trading, available-for-sale and held to maturity. Subsequent lessons go into detail on the accounting and reporting of the equity and cost methods.

Category	Definition	How is security reported on the Balance Sheet	How Unrealized Holding Gains and Losses are Recorded	How Realized Gains and Losses are Reported on the Income Statement
Trading [Mark-to-Market]	**Debt and Equity** securities bought and held principally for the purpose of selling them in the near term	Reported at **fair market** value, usually a current assets on the balance sheet	Unrealized gains and losses are included in **earnings** in the period they occur	Unrealized holding gains or losses will **already have been recognized**, and should not be reversed. **Dividends are income.**
Available-For-Sale **[Mark-to-Market]**	**Debt and Equity** securities not classified as trading or held-to-maturity	Reported at **fair market** value, and may be classified as current or noncurrent	Unrealized gains and losses are **excluded from earnings** - reported as OCI--unless the decline is considered to be "other than temporary" then--recognized in earnings	Realized gains and losses are **recognized** (gain or loss will be difference between selling price and carrying value less any permanent decline in value recognized). **Dividends are income.**
Held-to-Maturity **[No market revaluation]**	**Debt securities** that the organization has the **positive intent and ability** to hold to the maturity date	Reported at **amortized cost** and grouped with noncurrent assets on the balance sheet	Unrealized gains and losses are **excluded from earnings**--unless the decline is considered to be "other-than-temporary" or the Fair Value Option is selected	Realized gains and losses are **recognized** in accordance with amortized cost method. **No dividends on debt.**
Securities - Accounted for under the Equity Method	An **Equity** investment whereby the investor has **significant influence** over investee--generally >20% voting shares.	Reported in accordance with the **Equity Method** - if control >50% must consolidate	These securities are **not adjusted** for changes in market value unless the decline is considered to be "other-than-temporary" or the Fair Value Option is selected	Realized gains and losses from transactions are recognized for the difference between selling price and the equity basis of the stock. **Dividends are NOT income.**
Securities - Accounted for under the Cost Method	An **Equity** investment where there is **no significant influence** and it is a security with no readily determinable market value (privately held)	**At cost**. Cost basis is reduced if there is a liquidating dividend where the dividends declared exceed the investee's profits. Dividends and profits are measured from the date the investee was purchased.	There are no unrealized gains and losses because the cost method is not marked-to-market.	Realized gains and losses are **recognized** (gain or loss will be difference between selling price and carrying value less any permanent decline in value recognized). **Dividends are income. WATCH for liquidating dividends!**

II. **Held-to-Maturity Investments --** This classification includes only investments in debt securities that the investor intends to hold until the investment matures and has the ability to do so. This lesson presents the criteria necessary to be classified as Held-to-Maturity and the accounting and financial statement reporting for such investments. Coverage includes recognition of a premium or discount at the time of investment, the amortization of a premium or discount, financial statement presentation, and disposition of Held-to-Maturity investments.

A. **Criteria for this classification**

1. Applies only to investments in **Debt** securities because only debt has a maturity.

2. Applies when investor has:

   a. **Positive** intent to hold the securities to maturity; and

   b. **Ability** to hold the securities to maturity.

3. Held-to-Maturity classification is not appropriate if investor may sell due to need for cash or better investment opportunities, or if the debt can be settled (e.g., prepaid) and the investor would not recover all of the recorded investment.

4. Sale of Debt securities before maturity, that meet the following conditions, can be considered **held-to-maturity**:

   a. Sale is near enough to maturity date so that interest rate risk is substantially eliminated as a factor in pricing;

   b. Sale occurs after investor has collected (through periodic payments or prepayment) a substantial portion (at least 85%) of the principal outstanding at acquisition date.

B. Accounting and Reporting for this Held-to-Maturity classification

1. Record Investment at cost:

   a. Cost includes:

      i. Purchase price (e.g., per security cost);

      ii. Directly related costs incurred - brokerage fee, transfer fee, etc.

2. Carry and Report Held-to-Maturity Investments at Amortized Cost:

   a. Recognize periodic interest income

   > DR: Cash
   >
   > CR:Interest Income
   >
   > Interest Receivable (accrued interest collected on first interest date, if any)

   b. Fair Value Option: Normally, temporary changes in the fair value of investments held-to-maturity should not be recognized; however, GAAP permits an investor to elect the fair value option for most financial assets, including debt investments which the investor intends to hold to maturity.

   c. Report Held-to-Maturity investment in Financial Statements:

      i. Interest Income or Revenue (including increase/decrease from amortization of discount or premium)

      ii. Investment Held-to-Maturity (probably net of premium or discount) in Balance Sheet as:

         1. Current - if maturity is within one year (or operating cycle) of maturity;

         2. Noncurrent - if maturity is **not** within one year (or operating cycle) of maturity.

      iii. Investment Held-to-Maturity in Statement of Cash Flows is an Investing Activity.

III. Trading Investments - Overview -- This classification includes both debt and equity securities. All investments in this classification must be adjusted to fair value at the balance sheet date. The process for making that adjustment, as well as the required financial statement presentation and accounting for disposal (sale) of Held-for-Trading investments, are also presented.

A. Criteria for this classification

1. Applies to investments in both Debt and Equity securities;

2. Investor buys and holds for the purpose of selling in the "near term," generally with the objective of generating profits on short-term price changes.

B. Accounting and Reporting for this Held-for-Trading classification

1. Record Investment at cost.

    a. Cost includes:

    i. Purchase price (e.g., per security cost);

    ii. Directly related costs incurred - brokerage fee, transfer fee, etc.

2. Carry and Report Trading Securities at Fair Value

    a. For Debt Securities:

    i. Recognize periodic interest income.

    b. For Equity Securities:

    i. Recognize Dividends received as income.

    c. For Both Debt and Equity Securities, adjust to Fair Value at Balance Sheet date.

Example:
Determine the appropriate Carrying and Reporting Values for the following data:

Trading Investment	12/31/201X/Value Carrying	Fair	Lower of Carrying or Fair
Co. A	$100,000	$ 80,000	$ 80,000
Co. B	200,000	160,000	160,000
Co. C	50,000	75,000	50,000
Totals	$350,000	$315,000	$290,000

At what net amount should the Trading Investments be shown on 12/31/1X? $_____

Answer: $315,000 Fair Value of the aggregate Trading Investments classification.

What is the net amount of the adjustment necessary to reflect the correct amount at which the Trading Investments should be shown? $_____

Answer:	$35,000	
	Carrying Value	$350,000
	Fair Value	315,000
	Write-down	$ 35,000

C. Disposition (Sale) of Trading Investments:

1. If Debt Security, first recognize Interest Income and Amortization of Premium/Discount to date of sale;

2. Determining carrying value of investments to be sold:

  a. For Debt and Equity Securities = Fair Value

 3. Recognize (realized) gain or loss at date of sale, if any, as difference between sales price and carrying value of investments sold.

IV. Available-for-Sale Investments - Overview -- This classification includes all investments in debt and equity securities that are not classified as Held-to-Maturity or Trading, such as, for example, an equity security that the investor intends to hold indefinitely. This section presents the criteria necessary to be classified as Available-for-Sale and the accounting and financial statement reporting for such investments. Like the prior Trading classification, this classification includes both debt and equity securities. Therefore, the details related to both types of securities are not repeated here. The major difference between this lesson and the prior Trading section is that an unrealized holding gain or loss on an investment Available-for-Sale does not go on the income statement, but enters in the determination of Other Comprehensive Income, and subsequently shows up as (part of) Accumulated Other Comprehensive Income in Shareholders' Equity on the Balance Sheet.

 A. Criteria for this classification

  1. Applies to investments in both Debt and Equity securities.

  2. Includes all investments in Debt and (qualified) Equity securities not classified as Held-to-Maturity or Trading Investments.

 B. Accounting and Reporting for this Available-for-Sale classification

  1. Record Investment at cost

   a. Cost includes:

    i. Purchase price (e.g., per security cost);

    ii. Directly related costs incurred -- brokerage fee, transfer fee, etc.

  2. Carry and Report Securities Available-for-Sale at Fair Value:

   a. For Debt Securities:

    i. Recognize periodic interest income.

    ii. Recognize periodic amortization of Premium or Discount.

   b. For Equity Securities

    i. Recognize Dividends received as Dividend Income.

   c. For both **Debt and Equity Securities** adjust to Fair Value at Balance Sheet date:

    i. Determine Fair Value of Available-for-Sale Investments (of this classification) at balance sheet date (only).

    ii. Determine carrying Value of Available-for-Sale Investments (of this classification) at balance sheet date.

    iii. Adjusting Available-for-Sale Investments to Fair Value

     1. If Fair Value > Carrying Value:

      (a) Recognize (Unrealized) Holding Gain.

      (b) Gain is recording in Other Comprehensive Income.

     2. If Fair Value < Carrying Value:

      (a) Recognize (Unrealized) Holding Loss.

      (b) Loss is recognized in Other Comprehensive Income.

d. Assess Available-for-Sale Investments for Impairment.

   i. The individual securities classified as available for sale are assessed for impairment to determine if a decline in fair value below the amortized cost basis (debt) or cost (equity) is other than temporary using a two-step process:

      1. Determine if the fair value of an investment is less than its (amortized) cost; if so, the investment is impaired.

      2. Determine if the impairment is other than temporary.

   ii. If the investment is impaired and the impairment is other than temporary, an impairment loss equal to the difference between the investment's (amortized) cost and its fair value is recognized in current income as a realized loss.

      1. The fair value becomes the new (amortized) cost basis of the investment.

      2. Subsequent recoveries in fair value would not be recognized.

e. Financial Statement Presentation:

   i. Unrealized Holding Gain/Loss:

      1. Report as an item of Comprehensive Income, which is

      2. Included in Accumulated Other Comprehensive Income in Shareholders' Equity section of Balance Sheet, net of tax effects.

   ii. Available-for-Sale Allowance to Balance Sheet as adjustment to carrying value of Investment:

Available-for-Sale Investments	$200,000
Plus: Allowance to Increase to Fair Value	20,000
Available-for-Sale Investments at Fair Value	$220,000

   iii. Available-for-Sale Investments in Balance Sheet as Current and/or Noncurrent Asset. Available-for-Sale Investments generally will be classified as noncurrent assets, but those investments within one year (or operating cycle) of disposal will be classified as current assets.

   iv. Available-for-Sale Investments in Statement of Cash Flows as Investing Activity.

3. Disposition (Sale) of Available-for-Sale Investments:

a. If Debt Security, first recognize interest income and amortization of Premium/Discount to date of sale.

b. Determine carrying value of investment to be sold:

   i. For Debt and Equity Securities = Fair Value

c. Recognize (Realized) Gain or Loss at date of Sale, if any, as difference between sales price and carrying value of investments sold.

d. Any related unrealized (holding) gain or loss on securities sold that is in Accumulated Other Comprehensive Income at the date of sale is recognized in income.

Cost Method and Transfers Between Classifications

When an investment security is in a privately held company for which there is no market value, the investor may use cost method accounting for this investment. A cost method investment does not change in value unless there is a liquidating dividend. In addition, while holding investments, an investor's original intent or ability to exercise that intent may change and, therefore the classification of the investment, may change. This lesson discusses those issues.

After studying this lesson, you should be able to:

1. *Describe the accounting for a cost method investment.*

2. *Calculate the liquidating dividend for a cost method investment.*

3. *Identify the reasons an investor's intent with respect to his/her investments may change.*

4. *Describe the accounting treatment when reclassification changes occur.*

I. **Cost Method Investments**

A. The cost method of accounting for an equity investment is permitted if the investor cannot exert significant influence over the investee and there is no readily determinable fair value of the investment. In most cases, the cost method would be used because the investee is a privately held company.

B. The cost method requires that the initial investment be recorded at historical cost and is not subsequently adjusted unless there is a liquidating dividend or a permanent decline in value.

   1. The original cost of the investment, (historical cost) is the amount paid for the investment.

   2. Dividends are recorded like normal dividends and dividend income is recognized in earnings.

   3. Once investment is recorded, no further adjustments or changes are required, unless

      a. The fair market value of the investment has a permanent decline in value (such as the investee goes into bankruptcy). A permanent decline in value means that it is unlikely there would ever be a recovery of value. Under such a circumstance, a permanent write-down (or write-off) of the investment is required.

      b. There is a liquidating dividend. A liquidating dividend occurs when the dividends declared by the investee are in excess of the earnings of the investee since the acquisition by the investor. In other words, the investee is returning the capital rather than a dividend. This is an example of a return **of** capital rather than a return **on** capital.

      See the following example.

Example:
Liquidating dividend

Company ABC purchased 15% of the equity of Company XYZ for $500,000 on January 1, 20X1. During 20X1 XYZ Company had $200,000 of earnings and declared and paid $300,000 of dividends. Company XYZ paid more dividends than earnings and there is a $100,000 liquidating dividend ($200,000 - $300,000). Therefore when Company XYZ paid $45,000 ($300,000 x 15%) dividend to ABC, XYZ was distributing the earnings in the form of dividends plus return some of the capital back to ABC. This is a liquidating dividend.

The entry would be as follows:

Cash 45,000 (300,000 × 15%)

      Dividend Income   30,000 (200,000 × 15%)

      Investment in XYZ   15,000 (100,000 × 15%)

After the liquidating dividend the Investment in XYZ would have a balance of $485,000 ($500,000 - $15,000).

II. **Transfers Between Categories - Overview** -- The classification of an investment that gives the investor no significant influence over the investee may change as a result of a change in investor intent or the financial status of the investor. A change in classification requires that the security value be removed from the old classification and the appropriate value be assigned to the new classification. Because the old and new classifications may require different valuations, a gain or a loss may result from the transfer. This lesson presents the requirements necessary to transfer an investment from one classification to another and the appropriate treatment of a resulting gain or loss.

III. **Transfers Between Classifications**

  A. **Transfers result from**

    1. Changes in investor intent—for example, an investment that was initially classified as Held-for-Trading may be changed to Available-for-Sale because the investor now intends to hold the security indefinitely.

    2. Change in investor ability to hold-to-maturity—for example, an investment that was initially classified as Held-to-Maturity may be changed to Held-for-Trading because the investor now intends to sell the security in the near future to raise needed cash.

  B. The general rule is that transfers between classifications are accounted for at fair value (FV) at the date of transfer. That is, the value of the investment in the new category will be at fair value on the date of the transfer. The treatment of any unrealized gains or losses (G/L) is accounted for in accordance with the new classification.

    See the following illustration.

Transfer from → Transfer to ↓	Held-to-maturity	Available-for-sale	Trading
Held-to-maturity	NA	Establish HTM account at FV. Unrealized G/L in AOCI is amortized over remaining life of the debt.	Establish HTM account at FV. Unrealized G/L is recorded in income. very rare
Available-for-sale	Establish AFS account at FV. Unrealized G/L is recorded in AOCI.	NA	Establish AFS account at FV. Unrealized G/L is recorded in income. very rare
Trading	Establish Trading account at FV. Unrealized G/L is recorded in income.	Establish Trading account at FV. Unrealized G/L in AOCI is recorded in income.	NA

IFRS—Investments

This lesson summarizes the accounting for investments under IFRS No. 9 as it applies to investments, a major form of financial asset. The broader topic of accounting for financial instruments under IFRS, including financial liabilities, is covered in a later lesson in the subsection on Financial Instruments.

After studying this lesson, you should be able to :

1. *Describe how investments in each of the new categories are measured and reported.*

2. *Describe when transfers between categories are permitted and how they are treated.*

3. *Describe the new categories of investments and how investments are classified into those new categories under the new standard (IFRS No. 9).*

4. *Describe the conditions that determine whether or not an investment should be derecognized.*

I. **Introduction to IFRS No. 9**

A. **Historical Perspective**

1. In November 2009, the IASB issued IFRS No. 9, "Financial Instruments," to replace, in part, the previous international standard, IAS No. 39, "Financial Instruments: Recognition and Measurement." That November 2009 issuance replaces IAS No. 39 only as it relates to the classification and measurement of financial assets. It also established an effective date of January 1, 2013.

2. In October 2010, the IASB reissued IFRS No. 9 to incorporate new requirements on accounting for financial liabilities and to adopt as carry-over from IAS No. 39 the requirements for derecognition of financial assets and liabilities.

3. In August 2011, the IASB proposed pushing back the effective date of IFRS No. 9 from January 2013 until January 2015. In December, 2011, the IASB formally postponed the effective date of IFRS No. 9 until January, 2015, early adoption is permitted.

B. Between now and 2015 two sets of international standards (IAS No. 39 and IFRS No. 9) may be used in practice to account for investments (and other financial assets and liabilities).

C. We are of the view that it is highly unlikely that the AICPA will test two forms of IFRS and that the most recent standards will be the focus on the CPA exam. We suspect that this will be a lightly tested area until 2015.

D. The following table shows a high level summary of the differences between U.S. GAAP and IFRS.

	U.S. GAAP	IFRS
Classifications	Three classifications: 1. Held-to-Maturity 2. Available-for-Sale 3. Trading	Two classifications: 1. Held-to-Maturity - debt measured at amortized cost 2. Fair Value through profit or loss - debt at FV and all equity at FV
HTM valuation	Effective interest rate based on contractual cash flows and contractual life	Effective interest rate based on estimated cash flow and estimated life
Impairment of debt investment	An impairment loss on debt investment cannot be reversed	An impairment loss on debt investment can be reversed if there is objective evidence
Requirement for classification as HTM	Positive ability and intent to hold to maturity	Business model test - holding the instrument is to collect contractual cash flows Cash flow characteristic test - contractual terms of instrument provide cash flows on specific dates
OCI option	Gains/losses recorded in OCI only for available-for-sale securities. These gains or losses are recycled through profit or loss when the security is sold.	Entity may elect to record gains/losses to OCI at initial recognition of investment. This election is irrevocable and gains or losses are not recycled through profit or loss when sold.
Reclassification of debt instruments	Transfers from HTM when no longer have positive ability and intent	Transfer from HTM only when the business model objective changes
Transfers	Permits transfers into or out of trading classification	Does not permit transfers into/out of trading classification (FV through profit or loss)

II. Categories and Measurement Under IFRS No. 9

A. Categories of Investments

1. IFRS No. 9 establishes two categories of investments (as financial assets) for accounting purposes:

   a. Debt instruments (to be measured) at amortized cost;

   b. All other investments, including debt instruments not measured at amortized cost and all equity instruments and derivative instruments.

2. In order to be classified as a debt instrument at amortized cost, the instrument must not be a derivative debt instrument and meet the following two conditions:

   a. **Business model test --** The objective of the entity (its business model) is to hold the investment to collect the contractual cash flows; its business model is not to sell the instrument prior to its contractual maturity to realize changes in fair value.

   b. **Cash flow characteristic test --** The contractual terms of the investment give rise on specified dates to cash flows that are solely payments of principal and interest on the principal outstanding, where interest is only consideration for the time value of money and credit risk.

3. Investments (and other financial assets) that meet the foregoing conditions (i.e., business model test and cash flow characteristic test) are classified as debt instruments at amortized cost (except as noted in B.1., below); all other investments constitute the other classification.

4. Financial assets that have an embedded derivative instrument (i.e., that includes a derivative within the host instrument) are not separated (bifurcated) into different instruments for accounting purposes. If the host instrument is a financial liability, or a non-financial item, the bifurcation requirements are still required.

5. Classification is made at the time an investment is initially recognized.

B. Measurement of Investments

1. **An investment that meets the conditions of debt instrument at amortized cost** will be measured and reported at amortized cost **unless** conditions warrant the investor electing to measure the investment at fair value with changes in fair value recognized through profit or loss (net income).

   a. The fair value option would be available when its use would eliminate or significantly reduce a measurement or recognition inconsistency that would otherwise result from measuring assets or liabilities, or recognizing the gains or losses on them, on different basis.

   b. These measurement or recognition inconsistencies are sometimes referred to as "accounting mismatches."

2. If a debt instrument measured at amortized cost is sold or disposed of prior to maturity, the gain or loss on disposition must be separately present in the statement of comprehensive income with disclosure of the reasons for the disposal.

3. **All other investments in debt** (i.e., those not measured at amortized cost) must be measured at fair value, with changes in fair value reported through profit or loss (net income).

4. **All investments in equity** are measured and reported at fair value, with changes in fair value reported through profit or loss (net income)(FV-NI), except equity investments that the entity elects to report through other comprehensive income.

   a. Even investments in equity securities with no ready market must be reported at fair value; there is no cost method alternative as there is under U.S. GAAP. Cost, however, can be the best estimate of fair value.

   b. If the investor does not hold an equity investment for trading purposes, it may elect to report changes in fair value through other comprehensive income (FV-OCI).

      i. The election must be made when the investment is first recognized and is irrevocable;

      ii. Amounts recognized though other comprehensive income will never be reclassified to profit or loss (net income), even on disposal or impairment, but will remain in equity (e.g., transferred to retained earnings);

      iii. Dividends from these investments would be recognized in net income.

      iv. This category is analogous to the U.S. GAAP category "available-for-sale."

C. Transfers Between Classifications Under IFRS No. 9

1. Because there are only two categories of investments under IFRS No. 9, the only possible transfers are for debt instruments (there is no "amortized cost" for equity instruments); they are:

   a. From debt at amortized cost to fair value with changes recognized through profit/loss, or

   b. From fair value with changes recognized through profit/loss to debt at amortized cost.

2. The transfer between categories for investments in debt can be made only when the investor's business model objective for debt investments changes so that the (previous) category no longer applies.

    a. Such transfers, if appropriate, are treated prospectively in financial statements effective the first day of the first reporting period following the change in business model.

    b. Restatement of previously recognized gains/losses or interest income is not permitted.

    c. Transfers between classifications (reclassification) is not permitted based on changes in the characteristics of the instrument (e.g., the conversion option on an investment in convertible bonds lapses/expires).

3. A transfer between categories is not possible for investments in equity because equity investments have no amortized cost to enable that classification.

III. Derecognition of Investments

A. Derecognition of an investment (or other financial asset) is concerned with determining whether the investment or an element thereof (e.g., cash flows from an investment) should be written off.

B. Basically, an investment (or element thereof) should be written off when:

1. The investment asset (or an element thereof) has been transferred, and

2. Substantially all of the risks and rewards of ownership have been transferred.

C. An investment is considered transferred if either:

1. The entity has transferred the contractual rights to receive the cash flows associated with the investment, or

2. The entity has retained the contractual rights to receive the cash flows associated with the investment, but has concurrently assumed a contractual obligation to transfer those cash flows to another party under an arrangement that meets the following three conditions:

    a. The entity has no obligation to pay amounts to the eventual recipient unless it collects equivalent amounts on the original asset (investment), and

    b. The entity is prohibited from selling or pledging the original asset (other than as security to the eventual recipient), and

    c. The entity has an obligation to remit those cash flows without material delay.

D. Whether a transferred investment should be written off, depends on whether the transferring entity has relinquished substantially all of the risks and rewards of ownership.

1. If substantially all the risks and rewards of ownership have been transferred, the transferred investment should be written off.

2. If substantially all the risks and rewards of ownership have been retained, the transferred investment should not be written off.

3. If substantially all the risks and rewards of ownership have been neither transferred nor retained, treatment depends on whether control of the investment has been relinquished.

    a. If the entity no longer controls the investment, it should be written off.

    b. If the entity has retained control of the investment, it should not be written off.

IV. Disclosures Under IFRS No. 9 -- Basic disclosures required for investments (as financial assets) are set forth in a separate IFRS (No. 7), "Financial Instruments: Disclosures." Those requirements, which apply to all financial instruments, are not covered here. The most significant changes to those disclosure requirements (i.e., of IFRS No. 7) that are contained in IFRS No. 9 are presented here.

   A. Equity Investments at Fair Value Reported through Other Comprehensive Income (OCI) -- When equity investments are measured at fair value and reported through other comprehensive income (OCI), the entity must disclose:

   1. Identification of the investments that have been designated to be measured at fair value with changes in fair value reported through OCI and the reasons for choosing the OCI alternative for those investments;

   2. The fair value of each such investment at period end;

   3. Dividends recognized during the period on those equity investments, showing separately the amounts for investments held at the period end and those that were disposed of during the period;

   4. Transfers during the period from accumulated OCI to retained earnings and the reasons for those transfers;

   5. For equity investments reported through OCI that are disposed of (derecognized) during the period:

      a. The reasons for disposal;

      b. The fair value at the date of disposal;

      c. The gain or loss on disposal.

   B. Reclassifications Due To Changes in Business Model -- When an entity reclassifies investments between categories due to changes in its business model, it must disclose:

   1. The date and amount of each reclassification by category;

   2. A detailed explanation of the underlying change in business model and a qualitative description of the effects on the financial statements;

   3. If the reclassification is from fair value measurement to amortized cost measurement, it must disclose:

      a. For the period of reclassification, the fair value of the reclassified investments as of the end of the period and the gain or loss that would have been recognized during the period if reclassification had not occurred;

      b. For the remaining life of the investment, the effective interest rate at the date of reclassification and interest income recognized during each period.

   C. Gains or Losses on Sale of Investments Measured at Amortized Cost -- If debt instruments measured at amortized cost are sold or disposed of prior to maturity, any gain or loss must be recognized separately on the face of the financial statements.

   D. Additional disclosures are required when IFRS No. 9 is applied for the first time.

Equity Method

When an investment in equity securities gives the investor significant influence (but not control) over the investee, the investor must carry and report that investment using the full equity method of accounting. The only exception is if the investor elects the fair value option and chooses to report the investment at fair value. This lesson describes the application of the equity method of accounting.

After studying this lesson, you should be able to :

1. *Describe and illustrate the entries made by an investor using the equity method, including the impact on the investment account and the income recognized from the investee.*

2. *Describe the accounting when all or part of an equity method investment is disposed of.*

3. *Describe special disclosures required when the equity method is used.*

I. Equity Method - Overview -- The common accounting applied to an investment with >20% equity ownership (significant influence or control) is the equity method of accounting. The equity method requires the investor to periodically adjust the carrying value of the investment to (1) reflect changes in the investee's shareholders' equity (e.g., net income/loss dividends, etc.) and (2) recognize the effects of any difference between the cost of the investment assignable to the fair value of investee's amortizable assets and the book value of those assets (i.e., FV does not equal BV).

> **Note:**
> The investor can elect to record an equity ownership in an investee >20% but <50% at fair value and in some circumstances at cost. This lesson focuses on Equity Method accounting.

II. Investments Requiring the Equity Method -- The kinds of investments requiring the use of the equity method are:

A. Investments in voting equity securities; not non-voting equity or debt securities.

B. With sufficient ownership to give significant influence or control over the operating and financial policies of the investee.

> **Note:**
> This is a very popular topic on the CPA exam. Study time dedicated to this area will pay off!

1. Significant influence is presumed if there is 20% - 50% ownership of voting stock. Control is presumed when there is >50% ownership of voting stock. Although the Parent company will use equity method to account for the investment in its subsidiary, the Parent will consolidate the subsidiary for financial reporting purposes.

   a. Indicators of significant influence when ownership is <20%.

      i. Has representation on board of directors

      ii. Participates in investee policy making

      iii. Has material intercompany transaction

      iv. Is technologically interdependent with investee

      v. No other single investor has a material voting ownership of investee

2. Special indicators that the investor will **not** have significant influence and will use **Fair Value**:

   a. Investee opposes investment;

    b. Standstill agreement between investor-investee; this mean that the investor cannot acquire more stock or other attempts to exert significant influence;

    c. Significant influence or control is exercised by others; for example

        i. Investor A owns 35% of the voting stock, but Investor B owns the other 65% (has control) and does not cooperate with Investor A.

        ii. Investee is in bankruptcy or legal reorganization and under the control of the courts;

        iii. Investee is a foreign entity that operates under foreign government restrictions that preclude exercise of significant influence.

    d. Investor lacks information for use of equity method (very rare).

    e. Investor cannot obtain representation on investee Board of Directors.

C. If prior ownership with no significant influence is followed by additional purchase of equity shares resulting in significant influence, then:

    1. Switch from fair value to equity method; obtaining significant influence and therefore switching to equity method accounting is accounted for **retroactively;**

    2. Adjust investment and income (prior period adjustment) to what they would have been if equity method had been used from initial purchase.

III. Recording Initial Investment -- The initial investment in securities to be accounted for using the equity method will be recorded at cost.

A. Cost includes:

    1. Purchase price of the equity securities (e.g., price per share);

    2. Other directly related costs incurred in the acquisition (e.g., brokerage commission, transfer fee, etc.).

B. Entry:

DR: Equity Investment - Co. A
CR: Cash (or other consideration)

C. At the time of the initial investment, the investor must also:

    1. Determine book value (BV) of assets/liabilities of investee at date of investment;

    2. Determine fair value (FV) of assets/liabilities of investee at date of investment;

    3. Allocate any difference between cost of investment and book value of net assets of the investee to:

        a. FV of identifiable assets/liabilities, then any excess balance to

        b. Goodwill (or to gain if Cost < FV).

D. Subsequent to recording an investment that gives the investor significant influence over the investee, the investor must carry the investment on its books and report the investment in financial statements using either the Equity method or, at its option, using Fair Value (as provided by ASC 825).

E. Acquiring significant equity interest decomposing the purchase price

    1. It is assumed that the acquisition is considered an arms-length transaction negotiated by two independent parties. All **direct costs** related to the purchase are expensed because they are not considered an attribute of the acquiree. Direct costs are finder's fees, audit

fees, legal fees related to the acquisition. Direct costs are NOT costs to finance the acquisition, such as cost of borrowing or the fees to register the acquiring company's stock.

a. Combine **income statements** from the **date** of combination.

b. **Assets and liabilities** of the company acquired (the acquiree) are valued at **fair market value**.

c. The fair market value of the consideration transferred less the net fair market value of the identifiable assets acquired and liabilities assumed is **goodwill**. Complete a decomposition of the consideration transferred as shown below.

Fair value of the Business as a whole (Bus FMV) –

typically equals consideration transferred (Purchase Price (PP))

Unidentifiable intangible asset
(Goodwill)

Net Fair Market Value of assets acquired and liabilities assumed(FMV of Net assets)

Identifiable assets revalued to FMV
(tangible and intangible)

Net Book Value of assets acquired and liabilities

IV. **Summary of Equity Method** -- The affects of the equity method on an investor's investment (asset) and investment revenue are summarized in the following two T-accounts:

Note:
Dividends are NOT income.

A. Investment Account

(Equity) Investment in Investee X (on Balance Sheet)	
Original cost of Investment	
Pro rata share of investee's income since acquisition	Pro rata share of investee's losses since acquisition
Amortization of book value in excess of cost (i.e., on amounts allocated to write down nonfinancial assets)	Amortization of cost in excess of book value (i.e., on amounts allocated to identifiable assets, but not Goodwill)
Retroactive adjustment due to change from Fair Value to equity method (DR or CR)	Pro rata share of investee's dividends declared
	Impairment losses
	Disposal of investee stock (write off)

B. Equity Revenue Account

<table>
<tr><td colspan="2" align="center"><u>Investment (Equity) Income, Investee X (on Income Statement)</u></td></tr>
<tr>
<td>Pro rata share of investee's losses since acquisition</td>
<td>Pro rata share of investee's income since acquisition</td>
</tr>
<tr>
<td>Amortization of cost in excess of book value (i.e., on amounts to identifiable assets, but not Goodwill)</td>
<td>Amortization of book value in excess of cost (i.e., on amounts allocated to write down non-financial assets)</td>
</tr>
</table>

V. Equity Method Accounting

A. This section identifies and illustrates the basic steps in applying the equity method of accounting, including how the investor entity (1) recognizes its share of investee's net income or loss, (2) recognizes its share of investee's dividends, and (3) determines and accounts for any difference between the cost of its investment in the investee and the book value of the investee's net assets it acquired. The application of these steps (the equity method) affects both the investor's investment account (in the investee) and the revenue recognized from the investee by the investor. A chart is provided that summarizes the effects of the equity method on each of these accounts (investment and equity revenue).

VI. Equity Method Entries -- Under the equity method, the investor will recognize on its books and report in its financial statements changes in the investment (from original cost) to reflect the changing value of the investee's equity accounts. These changes include:

A. Investee Results of Operation (income/loss) - to be recognized by the investor when reported by the investee:

1. Investor recognizes (picks-up on its books) its proportionate share of investee's reported income/loss, excluding its share of any intercompany profits/losses in assets (e.g., in inventory, etc.).

   a. Entry (assuming investee has net income):

   > DR: Investment in Investee X
   >
   >   CR: Investment (equity) Income

   b. Entry (assuming investee has net loss):

   > DR: Investment (equity) Loss
   >
   >   CR: Investment in Investee X

2. If investee has outstanding cumulative preferred stock, any accrued dividends on that stock must be deducted (whether paid or not) before computing the common equity investor's share of reported net income/loss.

3. If investee reports prior period adjustment, investor picks-up its proportionate share as such (i.e., in investor's Retained Earnings).

4. If investee losses reduce the investment to zero, investor should discontinue applying the equity method unless investee's imminent return to profitability is assured.

5. If Investor elects to use the fair value method to measure and report an investment that otherwise would be accounted for using the equity method, the investors does NOT recognize its share of the investee's results of operation (or the effects of differences

between the cost of the investment and its fair value at acquisition; see D, below). The investee's results of operation are assumed to be reflected in the change in fair value of the investment (which is recognized in net income).

B. Investee Items of Other Comprehensive Income (OCI) -- If the investee reports changes to equity resulting from items of other comprehensive income, the investor recognizes (picks-up) its proportionate share of those items when reported by the investee.

   1. Items of other comprehensive income that might change equity would include:

      a. Unrealized gains/losses on available-for-sale securities;

      b. Foreign currency items;

      c. Pension and post retirement benefit items not recognized in period cost;

   2. Entry (assuming OCI items increased equity):

> DR: Investment in Investee X
>
>   CR: Other Comprehensive Income (to Accumulated OCI in equity)

C. Investee Dividends

   1. Investor recognizes (picks-up) its proportionate share of investee dividends as a reduction in its investment in the investee.

   2. For example, if the investee paid a cash dividend the investor entry would be:

> DR: Dividends Receivable/Cash
>
>   CR: Investment in Investee X

   3. If Investor elects to use the fair value method to measure and report an investment that otherwise would be accounted for using the equity method, the investors DOES recognize its share of the investee's cash dividends paid. Those cash dividends are considered income for the period to the investor.

> **Note:**
> Dividends under the equity method are "automatically" treated as liquidating (i.e., liquidating part of the investment).

D. Investee Book Value (BV) does not equal Investment Cost/Fair Value -- If the cost of investment to the investor and the fair value of the investee's assets/liabilities is different from the investee's book value at the date of investment, the investor will recognize periodic adjustment(s) to its investment account (and to the investment revenue account).

   1. Differences between the cost of the investment and the book value of the net assets to which the investment gives the investor a claim may be due to:

      a. Identifiable assets/liabilities carrying values on the books of the investee being different than the fair value of those assets/liabilities at the date of the investment.

      b. Goodwill being paid for by the investor.

   2. Investor adjustment - assuming the cost of investment exceeds the book value of the investment at the date of investment. (Note: See 5., below for when the book value > cost of investment.)

   3. Cost of investment > BV of net assets acquired (i.e., book value of investor's share of investee net assets);

   4. Investor makes entry for "depreciation" or "amortization" on its share of fair value in excess of book value as it relates to identifiable depreciable or amortizable assets; but **no** amortization of Goodwill.

    a. Entry: (assuming FV of depreciable assets > BV of those assets)

> DR: Investment (equity) Income
>
>   CR: Investment in Investee X

    b. Investor does not DR: "Expense," but reduces the amount of income picked-up from the investee, and reduces the carrying amount of the investment.

5. Investor adjustment - assuming the cost of investment is less than the book value of the investment at the date of investment (i.e., a bargain purchase).

    a. Allocate **any** difference to **FV of identifiable assets/liabilities** (e.g., reduce overvalued identifiable assets and/or increase undervalued liabilities), with any balance recognized as a gain in **earnings** in the period of investment.

    b. "Negative goodwill" is **not** recognized (as a deferred charge) and amortized.

6. If Investor elects to use the fair value method to measure and report an investment that otherwise would be accounted for using the equity method, the investors does NOT recognize the effects of any differences between the cost of the investment and its fair value at acquisition (or its share of operating results). Any difference between the cost of the investment and its fair value at acquisition is assumed to be reflected in the change in fair value of the investment (which is recognized in net income).

VII. Equity Method Revenue Recognized from Investment

A. The amount is recognized as

1. Investment (equity) Income/Loss (one amount).

VIII. Sale of Equity Method Investment -- Upon sale of all or part of an investment accounted for using the equity method, the following would apply:

A. Update investment and investment revenue accounts to date of sale by recording:

1. Share of investee income/loss to date of sale.

2. Depreciation/amortization on cost > BV (or BV > cost) to date of sale.

B. Gain/Loss on sale is the difference between selling price (SP) and book (carrying) value (BV) of the investment sold.

1. If SP > BV = Realize gain.

2. If SP < BV = Realize loss.

C. If sale is not for entire investment and results in the investor losing significant influence over the investee (e.g., < 20% ownership), the remaining investment should be accounted for at fair value with any difference between the carrying amount of remaining investment and its fair value recognized as a gain or loss in current income.

IX. Equity Method Disclosures -- When the equity method is used to report investments in common stock, the following disclosures are appropriate:

A. The name of each equity method investee and the percentage of ownership.

B. The name of any investee in which the investor own 20% or more (but not more than 50%) of the voting stock that is not accounted for using the equity method and the reason for that treatment.

C. The name of any investee in which the investor owns less than 20% of the voting stock that is accounted for using the equity method and the reason for that treatment.

D. Any difference between the carrying amount of the investment and the investor's share of the underlying claim to net assets and how that difference is treated.

E. When a bargain purchase gain is recognized, the amount of the gain recognized, the line item where the gain is recognized and a description of the transaction that resulted in the gain.

F. When there is a quoted market price for the common stock, the market value of each investment.

G. When the equity method is used for investments in corporate joint ventures that are material to the investor, summary information about the assets, liabilities and results of operation of those joint venture investees.

H. Possible effects of conversion or exercise of outstanding securities (e.g., options, convertible securities, etc.) on the investor's ownership claim.

IFRS—Equity Method

This lesson describes the U.S. GAAP/ IFRS differences in the application of the equity method of accounting.

After studying this lesson, you should be able to:

1. *Identify certain differences between the use of the equity method under U.S. GAAP and under IFRS.*

I. **Summary of Differences** -- Below is a summary of the differences in US GAAP and IFRS with respect to equity method accounting. Each of these differences are discussed more fully in this lesson.

U.S. GAAP	IFRS
No special term for investee	Investees are referred to as "associates"
Can apply fair value option to equity investee	Only certain investors (venture capitalists, mutual funds or unit trusts) can apply fair value option
No requirement for accounting policies to conform	Uniform accounting policies must be applied
It is encouraged to have reporting dates for investor and investee to be within 3 months	Reporting dates for investor and associate cannot be more than 3 months
Not required to adjust for significant transactions in the 3 month window	Required to adjust for significant transactions in the 3 month window
Can recognize investee losses if imminent return to profit is assured	Do not recognize losses
Impairment loss is measured as the carrying value less the fair value	Impairment loss is measured as the carrying value less the recoverable amount
Apply equity method until investment is sold	If investment is to be sold adjust to lower of fair value or carrying amount and reclassify as held-for-sale

II. **U.S. GAAP - IFRS Differences**

A. **Fair Value Option** -- Both U.S. GAAP and IFRS permit the use of the fair value option to measure investments which give the investor significant influence over an investee; however, the entities which may elect the fair value option are more limited under IFRS.

1. Under U.S. GAAP, any investor that has significant influence over an investee and would otherwise use the equity method of accounting may elect to carry and report the investment at fair value.

2. Under IFRS only certain types of investors that have significant influence over an investee and would otherwise use the equity method may elect to carry and report the investment at fair value.

   a. Under IFRS, an entity over which an investor has significant influence is called an "associate;" thus, the account would be "Investment in Associate."

   b. Only the following types of investors may elect to carry and report investments in associates using fair value:

      i. Venture capital organizations - private equity investment firms;

      ii. Mutual funds - an investment company offering a managed open-end portfolio of securities;

      iii. Unit trusts - an investment company offering a fixed (unmanaged) portfolio of securities with a fixed life.

B. Accounting Policies -- Under U.S. GAAP, the accounting policies used by an investee accounted for using the equity method do not have to conform to the accounting policies of the investor, as long as the investee accounting policies comply with U.S. GAAP. Under IFRS, in using the equity method the investor must apply uniform accounting policies to the investor and investee accounting for similar transactions and events

C. Like U.S. GAAP, IFRS presumes an investor that holds between 20% and 50% of the voting stock of an investee can exercise significant influence, unless there is evidence otherwise, and requires the use of the equity method for those investments.

    1. IFRS uses the term "associates" to refer to investees over which the investor has significant influence.

    2. The effects on the investment account and on the equity revenue account generally would be the same under IFRS as under U.S. GAAP, with these significant exceptions:

        a. Under IFRS, entities may have "Reserve" accounts, which don't exist under U.S. GAAP.

        b. Under IFRS, changes in reserve accounts of the associate (investee) are recognized by the investor under the equity method.

D. Under IFRS, the reporting dates (period ends) of the investor and its associates cannot be different by more than three months. Further, any significant transactions that occur during the up-to-three-month period must be adjusted to the accounts in recognizing the equity method effects. Under U.S. GAAP, the difference between reporting dates of the investor and investee should not be more than three months, but adjustments for significant transactions that occur during the intervening period do not have to be made to the investee accounts in applying the equity method. The entity may make adjustments for such a transaction, but it is only required to disclose such effects.

E. Under U.S. GAAP, when investee losses exceed the investor's investment, but imminent return to profitable operations by the investee appears assured, the investor may continue to recognize its share of investee losses (even if it has not guaranteed obligations of the investee or committed to provide further financial support). Under IFRS, when investee losses exceed the investor's investment, the investor should discontinue recognizing its share of investee losses even if the associate's (investee's) future profitability appears imminent and assured. However, if the investor has obligations or commitments to make payments on behalf of the associate, it may continue to recognize its share of losses to the extent of those obligations.

F. Under U.S. GAAP, if an investor determines that a decrease in the fair value of an equity investment is other than temporary, an impairment loss is measured as the excess of the carrying amount of the investment **over the fair value**. Under IFRS, if an investor determines that an equity investment is impaired, the impairment loss is measured as the excess of the carrying amount of the investment **over the recoverable amount**.

G. Under IFRS, if an equity method investment is to be sold, the investment is reported at the lower of (1) its fair value less cost to sell, or (2) the carrying amount as of the date the investment is classified as held-for-sale. Under U.S. GAAP, an investor continues to account for an equity method investment that is to be sold using the equity method of accounting until it loses significant influence over the investee.

Joint Ventures

Prior lessons have addressed accounting for investments in debt and equity securities for which there is a ready market. Because investments in joint ventures are not traded in a ready market, if at all, such investments are not covered in the prior lessons. This lesson covers accounting for and reporting of investments in joint ventures.

After studying this lesson, you should be able to:

1. *Define and Describe joint ventures.*

2. *Describe and illustrate accounting for joint ventures.*

3. *Identify how accounting for joint ventures under IFRS differs from accounting under U.S. GAAP.*

I. **Definition and Description** -- A comprehensive and generally accepted definition of a joint venture, particularly for accounting purposes, does not exist. Nonetheless, the following working definition incorporates the major, accepted characteristics of a joint venture.

> **Definition:**
> *Joint Venture*: An association of two or more entities that exercise joint control over an undertaking for profit generally set up for a limited purpose, a limited time, or both.

A. **Description**

1. The association created by a joint venture may be established by agreement or contract alone, or may take the form of a legal entity. For example, the joint venture may be formalized as a partnership, a corporation, or other business form (e.g., undivided interest entity).

2. Whatever the form, joint control by two or more investors is central to a joint venture association, generally with no single party having unilateral control. Usually, there are few investors/owners; often there are only two investors/owners. The joint venture agreement will specify how management will be shared, the responsibilities of the parties, and how the outcomes of the venture, including profits and losses, will be shared between or among the parties.

II. **Joint Venture Accounting**

A. **Introduction** -- Formal accounting for investments in joint ventures is specified only for corporate joint ventures - a joint venture organized as a separate corporation with the parties to the joint venture owning the equity of the separate corporation. The equity of the separately established corporation is not traded in any market, and certainly does not have a ready market. This fact separates the accounting for investments in joint ventures from the accounting for investments in debt and equity securities as described in prior lessons. Conventions derived from standards used for other entities are used in accounting for non-corporate joint ventures (e.g., partnerships).

B. **Accounting at Formation** -- An investor records its contribution of assets to a joint venture as an investment at the carrying value of the assets on its books at the time of contribution.

1. **Corporate Joint Venture Example** – See the following example.

> **Example:**
> **Facts:** Jay, Inc. and Vee, Inc. enter into an agreement to establish JV, Inc., a corporate joint venture. Each party will contribute cash and land or equipment to the venture. Jay contributes $50,000 cash and land with a carrying value of $25,000 and a fair value of $30,000.
>
> DR: Investment in JV, Inc., Joint Venture $75,000
>
>   CR:Cash $50,000
>
>   Land   25,000

2. **Partnership Joint Venture** -- When the joint venture is formed as a partnership, accounting by the investor/partner for contributions to form the joint venture would be the same as for a corporation, except that it would be recorded as Investment in JV Partnership, Joint Venture.

C. **Accounting Subsequent to Formation** -- Following the formation of a joint venture, the accounting by the investor will depend on the form of the joint venture (e.g., corporation or partnership) and, if a corporation, the relationship between the investor and the joint venture investee.

  1. **Corporate Joint Ventures** -- How an investor accounts for and reports its investment in the common stock of a corporate joint venture will be determined first by whether the joint venture entity is a variable interest entity (VIE) or not.

    a. If the joint venture is determined to be a variable interest entity and the investor determines that it is the primary beneficiary, the investor will consolidate the joint venture (because, as the primary beneficiary, it has effective control even though it does not hold a controlling equity interest).

    b. If the joint venture is not a variable interest entity (or the investor is not the primary beneficiary, if it is a VIE), the investor accounts for and reports its investment in the corporate joint venture using the equity method of accounting (because, generally, all investors in a joint venture can exercise at least significant influence).

    c. If, in a rare case, a single investor is able to unilaterally control a corporate joint venture that is not a VIE, that controlling investor would consolidate the joint venture.

  2. **Partnership Joint Ventures** -- An investor/partner in a joint venture in the form of a partnership would account for its investment as would any partner, with adjustments (equity method-like) for any intercompany items.

    a. Any intercompany profits/losses included in the assets resulting from transactions between the investor/partner and the partnership would be eliminated.

    b. The investment account of the investor would be increased (decreased) for the investor's share of joint venture profits (losses), after eliminating intercompany items, if any.

    c. The investment account of the investor would be decreased for distributions received from the partnership joint venture.

III. **IFRS - U.S. GAAP Differences** -- IFRS coverage of joint ventures is somewhat more extensive than U.S. GAAP coverage and provides an alternative reporting treatment (proportionate consolidation) generally not permitted by U.S. GAAP.

A. **IFRS Definition and Description** -- IFRS defines a joint venture as "a contractual agreement whereby two or more parties undertake an economic activity that is subject to joint control." IFRS distinguishes two types of joint arrangements:

1. **Joint venture** -- wherein the joint venture activity is carried out through a separate entity (corporation/company or partnership);

2. **Joint operation** -- wherein each party to the joint arrangement has rights to the separate assets and obligations relating to the arrangement; no separate entity is formed;

B. IFRS Accounting for Joint Arrangements

1. **Joint Venture – Use equity method** -- This method follows the conventional equity method (i.e., a one-line consolidation).

2. **Proportionate Consolidation Method** -- Under this method, the investor recognizes in its financial statements it share of the assets, liabilities, revenues (income) and expenses of the joint operation. These items and amounts may be recognized in one of two ways:

   a. Combined on a line-by-line basis with similar items in the investor's financial statements.

3. Reported as separate line items in the investor's financial statements; for example, separate line items for "Plant and Equipment" (of the investor) and "Interest in Plant and Equipment of Joint Operation."

Investor Stock Dividends, Splits, and Rights

As a result of holding an investment in equity securities, an investor may receive a stock dividend, a stock split ,or a stock right.

After studying this lesson, you should be able to:

1. *Describe each of these issues.*

2. *Summarize the appropriate accounting treatment for each.*

I. **Introduction** -- An investor who has an equity investment in another entity may receive a dividend on that stock, have the stock split, or hold a right to acquire other securities. This lesson describes each of these possibilities and summarizes the accounting treatment from the perspective of the investor - the recipient of the dividend, split or right.

II. **Stock Dividends Received by Investor**

   A. Investor receives additional shares of investee stock as dividend.

   B. Investor adjusts only **per share** (not total) cost (carrying value) of investment.

 Example:

Investment Carrying Value (Under Cost or Equity method) $100,000

Original number of shares = 1,000

Per share cost (carrying value) = $100,000/1,000 = $100

Stock Dividend of 10% received = 100 shares received

New Per Share Cost (Carrying Value) = $100,000/1,100 shares = $90.90 per share

---

   C. Upon subsequent sale (in part or total) write off shares at new per share **cost** (carrying value).

III. **Stock Split Received by Investor**

   A. Investor receives additional shares of investee stock in conjunction with investee decrease in par or stated value per share. In a reverse stock split the investor exchanges shares held for few shares of the investee in conjunction with investee increasing par or stated value per share.

   B. In either a stock split or a reverse stock split, the investor adjusts only per share (not total) cost (carrying value) of investment.

   C. Calculation/Treatment is the same as for Stock Dividend.

IV. **Stock Rights Received by Investor**

   A. Investor receives privilege (right) to purchase additional shares of investee at specific (option) price within a specific time; usually evidenced by a certificate called a stock warrant.

   1. If option price < market price, the stock right has a value.

   2. The value of the right is determined by allocating cost (carrying value) of investment between the shares of stock and stock rights based on relative fair market value.

3. Two alternative possibilities exist for determining the amount of the investment to be allocated to the stock rights:

   a. The per share market value of the rights is known/given (illustrated in B., below), or

   b. The per share market value of the rights is not known/given; the **theoretical** per share market value of the rights must be computed (illustrated in C., below).

B. **Market Value of Rights Known/Given** - Determine **cost** (carrying value) of stock rights (per right) assuming per share market value (MV) is given as follows:

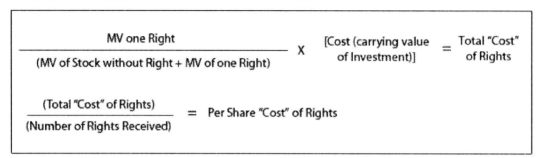

$$\frac{\text{MV one Right}}{(\text{MV of Stock without Right} + \text{MV of one Right})} \times [\text{Cost (carrying value of Investment)}] = \frac{\text{Total "Cost"}}{\text{of Rights}}$$

$$\frac{(\text{Total "Cost" of Rights})}{(\text{Number of Rights Received})} = \text{Per Share "Cost" of Rights}$$

C. **Market Value of Rights *not* Known/Given** - Determine theoretical market value of stock rights (per right) as follows:

1. Market Value (MV) of stock quoted **without value of right** (ex-right):

   (MV one Share of Stock w/o Right − Options Price w/Right) / Number of Rights to Buy One Share = Theoretical MV per right

2. Market Value (MV) of stock quoted **with right** (rights - on):

   (MV one Share of Stock w/Right − Option Price w/Right) / (Number of Rights to Buy One Share Plus (+) 1) = Theoretical MV per right

D. **Transfer share of investment carrying value between stock and (now) rights –** (assuming investment classified as Available-for-Sale)

   DR: X Securities Stock Rights – Available-for-Sale

      CR: Available-for-Sale Investment – X Securities

E. **Stock rights are equity securities --** Therefore, they must be classified as Trading- or Available-for-Sale and accounted for/reported as such.

F. **Disposition of stock rights**

1. **If sold** -- write off stock rights and recognize gain/loss.

2. Entry (assume gain):

   DR: Cash

      CR:X Securities Stock Rights Available-for-Sale

         Gain on Sale of Stock Rights

3. **If exercised** -- write off stock rights as (part of) cost of investment in securities purchased with the rights.

4. Entry:

> DR: Available-for-Sale Investment – X Securities
>
>   CR:X Securities Stock Rights – Available-for-Sale
>
>   Cash

5. **If allowed to lapse** -- write off stock rights and recognize loss.

6. Entry:

> DR: Loss on Expiration of Stock Rights
>
>   CR:X Securities Stock Rights Available-for-Sale

V. U.S. GAAP - IFRS Differences -- There are no significant differences between U.S. GAAP and IFRS in the treatment of stock dividends, stock splits and stock rights by the investor.

IFRS—Investment Property

Investment property is a separate category of investments under IFRS; there is not a comparable separate category under U.S. GAAP. This lesson summarizes the nature of and accounting for investment property under provisions of IFRS.

After studying this lesson, you should be able to:

1. *Define and describe what constitutes investment property.*

2. *Explain how investment property is measured and reported.*

3. *Identify the conditions under which property can be transferred into and out of the investment property category.*

4. *Describe the accounting for disposal of investment property.*

5. *Describe the special **disclosure requirements for investment property.***

I. **Introduction** -- A separate category of investments for "investment property" exists under IFRS standard, IAS 40, but not under U.S. GAAP. Assets that constitute investment property under IFRS likely would be included with the category "property, plant, and equipment" under U.S. GAAP. Further, unlike U.S. GAAP, which requires property, plant, and equipment to be measured and reported at cost, IFRS permits the use of either cost or fair value to measure and report the nonfinancial asset "investment property."

II. **Definition and Description of Investment Property**

   A. Investment property is property that consists of land, a building or part of a building, or both land and building, held by an owner, or lessee under a finance (capital) lease, for the purpose of earning rent, for capital appreciation, or for both rental income and capital appreciation.

   B. Examples of Investment Property - Investment property would include the following:

   1. Land held for long-term capital appreciation;

   2. Land held for undetermined future use;

   3. Building leased out under an operating lease;

   4. Vacant building held for leasing out under an operating lease;

   5. Property (land or building) that is being developed or constructed for future use as investment property.

   C. Examples of Property that would not be Investment Property - Investment property would not include the following:

   1. Property (i.e., land or building) held for use in production or supply of goods or services, or for administrative purposes;

   2. Property held for sale in the ordinary course of business or in the process of development or construction for such sale (i.e., land or building inventory);

   3. Property being developed or constructed on behalf of another party;

   4. Owner-occupied property, including property held for future use by the owner or employees and owner-occupied property awaiting disposal;

   5. Property leased to another entity under a finance (capital) lease.

   D. Property interest held by a lessee under an operating lease may be classified and accounted for as investment property provided the following conditions are satisfied:

1. The definition of investment property is otherwise met;

2. The operating lease is accounted for as if it were a finance (capital) lease;

3. The lessee measures the leased asset at fair value.

E. When an owner uses part of a property and the other part is held for rental or capital appreciation, if the parts can be sold or leased out separately they should be accounted for separately. Thus, the qualified part rented to others would be investment property and the owner-used part would not be. If the parts cannot be separately sold or rented, the property would not be investment property unless the part used by the owner is insignificant.

F. If services are provided in connection with the occupancy of a property and those services are relatively insignificant to the arrangement (e.g., cleaning or security), the owner may still treat the property as investment property.

G. Property rented or leased between a parent and its consolidated subsidiaries would not be investment property because at the consolidated level the property would be owner-occupied.

III. Measurement of Investment Property

A. Measurement at Recognition -- Investment property is initially measured at cost, including direct cost of acquisition (e.g., legal fees, transfer taxes, etc.). Direct cost does not included:

1. Start-up cost, including abnormal waste;

2. Initial operating losses.

B. Measurement Subsequent to Initial Recognition

1. An entity may elect to measure its investment property subsequent to acquisition using either:

   a. Fair value method (or model), or

   b. Cost method (or model).

2. Only one method - fair value or cost - must be used for all of an entity's investment property.

3. **Fair Value Measurement**

   a. Fair value is the price that would be received to sell an asset or paid to transfer a liability in an orderly transaction between market participants at the measurement date (IFRS No. 13);

   b. Fair value is determined as of each balance sheet date, and the asset adjusted to the new fair value;

   c. Gains or losses resulting from changes in fair value are reported in net profit or net loss (net income) of the period in which fair value changes;

   d. Example entry: Assume the fair value of land held as investment property increases during the period. The period-end entry would be:

DR: Land
CR: Unrealized gain on investment property

   e. Investment property measured at fair value should continue to be measured at fair value, even if market prices become less readily available.

4. **Cost Measurement**

   a. Under the cost method, investment property continues to be carried and reported at cost. However, fair value is required to be disclosed;

     b. If the property is depreciable, depreciation expense and accumulated depreciation are recognized;

     c. Investment property carried at cost is assessed for impairment and, if impaired, a loss and accumulated impairment are recognized.

   5. Changing from one method of measuring all investment property to another method is permitted only if it will result in a more relevant presentation. The Standard, IAS 40, states that it is highly unlikely to be the case for a change from fair value measurement to cost measurement.

IV. Transfers Into and Out Of Investment Property

  A. A transfer to or from the investment property classification would be made only when there is a change in use of the property as evidenced by the following kinds of events:

   1. Owner occupies property previously classified as investment property;

   2. Owner ceases to occupy property that otherwise meets the criteria of investment property;

   3. Property classified as investment property is readied for sale;

   4. Property is leased to another party under an operating lease.

  B. Transfers to or from investment property would be accounted for as follows:

   1. Transfers from investment property measured at fair value to owner-occupied property or inventory (e.g., land for sale) - fair value at the date of change is the amount at which the new category is recorded (i.e., its "cost").

   2. Transfers from owner-occupied property to investment property measured at fair value - difference between carrying amount of the property and its fair value should be treated as a revaluation under IAS No. 16.

     a. Revaluations adjust carrying value to approximate fair value at the balance sheet date;

     b. Increases in value are recognized in other comprehensive income and show up in the statement of financial position (balance sheet) as accumulated revaluation surplus;

     c. Decreases (that exceed prior increases) are recognized as an expense.

   3. Transfers from property inventory to investment property are measured at fair value with any difference between the prior carrying amount and fair value recognized in profit or loss (net income).

   4. Transfers to or from investment property measured at cost do not change the carrying amount of the property. Thus, for example, the cost and accumulated depreciation on property transferred to investment property from property, plant and equipment (or vice versa) would carry over to the new classification.

V. Disposal of Investment Property

  A. When investment property is disposed of (e.g., sold) or when it becomes worthless, it will be written off (derecognized).

  B. A gain or loss on disposal is the difference between proceeds received on disposal, if any, and the carrying amount written off.

  C. Any gain or loss on disposal will be recognized as income or expense in the income statement.

VI. Disclosures for Investment Property -- A number of specific disclosures for investment property are required. Some disclosures are required regardless of whether the fair value method or the cost method is used; other disclosures are specific to each method. The most important disclosures are identified here.

A. **Disclosures under either fair value or cost methods**

1. Whether fair value measurement or cost measurement is used;

2. If classification of property as investment property was difficult to make, the criteria used to distinguish property as investment property;

3. The amounts recognized in profit or loss related to investment property from:

   a. Rental income;

   b. Direct operating expenses, separately for investment property that generated rental income and investment property that did not.

4. Contractual obligations related to investment property (e.g., to develop, for repairs, for maintenance, etc.) ;

5. A reconciliation showing causes of the changes in the carrying amounts of investment property between the beginning and end of the period.

VII. Additional Disclosures Under the Fair Value Method

A. The methods and assumptions used in determining the fair value of investment property;

B. Whether or not fair value assigned to investment property is based on valuation made by a qualified independent valuer and, if so, the extent of that valuation and any adjustments thereto.

VIII. Additional Disclosures Under the Cost Method

A. The depreciation method used;

B. The useful life or depreciation rates used;

C. The gross carrying amount (cost) and accumulated depreciation and accumulated impairment losses at the beginning and end of the period;

D. The fair value of investment property or, at least, the range of estimates within which fair value falls.

Impairment of Debt and Equity Securities

This lesson presents the criteria for potential impairment of an investment in a debt or equity security. In general, an investment is potentially impaired if the fair value is less than the cost basis. There are different factors to consider if the investment is an equity security versus a debt security. However, both require an assessment of whether the impairment is other-than-temporary. This lesson presents how those impairment losses are recorded if the impairment is other-than-temporary. Once an impairment loss is recognized in earnings, the impairment loss cannot be recovered.

After studying this lesson you should be able to :

1. *Identify when losses associated with debt securities are recognized in earnings versus recognized in OCI.*

2. *Describe what is meant by other-than-temporary-impairment (OTTI).*

3. *State how impairment losses are measured for both debt and equity securities.*

I. All investments, including debt and equity securities should be tested for impairment annually or when factors indicate. In general, an investment is potentially impaired if the fair value is less than the cost basis. Application of impairment testing and the accounting for the decline in value is different for debt and equity investments. The first section discusses impairment for equity securities and the second section discusses impairment for debt securities.

II. **Equity Securities**

A. **Trading securities --** Trading securities are carried at fair value with changes in fair value recording in earnings. Therefore, any impairment in value is already recognized and no impairment testing is necessary.

B. **Available-for-sale securities (AFS) --** AFS securities are carried at fair value with the changes in fair value recorded in other comprehensive income. If the decline in the fair value of the AFS security is considered other-than-temporary, then the unrealized gains and losses in accumulated other comprehensive income (AOCI) should be transferred out of AOCI and recognized in earnings. Listed below are the two key factors to consider in the determination of whether the decline in value associated with the security is a loss other-than-temporary-impairment (OTTI):

1. Whether the security will recover in value. Taking into consideration:

   a. Length of time and extent to which the fair value has been less than cost;

   b. The financial condition of the issuer and the near term prospects of recovery.

2. Whether the investor has positive ability and intent to hold the security until recovery could occur.

C. If neither of the above factors indicate a recovery of the losses associated with the AFS security, then the losses in AOCI are reclassified to earnings and the AFS security is written down the fair value and that fair value becomes its new cost basis. All future considerations of impairment are based on the new cost basis. Recovery of the impairment loss is not allowed.

D. What is meant by other-than-temporary-impairment (OTTI)? The FASB purposefully uses the term OTTI and not the term "permanent." A decline in value need not be permanent – it would be very difficult to determine if a decline is permanent. The decline in value needs to meet the threshold of "not temporary" – which means there is no recovery anticipated in the foreseeable future and the entity has the ability to hold the security until there is a recovery in value.

E. Cost method investments -- Cost method investments do not have a readily determinable fair value. Therefore annual impairment testing is not required. However, if fair value is determined for a cost method investment for other purposes – then the entity must complete an impairment test. If a fair value measurement is not made for other purposes the entity must still complete an impairment test when factors indicate that there may be impairment. If the impairment is OTTI, the cost method investment is written down and a loss is recognized in earnings.

III. Debt Securities

A. If the fair value of the debt security is below the cost, you must evaluate whether the impairment is other-than-temporary. The decline in value is considered other-than-temporary if any of the following exist:

1. The holder has the intent to sell the impaired debt security.

    a. Recognized the OTTI in earnings. The impairment loss is the difference between the amortized cost and the fair value of the debt security.

2. It is more likely than not that the holder will be required to sell the impaired debt security before they can recover the amortized cost basis (i.e., the holder's need for cash for operations or other investment purposes will likely require that they sell the impaired debt security).

    a. Recognized the OTTI in earnings. The impairment loss is the difference between the amortized cost and the fair value of the debt security.

3. The holder does not expect to recover the entire amortized cost basis of the debt security, regardless of whether they intend to sell the security.

    a. Recognized in earnings the portion of the OTTI that is associated with credit losses.

    b. Recognize in OCI the portion of the OTTI that is associated with other factors.

B. Recovery of impairment losses is prohibited.

IV. Disclosure Requirements
-- There are significant disclosure requirements associated with impairment losses. The following items are required to be disclosed.

A. For each major security disclose the methodology and significant inputs to determine fair value and the measurement of credit losses.

B. Present the amounts recognized in earnings and in OCI.

Introduction to Intangible Assets

This lesson provides information on the accounting for intangible assets.

After studying this lesson, you should be able to:

1. *Define an intangible asset.*

2. *Identify the difference between a definite life and indefinite life intangible asset.*

3. *Describe how to test for impairment of definite life and indefinite life intangible assets.*

I. Introduction

Definition:
Intangible Assets: Long-term operational assets that lack physical substance or presence, but are currently used in the operation of a business and have a useful life extending more than one year from the balance sheet date.

A. Intangibles are similar to plant assets except that they lack physical substance. Many intangibles are legal rights. ASC 350 governs the accounting for intangibles by (1) dividing intangibles into definite or indefinite life intangibles, and (2) requiring that all intangibles be evaluated for impairment.

B. Sources of Intangibles -- Intangibles are either **acquired** from other parties or **internally developed**.

1. An acquired intangible is separately recognized in the accounts if either (1) the benefit of the asset is obtained through contractual or other legal rights (as in a patent), or (2) if the intangible is otherwise separable, i.e. can be sold, transferred, licensed, rented, or exchanged regardless of the acquirer's intent to do so.

2. Internally developed intangibles (such as organization costs) are expensed immediately if they are not specifically identifiable, have indeterminate values, or are inherent in a continuing business and related to the entity as a whole. Firms routinely expense the amount of internal expenditures devoted to the development of intangibles, most notably for patents, Research and Development (R & D), and goodwill. The only costs related to internally developed intangibles that are capitalized are registration fees and legal costs paid to outsiders.

C. Classification

1. Intangibles are **classified** as:

   a. Definite life intangibles (all of these are identifiable); or

   b. Indefinite life intangibles (further subdivided into identifiable intangibles and goodwill).

2. An intangible has a **definite** life either if the asset has a finite legal life or if the firm believes the useful life is finite. The useful life for amortization is set by economic factors (market and obsolescence) as well as by its legal life.

3. An intangible has an **indefinite** life if no legal, regulatory, contractual, competitive, or other factor limits the life. Indefinite means there is no foreseeable limit on the period of time over which the intangible is expected to provide cash flows. A renewable and very recognizable trademark is an example.

4. *Only definite life intangibles are amortized.* For example, some licenses and franchises that are renewable or even perpetual are not amortized because their benefits are indefinite in duration and no means exists to determine the useful life.

> **Example:**
> A city providing a perpetual license to run a ferry across a body of water.
> The same logic holds for land - this asset also has an indefinite life and is not depreciated, so this is not a new concept. Only now that concept is being applied to intangibles.

5. However, if an intangible has an indefinite legal life (e.g. trademark) but management believes that the asset has a finite life, then the asset is treated as a definite life intangible.

6. All intangibles are subject to impairment.

D. Summary Table

1. **FV** = fair value or market value;

2. **BV** = book value;

3. **R** = recoverable cost (nominal sum of net cash inflows over remaining life - the same value computed for plant asset - this is not a present value).

Definite Life Intangibles

Capitalize	Amortization	Impairment
External costs*	Over useful life	Same as assets in use
	Usually no residual value	Impairment if BV > R
	Usually SL method	Impairment Loss = BV − FV
*see below		

Indefinite Life Intangibles Other than Goodwill

Capitalize	Amortization	Impairment
External costs*	Do not amortize	Same as assets held for sale
		Impairment if BV > FV
		Impairment loss = BV − FV

Goodwill (also has indefinite life)

Capitalize	Amortization	Impairment
Price of firm acquired	Do not amortize	2 steps—see text
less fair value of net assets of firm acquired		

* External costs in the summary table above include amounts paid for registration, legal and accounting fees, outside design costs, consulting fees, successful legal defense costs, and also the cost of direct purchases of intangibles from others.
Costs of internally developed intangibles including salaries of employees working on patents, materials used, and overhead are expensed as incurred.

E. Amortization

1. Amortization of definite life intangibles is recorded just like depreciation expense. The debit is to an expense account such as amortization expense or selling, general and administrative expense (SG&A) for intangibles devoted to nonmanufacturing activities, and the debit is to work in process (and ultimately cost of goods sold) for manufacturing intangibles. The credit is usually made directly to the intangible rather than to a contra account.

Example:
DR: Amortization of copyright (SG&A) xx

CR: Copyright   xx

2. The straight-line method is typically used to compute amortization.

F. Residual Value -- For amortized intangibles, residual value is assumed to be zero unless:

1. The useful life to the firm is less than legal or economic life,

2. Another entity could obtain some benefit from the asset after the first firm was finished with it, AND

3. There is reliable evidence as to its amount (which would consist of a market for the asset at that time or a commitment from another firm to purchase the asset at end of its useful life).

G. Useful Life -- For amortized intangibles, if an asset is valuable only when it is used with other assets, the useful life of the other assets in the group can be a factor in setting useful life. For example, if a number of patents are used for one combined purpose, and the patents do not have any usefulness apart from the group, then the shortest useful life of the assets in the group sets the useful life for them all.

H. Changes in Classification -- If an amortized (definite life) intangible is later deemed to have an indefinite life, then amortization ceases. An impairment might result because fair value would now be used to test for impairment rather than recoverable cost.

I. Separate Recognition -- Many intangibles must be separately identified: trademarks and trade names, non-competition agreements, customer lists, order or production backlogs, copyrights and patents, secret formulas and processes, licensing agreements, and supply contracts. A major reason for identifying these is that intangibles with definite life are amortized. To include them in goodwill in an acquisition would mean they would not be amortized.

J. Types of Intangibles

1. **Marketing-related --** Trademarks, Internet domain names, non-competition agreements.

   a. Some of these items are indefinite life intangibles. Indefinite life intangibles include trademarks because they are renewable every 10 years indefinitely.

2. **Customer-related --** Customer lists, contractual relationships with customers.

   a. These are definite life intangibles because they could not have benefit periods of indefinite or unlimited life.

3. **Artistic-related --** Copyrights (these are not renewable).

   a. Definite life.

4. **Contract-related --** Franchises, licensing agreements, broadcast rights, service/supply contracts

    a. Some of these are definite life intangibles, and some are indefinite life intangibles (as in the case of a perpetual franchise or one that is renewable indefinitely).

5. **Technology-related** -- Patents (both product and process type) that have a 20-year life and give the holder the exclusive right to use, manufacture, or sell a product or process. Capitalize successful legal defense costs.

    a. These are definite life intangibles and although small modifications can lead to a new patent that effectively extends the life of the old (the BV of the old is added to the new), the new patent is still considered to have a definite life.

6. **Goodwill** -- Arises only from a business combination in which the fair market value of the entity purchased exceeds the fair market value of the entity's identifiable net assets (assets - liabilities). (More on goodwill in the next lesson!)

    a. Indefinite life and tested for impairment annually.

K. Revaluation of Book Value -- From time to time, the rights associated with an intangible asset must be legally defended. For example, a company might have a patent on a unique product. If a competitor infringes on the rights represented by the patent and manufactures a similar product, the company holding the patent might elect to defend those rights through legal action. Accounting for the legal costs of this action is dependent on the outcome of the legal action.

L. Successful Legal Defense -- If the rights associated with the intangible asset are successfully defended, the economic benefits associated with the intangible asset have been enhanced. Therefore, the related legal costs are recorded as an increase in the capitalized value of the intangible asset.

Example:
A firm owns a patent with a total capitalized cost of $45,000. At the beginning of the current year, the patent has been amortized four years of a total estimated nine year useful life. During the current year, the firm won a patent infringement suit concerning its patent. Legal costs amounted to $15,000. The legal costs are added to the book value of the patent. The book value at the beginning of the current year plus the $15,000 legal costs are amortized over the remaining five years of the patent's life.

Book value of patent at beginning of current year = $45,000 - $45,000(4/9) = $25,000

M. Unsuccessful Legal Defense -- If the rights associated with the intangible asset are unsuccessfully defended, the economic benefits associated with the intangible asset have likely been decreased to zero. Therefore, the related legal costs are recorded as legal expenses of the period incurred. In addition, the intangible is written off as a loss.

N. Impairment Test of Intangibles -- The procedure to test for impairment of an intangible asset is the same as for plant assets in use. The recoverable cost (R) of the intangible, the sum of net cash inflows attributable to using the asset, is compared to the BV of the intangible (cost less accumulated amortization). If R is less than BV then the asset is impaired and the asset is written down to FV (fair value). The impairment loss equals BV - FV. Subsequent amortization proceeds based on the new BV.

O. Impairment Test of Indefinite Life Intangibles Other than Goodwill

1. The procedure to test for impairment is the same as for plant assets held for sale. The FV is used to test for impairment AND measure the loss. An asset is impaired if BV exceeds FV.

2. Impairment losses cannot be reversed for either definite life or indefinite life intangibles. This aspect is not the same as for plant assets held for sale which can be written up to the extent of previous impairment losses.

Note:
Recoverable cost is not used to test for impairment for indefinite life intangibles because it could be argued that an indefinite life intangible could have recoverable costs given the potential for indefinite life.

II. Deferred Charges

A. Deferred charges are accounts that are difficult to classify. A variety of practice exists for these accounts. They should not be included in intangibles but are often listed close to intangibles in the balance sheet and are sometimes confused with intangibles.

B. Examples of Deferred Charges are listed below.

1. Long-Term Prepaid Insurance;

2. Long-Term Prepaid Rent;

3. Machinery Rearrangement Costs - Related to an assembly line for a manufacturing concern, the costs of an efficiency study. These costs are typically amortized over five to ten years;

4. Deferred Income Taxes - When transactions in the current or past periods give rise to future deductible temporary differences (which reduce future taxable income relative to future pretax accounting income), a deferred tax asset is created. Coverage of this topic is significantly expanded in a subsequent lesson;

5. Deferred bond issue costs - the costs of issuing bonds is recorded in a deferred charge and amortized over the term of the bonds.

III. Cash Surrender Value of Life Insurance

A. Firms that carry whole life insurance policies on key employees enjoy an annual increase in the investment portion of the policy. Cash surrender value is appropriately classified as an investment account but may be reported by some firms in Other Assets in the balance sheet.

Example:
The annual premium on a life insurance policy for a corporate executive is $800. In the third year, cash surrender value begins accumulation, at $200. Entry for third year premium:

Insurance Expense	600	
Cash Surrender Value of Life Insurance	200	
Cash		800

In subsequent years, the cash surrender value portion of the premium increases. The fourth year might be $300, for example. At the end of the fourth year, the balance in cash surrender value then would be $500.

Goodwill

This lesson provides information on the accounting for goodwill.

After studying this lesson, you should be able to :

1. *Describe how goodwill is created and initially measured.*

2. *Complete the steps to test for and measure goodwill impairment.*

I. Introduction

> **Definition:**
> *Goodwill*: The result of a business combination that is measured as the difference between the fair market value of the acquired company as a whole (the acquiree) and the fair market value of the identifiable net assets (assets - liabilities). The fair market value of the acquiree as a whole is often greater than the fair market value of the identifiable net assets. Goodwill is the excess of the fair market value of the entity as a whole over the fair market value of its identifiable assets.

B. Goodwill is the only intangible asset that is not identifiable. Goodwill is attributable to many different factors such as reputation, management skills, location, customer loyalty, etc. Goodwill is the value of the acquiree that cannot be attributable to specific identifiable tangible or intangible assets, or liabilities. Goodwill has an indefinite life because the going concern concept assumes that, in the absence of evidence to the contrary, the combined entity (acquirer and acquiree) will continue indefinitely.

C. Goodwill is recognized only when a buyer firm (the acquirer) obtains control of another enterprise. If a firm has never acquired another enterprise, then that firm would not have goodwill listed in its balance sheet.

D. In recording the acquisition of another business enterprise, the fair market value of the acquiree is compared to the fair market value of net identifiable asset of the acquiree. Any **excess** of entity fair value over fair value of identifiable assets is goodwill.

See the following example.

Example:
1. 100% ownership of Acquiree

Assume ABC Company acquired 100% of XYZ Company for $200,000, which is the FMV of XYZ as a whole. At the time of the acquisition, XYZ's net assets had a book value of $100,000.

The fair market value of the net identifiable assets of XYZ is $160,000, which means that XYZ has net assets with a fair market value greater than their book value.

In the acquisition of the XYZ Company, the ABC Company paid $40,000 for goodwill ($200,000 − $160,000), as illustrated in the model below.

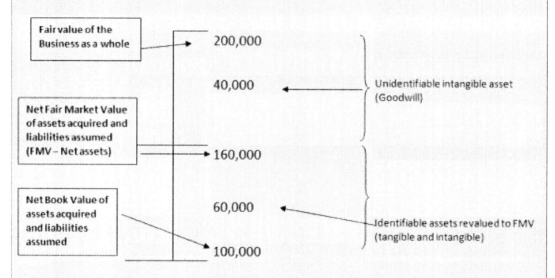

2. Now assume that ABC Company acquired 75% of XYZ Company for $150,000 and that the total value of the remaining 25% is $50,000. The diagram below depicts that the total goodwill is still $40,000, but goodwill is allocated between the controlling interest (acquirer ABC) and the noncontrolling interest (NCI). ABC Company, the controlling interest, is allocated $30,000 and the NCI is allocated the remaining 25%, or $10,000.

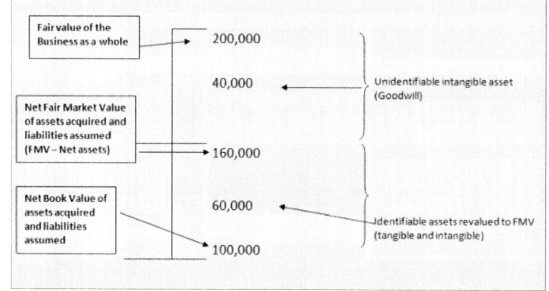

E. With reference to determining the **fair market value of net identifiable assets**, there are two notable points:

1. The use of the term "**net**" implies that all liabilities assumed in the acquisition have been subtracted from all assets acquired in the acquisition.

2. The use of the term "**identifiable assets**" implies that all identifiable assets are included, both tangible (such as property, plant, and equipment) and intangible (such as patents), including those that have a definite life and those that have an indefinite life.

F. Recoded goodwill remains on the books of the acquirer unless the acquiree is sold or the goodwill becomes impaired (as described in IV. below).

G. **Goodwill represents** an expectation on the part of the acquiring business enterprise that, because of synergies, there will be above normal earnings in the years immediately following the acquisition. If the acquiring company had created a new business, it would have had to develop a client base, reputation, and other favorable intangible characteristics. In acquiring an existing business enterprise, the acquiring company pays for the established client or customer base, the established business reputation, and other intangible characteristics.

H. **Goodwill Costs** -- Subsequent to acquisition, the costs to maintain, enhance, or repair purchased goodwill are expensed. The acquirer understandably wishes to maximize the return on its investment and often spends considerable sums to integrate the acquiree operations into its (acquirer's) operations. All such expenditures are expensed. They are not added to the recorded purchased goodwill.

IV. **Internally Developed Goodwill** -- Internally developed goodwill exists for most business entities. However, due to conservatism and objectivity/verifiability, internally developed goodwill is not recognized as an asset in the accounting records of a business entity. Internally developed goodwill cannot easily be measured or verified. This is a major reason that only purchased goodwill, resulting from an arm's length transaction, is recognized for accounting purposes.

V. **Bargain Purchases** -- Occasionally a firm acquires another enterprise for a price less than the fair value of the acquiree's net assets. This situation is referred to as a bargain purchase. The amount by which the fair value of the acquiree's net assets exceeds the price paid is recognized by the acquirer in the period of the acquisition as ordinary income.

> **Note:** A full description of the determination of goodwill and a bargain purchase amount resulting from a business combination is covered in the later lesson "Recognizing/Measuring Goodwill or Bargain Purchase Amount" as part of the Business Combination topic.

VI. **Goodwill Impairment**

A. **Goodwill**, like all indefinite life intangibles, **must be tested for impairment at least annually** or when certain circumstances indicate that its carrying value may be greater than its fair value (**called an impairment**).

1. When goodwill is recognized, it must be allocated to a reporting unit. A reporting unit is a component of an operating segment for which discrete financial information is available and regularly used by management for decision-making purposes.

2. Goodwill impairment testing must be done at the reporting unit level or one level below the reporting unit.

> **Note:**
> The CPA Exam typically does not ask the candidate to identify reporting units, but to know that goodwill is tested at the reporting unit level.

3. Prior to December 2011, a strictly quantitative two-step assessment was required to determine whether goodwill was impaired and, if so, the amount of any impairment.

4. **Effective for fiscal years beginning after December 15, 2011,** an entity may elect to use a qualitative assessment of whether impairment is likely to have occurred as a basis for determining if the quantitative two-step assessment is required. This qualitative assessment is often referred to as a "prestep."

a. The ability to use a qualitative assessment about the likelihood of goodwill impairment is intended to reduce the complexity and costs associated with assessing goodwill for impairment.

b. **Only if the qualitative assessment determines that is it more likely than not that an impairment has occurred, is the subsequent complex and costly two-step assessment required**.

c. The qualitative assessment (before the quantitative assessment) is optional; however, if the qualitative assessment indicates that the fair value of the reporting unit is more likely than not below the carrying value of the reporting unit, then the quantitative assessment is required. If the qualitative "prestep" is not completed, the entity must complete the quantitative two-step assessment.

B. Qualitative Assessment (prestep)

1. An entity is permitted, and may elect, to begin its determination of whether goodwill is impaired by performing a qualitative assessment.

2. The purpose of the qualitative assessment is to determine if it is more likely than not (i.e., a likelihood of more than 50%) that the fair value of the reporting unit with which the goodwill is associated has declined below the carrying value of that reporting unit, including its goodwill.

3. In evaluating whether it is more likely than not that the fair value of a reporting unit is less than its carrying value, an entity should consider all relevant events and circumstances, including:

   a. microeconomic conditions such as deterioration in general economic conditions, limited access to capital, fluctuation in exchange rates, or other adverse events in equity and credit markets;

   b. industry and market conditions such as deterioration in the industry environment, increased competition, decline in market-dependent multiples, change in the market for the entity's products or services, or a regulatory or political development;

   c. cost factors such as increases in raw materials, labor, or other costs that have a negative effect on earnings and cash flows;

   d. overall financial performance such as negative cash flows or actual or projected declines in revenues, earnings, or cash flows;

   e. entity-specific events such as changes in management, key personnel, strategy, or customers; contemplation of bankruptcy; or litigation;

   f. factors affecting a reporting unit such as changes in composition or carrying amount of its net assets, anticipation of selling or disposing all, or a portion, of a reporting unit, or recognition of goodwill impairment loss by a subsidiary that is a component of a reporting unit and

   g. if the reporting unit is publicly traded, a sustained decrease in share price (considered both in absolute terms and relative to the peer group).

4. **Qualitative Assessment Outcomes**

   a. After assessing the totality of the above kinds of events and circumstances, an entity determines that it **is not** more likely than not that the fair value of the reporting unit is less than its carrying value, then the quantitative steps of the goodwill impairment test **are unnecessary**.

   b. After assessing the totality of the above kinds of events and circumstances, an entity determines that it **IS** more likely than not that the fair value of the reporting unit is less than its carrying value, then the first step of the two-step quantitative assessment **must be performed**.

C. Quantitative Assessment—Step 1: Testing for Potential Impairment

1. If the qualitative assessment determines that it is more likely than not that the fair value of the reporting unit is less than its carrying value, then a quantitative assessment must be performed.

2. The first quantitative step used to identify potential goodwill impairment compares the fair value of a reporting unit with its carrying amount, including any deferred income taxes and previously recognized goodwill.

3. If the carrying amount of the reporting unit is greater than zero and its fair value exceeds that carrying amount, goodwill of the reporting unit is considered not impaired and the second quantitative step of the impairment test is not required.

4. If the carrying amount of the reporting units is greater than its fair value, the second quantitative step of the impairment test is required to measure the amount of the goodwill impairment loss.

Example:

Facts: Assume Firm A acquires firm B for $400 million when B's net identifiable assets have a fair value of $300 million. Subsequent to the acquisition, Firm B is considered a reporting unit. As a consequence of the acquisition, Firm A will recognize $100 million in goodwill, determined as cost of investment (fair value of B) $400 million − fair value of identifiable assets $300 million = $100 million goodwill.

One year later, as a result of its qualitative assessment, Firm A cannot rule out the possibility that the goodwill recognized when it acquired Firm B is impaired.

Example #1: No Potential Impairment

In carrying out step 1 of its quantitative assessment, Firm A determines that the fair value of Firm B, as a unit, is $420 million and that the carrying value of its investment in Firm B is $410 million. Since the fair value ($420 million) is greater than the carrying value ($410), there is no potential impairment and step 2 of the quantitative assessment is not required.

Example #2: Potential Impairment

Assume in carrying out step 1 of its quantitative assessment, Firm A determines that the fair value of Firm B, as a unit, is $340 million and that the carrying value of its investment in Firm B is $380 million. Since the fair value ($340 million) is less than the carrying value ($380), goodwill is potentially impaired and step 2 of the quantitative assessment is required to measure the impairment loss, if any.

D. Quantitative Assessment—Step 2: Measuring Impairment

1. When the first step of the quantitative assessment indicates the potential that goodwill is impaired, then this second quantitative step is required to measure the goodwill impairment.

2. Goodwill impairment is measured by comparing the (current) implied fair value of a reporting unit's goodwill with the carrying amount of that goodwill.

   a. The implied fair value of the goodwill is determined by assigning fair value to all of the assets and liabilities of a reporting unit, including any intangible assets, and comparing that net fair value with the fair value of the reporting unit as a whole.

   b. The excess of the fair value of a reporting unit over the fair value amounts assigned to its net assets is the implied goodwill of the reporting unit.

   c. The assignment of fair values to assets and liabilities, including any previously unrecognized intangible assets, is used only for the purpose of measuring goodwill impairment; those assigned values are not used to change the recorded values of recognized assets or liabilities, or to recognize any previously unrecognized assets or liabilities, including intangible assets.

3. If the carrying amount of goodwill exceeds the implied fair value of that goodwill, an impairment loss is recognized for the amount of the excess.

    a. The amount of loss recognized cannot exceed the carrying amount of the goodwill.

    b. After the impairment loss is recognized, the adjusted carrying amount is the new accounting basis for goodwill.

    c. Subsequent reversal of a goodwill impairment loss is not permitted.

 Example:
Assume the facts in Example 2 above, specifically:

Firm A acquires firm B for $400 million when B's net identifiable assets have a fair value of $300 million. Subsequent to the acquisition, Firm B is considered a reporting unit. As a consequence of the acquisition, Firm A will recognize $100 million in goodwill, determined as cost of investment (fair value of B) $400 million − fair value of identifiable assets $300 million = $100 million goodwill.

One year later, as a result of its qualitative assessment, Firm A cannot rule out the possibility that the goodwill recognized when it acquired Firm B is impaired. Therefore, it carries out a quantitative assessment.

In carrying out step 1 of its quantitative assessment, Firm A determines that the fair value of Firm B as a unit is $340 million and that the carrying value of its investment in Firm B is $380 million. Since the fair value ($340 million) is less than the carrying value ($380), goodwill is potentially impaired and step 2 of the quantitative assessment is required to measure the impairment loss, if any.

Step 2: The fair value of Firm B's identifiable net assets is determined to be $280 million.

Implied goodwill = Fair value of Firm B as a unit, $340,000 million − Fair value of Firm B's identifiable net assets, $280,000 million = $60 million implied goodwill.

Impairment loss = Carrying amount of goodwill $100 million - Implied value of current goodwill $60 million = $40 million impairment loss

Impairment Entry:

DR: Impairment Loss − Goodwill $40 million

    CR: Goodwill $40 million

E. Reporting Unit Book Value = Zero or Negative

1. If the carrying amount of a reporting unit is zero or negative, the second quantitative step must be performed to measure the amount of impairment loss, if any, when it is more likely than not that a goodwill impairment exists.

2. In evaluating whether it is more likely than not that the goodwill of a reporting unit with zero or negative book value is impaired, an entity should take into account:

    a. the events and circumstances described previously (IV. B.),

    b. whether there are significant differences between the carrying amount and the estimated fair values of its assets and liabilities, and

    c. the possible existence of significant unrecognized intangible assets.

VII. Goodwill Impairment Test Flowchart -- The following flowchart summarizes the required steps in carrying out the testing of goodwill for impairment.

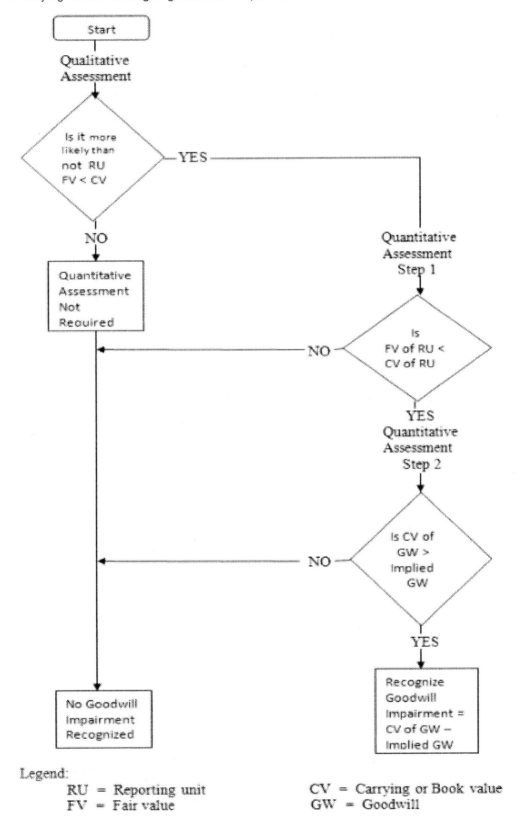

Legend:

RU = Reporting unit	CV = Carrying or Book value
FV = Fair value	GW = Goodwill

Intangibles and IFRS

This lesson presents the significant differences in the accounting for intangibles under IFRS and U.S. GAAP.

After studying this lesson you should be able to :

1. *Identify the major differences in the accounting for intangibles under IFRS and U.S. GAAP.*

I. Intangibles and IFRS

A. IFRS defines intangible asset as "an identifiable nonmonetary asset without physical substance." This definition has three key characteristic. (The definition and characteristics are very similar to U.S. GAAP.) The asset:

1. is controlled by the entity and the entity expects to derive future economic benefits;

2. lacks physical substance;

3. is identifiable to be distinguished from goodwill.

B. IFRS allows the intangible assets to be revalued to fair market value if there is an active market for the intangible asset. If the intangible is valued at fair value, the entire class of of intangible assets must be valued this way, not just select individual intangible assets. U.S. GAAP does not allow this.

C. IFRS allows reversal of impairment losses on intangible assets to the carrying value that would have been recognized had the impairment not occurred.

D. The method and amortization method of the intangible asset should be reviewed each annual reporting period. There is no requirement in U.S. GAAP that requires a review of the amortization method or life.

Intangible Assets	
IFRS	**U.S. GAAP**
Intangibles can be revalued to fair value if there is an active market	Revaluation to fair value is not permitted
Reversal of impairment loss is permitted	Reversal of impairment loss is not allowed
Estimated useful life and amortization method reviewed annually	Estimated useful life and amortization method reviewed when events or circumstances change

II. Goodwill and IFRS

A. IFRS IAS 36 requires goodwill impairment testing to use a single step quantitative test that is performed at the cash-generating unit (or group of cash-generating units). A company is likely to have more cash-generating units than reporting units. Therefore, more "buckets" of goodwill will be tested under IFRS than under U.S. GAAP within a given entity.

B. The test must be performed at least annually or whenever there is evidence that an impairment may have occurred. IFRS requires a one step impairment test. The carrying value of the cash-generating unit is compared to its recoverable amount. The impairment loss is the excess of the carrying amount of the cash-generating unit over the recoverable amount. The calculated value of the impairment loss reduces goodwill to zero. If there is additional value associated with the impairment loss, it is allocated to the other assets of the unit pro rata based on the carrying amount of each asset in the group. The unit is not reduced below the highest amount of its fair value less cost to sell, its value in use, or zero.

C. IFRS for small and medium-sized companies require goodwill to be amortized over the estimated useful life. If an estimate useful life is not reliably determinable, the goodwill should be assigned a life of 10 years.

D. Although other types of impairment loss are reversible under IFRS, goodwill impairment loss cannot be reversed. The IFRS believes that any subsequent increase in goodwill is more likely to be internally generated goodwill rather than a reversal of the impairment of the purchased goodwill. The IFRS (and U.S. GAAP) prohibit recording internally generated goodwill - therefore, goodwill impairment cannot be reversed.

Intangible Assets	
IFRS	**U.S. GAAP**
Goodwill is tested at the cash generating unit level	Goodwill is tested at the reporting unit level
One step test	A qualitative prestep and quantitative two-step test

Current Liabilities

This lesson is the first of several concerning recognition and reporting of current liabilities. The general nature and definition of liability are discussed, along with classification and valuation of liabilities.

After studying this lesson, you should be able to :

1. *Define liability, current liability, and noncurrent liability.*

2. *Categorize liabilities two different ways.*

3. *Determine the valuation of current and noncurrent liabilities.*

4. *Distinguish current from noncurrent liabilities.*

Definition:
Liabilities: Represent outsider claims to a firm's assets or are enforceable claims for services to be rendered by the firm.

I. **Liabilities in General**

A. **Definition of Liabilities**

1. Liabilities have three key elements, which are shown below. This definition is taken from the FASB's conceptual framework.

   a. Liabilities represent probable future sacrifices of economic benefits;

   b. Liabilities are obligations to transfer assets or provide services in the future;

   c. Liabilities are the result of past transactions or events.

2. It is important to note that, for a liability to be recognized in the accounts, it is not necessary to know the identity of the creditor, the exact amount that will be paid, or even the due date. Contingent liabilities, discussed later, are a category of liability for which one or more of these information items are not known as of the balance sheet date. However, the three elements from the conceptual framework above must be met by all liabilities if one is to be recognized in the accounts.

Example: 1. A firm signed a contract to perform services the following year. At the current balance sheet date, the firm has no liability because no resources have been exchanged. Only a contract has been signed. There is no past transaction that substantiates the liability as of the balance sheet date. There is no future obligation to provide services because neither party has executed the contract. None of the elements of the liability is met.

2. Do airline frequent flyer programs create liabilities for airline companies? The answer is yes, because all three parts of the definition of a liability are met. The airline has (1) an obligation to provide service (2) in the future (3) as a result of a past transaction (customers achieving the requisite miles or credit card purchases for a free flight). Airline companies accrue this liability. Again, none of the following is known at the time of the accrual: the identity of the creditor, amount to be paid, or due date.

B. Classification of Liabilities -- Liabilities are classified in two ways: (1) current liabilities (CL) or noncurrent liabilities (NCL), and (2) definite or contingent.

1. Most current liabilities (CL) are due within one year of the balance sheet. All other debt is noncurrent. Liabilities are presented on the balance sheet in increasing order of maturity. That is, current liabilities are presented first, and then, noncurrent liabilities are presented. CL include accounts payable, wages payable, income taxes payable, utilities payable, accrued payables, some notes payable, and many others. Noncurrent liabilities (NCL) include bonds payable, some notes payable, lease liabilities and pension liabilities.

2. Definite liabilities actually exist at the balance sheet. Contingent liabilities have some uncertainty at the balance sheet date. Their existence is contingent on an event that may or may not occur after the balance sheet. A contingent liability may be accrued as a definite liability, is disclosed as a contingency, or is not considered a liability at all. Most liabilities are definite. Examples of contingent liabilities include lawsuits, warranties and guarantees. Contingent liabilities are covered in a subsequent lesson.

C. Distinction between Current and Noncurrent Liabilities

1. **Current liabilities --** Are those that meet two criteria:

    a. Due in the coming year or the operating cycle of the business, whichever is longer;

    b. An obligation to be met by the transfer of a current asset or the "creation of another current liability."

        i. The operating cycle is the period from acquiring inventory and other resources, to sale, to receipt of cash from the receivable. Most firms have operating cycles much shorter than a year. One measure of the operating cycle is 365/inventory turnover + 365/AR turnover = number of days required to sell the inventory on hand + number of days required to collect receivables.

2. **Noncurrent liabilities --** Are defined by exclusion. That is, noncurrent liabilities are those that do not meet the criteria necessary for classification as a current liability.

 Example:
1. A bond payable liability is due four years from the balance sheet. This liability is classified as noncurrent.

2. If the bond liability matures serially, and a portion of the principal balance is due at the end of each year, then the amount due the following year is classified as a current liability in the balance sheet for the current year and is labeled: current maturities of long-term debt.

---

3. **Valuation of Liabilities**

    a. CLs are reported valued at the amount due, or nominal amount. Liabilities for services are measured at the amount received. For example, the unearned revenue (liability) for an amount received by an airline before a flight is provided is measured at the amount received for the ticket.

    b. NCLs are reported at the present value of all future payments (principal and interest), discounted at the prevailing rate of interest for similar debt on the date of issuance. Present value is the current sacrifice to retire the debt. Interest is the difference between the total future payments and present value. Interest is not recognized until time passes.

Caution: A CL and NCL reported in the balance sheet at equal values (for example, both $100,000) may require greatly different cash payment totals over their terms due to interest on the NCL principal.

---

    c. Although in theory all debt should be reported at present value, for practical reasons CL are not discounted because the difference between present and nominal (future) value is typically not material.

II. A Closer Look at Current Liabilities (CL)

  A. The essence of a CL is that it is expected to reduce the firm's liquidity within one year of the balance sheet date or operating cycle, whichever is longer. A CL payable with a current asset clearly will reduce the firm's liquidity. But what about the second part of the definition "creation of another CL"?

  B. CLs that are continuously refinanced (rolled over) by replacing them with other CLs due later (but within one year of the balance sheet date) must still be classified as CL, even though no current asset will be used to extinguish them in the year after the balance sheet date.

Example:

1. A note payable due 3/1/x2 is expected to be refinanced continuously on a 4-month basis, each time substituting a new 4 month note for the old. That is the intent of the debtor firm. The note due 3/1/x2 is classified as a CL in the 12/31/x1 balance sheet because it meets the second part of the CL definition.

Although the expectation is that no current asset will be used to retire the debt, there is no certainty that the debtor firm will be able to continue this practice. For example, the debtor firm cannot control the creditor who may decide not to refinance. Interest rates may increase substantially changing the strategy of the debtor firm.

Caution: Most liabilities due within one year of the balance sheet are CLs. But there are exceptions - some are classified as NCL.

2. A note is due 5 months from the balance sheet date but payable in the common stock of the debtor. The debtor does not reduce current assets in payment of this debt. A later lesson discusses another example - the refinancing of short-term debt on a long-term basis.

3. A bond liability due next year for which the firm has created a sinking fund investment (noncurrent asset) for bond retirement is classified as an NCL because payment will reduce noncurrent assets not current assets.

Caution: Most liabilities due later than one year after the balance sheet date are NCLs but there are exceptions - some are classified as CLs.

4. Long-term obligations callable on demand by the creditor are classified as current. Because the creditor can call in the debt, the debtor must report it as current. A creditor may require this provision in the debt contract to reduce the risk of losing principal. Such provisions also may be added in case the debtor violates a debt restriction. For example, a debt contract requires the debtor to maintain a current ratio (CA/CL) of 3.0 or more. If the ratio falls below 3.0, the debt is due on demand by the creditor, unless the debtor "cures" the violation within the next reporting period.

III. Definite Liabilities -- Definite liabilities are not dependent on any future event. The existence of these liabilities is determined by a current event or a past transaction or event. Definite liabilities include liabilities payable in definite amounts (e.g., accounts payable), those which can only be estimated (e.g., estimated income tax payable), and accrued liabilities that are recorded for expenses recognized before payment is made (e.g., utilities payable). Not all definite liabilities can be measured with certainty. Some are estimated and reported at an approximate amount.

A. Accounts Payable

1. These payables are also called trade payables. They represent the amount a business enterprise owes to suppliers and other entities that provide goods or services to the company.

2. These payables are typically for a short duration, usually 30 days. In some instances, the time period can be 45 or 60 days.

3. Accounts payable are recognized at the time of purchase or at the time that services are received by the business entity. In relation to purchased merchandise, the payable should be recognized at the point in which the merchandise is included in the company's inventory. The module on inventory discusses this issue in further detail (F.O.B. title test and goods on consignment). Several additional accounts such as purchases, purchases returns and allowances and others are created to accommodate the specifics of inventory purchasing.

B. Subsequent lessons provide additional examples of definite liabilities. For example, corporations often provide an estimate of fourth-quarter income taxes at year end:

Income tax expense	xxx	
Income tax payable		xxx

1. The amount recorded in this adjusting journal entry is an estimate of the amount due for the year; the exact amount often is subject to dispute because the process of preparing a corporation's income tax return is affected by ambiguities in the tax law and other issues. The first three quarterly payments also are estimates. Subsequent lessons consider income tax reporting in greater depth.

Specific Current Liabilities

This lesson considers several specific definite current liabilities. Recall that definite liabilities exist at the balance sheet. Additional examples appear in the context of other lessons.

After studying this lesson, you should be able to :

1. Record sales taxes payable from data about sales and the applicable tax rate.

2. Distinguish employer and employee payroll costs and which results in an employer expense.

3. Record payroll including employer payroll tax expenses, and payroll liabilities from both employer and employee sources.

4. Compute bonus liabilities with income tax effects.

I. **Sales Taxes** -- Firms collect sales taxes from their customers and periodically submit them to the state or local government. Between collection and submission of the tax, the firm has a liability to the government.

Example:
The sales tax rate is 10% and the total amount collected from customers for the month is $77,000. The summary entry to record sales and the sales tax is:

Cash	77,000	
Sales		70,000*
Sales Taxes Payable		7,000

* $77,000/1.10 = $70,000 The cash collected includes the sales tax.

The sales taxes payable account is debited when paid to the State, County, or City. Note that the firm reports only $70,000 of sales.

II. **Payroll Liabilities**

A. In their role as employers, firms incur definite current payroll-related liabilities from two different sources:

1. Employer costs including gross salary, employer share of fringe benefits, employer share of FICA and Medicare, and federal and state unemployment tax (FUTA and SUTA). The employer recognizes an expense for these costs.

2. Employee costs withheld from paychecks including income tax withholding, employee share of FICA, Medicare and fringe benefits, and also personal expenses such as parking, union dues and others. The employer does not recognize an expense for these costs but acts as a collection point resulting in an employer liability.

   a. Payroll tax liabilities are paid by the employer at specific dates set by law.

   b. Social security legislation levies the OASDI (Federal Old Age, Survivor, and Disability Insurance) tax, also called FICA (Federal Insurance Contribution Act) tax, on annual salaries and wages up to a certain annual salary limit per employee. In addition, the Medicare tax is levied on all salaries and wages without limit. Both employer and employee pay the same amount for both taxes.

c. Employers pay federal and state unemployment taxes. Both (1) Federal Unemployment Tax Act (FUTA) and (2) State Unemployment Taxes (SUTA) are levied on each employee's salary up to a certain limit per year. Only employers pay this tax.

Note: Because payroll tax rates and salary limits change, the CPA exam will provide approximate values. However, we recommend that you be aware of the general magnitude of such costs. Approximate rates and limits: FICA, 6.5% on the first $110,000 of salary per year; Medicare, 1.5% with no limit; FUTA, 6% on the first $7,000 reduced by up to 5.5% for contributions to SUTA; SUTA, 5.5% on first $7,000.

Caution: FICA, FUTA and SUTA all have salary limits beyond which no more tax is levied either for employer or employee (there is no limit for Medicare) for a particular year. Look for these limits in payroll problems and take care not to exceed them when computing these expenses for the employer and for FICA withholdings for the employee.

 Example:
Gross payroll is $60,000 for a month late in the year (gross pay limits for some employees have been exceeded). Use the approximate tax rates provided.

FICA tax, 7%, only $40,000 of gross pay subject to tax

Medicare tax, 1.5% of gross pay

State income tax withholding, $2,000 (based on withholding tables)

Federal income tax withholding, $18,000 (based on withholding tables)

State unemployment tax, 5%, only $20,000 of gross pay subject to tax

Federal unemployment tax, 1%, only $20,000 of gross pay subject to tax

Union dues withheld, $1,000

Health insurance premiums, $3,000 (1/3 paid by employees)

Retirement, $4,000 (1/4 paid by employees)

Salary or wage expense	65,000*
State inc tax withholding payable	2,000
Federal inc tax withholding payable	18,000
FICA tax payable (.07 x $40,000)	2,800
Medicare tax payable (.015 x $60,000)	900
Health insurance payable	3,000
Retirement payable	4,000
Union dues payable	1,000
Cash (net pay)	33,300

*$65,000 = $60,000 gross + 2/3($3,000 health) + 3/4($4,000 retirement).

Net pay = $60,000 − employee withholdings (excludes employer share of fringes) = $60,000 − $20,000 income tax − $2,800 FICA − $900 Medicare − $1,000 health − $1,000 retirement − $1,000 union = 33,300

The $65,000 expense includes only the employer's costs. The employees' net pay is reduced by their costs. Rather than increasing the expense debit, the net pay credit is reduced.

Remaining is to record the employer share of FICA and Medicare, and the employer's taxes for FUTA and SUTA. The next journal entry records these expenses. The two journal entries could be combined.

Payroll tax expense	4,900	
FICA tax payable (.07 × $40,000)		2,800
Medicare tax payable (.015 × $60,000)		900
FUTA tax payable (.01 × $20,000)		200
SUTA tax payable (.05 × $20,000)		1,000

The total employer expense for this payroll is $69,900 ($65,000 + $4,900).

III. Bonus Compensation Liabilities -- A bonus is an additional amount of compensation in excess of a base salary. Frequently, liabilities related to bonus compensation are dependent on operating results for the accounting period. The bonus may be based on income before or after the bonus, and before or after income tax effects. We recommend converting the problem statement directly into an equation. These types of problems require solving for up to two unknowns.

Example:
1. An employee's bonus is based on operating income after income taxes but before deducting the bonus. Operating Income before bonus and taxes is $90,000, the bonus rate is 10%, and the tax rate is 40%. Let B = bonus, T = tax.

$$B = .10 (\$90,000 - T)$$

$$T = .40 (\$90,000 - B)$$

$$B = .10 (\$90,000 - .40 (\$90,000 - B))$$

$$B = \$5,625$$

2. An employee's bonus is based on operating income after income taxes and bonus. Operating income before bonus and tax is $90,000, the bonus rate is 10%, and the tax rate is 40%. Let B = bonus, T = tax.

$$B = .10 (90,000 - T - B)$$

$$T = .40 (90,000 - B)$$

$$B = .10(90,000 - .40(90,000 - B) - B)$$

$$B = \$5,094$$

Deferred Revenue Principles

This is the first of two lessons about deferred or unearned revenues. This lesson provides the basic concepts that apply to all such accounts.

After studying this lesson, you should be able to:

1. *Identify deferred revenues and be able to record them correctly.*

2. *Determine the amount of revenue to be recognized, from given data about deferred revenues.*

3. *Compute the cash payments amount, from given data about deferred revenues.*

I. Deferred Revenues

> **Definition:**
> *A Deferred Revenue:* A liability recognized when cash is received before the service is provided or before the goods are shipped to customers.

A. Deferred revenues are liabilities representing cash received for goods not yet delivered or services to be performed. Recognition of revenue occurs when the firm provides the good or service at which point the deferred revenue (liability) is reduced. These liabilities often are reduced in adjusting entries. For example, a company may prepare an adjusting entry to recognize rent revenue and reduce unearned rent revenue.

B. Cash representing revenue that will be earned in the future is credited to one of the following accounts, which are simply different names for the same account:

1. Deferred revenue;

2. Unearned revenue;

3. Revenue received in advance.

C. Each of the above accounts is a liability. CPA exam questions in this area ask the candidate to determine the ending balances of two accounts:

1. Revenue to be recognized in income for the period; and

2. The amount of unearned revenue to be reported in the balance sheet.

D. Under the revenue recognition principle, revenue is not recognized unless it is (1) earned, and (2) realizable. In the case of deferred revenue, the cash collection occurs before the earnings process is complete. Such revenue is common for firms that require partial or full payment before providing service. Examples include real estate management companies (unearned rent), publishing companies (magazine subscriptions) and airline companies (flight liability).

E. A liability is recognized upon receipt of cash. As the service or good is provided, the liability is extinguished because the revenue is earned. In many cases, the contract need not be fully executed before some revenue is recognized. In these cases, the revenue is recognized based on the percentage of the total contract that has been provided.

II. Examples -- Several examples are provided to illustrate the variations in problems that may be encountered on the CPA exam.

Example: Duration Magazine Inc. collects subscriptions in advance from customers and records deferred revenue. As magazines are distributed over the subscription period, revenue is recognized. The beginning balance of deferred subscription revenue is $24,000. During the year, $87,000 of cash is collected. At the end of the year, the firm calculates from subscription data that the subscription value of magazines yet to be distributed is $37,000. The adjusting entry to record revenue for the period is:

Deferred Subscription Revenue	74,000	
Subscription Revenue		74,000*

* $24,000 + $87,000 − $37,000 = $74,000

Example:
Journal entries

A tenant pays a building management firm $24,000 for two years' rent on August 1, 20x3 ($1,000 per month). The rental period begins on that date and the building management firm has a calendar fiscal year. Provide the journal entries for 20x3.

Solution:

Aug 1, 20x3

Cash	24,000	
Unearned Rent		24,000

Dec 31, 20x3 (adjusting journal entry)

Unearned rent	5,000	
Rent revenue		5,000

$5,000 = $1,000 per month x 5 months August—December.

The 20x3 income statement will reflect $5,000 of rent revenue. The ending balance in unearned rent for 12/31/x3 is $19,000 ($24,000 − $5,000) of which $12,000 is a current liability (the portion relating to 20x4), and $7,000 is a noncurrent liability (the portion relating to 20x5).

See the following example.

Example:
Account balances given

The beginning and ending balances of unearned revenue for an airline company appear below. These amounts represent cash collected from customers for flights to be provided in the future.

	Beginning	Ending
Unearned Revenue	$300,000	$410,000

During the year, the firm collected $760,000 from customers for flights. How much revenue was recognized during the year?

Solution: Any operating account such as unearned revenue can be analyzed using a T account or an equation. The equation approach is illustrated below:

Beginning balance of unearned revenue + increase - decrease = Ending balance of unearned revenue

Unearned Revenue

Revenue recognized	Beginning balance – Cash received
	Ending balance

The increase for this account is the amount of cash received during the period; the decrease is the amount of revenue recognized.

Beginning balance	+	cash received	–	revenue earned	=	ending balance
$300,000	+	$760,000	–	?	=	$410,000

Solving for revenue earned yields $650,000. This amount is reported in the income statement.

Summary entries can be reconstructed:

Cash	760,000	
Unearned Revenue		760,000
Unearned Revenue	650,000	
Revenue		650,000

See the following example.

Example:
Reporting cash as revenue on receipt - In some cases, firms record all cash received as revenue and then make an adjusting entry (1) to recognize the amount of unrecognized revenue to report in the balance sheet, and (2) to adjust revenue.

At the beginning of the year, the balance in rent collected in advance (liability) was $56,000. During the year, the firm collected $520,000 in rent from tenants representing rentals of $2,000 per month. At year-end, 10 tenants had an average of eight months rent (at $2,000 per month) remaining on their contracts. The summary journal entries assuming that cash collected is recognized immediately as rent revenue are as follows:

Cash	520,000	
Rent Revenue		520,000
Rent Revenue	104,000	
Rent collected in advance		104,000

The ending liability balance (rent collected in advance)= 10 tenants × 8 months remaining on average × $2,000 per month = $160,000

Beginning balance	+	cash received	–	rent revenue earned	=	ending balance
$56,000	+	$520,000	–	?	=	$160,000

Solving for rent revenue earned for the year yields $416,000. Because the firm has already recorded $520,000 in revenue upon cash collection, the adjustment is $104,000: $520,000 rent recognized previously less the actual revenue earned of $416,000. In this case, the liability balance is directly computed; the amount of revenue recognized is computed as one of the components of the change in the liability account.

III. **Total Revenue to be Recognized** -- You may encounter situations in which firms require cash to be paid in advance for some services, while for other services the firm bills the customer after the service is provided. In this case, both unearned revenue and accounts receivable must be analyzed to uncover the total revenue to be recognized for the period.

Example:
The following amounts were taken from the comparative financial statements of a large local firm:

	12/31/x4	12/31/x3
Accounts receivable	$20,000	$12,000
Unearned revenue	34,000	28,000

The accounts receivable represents billings after service was provided to customers. Unearned revenue represents cash collected before service was provided. Total cash received from customers during 20x4: $126,000
What amount of service revenue was recognized during the period?

Solution: Accounts receivable is recognized when revenue is earned. The customer is billed after the service is provided. Unearned revenue is recognized when customers pay in advance, before service is provided. Cash received increases the unearned revenue account while reducing accounts receivable. Recognizing earned revenue has the opposite effect: it reduces unearned revenue while increasing the accounts receivable account.

Again, a T account or equation analysis helps. Although the amount of cash received on accounts receivable and the amount of cash received in advance from customers cannot be determined from the information provided, the total cash received from both sources is provided. The solution strategy is to set up the analysis of the two balance sheet accounts and place the revenue amounts on the same side of the respective equations:

Accounts receivable:

Beg. Bal + revenue earned − cash received = End. Bal

revenue earned = End. Bal + cash received − Beg. Bal

Unearned revenue:

Beg. Bal + cash received − revenue earned = End. Bal

revenue earned = Beg. Bal + cash received − end. Bal

Repeat the last equation for each account, insert the known amounts, recall that total cash received amounted to $126,000, and add the equations together.

AR:	revenue earned	=	End. Bal + cash received	−	Beg. Bal
		=	$20,000		$12,000
Unearned Rev:	revenue earned	=	Beg. Bal + cash received	−	end. Bal
		=	$28,000		$34,000
Sum:	revenue earned	=	$48,000 + $126,000	−	$46,000
		=	$128,000		

Therefore, total revenue to be recognized for 20x4 equals $128,000. However, from the information provided, the revenue cannot be broken down by source (customers paying in advance vs. customers paying after service is provided).

Short-cut approach: An alternative approach is to simply assume that one-half the total cash received relates to each of the two accounts (accounts receivable and unearned revenue). Again, an equation or T account may be used for the analysis; this time the account analysis can proceed separately for each account. Assume one-half of the cash (1/2 × $126,000 = $63,000) is applied to each account.

Accounts receivable:

Beg. Bal	+	revenue earned	−	cash received	=	End. Bal
$12,000	+	?	−	$63,000	=	$20,000

Unearned revenue:

Beg. Bal	+	cash received	−	revenue earned	=	End. Bal
$28,000	+	$63,000	−	?	=	$34,000

Total revenue earned = $71,000 + $57,000 = $128,000. Note however that the individual amounts of revenue, $71,000 and $57,000, are most likely not the actual revenue amounts by sources. Only the total is correct.

Specific Deferred Revenues

In this, the second of two lessons about deferred revenues, the focus is on specific examples of deferred revenue.

After studying this lesson, you should be able to:

1. *Record the appropriate journal entries for gift card programs.*

2. *Account for container deposits.*

3. *Determine the amount of revenue to be recognized for extended warranties.*

4. *Allocate the total revenue for an arrangement with more than one deliverable.*

I. Gift Certificates/Cards

A. When a retailer sells a gift certificate or gift card, it records an unearned revenue account (a liability). The transaction is a cash receipt for a possible future sale. When the card is used by a customer for a purchase, the liability is reduced, and sales (and cost of goods sold) are recognized.

B. In the case of forfeiture by a customer, the retailer still recognizes revenue, subject to certain legal constraints, if present. Some cards have definite expiration dates that allow for accurate determinations of forfeited cards. Other cards have no expiration dates. For these arrangements, after a certain amount of time and based on past experience, the retailer can assume that a certain percentage of cards will not be redeemed. To the extent that state law requires the firm to remit any or all of the forfeited gift revenue to the state, that portion of the gift card liability is not recognized as revenue.

Example: The beginning balance of a retailer's gift card liability (unearned revenue) for the current year is $4,600,000. During the year, $32,000,000 of gift cards were sold and $28,000,000 of cards were used by customers to purchase goods at a 60% average gross margin percentage. From past experience, the firm estimates that 20% of the beginning gift card liability balance has been forfeited by customers.

Journal entries for the year:

Receipt of cash:	Cash	32,000,000	
	Gift card liability		32,000,000
Customer redemption:	Gift card liability	28,000,000	
	Sales		28,000,000
	Cost of goods sold	11,200,000	
	Inventory		11,200,000
	$11,200,000 = $28,000,000(.40)		
Forfeiture:	Gift card liability	920,000	
	Forfeited card revenue*		920,000
	$920,000 = $4,600,000(.20)		

* This account is typically merged with sales in practice; no cost of goods sold is recognized.

The ending liability balance of $7,680,000 represents the remaining sales that could be recognized in the future on card redemptions. If forfeiture experience changes, the rate applied in the adjusting journal entry at year-end uses the new rate (change in estimate). Eventually, all cash received from customers for gift cards is recognized as revenue, unless state law requires that the firm remit all or a portion of forfeited card receipts to the state.

II. Container Deposits

A. In some industries, and for certain retail products, the seller requires a container deposit which is paid by the customer and reimbursed when the container is returned. Accounting for container deposits is similar to that for gift cards. The amount received from the customer is a liability until the container is returned. However, this liability is much less an unearned revenue account because containers are not meant to be sold. However, some containers are never returned and the deposit is forfeited - a non-sales revenue is recognized at this point. An expense is recognized for the cost of containers not returned by customers.

B. Sample journal entries

Receipt of deposit:	Cash
	Container deposit liability
Return of container:	Container deposit liability
	Cash
Forfeiture:	Container deposit liability
	Miscellaneous revenue
	Miscellaneous expense
	Inventory of containers

C. If there is a specified return period (e.g., one year), then the forfeiture entries are recorded after that period has elapsed. If not, and the firm honors returns indefinitely, an estimate of forfeitures is used for the forfeiture entries.

D. Are gift card and container deposit liabilities definite liabilities?

    1. The answer is yes. The firm has a liability at the point of receiving cash from the customer. The liability is not contingent on a future event. The firm has an obligation for the amount received. The liability will be extinguished regardless of action or inaction by the customer. These liabilities are not contingent on a future event.

III. Extended Warranties

A. Regular warranties are offered by many companies at no charge to the customer. They create contingent liabilities and are covered in another lesson. Extended warranties are offered for additional consideration and provide coverage beyond the regular warranty. When the customer pays for the extended warranty, another unearned revenue account (liability) is recorded. The reporting issue involves the timing of revenue recognition.

B. Accounting for extended warranties

    1. The unearned revenue is recognized as revenue over the life of the contract;

    2. Warranty expense (cost to service claims) is recognized as incurred;

    3. If the total cost of servicing claims over the contract life is estimable, then the revenue is recognized in proportion to costs incurred. Otherwise the straight-line method is used;

    4. Costs directly related to individual contracts (e.g., commissions) are capitalized and amortized over the life of the contract in the same proportion as revenue is recognized;

    5. Advertising and other indirect costs are expensed as incurred.

Example:
A firm's sales totaled $3,000,000 for the year. This figure includes $150,000 for 2-year extended warranty contracts covering the goods sold. The firm expects to incur a total of $120,000 cost in servicing warranty claims on these contracts. During year 1, $20,000 of warranty costs were incurred.

Journal entries for year 1:

Cash or Accounts receivable	3,000,000	
Sales		2,850,000
Unearned warranty revenue		150,000
Warranty expense	20,000	
Cash, inventory, other		20,000
Unearned warranty revenue	25,000	
Warranty revenue		25,000

$25,000 = ($20,000/$120,000)$150,000. One-sixth of expected total claims service has been performed. Therefore 1/6 of $150,000 is recognized as revenue. If the firm could not estimate the $120,000 total warranty cost, then $75,000 of revenue would be recognized ($150,000/2) using the straight-line approach.

The remaining $125,000 of warranty revenue ($150,000 − $25,000) is recognized in the second year of the contract, regardless of the actual cost incurred in the second year because the benefits cease at the end of the second year. At that point all the revenue is earned.

IV. Revenue Arrangements with Multiple Deliverables

A. Vendors often provide more than one product or service as part of a single arrangement. Not all items in the arrangement are necessarily delivered at the same time. The revenue for delivered items is separately recognized if the following two criteria are met:

1. The delivered item has value to the customer on a stand-alone basis; and

2. If the arrangement includes a general right of return relative to the delivered item, delivery of the undelivered item is considered probable and substantially in the control of the vendor.

B. If the criteria are not met for a delivered item, then the arrangement is treated as one unit and revenue recognition is deferred for the delivered item until all items are delivered.

Example:
A firm sells a machine and installation services to another firm. The machine is delivered. If the two criteria are met, then revenue is recognized for the machine and later for the installation when that is complete. (Note, if there is no right of return, then the second criterion does not apply.) If the two criteria are not met, the revenue for both items is recognized when the installation is complete.

C. Allocating the total arrangement price -- The total arrangement price is allocated to the individual items based their stand-alone selling prices (relative-selling price method). To determine the selling prices, the following hierarchy is used. Note that selling prices as set in an individual contract may not be representative of the stand-alone selling price to be used in the computation.

1. Vendor-specific objective evidence of selling price (VSOE) about the price of the item if sold separately by the vendor. If this information is not available, then use...

2. Third-party evidence of selling price (TPE) about similar or interchangeable items when sold separately by a third party on a stand-alone basis. If this information is not available, then use ...

3. Best estimate of selling price (for example, cost plus a reasonable profit margin).

D. The allocation of revenue to the individual items is not subject to change given new information - changes in estimate are not allowed.

Example:
Continuing with the previous example, assume that the selling price for the combined arrangement is $40,000. The machine, if sold separately, sells for $36,000. But the vendor does not sell installation services separately and thus has no separate selling price. Nor is there any TPE of price for the installation. The vendor therefore applies its normal profit margin to the cost of the installation and determines an estimate of the installation service selling price to be $8,000. The allocation of the $40,000 arrangement price is as follows:

To machine: $40,000[$36,000/($36,000 + $8,000)] = $32,727

To installation: $40,000[$8,000/($36,000 + $8,000)] =   7,273

Total revenue: $40,000

E. Multiple Software Deliverables -- For software, the total arrangement fee is allocated to the various items based on vendor-specific objective evidence of fair value, rather than selling price, regardless of contractually stated selling prices. Vendor-specific objective evidence of fair value is limited to the price charged when the same item is sold separately. If an item is not sold separately, the price is established by management.

1. **Residual Method** -- For multiple deliverable software items, when the vendor is able to determine the selling price for undelivered items but is unable to determine the price of the delivered items, the residual method is applied.

2. The allocation of the total arrangement price to the delivered items is the residual after subtracting the total selling price of the undelivered items. This results in the entire discount, if any, allocated to the delivered items. The amount allocated to the delivered items is recognized upon delivery. The amount allocated to the undelivered items is deferred until delivery.

3. For the residual method to be applicable, all other applicable revenue recognition criteria must be met, and the fair value of the undelivered items must be less than the total fee.

F. Exception -- If software within a multiple deliverable arrangement is an integral part of a bundle of products including nonsoftware products, then the previously discussed general guidance for revenue recognition for multiple deliverables is applied (using selling prices rather than fair value), rather than the residual method. The firm must use the relative-selling price method illustrated above.

1. The relative-selling price method is applied for all multiple deliverable situations in which software functions together with a tangible product to deliver the latter's essential functionality.

Notes Payable

This lesson is the first of two about notes payable accounting. The general principles applying to all notes payable are covered here.

After studying this lesson you should be able to :

1. *Choose the correct interest rate for the appropriate computation.*

2. *Determine whether a note is issued at a premium or discount.*

3. *Compute the total interest expense over the term of the note.*

4. *Compute interest expense for a period on a noncurrent note.*

5. *Apply the gross method and the net method.*

6. *Apply the effective interest and straight-line methods.*

7. *Record the initial issuance of notes payable at present value.*

8. *Distinguish simple interest notes and installment notes.*

9. *Compute and record interest expense on notes payable for multiple periods.*

10. *Record the relevant journal entries for notes issued in exchange for rights or other privileges.*

I. Notes Payable Reporting

A. Notes payable features

1. Short-term notes are classified as current liabilities if they meet that definition. Compared with accounts payable, short-term notes payable generally have a term of at least 30 days and bear interest. Short-term notes are typically reported at face value, rather than at present value.

2. Long-term notes are a major source of significant debt financing, especially for smaller firms. Long-term borrowing with notes involves one or a small number of creditors. Larger firms are more likely to use bonds for long-term debt financing, enabling a larger number of potential creditors to participate. Bonds generally have longer terms than notes. Long-term notes are reported at present value and are noncurrent liabilities if they meet that definition. The portion of the note principal to be paid off next year is classified as current.

B. Types of notes for accounting purposes

1. Simple interest notes have a face value that is also the maturity amount, the amount the debtor pays when the note matures (end of note term). The stated interest rate and face value determine the annual interest to be paid. A 5%, $10,000 (face value) note pays $500 interest per year, for example. Payments may be required at any specified interval including monthly, quarterly, semiannually, and annually. The $10,000 face value is paid at maturity.

2. Installment notes—each payment includes principal and interest—have no maturity value because the last payment reduces the note payable balance to zero. These notes are often used to purchase plant assets and may be secured by those assets. A mortgage note is an example.

3. Interest rates and principal. Both types of notes above involve two interest rates although often the two rates are the same on a given note.

4. The stated rate is the rate stated in the note and determines the cash interest due on the note each period.

5. The yield rate for the note (also called effective or market rate) is the rate on notes of similar risk and term. If the note is to be reported at present value, the yield rate is used for that computation.

6. When the yield rate exceeds the stated rate at time of borrowing, the note is issued at a discount which is recorded in a contra account to the note. When the yield rate is less than the stated rate, the note is issued at a premium and recorded in an adjunct account to the note. If the two rates are equal, the note is issued at face value. Discounts and premiums are much more common for bonds but the accounting is the same for notes and bonds.

7. The stated interest rate on a note is considered to be the fair rate (yield rate) unless (i) there is no stated rate, or (ii) the rate is clearly unreasonable, or (iii) the face value of the note is materially different from the fair value of consideration received for the note.

8. The discount or premium is amortized over the note term with the discount amortization increasing the net note liability and the premium amortization decreasing the net note liability.

9. The principal amount of the note is the amount borrowed and is the present value at the date of issuance. The total interest over the note term equals the difference between the total payments required under the note (principal and interest at the stated rate), and the principal amount.

10. Total interest also equals total cash interest over the term plus the discount or minus the premium at issuance.

C. Accounting for noncurrent notes payable

1. Noncurrent notes payable are issued for the present value of all future cash flows, including principal, and interest payments computed using the stated rate. The computation of present value uses the yield rate at the date of issuance. When notes are used to acquire nonmonetary items such as plant assets, the fair value of the property acquired or fair value of the note, whichever is more reliable, is used to record both sides of the transaction. If the fair value of the note is more reliable, the interest rate implicit in the note is used for recording the note, and interest expense over the term.

2. At subsequent balance sheet dates, notes are reported at the present value of remaining payments, again using the yield rate at the date of issuance.

3. Periodic interest expense is computed as the product of the yield rate at the date of issuance, and the beginning net note liability (present value). This approach is called the effective interest method and is required by GAAP. The difference between cash interest paid and interest expense recognized at each payment date is the amortization of discount or premium.

4. Another approach, called the straight-line method, amortizes the discount or premium equally each period. This approach is allowed only if it results in interest expense amounts not materially different from the effective interest method. The net note liability for this approach is only an approximation of the present value of the note.

5. The gross or net method of recording the note and interest expense are both acceptable. The gross method separates the face value (note payable) and discount or premium in different accounts. The net method uses one combined net account (note payable), which is the present value and net note liability under the effective interest method.

6. The fair value of notes must be disclosed - the estimate of the amount required to pay off the note at the balance sheet date. Notes are not typically traded on an exchange so an estimate must be made of the note's fair value using the current yield rate on similar notes. Also disclosed are the details of noncurrent notes such as interest rates, assets pledged, call and conversion provisions and restrictions, and the aggregate maturity

amounts for each of the five years following the balance sheet date. Firms may also choose the fair value option. This reporting option is illustrated in a lesson on bond accounting and is applied to notes in the same way.

7. Loan origination fees and points are amortized under the effective interest method.

II. **Examples** -- The examples in this and then next lesson illustrate the basic principles discussed above.

A. **Noncurrent Interest-Bearing Note Payable** -- An interest-bearing note payable is one in which the interest element is explicitly stated. These notes are recorded at the present value of future cash flows, using the market rate of interest as the discount rate. If the stated interest rate and the market interest rate are the same, the present value of the future cash flows is equal to the face amount of the note. If the stated interest rate and the market rate of interest are not equal, the present value of the future cash flows is not equal to the face amount of the note. In this instance, a discount or premium will be recorded, and the amortization of the related premium or discount will be completed using the effective interest method.

 Example: Interest-Bearing Long-Term Notes Payable where Stated and Market Rates Unequal.

The Montana Company paid for legal services received by giving the law firm a $10,000 three-year, 6% note payable (interest payable at the end of the year) on January 1 of Year One. The market rate of interest for a note of this type is 10%. The value of the legal services is not specified. Therefore the present value of the note is used as the amount to record both sides of the transaction. In some cases, the stated rate is intentionally lowered to ease the cash flow requirements of the debtor firm during the note term.

Present Value of Future Cash Flows:

$10,000 × .75131 (PV of $1, N = 3, I = 10%)　　　= $7,513

$600 × 2.48685 (PV of an Annuity, N = 3, I = 10%)　= <u>1,492</u>

Total Present Value of Future Cash Flows　　　　$9,005

Debt Amortization Schedule

Date	Cash Interest	Interest Expense	Discount Amortized	Unamortized Discount	Carrying Value
1/1/Y1				$995	$9,005
12/31/Y1	$600	$900	$300	$695	$9,305
12/31/Y2	$600	$931	$331	$364	$9,636
12/31/Y3	<u>$600</u>	<u>$964</u>	<u>$364</u>	$0	$10,000
Totals	$1,800	$2,795	$995		

Entries:

Year 1:	Legal Expenses	$9,005	
1/1/1	Discount on Note Payable	$995	
	Note Payable		$10,000

This discount account is contra to Note Payable

12/31/1	Interest Expense	$900	
	Discount on Note Payable		$300
	Cash		$600
Year 2:	Interest Expense	$931	
12/31/2	Discount on Note Payable		$331
	Cash		$600
Year 3:	Interest Expense	$964	
12/31/3	Discount on Note Payable		$364
	Cash		$600
	Note Payable	$10,000	
	Cash		$10,000

In this example, we illustrate the gross method. The note payable is listed at face value, with separate accounting of the discount. The net method is also acceptable and would record the note payable initially at $9,005 with no discount recorded. Interest expense for Year 1 is .10 × $9,005 (balance at beginning of Year 1). Interest expense is based on the net note at the beginning of each period, regardless of whether the gross or net method is used. The yield rate (10%) is used to compute interest.

The legal expenses are recorded at the present value of the future payments. The value of the services is defined by the present value of $9,005 because the law firm accepted the note. The worth of the note is its present value using the market rate of interest (10%). That present value includes the present value of both the face amount and the interest payments. The stated rate of 6% is used only to compute the interest payments. Interest expense is based on the market rate of 10%.

The total interest expense over the note term ($2,795) is the difference between the principal of $9,005 and the sum of the future payments of $11,800 (3 x $600 + $10,000). It also equals the sum of the $1,800 cash interest over the term (3 × $600) and the $995 discount. The discount represents additional interest because the firm received only $9,005 worth of services but must pay $10,000 at the note's maturity.

If the straight-line (SL) method of amortization had been chosen, the journal entry for the three interest payments would be the same, as follows:

Interest expense	932	
Discount on note payable	332	(995/3)
Cash	600	

III. **Joint and Several Liability Arrangements** -- Joint and several obligations arise when more than one entity agrees to be liable for the entire amount of an obligation. If one of the entities is unable to make payment with the liability is due, each of the other entities is fully liable for the debt. Such arrangements may arise through a borrowing that involves a note payable.

A. A firm in such an arrangement for which the total amount of the debt is fixed at the reporting date, reports the obligation at the sum of:

  1. The amount the firm agreed to pay (the required amount according to the arrangement); and

  2. Any additional amount the firm expects to pay on behalf of the others in the arrangement.

B. If there is an amount within the range for the second part (b.) that is a better estimate than any other in the range, then that amount is used for (b.). If not, the minimum amount in the range is used.

C. There is no corresponding international standard although joint and several liabilities are treated as contingencies under IFRS.

IV. Specific Types of Notes Payable

A. Non-interest-Bearing Notes Payable -- A non-interest-bearing note payable is one in which the interest element is not explicitly stated but rather is included in the face amount of the note. These notes are recorded at the present value of future cash flows, using the market rate of interest as the discount rate. In this instance, a discount related to the note will be recorded and amortized using the effective interest method.

Example:
A firm purchases a used plant asset by issuing a one-year, $10,165 face value note. The note pays no cash interest. The purchase occurred on July 1, Year 1 for this calendar-year firm. The plant asset has a market value of $9,500. The implied market rate of interest is 7% as shown below. A noninterest-bearing note is another example for which the stated rate (0% here) is less than the yield rate.

$10,165(PV of $1, I=?, N=1) $\qquad$ = $9,500

(PV of $1, I=?, N=1) = $9,500/$10,165 $\qquad$ = .93458

This present value factor corresponds to I = 7%.

The purchaser included the 7% interest in the face value of the note. (Net method is shown.)

July 1, Year 1	Equipment	9,500	
	Note Payable		9,500
December 31, Year 1	Interest Expense $9,500(.07/2)	332.50	
	Note Payable		332.50

Interest expense is based on the beginning net liability balance

June 30, Year 2	Interest Expense	332.50	
	Note Payable		332.50
	Note Payable	10,165	
	Cash		10,165

Total interest on the note = $665 = $332.50(2) = $10,165 − $9,500. This solution illustrates the net method. There is no separate accounting for the discount. The gross method could also have been used. The straight-line method is inappropriate in this example given the magnitude of the difference between the stated and yield rates.

B. Installment Note

 Example: On 1/1/x5, a firm purchased a building by paying $100,000 down and signing a $400,000, 6%, 10-year secured mortgage note. The note calls for annual payments beginning 12/31/x5. The prevailing interest rate for a note of this type is 10%. Each payment includes principal and interest, and the note is fully paid with the last payment. The gross or net method can be used as always but the straight-line method is not appropriate because each payment reduces principal. Using SL would associate equal amounts of discount to each period when the amount of principal outstanding is declining each period.

The annual payment (pmt) is computed using the stated rate and total note amount as indicated in the note:
400,000 = pmt(PV annuity, i=.06, n=10) = pmt(7.36009)
400,000/7.36009 = pmt = $54,347

The amount borrowed is the present value of all payments required on the note using the prevailing or yield rate of 10%. The problem is silent on the fair value of the building. Therefore, the present value of the note (at the yield rate) is used for recording both the note and building.

Amount borrowed = $54,347(PV annuity, i=.10, n=10) = $54,347(6.14457) =$333,939

Journal entries (net method):

1/1/x5	Building	433,939	
	Cash		100,000
	Mortgage note payable		333,939
12/31/x5	Interest expense	33,394	333,939(.10)
	Mortgage note payable	20,953	
	Cash		54,347
12/31/x6	Interest expense	31,299	(333,939 − 20,953)(.10)
	Mortgage note payable	23,048	
	Cash		54,347

The ending 20x5 balance of the note payable is $312,986 = $333,939 − $20,953, the principal portion of the first payment. The total balance is reported as follows: (1) $23,048 current liability (CL), and $289,938 noncurrent (NCL) = $312,986 − $23,048. The portion of the liability to be paid in 20x6 is the amount classified as current for 20x5 ($23,048).

The ending 20x6 balance of the note payable is $289,938 = $333,939 − $20,953 − $23,048. This balance also can be computed as $54,347(PV annuity, i=.10, n=8) because there are eight payments remaining at this point.

Total interest over the 10 year note term equals the difference between the total payments on the note less the amount borrowed = (10 × $54,347) − $333,939 = $209,531.

C. Note in Exchange for Rights or Other Privileges

C. Note in Exchange for Rights or Other Privileges -- A firm may borrow from a customer and ask for an interest rate less than the prevailing rate in exchange for a reduced price on goods or services to be sold to the customer. Part of the consideration received on the borrowing is a prepayment by the customer for the reduced price. The note is recorded as

always using the prevailing rate. The difference between the amount borrowed and the present value of the note is unearned revenue.

Example:

At the beginning of 20x4, Duke Inc. borrowed $40,000 by issuing a three-year noninterest-bearing note with face value of $40,000. The prevailing rate on similar notes is 10%. In exchange, Duke agrees to provide the creditor (customer of Duke) with goods at a reduced price over four years.

The present value of the note is $40,000(PV1, i=.10, n=3) = $40,000(.75131) = $30,052.

Journal entries (gross method):

1/1/x4			
Cash	40,000		
Discount on note	9,948		40,000 - 30,052
Note payable		40,000	
Unearned revenue		9,948	

Duke receives an interest-free loan in exchange for reducing the prices on its goods to the creditor firm which is also Duke's customer. The loan is in substance only for $30,052 and is the basis for interest expense recognition. The remaining $9,948 received by Duke is a prepayment by the customer for reduced prices on the goods it will buy from Duke.

12/31/x4			
Interest expense	3,005		.10(30,052)
Unearned revenue	2,487		9,948/4
Discount on note		3,005	
Sales revenue		2,487	

The remaining journal entries for interest proceed as illustrated in other examples. The ending net balance of the note immediately before payment will be $40,000 because the discount will be fully amortized. The recognition of sales revenue proceeds as above over four years assuming the customer purchases equivalent amounts of goods each year.

Bond Accounting Principles

In this lesson, the first of several about accounting for bonds, the basic principles of recording bonds and recognizing interest are illustrated. Being able to apply present value is a prerequisite.

After studying this lesson, you should be able to:

1. *Identify the seven items of information required to account for a bond issue.*

2. *Compute the selling price of a bond issue.*

3. *Determine whether a bond will sell at a premium or discount, without computing the bond price.*

4. *Apply the effective interest method of amortizing bond discount and premium.*

5. *Decide when the straight-line method of amortizing bond discount and premium is appropriate.*

6. *Apply the straight-line method of amortizing bond discount and premium.*

Study Tip: This is a major topic on the CPA exam. A bond is a long-term debt instrument issued to many different creditor/investors. A bond contrasts with a note that represents the debt for a borrowing from a single creditor. Bond issuance allows more capital to be raised because it can attract many more creditors. The main issues are recording the bond at issuance, recognizing interest expense, and recognizing any gain or loss on retirement.

I. Bond Basics

Definition:
Bond: A **bond** is a financial debt instrument that typically calls for the payment of periodic interest (although a zero coupon bond pays no interest), with the principal being due at some time in the future. The bondholder (creditor or investor) pays the issuing firm an amount based on the stated and market rates of interest and receives interest and the face amount in return, over the bond term.

A. There are seven items of information that must be known to account for a bond:

1. **Face (maturity) value** -- The amount paid to the bondholder at maturity. This amount is often $1,000.

2. **Stated (coupon) interest rate** -- The rate at which the bond pays cash interest. The rate is stated on the bond. If the rate is 6% and the bond's face value is $1,000, then one bond pays $60 interest each year.

3. **Interest payment dates** -- The dates the bond pays the cash interest. Two interest payment dates per year is the norm.

4. **Market (yield, effective) interest rate** -- The rate equating the sum of the present values of the cash interest annuity and of the face value single payment, with the bond price. If a 6%, $1,000 bond was issued for $900, the market rate of interest equates the $900 amount with the present value of the annuity of $60 (or $30 twice a year), and the

$1,000 face value to be paid in the future. The market rate is the true compounded rate of return on the bond. This rate is determined by the market and does not appear on the bond.

5. **Bond date** -- The first possible issuance date. This date is listed on the bond.

6. **Issuance date** -- The date the bonds are actually issued. This date cannot be earlier than the bond date but frequently is later. This information is not on the bond.

7. **Maturity date** -- The date the maturity value is paid, the end of the bond term.

B. **Other terminology**

1. **Bond term** -- The period from issuance date to maturity date.

2. **Bond issue costs** -- The cost of printing, registering, and marketing the bonds.

3. **Accrued interest on bond sale** -- The amount of interest, based on the coupon interest rate for the period, between the issuance date and the immediately preceding interest payment date.

4. **Bond price** -- The current market price of a bond exclusive of accrued interest.

5. **Bond proceeds** -- The sum of the bond price and any accrued interest.

C. **Types of bonds** -- There are several classifications of bond issues. The most important for the exam are:

1. **Secured vs. unsecured (debentures)** -- A secured bond issue has a claim to specific assets. Otherwise, the bondholders are unsecured creditors and are grouped with other unsecured creditors. An unsecured bond is backed only by the credit rating of the issuing firm and is called a debenture.

2. **Serial vs. single maturity term** -- A serial bond matures serially, that is at regular or staggered intervals. The principal is paid gradually rather than all at once, as is the case with a single maturity or term bond.

3. **Callable vs. redeemable** -- An issuer can retire callable bonds before maturity at a specified price. The bondholder can require a redeemable bond to be retired early.

4. **Convertible vs. nonconvertible** -- A convertible bond can be converted into capital stock by the bondholder; a nonconvertible bond cannot.

D. **Determination of Selling Price of the Bond (Initial Book Value)** -- The selling price of a bond is equal to the present value of future cash flows related to the bond financial instrument (principal and cash interest). The discount rate used for this calculation is the market rate of interest on the date the bonds are issued.

1. **Stated Rate > Market Rate** -- If the stated interest rate is greater than the market rate of interest, the bonds will sell at a premium. (Premium: stated rate > market rate)

   a. **The premium** -- Is the amount received above face value and is recorded in Premium on Bonds Payable, an adjunct account to Bonds Payable. If a $1,000 bond sells for $1,100, then the premium is $100. The bond sells at a premium because the bond is paying a higher stated rate than required on the market. The price increases (and yield rate decreases) to the point at which the yield rate equals the market rate for similar bonds. The more a bondholder pays for a bond, the lower the yield rate.

2. **Stated Rate < Market Rate** -- If the stated interest rate is less than the market rate of interest, the bonds will sell at a discount (Discount: stated rate < market rate).

   a. **The discount** -- Is the amount below face value and is recorded in Discount on Bonds Payable, a contra account to Bonds Payable. If a $1,000 bond sells for $950, then the discount is $50. The bond sells at a discount because the bond is paying a lower stated rate than required on the market. The price decreases (and yield rate increases) to the point at which the yield rate equals the market rate for similar bonds. The less a bondholder pays for a bond, the higher the yield rate. Discounts are more common than premiums.

3. **Stated Rate Equals Market Rate** -- If the stated rate and market rate are equal, the bond sells at face value and no premium or discount is recorded. (Sell at face value: stated rate = market rate)

 Example:
A bond issued at a discount:

A 6%, $1,000 bond dated 1/1/x7 is issued on that date to yield 8%. The bond pays interest each June 30 and December 31 and matures four years from issuance. The bond price equals:

$1,000(PV of $1, I = 4%, N = 8)

+ .03($1,000)(PV of $1 annuity, I = 4%, N = 8)

= $1,000(.73069) + $30(6.73274)

= $933

The price (present value) is computed using the market rate of interest. 4% is used rather than 8% because the bonds pay interest semiannually. The 3% interest rate is used only to compute the semiannual interest payment. The bond sells at a discount because investors can earn 8% on competing bonds. The price of these bonds must fall in order for them to be issued. The stated rate cannot be changed, so the only variable left to change is the price. The bondholder is paying less than face value but will receive face value in return. Thus, the yield rate exceeds the coupon interest rate.

Bond prices are expressed in percentage of face value. This bond was issued at 93.3, or 93.3% of face value. Bond prices are always quoted exclusive of any accrued interest.

The entry to record the issuance of the bond is:

Cash	933	
Discount on Bonds Payable	67	
Bonds Payable		1,000

The noncurrent liability section of the balance sheet immediately after issuance would disclose:

Bonds Payable	$ 1,000
Less Discount on Bonds Payable	(67)
Net Bonds Payable	$ 933

The $933 amount is the net bond liability or book value of the bond issue. The bonds payable account is always measured at face value. The discount and premium are contra or adjunct accounts that reduce or increase the net liability to present value. With interest rate changes after issuance, the fair value of the bond most likely is not $933. In the last year of the bond term, the net liability is reported as a current liability, often called "current maturities of long-term debt."

E. Amortization of Premium / Discounts

1. The discount or premium on a bond issue is amortized over the bond term. The book value of the bond issue must equal face value on the maturity date because that is the amount paid to retire the bonds.

2. The amortization of premiums and discounts is accomplished through the use of the *effective interest method*. Due to materiality, many companies employ the *straight-line amortization method*. The straight-line method is acceptable only if the results do not depart materially from the effective interest method.

Note:
Both methods of amortization are tested on the exam. Questions with more involved requirements often use the straight-line method because the amounts are easier to compute.

3. **Effective interest method --** This method first computes interest expense based on the beginning book value of the bond and the market rate at issuance. The difference between interest expense and the cash interest paid is the amortization of the discount or the premium. The market rate at issuance is always used. The rate is not changed after issuance because it represents the true interest rate over the bond term. The amortization of discount or premium is a "plug" figure.

Example:
Using the previous example of computing the bond price, the June 30 entry in year of issuance under the effective interest method is:

Interest Expense $933(.04)   37

Discount on Bonds Payable   7

Cash $1,000(.03)   30

The net book value of the bonds is now $940 ($933 + $7). That is the amount on which interest expense at December 31 is computed. Under the effective interest method, the book value changes with each interest entry. Therefore, each entry recognizes a different amount of interest expense. But the ratio of interest expense to beginning book value is constant and equals the effective interest rate. The resulting book value is the present value of remaining cash payments using the yield rate at issuance.

4. **Straight-line (SL) method --** This method recognizes a constant amount of amortization each month of the bond term. The straight-line method should not be used when (a) the term to maturity is quite long and there is more than a minor difference between the market and stated rates, or (b) when there is a very significant difference between the market and stated rates regardless of the length of the term. An example of (b) is a zero coupon bond. Such bonds pay no interest (stated rate = 0). However, they yield competitive rates. The effective interest method must be used for these bonds.

Example:
Using the previous example of computing the bond price, the June 30 entry in year of issuance under the straight-line method is:
(note : The interest expense amount is a "plug" figure.)

Interest Expense   38

Discount on Bonds Payable   8 ($67/48 months)(6 months)

Cash $1,000(.03)   30

The bond term is 4 years long or 48 months. Six months have elapsed since the issuance of the bonds. The entry at each interest date is the same as the one above for the straight-line method. The interest expense is the same amount for each entry, but the ratio of interest expense to beginning book value changes because book value changes each period with the amortization of discount. The resulting book value is only an approximation to the present value of remaining payments.

II. Purpose of Amortization -- The purpose of amortization of the premiums and discounts is to adjust interest expense to reflect the market rate of interest and to ensure that the book value at maturity equals face value. Through adjustment of the selling price of the bonds (that is, the bonds are issued at a premium or a discount), all bonds ultimately "pay" the market rate of interest.

A. Amortize Premium

1. When a premium is amortized, the bond interest expense is adjusted downward to reflect the lower market rate of interest. An example entry is:

Interest Expense	xx	
Premium on Bond	xx	
Cash		xx

2. Cash interest exceeds interest expense because the firm received an amount exceeding face value but will pay back only face value. The total interest cost to the firm over the bond term is the total cash interest paid less the total premium, which is retained by the firm.

B. Amortize Discount

1. When a discount is amortized, the bond interest expense is adjusted upward to reflect the higher market rate of interest. An example entry is:

Interest Expense	xx	
Discount on Bond		xx
Cash		xx

2. Interest expense exceeds cash interest because the firm received an amount less than face value but will pay back face value. The total interest cost to the firm over the bond term is the total cash interest paid plus the total discount.

Bond Complications

This lesson incorporates additional aspects into accounting for bonds.

After studying this lesson, you should be able to:

1. Record the issuance of a zero coupon bond, and subsequent interest expense.

2. Compute and record accrued interest for bonds issued between interest dates.

3. Account for bond issue costs at the issuance of the bonds and throughout the bond term.

I. **Zero Coupon Bonds** -- These bonds pay no interest (coupon rate is zero) but the accounting procedure remains the same except that no cash interest is paid during the term. The entire amount of interest is included in the face value, just like a noninterest-bearing note. Zero coupon bonds, and also "deep-discount" bonds with very low coupon rates, are issued at a large discount.

 Example:
$400,000 (face value) of zero coupon bonds are issued to yield 5% on January 1, Year 1. The bonds mature in 20 years.

Issue price = $400,000(PV $1, i=5%, n=20) = $400,000(0.37689) = $150,756

Journal entries:

1/1/year 1	Cash	150,756	
	Discount on bonds	249,244	
	Bonds payable		400,000
12/31/year 1	Interest	7,538	$150,756(.05)
	Discount on bonds		7,538

The SL method is not appropriate for this type of bond.

II. **Bonds Issued between Interest Dates** -- When bonds are issued between interest dates, the total cash received by the company issuing the bonds will be equal to the selling price of the bonds plus interest accrued since the last interest date. This sum is called the proceeds. The accrued interest computation uses the stated rate. The purpose of collecting accrued interest from the bondholder on issuance (if the bond is issued between interest dates) is to facilitate the trading of bonds and to guarantee that the bondholder receives interest only for the period of time the bonds are held. By requiring the investor to pay for the interest accrued since the last interest date, the issuing company can issue "full" interest checks to all bondholders at the next interest date.

See the following example.

Example: A bond issue dated January 1 and paying interest each June 30 and December 31 is issued on April 30. The issuing firm collects 4 months of interest from January 1—April 30. Then, on June 30, the firm pays 6 months of interest. If the original bondholder holds the bonds on June 30, the bondholder receives 6 months of interest because the bond automatically pays 6 months of interest on that date. But the bondholder is entitled to only 2 months of interest because that is the period the bonds were held. The bondholder nets 2 months of interest:

   6 months of interest received on June 30

   − 4 months paid at purchase

   = 2 months earned interest

When bondholders sell bonds to other investors on the bond market, there is no effect on the firm's accounting. The buyer pays the seller for accrued interest since the last interest payment date.

The issuance of bonds between interest dates affects the entry for issuance. Accrued interest payable is credited for the interest collected from the bondholders and cash is increased by this amount. There is no interest expense recognized at this point because the bond term has just begun. Accrued interest has no effect on the premium or discount to be recorded.

The interest expense entries under the straight-line method also are affected. The bond term reflects a shorter period of time.

Example: Bender Inc. issued $8,000 of 8% bonds at 105 on March 1. The bonds pay interest each December 31 and June 30 and are dated January 1, Year 1. The bonds mature five years after the bond date. The first three entries under the straight-line method are:

March 1, Year 1

Cash $8,000(1.05) + .08(2/12)($8,000)	8,507	
Premium on Bonds Payable ($8,000).05		400
Accrued Interest Payable .08(2/12)($8,000)		107
Bonds Payable		8,000

June 30, Year 1

Interest Expense	185	
Premium on Bonds Payable ($400/58 months)(4months)	28	
Accrued Interest Payable	107	
Cash .08(6/12)($8,000)		320

(There are 58 months in the bond term, or 4 years and 10 months, and 4 months have elapsed since the bond issuance, requiring 4 months of amortization.) The accrued interest is a separate resource. It is not included in the price and has no effect on the discount or premium.

December 31, Year 1

Interest Expense	279	
Premium on Bonds Payable ($400/58 months)(6 months)	41	
Cash .08(6/12)($8,000)		320

The remaining entries in the bond term are identical to the December 31 entry.

III. Bond Issue Costs -- These costs include legal costs, printing costs, and promotion costs. They are capitalized as a noncurrent deferred charge (asset account) and amortized to expense over the term of the bonds using the straight-line method. The rationale for capitalization is that the issue costs will provide benefits the entire bond issue. This is an example of the matching concept. The costs are not netted against the proceeds. Like accrued interest, bond issue costs have no effect on the premium or discount recorded.

Example:

Assume Bender Inc., from the previous example, incurred $580 of bond issue costs in the issuance of the bonds. The bond term is 58 months. The entries in addition to those given previously are:

March 1, Year 1

Bond Issue Costs	580	
Cash		580

June 30, Year 1

Bond Issue Expense ($580/58 months)(4 months)	40	
Bond Issue Costs		40

December 31, Year 1

Bond Issue Expense ($580/58 months)(6 months)	60	
Bond issue costs		60

When bonds are retired early, any remaining unamortized bond issue costs increase the loss on retirement, or decrease the gain, because the asset no longer has any future benefit.

Bond Fair Value Option, International

This lesson addresses the use of the fair value option for bond accounting, and international accounting aspects of bonds.

After studying this lesson, you should be able to:

1. Prepare a bond amortization schedule.

2. Determine when the fair value option can be chosen, for both U.S. and international accounting standards.

3. Apply the fair value option to determine the periodic unrealized gain or loss.

4. Report the unrealized gain or loss in the correct financial statement.

5. Identify differences between U.S. and international principles as they apply to bond accounting.

I. **Amortization Tables** -- Firms often prepare an amortization table for the entire bond issue. The following is an example of an amortization table showing the use of the effective interest method for more than one period. Only the first two years are shown. One line of an amortization conveys the same information as the journal entry for that year.

Example:
On January 1, 20A, the Idaho Company issued bonds with a face value of $100,000 and a stated interest rate of 7%. The bonds will mature on December 31, 20E. Interest on the bonds is paid each December 31. The market rate of interest on January 1, 20A was 8%.

Selling Price of the Bonds

$100,000 × .68058 (Present Value of $1, N = 5, I =8%)	$68,058
$7,000 × 3.99271 (Present Value of Annuity, N = 5, I= 8%)	27949
Total Price	$96,007

Partial Amortization Schedule:

Date	Cash Interest	Effective Interest	Discount Amortized	Unamortized Discount	Carrying Value of Bonds
1/I/20A				$3,993	$96,007
12/31/20A	$7,000	$7,681	$681	$3,312	$96,688
12/31/20B	$7,000	$7,735	$735	$2,577	$97,423

Under the effective interest method, the carrying value of the bonds at the beginning of the year is used to compute interest expense. The 20A interest expense of $7,681 equals ($96,007 × .08). The 20B interest expense of $7,735 equals ($96,688 × .08).

A. When interest payment dates and fiscal year end do not coincide, the portion of the interest period that falls within a reporting period is used to compute interest expense. The effective interest method "straight-lines" the interest calculation during an interest period.

> **Example:**
> If the Idaho bonds above were issued on March 1, Year A, the amount of interest recognized and discount amortized would be 10/12 of the amounts in the 12/31/20A row of the amortization table above. Also, interest payable is credited at 12/31/A for 10/12 of $7,000, rather than cash.

II. Fair Value Option (FVO)

A. The FVO allows certain financial assets and liabilities to be reported at fair value, with unrealized gains and losses reported in earnings in the year they occur. This option reduces the accounting mismatch inherent in using fair value for assets and a different measurement basis for liabilities. The option allows for more consistent reporting and reduces earnings volatility because the effect of interest rate changes on investments in debt securities is opposite that on liabilities such as bonds payable.

B. The firm makes an irrevocable decision to choose the FVO on the date of issuance. The choice is by debt instrument. The option can be applied to all or a subset of debt instruments, even within the same type.

    1. If the option is not chosen, then the accounting proceeds as discussed previously.

    2. If the option is chosen, then the accounting also proceeds as discussed above but in addition, the firm increases or decreases the resulting book liability to fair value.

        a. Fair value is the quoted market price of the security. If that is not available, the current market rate of interest on similar debt instruments is used to estimate fair value.

        b. The required change in the fair value adjustment (FVA: adjunct or contra account) for the period is recognized as an unrealized gain or loss and is included in income from continuing operations.

            i. If the required fair value adjustment has increased, the firm recognizes an unrealized loss. The amount required to pay off the liability relative to the book value under the effective interest method at the balance sheet date has increased.

            ii. If the required fair value adjustment has decreased, the firm recognizes an unrealized gain.

            See the following example.

Example: Fair value option applied.
Amortization Schedule

Date	Cash Interest	Interest Expense	Premium Amortization	Unamortized Premium	Net Liability
1/1/x1				4213	104213
12/31/x1	7000	6253	747	3466	103466
12/31/x2	7000	6208	792	2674	102674
12/31/x3	7000	6160	840	1834	101834
12/31/x4	7000	6110	890	944	100944
12/31/x5	7000	6056	944	0	100000

12/31/x1	Interest expense	6,253	
	Premium	747	
	Cash		7,000

The resulting 12/31/x1 book value is $103,466 (see amortization schedule).

Now assume that the fair value of the bond issue at 12/31/x1 is $102,200 (interest rates have increased). The book value of the bond issue is reduced to that amount using a fair value allowance account (FVA), which can be an adjunct or contra account to bonds payable.

Required fair value adjustment (FVA) = $103,466 − $102,200 = $1,266 dr.

12/31/x1	FVA	1,266	
	Unrealized gain		1,266

Financial Statement Effects

Income Statement		Balance Sheet	
Interest expense	$6,253	Bonds payable	$100,000
Unrealized gain	1,266	Premium	3,466
		FVA	(1,266)
		Net liability (fair value)	$102,200

12/31/x2

The fair value of the bond issue at 12/31/x2 is $103,136 (interest rates have decreased). From the amortization schedule, the book value, had the FVO not been chosen is $102,674 (see amortization schedule).

Required FVA = $103,136 − $102,674 =	$462 cr.
FVA before adjustment	1,266 dr.
Adjustment to FVA	$ 1,728 cr.

Unrealized loss	1,728	
FVA		1,728

The loss of $1,728 also equals the sum of (1) increase in fair value for the period ($103,136 − $102,200), plus (2) $792 amortization of the premium for the period. Both factors cause the difference between fair value and the net liability per the amortization schedule) to increase.

III. U.S. GAAP - IFRS Differences

A. Most aspects of bond accounting are the same for international accounting standards and U.S. standards. For example, the effective interest method is required although the SL method can be used if its results are not materially different. The effective interest rate at issuance and other details of the bond issue must be disclosed. However, there are differences in accounting for debt issue costs, and in applying the fair value option (FVO).

B. IFRS require the effective interest method in all cases, and the amortization period is the expected term of the bond, as opposed to the contractual period as per US standards.

C. Debt issue costs, called transaction costs under international accounting standards, are treated as a reduction in the proceeds from the debt. This is in significant contrast with the U.S. treatment which capitalizes them as an asset and then amortizes them over the bond term.

1. The international treatment reduces any premium and increases any discount because proceeds are reduced. If the liability is not reported at fair value, the effective rate of interest is increased (because proceeds are reduced) with a corresponding effect on periodic interest expense.

 Example: On 1/1/x1, 20, 5%, $1000 bonds are issued at 97.5. The bonds mature in ten years and pay interest each June 30 and December 31. $700 of bond issue costs were incurred.

Calculation of the effective interest rate "m":

.975($20,000) − $700 = $20,000(PV $1, m, n=20) + (.05/2)($20,000)(PV $1 annuity, m, n=20)

$18,800 =$20,000(PV $1, m, n=20) + $500(PV $1 annuity, m, n=20)

Using a spreadsheet program or business calculator, m is computed to be approximately 5.8%. If there were no debt issue costs, m would have been 5.3%.

Journal entries:

1/1/x1	Cash	18,800	
	Discount on bonds	1,200	
	Bonds payable		20,000

6/30/x1	Interest expense	545	18,800(.058/2)
	Discount on bonds		45
	Cash		500

Note that the $700 debt issue costs amount is not capitalized as they would be under U.S. standards. Rather, they reduce the proceeds and increase the discount $700.

D. Fair value option -- This option also is available under international standards but is less of a free choice compared with U.S. standards. The option works the same way. The choice is irrevocable and unrealized gains and losses are recognized in income.

1. However, the option is limited to financial assets and liabilities that are managed and evaluated as a group on a fair value basis as part of a risk management or investment strategy. The entity cannot arbitrarily choose which liabilities will receive the optional accounting treatment. As such, the application of the FVO is more faithful to the underlying purpose of reducing the effect of different accounting measurements on financial assets and liabilities.

Convertible Bonds

The purpose of this lesson is to discuss and illustrate the accounting for convertible bonds.

After studying this lesson, you should be able to:

1. Record the issuance of a convertible bond issue.

2. Compute and record interest expense during the bond term.

3. Provide the journal entry for the conversion of the bonds using the book value method or the market value method.

4. Account for induced conversion of convertible bonds.

5. Record convertible bonds that can be settled in cash.

6. Identify and account for a beneficial conversion feature.

I. **Introduction** -- In an effort to increase the marketability of a bond issue (or increase its equity capital later), a firm may include a convertibility feature in the terms of the bond entitling the holder of the bond to convert the bond into common or preferred stock. The accounting issue here is to correctly account for the conversion. No part of the bond price is allocated to the conversion feature, in direct contrast with bonds issued with detachable stock warrants (discussed in the next lesson).

II. **The Issue**

   A. As will be discussed, an investor could purchase a bond with detachable stock warrants and could hold two securities, one debt security and one equity security. If an investor purchases a convertible bond payable, the investor is purchasing a single debt security that may be converted to an equity security.

   B. When a convertible bond is issued, the entire proceeds are treated as the selling price of the bond. In other words, no proceeds will be allocated to the conversion feature. Accounting for the bonds is unaffected by the conversion feature until conversion takes place.

III. **Two Methods are Allowed by GAAP**

   A. **Book Value Method (the most common)** -- Upon conversion, the remaining book value of the bonds (face value plus unamortized premium or less unamortized discount) is transferred to the capital stock account and contributed capital in excess of par account. No gain or loss is recorded.

      1. If conversion occurs between interest dates, interest expense and amortization of discount or premium is recognized to the point of conversion, for both book value and market value methods.

   B. **Market Value Method** -- Upon conversion, the market value of the stock or bonds, whichever is more reliable, is allocated to the capital stock account and contributed capital in excess of par account. A gain or loss is recorded equal to the difference between the total market value recorded, and the remaining book value of the bonds.

   See the following example.

Example:
A firm has $10,000 of convertible bonds outstanding with a book value of $9,200. Each bond is convertible into 30 shares of $20 par value common stock with a current market value of $32 per share.

Conversion entry under the book value method:

Bonds Payable	10,000	
Discount on Bonds Payable ($10,000 − $9,200)		800
Common Stock (10 bonds)(30)($20 par)		6,000
Contributed Capital in Excess of Par, Common		3,200

No gain or loss is recognized because the book value of the bonds is simply transferred to the stock accounts.

Conversion entry under the market value method:

Market Value of Stock Issued on Conversion = (10 bonds)(30)($32) = $9,600

Bonds Payable	10,000	
Loss on Conversion of Bonds	400	
Discount on Bonds Payable ($10,000 − $9,200)		800
Common Stock (10 bonds)(30)($20 par)		6,000
Contributed Capital in Excess of Par, Common		3,600*

* $9,600 − $6,000 = 3,600. The total value to be recorded in the owners' equity accounts is $9,600, the market value of stock issued.

The loss of $400 is caused by the issuance of $9,600 worth of stock to retire only $9,200 of debt (at book value).

IV. Induced Conversion -- After the convertible bonds are issued, the issuing firm may decide that its financial position would be improved if the bonds were converted. The issuer may then offer additional consideration to the bondholders to encourage them to convert, thus changing the original terms of the bond for a limited period of time.

A. Examples of additional consideration include an increase in the number of shares per bond on conversion, issuance of warrants, and cash. On conversion, the issuer recognizes an expense for the excess of the common stock and other consideration provided to the bondholder, over the fair value of the common stock that would have been issued under the original bond terms. The measurement date for fair value is the date the bondholders accept the offer of inducement. Either method of recording the conversion can be applied (book value method or market value method). The amount of expense recorded is the same.

See the following example.

Example:
Refer to the previous example. Several years after the bonds were issued, the issuing firm increases the number of shares issuable per bond on conversion from 30 to 35 for a limited time, to induce conversion. The bonds are converted when the market price of the stock is $32. Assume the previous $9,200 bond net book value at date of conversion. The entry for conversion under the book value method is as follows:

Bonds Payable	10,000	
Expense for bond conversion	1,600*	
Discount on Bonds Payable ($10,000 − $9,200)		800
Common Stock (10 bonds)(35)($20 par)		7,000
Contributed Capital in Excess of Par, Common		3,800

* (10 bonds)(35 − 30)$32, the fair value of the increase in consideration used for inducement.

If $1,600 cash were used as the inducement, cash would be credited rather than increasing the contributed capital accounts as was the case above.

Bonds with Detachable Warrants

Bonds sold with detachable warrants provide the option to purchase stock of the issuer. This lesson covers the accounting aspects of this type of bond issue.

After studying this lesson, you should be able to:

1. *Allocate the bond price to the bond issue and the warrants.*

2. *Distinguish the two cases that arise for determining the allocation to the bond issue.*

3. *Contrast the U.S. and international accounting treatment of bonds with detachable stock warrants, and convertible bonds.*

I. **Introduction** -- In an effort to increase the marketability of a bond issue, a firm may include detachable stock warrants (also called rights) with the bonds entitling the holder of the warrants to purchase stock at a fixed price within a limited time period. The bonds may pay somewhat lower interest or their price may be increased somewhat, relative to bonds without warrants. The accounting issue here is to determine the allocation of the bond price to the bond and to the warrants.

II. **The Issue** -- When bonds are sold with detachable stock warrants, the issuing company is actually selling two securities in a single transaction. The bond price must be allocated between the bonds payable and the stock warrants based on their fair values. Any accrued interest is treated as with ordinary bonds. The portion of the bond price allocated to the bonds then determines if there is a discount or premium. The portion of the bond price allocated to the warrants is recorded in an owners' equity account. If bonds are sold with nondetachable warrants, there is no allocation of the bond price to the warrants.

> **Note:** Bonds with detachable warrants may sell for a price above 100, but after allocating a portion of the proceeds to the warrants, an amount less than face value may be allocated to the bonds resulting in a discount. Thus, a price exceeding 100 does not necessarily imply a premium when warrants are attached to the bonds.
> Do not allocate any accrued interest to the bonds or warrants. Only the bond price is allocated to the bonds and warrants. The accrued interest is treated as with ordinary bonds, as a separate liability at issuance of the bonds.

III. **Recording the Issuance** -- Allocation of bond price

   A. Fair Market Value of Bonds and Stock Warrants Can be Determined. If both fair market values are known, the proceeds are allocated based on the respective fair market values of the securities.

   B. Fair Market Value of One Security Can be Determined. If the fair market value of only one security is known, proceeds equal to the fair market value are allocated to that security, and the incremental proceeds are allocated to the remaining security.

   C. **Examples** -- A firm issued $10,000 of 6% bonds with detachable stock warrants. Each $1,000 bond has 8 warrants attached. Each warrant entitles the holder to purchase one share of $9 par common stock for $30. The bonds sell for 107 at an interest date; therefore there is no accrued interest.

   See the following example.

Example:
1. The fair values of both securities can be estimated

Assume that the market value of the warrants is $20 each shortly after sale, and the market value of the bonds is 98 without the warrants.

Market Value of Warrants: 10 bonds(8 warrants)($20)		$ 1,600
Market Value of Bonds: .98($10,000)		9,800
Total Market Value		$11,400

Allocation of $10,700 bond price ($1.07 × $10,000):

To Warrants:	($1,600/$11,400)$10,700 =	$ 1,502
To Bonds:	($9,800/$11,400)$10,700 =	9,198
Total	Allocation	$10,700

Entry:			
Cash 1.07($10,000)	10,700	
Discount on Bonds $10,000 − $9,198	802	
Detachable Stock Warrants (OE)		1,502
Bonds Payable		10,000

2. Only the value of the warrants is known ($20 per warrant)

Allocation of $10,700 bond price ($1.07 × $10,000):

To Warrants:	10 bonds(8 warrants)($20)	$1,600
To Bonds:	(remainder)	9,100
Total	Allocation	$10,700

Entry:			
Cash 1.07($10,000)	10,700	
Discount on Bonds $10,000 − $9,100	900	
Detachable Stock Warrants (OE)		1,600
Bonds Payable		10,000

IV. Accounting after Issuance -- Subsequent accounting for the bonds is unaffected by the warrants. The discount or premium is amortized as before. If the warrants are exercised, cash is debited at the exercise price of $30. The detachable stock warrants account also is debited (closed). Credited are common stock and contributed capital in excess of par. If any of the warrants expire without being exercised, the balance in the detachable stock warrants account is closed (debited) to contributed capital from expiration of stock warrants.

See the following example.

Example:
Using the previous example (both market values known), assume all warrants are exercised:

Entry:			
Cash − 10 bonds(8 warrants)($30)		2,400	
Detachable stock warrants		1,502	
Common stock − 10 bonds(8 warrants)($9 par)			720
Contributed capital in excess of par, common			3,182

Now, instead, assume that the warrants expire (because the stock price did not increase above $30).

Entry:			
Detachable stock warrants		1,502	
Contributed capital from expired warrants (OE)			1,502

The $1,502 of the bond price allocated to the warrants is maintained in the permanent contributed capital from expired warrants account.

V. U.S. GAAP - IFRS Differences

A. International accounting standards require that compound securities including bonds with warrants and convertible bonds be separated into their debt and equity components for reporting purposes. This is an example of reporting the economic substance of the transaction rather than being constrained by its legal form. Recall that U.S. accounting does not separate the debt and equity feature for convertible bonds in most cases.

1. In general, international standards require that any compound security that has both debt and equity characteristics be reported as separate components. U.S. standards require this reporting for bonds issued with detachable stock warrants and some other securities, but no corresponding general rule currently exists.

2. For international reporting, the total price of the compound security must be allocated first to the debt component, with the remainder to the equity component as a residual (credit). In the case of a convertible bond (or bonds issued with warrants), the firm estimates the fair value of the bonds without the conversion feature or warrants by using the prevailing rate on similar bonds without such features to discount the future cash flows on the bond alone. That amount is allocated to the bond issue enabling a determination of discount or premium. The remaining portion of the bond price is a residual allocated to the equity feature (conversion feature or warrants). This ordering of allocation (debt first) is consistent with the definition of equity as a residual amount after deducting liabilities from assets. Not allowed is an estimation of the fair value of the equity component, with the residual going to the debt component.

3. Conversion of convertible bonds. The equity component recognized at issuance is closed (debited) on conversion, along with the bonds payable account and any remaining discount or premium. The final capital accounts (stock and contributed capital) are credited in this journal entry. For example, assume that the account "Conversion feature (OE)" was credited upon issuance of a convertible bond. When the bond is converted, the following journal entry is recorded.

See the following example.

Bonds payable	face value
Conversion feature (OE)	amount from issuance
Bond discount	unamortized amount
Common stock	at par
Contributed capital in excess of par	to complete entry*

* only the book value method is used; the current market value of the stock is not used to record the contributed capital accounts and no gain or loss is recognized.

4. If the bonds are not converted, the Conversion feature (OE) account remains as part of the contributed capital accounts of the issuer as is the case for detachable stock warrants not exercised, under U.S. standards.

B. Bonds issued with stock warrants -- U.S. standards require that the allocation of the bond price to detachable stock warrants be based on fair value. As noted above, international standards require that the fair value of the bonds first be estimated, with the residual going to the warrants. This may result in a somewhat different allocation compared with the U.S. approach when the value of the warrants is separately determinable. Also, the international approach is the same for both detachable and nondetachable warrants. U.S. standards allocate a value only to detachable warrants.

C. Induced conversion -- Contrary to the U.S. approach which recognizes an expense for the inducement, international standards do not. Because the issuance of the convertible bond generates a recorded OE component, there is no further adjustment for the inducement.

Refinancing Short-Term Obligations

Current liabilities can be reclassified as noncurrent under the accounting principles covered in this lesson.

After studying this lesson, you should be able to:

1. *List the three ways a firm can reclassify current liabilities to noncurrent status under GAAP.*

2. *Highlight the critical difference between U.S. and international standards with regard to this type of reclassification.*

I. Introduction

A. Definition -- Recall that the definition of a current liability includes "the incurrence of other current liabilities." This means that if a firm refinances a current liability with another current liability, the liability remains classified as current even though no current asset may be required for extinguishment in the coming year. The reason for this requirement is that the debtor firm cannot guarantee it will be able to continue to refinance on a short-term basis indefinitely.

B. Refinancing ST Obligations -- Many firms have a preference for classifying liabilities as noncurrent rather than current to improve their reported liquidity position and reduce the perceived immediate riskiness of the firm. Refinancing on a current basis is of no help here, but if a current liability is refinanced on a long-term basis, the classification of a current liability can be successfully changed to noncurrent.

C. An accounting standard was adopted to curb reporting abuses in this area. It established requirements for reclassifying current liabilities as noncurrent. Now there are definite criteria which must be met before a liability due within one year of the balance sheet date can be reclassified as noncurrent.

D. The Situation -- The situation to be addressed is best explained through an example. On December 31, 20x7, the Bulldog Company had a short-term note payable that matures on April 1, 20x8. The Bulldog Company plans to refinance this short-term obligation as a long-term obligation on April 1, 20x8. The questions at hand involve the classification of the note payable on the December 31, 20x7 balance sheet. Should the note be classified as a current liability? Should be the note be classified as a long-term liability? If so, what conditions should be met to justify the reclassification?

II. Criteria for Reclassifying Current Liabilities as Noncurrent Liabilities -- Reclassification of a current liability to noncurrent status is possible provided two conditions are met. These conditions are described below.

A. Intent -- The intent to refinance the short-term obligation as a long-term obligation must be proven. This proof might be in the form of board of directors' meeting minutes or through written correspondence with the financial institution.

B. Ability

1. The firm must also be able to refinance the obligation and demonstrate that ability before the issuance of the financial statements. There are three ways to meet this requirement. Each must occur in the period between the balance sheet date and the date the financial statements are issued or are available to be issued, if the liability is to be reclassified as noncurrent.

   a. Actually refinance the liability on a long-term basis. In this case, the firm replaces the current liability with a noncurrent liability.

    b. Enter into a noncancelable refinancing agreement supported by a viable lender. The agreement must extend more than one year beyond the balance sheet date. The purpose of the agreement is to refinance the liability on a noncurrent basis.

    c. Issue equity securities replacing the debt.

  2. The details of the refinancing arrangement must be disclosed in the footnotes.

Example:

On December 31, 20x7, the Bulldog Company reports a current note payable that matures on April 1, 20x8. The note is payable to an equipment dealer. The 20x7 financial statements are issued March 4, 20x8. If any of the following transactions or events occur, then the original note is classified as long term in the 20x7 balance sheet:

1. On February 22, 20x8, Bulldog issues another note payable maturing in 20x9 to replace the existing note.

2. On March 1, 20x8, Bulldog signs a noncancelable refinancing agreement with a lender capable of honoring the agreement. The agreement requires the lender to pay the original note in return for a note from Bulldog due after December 31, 20x8 (at a higher interest rate). The refinancing need not occur before the issuance of the financial statements. Only the agreement must be set in place by that time.

3. In February, Bulldog issues shares of its common stock to the equipment dealer in full payment of the note. (If this occurs before the balance sheet date, then Bulldog has no liability to reclassify.)

However, if the firm extinguishes the original note in February by paying cash, and then replenishes the cash with the issuance of a long-term note, the original note remains a current liability in the 20x7 balance sheet because current assets were used for extinguishment.

Also, if a refinancing agreement is cancelable by either party, then there is no reclassification of the note because then there is no guarantee that current assets will not be used in 20x8 to pay the note.

Finally, if the firm enters into a revolving credit agreement whereby one current liability is continually replaced with another current liability, even though no current assets may actually be used for a significant time period, the agreement does not allow reclassification of the liabilities to noncurrent status. This arrangement falls within the definition of a current liability.

Note: The amount of short-term debt that can be classified as noncurrent cannot exceed the amount available under the agreement (or the amount refinanced or extinguished through issuing stock). The maximum amount may also be limited to the value of collateral put up by the debtor. For example, the amount of a $60,000 note to be refinanced with another lender might be limited to $40,000, the amount of collateral put up by the debtor. In this case, only $40,000 could be classified as noncurrent.

III. U.S. GAAP - IFRS Differences

  A. International standards require that the debtor firm must exhibit its ability to refinance the current liability by taking action or having an agreement in-place <u>before</u> the balance sheet date. If the action is delayed until after the balance sheet date but before the financial statements are issued or available to be issued, the current liability is not reclassified. This is in contrast with U.S. standards. The options available under international standards for refinancing a current liability to noncurrent status then are:

    1. The refinancing of the current liability on a long-term basis must occur before the balance sheet date.

2. If a refinancing agreement is the chosen method, the refinancing agreement must be in place before the balance sheet date and the intent of the firm must be to refinance the obligation on a long-term basis within one year of the balance sheet date. An existing loan facility and intent of the firm to roll-over the debt suffices as well.

3. Issuing equity securities to extinguish the liability before the balance sheet is not an option because the firm would have no current liability to report at the balance sheet date. Rather than reclassify the current liability, the liability would be retired.

Debt Retirement

The debt retirement topic is usually tested in the context of bond retirements. The general accounting principles are discussed in this lesson. It also reinforces the basic principles by illustrating a comprehensive example .

After studying this lesson you should be able to :

1. *Apply both the effective interest and straight-line methods when recording a bond retirement.*

2. *Complete the retirement by recording the removal of all relevant bond accounts.*

3. *Record the journal entry to update premium or discount amortization and bond issue cost amortization for a full or partial retirement.*

4. *Compute the bond price on the date of retirement.*

5. *Recognize when a gain or loss is to be recorded.*

6. *Complete the recording of a bond retirement by removing the correct amount of relevant bond account balances at the date of retirement.*

7. *Record the amortization of discount or premium and bond issue costs to the date of retirement on the portion of a bond issue retired.*

I. Accounting Principle

A. When debt is retired at maturity, any discount or premium, and debt issue costs, are fully amortized. The final payment extinguishes the liability at its maturity value, which is also the net liability amount at maturity. No gain or loss is recognized.

> **Note:**
> This topic, in the context of bonds payable, is frequently tested on the CPA exam.

B. Firms may retire their debt at any time (before maturity) unless the debt agreement prohibits it. An accounting issue arises when debt is retired before it matures because interest rates may have changed since the debt was issued. The result is that the firm must pay an amount reflecting the new market rate of interest to retire the debt. This amount may be more or less than the book value of the debt, which still reflects the market rate of interest at date of issue. The accounting issue here is the computation and classification of the gain or loss on retirement of debt.

C. Most gains and losses on debt retirement are included in income from continuing operations.

D. When interest rates have increased since debt was issued, the market price of the debt security decreases (interest rates and debt prices are inversely related). The price the firm will have to pay to retire the debt thus declines below book value. Firms can record sizable gains when they retire their own debt early if interest rates have increased.

E. Conversely, when interest rates have declined, the market price of the debt security increases causing a loss on early retirement.

F. Debt is considered extinguished when one of two conditions is met. Those conditions are described below.

1. The debtor pays the creditor and is relieved of any obligation related to the debt.

2. The debtor is legally released from being the primary obligor of the liability. This legal release may be done by the creditor or by the courts. (An example is the release from a mortgage note upon sale of the related property.)

G. If the debtor firm places assets into an irrevocable trust for the purpose of retiring debt (in-substance defeasance), the liability nonetheless remains on the balance sheet, along with the assets, separately reported. The liability is not extinguished nor is a gain or loss recorded.

II. Accounting for Debt Extinguishment

A. Extinguishment of debt can be accomplished in a variety of ways. The company can simply pay off the debt. Also, debt may be replaced by a new debt issue (a refinancing, also called a refunding). For a refunding, the present value of the new debt issue is used as the price of retiring the old issue. Alternatively, the company may purchase a bond issue on the open market and retire the bonds payable. Finally, the company may retire callable bonds by exercising the "call" feature of the bonds if the bonds are callable, and pay the call price.

B. Regardless of the method however, the accounting is the same:

1. Record interest and amortization of discount or premium, and amortization of debt issue costs, to the date of extinguishment. Accrued interest from the most recent interest payment date will be included in the proceeds.

2. Remove the related debt accounts at their remaining amounts (face value, unamortized discount or premium, and any unamortized debt issue costs)

3. Record the gain or loss. Unless the gain or loss is both unusual and infrequent, it is classified as an ordinary gain or loss.

   a. A gain occurs when the market value of the cash, other asset, or debt instrument used to retire the original debt is less than the book value of the original debt less unamortized debt issue costs. (Unamortized debt issue costs reduce the gain.)

   > Gain = debt book value − unamortized debt issue costs − cash paid

   b. A loss occurs when the market value of the cash, other asset, or debt instrument used to retire the original debt is more than the book value of the original debt less unamortized debt issue costs. (Unamortized debt issue costs increase the loss.)

   > Loss = cash paid − debt book value + unamortized debt issue costs

Example:
The Washington Company exercised its **call** privilege related to an outstanding bond payable. The book value of the bond payable was $105,000, including unamortized premium on bond payable of $5,000. The call price was $104,000. The entry to record the transaction is shown below.

Bonds Payable	$100,000	
Premium on B/P	$ 5,000	
Cash		$104,000
Gain		$ 1,000

III. U.S. GAAP - IFRS Differences

A. The accounting for debt retirement is essentially the same for both sets of standards.

B. International standards use the term "derecognition" of the liability as well as "extinguishment" of debt when a liability is retired. A liability is extinguished or derecognized only when the obligation is discharged, canceled or expired. The terminology for what constitutes an extinguishment is somewhat different between U.S. and international standards, but the meaning and effect is essentially the same. The focus of both is on the economic substance of the transaction.

C. Gains and losses on debt extinguishment are reported in "other income," the same category as interest expense, on international income statements.

D. In-substance defeasance is treated the same way as for U.S. standards. It is not accounted for as an extinguishment of debt or derecognition of the assets used for that purpose.

E. Some modifications of terms restructuring are treated as debt extinguishments for international accounting. This topic is discussed in the lessons on troubled debt restructurings.

IV. Debt Retirement Examples

A. More involved Example of Bond Retirement

Example:
$10,000 of bonds were issued 5/1/Year 1 at 91. The bonds mature 12/31/Year 6. The straight-line method is used. Bond issue costs of $680 were incurred on issue. The bonds pay interest each December 31. On 1/1/Year 4, 60% of the issue was retired at 97.

The bond term is 5 years and 8 months, or 68 months. The bonds are retired when 3 years or 36 months remain in the bond term. The original discount was $900 (.09 x $10,000).

Entry for retirement:

Bonds Payable .60($10,000)	6,000	
Loss	322	
Bond Discount .60($900)(36/68)		286
Bond Issue Costs .60($680)(36/68)		216
Cash .97(.60)($10,000)		5,820

1. **Exam Note --** The CPA exam has previously asked the following type of question in relation to an early retirement of bonds: "In computing the gain or loss on the above bond retirement, the price paid for the bonds is compared to which of the following values?" This question refers to the computation of the gain or loss. The loss in the above example is the difference between the cash paid to retire the debt and the book value of the debt retired less the unamortized bond issue costs on the portion of the debt retired:

Cash paid to retire debt	$5,820
Book value of debt retired 6,000 − 286 =	5,714
Less unamortized bond issue costs (216)	(5,498)
Equals loss	322

The answer to the question is $5,498.

B. Comprehensive Example of Bond Retirement:

Example: This example serves to provide a thorough review of both bond accounting and bond retirement accounting. It includes both the effective interest and straight-line (SL) methods, and illustrates the accounting for partial retirement (less than 100% of the bond issue).

Partial Amortization Schedule (Effective Interest Method)

Date	Cash Interest	Interest Expense	Discount Amortization	Unamortized Discount	Net Liability
1/1/x1				3993	96007
12/31/x1	7000	7681	681	3312	96688
12/31/x2	7000	7735	735	2577	97423

On 4/1/x3 the firm retires one-fourth of the bond issue at 102.

Effective Interest Method
There are 2 years and 9 months remaining in the bond term at 4/1/x3, or 33 months of the total of 60 months in the term. The journal entries are dated 4/1/x3. The three entries shown for each method can be combined.

Entry to accrue interest and amortize the discount and bond issue expense on 1/4 of the bond issue for three months:

Interest expense	487		(3/12)(.08)($97,423)(1/4)
Cash		438	(3/12)(.07)($100,000)(1/4)
Bond discount		49	amortization for 3 mo.
Bond issue expense	63		(3/12)($5,000)(1/4)(1/5)
Bond issue cost		63	amortization for 3 mo.

Interest expense is computed based on the most recent net liability balance ($97,423). Accrued interest of $438 is paid based on the coupon interest rate. The bond issue expense is based on 3/12 of a year on 1/4 of the issue, with the amortization over 5 years.

Entry to remove amounts from affected accounts, recognize the gain or loss, and record the cash payment:

Bonds payable	25,000		
Loss	1,783		
Bond discount		595	$2,577(1/4) − $49
Bond issue costs		688	$5,000(33/60)(1/4)
Cash		25,500	1.02($25,000)

The $49 of amortization from the first entry is subtracted above when removing 1/4 of the remaining discount in the second entry because $2,577 is the remaining discount on all the bonds at 12/31/x2 from the spreadsheet. The $49 has already been removed in the first entry and accounts for the three months of 20x3. The credit of $595 is the amount of discount remaining on 1/4 of the bonds at 4/1/x3 after the first entry is recorded.

The bond issue cost remaining is 33/60 of the amount for 1/4 of the issue because 33 months remains in the bond term at the time of the retirement.

Loss = cash paid − debt book value + unamortized debt issue costs

Loss = $25,500 − ($25,000 − $595) + $688 = $1,783

The remaining 75% of the bond issue continues but the amounts in the full amortization schedule are reduced to 75% of their original amounts.

No entries are recorded for the remaining bonds on 4/1/x3, the early retirement date.

Straight-line Method

The same three entries for the SL method are as follows.

Interest expense	488		
Cash		438	same as in previous set of entries
Bond discount		50	(3/12)($3,993)(1/4)(1/5)
Bond issue expense	63		same as in previous set of entries
Bond issue cost		63	

Note that the SL method is applied the same way to amortize both the discount and bond issue costs.

Bonds payable	25,000		
Loss	1,737		
Bond discount		549	$3,993(33/60)(1/4)
Bond issue cost		688	same as in previous set of entries
Cash		25,500	same as in previous set of entries

The SL method allows a direct calculation of the remaining discount at time of retirement, using the original discount amount, fraction of bond term remaining, and fraction of bond issue retired.

Loss = cash paid − debt book value + unamortized debt issue costs

= $25,500 − ($25,000 - $549) + $688 = $1,737

Troubled Debt

After studying this lesson, you should be able to :

1. *Determine the new interest rate to be applied by the debtor firm in a troubled debt restructure for which the sum of restructured cash flows exceeds the original debt amount.*

2. *Identify the similarities and differences in accounting for troubled debt restructures under U.S. and international standards.*

3. *Account for two types of loan modifications under international standards.*

4. *Record interest expense during the restructured debt term.*

5. *Account for a modification of terms troubled debt restructure when the restructured flows are less than the book value of the liability being restructured.*

6. *Record a settlement troubled debt restructure for both debtor and creditor.*

7. *Categorize a troubled debt restructure into one of three types.*

8. *Identify when a debt restructure is troubled.*

I. Introduction

A. Restructuring of debt is commonplace. Extension of terms, changes in interest rates, and other aspects of the debt agreement are examples. The creditor is said to grant a *concession* when it agrees to terms that are less favorable than under the original debt agreement. A troubled debt restructuring (TDR) occurs in these cases. For a restructuring to be considered a TDR, the creditor must conclude *both* of the following:

1. The creditor granted a concession;

2. The debtor is in financial difficulty, which means that without the concession, it is likely that the debtor will default.

B. The accounting for the restructure depends on whether the debt is settled (a settlement) or whether it continues (a modification of terms). The accounting for settlements by the creditor and debtor is parallel, but is significantly different for a modification of terms. A TDR is a formal restructure. A loan impairment is recorded by the creditor for TDRs and whenever the creditor believes it will receive less than under the original agreement.

C. In all TDR cases, the present value of the consideration paid under the restructured agreement is less than the carrying value of the debt at date of restructure.

1. If the debt is settled, the market value of consideration transferred is less than the carrying value of the debt at date of restructure (creditor grants a concession);

2. If the debt is modified, the present value of the restructured cash flows is less than the carrying value of the debt at date of restructure (creditor grants a concession).

II. Background

A. In a troubled debt restructure, the creditor is attempting to make the best of a bad situation. The debtor is having difficulty living up to the terms of the initial debt agreement. In order to salvage the case, the creditor works with the debtor to restructure the debt agreement.

B. The creditor makes a concession that would not otherwise be made. The creditor typically believes that more is to be gained by voluntarily reducing the payments required under the agreement, or by extending the terms, than by forcing the debtor into bankruptcy.

1. In a settlement restructure, the concession is the acceptance of assets, or equity securities, with a market value less than the book value of the receivable from the debtor, in full payment of the debt;

2. In a modification of terms restructure, the concession is the acceptance of revised debt terms that result in a new present value of remaining cash flows that is less than the book value of the receivable from the debtor.

C. Either way, the creditor accepts consideration with a value less than the liability's book value. Debt restructuring is common. But only when the creditor makes a concession is the restructuring a "troubled" debt restructuring. A settlement TDR is simply an extinguishment of debt at a gain and is not inconsistent with normal noncurrent debt accounting. However, accounting for modification of terms TDRs diverges from the usual procedure.

III. **Debtor and Creditor Recording and Reporting of Settlement Troubled Debt Restructures**

A. **Debtor** -- In settlement restructures, the debtor:

1. Records a gain equal to the book value of the debt, including any unpaid accrued interest, less the market value of consideration transferred in full settlement of the debt;

2. Records an ordinary gain or loss on the disposal of nonmonetary assets transferred in full settlement of the debt;

3. Removes the debt from the books;

4. Records any stock issued in settlement at the market value.

B. **Creditor** -- In settlement restructures, the creditor:

1. Records an ordinary loss equal to the difference between the book value of the receivable and the market value of assets or stock of the debtor received;

2. Removes the receivable from the books;

3. Records assets received at market value.

Example:
On January 1, a debtor owed a creditor a $10,000 note due on this date. In addition, $1,000 of unpaid interest from the previous year was also due. (A 10% original interest rate is implied.) The debtor could not pay the entire amount and the two parties agreed on a restructure in which the debtor would transfer land (cost, $4,000; market value, $2,000) and issue stock (market value and total par value, $5,000) in full settlement of the debt.

Debtor			Creditor		
Note Payable	10,000		Investment in Stock	5,000	
Interest Payable	1,000		Loss on Debt Restructure	4,000	
Loss on Land Disposal	2,000		Land	2,000	
Gain		4,000	Note Receivable		10,000
Capital Stock		5,000	Interest Receivable		1,000
Land		4,000			

The debtor's gain is the difference between the book value of the debt settled ($11,000 which includes interest) less the market value of items transferred ($2,000 land + $5,000 stock). This equals the creditor's loss on restructure (and equals the concession) because the two parties reported the same book value for the debt and receivable plus interest. The debtor's loss on disposal is the loss that would be recorded had the land been sold for cash.

IV. Debtor Reporting of Modification of Terms Troubled Debt Restructure

A. For debtor accounting purposes, there are two very different cases for modification of terms TDRs. The cases are distinguished by the relationship between the pre-restructure book value of the debt, and the nominal sum of restructured future cash flows. The book value of the original debt always includes unpaid accrued interest.

1. In modification of terms restructures in which the nominal sum of the restructured flows is *less than or equal* to the book value of the debt plus accrued interest, the debtor:

   a. Reduces the carrying value of the debt to the nominal sum of restructured cash flows;

   b. Records a gain for the difference between the book value and the nominal sum of restructured cash flows;

   c. Records no further interest; all future cash payments are returns of principal.

2. In modification of terms restructures in which the nominal sum of the restructured flows is *greater* than the book value of the debt plus accrued interest, the debtor:

   a. Records no gain or loss and does not change the carrying value of the debt;

   b. Computes the new rate of interest equating the present value of restructured cash flows and the book value of the debt;

   c. Records interest expense based on the new rate for the remainder of the loan term.

V. SUMMARY TABLE FOR LOAN IMPAIRMENTS AND TDRS

(bv = book value of the liability including unpaid accrued interest)	Creditor	Debtor
TDR (1) Settlement	Creditor accepts assets with market value < bv. Record loss	Gain
TDR (2) Modification of terms: sum of new flows < bv	Loan impairment	Gain, new debt bv = sum of new flows (not pv)
TDR (3) Modification of terms: sum of new flows > bv	Loan impairment	No gain; recognize interest at lower rate

VI. Examples of Modification of Terms TDRs -- This and the next lesson provide examples of modification of terms troubled debt restructurings.

See the following example.

Example:

Debtor accounting for modification of terms. *Nominal sum of restructured flows less than book value.* On January 1, Year 1 a debtor owed a creditor a $10,000 note due on this date. In addition, $1,000 of unpaid interest from the previous year was also due. The debtor could not pay the entire amount and the two parties agreed on a restructure in which the debtor would make the following payments:

		Restructured cash flows
December 31, Year 1	Interest	400
	Principal	3,000
December 31, Year 2	Interest	400
	Principal	3,000
Total restructured cash flows		6,800

The "interest" cash flows are not really interest because all flows are returns of principal in this case. However, restructuring agreements may refer to such smaller flows as interest. The nominal sum of $6,800 is less than the $11,000 book value of debt.

Entries for Debtor:

January 1, Year 1	Interest Payable	1,000	
	Note Payable	10,000	
	Gain		4,200
	Note Payable		6,800

This entry reduces the carrying value of the debt to $6,800. The gain is the difference between the book value of the old debt plus interest ($11,000) and the nominal sum of restructured flows. The old debt accounts are closed and a new note payable is recorded. An alternative is to simply reduce the old note account $3,200 and close the interest payable account.

December 31, Year 1	Note Payable	3,400	
	Cash		3,400
December 31, Year 2	Note Payable	3,400	
	Cash		3,400

The accounting for this case (sum of new flows < book value) is a significant departure from the normal procedure for noncurrent debt accounting which would report the new note payable at present value, rather than nominal value as in this situation.

VII. Troubled Debt - Modification 2, International

A. Examples of Modification of Terms TDRs when Sum of New Flows > BV of Debt --

See the following example.

Example: Debtor accounting for modification of terms. *Nominal sum of restructured flows greater than book value.* On January 1, Year 1 a debtor owed a creditor a $10,000 note due on this date. In addition, $1,000 of unpaid interest from the previous year was also due. Note that the implied interest rate on the loan is 10%. The debtor was unable to pay the total amount and the parties agreed to a restructure in which the debtor would make a single lump sum payment of $11,440 on December 31, Year 1. In this case, the nominal sum of restructured cash flows ($11,440) exceeds the book value of $11,000. Thus, there will be interest paid at the end of Year 1. The new interest rate is found as:

(PV of $1, I = ?, N = 1)($11,440) = $11,000

(PV of $1, I = ?, N = 1)($11,440) = $11,000/($11,440) = .96154

This present value factor corresponds to 4%, indicating the concession made by the creditor. Rather than earning 10%, the creditor will earn only 4%. Another way to consider the concession is to compute the present value of the restructured flows using the original interest rate:

$11,440(PV of $1, I = .10, N = 1) = $11,440(.90909) = $10,400

This amount is less than the $11,000 book value of the debt and thus again the debtor is making a concession.

Entries for Debtor:

January 1, Year 1	No entry needed		
December 31, Year 1	Interest Expense .04($11,000)	440	
	Note Payable	10,000	
	Interest Payable	1,000	
	Cash		11,440

B. The previous example for modification of terms with sum of restructured flows exceeding the book value of the debt to be restructured illustrates a restructure agreement requiring only a single payment. Other examples might require only an annuity of payments. Either way, only one present value factor is used and the calculation of the new interest rate is straightforward.

C. Many restructurings include both single payments and annuities as restructured flows. In these cases, there are two "unknowns" in terms of present value factors. The candidate may be called upon to set up the solution for such a situation, and explain how to solve for the new effective rate. It is even possible that a simulation may enable the actual calculation. The following example is an illustration.

See the following example.

Example: On 1/1/x1 a debtor owed a creditor a $6,573 (face) noninterest-bearing note due on this date. The interest rate implied on this note was 8%. The debtor was unable to pay the total amount and the parties agreed to a restructure in which the debtor would make the following restructured payments: (1) restructured face value of $5,000 due 12/31/x6, (2) annual interest payments at 10% of the new face value, beginning 12/31/x1.

In this example, the sum of restructured cash flows is $8,000 [$5,000 + (6 x $500)] which exceeds the debt book value ($6,573). Is this a troubled debt restructure?

Yes; there are two ways to answer this question.
(1) Use the original interest rate of 8% to determine the present value of new flows. If that present value is less than $6,573, then the creditor is making a concession.

PV of new flows = $5,000(pv of $1, i=.08, n=6) + $500(pv $1 annuity, i= .08, n=6)

PV = $5,000(.63017) + $500(4.62288) = $5,462 < $6,573 therefore, the restructuring is a troubled debt restructure.

(2) Compute the new effective rate (m) implied by the new flows. If that rate is less than 8%, then the creditor is making a concession.

$5,000(pv of $1, m, n=6) + $500(pv $1 annuity, m, 6) = $6,573

The solution for m can be computed using the internal rate of return (IRR) function within standard spreadsheet programs. See below. m = 4% which is less than 8%. Therefore, the restructuring is a troubled debt restructure.

Spreadsheet solution for m. The original liability balance is placed into cell A1 as a negative amount (the "investment"). Each succeeding cell is a separate cash flow in which each new cell indicates a new period. The next five cells are the annual interest payments of $500. The cash flow for 20x6 (cell A7) includes both principal ($5,000) and interest because they occur simultaneously. In cell B7 the IRR function is inserted and the spreadsheet formula returns 4% for m in that cell.

	A	B
1	− 6573	
2	500	
3	500	
4	500	
5	500	
6	500	
7	5500	=IRR(A1:A7)

The first two required journal entries are:

12/31/x1	Interest expense	263	(6,573)(.04)
	Note payable	237	
	Cash		500
12/31/x2	Interest expense	253	($6,573 − $237).04
	Note payable	247	
	Cash		500

At 12/31/x6, the note balance is $5,000 and is retired with the final payment of that amount.

VIII. U.S. GAAP - IFRS Differences

A. International accounting standards treat **settlements** of debt the same way as do U.S. standards although the term "troubled" is not used. The transaction is an extinguishment of debt with a gain recognized by the debtor in profit or loss if the settlement is troubled.

B. International accounting standards do not identify **modifications** of loans as "troubled." Rather, there are two cases based on whether the modification is (1) significant, (2) not significant. These do not correspond to the two modification of terms cases under U.S. standards.

    1. **Significant Modification** -- When the modification of the original loan is considered significant, the transaction is treated as an extinguishment of the old debt and recognition of the new debt. The new debt is recorded at fair value. Any gain or loss is fully recognized and any costs or fees reduce the gain or increase the loss on retirement. This is consistent with the normal application of noncurrent liability accounting.

        a. A modification is significant if the difference between the present values of the two debts (computed with the original rate of interest) is 10% or more of the present value of remaining cash flows on the old debt. The original rate is used only for purposes of determining the 10% threshold. The rate used to record the new debt and recognize subsequent interest is the effective rate of interest on similar debt.

Example: Significant Modification

On January, 1, 20x2, DCo. owes a 6%, $50,000 note due four years from this date, along with one year of unpaid interest for 20x1 ($3,000 = .06 x $50,000). DCo. is experiencing significant financial difficulty and appeals to the creditor to restructure the loan. The creditor agrees in order to help DCo. avoid bankruptcy. The term is left unchanged but the interest rate is reduced to 4%, with interest payments due annually each December 31, and the principal is reduced to $30,000. The one year of unpaid interest is not forgiven but rather is required to be paid immediately. The creditor charges $1,900 to restructure the loan payable in cash.

The present value of the new loan arrangement using the original 6% rate is as follows:

pv = 30,000(pv of $1, i=6%, n=4) + .04(30,000)(pv $1 annuity, i=6%, n=4) + 3,000

pv = 30,000(.79209) + 1,200(3.46511) + $3,000 = 30,921

The present value of the new loan arrangement at 6% is $30,921, or approximately 58.3% of the $53,000 present value of the original loan. The 10% threshold is exceeded and thus the transaction is treated as an extinguishment of the original loan. The new loan is to be recognized at fair value. The comparison of present values computed under the original loan's interest rate is solely for the purpose of determining whether the modification is substantial (exceeds the 10% threshold).

Assume that the market rate of interest on the new loan is 13% given DCo.'s financial condition. The new loan is reported at its fair value, the present value of future cash flows at 13%.

New loan initial book value =

  = 30,000(pv of $1, i=13%, n=4) + .04(30,000)(pv $1 annuity, i=13%, n=4)

  = 30,000(.61332) + 1,200(2.97447) = 21,969

Note payable	50,000		
Interest payable	3,000		
Note payable		21,969	
Cash		4,900	($3,000 interest + $1,900 costs)
Gain		26,131	

The above journal entry illustrates the net method. If the gross method were used, the new note payable would be recorded at $30,000 with a discount of $8,031 debited. Either way, interest expense on the restructured note is based on the net note balance at the beginning of each period, calculated at 13%.

2. Not A Significant Modification. If the 10% threshold is not met, then the difference in present values is deferred and amortized over the new debt term. The new debt is not measured at fair value but rather takes on the original loan book value plus or minus the loss or gain. Any costs or fees adjust the carrying value of the debt and are thus amortized over the new debt term. A deferred gain is a liability and its amortization is reported in other income.

 Example:
Not A Significant Modification

A firm in financial difficulty includes in its liabilities a 4%,$80,000 loan due six years from the current balance sheet date, December 31, 20x4. The interest due on that date is paid. On the next day (1/1/x5) the firm restructures the loan with the creditor. The term is shortened to four years, principal reduced to $75,000, and the interest rate is reduced to 3% with interest payments due annually each December 31 beginning one year from the restructuring date.

The present value of the new loan using the original 4% rate is as follows:

pv = 75,000(pv of $1, i=4%, n=4) + .03(75,000)(pv $1 annuity, i=4%, n=4)

pv = 75,000(.85480) + 2,250(3.62990) = 72,277

There is less than a 10% difference between the two present values ($72,277/$80,000 = 90.3%).

Note payable	80,000	
Note payable		72,277
Deferred gain		7,723

The original interest rate of 4% continues to be applied to the new debt balance for purposes of computing interest expense.

Debt Covenant Compliance

Several aspects of debt covenants are discussed in this lesson.

After studying this lesson, you should be able to:

1. Describe the basic content of a debt covenant.

2. Articulate the reasons for debt covenants.

3. List several attributes that serve as the restriction included in debt covenants.

4. Note different ways in which compliance with a debt covenant can be demonstrated.

5. Be aware of the possible responses by the creditor in the event of noncompliance.

6. Reclassify debt, if needed, in the event of noncompliance.

I. Background - Debt Covenants

A. A debt covenant is a part of the larger contract underlying the debt instrument. A bond indenture (contract) details the rights and duties of the issuing firm (debtor, borrower) and the bond holder (creditor, lender), for example. A covenant, also called a restriction, is a section of the contract that describes the responses available to the creditor if certain events or conditions occur, such as the debtor's current ratio declining below a certain level. The covenant may allow the creditor to call the debt (demand immediate payment). Covenants also protect the debtor from such actions should the conditions not occur (debtor maintains compliance with the covenant).

B. Covenants can be established either unilaterally by the creditor, or through negotiation between creditor and debtor. Firms emerging from corporate reorganization or bankruptcy may be subject to more stringent covenants. A description of the covenant is disclosed in the notes to the debtor's financial statements.

C. Covenants are one form of protection for the creditor. Others include requiring the issuing firm to redeem bonds according to a prespecified schedule (sinking fund debentures), requiring the issuing firm to accumulate a sinking fund for the eventual retirement of bonds, and structuring the bonds as serial bonds.

II. Specific Attributes Used in Covenants

A. A wide variety of measures is used in debt covenants. Typically, a minimum or maximum value for the measure is the condition beyond which the debtor is in violation. The following list provides examples.

1. Current ratio (current assets/current liabilities), a measure of liquidity. If the debtor's current ratio falls below 2.0 for example (a minimum level), the debtor has violated the covenant. The creditor then has the right to respond in specific ways defined in the contract. This aspect is discussed below.

2. Working capital (current assets - current liabilities). A minimum level is specified in the covenant.

3. Income measures such as net income before tax, net income, income from continuing operations, and EBITDA (earnings before interest, taxes, depreciation, and amortization). The covenant specifies a minimum absolute level, or possibly one based on a percentage of the previous year's amount.

4. Interest coverage ratio (EBITDA/interest expense). A minimum level is specified.

5. Retained earnings balance, or total owners' equity balance. A minimum level is specified.

6. Debt to equity ratio. A maximum level is specified.

7. Total debt. A maximum level is specified.

8. Interest expense. A maximum level is specified.

9. Total assets or net assets. A minimum level is specified.

III. U.S. GAAP - IFRS Differences

A. If the debtor firm breaches a debt covenant causing the debt to be payable on demand, it is classified as current, unless the creditor agrees, by the balance sheet date, to allow a "grace" period ending at least one year after the balance sheet, during which the creditor can cure the breach and during which the debtor cannot demand payment.

B. For subjective acceleration clauses, U.S. standards require current classification when relevant conditions are present because the callable on demand feature cannot be controlled by the debtor. International standards have no such requirement.

Owner's Equity Basics

This lesson begins several addressing the accounting for owners' equity (OE) by a corporation. The overview of this large area is provided here. This lesson continues with the basics by addressing the rights of stockholders, and the categories of capital stock found in the owners' equity section of the balance sheet.

After studying this lesson you should be able to:

1. *Identify terminology differences for OE between U.S. and international reporting.*

2. *Apply stock dividends and splits to the computation of the number of shares in each category.*

3. *Compute the number of shares in the authorized, issued, outstanding, and treasury states or categories.*

4. *List and distinguish the rights of common and preferred shareholders.*

5. *Define several terms within the OE category.*

6. *List several different accounts that fall under "additional paid in capital."*

7. *Compare the corporate form of business organization to other forms of business organization.*

8. *Identify OE accounts from a list that includes other types of accounts.*

9. *Distinguish the two major types of OE.*

Definition:
Owners' Equity: The owners' equity (OE) accounts represent the residual interest in the net assets of an entity that remain after deducting its liabilities.

I. Two Main OE Categories

A. OE can be divided into two main categories: (although there are other minor subcategories that do not fall into the two main ones.)

1. Earned; and

2. Contributed.

B. Earned Capital -- There is no one measurement basis for earned capital (retained earnings) because all of the measurement bases that are reflected in net income are also reflected in retained earnings.

C. Contributed Capital -- The primary measurement basis for contributed capital is the historical value of direct investments made in the firm by investors, in return for shares of capital stock.

D. Equation

Total owners' equity = total assets − total liabilities.

1. This equation can also be used for changes in the three types of accounts during a period.

 Example:
(Changes in account balances—find unknown OE change) The following changes in a firm's account balances occurred during the year:

	Increase
Assets	$8,900
Liabilities	2,700
Capital stock	6,000
Additional paid-in capital	600

Assume a $1,300 dividend payment and the year's earnings were the only changes in retained earnings for the year. Net income for the year can be found as follows:

Increase in Assets	=	Increase in Liabilities + Increase in OE
$8,900	=	$2,700 + $6,000 + $600 + net income − $1,300
Net income	=	$900

II. Presentation of Equity Accounts

A. Major Account Types -- For a corporation, the major account types in OE are:

1. Preferred stock, the total par value of issued preferred stock;

2. Common stock, the total par value of issued common stock unless the stock is no-par stock and a stated value is not used;

3. Additional paid-in capital, preferred. This account reports the amount received for preferred stock issuances in excess of the par value;

   a. "Additional paid-in capital" is also referred to as "contributed capital in excess of par."

4. Additional paid-in capital, common. This account reports the amount received for common stock issuances in excess of the par value;

   a. In general, "Additional paid-in capital" is a category of OE used for several different sources such as paid-in capital from treasury stock transactions, stock award plans, and others.

5. Retained earnings, the net of the firm's earnings to date less dividends to date, plus or minus other items including prior period adjustments and certain accounting changes.

6. Accumulated other comprehensive income, the running total of all other comprehensive income items through the balance sheet date. See the lesson on the statement of comprehensive income.

7. Treasury stock which is the cost or par value of the common stock of a firm purchased by that firm, depending on the method used by the firm. Treasury stock of Coca-Cola Company, for example, is stock of Coca-Cola purchased by Coca-Cola. This account is a negative or contra OE account.

B. Types of Ownership

1. The types of ownership, and therefore the types of accounts recorded in OE, include

    a. A sole proprietorship;

    b. The partnership form of business;

    c. The corporate form of business.

> **Note:**
> This lesson stresses the corporate form of ownership because that form is emphasized on the CPA exam.

2. Sole Proprietorship

    a. With a proprietorship, the ownership of the business enterprise consists of a single individual or party.

3. Partnership

    a. With a partnership, the ownership of the business enterprise consists of two or more participants.

4. Corporation

    a. With the corporate form of business, the stock may be closely held by a small number of investors or, in the case of a publicly traded company, the stock may be held by a large number of investors with the stock traded on an organized exchange.

    b. The stockholders' section of the corporate balance sheet includes the contributed capital accounts, such as common stock and contributed capital in excess of par, the retained earnings account and others referred to above.

    c. Capital stock (preferred or common) is the means by which ownership is conveyed. If there is only one class of stock, it is common stock.

5. Advantages and disadvantages of the corporate form of business

    a. Shareholders have limited liability; the corporation is a separate legal entity. Shareholders are not liable for the actions of the corporation and can lose only their investment. Partners and sole proprietors have unlimited liability. If the business cannot satisfy its debts, the creditors can seek relief from the owners of those types of businesses.

    b. A firm "goes public," i.e. becomes a corporation, because it is easier to raise significant amounts of capital. Any investor in the world can purchase shares of a publicly traded corporation. Current shareholders can likewise sell their shares easily. In contrast, each time the ownership composition of a partnership changes, the partnership agreement is redrawn.

    c. Lack of mutual agency for a corporation. The actions of one shareholder (unless an officer of the corporation) does not bind the corporation or other shareholders. In contrast, each partner's actions binds the partnership.

    d. Double taxation of corporate profits. A corporation must pay income taxes and file an annual tax return. Dividends to shareholders are taxed on their personal returns. This double taxation is mitigated to some extent through the dividends received deduction if a shareholder of one corporation is another corporation (discussed in the taxation section of this review course). In contrast, partnerships and sole proprietorships file only an information return. The owners pay income tax on their portion of the income from the business.

    e. Corporations are subject to a great deal more regulation, including SEC reporting requirements for publicly held corporations.

6. Hybrid organizations -- These organizations have some of the characteristics of both corporations and partnerships or sole proprietorships.

    a. S corporation. This is a classification for tax purposes. If the relevant tax rules are followed, limited liability is retained but the income is taxed only once, at the owner level.

    b. Limited liability companies allow all owners to be involved in the management of the business with each being liable only to the extent of their investment. Double taxation is avoided.

    c. Limited liability partnerships are less generous with respect to the limited liability feature.

III. Legal Capital -- "Par" value is the minimum legal issue price for capital stock in most states and appears on the stock certificate.

  A. No Par Value Alternatives -- If the stock has no par value, two alternatives exist:

    1. The firm may designate a stated value which serves the same function as par value except that it does not appear on the certificate.

    2. The firm may not use a par value at all, in which case the stock is referred to as no par stock.

  B. Measured at Par or Stated

    1. The preferred stock and common stock accounts are always measured at par or stated value.

    2. Any excess of issuance price over the par value is credited to additional paid-in capital (preferred or common).

  C. No Par Stock Credited -- If the stock is no-par stock, then the entire issuance proceeds is credited to the capital stock account and there is no additional paid-in capital account (contributed capital in excess of par).

  D. Legal Capital -- The legal capital or minimum capital of a corporation is usually the par value of the stock or the stated value of the stock issued.

    1. **Establishes Minimum Investment --** This legal requirement establishes the minimum investment necessary to become a part of the ownership group of a corporation.

    2. **Protection for Creditors --** Legal capital provides a measure of protection for the creditors of the corporation.

      a. Dividends may not be paid from legal capital;

      b. If there were no such protection, management could liquidate the corporation by paying back the shareholders their investment, leaving the creditors with assets that might not be worth their book value.

      c. In many states, firms may not pay dividends to common stock in an amount that would cause total assets to be less than total liabilities plus the liquidation preference of preferred stock. The liquidation preference of preferred stock is the amount payable on liquidation of the company.

  E. Stock Not Discounted -- In most states, stock cannot be sold at a discount.

    1. If stock is sold at a discount, a contingent liability equal to the difference between the par or stated value and the acquisition cost of the stock is borne by the original shareholder.

    2. This requirement is an attempt to provide some legal protection for creditors.

  F. Treasury Stock Transactions -- Another attempt to provide some protection for creditors is a limit on the amount of treasury stock transactions.

    1. In many states, treasury stock may not be purchased in excess of the amount of unrestricted or unappropriated retained earnings.

    2. The corollary of this constraint is that the cost of treasury stock is a restriction on retained earnings.

Example:
A firm has $100,000 of assets, but only $30,000 is liquid current assets.

Total debt equals $70,000.

The firm has no retained earnings.

The legal capital of the firm is $30,000.

Although the firm has sufficient recorded assets to cover the creditor and shareholder interests, if the $30,000 of liquid assets was paid to the shareholders, buying out their interests, the $70,000 book value of remaining assets may not be sufficient to cover the creditors' claims because the assets may have a market value significantly less than $70,000.

The creditors would incur a loss.

This would be in direct violation of the order of rights upon liquidation of a corporation: Stockholders receive assets after all the creditors are satisfied.

IV. Rights of Shareholders, States of Stock

A. Common Stock Rights -- In return for purchasing a share of common stock, the common shareholder receives the following rights:

1. Voting Rights

a. Common shareholders have the right to participate in the decision-making process of a corporation by voting for the board of directors, the external auditors, and other major issues.

b. That is, the shareholders have a right to participate in major operating and financing decisions through the exercise of voting rights.

c. They do not, however, have the right to participate in day-to-day management functions.

2. Dividend Rights

a. Common shareholders have rights related to the receipt of dividends.

b. The dividend rights of common shareholders are subordinate rights in that preferred shareholders receive their dividend allocation prior to any allocation to the common shareholders.

c. Dividends are not mandatory.

d. They must be declared by the Board of Directors before the firm is liable to the shareholders for dividends.

3. Preemptive Rights

a. The preemptive rights of common shareholders allow current shareholders to maintain their existing percentage of the firm in the event of a new stock issuance by the firm.

b. Preemptive rights are not always present, depending on state law and the corporate charter.

c. The preemptive right is important to shareholders owning an appreciable percentage of the firm.

    d. Without the preemptive right, management could issue shares in an effort to reduce the percentage ownership (and influence) of a shareholder who disagrees with the current management over major issues affecting the direction of the firm.

 Example:
A firm plans to issue 100,000 shares of common stock.

A shareholder currently owns 2% of the outstanding common stock.

The shareholder must be allowed to purchase 2,000 of the new shares if the preemptive right is present.

The shareholder cannot be compelled to make the purchase, however.

    4. **Rights Related to Liquidation** -- In the event of liquidation, common shareholders are again in a subordinate role.

        a. The creditors are satisfied first.

        b. Then, the preferred shareholders are eligible to receive the liquidation values for the preferred shares.

        c. Finally, the remaining assets are distributed to the common shareholders. The common shareholders are the very last to receive assets on liquidation. They have the residual interest in the firm.

        d. Positive total owners' equity does not necessarily imply that any shareholders will receive assets upon liquidation. If the fair value of assets is less than total liabilities at liquidation, no shareholder would receive any assets.

B. Preferred Stock Rights -- Preferred stock is called "preferred" because these shares typically are paid dividends before common stock. Preferred shareholders, however, usually give up their right to vote in return for the dividend preference.

    1. **The rights of preferred shareholders are**

        a. Nonvoting -- Typically, preferred shareholders do not have voting rights. That is, preferred shareholders are not participants in the major operating and financing decisions made by the company.

        b. Dividend Preferences -- In relation to dividends, preferred shareholders receive their dividend allocation first. Then, the remainder of the dividend is allocated to common shareholders.

        c. Additional Features -- This dividend preference for preferred shareholders can be enhanced by additional features such as with cumulative preferred stock and participating preferred stock. The process of allocating dividends to the two types of stock is illustrated in a later lesson.

        d. Dividends in Arrears

            i. If preferred stock is cumulative and dividends for a year are not paid, then the dividends are said to be in arrears.

            ii. No dividends may be paid to any other class of stock, including the current preferred stock dividend requirement, until the dividends in arrears are paid.

            iii. This is how the dividend preference for preferred stock is preserved. However, there is no liability for dividends in arrears until the dividends are declared.

            iv. Undeclared dividends in arrears are disclosed in the footnotes until the dividends are paid.

e. Liquidation Preferences

    i. In the event of liquidation, the creditors are paid first.

    ii. Secondly, the preferred shareholders receive their specified liquidation values per share. This amount may be different from par value, or the value paid for the shares. The liquidation preference per share of preferred stock must be disclosed in the equity section of the balance sheet when the preference exceeds par value. There is no preemptive right for preferred shareholders because preferred stock does not vote in the affairs of the corporation.

    iii. Finally, any remainder is allocated to the common shareholders.

C. Number of Common Shares Issued, Outstanding, and in the Treasury

1. **Common Stock --** When a corporation is formed, the total number of shares that may be issued is called the *authorized shares* . This amount can be increased only by vote of the shareholders. For common stock, this total can be broken down into:

   a. Number issued: The number of shares ever issued by the firm but not retired

   b. Number outstanding: The number of shares currently held by stockholders

   c. Number in the treasury: The number of shares purchased by the issuing firm and not yet reissued. Treasury shares are included in the number of issued shares:

   > \# Issued shares = \# Outstanding shares + \# Treasury shares

   > **Note:** The number of issued shares is always greater than or equal to the number of outstanding shares if the firm has treasury stock.

2. **Treasury Not Outstanding --** Cash and property dividends are not paid on treasury stock because treasury shares are not outstanding.

3. **Shares Outstanding --** Earnings per share and most other per-share calculations are made on shares outstanding because these shares represent the "active" shares -- those in the hands of the investors. These are the shares that vote and receive dividends.

4. **Dividends and Splits --** Stock dividends and splits not substantive transactions. They do not cause a change in the firm's assets or relative ownership in the firm. They are retroactively applied to all issuances of stock preceding the stock dividend or split.

   See the following example.

Example:
1. Shares outstanding computation

A corporation had 70,000 shares of common stock authorized and 30,000 shares outstanding at the beginning of the year. During the year, the following events occurred:

January	Declared 10% stock dividend
June	Purchased 10,000 shares for the treasury
August	Reissued 5,000 shares
November	Declared 2-for-I stock split

At the end of the year, the number of outstanding shares of common stock are:

$$(30,000(1.10) - 10,000 + 5,000)2 = 56,000$$

Stock dividends and splits are applied retroactively to all shares outstanding and are applied to all substantive changes in shares outstanding that occur before the stock dividend or split.

2. Number of shares issued and outstanding calculation

Of the 12,500 shares of common stock issued by a firm, 2,500 shares were in the treasury at the beginning of the year. During the year, the following transactions occurred in chronological order:

a. 1,300 treasury shares were reissued under a stock compensation plan

b. A 3-for-1 stock split took effect

c. 500 shares of treasury stock were purchased

Issued shares include outstanding shares and treasury shares. Treasury shares are issued but not outstanding. Stock splits are applied to all outstanding shares because a split reduces the par value of each share of issued stock. Treasury shares must be adjusted for splits because treasury shares typically are reissued.

Number of shares issued at year end: 12,500(3) = 37,500

Number of shares outstanding at year end: (10,000 + 1,300)3 - 500 = 33,400

3. Number of shares issued and outstanding computation

A firm issued 10,000 shares of common stock. Of these, 500 were held as treasury stock at December 31, 20x3. During 20x4, transactions involving the firm's common stock were as follows:

May - 100 shares of treasury stock were sold.

August - 1,000 shares of previously unissued stock were sold.

November - A 2-for-1 stock split took effect.

Laws in the firm's state of incorporation protect treasury stock from dilution. At December 31, 20x4, the number of common stock issued and outstanding:

Issued = (10,000 + 1,000)2 = 22,000

Outstanding = (9,500 + 100 + 1,000)2 = 21,200

The treasury shares are already issued. Therefore, in the calculation of issued shares, no separate adjustment for treasury shares is needed.

D. Disclosures

1. Footnote disclosures for equity can be extensive if the entity has several classes of stock. The following are required disclosures.

   a. Rights and preferences of each class of stock including liquidation preferences and voting rights;

   b. Number of shares authorized, issued and outstanding for each class of stock;

   c. Par value for each class of stock;

   d. Treasury shares;

   e. Restrictions regarding dividends and dividends in arrears;

   f. Call and conversion information.

E. U.S. GAAP—IFRS Differences

1. International and U.S. accounting for stockholders' equity are very similar. Some areas are not addressed by international standards and the U.S. treatment is typically prescribed in these situations. In terms of presentation on the balance sheet, OE is often presented before liabilities in international statements. Owners' equity in international statements has three main categories: issued share capital, retained earnings, and other equity including reserves. The term "reserve" is not commonly used in U.S. financial reporting.

2. **Terminology differences**

   a. Common stock and its account in the ledger are referred to as "ordinary shares" for international accounting.

   b. Preferred stock is referred to as "preference shares."

   c. Paid-in capital in excess of par (or additional paid-in capital) is referred to as "share premium."

   d. The term "reserve" is commonly used.

3. **Reserves**

   a. In some international jurisdictions, reserves are similar to retained earnings appropriations under U.S. GAAP in that they restrict dividends. Paid-in capital, for example, is typically off-limits for dividends as well as amounts paid for treasury stock (capital redemption reserve). Firms may set up a reserve account for that purpose (a credit to an OE account). Likewise, the revaluation surplus or reserve from upward revaluation of plant assets is not available for dividends.

   b. The items reported in other comprehensive income are referred to as "reserves" for international accounting. For example, the net unrealized gain or loss on available-for-sale securities under the fair value method is referred to as "investment revaluation reserve." Another is the revaluation reserve from upward revaluation of plant assets.

   c. Depending on the jurisdiction, a firm may be required to establish a reserve, called a statutory or legal reserve, based on the requirements of the law. These reserves may be required for protection of creditors. The reserve is created in an account similar to an appropriation under U.S. standards.

4. **Disclosures**

   a. In addition to the usual disclosures involving equity as per U.S. statements, international disclosures also include amounts of capital not yet paid in, restrictions on the repayment of capital, and changes in reserve accounts.

b. The amount of treasury stock can be disclosed either in the OE section of the balance sheet or in the notes.

c. If a firm reserves shares for future issuance under stock options or subscription contracts, the number of shares, terms and amounts are disclosed. A firm must have sufficient shares to satisfy these commitments. The reserved shares are not available for other transactions.

Stock Issuance

The different ways that stock is issued are addressed in this lesson.

After studying this lesson, you should be able to:

1. Prepare the journal entry for the issuance of par stock, no-par stock with stated value, and true no-par stock, for cash.

2. Record a stock subscription and defaults by subscribers.

3. Classify the stock subscriptions receivable account.

4. Record the journal entry for stock issued in exchange for a nonmonetary asset or service.

5. Allocate the total issuance proceeds to several securities in a basket sale.

6. Account for stock issuance costs.

I.   There are Several Types of Stock Issuance Transactions

    A.   Cash Transaction -- In recording a cash sale of common stock, the corporation will credit the stock account for the par or stated value of the stock sold. Any remainder is recorded in an account such as contributed capital in excess of par value or in excess of stated value.

        1.   Entry for issuance of par (or stated) value common stock:

	(issue price) × (# of shares issued)	
Cash		
Common stock		(par or stated value) × (# of shares issued)
Contributed capital in excess of par(common)		(remaining amount*)
*(issue price - par or stated value) x (# of shares issued)		

    B.   Preferred stock -- Is handled the same way; the issuance of preferred stock credits the Preferred stock account and contributed capital in excess of par (preferred).

    C.   True No Par Stock -- When the stock is true no-par stock (without stated value),

        1.   The entire proceeds from issuance of stock are credited to the common stock account;

        2.   No contributed capital account is recorded.

> **Note:**
> If the stock has no par value but a stated value is specified, the contributed capital account is titled: Contributed capital in excess of stated value (common).

    D.   Stock Sold on a Subscription Basis

        1.   Sale of stock on a subscription basis requires a contract specifying

            a.   Share price;

            b.   Number of shares;

            c.   And the payment dates.

2. **When stock is sold** on a subscription basis, the implication is that the selling price of the stock will be received in a series of payments from the shareholder. Once the full amount is received, the stock will be issued.

3. **At the signing of the contract** -- Subscribers may make their first payment.

4. **Initial payment**

Cash	amount of payment
Stock subscriptions receivable	sum of remaining payments
Common stock subscribed	(par) × (# of shares subscribed)
Contributed capital in excess of par	(contract price − par) × (# shares)

5. **Subsequent payments**

Cash	amount of payment
Stock subscriptions receivable	amount of payment

6. **Issuance of shares after final payment**

Common stock subscribed	(par) × (# of shares subscribed)
Common stock	(par) × (# of shares subscribed)

7. **Account classifications** -- Stock subscriptions receivable: contra-common stock subscribed (contra OE). However, if the subscription is fully paid before the financial statements are issued or available to be issued, then the account is classified as an asset.

8. **Common stock subscribed** -- Owners' equity.

9. **Recorded at Signing** -- Note that the contributed capital in excess of par is recorded when the contract is signed indicating that, in all probability, the shares will be issued.

10. **Credited Upon Final Payment** -- Common stock is not credited until the final payment is made because the shares are not issued at that time.

11. **Default by subscriber** -- If the subscriber fails to make all the payments and defaults, the journal entry to record the default depends on the contract and applicable state law.

12. Possibilities include:

    a. Return all payments to subscriber;

    b. Issue shares in proportion to payments made;

    c. The subscriber receives no refund or shares.

See the following example.

Example: An individual subscribes to 200 shares of $10 par common stock at a subscription price of $15. After making payments totaling $1,200, the subscriber defaults.

Summary entry before default:

Cash	1,200	
Stock subscriptions receivable	1,800	
Common stock subscribed		2,000
Contributed capital in excess of par		1,000

Default assumption (1), return all payments to subscriber:

The above entry is reversed.

Default assumption (2), issue shares in proportion to payments made:

$1,200/$15 = 80 shares fully paid. Required ending balances:

Common stock: 80($10)	= $800
Contributed capital in excess of par: 80($15-$10)	= $400

Common stock subscribed	2,000	
Contributed capital in excess of par	600	
Subscriptions receivable		1,800
Common stock		800

OE increases $1,200 as a result of this entry.

Default assumption (3), no refund or shares to subscriber:

Common stock subscribed	2,000	
Contributed capital in excess of par	1,000	
Subscriptions receivable		1,800
Contributed capital from default		1,200*

*equals amount paid in by subscriber

E. Stock Issued in Exchange for Nonmonetary Consideration

1. **Value Most Clearly Determined** -- When stock is sold and a nonmonetary asset is received, the recording of the transaction will be based on the fair market value of the stock sold or the fair market value of the asset received (or services received), whichever can be most clearly determined.

2. **Small Number of Shares** -- When the stock is actively traded, and the number of shares issued is small in relation to the number of shares already outstanding, generally the market price of the issued shares is the more reliable of the two measures.

3. **Significant Number of Shares** -- If the number of shares issued is significant, then the market value of the consideration received may be a better measure because the issuance of a large number of shares could affect the market price of the stock.

Example:
1. A firm issued 300 shares of $5 par common stock for used equipment.

2. The market value of the equipment is not easily determinable.

3. The firm's stock was quoted at $30 a share on a national stock exchange.

4. The firm has hundreds of thousands of shares outstanding.

Equipment 300($30)	9,000	
Common stock 300($5)		1,500
Contributed capital in excess of par - common		7,500

If services are received in exchange for stock issuance, the debit is to an expense.

II. Basket Sale

A. A basket sale occurs when two or more securities are bundled together and sold in a single transaction.

B. The total amount received must be allocated to the individual securities sold.

C. **Allocating Methods** -- For example, common stock and preferred stock might be bundled together and sold in a single transaction. In allocating the proceeds to the common stock sold and the preferred stock sold, the company will use the proportional method or the incremental method.

1. **Proportional Method** -- When both securities have established market values, the allocation will be based on their respective fair market values.

2. **Incremental Method** -- When only one security has an established fair market value, that security is assigned proceeds equal to the known fair market value. Any incremental proceeds are allocated to the remaining security sold.

Example:
100 shares of a firm's $10 par common stock, along with 50 shares of the firm's $12 par preferred stock are issued as a unit for a total consideration of $4,200.

1. The market prices of the shares are: common, $35; preferred, $20.

		Total market values:		Allocation of proceeds:	
Common	$35(100)	$3,500	($3,500/$4,500)$4,200	$3,267
Preferred	$20(50)	1,000	($1,000/$4,500)$4,200	933
Total		$4,500		$4,200

Entry to record issuance:

Cash	4,200	
Preferred stock 50 × $12		600
Contributed capital in excess of par-preferred ($933 − $600)		333
Common stock 100 × $10		1,000
Contributed capital in excess of par-common ($3,267 − $1,000)		2,267

2. The market price for the common stock is $35. The preferred stock does not sell actively and no current quote is available.

Total allocation to common = $35(100) = $3,500

Remaining amount of proceeds to preferred: $4,200 − $3,500= $700

<u>Entry to record issuance:</u>

Cash	4,200	
Preferred stock 50 × $12		600
Contributed capital in excess of par-preferred ($700 − $600)		100
Common stock 100 × $10		1,000
Contributed capital in excess of par-common ($3,500 − 1,000)		2,500

III. Stock Issue Costs are Treated as a Reduction in the Proceeds of the Stock Issuance -- This reduces the contributed capital in excess of par account.

A. **Rationale --** There is no future benefit of the issue costs -- the costs have served their purpose as soon as the stock is issued. No future periods benefit. This view emphasizes the balance sheet.

> **Note:** In contrast with stock issue costs, debt issuance costs (e.g., bond issue costs) must be recorded in a deferred charge, and amortized over the debt term. Offsetting against the proceeds is not allowed for debt. For stock issue costs, there is no term over which to amortize the costs.
> **Note:** The annual costs of maintaining the stockholder records and processing dividends are expensed as incurred.

Example:
A firm issued 100 shares of $5 par common stock for $26 per share and incurred $75 of stock issue costs.

Cash (100 × $26) − $75	2,525	
Common stock		500
Contributed capital in excess of par, common		2,025

There is no further accounting for the issue costs.

Preferred Stock

The accounting treatment for the issuance, redemption, retirement and conversion of preferred stock is addressed by this lesson.

After studying this lesson, you should be able to:

1. *Prepare the journal entries for the issuance and retirement of preferred stock.*

2. *Record the conversion of convertible preferred stock.*

3. *Identify the type of preferred stock that is classified as debt.*

I. Issuance

A. Preferred stock often has a larger par value than common stock, and has a dividend stated in dollar terms or a percentage of face value. An issue of 6%, $100 par preferred stock is equivalent to an issue of $6, $100 par preferred stock for example. Upon issuance, any excess of proceeds over total par value of shares issued is credited to contributed capital in excess of par.

Cash	issue price less any issue costs
Preferred stock	total par value
Contributed capital in excess of par-preferred	difference

B. Convertible preferred stock allows the preferred shareholder to convert the preferred shares to common shares. The journal entry for issuance of convertible preferred stock does not allocate any of the proceeds to the conversion feature. As with convertible bonds, the securities are recorded at issuance in the same way nonconvertible securities would be.

C. Preferred stock with warrants. Preferred stock, like bonds, may be issued with warrants for the purchase of common stock entitling the holder to purchase common stock at a fixed price. The same procedure for bonds with detachable warrants is applied. The issue price of the preferred stock is allocated to (1) the preferred stock accounts, and (2) another OE account for the common stock warrants. The allocation is based on fair value. When the warrants are exercised, cash is debited, the warrant account is closed, common shares are issued, and the common stock accounts are established.

II. Calling and Redeeming Preferred Stock -- When preferred stock is called (by the issuer) or redeemed (by the stockholder) or is acquired and retired, all related OE accounts are removed. Callable preferred stock can be called in by the issuer at a specified price during a specified period. No gain or loss is recognized for these events because the transactions are between the firm and its owners.

A. Any **debit difference** is recorded in retained earnings;

B. Any **credit difference** is recorded in a contributed capital account.

C. Any **dividends in arrears** must be paid when the shares are acquired (retained earnings is debited).

D. **The general journal entry is:**

Preferred stock	par value of stock called or redeemed	
Contributed capital in excess of par	amount recorded on original issuance*	
Retained earnings	if difference is a debit	
Cash		amount paid to the shareholders
Contributed capital from retirement of Preferred stock		if difference is a credit

*this amount is limited to the original recorded amount on the shares now acquired back by the issuing firm.

 Example: 100 shares of 6%, $50 par callable cumulative preferred stock with two years of dividends in arrears are called at $53. The shares were issued for $51 a share.

Journal entries:

Retained earnings 2(.06)($50)(100)	600	
Cash (for dividends in arrears)		600
Preferred stock ($50)(100)	5,000	
Contributed capital in excess of par, preferred ($51-$50)100	100	
Retained earnings ($53 − $51)100	200	
Cash $53(100)		5,300

III. **Conversion of Preferred Stock --** When convertible preferred stock is converted into common stock, the preferred stock accounts are transferred to the common stock accounts. Again, there is no gain or loss.

   A. **Retained Earnings Debited --** If the total recorded value of the preferred stock is less than the par value of the common stock issued on conversion, retained earnings is debited for the difference.

   B. **The general journal entry is:**

Preferred stock	par value of stock converted	
Contributed capital in excess of par	amount recorded on original issuance*	
Retained earnings	if needed	
Common stock		par value of common stock issued
Contributed capital in excess of par, common		if difference is a credit

* this amount is limited to the original recorded amount on the shares now being converted to common.

Example: 100 shares of 6%, $50 par convertible preferred stock is converted into $10 par common stock at a rate of two shares of common per share of preferred. The preferred stock was for $51 a share.

Journal entry:

Preferred stock ($50)(100)	5,000	
Contributed capital in excess of par, preferred ($51-$50)100	100	
Common stock 100(2)($10)		2,000
Contributed capital in excess of par, common		3,100

If each share of preferred stock was convertible into six shares of common stock, the conversion entry would be:

Preferred stock ($50)(100)	5,000	
Contributed capital in excess of par, preferred ($51-$50)100	100	
Retained earnings	900	
Common stock 100(6)($10)		6,000

IV. Redeemable Preferred Stock

A. Redeemable preferred stock may require the issuing firm to (1) redeem the stock (purchase the stock from the shareholder) at a specified future date at a specified price, or (2) redeem the stock at the option of the shareholder. A preferred stock or other financial instrument issued in the form of shares is mandatorily redeemable if the issuer is unconditionally required to redeem the instrument by transferring its assets at a specified or determinable date(s) or when an event certain to occur takes place. If the obligation to redeem is dependent on a future uncertain event, the instrument is considered to be mandatorily redeemable when that event occurs, or when the event becomes certain to occur.

    1. Only the first of the two types noted above is considered mandatorily redeemable.

B. Balance sheet classification -- Mandatorily redeemable financial instruments (such as redeemable preferred stock) must be classified as debt (rather than owners' equity) unless the redemption is required to occur only if the issuing firm goes out of business. Such items are not to be presented between the liabilities section and the equity section of the statement of financial position. Rather, they are to be presented as liabilities. In the past, GAAP did not require redeemable preferred stock to be classified as debt, and SEC rules required such stock to be disclosed between the liabilities and owners' equity sections - the "mezzanine."

    1. At the end of each year the liability is reported at the present value of the amount to be paid at maturity. The implicit rate at date of issuance is used for the discounting. Interest expense is recorded for the amount of cash dividends paid, as adjusted for the change in present value for the maturity amount.

    2. If either the maturity date or maturity value (redemption price) is not known, the fair value is used for balance sheet reporting and the change in fair value is used for interest expense measurement.

V. U.S. GAAP—IFRS Differences

A. Under international standards, when (1) preferred stock provides for mandatory redemption for a fixed or determinable amount at a fixed or determinable date, or (2) gives the holder the right to require the issuer to redeem the stock at or after a particular date for a fixed or determinable amount, then it is classified as a liability. As such, more preferred stock is reported as debt for international reporting.

      1.   Under international standards, the feature that makes an item debt is that the issuer is currently, or can be required to, deliver cash or other financial instrument to the holder of the instrument with terms that are potentially unfavorable to the issuer.

B. If a preferred stock issue does not explicitly meet either of the two criteria above but is expected to meet one later during its term, then again it is treated as a liability.

      1.   An example is preferred stock with a dividend that increases over time such that the issuer will be required to redeem the preferred stock. Another is if the holder has the option to require redemption if a future event occurs, and that event is probable, then the instrument is classified as debt.

Treasury Stock

Accounting generalizations and the specifics of the cost method are covered in this lesson. It also addresses the specifics of the par method and compares it to the cost method. Share retirement and donated stock also are covered.

After studying this lesson, you should be able to:

1. *Record the receipt by a corporation of donated stock.*

2. *Describe the accounting for share retirement.*

3. *Identify the differences between the cost and par methods.*

4. *Record the journal entries for purchase and reissuance of treasury stock under the par method.*

5. *Note the two methods of accounting for treasury stock.*

6. *Record the purchase and reissuance of treasury stock under the cost method.*

7. *Identify the main accounting aspects of all treasury stock transactions.*

8. *List the reasons why firms buy their stock back.*

Exam note: CPA exams in the past have listed a firm's treasury stock in the investment section of the balance sheet in questions calling for the candidate to identify errors. This requires the candidate to recognize that treasury stock is not an asset of the firm. It is reported as a contra-owner's equity account. These questions are solved by reducing the investment account by the amount recorded as treasury stock, and reinstating the treasury stock account as a reduction from total OE.

I. **Why Firms Buy Their Stock --** The following motivations provide a representative list.

   A. To offset the dilution from the issuance of stock under stock-based compensation agreements;

   B. To provide shares to meet stock-based compensation agreement commitments;

   C. To distribute "profits" without paying dividends thus lowering the tax for shareholders who relinquished their shares. They will pay capital gains rates rather than ordinary rates on dividend income;

   D. To combat a hostile takeover by acquiring shares of "neutral" shareholders thus concentrating shares in the hands of "friendly" investors;

   E. To take advantage of a temporarily low stock price;

   F. To establish a market price for the stock;

   G. To increase earnings per share;

   H. To reduce future cash dividends.

II. **Accounting Generalizations About Treasury Stock --** The following statements hold regardless of the method used to account for treasury stock.

   A. No one owns treasury stock -- there is no shareholder for this stock.

B. Treasury stock is not an asset.

C. A firm cannot record any income account in a treasury stock transaction.

D. A firm cannot profit from treasury stock transactions.

E. The treasury stock account is debited upon purchase of treasury stock. The account is a contra OE account, not an asset account. The common stock account is not affected by treasury stock transactions because treasury stock is considered issued stock.

F. Treasury stock reduces the number of shares outstanding but not the number of shares issued, because treasury stock is issued stock.

G. When treasury stock is purchased, earnings per share increases because the denominator of EPS is reduced with no effect on the numerator.

H. The net assets and owners' equity of the firm decrease by the cost of treasury shares purchased.

I. Retained earnings can be decreased in some cases, but never increased by treasury stock transactions.

III. Accounting for Treasury Stock

A. There are two methods available to account for treasury stock

1. Cost Method which records the treasury stock account at the cost of shares reacquired;

2. Par Value Method which records the treasury stock account at the par value of shares reacquired.

B. Owners' equity is reduced by the same amount, regardless of which method is used, but the balances of certain OE accounts are different under the two methods.

IV. Cost Method

A. Description of the cost method -- At purchase, treasury stock is debited for cost. The contributed capital in excess of par account that was credited when the stock was issued is not affected. Reissuances credit the treasury stock account at cost, and the difference between the purchase price and reissue price is recorded in contributed capital from treasury stock.

B. Journal entry example: (The par of common stock is $5, original issuance price was $20, a total of 700 shares have been issued, and retained earnings is $4,000.)

See the following example.

Purchase 200 shares of treasury stock for $25 a share:

Treasury stock (cost) 200 × $25	5,000	
Cash		5,000

Reissue 50 shares of treasury stock for $30 a share (greater than cost):

Cash 50 × $30	1,500	
Contributed capital from treasury stock ($30 − $25)50		250*
Treasury stock 50 × $25		1,250#

* Excess of reissue price over cost of treasury stock

\# FIFO, average or specific identification can be used to measure the cost of treasury stock sold when there is more than one cost represented in the treasury stock account.

Reissue 50 shares of treasury stock for $18 a share (less than cost):

Cash 50 × $18	900	
Contributed capital from treasury stock	250*	
Retained earnings	100#	
Treasury stock 50 × $25		1,250

* Reduces the balance to zero

\# The total excess of cost over reissue price is 50($25 − $18) = $350. The contributed capital from treasury stock account accounts for $250 of that amount. The remainder is taken from retained earnings.

V. Balance sheet presentation -- Treasury stock is subtracted at the very bottom of the OE section of the balance sheet. The balance is $2,500 (100 treasury shares remaining x $25 cost). The common stock and original contributed capital in excess of par accounts are unaffected.

OE section:	
Common stock 700($5)	$ 3,500
Contributed capital in excess of par 700($20 − $5)	10,500
Contributed capital from treasury stock	0
Retained earnings $4,000 − $100	3,900
Less treasury stock at cost	($2,500)
Total OE	$15,400

VI. Par Value Method

A. This is the second of two methods allowed for treasury stock accounting. The first is the cost method, covered in the previous lesson.

B. **Description of the par value method** -- At purchase, the treasury stock account is debited for par value, and the contributed capital in excess of par account that was credited when the stock was issued is debited for the original amount recorded. Reissuances are treated as a regular issuance of stock except that treasury stock is credited, rather than common stock.

C. **Journal entry example** -- The initial data for the cost method (previous lesson) is used (par of common stock is $5, original issuance price was $20, a total of 700 shares have been issued, and retained earnings is $4,000) **but**, the transactions in this section are not the same as for the cost method so that the main aspects of the par method can be shown.

Purchase 100 shares of treasury stock for $15 a share (less than original price):

Treasury stock (par) 100 × $5	500	
Contributed capital in excess of par, common ($20 − $5)100	1,500	
Contributed capital from treasury stock ($20 − $15)100		500
Cash		1,500

This entry reduces the original contributed capital in excess of par as if the stock were going to be retired.

Purchase 100 shares of treasury stock for $22 a share (greater than original price):

Treasury stock 100 × $5	500	
Contributed capital in excess of par, common ($20 − $5)100	1,500	
Contributed capital from treasury stock ($22 − $20)100	200	
Cash 100 × $22		2,200

It is important to remember that the contributed capital in excess of par account is always reduced by the original amount received when the stock was issued ($1,500).

The excess of the cost ($22) over original issue price ($20) is first taken from any previous contributed capital from treasury stock transactions. In this case, $500 is available from the previous treasury stock purchase.

If this amount were insufficient to complete the debit side of the entry, retained earnings would be reduced by the remaining amount. (If the purchase price had been $28, then retained earnings would be reduced by $300.)

Reissue 150 shares of treasury stock for $18 a share:

Cash 150 × $18	2,700	
Contributed capital in excess of par ($18 − $5)150		1,950
Treasury stock 150 × $5		750

This entry is essentially the same as for the issuance of unissued stock. The only difference is that treasury stock, rather than common stock, is credited.

D. **Balance sheet presentation** -- Treasury stock is reported as a subtraction from the common stock account in the balance sheet. The balance is (50 treasury shares remaining x $5 par) = $250. The common stock and original contributed capital in excess of par accounts are unaffected. Assume that 700 shares of common stock have been issued. The balance sheet would show:

OE section:	
Common stock 700 ($5)	$ 3,500
Less treasury stock at cost (50 × $5)	(250)
Common stock outstanding	3,250
Contributed capital in excess of par	
700($20-$5) − $1,500 − $1,500 + $1,950	9,450
Contributed capital from treasury stock	
$500 − $200	300
Retained earnings	4,000
Total OE	$17,000

(The total OE for the cost and par value method examples are not equal because the transactions were different. If the transactions were the same, the total OE would be the same although the component balances other than the common stock account could be different.)

VII. Comparison of Cost and Par Value Methods

A. When treasury shares are purchased at a cost greater than par but less than original issue price, what is the relative impact of the cost and the par value methods on additional paid-in capital and retained earnings?

   1. **Cost Method** -- Under the cost method, when treasury stock is purchased for an amount less than original price, the treasury stock account is debited. This is a contra OE account. Additional paid-in capital and retained earnings are unaffected.

   2. **Par Value Method** -- Under the par value method, the treasury stock account is debited for par value, and additional paid-in capital is debited for the amount in proportion to the original issue price. Because less was paid for the treasury stock than was received on original issuance, retained earnings is unaffected. Rather, additional paid-in capital from treasury stock is credited for the difference, but not by as much as the debit to the original issuance additional paid-in capital account.

   3. Therefore, additional paid-in capital decreases under the par value method relative to the cost method, but there is no difference in the effect on retained earnings under the conditions imposed.

B. Use of the contributed capital from treasury stock account when treasury shares are reissued or purchased:

	Cost Method	Par Value Method
Increase in contributed capital from treasury stock	Reissue at a price exceeding cost	Purchase at a price less than original issue price
Decrease in contributed capital from treasury stock	Reissue at a price less than cost	Purchase at a price exceeding original issue price

C. Share Retirement

   1. Sometimes firms retire their shares after purchasing them on the market, rather than treating them as treasury shares. Retired shares are placed back into the authorized but unissued category. Accounting for the purchase and retirement of shares is the same as

the purchase of treasury shares under the par value method, except that common stock account is used instead of the treasury stock account.

a. If the purchase price is less than the original issue price, then contributed capital from stock retirement is credited.

b. If the purchase price is greater than the original issue price, then contributed capital from stock retirement is debited until exhausted, and retained earnings is debited for the remainder, if any.

2. Subsequent issuance of the retired shares is recorded as a normal stock issuance, because the retired shares were treated as unissued.

Dividends

This lesson considers cash and other property dividends, which are distributions of the firm's earnings (reduction in retained earnings).

After studying this lesson, you should be able to:

1. *Identify the important dates for recording dividends.*

2. *State the accounting treatment of dividends in arrears.*

3. *Record a property dividend using the correct amount.*

4. *Prepare the journal entries for declaration and payment of a scrip dividend.*

5. *Note the main difference between liquidating dividends and other cash and property dividends.*

I. **Cash and Other Property Dividends**

   A. Cash, and other property dividends reduce the distributing firm's assets and retained earnings. A liability is recognized for these liabilities on the date of declaration. Stock dividends also reduce retained earnings but do not involve a distribution of assets. No liability is recognized for stock dividends.

      1. **Relevant dates --** In relation to dividends, there are three important dates.

         a. First, the declaration date is the date the board of directors formally declares the dividend. This is the most important date in terms of the effect on the firm's resources and therefore its balance sheet. At this date, the firm recognizes a liability and a reduction in retained earnings.

         b. Secondly, the date of record is simply a cut-off date. The shareholders of record on this date will be the recipients of the dividend payments. This date is used because it requires a certain amount of time to compile the list of shareholders as of a particular date.

         c. Finally, the payment date is the date the dividends are actually distributed to the shareholders.

   B. **Cash Dividends**

      1. The distribution of earnings will take the form of a cash distribution. The related liability will be recognized on the date of declaration. The typical entries related to a cash dividend are shown below.

Date of Declaration: Retained Earnings	xx	
Dividends Payable		xx

      2. Some firms debit the temporary account Dividends Declared rather than debit retained earnings directly. At year-end, the Dividends Declared account is closed to retained earnings.

Date of Record:	No Entry	
Date of Declaration: Retained Earnings	xx	
Dividends Payable		xx

C. Dividends in Arrears -- Unpaid dividends for a particular year on cumulative preferred stock. Dividends are not required to be paid but are said to accumulate if unpaid. However, no liability is recognized for dividends in arrears until there has been a dividend declaration. The cumulative feature of preferred stock simply means in the event of a dividend declaration, preferred shareholders are entitled to be paid the dividends in arrears before any distribution related to the current period occurs. Dividends in arrears are disclosed in the footnotes.

D. Other Property Dividends

1. In this type of dividend, the distribution of earnings will take the form of a non-cash distribution. In other words, a non-cash asset will be distributed to the shareholders. The most common type of asset distributed in a property dividend is an investment in securities of other firms. Few other assets are so easily distributable to a large number of shareholders. The related liability and the gain or loss on disposal of the asset will be recognized on the date of declaration. The dividend is recorded at the market value *at declaration date*. The typical entries related to a property dividend are shown below.

Date of Declaration: Retained Earnings	xx	
Dividends Payable		xx

2. The above entry is recorded at the market value of the asset to be distributed. In other words, retained earnings is reduced by the true economic sacrifice of declaring the dividend, at the time of making the commitment to distribute the asset. The liability is also measured at market value.

Asset	xx	
Gain on Disposal		xx
	OR	
Loss on Disposal	xx	
Asset		xx

3. Remaining entries:

Date of Record:	No Entry	
Date of Payment: Dividends Payable	xx	
Asset		xx

4. The credit to the asset is for the adjusted book value, which equals the market value on the declaration date. Ignoring income tax effects, the net reduction in retained earnings resulting from a property dividend is the book value of the asset to be distributed. Retained earnings is reduced by the market value of the asset distributed, but the gain or loss decreases or increases that effect to a net amount equaling the book value of the asset distributed.

    See the following example.

Example:
A firm declares and pays a property dividend. The book value of the asset distributed is $4,000, and the market value is $6,000.

Retained Earnings	6,000	
Dividends Payable		6,000
Asset	2,000	
Gain on Asset Distribution		2,000
Dividends Payable	6,000	
Asset		6,000

Retained earnings is decreased a net of $4,000 ($6,000 from recording the dividend − $2,000 gain on asset), an amount equaling the book value of the asset.

II. **Scrip Dividends** -- A scrip dividend is first distributed in note payable (scrip) form because the firm does not have the cash at the date of declaration to pay the dividend but wants to assure the shareholders that the dividend is forthcoming.

   A. **Interest Paid** -- Interest is paid on the note until cash is paid.

   B. **General entries**

   At declaration:

Retained earnings	amount of dividend declared
Scrip dividend payable	a liability account

   At payment:

Scrip dividend payable	amount of dividend declared
Interest expense	
Cash	dividend plus interest

   C. **Interest expense** is computed from the date of declaration to the date of payment using the interest rate in the note. The principal amount is the amount of dividend declared.

   D. **Partial Payment** -- If a partial payment is made after declaration (to shareholders of record), then the interest expense is computed from the date of that partial payment to the date the final payment is made. The principal amount on which interest is computed is the amount of the final payment.

   E. **Returns on Capital** -- Cash, property, and scrip dividends are returns on capital. They are distributions of earnings, not contributed capital.

III. **Liquidating Dividends** -- A liquidating dividend is a return **of** capital, rather than a return **on** capital. It is a return of contributed capital -- an amount invested by the shareholder.

   A. **Reduces Contributed Capital Account** -- The liquidating portion of a dividend reduces a contributed capital account, rather than retained earnings, and must be disclosed as a liquidating dividend.

   B. **Capital Account Debited** -- Rather than debiting retained earnings for the liquidating portion, a contributed capital account is debited.

C. Liquidating Dividend Occurrence -- One situation in which a liquidating dividend occurs is the payment of a dividend in excess of earnings by a firm in the extractive industries.

1. In this case, because the depletable resource will not be replaced (as would be the case for depreciable assets), a dividend equal to net income plus depletion can be distributed without harming the ability of the firm to maintain capital.

> **Example:**
> **1.** A firm has net income of $10,000 which reflects $2,000 of depletion. A dividend of $12,000 can be paid because the depletable resource will not be replaced. If $12,000 of dividends is declared, the entry is:
>
> | | | |
> |---|---|---|
> | Retained earnings | 10,000 | |
> | Contributed capital | 2,000 | |
> | Dividends payable | | 12,000 |
>
> The liquidating portion is $2,000.
>
> **2.** (Liquidating dividend) A firm in the extractive industries declared a cash dividend of $40,000. The dividend is legal in this state. The following data pertain to the firm just prior to the dividend:
>
> | | |
> |---|---|
> | Accumulated depletion | $10,000 |
> | Capital stock | 50,000 |
> | Additional paid-in capital | 15,000 |
> | Retained earnings | 30,000 |
>
> Retained earnings is used first as a source of capital for the dividend ($30,000 of the $40,000 total dividend).
>
> The remaining $10,000 reduces additional paid-in capital and is a liquidating dividend.
>
> The accumulated depletion justifies the liquidating portion because it is a recognized reduction in net income that represents the allocated cost of an investment that will not be replaced. Dividends in excess of income are allowed to the extent of accumulated depletion less any prior liquidating dividends.

IV. U.S. GAAP - IFRS Differences

A. There is no recognition of dividends declared after the balance sheet date but before the financial statements are authorized for issue. No liability or reduction in retained earnings is recorded. This is the case for both international and U.S. reporting.

B. However, for international reporting, the amount of dividends proposed (but not formally approved) or declared before the financial statements were authorized for issue must be disclosed. This disclosure can be made within the OE section of the balance sheet or in the notes. There is no recognition until declaration.

Stock Dividends and Splits

This is the second lesson about dividends. Stock dividends reduce retained earnings but cause no reduction in the firm's assets.

After studying this lesson, you should be able to:

1. *Identify the differences between cash dividends, stock dividends, and stock splits.*

2. *List the effects of stock dividends on shares outstanding, and on the accounts.*

3. *Record large and small stock dividends.*

4. *Note the effects of stock splits on the accounts.*

I. **Stock Dividends --** A stock dividend is a distribution by a firm of its stock to its shareholders in proportion to their existing holdings. The shareholder does not pay for these shares. Stock dividends do not involve a future transfer of assets or a future provision of services. Therefore, in relation to stock dividends, no liability is recorded. Each investor simply holds more shares, but each share is worth proportionately less than before the dividend. Each investor maintains the previous ownership percentage. In theory, the stock price should fall by the amount necessary to maintain the predividend market capitalization of the firm.

> **Example:**
> If a firm has 10,000 shares of common stock outstanding and issues a 5% stock dividend, then 500 shares are distributed to the current shareholders at no cost to them.
>
> If a specific shareholder owned 2,000 shares, he or she would receive 100 shares (2,000 × .05).

A. **Effect of Dividend --** The effect of a stock dividend is to increase the number of shares issued and outstanding.

B. **EPS Decreased --** Earnings per share is decreased by a stock dividend.

C. **Stock Dividend Purpose --** Stock dividends are distributed to reduce the market price of the firm's stock and also to reduce demand by shareholders for cash dividends.

D. **Permanent Capitalization --** A stock dividend is a permanent capitalization of retained earnings into contributed capital.

E. **Accounting for Dividends --** Accounting for stock dividends depends on the size of the stock dividend (small or large).

1. **Small stock dividend --** (% of dividend is less than 20%-25%) Capitalize at market price.

   See the following example.

Example:
Assume a firm has 20,000 shares of $5 par common stock outstanding and declares a 5% stock dividend when the market price is $20 per share.

This is a small stock dividend because 5% is less than 20%-25%.

Entry:

Retained earnings 20,000(.05)($20)	20,000	
Common stock 20,000(.05)($5)		5,000
Contributed capital in excess of par, common		15,000

2. **Market Price Measure** -- The market price of the stock at the **declaration date** is used to measure the stock dividend because that is the date on which the commitment to distribute the dividend is made.

   a. **Market to Pay Dividend** -- Market price is used on the assumption that the market price of the stock will not change given the small size of the dividend, and the shareholder then can sell the shares received while maintaining the predividend market value of the investment. In effect, the firm is using the market to pay the dividend.

   b. **Debit to Retained Earnings** -- Under the above assumption, the debit to retained earnings is the value of the stock distributed and therefore represents the amount of retained earnings to be permanently capitalized to contributed capital. This amount of retained earnings will never be available for cash dividends.

3. **Large stock dividend** -- (% of dividend is greater than 20%-25%) Capitalize at par value.

Example:
Assume a firm has 20,000 shares of $5 par common stock outstanding and declares a 40% stock dividend when the market price is $20 per share.

This is a large stock dividend because 40% is greater than 20%-25%.

Entry:

Retained earnings 20,000(.40)($5)	40,000	
Common stock		40,000

In this case, the assumption cannot be made that the market price of the stock will remain unchanged because of the large dilution in the number of shares outstanding.

Thus, only the par value of shares issued is permanently capitalized. Subsequent changes in market price do not affect the accounting.

   a. Large stock dividends also can be accounted for as a stock split effected in the form of a stock dividend. The debit would be to contributed capital in excess of par, rather than retained earnings in the above example. As such, retained earnings is not capitalized to permanent capital if this alternative is chosen.

4. **Change in Total OE** -- Neither type of stock dividend causes a change in total OE, but retained earnings is reduced and contributed capital is increased (except for a large stock dividend accounted for as a stock split).

a. **No Liability Recorded** -- It is important to remember that no liability is recorded for a stock dividend because it does not involve the distribution of goods or services, and therefore, does not meet the definition of a liability.

II. **Stock Splits** -- A stock split is not a dividend. Rather it is an adjustment to par value and number of issued shares.

A. **A 2-for-1 split** halves the par value and doubles the number of shares. The reason firms split their shares is to reduce the market price and make the shares available to a larger number of shareholders.

B. **No accounting entry** is needed although firms may make a memo entry to record the split.

1. **No Change in OE** -- There is no change in any account balance within owner's equity.

C. **Dividend/Split Similarity** -- Although both a 100% stock dividend and 2-for-1 stock split double the number of shares outstanding, there are few other similarities.

1. **Comparison Dividend/Split** -- Comparison of a 100% stock dividend and 2-for-1 stock split.

	100% stock dividend	2-for-1 stock split
Effect on total OE	None	None
Effect on retained earnings	Decrease	None
Effect on par value	None	Cut in half
Effect on shares outstanding	Double	Double
Effect on contributed capital	Increase	None
Effect on common stock account	Increase	None

III. **Additional Aspects**

A. Treasury shares usually do not receive stock dividends. However, if the treasury shares were intended to be used to meet a commitment under a stock option plan for example, then the treasury shares would be adjusted for the stock dividend.

B. Real estate trusts and other firms may declare dividends that may be paid in cash or shares at the election of the shareholders with a potential limitation on the total amount of cash that all shareholders can elect to receive in the aggregate. For this type of distribution, the stock portion of the distribution is treated as a stock issuance, not a stock dividend.

Dividend Allocation

The last lesson about dividends considers the order and allocation of dividends between preferred and common stock.

After studying this lesson, you should be able to:

1. *Allocate dividends when there are dividends in arrears.*

2. *Determine the dividends to common when the firm has partially participating preferred stock.*

3. *Calculate the dividends to both classes of stock when the firm has fully participating preferred stock.*

I. Introduction

A. Nonparticipating preferred stock is entitled only to the annual dividend percentage noted in the stock certificate -- the annual dividend requirement.

B. When the full amount of preferred stock dividend is not paid on cumulative preferred stock for any given year, the unpaid dividends are in arrears and must be paid before any other dividend.

C. If the preferred stock is noncumulative and the current year dividends are not paid, then they are never paid.

D. When preferred stock does not participate beyond its annual percentage or amount, the order of dividend payments is:

1. Preferred: Any dividends in arrears (only if preferred stock is cumulative);

2. Preferred: Current period dividend;

3. Common: Remainder.

Example:
a. A firm has 200 shares of 5%, $100 par cumulative nonparticipating preferred stock.

b. The annual dividend requirement on the stock is $1,000 (.05 × 200 × $100).

c. This preferred stock might also be referred to as $5 preferred stock (rather than 5%) indicating the annual dividend per share.

d. The firm also has 4,000 shares of $10 par common stock outstanding.

e. Two years of dividends are in arrears and $7,000 of dividends are declared.

f. The dividend allocation is (P = preferred; C = common):

		P	C
i. Preferred:	arrears	$2,000	
ii. Preferred:	current	1,000	
iii. Common:	remainder		$4,000
Total		$3,000	$4,000

II. Preferred Stock is Participating -- When preferred stock is participating, the stock may receive dividends in addition to the annual current dividend requirement. When preferred participates, common receives a matching amount. Preferred stock may be fully or partially participating.

A. Fully Participating

1. After any dividends in arrears are allocated, the remaining dividends are allocated based on the total par value of the preferred and common stock outstanding.

2. If total dividends are not sufficient to provide common with a matching amount equal to the preferred percentage times total par value of common, then there is no participation and common receives all the dividends after the current year preferred dividend requirement and any dividends in arrears are allocated.

B. Partially Participating

1. The preferred stock receives dividends up to an additional percentage.

   a. Common stock receives a matching amount equal to the preferred percentage times total par of common stock outstanding before the preferred stock receives its additional allocation.

   b. Common stock receives any dividends in excess of the additional amount allocated to common.

2. If the total dividends declared are not sufficient to provide the maximum additional participating percentage to both preferred and common (after common receives its share based on the preferred percentage), then each class of stock receives a share of the remainder in proportion to total par.

3. The steps in the allocation are:

   a. Preferred: Any dividends in arrears;

   b. Preferred: Current period dividend;

   c. Common: Matching amount: preferred percentage x total par of common outstanding;

   d. Preferred: Additional percentage;

   e. Common: Remainder.

III. Examples -- Common information: A firm has 200 shares of 5%, $100 par cumulative participating preferred stock. The annual dividend requirement on the stock is $1,000 (.05 x 200 x $100). The firm also has 4,000 shares of $10 par common stock outstanding.

		Percentage
Total par value of preferred stock outstanding:	$20,000	1/3
Total par value of common stock outstanding:	40,000	2/3
Total par value	$60,000	

See the following example.

Example:
1. Fully participating

The preferred stock is fully participating. Two years of dividends are in arrears and total dividends declared are $11,000.

	P	C
a. Preferred: Arrears	$2,000	
b. Preferred: Current	1,000	
c. Common: Matching amount .05($40,000)		$2,000
Dividend remaining =		
$6,000 ($11,000 − $5,000 allocated above)		
d. Preferred: Participation (1/3)($6,000)	2,000	
e. Common: Participation (2/3)($6,000)		4,000
Total	$5,000	$6,000

If total dividends were less than $5,000 but more than $3,000, then common would receive the entire amount above $3,000. There would be no dividends available for participation to either class of stock because common did not receive its matching amount.

2. Partially participating

The preferred stock is participating to a maximum additional percentage of 4% (for a total of 9%). Two years of dividends are in arrears and total dividends declared are $14,000.

	P	C
a. Preferred: Arrears	$2,000	
b. Preferred: Current	1,000	
c. Common: Matching amount .05($40,000)		$2,000
Dividend remaining =		
$9,000 ($14,000 - $5,000 allocated above)		
This amount is less than 4% of total par of both		
classes of stock: ($2,400 = .04 × $60,000)		
d. Preferred: Participation (.04)($20,000)	800	
e. Common: Remainder ($9,000 − $800)		8,200
Total	$3,800	$10,200

If the remaining dividends after Step 3 were less than $2,400, then the remaining dividends are allocated in proportion to total par value. Using the same information except that total dividends declared are $6,800:

	P	C
a. Preferred: Arrears	$2,000	
b. Preferred: Current	1,000	
c. Common: Matching amount .05($40,000)		$2,000

Dividend remaining

$1,800 ($6,800 − $5,000 allocated above)

This amount exceeds 4% of total par of both

classes of stock: ($2,400 = .04 × $60,000)

Therefore the remaining dividend is

allocated in proportion to total par value.

d. Preferred: (1/3)($1,800)	600	
e. Common: (2/3)($1,800)		1,200
Total	$3,600	$ 3,200

Stock Rights, Retained Earnings

Accounting for stock rights, and the retained earnings statement are the focus of this lesson.

After studying this lesson, you should be able to:

1. *Account for stock rights issued to existing shareholders, and for rights issued to outside parties.*

2. *Articulate the reasons for retained earnings appropriations and restrictions.*

3. *Record retained earnings appropriations.*

4. *Prepare a statement of retained earnings.*

5. *Describe each item found in the statement of retained earnings.*

I. **Stock Rights** -- This section covers the issuance of stock rights to existing shareholders and to outside parties for services. A later section covers stock option plans for employees. The main question is whether the issuance of the rights is an event to be recognized in the accounts.

> **Definition:**
> *A Stock Right*: Gives the holder the option to purchase a certain number of shares of the issuing firm at a specified price during a specified time period.

A. Stock rights are often used to convey preemptive rights.

B. The existing shareholders are given rights (via a stock warrant) to purchase their pro rata number of shares to keep their current percentage in the firm.

C. The rights have an expiration date and must be exercised by this date.

> **Entries:**
> At issuance of rights: No journal entry is made. No resources have been transferred.
>
> At exercise of rights: The usual entry to record the issuance of stock is made. The issue price is the exercise price as specified in the stock warrant, not the market price on the date of exercise.
>
> If rights lapse: No entry is made if the shareholder does not exercise the rights.

D. **Stock Rights Issued to Outside Parties for Services**

> At issuance of rights: Record an expense and owners' equity account equal to the difference between the market price and exercise price, times the number of shares under option.
>
> At exercise of rights: Record the stock issuance at the exercise price and remove the OE account credited at issuance of the rights.

See the following example.

Example:
A firm issues 300 rights to an attorney for services rendered to the firm. Three rights entitle the holder to purchase one share of the firm's $5 common stock for $20. The market value of the stock on the day the rights were issued was $30.

Entries:

At issuance:

Legal expenses ($30 − $20)(300/3)	1,000	
Stock rights outstanding (OE)		1,000

The $1,000 recorded amount represents the opportunity cost to the firm of committing to an issuance of 100 shares of stock for $20 when the market price is currently $30. Subsequent changes in market price do not enter into the accounting.

At exercise:

Cash (300/3)($20)	2,000	
Stock rights outstanding	1,000	
Common stock (300/3)($5)		500
Contributed capital in excess of par, common		2,500

II. Appropriations of Retained Earnings

A. Unappropriated Retained Earnings

1. **Available for Declaration** -- This portion of retained earnings is available for dividend declaration. In other words, the future use of this amount of retained earnings has not been determined.

2. **No Specific Purpose** -- Unappropriated retained earnings have not been earmarked for a specific purpose.

3. **Not All Are Paid** -- Not all unappropriated retained earnings must be paid in dividends, however.

B. Appropriated Retained Earnings

1. **Declared Off-Limits** -- This amount of retained earnings has been declared off-limits for dividends so that funds may be conserved for a specific purpose or objective.

   a. **Financial Planning** -- The purpose might be related to financial planning, such as debt retirement or plant expansion.

   b. **Legal Requirement** -- The purpose or objective might be related to some legal requirement, such as the appropriation of retained earnings related to treasury stock transactions.

   c. **Contractual Obligation** -- Finally, the purpose of the appropriation might be related to a contractual obligation, such as a clause in a loan agreement requiring the appropriation.

2. **End Result** -- The end result of appropriated retained earnings is quite simple. When retained earnings are appropriated, the amount of unappropriated retained earnings declines, and the amount of possible dividend declarations declines as well.

C. Formal Communication -- A retained earnings appropriation is management's formal communication that a portion of retained earnings has been declared off-limits for dividends.

D. Appropriation Entry -- The entry for an appropriation is:

Retained earnings	amount appropriated
Retained earnings, appropriated for X purpose	amount appropriated

1. **No Reduction** -- This entry does not reduce total retained earnings nor does it necessarily reduce dividends.

2. **When Purpose Fulfilled** -- When the purpose for which an appropriation is made has been fulfilled, the above entry is reversed, reinstating the amount to unappropriated retained earnings.

   a. **No Effect** -- The entry to reverse the appropriation also has no effect on total retained earnings.

E. Partition Retained Earnings -- Retained earnings appropriations have no effect on assets. They do not "reserve" assets. They simply partition retained earnings into two parts.

III. Restrictions on Retained Earnings

Definition:
Restriction on Retained Earnings: A constraint placed on a certain portion of retained earnings by an external party.

A. Effect Like Appropriation -- It has the same effect as an appropriation and may be accompanied by an appropriation.

Example:
States Restrict: States often restrict retained earnings in the amount of the cost of treasury stock held by the firm. This is a protection for the creditors. It forces the firm to maintain its legal capital.

Bondholders Restrict: Bondholders often restrict retained earnings through the debt agreement or bond covenant. This is also a protection for the creditors but this time is protection for a specific group of creditors - the bondholders themselves who want the firm to conserve cash so that their claims can be met.

B. Disclosure -- Both restrictions and appropriations are disclosed in the notes to the financial statements.

Note: Both restrictions and appropriations may cause the amount of dividends to be reduced. However, a firm need not appropriate retained earnings or be subject to a constraint on retained earnings in order to lower the amount of dividends paid. The firm simply needs to reduce the amount of dividends declared. However, an appropriation supports this decision and may make such a decision more acceptable to shareholders.

Example:
If total retained earnings is $400,000, and a $100,000 appropriation is recorded, and the firm was planning to declare only $150,000 in dividends, the appropriation does not reduce dividends although it may still accomplish its communication objective.

IV. Statement of Retained Earnings

A. Purpose -- The purpose of the Statement of Retained Earnings is to provide the reader of the financial report with a detailed account of increases and decreases in retained earnings that were recorded in a given accounting period. The retained earnings statement may be shown separately, or more frequently, as part of the statement of changes in equity (see separate lesson on that topic).

1. **A typical Statement** of Retained Earnings is shown below.

The Tiger Company

Statement of Retained Earnings

For the Year Ended December 31, 20x7

Retained Earnings, January 1, 20x7	XX
Prior Period Adjustment	(±) XX
Change in Accounting Principle - Catch-Up Adjustment	(±) XX
Restated Balance, January 1, 20x7	XX
(±) Net Income	(±) XX
(−) Cash and Property Dividends Declared	(−) XX
(−) Stock dividends	(− XX
(=) Retained Earnings, December 31, 20x7	XX

Footnote: The retained earnings balance on December 31, 20x7 is $XX. Of that amount, $YY has been appropriated for...

B. Adjusted for Prior Adjustments

1. As you can see, the beginning retained earnings balance is adjusted initially for any prior period adjustment (corrections of errors in prior year net income) recorded during the year and for the catch-up adjustment related to changes in accounting principle.

2. **Restated Balance** -- The restated balance is increased by reported income and decreased by any dividend declarations that occurred during the year.

Book Value Per Share, Quasi-Reorganization

This lesson includes miscellaneous OE items such as the book value per share ratio, and accounting for quasi-reorganizations.

After studying this lesson, you should be able to:

1. *Analyze the effect of transactions on book value per share.*

2. *Identify the reasons and effects of a quasi-reorganization.*

3. *Record the journal entries for a quasi-reorganization.*

4. *Prepare the post-reorganization Balance Sheet.*

5. *Compute book value per share.*

I. **Book Value Per Share (of common stock)** -- Among the ratios tested on the CPA exam, book value per share has appeared with relative frequency. Its calculation tests a number of details concerning owners' equity.

> **Definition:**
> *Book Value per Share Ratio Equals*: Common stockholders' equity per share of outstanding common stock at the end of the period.

1. **Common Stockholders' Equity** -- Common stockholders' equity is total OE after preferred dividend claims are removed.

2. **Statistic Represents** -- The statistic represents the historical value of the firm per common share and may be used as a benchmark for comparisons with market value per share.

   a. **Unlikely Book Value Paid** -- However, it is very unlikely that book value per share would ever equal market value per share for most firms.

B. **Equations**

> Book value per share outstanding =
>
> Common stockholders' equity/ending common shares of common stock outstanding
>
> Common stockholder's equity =
>
> Total OE − liquidation preference of preferred stock − preferred stock dividends in arrears

C. **Amount Payable** -- The liquidation preference of preferred stock is the amount payable on liquidation of the company. It must be paid before the common stock receives any assets.

See the following example.

Example:
1. Book value per share

The stockholders' equity section for a firm's balance sheet shows:

6% noncumulative preferred stock, $100 par (liquidation value $105 per share)	$10,000
Common stock	33,000
Retained earnings	12,500
Treasury stock	(6,000)
Total OE	$49,500

At the end of the period, the firm has 100 shares of preferred stock outstanding, 3,300 shares of common stock issued, and 300 common treasury shares.

Book value per share is $13.00 = ($49,500 − 100($105)) / 3,000. Only 3,000 shares of common are outstanding.

If the preferred stock was cumulative and there were dividends in arrears, they also would be subtracted from total owners' equity in the numerator.

The par value of preferred stock is not used in the calculation if it is different from the liquidation preference, as is the case here.

2. Book value per share—effect of treasury stock purchase:
A firm purchased treasury shares at a cost exceeding the original issuance but less than book value per share. This transaction reduces total stockholders' equity but increases book value.

Explanation:
The purchase of treasury stock at any price decreases total owners' equity.

When the purchase price per share is less than book value per share, then the denominator of book value per share decreases by a greater percentage than does the numerator, and book value per share increases.

Assume that the total owners' equity and number of shares before the treasury stock purchase is $4,000 and 400 respectively. Book value per share is $10. The firm purchases 20 shares of treasury stock for $8 (less than book value). The new book value per share is: ($4,000 − $160)/ (380) = $10.11. Book value per share has increased.

II. **Quasi Reorganization** -- An alternative to bankruptcy in some cases, quasi-reorganization allows a firm a fresh start and new, more conservative asset values.

   A. **Conditions** -- Operating losses have created a deficit in retained earnings (negative balance) and certain asset values are overstated.

      1. **Positive Prospects** -- However, the firm has positive prospects for the future but will be unable to pay dividends until the deficit is absorbed by future income.

      2. **Updated Balance Sheet** -- Rather than continue with unrealistic asset values and negative retained earnings (the inability to pay dividends will hurt the firm's ability to raise capital), a quasi-reorganization will provide an updated balance sheet with no retained earnings deficit.

   B. **Requirements for a Quasi-reorganization**

      1. **Approval** -- Shareholder and creditor approval.

      2. **Balance Becomes Zero** -- The retained earnings balance must be zero immediately after the quasi-reorganization.

3. **No Negative Balance After** -- No contributed capital account can have a negative balance after the quasi-reorganization.

4. **Assets Down to Market** -- Assets must be written down to market value (asset write-ups are possible but would be rare).

5. **Dated Years After** -- Retained earnings must be dated for a period of 3 - 10 years after the quasi-reorganization to indicate that the balance reflects income earned after the quasi-reorganization.

C. Accounting Steps

1. Write **assets down to market** value, further reducing retained earnings (increasing the deficit).

2. **Reduce contributed capital** to absorb the retained earnings deficit.

3. **Change Value/Number Shares** -- If needed, change par value or the number of shares of common stock to absorb the remaining deficit.

Example: A firm has the following balance sheet (abbreviated):

Assets	$10,000	Liabilities	$4,000
		Common stock ($1 par)	3,000
		Contributed capital in excess of par	5,000
		Retained earnings	(2,000)

Certain plant assets with a book value of $5,000 are worth only $1,000. The firm elects to reduce par value to accomplish the quasi-reorganization.

Entries:

Retained earnings	4,000	
Plant assets		4,000

The retained earnings deficit is now $6,000.

Contributed capital in excess of par	5,000	
Retained earnings		5,000

The retained earnings deficit is now $1,000.
The common stock is reduced to $2,000 to absorb the remaining deficit.
This means that par value must be reduced to $.67

$2,000 = (3,000 shares)(new par value)

$2,000/3,000 = $.67 = new par value

Common stock	1,000	
Retained earnings		1,000

The balance sheet immediately following the quasi-reorganization is:

Assets	6,000	Liabilities	4,000
		Common stock ($.67 par)	2,000
		Contributed capital in excess of par	0
		Retained earnings	0

General Revenue Recognition

The first lesson on revenue reviews the definition and recognition criteria for revenue, and highlights the major recognition methods. The installment method is covered in detail.

After studying this lesson, you should be able to:

1. *Define revenue.*

2. *State the general revenue recognition criteria.*

3. *Explain when major revenue recognition methods are applied.*

4. *Record deferred and recognized gross profit under the installment method.*

5. *Account for repossessions under the installment method.*

6. *Point to general differences in revenue recognition between U.S. and international standards.*

Definition:
Revenue: Inflows or other enhancements of assets of an entity or settlements of its liabilities (or a combination of the two) from delivering or producing goods, rendering services, or other activities that constitute the entity's ongoing major or central operations.

I. **Criteria for Revenue Recognition**

A. Revenues are recognized in the accounting year in which the following three criteria are met, regardless of when the cash is collected.

1. The goods and services have been provided to the customer or client (the revenue is earned).

2. The company is reasonably assured of collecting receivables (the revenue is realizable).

3. The company can determine the expenses incurred in providing the goods and services. This criterion is not a constraint on recognition in most situations. "Earned" and "realizable" are the primary criteria.

B. The SEC refined these criteria. Under SEC guidance, revenue is recognized when the following four criteria are met:

1. Persuasive evidence of an arrangement with a customer leading to revenue exists;

2. Delivery has occurred or services have been provided;

3. The seller's price is fixed or determinable;

4. Collectibility is reasonably assured.

C. The first two are expansions of the "earned" criterion and the last two are expansions of the "realizable" criterion.

D. For SEC guidance, delivery of goods (see 2., above) is not considered complete until the customer has accepted the goods (requiring evaluation of the performance of the goods, which may require installation before such evaluation), taken title, and assumed the risks and rewards of ownership. Thus the "earned" criterion is met only when the seller has no more obligation to the buyer under the arrangement.

E. The "deposit method" is invoked when the customer pays the seller before the seller has transferred the goods to the buyer. The sale is not complete until the goods are shipped. The seller records a liability for the amount received until the goods are shipped, at which time the deposit liability is extinguished and the revenue is recognized.

F. Criteria Not Met -- When one or more of the three criteria above are not met, revenue is deferred.

1. **Certain Methods Accepted --** Certain established methods of revenue recognition have achieved acceptance in the business community that allow for some latitude in applying these three criteria. The major revenue recognition methods are listed below, along with the criterion that causes revenue to be postponed until it is met.

Method	Last Criterion to be Met
Point of sale method (ordinary sale)	Seller performance (providing the good)—"earned"
Installment method	Receipt of cash --"realizable"
Cost recovery method	Receipt of cash in the amount of cost—"realizable"
Percentage of completion method	Seller performance (work is progressing)—"earned"
Completed contract method	Seller performance (completion)—"earned"
Sales with right of return	Expiration of return right or ability to estimate returns—"earned"

Example:
The cost recovery method does not recognize any income until sufficient cash is received from the customer to cover the cost of the item sold. Thus, the last criterion to be met is receipt of cash (realizable). The firm has performed, and expenses are estimable. It is the receipt of cash that is "holding up" the recognition of profit. In contrast, when the seller allows a right of return, until the right expires, the seller has not completed its performance (earned). Each of the above methods is acceptable under GAAP provided that certain requirements are met. In this and the next few lessons, alternatives to the point-of-sale method are discussed.

II. Installment Method of Revenue Recognition

A. Installment Sales Basis

1. The installment basis is a version of the cash basis of accounting. The method is typically employed in one of two situations.

   a. Collectibility Questionable -- The collectibility of receivables might be questionable. If so, these questions might warrant use of the installment sales basis.

   b. Extended Time Period -- If receivables will be collected over an extended time period, the installment sales basis might be appropriate.

2. **Gross Profit Formula**

   a. In applying the installment method, the gross profit percentage is calculated for merchandise sold.

   b. This percentage is: (sales - cost of goods sold) / sales.

c. When cash is collected, the amount received is divided between recovery of cost and gross profit received. If no cash is received, no profit is recognized.

d. The amount of recognized gross profit = (cash received in period) x (gross profit percentage). The remaining portion of the cash received is considered a return of cost.

Caution: Not all installment sales are required to be accounted for under the installment method of revenue recognition. Rather, only if the collectibility is uncertain or if the term is very long should some method that bases revenue recognition on cash received be used, such as the installment method or cost recovery method.

Example:

Installment method of revenue recognition: A firm sells goods with a total sales value of $80,000. The cost of the items sold is $60,000. During the year, the firm collects $25,000. The firm is uncertain about collecting the remaining sales price and elects to use the installment method of revenue recognition. The entries and balance sheet disclosure for the seller are shown below for this method. The gross profit percentage is 25%: ($80,000 − $60,000)/ $80,000.

During the year:

Installment accounts receivable	80,000	
Installment sales		80,000
Cost of goods sold	60,000	
Inventory		60,000
Cash	25,000	
Installment accounts receivable		25,000

End of year adjusting entries:

The income statement accounts are closed, gross profit is deferred, and a portion of the gross profit is recognized.

Installment sales	80,000	
Deferred gross profit (contra receivable)		20,000
Cost of goods sold		60,000
Deferred gross profit(.25 × $25,000 cash)	6,250	
Recognized gross profit (to income statement)		6,250

Explanation: The firm is able to recognize gross profit, at the 25% rate, only on cash collected from the customer. Each $1 of cash collected is $.75 return of cost and $.25 gross profit. Cash collected includes any down payment or other cash paid by the customer.

The recognized gross profit account is an income statement account. Income increased only $6,250 this year because of the sale. The remaining $13,750 ($20,000 − $6,250) is deferred to the next period. When more cash is collected, more gross profit is recognized and the amount deferred is decreased.

Gross profit is not net income. The expenses below gross margin must also be taken into account when computing net income. Some firms prefer to disaggregate recognized gross profit into sales and cost of goods sold for reporting. In the example above, the firm would report $25,000 of sales and $18,750 of cost of goods sold ($25,000 × .75). Under this alternative reporting, gross margin is increased $6,250.

Balance sheet presentation of the receivable:

Accounts receivable $80,000 - $25,000	$55,000
Less deferred gross profit	(13,750)
Equals net accounts receivable	$41,250

The net accounts receivable of $41,250 equals the cost of the inventory yet to be recovered: $41,250 = (1 − .25)($55,000). The receivable must be shown at cost.

To report the receivable at sales value ($55,000) would imply that the remaining $13,750 of gross profit had been recognized.

Exam note: The CPA exam frequently asks for the amount of deferred gross profit on the installment sales method. In the above example, that amount is $13,750. Also, the gross profit percentage often changes each year. When sales from more than one period are given, be sure to apply the gross margin method that applies to each year's sales.

Example:
Data for a firm using the installment method of revenue recognition follow:

Year	Sales	Cost of goods sold	Cash collected	
1	$3,000	$2,000	Year 1 sales $	500
2	$4,500	$2,250	Year 1 sales	1,500
			Year 2 sales	2,000

What is the amount of deferred gross profit to be reported at the end of year 2?

Solution:

The gross profit percentages are:

Year 1: ($3,000 − $2,000)/$3,000 = 1/3

Year 2: ($4,500 − $2,250)/$4,500 = 1/2

Deferred gross profit at 12/31/Year 2 = ($3,000 − $500 − $1,500)(1/3) + ($4,500 − $2,000)(1/2)= $1,583

This amount would be subtracted from gross accounts receivable at year-end ($3,500) in deriving the net accounts receivable balance ($1,917).

B. Repossession -- Occasionally, an item sold is repossessed due to nonpayment by the customer. Under the installment method of revenue recognition, the remaining receivable and deferred gross profit balances are closed, the repossessed inventory is recorded at fair value, and a gain or loss is recorded.

Example:
Goods costing $8,000 were sold for $20,000 in a previous year. The installment method was used to recognize revenue because cash receipts were uncertain. As of the beginning of the current year, cash collections from previous years on the sale totaled $14,000. The gross margin percentage is $12,000/$20,000 or 60%. The goods are repossessed and have a fair value of $1,000 at the time of repossession.

Account balances at the beginning of the current year

Installment accounts receivable	$6,000	($20,000 - $14,000)
Deferred gross profit	(3,600)	($6,000 x .60)

Journal entry for repossession:

Inventory	1,000	
Deferred gross profit	3,600	
Loss on repossession	1,400	
Installment accounts receivable		6,000

The loss equals the difference between the fair value of the inventory ($1,000) and the net installment receivable ($2,400).

III. U.S. GAAP - IFRS Differences

A. The definition of revenue for international standards is substantively the same as for U.S. standards although the wording is somewhat different.

1. International definition: revenue is the gross inflow of economic benefits during the period arising in the course of ordinary activities when those inflows result in increases in equity, other than increases relating to contributions from equity participants.

2. U.S. GAAP distinguishes revenue and gains; IFRS revenues include gains.

B. International standards specifically define the sources of revenue (listed below). In contrast, U.S. standards do not.

1. Sale of goods;

2. Rendering of services;

3. Use by others of the entity's assets yielding interest, royalty and dividend revenue (equity method dividends are not revenue as per U.S. standards).

C. International standards are much less specific with respect to recognition of revenue in special industry situations. There are fewer exceptions; international practice relies more on general principles.

D. Revenue is recognized under international standards when the following criteria are met:

1. The amount of revenue and costs associated with the transaction can be measured reliably;

2. It is probable that the economic benefits associated with the transaction will flow to the seller;

3. For the sale of goods, the seller must have transferred to the buyer the risks and rewards of ownership, and does not effectively manage or control the goods (a significant right of return is an example);

4. For the rendering of services, the stage of completion can be measured reliably.

E. In comparison, the U.S. principle focuses on when the earnings process is complete and whether cash will be collected, whereas the international definition is focused on when the transfer of risks and rewards of ownership take place. However, the two definitions usually lead to the same result.

F. **Biological and Agricultural Assets --** When the future economic benefits are probable and can be reliably estimated for these assets, gains and losses from increases and decreases in the fair value (less estimated selling costs and taxes) are recognized as they occur, before the sale takes place.

Other Revenue Situations

This lesson illustrates the cost recovery method, revenue recognition under a right of return, and revenue recognition in other specific business contexts.

After studying this lesson, you should be able to:

1. *Identify when the cost recovery method may be used.*

2. *Apply the cost recovery method.*

3. *Determine when revenue is to be recognized under a right of return.*

4. *Apply the milestone method of revenue recognition.*

5. *Recognize the appropriate amount of revenue for an initial franchise fee.*

I. Cost Recovery Method

A. The cost recovery method is more conservative than the installment method. No gross profit is recognized on cash collections until the cost of the item sold is fully recovered. After that point, all collections constitute gross profit.

1. **Justification for Use** -- Justification for the use of the cost recovery basis is identical to the reasons used to justify the installment sales basis - uncertainty about cash collection (realizable criterion).

2. **Similar to Installment** -- The journal entries are essentially the same although gross profit is recognized more slowly under the cost recovery method.

 Example: Merchandise with a cost of $60,000 is sold for $90,000 in Year 1. Cash collections will have to exceed $60,000 before any gross profit is realized. All gross profit is deferred until $60,000 cash is collected.

Cash collected in Year 1 is $40,000. Therefore, gross profit recognized is zero and deferred gross profit is $30,000.

Cash collected in Year 2 is $30,000. Therefore, gross profit recognized is $10,000 because total cash collected is $70,000 to this point. From here on, all cash collected is gross profit.

Cash collected in Year 3 is $20,000. Therefore, gross profit recognized is $20,000.

Note: The installment method would have recognized some profit in Year 1. The entries for the cost recovery method are similar to the installment method and use the same accounts. The adjusting journal entry deferring the total gross profit for the year of sale is the same. But adjusting entries for gross profit recognition (and closing of deferred gross profit) are recorded only when total cash receipts exceed cost. Thus, only the timing of recognizing gross profit differs.

II. Revenue Recognized at the Completion of Production

A. Certainly for most products, revenue is not recognized at the completion of production. However, for products such as precious metals and certain agriculture products, if three conditions are met, the revenue should be recognized at the completion of production. These three conditions are listed below.

1. There is a relatively stable market for the products;

2. Any related marketing costs are nominal;

3. The units produced must be homogeneous.

B. **Limited Applicability** -- At completion of production, the usual uncertainties as to sale (and collection of cash) are absent, allowing revenue recognition to take place before sale. This method has very limited applicability.

III. Sales with a right of return

A. Sellers often provide a right of return. The amount of net sales recognized for a period depends on whether six criteria (listed in B., below) are met.

1. Sales are recognized at the point of sale if the six criteria (listed below) are met; **or**

2. After the point of sale, when the return privilege expires, if the six criteria are not met. In this case, the sale may not be recognized as revenue until the period following the physical sale.

B. **Six Criteria** -- Revenue is recognized at the point of sale if all of the following six criteria are met:

1. The seller's price to the buyer is substantially fixed or determinable at the date of sale;

2. The buyer has paid the seller, or the buyer is obligated to pay the seller, and the obligation is not contingent on the resale of the product;

> **Note:**
> The last criterion is the most important for you to remember. If returns are not estimable as of the balance sheet date, then no sales with a right of return still effective can be recognized. (The same holds for the other five criteria as well.) The six criteria are expansions of the general earned and realizable criteria for revenue recognition.

3. The buyer's obligation to the seller would not be changed in the event of theft, physical destruction, or damage to the product;

4. The buyer acquiring the product for resale has economic substance apart from that provided by the seller;

5. The seller does not have significant obligations for future performance to directly bring about resale of the product by the buyer;

6. The amount of future returns can be reasonably estimated.

C. **Recognition when all six criteria are met**

1. Reported net sales for the year equals total sales less actual returns on those sales during the year less estimated returns at year-end.

2. Accounts receivable is reported net of deferred gross profit on the estimated returns at year-end. The journal entries are similar to those for the installment method.

D. **Recognition when all six criteria are not met**

1. If all six criteria are not met, revenue recognition is postponed until the return privilege has substantially expired, or the six criteria have been met. Reported net sales equals total sales less actual returns on those sales during the year less sales with a return privilege that is still effective.

2. Accounts receivable is reported net of deferred gross profit on sales with a return privilege still effective.

See the following example.

> **Example:**
> **1.** Of a firm's total sales of $50,000 for the period, $20,000 have a return privilege that has not expired as of the balance sheet date. The six criteria for recognizing revenue with a right of return have been met and the firm estimates that remaining returns will amount to $5,000 during the next year on the current year's sales. Total recognized net sales for the year are $45,000. Actual returns on the period's sales also would reduce net sales.
>
> **2.** Of a firm's total sales of $50,000 for the period, $20,000 have a return privilege that has not expired as of the balance sheet date. The six criteria for recognizing revenue with a right of return have NOT been met. Total recognized net sales for the current year are only $30,000. Even though it is most likely that some of the remaining $20,000 of sales will not be returned, GAAP requires the most conservative possible accounting if the six criteria are met: no sales are recognized. Next year, when the return privilege expires, any unreturned sales will be recognized as sales in that year.

IV. Goods on Consignment

A. Recognized Revenue -- The consignor (owner of the goods) recognizes revenue when the goods are sold by the consignee.

B. Selling Expenses -- Any amounts paid to the consignee for handling and selling the consignor's goods are treated as selling expenses by the consignor.

C. Revenue not Recognized -- Revenue is not recognized when the consignor merely ships goods to the consignee.

V. Initial Franchise Fee

A. Recognized as Revenue -- When the franchisor (for example, McDonald's Corporation) sells a franchise to a franchisee, the latter can sell the franchisor's products under the franchise agreement. The franchisor charges an initial fee and continuing fees. The initial franchise fee is recognized by the franchisor as revenue when all material services or conditions have been substantially performed or satisfied by the franchiser. These services include training of the franchisee and constructing the facilities, for example. The fee is recorded as unearned revenue until it is recognized as revenue.

B. Commencement of Operations -- The commencement of operations by the franchisee is generally presumed to be the earliest point at which performance has been completed.

C. Questions About Collectibility -- If there are questions about the collectibility of the initial franchise fee or if the amount will be collected over an extended time period and no estimate of uncollectibility can be made, it is appropriate to employ the installment sales basis or the cost recovery basis to recognize the revenues related to the initial franchise fee.

D. Extended Time Period -- If the goods and services related to the initial franchise fee are to be provided over an extended time period, it is appropriate to employ the percentage of completion method or the completed contract method to recognize the revenues related to the initial franchise fee.

E. Accrual Basis -- The revenues and expenses related to continuing franchise fees should be accounted for under the accrual basis of accounting. The franchisor typically recognizes the revenue as it provides goods and services (including advertising) to the franchisee. The related costs are matched against this revenue in the same period the revenue is earned.

VI. Milestone Method for R and D Arrangements

A. Payments to a firm (vendor) conducting research for other entities may be contingent on achieving milestone events such as successful completion of the testing phase of a new product. The recognition of these payments as revenue in their entirety in the period the milestone is achieved is called the milestone method. There often are several milestones in an arrangement.

B. Revenue is recognized at milestones only if the milestone meets the following criteria to be considered substantive (complete). The consideration earned by achieving the milestone must :

1. Be commensurate with either (a) the vendor's performance in achieving the milestone, or (b) the enhancement of the value of the item delivered as a result of achieving the milestone. In other words, the consideration must in-line with the value provided by the vendor;

2. Relate only to work already performed;

3. Be reasonable relative to all deliverables and payment terms in the arrangement.

C. Each milestone is evaluated separately and must be substantive in its entirety. As a result, milestones and resulting revenue recognition can occur at different times for an arrangement.

D. Choosing the milestone method is an accounting policy choice. Other appropriate methods may be applied provided that they do not recognize the consideration as revenue in its entirety. However, the firm must be consistent in its application of chosen method for similar arrangements.

Contract Accounting

This lesson about contract accounting covers the rationale for the applicable methods and the journal entries for the typical case. It also addresses the accounting for losses on a contract .

After studying this lesson, you should be able to:

1. *Record the loss when a contract turns unprofitable under both methods of accounting.*

2. *Apply the cost recovery method to a long term contract under international accounting standards.*

3. *Account for a single period loss on a profitable contract.*

4. *Distinguish the two types of losses on contract.*

5. *Close the contract accounts under both methods.*

6. *Prepare the financial statement presentation of the accounts.*

7. *Record annual gross profit under the percentage of completion method.*

8. *Record the three summary journals each year for a contract under both methods.*

9. *Determine when to use the percentage of completion method and the completed contract method.*

I. **Methods of Revenue Recognition for Long-Term Contracts** -- Long-term contracts pose a unique revenue recognition problem. The seller/contractor performs its obligation over a long period of time. Cash collection generally is not an issue because projects generally are financed by third parties. Should the contractor recognize revenue as work progresses, or wait until the entire project is complete? Because of the long-term nature of construction contracts, the answer to this question has a significant impact on the contractor's income during the contract period. Two methods are used for revenue recognition in this context:

   A. **Completed contract method** -- No profit is recognized until the contract is complete. This method is required if estimates of the degree of completion at interim points cannot be made.

   B. **Percentage of completion** -- Recognize profit in proportion to the degree of completion. This method is required if estimates of the degree of completion at interim points can be made **and** reasonable estimates of total project cost (and therefore profitability) can be made, **and** when the buyer and seller can be expected to perform under the contract.

II. **Basic Illustration** -- The following example provides an illustration of both methods. A later lesson considers the effect of losses on contracts.

   A. A contractor begins construction of a building for a client. The contract price is $10,000. Data for two years follows. The estimated remaining cost is updated at the end of each year. The project is incomplete at the end of year 2 because costs remain for completion after year 2. Each year for each contract, four different types of journal entries are recorded.

   See the following example.

	Year 1	Year 2
Cost incurred in Year	$2,000	$4,000
Estimated remaining cost to complete at end of year	6,000	1,500
Progress billings in year	1,000	3,500
Collections on billings in year	800	3,000

III. Year 1

A. The first three summary journal entries for Year 1 are the same for both methods:

Construction in progress (inventory)	2,000	
Materials, cash etc.		2,000
Accounts receivable	1,000	
Billings		1,000
Cash	800	
Accounts receivable		800

B. Construction in progress is an inventory account and a current asset. Although the contract may run for several years, the operating cycle of a construction firm is the length of its contracts. Thus, the inventory account is classified as a current asset. Construction in progress is debited only when costs are incorporated into the project. Purchases of materials for the project are recorded in the materials account.

C. Billings is contra to construction in progress. In the balance sheet, if the balance in construction in progress exceeds cumulative billings to date, the net difference is a current asset: Excess of construction in progress over billings on contracts. If cumulative billings exceed the construction in progress balance, the difference is disclosed in the current liability section. By subtracting billings from construction in progress, the seller is transferring its equity in the project from the physical asset to the financial asset (to accounts receivable and then ultimately to cash).

D. The completed contract method recognizes no profit in Year 1 (or even in Year 2). The percentage of completion recognizes profit each year. Completed contract records no further entries for the first two years.

E. The fourth entry (below) is recorded for percentage of completion only, and is an adjusting entry. This entry records the profit on the project for the year based on the percentage of completion, which is 25% at the end of Year 1. 25% = ($2,000/($2,000 + $6,000)). The expected total cost of the project is $8,000 at the end of Year 1 and $2,000 of cost has been incurred.

F. Adjusting entry for percentage of completion only:

Construction in progress	500	
Construction expenses	2,000	
Construction revenue		2,500

G. $2,500 revenue = 25%($10,000). The project is 25% complete allowing 25% of the total revenue to be recognized. The $2,000 of construction expense is the cost incurred in the period. The $500 profit can be directly computed as the percentage of completion times the total estimated profit: .25($10,000 − $8,000) = $500. The $500 profit is recorded in the inventory account because it represents the increase in the value of the inventory. When $500 of profit is recognized, the net assets of the seller must also increase.

H. Caution -- The total estimated cost of the project at the end of any year equals cost incurred to date + estimated remaining costs to complete at year-end. This amount generally must be computed by the candidate. This amount is the denominator of the percentage of completion and also is used to compute profit to date. For example, the $8,000 figure would not be provided for the candidate. This amount changes each year of the project.

I. The balance sheet and income effects for both methods at the end of Year 1:

	Completed contract	Percentage of completion
Income statement		
Recognized gross profit	$ 0	$ 500*

*The $2,500 revenue less $2,000 expense also can be reported.

Balance sheet (current assets)	Completed contract	Percentage of completion
Accounts receivable	200	200
Construction in progress	$2,000	$2,500
Less billings	(1,000)	(1,000)
Excess of construction in progress over billings	1,000	1,500

If no losses are expected, the balance in construction in progress at any balance sheet date is:

Completed contract:	total cost to date
Percentage of completion:	total cost to date
	+ total recognized gross profit to date

The construction in progress and billings accounts are separate accounts. Billings is subtracted from construction in progress only for reporting in the balance sheet.

IV. Year 2

A. The first three journal entries are the same as the first year's except for the amounts. Both methods record these entries. These entries are not shown; the amounts are: $4,000, $3,500, and $3,000.

B. The fourth entry (for percentage of completion below) shows how the profit for the second year is computed as the total profit to date less the profit recognized in earlier years. Thus in the fourth year of a project, the profit recognized is total profit through the fourth year less the profit for the first three years. After the first year, there is no direct way to compute profit for the year because total profit through the end of each year uses the estimated remaining cost amount, which varies each year.

C. The percentage of completion at the end of Year 2 = cost to date/total estimated cost = ($2,000 + $4,000)/($2,000 + $4,000 + $1,500) = $6,000/$7,500 = 80%.

D. Note that the estimated remaining cost to complete ($1,500) is the only difference between the numerator and denominator.

Profit recognized in Year 2 = total estimated profit through Year 2

− profit recognized in previous periods

= .80($10,000 − $7,500) − $500

= $1,500

Adjusting entry for percentage of completion only:

Construction in progress	1,500	
Construction expenses	4,000	
Construction revenue		5,500

$5,500 = .80($10,000) − $2,500 revenue in Year 1

V. End of Contract—Year 3

A. Assume that total cost incurred by the contractor for the project was $7,500 with completion occurring in Year 3. Under percentage of completion, the final adjusting entry (fourth entry in year) would record profit for that year and update the construction-in-progress account. That entry is:

Construction in progress		500	
Construction expenses	$7,500 − $6,000	1,500	
Construction revenue	$10,000 − $8,000		2,000

B. The entries to complete the contract and close the accounts are:

Completed Contract:			Percentage of Completion:		
Billings	10,000		Billings		10,000
Construction expenses	7,500		Construction in progress		10,000
Construction in progress		7,500			
Construction revenue		10,000			

C. Only in the final year of the contract is profit recognized under the completed contract method. At completion, $2,500 of profit is recognized (revenue less expenses). Under the percentage of completion method, the construction in progress account balance is total cost plus total profit, or $7,500 + $2,500 = total contract price of $10,000. The billings account reflects the full contract price under both methods.

VI. Contract Accounting, Losses

A. Losses on Contracts

1. For accounting purposes, there are two kinds of losses on long-term contracts: (1) overall losses, and (2) single period losses.

2. They require very different accounting. In particular, a single period loss is treated exactly the same way as profit during the year, for both percentage of completion and completed contract methods. Overall losses require very different reporting.

B. Overall Losses -- GAAP requires, for both methods (percentage of completion and completed contract), that when an overall loss on a contract is anticipated, the loss be recognized in full. An overall loss occurs when the total estimated costs of the project exceed the contract price.

Example:

Year 3 is added to the data for the basic illustration in the previous lesson. The information for years 1 and 2 are the same as before. Through year 2, a total of $2,000 profit was recognized.

	Year 1	Year 2	Year 3
Cost incurred in Year	$2,000	$4,000	$2,400
Estimated remaining cost to complete at end of year	6,000	1,500	1,800

At the end of Year 3 the overall anticipated loss is $200:

= total estimated project cost − contract price

= $2,000 + $4,000 + $2,400 + $1,800 − $10,000 = $200

The loss is recognized in full for both methods. Any previous profit under percentage of completion is removed from the construction in process account. In the first two years under percentage of completion, recognized revenue was $8,000 and recognized profit was $2,000 from the previous example. The adjusting entries to record the loss are:

Adjusting entry for percentage of completion:

Construction expenses	2,435#	
Construction in progress		2,200*
Construction revenue		235^

The loss recorded by this entry is $2,200, the difference between the revenue and expense.

\# A plug figure. When an overall loss is anticipated, the amount recorded as construction expense is no longer the year's incurred cost

* $2,000 profit in Years 1 and 2 plus the overall loss of $200

^ The percentage of completion is now ($2,000 + $4,000 + $2,400)/($2,000 + $4,000 + $2,400 + $1,800)= .8235. .8235($10,000) − $8,000 previous revenue = $235

The construction in progress account balance is now total cost to date less the overall loss. The same holds for completed contract. No previous profit must be removed however, and the entry under the completed contract method is:

Loss on construction contract	200	
Construction in progress		200

C. Single Period Loss -- When the total profit through the end of a given year is less than the profit recognized in previous years, a loss has occurred in the given year although there is no overall loss. In the current example under percentage of completion, the firm has recognized

$2,000 of profit through the first two years. If the normal computation of profit resulted in total profit through Year 3 of $1,700, then a single period loss of $300 has occurred. The entries are the same as before. The adjusting entry for profit is computed as usual. The only difference is that construction in progress is credited (reduced) for $300, rather than debited.

1. The completed contract method is unaffected by single period losses.

D. U.S. GAAP—IFRS Differences

1. International standards require the percentage of completion method when the contractor can reliably estimate total costs although international standards are less specific regarding how to measure the stage of completion. Both sets of standards require full recognition of an estimated overall loss in the year that determination is made.

2. In contrast with U.S. standards however, when the percentage of completion method is not appropriate, the completed contract method cannot be used. Rather, the cost recovery method (also called the zero-profit method) is applied. This approach is also applied to long-term service contracts when the total estimated cost of providing the service cannot be estimated reliably.

   a. In this context, the cost recovery method requires that the contractor recognize construction expense equal to the revenue recognized, thus generating no gross profit. The amount of revenue recognized is computed as per the percentage of completion method. This is the same journal entry for recognition of profit under the percentage of completion method except there is no debit to construction in progress.

Example:

The basic illustration for U.S. standards in the previous lesson (no losses) is used to illustrate the cost recovery method. Before the contract is completed, only the fourth journal entry each year is different compared with the percentage of completion method. Only the fourth journal entry is shown here for both methods.

Contract data: contract price, $10,000.

Year 1 cost incurred, $2,000. Year 2 cost incurred, $4,000.

Fourth journal entry under percentage of completion (from previous lesson):

Year 1			Year 2		
Construction in progress	500		Construction in progress	1,500	
Construction expenses	2,000		Construction expenses	4,000	
Construction revenue		2,500	Construction revenue		5,500

Fourth journal entry under cost recovery method (international standards):

Year 1			Year 2		
Construction expenses	2,000		Construction expenses	4,000	
Construction revenue		2,000	Construction revenue		4,000

Under the cost recovery method, there is no debit to construction in progress. This approach yields the same gross profit (zero) as the completed contract method but the latter records no revenue or expense until the project is complete.

---

3. When the project is completed, the total profit on the contract is recognized as a debit to construction in progress and the remaining cost incurred and revenue are recognized.

Example:

Again using the basic illustration for U.S. standards above (no losses), Year 3, the cost recovery journal entry before closing the contract is as follows. The total contract price was $10,000 and the cost incurred in Year 3 was $1,500. Total contract cost is $7,500. The entry for international standards is:

Construction in progress	2,500	$10,000 − $7,500
Construction expenses	1,500	
Construction revenue		4,000

10,000 − $2,000 − $4,000

The $4,000 construction revenue is the difference between total contract price and the revenue recognized in the first two years. The entire profit for the project is recognized in the final year (Year 3) of the contract.

---

4. The cost recovery (zero- profit) method is invoked when total project cost cannot be estimated, and also for any other reason causing completion of the contract to be uncertain.

   a. Other causes include (1) a finding that the contract is not enforceable, (2) if completion is dependent on pending litigation, and (3) if the contractor cannot complete the contract due to internal problems such as pending bankruptcy.

5. International standards distinguish fixed fee contracts (use the percentage of completion method) and cost-plus contracts for which the percentage of completion method is not used. In a cost-plus contract, the total cost of the project is variable with the customer taking the risk for cost increases. The amount of revenue recognized by the contractor in any period is the cost incurred plus the agreed-upon percentage markup above cost.

Costs and Expenses

This lesson considers the general principles for recognizing expenses and losses before and after expenditures are made. Many of the FAR lessons consider specific costs and expenses. Advertising costs and property taxes are illustrated here.

After studying this lesson, you should be able to:

1. *Recognize that cost is a general term encompassing other specific accounting terms.*

2. *Distinguish assets, expenses and losses.*

3. *Describe how conceptual framework concepts affect the recognition of assets, expenses and losses.*

4. *Determine when advertising costs are expensed, and when they are capitalized.*

5. *Prepare the journal entries relevant to property taxes assessed for an annual period.*

I. **General Concepts**

A. **Cost** -- Costs are the economic sacrifices incurred by firms for goods and services used in their business. Costs are measured at the cash equivalent or fair value of consideration transferred, or liability assumed, for the good or service. The conceptual framework description of cost is "... the value of cash or other resources given up (or the present value of an obligation incurred) in exchange for a resource measures the cost of the resource acquired."

   1. For accounting purposes, a cost can cause the recognition of an asset, expense, loss, or liability. Many costs, as evidenced by expenditures, are first recognized as assets, and then later expensed or written-off as a loss. Only the expense and loss dispositions enter into the determination of income. Expenses and losses are the portions of costs that no longer have future value.

B. **Expense vs. Loss**

   1. Both expenses and losses are debited when they are recognized and both reduce net income.

   2. Only expenses provide a benefit to the firm. Expenses are outflows of resources that are incurred in production or other activities central to the ongoing **primary** operations of the entity. Examples include salary expense, rent expense, and many others. In each case, the firm obtains a benefit.

   3. Losses provide no benefit to the primary operations of the entity. Losses are **incidental** to the primary operations. Losses are recognized when it becomes evident that a previously recognized future benefit (an asset) has been reduced. When assets are "written off" as worthless, a loss is recognized. Losses also occur from casualties. The loss represents the amount of asset reduction for which there is no benefit. Losses also arise from the sale of assets for less than book value or the retirement of liabilities for more than book value.

II. **Timing of Cash Payment** -- The incurrence of cost can occur before, at the same time, or after expense or loss recognition. Over the life of the resource obtained, total cost and total expenses (plus losses) will be of equal amount. But for any reporting period, the amounts are often different.

A. When cash payments precede expense recognition, an asset typically is recorded because payment of the good or service occurs before its use in the business. Over the period of the asset's benefit, an expense is recognized. Examples include plant assets (depreciation) and prepaids (rent expense, insurance expense). These items are called deferrals. (Payment before expense.)

B. When expenses precede cash payments, a liability typically is recorded. The liability is paid at a later date. The service or good is received and used before payment. These items are called accruals. (Payment after expense.)

III. Matching

A. The matching principle is frequently used to determine the amount of expense to be recognized for a given period. This is an income statement emphasis and is a major underlying concept used for determining the timing of expense recognition. The principle states that expenses are to be recognized in the same period as the related revenues. The revenues drive the recognition of expense. The wording of the principle presumes a causal relationship but depending on the expense, the strength of the relationship between expenses and revenues varies. The following is a list of expense categories from strong to weak relationship with revenue.

1. **Expenses with a direct causal link to revenues --** Cost of goods sold, and sales commissions based on sales revenue are examples. The link between revenues and expenses is the strongest for this category. For example, when inventory is sold, cost of goods sold is recognized for the cost of the item sold. Before sale, the inventory is reported as an asset.

2. **Expenses associated with revenues in a specific time period --** Salaries, property taxes and other similar costs are examples. These costs are only indirectly related to revenues produced in the same period because they serve many different efforts. The presumption is that they contributed to the overall effort of generating revenues in that period.

3. **Expenses associated with benefits over more than one period --** This category includes depreciation and amortization expenses that are allocated on a systematic and rational basis to time periods or units of production (if the asset is involved in manufacturing). Long-term prepaids are included in this category. As they expire, they give rise to operating expenses including rent and insurance.

4. **Expenses recognized in the period incurred --** Examples are advertising and R&D (research and development) expense. The relationship between these costs and revenues is not determinable. There is no way to determine whether these expenditures have future benefit (with some exceptions).

IV. Asset and Liability Definitions vs. Matching

A. Relative to matching, the recent emphasis has been on determining whether an asset or liability is to be recognized. The conceptual framework definitions are followed in this regard. This is a balance sheet emphasis and is a concept competing with matching as a major underlying concept used for determining the timing of expense recognition. An expense is a derived concept, based on the decrease in an asset or increase in a liability.

B. Interperiod tax allocation is an example of the balance sheet emphasis. The firm directly determines its income tax liability and the change in deferred tax accounts for the period. Income tax expense is the net change in these assets and liabilities. The firm is not attempting to match income tax expense with the benefits of operating in the U.S.

1. Accounting for R&D is another example. Because future benefit is not probable for most R&D efforts, there is insufficient justification for recording an asset, which is a probable future benefit controlled by the firm as a result of a past transaction. Here the focus is on

whether there is an asset. The definition is not met; therefore an expense is recognized. The firm is not attempting to match R&D expense with the future revenues of inventions developed from current R&D efforts.

2. Another example is the use of the successful efforts method of accounting for natural resource exploration costs. This method capitalizes (debits an asset) only the costs of successful explorations (finding the resource). Unsuccessful efforts are expensed.

C. Matching, however, continues to be the justification for other practices including accounting for bond issue costs, the full costing method of accounting for natural resource exploration costs, and capitalization of interest. In these cases, assets are not enhanced. However, an asset is recorded in each case so that its cost can be matched against the related future revenues.

D. In many other situations, both concepts (matching, and the definitions of asset and liability) lead to the same accounting. For example, the recognition of estimated warranty expense in the year of sale both matches the expense in the year of sale, and records the probable obligation of the firm to transfer resources in the future as a result of a past transaction.

V. Advertising Costs

A. Advertising costs include the costs of content production and communicating that content.

B. The general principle is that advertising costs are either (1) expensed as incurred or (2) when the advertising first occurs. This is a policy choice and must be consistently applied. Although the advertising may be for an extended period of time, both alternatives reflect the lack of probable future benefit and are consistent with accounting for R & D.

1. The second alternative assumes that the cost of advertising has been incurred and the advertising service will take place in the future. Examples are the first television commercial to be aired, and the first appearance of an advertisement in a newspaper.

C. Tangible assets such as catalogues and billboards are recognized as prepaids and amortized to advertising expense until they are no longer owned or expected to be used.

D. Accounting for certain direct response advertising programs is different. Direct response advertising is a promotional method designed to encourage prospective customers to respond directly to the advertiser. Methods include the use of coupons, toll-free telephone numbers and Internet links.

1. Direct response advertising costs are capitalized if the main purpose is to produce sales from customers who respond directly to the advertising, and if it is probable that future benefits will result and extend beyond the current period.

2. Capitalized costs are amortized as advertising expense over the expected period of benefit. Expiration of an offer is an example of the end of an amortization period.

3. The firm must be able to support the contention that there are future benefits from this form of advertising through past experience.

4. The types of costs that are capitalized include:

a. Incremental direct costs such as the costs of logos, advertisements on the Internet and others;

b. Salary costs of employees directly involved in the advertising activities including developing the concepts, artwork, advertising copy etc. ;

c. Assets used as prizes directly related to direct response advertising programs.

5. Not capitalized are indirect costs such as facility costs and depreciation.

VI. Property Taxes

A. Property taxes are levied by state and local governments based on the assessed valuation of property as of a given date. The tax becomes a lien against the property on the date specified by law and thus legally the liability comes into existence on that date. From the perspective of the taxing authority, property taxes do not "accrue" over time. The fiscal periods of the taxing authority and the firm paying the tax (the property owner) often do not coincide.

B. The issues then are (1) what is the period over which to recognize the tax, and (2) what is the amount of any liability or prepayment for balance sheet reporting.

C. Accounting Principles

1. The tax-paying firm accrues the property tax monthly as expense over the fiscal year of the taxing authority because the expense should be recognized in the same period the firm benefits from the services provided by the governmental unit (taxing authority).

   > **Note:**
   > This is the most important point to remember.

2. Until the amount of the tax bill for the year is known, the firm estimates the annual amount for purposes of recording the monthly property tax expense.

3. When the amount of the tax bill for the year becomes known, the difference between the estimated annual amount and the actual annual amount is treated as an increase or decrease to the monthly property tax expense amount based on the annual estimate.

4. Until the tax is paid, the firm records a liability for the recognized expense to date. When the tax is paid, the liability is extinguished and a prepayment of tax is recognized for the remaining months of the taxing authority's fiscal year. That prepayment is reduced as the expense for the remaining months is recognized.

Example:
The county where a calendar-fiscal year firm is located has a June 30 fiscal year-end. The firm will accrue property taxes monthly and estimates the tax for the current tax fiscal year (July 1, 20x4—June 30, 20x5) to be $12,000 based on the previous year's bill. In December the actual tax bill is received showing $12,700 as the actual amount. The firm pays the tax bill on December 26, 20x4 before the December 31, 20x4 due date. The county's billing practice thus requires property owners to pay first half of the annual year tax in arrears (last six months in 20x4) and to prepay the last half (first six months of 20x5).

End-of month journal entries for July—November 20x4 (5 monthly entries)

Property tax expense	1,000	
Property tax payable		1,000

(Estimated property tax $12,000/12 months)

December 26, 20x4 entry

Property tax payable	5,000	
Prepaid property tax	7,700	
Cash		12,700

(To record payment, remove payable (5 months × $1,000) and recognize prepayment)

December 31, 20x4 entry

Property tax expense	1,100	
Prepaid property tax		1,100

(To record December property tax expense ($12,700 − $5,000)/7 months)

Starting with December, the remaining portion of the total actual property tax expense amount is allocated evenly over the remaining 7 months of the county's fiscal year. This is a change in estimate and is handled prospectively. The previous five months' estimated expense amounts are not retrospectively adjusted.

In the 20x4 balance sheet, the firm reports $6,600 of prepaid property tax as a current asset ($7,700 − $1,100 or 6 × $1,100). The property tax expense is accrued by the firm over the county's fiscal period. The firm will recognize $6,600 of property tax expense for the first six months of 20x5 ($1,100 monthly).

VII. Costs and Expense under IFRS

A. In general, the recognition of costs and expenses under IFRS is similar to US GAAP. One main difference related to the topics covered in this lesson relate to advertising and promotional expenses. U.S. GAAP permits capitalization of certain direct response advertising costs. IFRS does not allow capitalization of these costs - all must be expensed as incurred.

Costs and Expenses	
IFRS	**U.S. GAAP**
All advertising and promotional costs are expensed as incurred	Certain direct response advertising cost can be capitalized

Compensated Absences

Accounting by the employer for vacation and holiday pay programs is the focus of this lesson.

After studying this lesson, you should be able to:

1. *Explain the relevance of the four criteria for recognizing compensated absence expense and obligation.*

2. *Record the journal entry for recognizing the annual expense.*

3. *Note the exception for sick leave benefits.*

4. *Prepare the journal entry for payment, including situations for which the rate of pay has changed.*

I. **Compensated Absences**

A. Compensated absences include vacation, holiday and sick leave periods for which the employee is compensated. GAAP requires that accrual accounting be applied if certain criteria are met. The expense of these benefits is accrued during the period employees earn these benefits if all of the following four criteria are met:

1. The obligation is attributable to services rendered as of the balance sheet date;

2. The rights vest (benefits are no longer contingent on continued employment) or accumulate (carry over to future periods);

3. Payment of the obligation is probable;

4. The amount of the obligation is estimable.

B. Some benefits do not require accrual. For example, some holiday pay benefits, military leave and maternity leave benefits do not accumulate if the employee does not use these benefits. Therefore, no accrual is required. In general, if the probable and estimable criteria are not met, there is no accrual. Such expenses are recognized when paid (pay-as-you-go).

C. Vesting is more valuable to the employee than accumulation because the employee can leave the firm and be paid the benefits if they are vested. However, if benefits accumulate, the employee does not lose the benefits if the holiday or vacation is not taken by the balance sheet date. Limits on accumulation (for example, at most 10 weeks of vacation pay can be accumulated for some firms) place a cap on the amount of liability accrued.

II. **Measurement of the Accrual** -- The measurement of the accrual can be based on current or future wage rates although typically current rates are used. Current rates result in a lower expense accrual and do not telegraph future pay raises.

A. If current rates are used for the accrual, and a pay raise is enacted between the accrual of the expense and its payment, the effect of the raise is treated as a change in estimate and is recognized currently and prospectively, retroactive application does not apply.

B. The liability is not discounted but rather is reported at nominal (future) value.

See the following example.

Example:
At year-end, employees had earned a total of $35,000 worth of vacation and holiday pay. Of that amount, $12,000 of vacation and holiday pay was paid during the year.

Adjusting entry at year-end:

Salary Expense	23,000	
Liability for Compensated Absences		23,000

Next year, there is an across the board 4% pay rate increase. The remaining holiday and vacation pay is paid.

Liability for Compensated Absences	23,000	
Salary Expense .04($23,000)	920	
Cash		23,920

III. **Sick Pay Benefits** -- Accumulated sick pay benefits need not be accrued (but may be) because the event causing payment (illness) cannot be predicted. However, if unused sick pay benefits are routinely paid to employees (for example, upon leaving the firm), then accrual is required because in this case the benefits vest.

IV. **Benefits not Accrued** -- In practice, not all earned compensated absence benefits are accrued because not all earned benefits are taken by employees. For example, not all vacation pay benefits are taken because some employees let a portion of their benefits lapse.

Example:
The beginning balance of the liability for compensated absences for the year is $50,000. During the current year, $25,000 of additional benefits were earned. The firm estimates that 15% of benefits earned each year will not be paid. Benefits paid for the year totaled $35,000.

Journal entries:

Liability for compensated absences	35,000	
Cash		35,000
Salary expense	21,250	
Liability for compensated absences		21,250

$21,250 = .85($25,000). The expense recognized reflects the amount earned in the period that will probably be paid.

The ending liability balance is $36,250 (= $50,000 - $35,000 + $21,250) and represents the expected future payment for compensated absence benefits earned through the end of the current year.

Pension Principles, Reporting

This lesson begins several by describing the basic principles underlying accounting for defined benefit pension plans.

After studying this lesson, you should be able to:

1. *Distinguish defined contribution and defined benefit pension plans.*

2. *Account for defined contribution plans.*

3. *Describe the inputs to a pension benefit formula and the relevance of the formula to accounting for defined benefit pension plans.*

4. *List the main attributes of accounting for defined benefit pension plans.*

5. *Define projected benefit obligation.*

6. *Explain the two separate sides of the pension plan.*

7. *Calculate reported pension liability.*

8. *Note the components of pension expense.*

I. **Types of Pension Plans** -- (1) defined contribution plans, and (2) defined benefit plans.

A. There are two main types of pension plans:

> **Definition:**
> *Defined contribution plans*: The amount of the employer contribution is defined by contract. For example, the employer contributes 5% of gross salary to the plan each month.

1. The benefits paid during retirement are dependent on the return on the pension fund assets and therefore are not defined. The employee bears the risk of fund performance in this type of plan. The sponsoring firm has no obligation to the employee beyond the total annual contribution. A 401K plan is an example of a defined contribution plan. Earnings are tax exempt until withdrawals are made.

2. Accounting for defined **contribution** plans is simple: The amount of annual pension expense recognized is the required contribution. Any shortfall represents a liability until the employer covers it. If the payment is not expected to be within one year of the balance sheet date, the liability is discounted to present value. Amendments to the plan that change benefits earned previously are immediately expensed.

3. The sponsor must disclose a description of the plan, the covered employee groups, information about how contribution amounts are determined, and any factors affecting comparability between periods.

> **Definition:**
> *Defined benefit plans*: The benefits paid during retirement are based on a formula and therefore are defined.

4. The contribution to the pension fund is not defined. The employer bears the risk in this type of plan because the benefit is defined.

B. Defined contribution and benefit plans can be **contributory** or **noncontributory**.

1. In a contributory plan, contributions to the pension plan are made by the employer and the employees. In noncontributory plans, contributions to the pension plan are made by the employer only.

C. Defined Benefit Plans -- These plans are the focus of the lessons pertaining to pension accounting. Because the benefit during retirement is defined, the determination of annual pension expense and the ending pension obligation for a given year is complicated by the need to estimate many factors including turnover, final salary, life expectancy, and others.

D. Accounting for Defined Benefit Plans -- Is based on accrual accounting: pension expense is recognized as benefits are earned and the pension obligation is recognized for unpaid benefits. The cash basis of accounting ("pay-as-you-go"), which would recognize pension expense when retirement benefits are paid, is not permitted. One of the costs of generating current period revenue is the provision, by the employer, of employee pension benefits. That cost is matched as pension expense against the revenues it helped generate. Also, the definition of a liability is met because pension benefits are promised as credits are earned during the employee service period.

> **Exam note:**
> Essentially all pension questions on the CPA exam pertain to defined benefit plans.

E. Trustee -- Many firms sponsoring defined benefit plans use a trustee or insurance company to disburse retirement checks. The sponsoring firm makes periodic funding contributions to the trust company. Those contributions and the earnings on them comprise the pension plan assets available for payment of retirement benefits. The periodic trustee report provides detailed information about the funding of the pension plan and benefit payments made by the plan. Information from the trustee is the basis for the asset "side" of pension accounting. Information on the fund balance and actual return on plan assets for a period is provided by the trustee report.

F. Benefit Formula -- The pension benefits that an employee is entitled to at retirement are explicitly stated in the pension plan. The estimated future benefits are the primary input into the determination of the pension obligation. The benefit level is based on the benefit formula which includes such variables as:

1. Years of service;

2. Age at retirement; and

3. Highest salary attained.

 Example: The annual benefit payment for a defined benefit plan is:

(years of service/40)(final or highest annual salary)(age at retirement/65).

The annual benefit may not exceed final salary.

An employee retiring at age 60 after 25 years of service with a final salary of $80,000 will receive an annual pension benefit of $46,154 = (25/40)(80,000)(60/65).

G. Actuary -- The *actuarial* present value of those pension checks at the reporting date (well before employees have retired) is the foundation for pension accounting. Present value calculations are performed by actuaries who typically work for insurance companies and are highly trained in the mathematics relevant to employee benefits. The management of the sponsoring firm works with the actuary providing the employee information required to make estimates of life expectancy, turnover, final salary, the discount rate used for computing present values, and other amounts. Actuarial information is the basis for the liability and expense "side" of pension accounting. This information is conveyed to the firm by the report of the actuary. Without the actuary, accounting for defined benefit pension plans would not be possible.

II. Accounting for Defined Benefit Pension Plans -- is characterized by the following special attributes

> **Delayed recognition of certain items in pension expense** -- Gradual recognition through amortization rather than immediate recognition.
> **Net cost reporting of pension expense** -- This expense (or component of inventory cost for manufacturing personnel) is the net sum of five components, one or more of which can be negative (decrease in pension expense).
> **Offsetting in the balance sheet** -- The pension obligation and pension plan assets are not recognized separately in the balance sheet; rather they are offset yielding one much smaller reported net asset or liability.

The two main accounting reporting issues are:

A. The determination and reporting of annual pension expense;

B. The determination and reporting of the ending pension obligation for the period.

1. For the **current year**, the firm must report:

    a. **Pension expense** -- The cost to the firm of providing the pension benefits earned during the year. This amount is reported in the income statement and has five independently computed components.

    b. **PBO (projected benefit obligation)** -- The present value of unpaid pension benefits promised for work done through the balance sheet date, as measured by the benefit formula. PBO reflects future salaries if they are used in the formula, but PBO reflects service credits earned only through the balance sheet date. This major liability is reported only in the footnotes, not in the balance sheet (off-balance sheet). PBO is an actuarial present value that takes into account such variables as life expectancy, estimated final salary, years of service, turnover, interest rates, etc. An actuarial firm provides this information.

    c. **Pension assets at market value** -- The current ending plan assets (with the trustee). This is the fund available for retirement benefits. Like PBO, plan assets are reported only in the footnotes, not the balance sheet (off-balance sheet). The ending plan asset balance equals: contributions made by the sponsoring firm to date + investment return to date (interest, dividends, stock appreciation, recognized gains and losses) - benefits paid to date.

    d. **Pension liability** -- The difference between ending PBO and plan assets at the balance sheet date, reported in the balance sheet. Pension liability (PBO - assets) is the amount underfunded. If the plan is overfunded (assets exceed PBO), then pension asset is reported (assets - PBO). The pension liability (or asset) amount is also called "funded status" and represents the critical reporting value for pensions. If PBO is $40 million and plan assets at market value are $30 million, the pension fund is underfunded by $10 million. The pension liability of $10 million is the only amount reported in the balance sheet. Both PBO and assets are measured as of the balance sheet date.

        i. **Classification of liability or asset**

            1. The portion of pension liability classified as current is the excess of benefits payable for the coming year over the fair value of plan assets - this is the amount of payments that cannot be paid out of existing plan assets. The remainder is a noncurrent liability.

            2. If PBO is less than plan assets, the reported pension asset is classified as noncurrent because it is restricted and not available for other purposes.

ii. When a firm has more than one defined benefit pension plan, the pension assets for those plans with plan assets at fair value > PBO are aggregated into one asset for reporting, and vice versa for plans with pension liabilities. Offsetting is not permitted because one plan's assets cannot be used to pay another plan's benefit payments.

> **Note:** Two additional liability measures are reported in the footnotes: **ABO** (accumulated benefit obligation) - the present value of unpaid pension benefits through the balance sheet using current salaries. This calculation is the same as for PBO except that the latter uses future salaries.   **VBO** (vested benefit obligation) - the present value of vested benefits;   In most situations, the following relationship holds: PBO > ABO > VBO.

C. Two important estimates -- In pension accounting are:

1. Discount rate - the rate used for all actuarial present value pension calculations. It is the rate at which the pension obligation could be settled and is pegged at the market rate of interest;

2. Expected rate of return - the rate used to compute expected return on plan assets, one of the components of pension expense.

D. The two rates are independent although generally similar in magnitude.

E. Pension expense for a period -- (Assume a calendar fiscal year) Is the sum of five components:

1. **Service cost (SC)** -- The actuarial present value of pension benefits earned during the current period. This amount is the increase in pension expense due to service provided during the year. Service cost is an immediate increase in PBO.

2. **Interest cost** -- = growth in PBO for the period due to the passage of time = (discount rate)x(PBO at Jan. 1). This component is based on benefits earned through the end of the previous year. PBO is a present value. Because PBO is not paid until retirement benefits are paid, it grows by the interest rate as would any unpaid liability. That liability increase must be paid by the firm; therefore, the increase in PBO is part of annual pension expense.

3. **Expected return on plan assets** -- = (expected rate of return)x(plan assets at Jan. 1 at market value). This component **reduces** pension expense. The return on plan assets is the amount of the pension fund that is not paid by the sponsoring firm. Rather, investment returns on the assets provide a significant portion of the amounts paid to retirees. Expected return is used for component 3 rather than actual return to smooth the volatility in pension expense. Expected and actual return on plan assets for the period are generally not the same.

4. **Amortization of prior service cost** -- (PSC) (Discussed later). This component causes pension expense to be increased gradually by the effect of amendments to the plan, which grant an increase in the value of pension benefits for service already provided by the employees.

5. **Amortization of net gain or loss** -- (Discussed later). This component causes pension expense to be gradually increased or decreased by (a) changes in PBO caused by estimate changes or experience changes, and (b) differences between expected and actual return on plan assets.

F. Each component is **computed independently**.

1. Components 1 and 2 always increase pension expense.

2. Component 3 always reduces pension expense.

3. Component 4 almost always increases pension expense because benefits are usually increased by plan amendments. In rare cases, a pension plan modification may reduce pension benefits in which case component 4 would reduce pension expense.

> **Note:**
> Components 1-5 are not generally known by their numbers. Be able to recognize each component by name.

4. Component 5 decreases pension expense for gains (PBO decreases and when actual return exceeds expected return), or increases pension expense for losses (PBO increases and when actual return falls short of expected return).

G. Pension expense for a period reflects changes in PBO and assets during the period, along with amortizations of changes in PBO and assets occurring in previous periods. Pension expense is affected by PBO and assets (the two "sides" of pension accounting), but does not affect PBO or assets. In other words, PBO and assets are known before pension expense is computed.

Pension Expense

This lesson highlights the first three components of pension expense to illustrate the model for accounting for defined benefit pension plans. It also focuses on the general effects of delayed recognition on the reporting process, and illustrates accounting for prior service cost. The lesson continues with the application of delayed recognition to the second aspect requiring this procedure: pension gains and losses.

After studying this lesson, you should be able to :

1. *Apply two methods for amortizing pension gain or loss for the year.*

2. *Compute the amount subject to amortization for the following year.*

3. *Record the net pension gain or loss for a year.*

4. *Distinguish the two computations required each year.*

5. *Describe the composition of the pension gain or loss amount that is subject to amortization.*

6. *Apply two methods of amortizing prior service cost and record the resulting journal entry.*

7. *Record prior service cost.*

8. *Explain how prior service cost arises and interpret the initial recognized amount.*

9. *Describe the effects of delayed recognition on the accounting and reporting by the employer.*

10. *Note the two aspects of pension accounting subject to delayed recognition.*

11. *Recall the important aspects of reporting regarding pension plans.*

12. *Determine the financial reporting and footnote disclosure for the sponsor.*

13. *Record pension expense and funding contribution.*

14. *Calculate the first three components of pension expense.*

I. **Accounting for Pension Expense—Components 1-3**

A. The first three components of pension expense occur each year. This example illustrates the first three components, resulting journal entries, and financial statement reporting. The last two components are independent of these and are discussed later. Recall that the first three components are (1) service cost, (2) interest cost, (3) expected return on plan assets.

B. **20x1**

1. **Component 1, service cost --** 20x1 is the first year of a defined benefit plan. Service cost (SC) for 20x1, as computed by the actuary, is $3,000 (the present value of benefits earned in 20x1 taking into account estimated final salary, years of service, age at retirement, life expectancy, and other factors).

2. Discount rate is 5%, expected rate of return on plan assets is 6%.

3. Funding contribution to trustee is $2,000 (assume year-end).

4. **Component 2, interest cost --** There is no PBO at January 1, 20x1, because the plan was not in existence before that date. Therefore, there is no interest cost (component 2) for 20x1.

5. **Component 3, expected return** -- There was no pension fund at January 1, 20x1, so there is no expected return (component 3). SC is the only component for the first year. PBO at year-end is $3,000, the present value increase in PBO due to service credits earned in 20x1.

    a. **Journal Entries** -- When only components 1-3 are present, the sponsoring firm makes only two journal entries each year (the first is an adjusting entry):

Pension expense	3,000	
Pension liability		3,000
Pension liability	2,000	
Cash		2,000

    b. These two entries cause:

        i. Income from continuing operations before tax to decrease $3,000;

        ii. Cash to decrease $2,000; (The cash is no longer available to the sponsoring firm because it has been placed into the pension fund.)

        iii. Reported pension liability to increase $1,000 ($3,000 − $2,000), the amount by which the plan is underfunded.

    c. There is no journal entry on the sponsoring firm's books when retirement benefits are paid - these amounts are paid by the trustee. However, both PBO and plan assets are reduced by benefits paid.

    d. In the first entry above, pension expense causes pension liability (PBO − assets) to increase because SC is a direct increase to PBO. The funding contribution causes pension liability (PBO - assets) to decrease because assets reduce the pension liability.

> PBO at 12/31/x1 is $3,000, the present value of benefits earned to date. The $3,000 amount is also SC because this is the first year of the plan.
>
> Assets at 12/31/x1 = $2,000 (from funding in 20x1)
>
> Pension liability = $1,000 = $3,000 (PBO) − $2,000 (assets)
>
> = $1,000 = $3,000 (credit in entry for pension expense) − $2,000 (debit in entry for funding)

    e. The pension plan is underfunded $1,000 - the amount of the reported pension liability. PBO of $3,000 and assets of $2,000 are reported in the footnotes. Pension expense of $3,000 is reported in the income statement.

    f. The Employee Retirement Income Security Act of 1974, as amended requires that employee pension benefits vest within a certain period (5 or 7 years is typical). **Benefits are vested** if they are not contingent on continued employment. The Act also requires that firms provide minimum funding of pension plans. In addition, amounts funded by the employer are tax deductible, but only up to a maximum amount. Cash flow considerations also constrain the amounts funded.

C. 20x2

1. SC = $3,300 = the present value of benefits earned in 20x2. (This amount is larger than for 20x1; the increase may be due to an increase in the number of employees covered by

the plan, higher future salaries, 20x2 is one year closer to the payment of retirement benefits, and other factors.). Again, this amount is provided by actuary.

2. Expected return = .06(fund balance at 1/1/x2) = .06($2,000) = $120. Assume expected return and actual return are the same in this example (otherwise, component 5 will come into play).

3. Funding in 20x2 is $3,000 (year-end).

Pension expense (end of 20x2):

1. SC	$3,300
2. Interest cost = (.05)($3,000 PBO at 1/1/x2)	150
3. Expected return on plan assets (.06)($2,000 assets at 1/1/x2)	(120)
Pension expense	$3,330

Journal Entries:

Pension expense	3,330	
Pension liability		3,330
Pension liability	3,000	
Cash		3,000

---

a. Pension expense increases the pension liability (PBO − assets) by $3,330 because:

   i. SC and interest cost directly increased PBO by $3,450 ($3,300 + $150);

   ii. Expected return increased assets by $120 which reduces pension liability;

b. The net effect on pension liability therefore is $3,330.

c. To this point of coverage, ending PBO is the sum of service cost to date and interest cost to date, less benefits paid to date.

PBO 12/31/x2 = $3,000 SC(20x1) + $3,300 SC(20x2) + $150 interest cost (20x2) = $6,450. PBO is the actuarial present value of benefits earned for the first 2 years, based on the benefit formula. If the firm invested $6,450 at end of 20x2 at the discount rate of 5%, then there would be just enough to cover all benefits earned through 20x2. (Benefits will be paid much later, during the retirement period.)

---

d. Assets at 12/31/x2 = $2,000 beginning balance + $120 (20x2 actual return) + $3,000 20x2 funding = $5,120.

   i. Plan assets always reflect actual return. Pension expense uses expected return. These amounts are the same in this example but will be different for the coverage of component 5 (discussed later).

Pension liability at 12/31/x2 = $6,450 (PBO) − 5,120 (assets) = $1,330 = $1,000 (1/1/x2 balance) + 3,330 (pension expense entry) − 3,000 (funding entry)= $1,330

---

e. The pension plan is underfunded $1,330 - the amount of the reported pension liability. PBO, and assets are reported in the footnotes. Pension expense of $3,330 is reported in the income statement.

> **Note:**
> Time permitting, verify the ending pension liability balance by computing both ways as shown above. If the amounts are different, you know an error has been made.

II. Reporting By the Pension Plan

A. The entity that administers pension plans is required to separately provide accrual-based financial statements for the plans they administer. Typically an insurance company or trust company provides this service but the reporting requirements apply as well to firms that administer their own plans. This reporting requirement is in addition to the reporting by plan sponsors (which constitutes the bulk of the coverage on pensions) although there is significant overlap between the two sets of reports.

B. Requirements for the annual accrual basis financial statements for defined contribution plans:

1. A statement of net assets available for benefits as of the end of the plan year;

2. A statement of changes in net assets available for benefits for the year then ended;

3. A statement of cash flows is not required but encouraged;

4. A general description of the plan agreement including vesting, allocation provisions, the disposition of forfeitures, and a description of significant plan amendments adopted during the period.

C. Requirements for the annual accrual basis financial statements for defined benefit plans:

1. A statement reporting net plan assets at fair value available to pay pension benefits at the beginning or end of the year (end of year preferable).

2. A financial statement reporting the changes for the year in net plan assets at fair value available to pay pension benefits;

3. A statement of the actuarial present value of accumulated plan benefits as of at the beginning or end of the year (using the same date as plan assets in 1).;

4. Additional information about factors affecting the change in actuarial present value of accumulated plan benefits from the previous year;

5. The term "accumulated plan benefits" is used because this reporting requirement applies to other types of employee benefits, in addition to pension plans;

6. A statement of cash flows is not required but encouraged;

7. A general description of the plan including vesting and benefit provisions, plan amendments adopted in the current year, funding policy, and a description of the priority order of participant's claims upon plan termination.

I. Delayed Recognition—Components 4 and 5

A. Components 1-3 of pension expense are recognized immediately, but components 4 and 5 are subject to delayed recognition in pension expense. The items causing these last two components are recognized immediately in pension liability and other comprehensive income (OCI), however.

B. Defined benefit pension plans are subject to **two significant changes**:

1. **Prior service cost (PSC)** -- This is an immediate increase in PBO from the retroactive application of an increase in benefits for service already rendered (from plan amendments or from retroactive application to employee service before the plan's adoption). It is called "prior" service cost because the service cost of previous years has been increased. For example, a defined benefit pension plan provides benefits equal to 2% of final salary for each year of service. The plan is later amended to increase the rate

2.10% and the amendment is retroactive. The present value of the increased benefits (.10%) earned prior to the amendment is PSC. Employees have already rendered the service for a PSC grant. In rare cases, a retroactive grant may decrease the benefits for service already rendered.

2. **Pension gains and losses** -- There are two sources of pension gains and losses: (a) changes in PBO due to estimate changes and experience changes, and (b) the difference between expected and actual return. For example, if employee turnover decreases or life expectancy increases, then future benefits will exceed the previous estimates used to compute PBO. The increase in PBO is called an actuarial loss or PBO loss. Also, recall that component 3 of pension expense is expected return. If actual return exceeds expected return, the difference is a gain, and vice versa. The gains and losses from both sources are netted into one amount at the beginning of each year.

C. **PSC, and PBO gains and losses** -- These are immediate changes to PBO, and therefore to pension liability (PBO - assets). Asset gains or losses also affect the pension liability because component 3 is expected return. The impact on pension liability is recognized immediately along with an equal effect on Other Comprehensive Income (OCI), but due to the long-run nature of pension costs, and the desire to decrease the volatility of reported pension expense, these two pension plan changes are not immediately recognized in pension expense. Rather, they are recognized on a delayed basis by gradually amortizing them as components 4 and 5. Also, for gains and losses, delayed recognition allows for the canceling out of opposite items without bringing significant amounts into pension expense. A gain of $10 combines with a $7 loss to yield a $3 net gain for example.

D. Recall that comprehensive income (CI) is the sum of net income (NI) and other comprehensive income (OCI) for a period:

CI = NI + OCI

E. CI is a "global" measure of income. Its purpose is to report most changes in owners' equity other than transactions with owners. OCI items are similar to items currently recognized in net income, but which are not so reported. Rather, they bypass the income statement and are recorded directly into an owners' equity account. An unrealized gain or loss on securities available-for-sale is an example of an OCI item. PSC, and pension gains and losses are others. They cause OCI, and therefore CI to change, but not NI.

Example: The present value of a PSC amendment is $40,000. PBO therefore is increased by $40,000 immediately. In the same year, the actuary recomputes PBO because of new information on turnover, which has increased. The result is a decrease in PBO of $10,000 (with higher turnover, pension benefits will decrease because employees will remain with the firm a shorter time than previously expected).

The net result is that PBO is increased $30,000 ($40,000 − $10,000) and OCI is decreased $30,000 for the year. CI is also decreased $30,000 for the year. If it were not for delayed recognition, the entire $30,000 would have increased pension expense thus reducing net income. Instead, OCI is reduced immediately by the full change in PBO.

II. **Component 4 of Pension Expense—Amortization of Prior Service Cost (PSC)** -- The amortization of the initial present value amount for PSC is component 4 of pension expense. In most cases, component 4 increases pension expense although retroactive amendments have decreased pension benefits.

A. Amortization is computed using one of two methods (a free choice but the firm must be consistent):

1. Straight-line method (amortize PSC over the average remaining service period of employees covered by the amendment);

2. Service method (amortize an equal amount of PSC per service-year, more amortization is recognized when more employees are working).

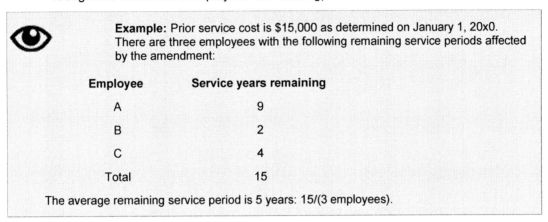

Example: Prior service cost is $15,000 as determined on January 1, 20x0. There are three employees with the following remaining service periods affected by the amendment:

Employee	Service years remaining
A	9
B	2
C	4
Total	15

The average remaining service period is 5 years: 15/(3 employees).

B. Straight-line method

1. Amortization each year is $3,000 ($15,000/5). Pension expense is increased $3,000 for the years 20x0—20x4. After that, unless another prior service grant is awarded, pension expense will no longer reflect this component. Only the initial PSC amount is amortized—as component 2 (interest cost) automatically includes interest on the growth in PSC because the $15,000 is included in PBO.

C. Service method

1. A constant amount of amortization is recognized for each service year: $1,000 = $15,000/15. For the first two years (20x0 and 20x1), all three employees are working (three service years). Therefore, 3($1,000) or $3,000 of PSC is amortized (included in pension expense). The amortization (component 4) for each year is shown below.

Year	Service Years	Calculation	Amortization
20x0	3	3($1,000)	$3,000
20x1	3	3($1,000)	$3,000
20x2	2(B is retired)	2($1,000)	$2,000
20x3	2	2($1,000)	$2,000
20x4	1 (C is retired)	1($1,000)	$1,000
20x5	1	1($1,000)	$1,000
20x6	1	1($1,000)	$1,000
20x7	1	1($1,000)	$1,000
20x8	1	1($1,000)	$1,000
			$15,000

2. The rationale for delayed recognition of PSC is that the firm will receive a benefit from the retroactive increase in pension benefits (higher morale, lower demands for future pay increases, etc.). The cost of the amendment should be matched against the benefits to be received in the future. The service method is preferable in this regard because more cost is included in pension expense when more employees are working.

> **Note:**
> The two methods always yield the same amortization amount for the first year (in this example, $3,000).

III. An Expanded Formula for PBO Now Includes PSC

> PBO ending amount= SC to date + interest cost to date − benefits paid to date + PSC

A. Journal entries for recognition of PSC, and its amortization

1. Recognition of PSC:

PSC-OCI	15,000	
Pension liability		15,000

2. Pension liability (PBO − assets) is increased immediately because PBO is increased immediately. The account PSC-OCI represents a specific OCI item (the "OCI" in the account title simply indicates that PSC is included in OCI). OCI is immediately reduced by $15,000 because the cost of the pension plan has increased that amount. All OCI items are merged into one net change in owners' equity called Accumulated Other Comprehensive Income (AOCI).

3. Amortization of PSC in 20x0 (same amount for each method). This entry is in addition to the entry to record the components 1-3 and may be merged with that entry:

Pension expense	3,000	
PSC-OCI		3,000

4. The above entry reclassifies a part of PSC-OCI to pension expense - this is delayed recognition. Pension expense is increased $3,000 by this entry. The $3,000 amount is called a reclassification adjustment because a portion of the $15,000 reduction in OCI has now been transferred to net income. This journal entry has no effect on CI for the year because net income has been reduced and OCI has been increased (credited).

IV. Formal vs. Informal Record

A. Formal record -- The pension information maintained in the accounts is called the formal record. These accounts include pension expense, pension liability, PSC-OCI, Pension gain/loss-OCI.

B. Informal record -- Any pension information not formally recorded in the accounts. These amounts include PBO and assets at market value.

I. Component 5 of Pension Expense—Amortization of Net Gain or Loss

A. This component may cause pension expense to decrease (for a net gain) or to increase (for a net loss). Each fiscal period begins with one net gain or loss because all gains and losses are merged into one amount. Gains and losses cancel each other.

B. Component 5 is the amortization of the net gain or loss at the **beginning** of the year.

C. The net gain or loss at the beginning of a year is the net sum of all previous gains and losses less previous amortization. The following table illustrates the two sources of gains and losses.

	PBO Change	Asset Return
Gain	decrease in PBO from increase in expected or actual turnover, decrease in life expectancy, etc.	Actual return > expected return
Loss	increase in PBO from decrease in discount rate, decrease in turnover, etc.	Actual return < expected return

1. PBO gains and losses stem from both (1) experience not equal to a prior estimate, and (2) change in estimate of future events. No distinction is made between these two types for purposes of component 5.

> **Example:**
> The current year began with no net gain or loss. There is no component 5 for the current year because there is no net gain or loss to amortize as of the beginning of the year.
>
> At the end of the current year, the actuary informs the sponsoring firm that PBO has increased $14,000 due to a decrease in expected turnover and actual return exceeded expected return by $4,000. The ending net loss is $10,000 for the current year ($14,000 PBO loss − $4,000 asset gain).
>
> The **net loss** of $10,000 is the source of amortization (component 5) for the next year.

D. There are **two computations** for component 5 each year:

1. Determining the amortization of the net gain or loss at the beginning of the current year to include in pension expense for the year. There are two methods of amortization allowed: (1) minimum (corridor) amortization (most popular) and (2) SL amortization. Both use average remaining service period of employees as the denominator. The firm must be consistent in its application. If corridor amortization is not chosen, any consistently applied method resulting in an amortization amount is acceptable. SL is the most popular choice for the second alternative.

> **Note:**
> The final (complete) formula for PBO at a balance sheet date is:
> PBO = SC to date + interest cost to date − benefits paid to date + PSC + net PBO gain or loss to date.

2. Determining the net gain or loss at the end of the current year for amortization the following year. The ending net gain or loss = beginning net gain or loss - amortization of beginning net gain or loss ± PBO gain or loss for the current year + or - asset gain or loss for the current year.

II. Full Example -- This example illustrates all of the computational aspects for component 5 of pension expense and also provides an overall review of defined benefit pension accounting in a comprehensive context.

A. Assumed data at 12/3/x4

1. PBO, $50,000;

2. Assets, $30,000;

3. There is no net gain or loss at the end of 20x4;

4. Average remaining service period of employees covered by the plan is 10 years. Assume this value remains constant over the next several years as employees retire and new employees are hired;

5. Discount rate, 5%;

6. Expected long-term rate of return, 6%.

B. 20x5 (end of year) -- There is no component 5 (amortization) for 20x5 because there is no net gain or loss at 1/1/x5.

C. Assumed Data

1. Ending PBO after including SC, interest cost, and subtracting benefits paid for 20x5, but before PBO loss, $90,000;

2. PBO loss from change in estimated turnover, $15,000;

3. PBO after including PBO loss, $105,000 ($90,000 + $15,000);

4. Ending assets at market value, $75,000;

5. Ending pension liability = $105,000 PBO − $75,000 assets = $30,000;

6. Actual return on assets, $2,000.

D. Computation of Net Loss at 12/31/x5

Asset gain = actual return $2,000 − expected return ($30,000 × .06 = $1,800) =	($200)
PBO loss	15,000
Net loss	$14,800

1. The net loss of $14,800 is the amount subject to amortization for 20x6. The entry to record the net loss (alternatively, the gain and loss can be recorded separately):

Pension gain/loss-OCI 14,800	
Pension liability	14,800

2. This entry, like the one recording PSC-OCI, recognizes the net loss as a component of OCI and increases the pension liability. "Pension gain/loss-OCI" is so named to indicate the account can be a gain or loss. The PBO loss immediately increased the pension liability (PBO − assets). The journal entry to record pension expense (first 3 components) used expected return thus reducing pension expense by $1,800. As a result, pension liability was not reduced by actual return, which was $200 more. Therefore, the pension liability must be reduced an additional $200. That amount is netted against the PBO loss resulting in the $14,800 increase in the pension liability.

E. 20x6 (end of year)

1. The $14,800 net loss from 20x5 is the amount subject to amortization yielding component 5 of pension expense for 20x6. The results of applying the two allowable methods are as follows.

    a. SL method: amortization = $14,800/10 years = $1,480. If this method is chosen, component 5 of pension expense is a $1,480 increase (because this portion of the loss is being recognized in pension expense—a loss represents an increase in the firm's pension cost).

b. Corridor (minimum) method. The amount of the $14,800 subject to amortization is the amount outside the corridor. The corridor is plus or minus 10% of the larger of PBO and assets, both at the beginning of the year. This method results in lower amortization relative to the SL method allowing for more cancellation of gains and losses over time.

Amortization =

($14,800 − .10(larger of $105,000 PBO at Jan. 1, or $75,000 assets at Jan. 1)) / 10 years =

($14,800 − .10($105,000)) / 10 = $430.

If this method is chosen, component 5 of pension expense is a $430 increase.

F. Assume the Following Data

1. SC is $8,000 for 20x6;

2. The firm chooses corridor amortization of net gain or loss;

3. Benefits paid to retirees during the year, $12,000;

4. Funding contribution, $15,000;

5. Actual return on assets, $400.

6. PBO gain from reduction in rate of compensation increase (reduces estimated final salaries), $22,000 (year-end).

7. Amounts to be determined by firm (candidate for CPA exam):

   a. Interest cost for 20x6 = .05($105,000) = $5,250;

   b. Expected return on plan assets = .06($75,000) = $4,500;

   c. Asset loss for 20x6 = $4,500 expected return − $400 actual return = $4,100;

   d. Pension expense for 20x6 = $8,000 SC + $5,250 interest cost − $4,500 expected return + $430 amortization of net loss = $9,180. If there were unamortized PSC, the amortization of PSC would be added to this total;

   e. Ending PBO = $105,000 beginning PBO + $8,000 SC + $5,250 interest cost - $22,000 PBO gain − $12,000 benefits paid = $84,250;

   f. Ending assets at market value = $75,000 beginning assets + $400 actual return + $15,000 funding - $12,000 benefits paid = $78,400.

G. Journal Entry to Record the PBO Gain and Asset Loss ($22,000 − 4,100 = $17,900)

Pension liability	17,900	
Pension gain/loss-OCI		17,900

H. Journal Entry to Record Pension Expense

Pension expense	9,180	
Pension liability		8,750
Pension gain/loss-OCI		430

1. $8,750 = $8,000 SC + $5,250 interest cost − $4,500 expected return. The $430 amortization of the net loss from the previous period increases pension expense with no additional effect on the pension liability. The recording of the loss increased pension liability that year.

I. Journal Entry to Record Funding

Pension liability	15,000	
Cash		15,000

Computation of net gain at 12/31/x6

Net loss, 1/1/x6	$14,800
Amortization	(430)
Asset loss	4,100
PBO gain	(22,000)
Net gain	(3,530)

J. This example illustrates how a net loss can turn into a net gain in one period. The ability of gains and losses to cancel each other supports corridor amortization.

K. Verification of Ending Pension Liability (via components and journal entry effects)

1. Ending PBO − ending assets: $84,250 − $78,400 = $5,850;

2. Ledger account: $30,000 beginning 20x6 balance − $17,900 recording net gain for 20x6 + $8,750 pension expense entry − $15,000 funding entry = $5,850.

L. 20x7 (end of year)

1. To complete the example, only component 5 is illustrated:

2. Calculation of component 5:

   a. SL method: amortization = $3,530/10 years = $353, decreases pension expense. This amount is shown for illustration. The firm chose corridor amortization for 20x6 which also should be chosen for 20x7 for consistency.

   b. Corridor (minimum) method: the corridor amount = .10(larger of $84,250 PBO at January 1, or $78,400 assets at January 1) = $8,425. Because the $3,530 net gain is not outside (larger than) the corridor amount, there is no amortization required under this method. Because the firm chose this method, there is no component 5 for 20x7.

3. If there were no PBO gain or loss for 20x7, and actual return equals expected return, the net gain of $3,530 is carried over to 20x8. The corridor amount will most likely change because the ending balance of both PBO and assets typically changes each year.

Settlements, Curtailments, International

The last lesson on pension accounting provides guidance on other issues in pension accounting and describes the main differences between U.S. and international standards regarding pension accounting.

After studying this lesson you should be able to :

1. *Describe the international approach to accounting for prior service cost.*

2. *Note terminology differences between U.S. and international standards.*

3. *Distinguish accounting for pension gains and losses between the two sets of standards.*

I.   U.S. GAAP - IFRS Differences

A. In many significant ways, international and U.S. pension accounting standards are the same. For example, pension expense has the same five components, and the plan obligation and plan assets are not reported on the balance sheet. However, because the governments of many countries provide significant contributions, pensions may have less of a material impact on sponsors' financial statements in these countries. Accounting differences are discussed below.

B. **Terminology and presentation**

1. PBO for U.S. standards is called defined benefit obligation (DBO) for international standards.

2. Pension liability or asset reported in the balance sheet (for U.S.) is called defined benefit liability or asset (international).

3. PSC is prior service cost for U.S., but is called past service cost for international accounting.

4. For international reporting, pension expense need not be reported as a single amount. The expense components may be reported in different line items within the income statement. Interest expense and expected return, for example, can be included with other interest expense and investment income. In general, other than service cost, the components can be reported as financing income and expense.

C. A multiemployer plan has two or more unrelated firms contributing assets to the same plan for the payment of pension benefits of the employees of the participating firms. Under U.S. standards, each participant firm accounts for the plan as a defined contribution plan. Pension expense is simply the required contribution for the period, and any unpaid amount at year-end is reported as a liability. International standards allow such plans to be accounted for as defined benefit plans if there is sufficient information.

D. Accounting for pension gains and losses. Under IFRS, gains and losses from both sources (liability, assets) are recognized immediately in DBO and OCI. This is the treatment under U.S. standards. However, under IFRS, gains and losses are not subsequently amortized into pension expense. Net income is never affected. Rather, pension gains and losses are treated as permanent owners' equity items.

See the following example.

Example:
An actuarial loss of $1,000,000 million is recorded as follows:

Pension gains/losses-OCI	1,000,000	
Defined benefit liability		1,000,000

E. Accounting for past service cost (PSC). Under international standards, PSC is expensed immediately in pension expense at the amendment date for the amount vested. The remainder (unvested portion) is treated as unrecognized PSC (as per alternative 2 for actuarial gains and losses above) and amortized on a straight-line basis over the remaining period to vesting (which varies by individual employee). The unrecognized PSC is a contra liability.

1. Journal entry for $200,000 PSC, $160,000 of which is vested.

Pension expense	160,000	
Unrecognized PSC	40,000	
Defined benefit liability		200,000

2. Later, journal entry for amortization of $4,000 of unrecognized PSC:

Pension expense	4,000	
Unrecognized PSC		4,000

3. The unrecognized (unvested) portion is not recognized in OCI. Thus, the pension-related component of AOCI for international standards includes only pension gains and losses. For U.S. standards, AOCI includes the full amount of PSC initially without respect to vesting, as well as pension gains and losses.

F. Defined benefit liability or asset. The liability or asset reported in the balance sheet will have a different balance under international standards relative to U.S. standards.

1. Due to delayed recognition of pension gains and losses (under one of the acceptable alternatives), and to unvested PSC, reported defined benefit liability or asset will not equal the difference between DBO and plan assets at fair value (funded status). This is at odds with US standards which define reported pension liability or asset as the difference between PBO and plan assets at fair value. The difference is the unrecognized items.

2. The resulting reported defined benefit liability amount reflects the following:

> DBO
>
> − Plan assets at fair value
>
> = Funded status
>
> + Unrecognized net pension gain or − unrecognized net pension loss
>
> − Unrecognized PSC
>
> = Defined benefit liability

3. If the reported account is an asset (defined benefit asset), the amount reported is the lower of (a) the above computation, and (b) the total of:

   a. Unrecognized actuarial losses and unrecognized PSC; and

    b. The present value of economic benefits from refunds from plan or reductions in future contributions.

4. International standards do not address the classification of the defined benefit liability or asset. Under U.S. standards, it is possible for the liability to be classified into current and noncurrent components but the asset is always noncurrent.

Nonretirement Postemployment Benefits

This lesson describes the accounting for nonretirement benefits for individuals previously employed by the firm. The criteria for compensated absences are applied to this type of benefit as well.

After studying this lesson, you should be able to:

1. *List specific benefits covered by this accounting.*

2. *Note the criteria required for accrual.*

3. *Compare accounting for this type of benefit with that of compensated absences.*

4. *Prepare the journal entries for accrual and payment of benefits.*

I. Accounting Guidelines

A. Employers may provide benefits to former and inactive employees after their employment ends but before they retire. Beneficiaries and dependents of the employees also may be covered. These benefits include salary continuation, severance pay, supplemental unemployment benefits, job training, counseling and disability benefits for inactive or former employees, continuation of health care and insurance coverage, and wages for disability or terminated employees. The principles discussed in this section do not apply to pensions, share-based compensation or postretirement benefits.

B. As with accounting for pensions and postretirement benefits, accrual accounting is required. The expense and associated liability is recorded when employees earn the benefits, not when the benefits are paid.

C. The accrual of a liability for employment benefits is necessary in two situations:

1. When the benefits meet the following four criteria. The accounting standard mandating accrual of the expense for compensated absences (discussed in a previous lesson) was later extended to nonretirement postemployment benefits. These are the same four criteria used for compensated absences.

   a. The employer's obligation relating to employees' rights to receive compensation for future absences is attributable to employees services already rendered;

   b. The obligation relates to rights that vest or accumulate;

   c. Payment of the compensation is considered probable;

   d. The amount of the compensation can be reasonably estimated;

2. When the benefits do not meet the four conditions above, the accounting standard for contingencies applies. If it is probable that a postemployment liability has been incurred as of the date of the financial statements, and the amount of the future compensation payment can be reasonably estimated, then the expense and liability is recorded in that period.

II. In Comparison With Compensated Absences

A. Nonretirement postemployment benefits are less uniform and repetitive compared with compensated absences because specific events such as plant closings and restructurings often are the cause of the benefits. As such, they may be subject to more estimation uncertainty.

B. Earned benefits are more likely not to be accrued given that the benefits may not vest or accumulate.

C. When these benefits are part of a restructuring, the expense and liability is recognized only when the restructuring is approved by management, all details are determined, and employees are notified. The postemployment benefits expense may be reported as part of a larger restructuring charge.

D. If the expense is not accrued because of the lack of ability to estimate the costs, a footnote describes the benefits and the reasons for nonrecognition.

 Example:
At the beginning of the current year, the balance in liability for postemployment benefits is $1.4 million. During the current year:

a. $0.8 million in salary continuation benefits was paid to former employees (this amount was included in a previous year's accrual).

b. At year-end, the firm estimates that earned benefits for the year total $1 million and consist of the following: (1) $0.7 million in counseling benefits (vested), (2) $0.3 million in salary continuation benefits (accumulated). Of this amount, the firm estimates that 90% will be paid.

Journal entries for current year:

Liability for postemployment benefits	0.8 million	
Cash		0.8 million
Postemployment benefits expense	0.9 million	($1.0 million x .90)
Liability for postemployment benefits		0.9 million

Retirement Benefits

This lesson covers the accounting for retirement benefits other than pensions. The most significant benefit in this category is postretirement health care. The accounting is essentially the same as for defined benefit pension plans.

After studying this lesson, you should be able to:

1. *Explain EPBO and its relevance to the reported obligation.*

2. *Describe how APBO is computed and what it represents.*

3. *Express how to measure the reported liability and expense.*

4. *Determine an employee's full eligibility date and explain how it affects the measurement of the plan obligation and reported liability.*

5. *Identify the differences in the components of the expense between pension accounting and postretirement benefit accounting.*

I. Potential Benefits

A. In addition to pensions, many firms provide other postretirement benefits to retirees based on the service they provided during their years as employees. Such benefits are often referred to as "OPEB" or other postemployment benefits. These benefits may include one or more of the following:

1. Health care or Medical Care Benefits;

2. Dental Care Benefits;

3. Eye Care Benefits;

4. Life Insurance Benefits;

5. Benefits related to Legal Services;

6. Benefits related to Tax Services;

7. Benefits related to Tuition Assistance;

8. Benefits related to Day Care;

9. Benefits related to Housing Assistance.

B. By far, the largest in magnitude in terms of cost is postretirement health care coverage. The recipients of these benefits may include retirees, their spouses, and their other dependents and beneficiaries. This is in contrast to pensions in which only the employee receives the benefit.

II. Accounting for Postretirement Benefit Plans

A. **Liability Reporting** -- As with pensions, the primary measure of the postretirement benefit obligation is netted against plan assets. The difference, postretirement benefit liability, is reported in the balance sheet.

B. The primary measure of postretirement benefit obligation is **Accumulated Postretirement Benefit Obligation (APBO)**. It is used and reported the same way as PBO in pension accounting, but is computed differently.

1. **First** -- Expected Postretirement Benefit Obligation (EPBO) is computed. This is the present value of benefits expected to be paid based on the level of coverage the employees are expected to attain. Postretirement health care plans provide services

based on years of service, retirement age, and other variables. An employee may receive 50%, 75%, or 100% coverage during retirement, for example, depending on age at retirement and years of service. EPBO is estimated each year based on the coverage expected to be attained by each employee and based on estimates of health care costs during the employee's retirement.

    a. EPBO is the present value of benefits to be paid by the firm, after deducting the contributions of the employee and any Medicare or other government-sponsored plan payments. In contrast to pension accounting, there is no benefit formula. Rather, EPBO reflects the level of service expected to be attained by the employee.

  2. **Second --** APBO is computed as the fraction of EPBO earned by the employee as of the balance sheet date. For example, Pat is expected to attain a coverage level of 75% of full coverage. If Pat must work for 20 years to obtain that level, and Pat has worked 12 years as of the balance sheet date, APBO for Pat is (12/20) x EPBO. Remember that EPBO is the present value of the total cost expected to be paid by the firm and includes service projected all the way to retirement. The measurement of APBO stops at the balance sheet date. EPBO is used only to compute APBO.

C. Postretirement benefit liability as reported in the balance sheet = APBO − plan assets at market value. APBO and plan assets are reported in the footnotes only, not in the balance sheet.

D. Postretirement Benefit Expense -- As with pensions, postretirement benefit expense has five components, and one additional component (which is also present in some pension plans but has essentially disappeared from pension accounting). Except for a few differences, postretirement benefit expense is computed the same way as pension expense. Delayed recognition applies to components 4-6.

  1. **Service cost (SC) --** The increase in APBO attributable to service provided in the period. SC is recognized only during the attribution period - the period to full eligibility (see below). This often occurs before retirement, in contrast with pension accounting.

  2. **Interest cost --** The increase in APBO due to the passage of time = (discount rate) × (APBO at January 1).

  3. **Expected return on assets --** (expected rate of return) × (assets at January 1).

  4. **Amortization of prior service cost (PSC) --** The same two amortization methods allowed in pensions are allowed for PSC in postretirement benefit plans.

    a. Initial full recognition of PSC is recorded in PSC-OCI and postretirement benefit liability, as is the procedure for pensions.

  5. **Amortization of net gain or loss at January 1 --** The same two amortization methods allowed in pensions are allowed for postretirement benefit expense. Changes in APBO and the difference between actual and expected return on plan assets are the two sources for gains and losses, as with pensions. However, firms may recognize postretirement benefit gains or losses immediately, with some limitations. This option is not permitted for pensions.

    a. Initial full recognition of postretirement benefit gains and losses is recorded in postretirement benefit gain/loss-OCI and postretirement benefit liability, as is the procedure for pensions.

  6. **Amortization of transition obligation --** Before accrual accounting was mandated for postretirement benefits, most firms used cash basis accounting for postretirement benefits. As a result, most if not all, of APBO at the date of transition to accrual accounting (in 1992) was not recognized. Many firms elected to recognize immediately that entire amount as an accounting change, decreasing income in the year of transition. For these firms, there is no component 6. Those that did not recognize the transition obligation (APBO at transition) immediately in income, chose the other available option at

the time which was to amortize the initial APBO amount over average remaining service period (if less than 20 years, the firm may use 20 years) on a straight-line basis (similar to amortization of PSC if SL is used). The result is component 6 of pension expense. Under either option, the entire transition obligation was recognized in postretirement benefit liability.

III. Full Eligibility

A. In contrast with pensions, employees often reach full eligibility before retirement. In these cases, no additional benefits are earned beyond the full eligibility date. (With pensions, each year of service typically increases the retirement benefit.) An employee is fully eligible for the benefits expected to be received when the employee renders the necessary years of service and meets any other requirements necessary to receive those benefits. Full eligibility does not mean that the employee will receive full benefits. Rather, it means that the employee has reached the service level required to receive the benefits that will most likely be granted to the employee during retirement.

Example: A postretirement health care plan provides 50% of full postretirement health care coverage for 20 years of service rendered after age 40, 70% coverage for 25 years of service after age 40, and 100% coverage for 30 years of service after age 40. If an employee hired at age 35 is expected to retire at age 62, then the employee is expected to work 22 years after age 40. This employee therefore is expected to be eligible to receive 50% of full health care coverage during retirement. Note that, depending on the plan, the attribution period may not begin with the date of employment.

The employee's full eligibility date is age 60, at which time the requisite 20 years of service after age 40 has been rendered. Service cost, the first component of postretirement benefit expense, for this employee, is attributed to service from age 40 to age 60. After that point, SC no longer is computed for the employee, but interest cost continues. The period during which the employee earns benefits toward full eligibility is 20 years.

APBO is a fraction of EPBO. The fraction is the number of years of the full eligibility period actually served by the employee as of the balance sheet date. When our employee above, who is expected to receive 50% of full coverage, reaches the age of 45, the employee will have rendered 5 years of the total period to full eligibility. On this date, APBO = (5/20)EPBO. The next year APBO = (6/20)(EPBO).

Note, however, that EPBO increases each year with the passage of time, as does APBO. When the employee reaches full eligibility at age 60, no more service cost is computed. At that point, APBO = EPBO, and both grow with interest cost until the employee retires at age 62.

See the following example.

Example:
Assume the following data for the current year(assumes one covered employee for simplicity):

EPBO at Jan. 1 of the current year, $4,000

Plan assets at Jan. 1, $1,000;

Discount rate, 6%;

Expected rate of return on assets, 7%;

Actual return on plan assets, $70;

Funding (year-end), $900;

Years required to full eligibility, 20 years;

Years worked as of Jan. 1, 9 years;

APBO, Jan. 1 = $4,000(9/20) = $1,800;

Postretirement benefit liability reported in the balance sheet, Jan. 1 = $1,800 APBO − $1,000 assets = $800;

EPBO, Dec. 31 = $4,000(1.06) = 4,240 (6% growth due to interest;)

APBO, Dec. 31 = $4,240(10/20) = $2,120 (one more year of service provided);

Assets, Dec. 31 = $1,000 beginning assets + $70 actual return + $900 funding = $1,970.

Postretirement benefit expense:

1. SC = $4,240(1/20) (the portion of ending EPBO attributable to service in the current year) =	$212
2. Interest cost = $1,800(.06) (growth in APBO for the year) =	108
Expected return on plan assets = $1,000(.07) =	(70)
Total	$250

Postretirement benefit expense	250	
Postretirement benefit liability		250

Postretirement benefit liability	900	
Cash		900

Ending balance of postretirement benefit liability ($150) computed two ways:
$2,120 ending APBO − $1,970 ending assets = $150

$800 beginning balance + $250 increase from pension expense entry − $900 decrease from current year funding = $150

See the following example.

IV. Example - Ending Postretirement Benefit Liability:

Example: The previous example illustrated the relationship between APBO and EPBO for a single employee. In practice, the actuary provides the underlying amounts relevant to the reported obligation and for computing postretirement benefit expense across the entire employee group. The following example uses data at the firm level.

Data for the postretirement health care plan for a firm is as follows, for the current year (in millions):

Service cost	$100
Accumulated postretirement benefit obligation, Jan. 1	800
Plan assets at fair value, Jan. 1	200
Prior service cost ($100 initial amount, $10 amortization per year)	80
Net loss at Jan. 1 (current year amortization, $4)	56
APBO gain (actuarial gain), Dec. 31	40
Retiree benefits paid	120
Funding contribution (year-end)	240
Return on plan assets, actual	19
Discount rate	5%
Expected return on plan assets	6%

Required: (1) record postretirement benefit expense and any other required journal entries, (2) determine ending postretirement benefit liability using two different calculations, and (3) determine the amount of net gain or loss to carry over to the next year.

Solution:
(1) Postretirement benefit expense:

1. SC	$100
2. Interest cost (.05)($800)	40
3. Expected return (.06)(200)	(12)
4. Amortization of PSC	10
5. Amortization of net loss	4
Total	$142

Postretirement benefit expense	142	
Postretirement benefit liability		128
PSC-OCI		10
Postretirement benefit gain/loss-OCI		4

Postretirement benefit liability	240	
Cash		240

Asset gain for the year = $19 actual return − $12 expected return = $7

APBO gain =   <u>40</u>

Total gain for period $47

Postretirement benefit liability   47

    Postretirement benefit gain/loss-OCI   47

(2) Beginning postretirement benefit liability = $800 beginning APBO - $200 beginning assets = $600

Ending APBO = $800 beginning APBO + $100 SC + $40 Interest cost − $120 benefits paid - $40 APBO gain = $780

Ending assets = $200 beginning assets + $240 funding + $19 actual return − $120 benefits paid = $339

(3) Ending postretirement benefit liability
$780 ending APBO − $339 ending assets = $441

$600 beginning balance + $128 (pension expense entry) − $240 (funding entry) − $47 current year gain entry = $441

V. Disclosures

A. The disclosures required for postretirement benefit plans are essentially the same as covered for defined benefit pension plans. Where PBO (projected benefit obligation) for pension plans is disclosed for example, APBO and EPBO are disclosed for postretirement plans. As with pension plans, the components of postretirement benefit expense are disclosed. And where the rate of compensation increase is disclosed for pensions, the expected rate of increase in future medical and dental benefit costs is disclosed for postretirement benefit plans.

B. Many firms are combining these disclosures. Review the listing of disclosures in the section on defined pension benefit plans.

VI. U.S. GAAP - IFRS Differences

A. The international accounting standard applicable to defined benefit pension accounting also applies to postretirement benefits. The lessons on pension accounting provide details about the differences between international and U.S. standards. These differences apply as well to postretirement benefits.

B. Firms use appropriate account titles to distinguish pension expense and post retirement benefit expense, and DBO for pensions and the analogous obligation measure for retirement benefits.

C. In many countries, funding is on a pay-as-you-go basis which reduces or eliminates component 3 of postretirement benefit expense, expected return on plan assets. The fund (the basis for expected return) is nonexistent or very small.

D. Both international and U.S. standards allow for immediate recognition of postretirement benefit gains and losses (in contrast with pensions). But for international accounting, the immediate recognition is in OCI whereas for U.S. standards the immediate recognition causes postretirement benefit expense to change immediately.

Stock Options

This is the first of several lessons concerning stock-based compensation. Stock options are one type of compensation plan.

After studying this lesson, you should be able to:

1. *Modify the accounting for stock options for graded vesting plans.*

2. *Explain how stock option plans affect the recording of deferred income tax.*

3. *Record the periodic compensation expense for a performance plan, allowing for changes in the incentive and forfeitures.*

4. *Compute the total compensation expense for a performance stock option plan.*

5. *List the variables used as inputs to compute the fair value of an option.*

6. *Prepare the entry for the exercise and expiration of options.*

7. *Include forfeitures in the accounting.*

8. *Record the journal entries to record periodic compensation expense.*

9. *Measure total compensation expense for the plan.*

10. *Describe the important amounts and dates for a fixed stock option plan.*

11. *Account for noncompensatory plans.*

I. **Stock Purchase Plans Open to All Employees**

A. Before discussing stock option plans, plans for the rank and file are presented as a background to this significant reporting area. In this type of plan, employees purchase stock directly from firms, they may receive a small discount, and the employer may match a portion of the purchase.

1. **Noncompensatory Plans**

a. Such plans are considered **noncompensatory** (no significant compensation is provided) if all apply:

i. Essentially all employees can participate;

ii. Employee must decide within one month of the firm setting the price for the stock whether to enroll in the plan;

iii. Discount does not exceed the employer cost savings inherent in issuing directly to employees (≤5% market price meets this criterion);

iv. Purchase price must be based solely on the market price of the stock;

v. Employees can cancel their enrollment before purchase date and obtain a full refund.

2. **Matching Portion --** If noncompensatory, the shares are recorded as any other stock issuance. The only expense is the portion paid for by the firm (the matching portion), if any.

Compensation expense	amount paid by firm
Cash	amount paid by employee
Common stock	par of stock issued
PIC-CS	price − par of stock issue

3. **Compensatory Plan** -- If not all 5 criteria are met, then the plan is compensatory. For example, if the discount is substantial, then that amount is recorded as expense.

Compensation expense	discount from market price on date of purchase
Cash	discounted price
Common stock	par of stock issued
PIC-CS	remainder

B. The remaining parts of this section pertain to incentive plans for selected employees - typically upper management. The terms of these plans provide an incentive for the employee to provide significant value and be well-compensated.

II. Stock Option Plans

> **Definition:**
> *A Stock Option Plan*: Provides an employee with the option to purchase shares of employer firm stock at a fixed price in the future, after a reasonable service period. The options expire beyond a certain point.

A. The value of such a grant stems from the potential for the stock price to increase. The ability of employees to influence the stock price provides the incentive.

B. **Basic Example** -- On 1/1/x1, selected executives of Flowers Inc. are granted the option to purchase 10,000 shares of the firm's $1 par common stock for $5 per share during the two-year period beginning 1/1/x5 and ending 12/31/x6 (exercise period). The market price of the stock on the grant date also is $5. To maintain their eligibility for the option plan, the employees must continue to be employed by the firm for the four years after the grant date.

1. **Features of the Plan**

   a. The $5 fixed price of the stock is called the option price or exercise price;

   b. The four-year period before the option can be exercised is called the service period, vesting period and amortization period;

   c. During the service period, compensation expense is recognized;

   d. To fully exercise the option, the employees must pay $50,000 for the 10,000 shares;

   e. The options vest at the end of the service period; (The ability to exercise the option is no longer contingent on continued employment with the firm at this point.)

   f. This type of plan is called a "fixed" plan because the relevant terms are set at the grant date;

   g. This plan illustrates "cliff" vesting because all options vest at the same time.

C. Measuring Compensation Expense

1. To measure compensation expense, the FASB chose the more reliable of the following (1) value of employee services to be received, and (2) value of options provided. Because the value of the employee services cannot be directly measured, GAAP requires that the fair value of the options granted be estimated using an option-pricing model. Various option-pricing models are available that use the following six variables at grant date to determine the value of the option (including Black-Scholes, lattice, and others):

    a. Exercise price (option price) − *higher fair value with lower option price (less must be paid to obtain the shares)*;

    b. Expected average life of the option (service period + exercise period) − *higher fair value with longer option period (there is a greater chance the stock price will increase and the time value of money is greater)*;

    c. Current stock price − *higher fair value with higher price (the fair value of the option is in part a function of current stock price)*;

    d. Expected volatility of the stock − *higher fair value with greater volatility (there is a greater chance of price increase − decreases don't hurt the holder)*;

    e. Risk-free rate of interest − *higher fair value with higher interest rate (the option holder can invest the exercise price and earn interest during service period)*;

    f. Dividend yield at the grant date − *higher fair value with lower dividend yield (dividends foregone reduce the time value of money)*.

2. **Fair Value Method** -- Assume that Flowers's choice of option-pricing model at grant date establishes the fair value of one option to be $2.20. Note that the market price of the stock at grant date is not used for measuring the cost of the option plan to the firm.

    a. Total compensation expense for the four-year service period is $22,000 (10,000 × $2.20). This amount is allocated on a straight-line basis. The following journal entries illustrate the accounting.

    ```
    12/31/x1, x2, x3, x4

    Compensation expense     5,500        $22,000/4
        PIC-stock options              5,500
    ```

    b. If stock options vest immediately at grant, then the entire compensation expense as measured by the option's fair value is recognized immediately.

    c. When the firm issues a stock dividend or splits its stock, unexercised options are adjusted. The number of shares under option, fair value and exercise price are proportionately adjusted. For example, a two-for-one split doubles the number of shares under option, and halves the fair value and exercise price. The total fair value and compensation expense to be recognized remain unchanged.

D. Compensation Expense is Reported as a component of income from continuing operations. For manufacturing firms, a portion may be allocated first to an inventory account and then to cost of goods sold. PIC-stock options is an owners' equity account which will be closed to another contributed capital account upon exercise.

See the following example.

At exercise		
Cash	50,000	10,000($5)
PIC-stock options	22,000	5,500(4)
Common stock		10,000 10,000($1)
PIC-CS		62,000

1. **Net Effect** of the accounting:

   a. Earnings is reduced $5,500 for each year in the service period;

   b. Retained earnings is reduced $22,000 from compensation expense;

   c. Contributed capital increases $72,000 = the fair value of the options at grant date ($22,000) + cash paid in by employee ($50,000);

   d. Net effect on total OE = $72,000 − $22,000 = $50,000 = cash increase.

2. Essentially, retained earnings is converted into permanent capital for the amount of the fair value of the option, but its placement on the income statement is the key idea. The firm increases its permanent value by the value of the manager's services.

E. **Expiration of Options** -- When the market price fails to increase above the option price (here $5), the options expire. There is no retroactive adjustment and the compensation expense remains (because there was value at grant date), and the PIC-stock options account is simply renamed.

   1. Assume all 10,000 options expire—entry at end of exercise period:

PIC-stock options	22,000	
PIC-expired stock options		22,000

   2. Net effect of all the journal entries is to reduce retained earnings by $22,000 (through compensation expense), and increase permanent capital by the value of the grant ($22,000).

F. **Forfeitures** -- The above example did not include forfeitures. Firms must incorporate an estimate of forfeitures if probable and estimable because the expense must be based on the number of options expected to vest. This reduces the total amount of compensation expense to recognize.

Example: If as of the grant date, 10% of the 10,000 options are expected to be forfeited, then only 90% of the $22,000 total fair value is used for the accounting (.9 x $22,000 = $19,800). The entries would be the same except use $19,800 in place of $22,000, and 9,000 options in place of 10,000.

If there is a change in estimated forfeitures, the amount of compensation expense in the year the change is determined is increased or decreased by the effect of the change on all previous years and current year (but no retroactive application). The year of the change receives the entire "catch up" adjustment.

The result is that the amount of compensation expense recognized through the end of that year reflects the amount of expense that would have been recognized using the new estimate all along. In effect, the new estimate is applied to periods before it was known. This procedure is contrary to the usual approach to estimate changes that would allocate the remaining expense over the remaining service period.

Example: Assume in the Flowers example that initially there were no forfeitures expected, but in 20x3 new information implies that a total of 10% of the options will be forfeited. The entries for the first two years are as above. Relevant amounts (assume net method) at the end of 20x2:

PIC-stock options balance, $11,000 (5,500 × 2)

Compensation expense recognized to date, $11,000

New estimate of total compensation expense, $19,800 (.9 × $22,000)

12/31/x3

Compensation expense	3,850		$19,800(3/4) − $11,000
PIC-stock options		3,850	

By the end of 20x3, 3/4 of the total compensation expense is recognized. The more typical estimate change procedure would have allocated the last two years of expense ($19,800 - $5,500 - $5,500) evenly over the last two years, or $4,400 per year. This approach is not permitted.

12/31/x4

Compensation expense	4,950		$19,800(1/4) (SL)
PIC-stock options		4,950	

Total compensation expense recognized over the 4 years = $11,000 + $3,850 + $4,950 = $19,800.

Constant percentage of estimated forfeiture: A quick calculation of total compensation cost is possible if the firm anticipates a constant percentage of estimated forfeitures each year during the service period. For example, a plan grants 100,000 options on 1/1/x1. The fair value of each option is $2.45, service period is four years, and the anticipated forfeiture rate is 4% per year during the service period.

Total compensation expense = $100,000($2.45)(1 − .04)^4 = $208,090$

Inability to estimate forfeitures: If the firm is unable to estimate forfeitures and forfeitures occur, the expense recognized in previous periods on the forfeited shares is reversed in the current period. This procedure reduces the compensation expense otherwise recognized in the current period.

III. U.S. GAAP – IFRS Differences

A. International and U.S. standards are similar for stock-based compensation plans. However, they have a larger effect on the financial statements of U.S. firms because share-based compensation is less common outside the U.S.

B. Deferred tax asset

1. The increase in the deferred tax asset for a stock award or stock option plan under U.S. standards is based on the cumulative compensation expense to date. That amount is used as the estimate of the future tax deduction and is the basis for increasing the deferred tax asset.

2. Under international standards, the deferred tax asset is increased only when the option has intrinsic value (market price > option price) during the service period. Under this approach, if there is no intrinsic value, there is no estimated tax deduction and no increase in deferred tax asset is recognized.

C. Graded vesting options -- Under international standards, each group of options must be accounted for separately. As a result, the straight-line averaging approach is not allowed.

Stock Awards

This lesson discusses another type of stock-based compensation plan. The calculation of total compensation expense is more direct under stock awards, relative to stock options.

After studying this lesson, you should be able to:

1. *Compute total compensation expense.*

2. *Record periodic compensation expense using the gross or net methods.*

3. *Prepare the journal entry for vesting.*

4. *Modify the recording of compensation expense for forfeitures.*

5. *Explain the essential elements of a stock award plan.*

I. **Stock Award Plans (Restricted Stock)**

A. Under stock award plans, stock is awarded for continuing employment but the employee cannot sell the stock (the main restriction) until the award is vested - and the employee may not receive the shares until vested. Employee acquires the normal rights of shareholders at grant.

B. For such plans, total compensation expense is the number of shares awarded multiplied by the market price of the stock at grant date (the fair value at that date). This amount is recognized as expense over the period the employee provides the service for which the grant was awarded. When the award vests, there is no additional incentive and expensing is complete. Changes in stock price after the grant have no effect on the accounting. If the award vests immediately at grant, then the entire compensation expense is recognized immediately.

See the following examples.

Example:
January 1, 20x1, 500 shares of restricted stock are granted to each of two employees (1,000 shares in total). The stock is $1 par common stock and the market price is $6 on the grant date. The employees must work 3 years at which time the award is vested. This example shows the "gross" method whereas the previous illustrations of accounting for stock options used the "net" method. Both are acceptable and yield the same financial reporting.

Total compensation expense = $6,000 (1,000 × $6)

1/1/x1 (Grant date)

Deferred comp expense	6,000	
Common stock		1,000
PIC-CS		5,000

Deferred compensation expense is a contra OE account. The effect of the above entry on total OE is zero.

12/31/x1, x2, x3

Compensation expense	2,000	
Deferred comp expense		2,000

Under the "net" method, the firm makes no entry on 1/1/x1. At each 12/31, compensation expense is debited for $2,000 and a PIC account is credited. (PIC-stock award)

12/31/x3 (Vesting)

No entry is needed under the "gross" method because the full amount of compensation expense is recorded, deferred compensation expense is closed, and the stock was recorded at grant date. Under the "net" method, the vesting entry replaces the PIC account created during the service period and the permanent OE accounts are credited:

PIC-stock award	6,000	
Common stock		1,000
PIC-CS		5,000

The net effect of the accounting:
An expense equal to the value of the stock at grant date is recognized;

Contributed capital increases by that amount;

Retained earnings is reduced by the same amount permanently;

There is no net effect on OE. (The firm did not pay or receive anything that can be objectively measured.)

Forfeitures: If employees do not continue employment through the vesting date then the expense recognized on those awards is reversed. The effect is to reduce compensation expense in the current year by the amount of compensation expense recognized in previous years' on the forfeited stock. Reversal is recorded because the stock is taken back - ultimately the firm did not give anything to the employee in this case. The forfeiture is treated as an estimate change; retrospective application is not permitted.

Example: One of the two employees in the example above leaves the firm at the end of 20x2. The deferred compensation expense balance is $4,000 ($2,000 for the employee leaving) before recognizing compensation expense.

12/31/x2

Common stock	500	
PIC-CS	2,500	
Deferred comp expense		2,000
Compensation expense		1,000

The above gross method entry "takes back" the $1,000 of compensation expense recognized on this employee in 20x1, and removes the contributed capital accounts for the employee. The entries continue for the remaining employee. Under the net method, PIC-stock award is debited $1,000 and compensation expense credited $1,000.

12/31/x2, x3

Compensation expense	1,000	
Deferred comp expense		1,000

The $1,000 compensation expense for remaining two years before removing the prior expense recognized on forfeited shares = (500 remaining shares)($6)/(3 year service period) = $1,000. Another way to calculate this amount is: ($6,000 original total compensation expense − $2,000 expense for x1 − $2,000 expense for x2 and x3 on forfeited shares)/2.

For 20x2, there is no net compensation expense ($1,000 decrease and $1,000 increase), and in 20x3, $1,000 of compensation expense is recognized. With the $2,000 recognized in 20x1, a total of $3,000 of compensation expense is recognized for one employee for which the award vested. At this point, the deferred compensation expense balance is zero and there are no further entries.

If the firm is able to estimate forfeitures, the procedure followed for stock options is applied to stock awards as well. The initial total compensation expense amount is reduced by estimated forfeitures before allocating to the service periods. There is no need to reverse previous compensation expense amounts in this case.

Stock Appreciation Rights

The final lesson pertaining to stock-based compensation addresses the accounting for a plan that bases total compensation on the increase in the firm's stock price over a period of years. A liability is recorded under certain circumstances.

After studying this lesson, you should be able to:

1. *Explain when a liability is recorded for an SAR.*

2. *Compute and record periodic compensation expense.*

3. *Modify the calculation of periodic compensation expense for forfeitures.*

4. *Identify the period over which compensation expense is computed.*

I. **Stock Appreciation Rights (SARs)**

   A. These plans are different from stock option plans: (1) employee receives the difference between the stock price at grant date, and the stock price at exercise date, (2) pays nothing, (3) the SAR specifies payment of the benefit in either cash or stock (employee may have a choice). The accounting issue is whether the arrangement involves debt or equity.

   B. If the SAR plan allows the employer to issue stock, then the SAR is accounted for as a stock option plan. The fair value of the SAR is estimated at grant date and the total fair value is allocated to compensation expense over the service period.

   C. If the SAR plan specifies that payment is in cash, or allows employee to choose cash payment:

   1. The firm records a liability rather than paid-in-capital when compensation expense is recognized;

   2. For each year in the service period, the fair value of each right is reestimated in light of new information using an option pricing model;

   3. Compensation expense is recorded each year based on the fair value at the end of the period (fair value is reestimated each year through exercise), for the portion of the service period elapsed using the catch up procedure for stock options. Expense recognition continues through the exercise date.

   4. Expected forfeitures are built into the calculation of total compensation expense as illustrated previously for stock options;

   5. At exercise date, the fair value of the SAR equals the difference between price at grant date and the price paid for the stock.

      See the following example.

Example: On 1/1/x1, several executives are granted SARS on a total of 10,000 shares which, at exercise, pay cash equal to the difference between the $5 per share market price at grant date and the market price at exercise. The market price of the stock on the grant date is $5. To continue owning the SARs, the employees must work for 4 years at which time the SARs are exercisable, for the 2 years following that date.

Fair value per SAR:

12/31/x1 $3

12/31/x2 4.50

12/31/x3 2.80

12/31/x4 3.50

12/31/x5 3.90

1/1/x1

no entry

12/3/x1

Compensation expense 10,000($3)/4	7,500	
Liability under SAR plan		7,500

12/3/x2

Compensation expense 10,000($4.50)(2/4) − $7,500	15,000	
Liability under SAR plan		15,000

12/3/x3

Liability under SAR plan 10,000($2.80)(3/4) − $22,500	1,500	
Compensation expense		1,500

(Through this date, $21,000 of compensation expense has been recognized: $21,000 = 10,000($2.80)(3/4) = $7,500 + $15,000 - $1,500) Note that both the liability and compensation expense are reduced this year.

12/3/x4

Compensation expense 10,000($3.50)(4/4) − $21,000	14,000	
Liability under SAR plan		14,000

The SARs have vested, but the liability and expense continue to be adjusted until exercise or lapsing because the firm must report the liability at the amount of probable payment.

12/3/x5

Compensation expense 10,000($3.90) − $35,000	4,000	
Liability under SAR plan		4,000

During 20x6, the SARs are exercised at which time the executives choose to receive the appreciation in cash. The market price at exercise date is $8.40 (fair value of SAR is $3.40, the difference between $8.40 and $5 price at grant).

Liability under SAR plan 10,000(3.40) − $39,000	5,000	
Compensation expense		5,000
Liability under SAR plan	34,000	
Cash 10,000($8.40 − $5)		34,000

Total compensation expense recognized over the entire period is $34,000. If the SAR had no value at the end of exercise period (because the market price was not greater than $5), the entire liability is extinguished and compensation expense is reduced by the same amount as the liability balance at that time.

II. Summary/Recap on Expirations/Forfeitures

A. The following table provides a summary for the accounting for expirations and forfeitures across the various types of stock compensation plans.

	Expiration	Forfeiture
Stock awards	Not applicable	Reverse prior expense
SARs	Not applicable	Catch-up

Interperiod Tax Allocation Basics

The first lesson of several about accounting for income tax provides the big picture of the area and the major issues. Terminology is emphasized so that later lessons can be understood within the context of the larger issues.

After studying this lesson, you should be able to:

1. *Note that the emphasis of interperiod tax allocation measurement is on the appropriate recognition of assets and liabilities.*

2. *Explain how income tax expense is computed in general.*

3. *Identify the major categories of differences between tax accounting and financial reporting.*

4. *Define taxable income, income tax liability, current and deferred income tax provision, and other terms.*

I. Accounting for Income Taxes - Theoretical Considerations

A. The theoretical considerations of accounting for income taxes include the accrual basis of accounting, the matching principle, and the proper recognition of assets and liabilities.

B. Income tax expense is recognized when it is incurred, regardless of when the payment is actually made to the Internal Revenue Service. The process of recognizing income tax expense is called interperiod tax allocation. This process ensures proper matching of income tax expense with revenues.

C. However, GAAP de-emphasizes the matching concept. Rather, it adopted the asset/liability approach for measurement of income tax effects.

   1. The emphasis is on the correct measurement of the income tax assets and liabilities.

   2. Deferred tax assets and liabilities are now measured directly, along with the income tax liability.

   3. Income tax expense is now a derived amount—a **plug** figure.

D. This does not mean that income tax expense for a period does not reflect the income tax cost of transactions in the period. Rather, it means that greater emphasis is placed on measuring the changes in balance sheet accounts than in the income statement account - income tax expense.

> **Example:**
> If future enacted tax rates have changed, the measurement of the deferred tax assets and liabilities will reflect the future tax rates because those are the rates that will be in effect when the deferred tax assets and liabilities are realized and paid. A pure matching approach would apply the current tax rate to a measure of pretax accounting income and directly measure income tax expense. The deferred tax asset and liability would be derived concepts.

E. **Summary** -- The main effects of applying the asset/liability approach are:

   1. Income tax expense for the period reflects the amount that will ultimately be payable on the year's transactions.

   2. The income tax payable account, deferred tax asset account, and deferred tax liability account report the remaining tax receivables and obligations facing the firm from transactions that have already occurred as of the balance sheet date.

3. Income tax expense is an amount derived from the changes in the tax-related assets and liabilities. It is no longer a directly computed value.

II. **Terminology and Definitions** -- Several terms and definitions are provided early in the discussion to help you with the concepts and procedure.

A. **Taxable Items** -- Amounts that cause income tax to increase. This is an Internal Revenue Code term and typically refers to revenues that cause taxable income to increase.

B. **Deductible Items** -- Amounts that cause income tax to decrease. This is an Internal Revenue Code term and typically refers to expenses that cause taxable income to decrease.

C. **Pretax Accounting Income** -- Income before income tax for financial accounting purposes determined by applying GAAP. This title is not used on the income statement (which uses titles such as income from continuing operations, income before discontinued operations, and others). Rather, for convenience and to focus on the issues, pretax accounting income traditionally has been used as a single measure of income before tax for accounting purposes. "Pretax financial income" is the term used by FASB for this amount .

D. **Taxable Income** -- Income before tax for tax purposes. This is the analogue of pretax accounting income. Taxable income is the amount to which the tax rates are applied in determining the income tax liability for the year.

E. **Income Tax Liability** -- The amount of income tax the firm must pay on taxable income for a year. Firms pay this liability in estimated quarterly installments with the last installment due early in the year following the tax year.

F. **Income Tax Expense** -- The account reported in the income statement that measures the income tax cost for the year's transactions. Income tax expense equals the income tax liability plus or minus the net change in the deferred tax accounts for the period.

G. **Current Income Tax Provision** -- Also called current portion of income tax expense and current provision for income tax. This term is used in the income statement to refer to the amount of income taxes due for the year. This amount is the same as the income tax liability for the year.

H. **Deferred Income Tax Provision** -- The amount of income tax expense that is not currently due. This amount equals the net sum of the change in the deferred tax accounts.

Example:
Assume the following year-end income tax accrual entry. For simplicity, we assume that the entire year's tax liability is paid early the following year.

Income Tax Expense	40,000	
Deferred Tax Asset	6,000	
Deferred Tax Liability		9,000
Income Tax Payable		37,000

Current income tax provision:	$ 37,000 (income tax liability)
Plus deferred income tax provision	<u>3,000</u> *
Equals total income tax expense	$ 40,000

$9,000 increase in deferred tax liability less $6,000 increase in deferred tax asset

---

I. **Permanent Difference** -- An amount that appears in the tax return or income statement but never both. These include items of revenue or expense that are never taxable or deductible; also taxable and deductible items that never appear in the income statement. This type of difference is also called a nontemporary difference.

> **Example:**
> A fine or penalty is never deductible but is treated as an expense or loss for income statement purposes. Permanent differences do not enter into the process of interperiod tax allocation. They have no deferred tax consequences.

J. Temporary Difference -- An item of revenue or expense that, over the total life of the item, will affect pretax accounting income and taxable income in the same total amount, but will be recognized in different amounts in any given year for financial reporting and tax purposes.

> **Example:**
> Depreciation can be different in any given year for income reporting and tax purposes, but total depreciation is the same over the life of the asset under the two reporting systems.

K. Net Operating Loss -- Negative taxable income (strictly a tax term). A net operating loss can be carried back 2 years to reduce taxable income in those years for a refund of taxes, and carried forward 20 years to reduce taxable income and therefore the tax liability in future years.

L. Deferred Tax Asset -- The recognized tax effect of future deductible temporary differences. These differences, caused by transactions that have occurred as of the balance sheet date, will cause future taxable income to **decrease** relative to pretax accounting income.

M. Deferred Tax Liability -- The recognized tax effect of future taxable temporary differences. These differences, caused by transactions that have occurred as of the balance sheet date, will cause future taxable income to **increase** relative to pretax accounting income.

N. Interperiod Tax Allocation -- The process of measuring and recognizing the total income tax consequences of transactions in the year. Only temporary differences and net operating loss carryforwards enter into this process. Interperiod tax allocation gives rise to deferred tax accounts because the total tax consequence of the period's transactions is not equal to the current income tax liability. The current tax liability (measured at the current tax rate) measures a part of that total, but there will be additional tax consequences in the future because of transactions that have occurred as of the balance sheet date. Hence the need for the deferred tax accounts. Deferred tax accounts are measured at the **future enacted** tax rate.

III. Three Types of Differences - Between GAAP and Income Tax Law

A. The three main categories of differences between the two reporting systems in terms of their effect on accounting for income taxes are:

1. Permanent differences;

2. Temporary differences; and

3. Net operating losses.

B. For interperiod tax allocation, temporary differences are the most important.

Permanent Differences

One of the two major types of differences between tax accounting and financial reporting is discussed here. This type of difference does not cause a deferral of tax and is treated in a more straightforward way relative to temporary differences.

After studying this lesson, you should be able to:

1. *Describe the general effect of permanent differences on the measurement of income tax expense.*

2. *List important specific permanent differences.*

3. *Note how each specific difference affects the tax accrual entry.*

I. **Nature of Permanent Differences**

A. The permanent differences are those, due to the existing tax laws, that will not reverse themselves over an extended period of time. In other words, these differences never reverse, and the passage of time will not cause the differences to disappear. The treatment of permanent differences under the two reporting systems is **permanently** different. Some of the more common permanent differences follow.

B. For purposes of the CPA exam, our recommendation is to be familiar with the most common specific permanent differences. There are far fewer of these relative to temporary differences. Also, be able to identify a new difference as permanent, if given sufficient information about how the item is treated for financial reporting and for tax.

II. **Specific Permanent Differences**

A. **Tax-Free Interest Income --** An example of this difference is the interest income earned on an investment in a state or municipal bond. The interest income is included in pretax accounting income, but not in taxable income.

B. **Life Insurance Expense --** The insurance premiums on a life insurance policy for a key employee where the firm is the beneficiary are not deductible from taxable income, but are an expense for financial reporting.

C. **Proceeds on Life Insurance --** In the event of the death of the key employee, the proceeds from the insurance policy are not taxable, but are included as a gain for financial reporting purposes.

D. **Dividends Received Deduction --** The dividends received deduction is a deduction for tax purposes equal to 80% (amount subject to change) of qualified dividends received. It is an amount of dividends received that is not subject to tax. However, the entire amount of dividends received is included in pretax accounting income. There is no similar deduction for financial reporting purposes.

E. **Fines and Penalties --** Many fines, penalties and expenses resulting from a violation of law are not deductible for tax purposes, but are recognized as an expense or loss for financial reporting purposes.

F. **Depletion --** GAAP depletion (cost depletion) is based on the cost of a natural resource used up. Tax depletion is based on revenues of resource sold. The difference in any year is a permanent difference.

III. **General Rule for Accounting for Permanent Differences --** For each of the differences listed above, an item is recognized in one system of reporting but not in the other. The difference never reverses as it does with temporary differences. But the income tax law is what ultimately determines whether an item is considered for tax purposes. Hence the rule for permanent differences: **The effect of a permanent difference on income tax expense is the same as its effect on the income tax liability for the period.**

> **Example:**
> Pretax accounting income is $20,000 and taxable income is $22,000. The only difference is a $2,000 fine that is recognized for accounting purposes but is not deductible for tax purposes. If the tax rate is 30%, the income tax accrual entry is:
>
> Income Tax Expense ($22,000 × .30) 6,600
>
>   Income Tax Payable   6,600
>
> The fine will never be deductible for tax purposes. Therefore, financial reporting treats the item giving rise to the permanent difference (through income tax expense) in the same way the tax code treats the item - it is not deductible. Permanent differences are not considered when computing the balances of deferred tax accounts. Permanent differences are not allocated - they do not affect the process of interperiod tax allocation.

Temporary Differences

This lesson discusses the basics of accounting for the more involved type of difference between tax accounting and financial reporting.

After studying this lesson, you should be able to:

1. *Explain the basic nature of an item causing a temporary difference.*

2. *Identify specific temporary differences.*

3. *Note that both revenues and expenses can be recognized for financial reporting before or after they are recognized for tax reporting.*

4. *Define originating and reversing temporary differences.*

5. *Categorize temporary differences into taxable and deductible differences.*

6. *Calculate taxable income from pretax accounting income and additional information.*

I. Nature of Temporary Differences

A. In contrast with permanent differences which never reverse over time, temporary differences do reverse. The temporary differences are actually timing differences. These are the differences involved with the process of interperiod tax allocation—the recognition of deferred tax accounts.

> **Example:**
> A firm provides services for a client for a fee of $4,000. The service is provided near the end of the year. The client is expected to remit the fee early the following year. For financial accounting purposes, the $4,000 of revenue is recognized in the year the service is provided but for tax purposes is taxable in the year the fee is received. Over the two years, both systems recognize the same amount of revenue. The temporary difference of $4,000 originated in the first year, and reversed in the second. At the end of the first year, the firm has a future difference of $4,000. That is the basis for the recorded deferred tax account at the end of the first year.

1. The only difference between the two reporting systems (GAAP and tax) is one of timing of recognition.

2. The concept of future temporary differences is one way to refer to the underlying differences leading to the deferred tax accounts. Another is in reference to an item's tax basis compared with its amount for financial reporting purposes. For example, the cost of a plant asset is $100,000 and for financial reporting the asset has been depreciated $15,000 through the current balance sheet date (book value $85,000). The asset has been depreciated $25,000 for tax purposes through the balance sheet date. For tax purposes, this asset is said to have a tax basis of $75,000. The difference between the book value and tax basis is $10,000, which also is the future taxable difference. The $10,000 difference is the amount that enters into the computation of the deferred tax liability at the end of the current year.

II. Some Temporary Differences -- Some of the more frequently observed temporary differences are listed and described below. In most cases, a balance sheet account reflects the amount of the difference to reverse in the future.

A. **Taxable After Recognized for the Books** -- Revenues or Gains that are Taxable after they are Recognized in Financial Income.

Example:
1. An example of this type of difference involves the use of the Installment Sales Basis of Accounting for income tax purposes. The accrual basis of accounting is used by the entity for financial reporting purposes, while a version of the cash basis, the Installment Sales Basis, is used for income tax purposes. The net installment accounts receivable at year-end reflects the future temporary difference.

2. The use of the equity method to recognize income from investments in equity securities is another example. The equity method is used for financial reporting purposes, and the amount of income reported on the income statement corresponds to the percentage of stock owned in the investee multiplied by the reported earnings of the investee. Investment income recognized for tax purposes will be equal to the dividends received in a given year (after the dividends received deduction, if applicable).

B. Deductible After Recognized for the Books -- Expenses or Losses that are Deductible after they are Recognized in Financial Income

Example:
An example of this type of difference involves the recognition of warranty expense. For financial reporting purposes, warranty expense is usually estimated and recognized in the year the related merchandise is sold. For tax purposes, warranty expense is recognized in the year the defective products are returned by the customers. The warranty liability reflects the future temporary difference.

C. Taxable Before Recognized for the Books -- Revenues or Gains that are Taxable before they are Recognized in Financial Income

Example:
1. An example of this type of difference involves the recognition of rent revenue or subscription revenue. For financial reporting purposes, the rent revenue or subscription revenue is recognized in the year that it is earned. For tax purposes, the rent revenue or subscription revenue is recognized in the year that the related cash payment is received. The unearned subscription revenue account reflects the future temporary difference.

2. On September 1, 20x7, the Dolphin Company rented a vacant warehouse to the Raider Company. The lease term was one year, from September 1, 20x7 through August 31, 20x8. The warehouse annual rental fee was $24,000, which was paid in full on September 1, 20x7. For financial reporting purposes, $8,000 rental revenue will be reported in 20x7, and $16,000 rental revenue will be reported in 20x8. For tax purposes, the entire $24,000 will be reported on the 20x7 tax return. The total rent revenue is the same under the two systems of reporting but the timing of recognition is different in each year affected. At the end of 20x7, the $16,000 balance in unearned rent (a liability) equals the future temporary difference to reverse in 20x8.

D. Deductible Before Recognized for the Books -- Expenses or Losses that are Deductible before they are Recognized in Financial Income:

Example:
An example of this type of difference is depreciation recorded for income tax purposes. For financial reporting purposes, depreciation is recorded over the estimated useful life of an asset. For tax purposes, depreciation is recorded over shorter time frames called recovery periods. In addition, for tax purposes, an accelerated depreciation method is typically employed.

III. Categorizing Temporary Differences

A. Originating/Reversing

1. When an item causing a temporary difference first occurs, the difference is called an originating difference.

2. In later years, the difference attributable to the item is called the reversing difference.

B. Future Differences -- The classification of temporary differences is based on the future reversal rather than the originating amount because deferred tax asset and liability balances reflect the future tax consequences of transactions that have already occurred.

C. Two Categories -- For purposes of interperiod tax allocation and recording the annual income tax accrual entry, temporary differences are classified into two categories.

1. The first category, called **Taxable Temporary Differences**, involves differences that initially cause a postponement in the payment of taxes.

   a. In the year of origination, the item causes taxable income to decline relative to pretax accounting income.

   b. When the item reverses, the item causes future taxable income to exceed pretax accounting income. This is why these differences are called taxable differences. They increase taxable income relative to pretax accounting income in the future.

   c. Future taxable differences give rise to deferred tax liabilities.

2. The second category, called **Deductible Temporary Differences**, involves differences that initially cause a prepayment of taxes.

   a. In the year of origination, the item causes taxable income to increase relative to pretax accounting income.

   b. When the item reverses, the item causes future taxable income to be less than pretax accounting income. This is why these differences are called deductible differences. They reduce taxable income relative to pretax accounting income in the future.

   c. Future deductible differences give rise to deferred tax assets.

D. Examples of Taxable Temporary Differences -- future taxable income > future pretax accounting income):

1. Depreciation

 Example: For financial reporting and tax purposes, depreciation on a plant asset purchased Year 1 will be:

Year	Book Depreciation	Tax Depreciation
1	$10,000	$16,000
2	10,000	9,000
3	10,000	5,000
Totals	$30,000	$30,000

At the end of Year 1, the firm has a future taxable difference of $6,000, the difference between depreciation for Years 2 and 3 under the two systems. ($20,000 − $14,000). At the end of Year 1, the firm knows that its future taxable income will exceed pretax accounting income by $6,000 because of transactions that have occurred through the end of Year 1.

At the end of Year 1, the tax basis of the asset is the book value for tax purposes and equals $14,000 (cost of $30,000 − $16,000 depreciation in Year 1). The net book value for balance sheet purposes is $20,000 ($30,000 − $10,000). The difference between the two book value amounts is the future temporary difference of $6,000.

2. Installment Sales

Example: During Year 1, a firm sells $6,000 worth of goods on the installment basis. For financial reporting purposes, the firm uses the point-of-sales method to record revenue and recognizes the entire $6,000 in Year 1. For tax purposes, the firm uses the installment method, which postpones revenue recognition until cash is received. No cash is received in Year 1 on the sale and the firm has no tax liability for this amount.

At the end of Year 1, the firm has a future taxable difference of $6,000. In a later year, when cash is received, the firm's taxable income will exceed pretax accounting income by $6,000 because of transactions that have occurred through the end of Year 1.

The future temporary difference is found on the balance sheet in the Installment Receivable account, which has a balance of $6,000, the amount not yet collected.

E. Examples of Deductible Temporary Differences -- (future taxable income < future pretax accounting income)

Example:

1. Warranty expense. On sales for Year 1, the firm recognizes $8,000 of estimated warranty expense. Also during Year 1, $1,000 was spent servicing warranty claims. The firm can deduct only the $1,000 on its Year 1 tax return because tax law limits the deduction to the actual cost of claims service. At the end of Year 1, the firm has a $7,000 future deductible difference. Next year, when the remaining claims are serviced, the firm's taxable income will fall by $7,000 relative to pretax accounting income.
The future temporary difference is found in the warranty liability, which has a balance of $7,000, the amount of future claims expected.

2. Revenue received in advance. During Year 1, the firm collected $22,000 in advance of providing its services to customers. By the end of the year, the firm had performed $10,000 worth of service. The full $22,000 is taxable in Year 1 but only $10,000 of revenue is recognized in the income statement. At the end of Year 1, the firm has a $12,000 deductible difference. Next year, when the remaining service is provided, the firm's pretax accounting income will increase $12,000 with no effect on taxable income. Future taxable income will be less than pretax accounting income.

The future temporary difference is found in the unearned revenue account, which has a balance of $12,000, the amount of paid services yet to be provided.

IV. Relationship Between Pretax Accounting Income and Taxable Income

A. Frequently, examination problems provide only one of the two income measures. Also, some firms maintain only one set of records and adjust pretax accounting income to derive taxable income. The adjustment process is shown below:

Pretax accounting income	$ xx
Plus and minus originating temporary differences	xx
Plus and minus permanent differences for the period	xx
Equals taxable income	$ xx

B. This approach simplifies the process of computing taxable income because it focuses only on the differences between the two income measures.

Example:
The four temporary differences in the previous examples are repeated below, along with additional information for Year 1.

Pretax accounting income	$100,000
Fines and penalties	9,000
Municipal bond interest received	14,000
Depreciation deduction	16,000
Depreciation expense recognized for books	10,000
Taxable installment sales	0
Installment sales revenue recognized for books	6,000
Warranty deduction	1,000
Warranty expense recognized for books	8,000
Taxable service revenue	22,000
Service revenue recognized for books	10,000

Computation of taxable income:		Balance sheet account:
Pretax accounting income	$100,000	
Plus nondeductible fines and penalties	9,000	
Less nontaxable municipal bond interest received	(14,000)	
Excess of tax over book depreciation	(6,000)	Equipment book value
Excess of book over tax sales revenue	(6,000)	Installment receivable
Excess of book over tax warranty expense	7,000	Warranty liability
Excess of tax over book service revenue	12,000	Unearned revenue
Taxable income	$102,000	

The first two adjustments, fines and penalties, and municipal bond interest are permanent differences. Pretax accounting income was reduced by fines and penalties but they are not deductible for tax purposes and therefore must be added back in computing taxable income. The opposite is true for municipal bond interest. It is included in pretax accounting income but is not taxable and therefore is subtracted in computing taxable income.

The remaining adjustments are all temporary differences. The originating differences are used to convert pretax accounting income to taxable income. The reversing differences will enter into the recognition of deferred tax accounts. For example, $16,000 of depreciation is deducted for tax purposes but pretax accounting income reflects only $10,000 of depreciation. Thus, an additional $6,000 must be subtracted in computing taxable income.

Tax Accrual Entry

This lesson integrates previous lessons on accounting for income tax by illustrating the tax accrual entry. This entry recognizes the firm's tax liability, changes in deferred tax accounts, and income tax expense.

After studying this lesson, you should be able to:

1. *Identify the types of differences causing deferred tax assets and liabilities.*

2. *Record the tax accrual entry when there are no beginning balances in deferred tax accounts.*

3. *Compute income tax expense as a derived amount.*

4. *Note that it is the future temporary differences which are involved in computing deferred tax account balances.*

I. General Tax Accrual Entry

A. The previous definitions and categorization of differences as permanent and temporary are used in this lesson to develop the year-end tax accrual entry.

B. The following entry is a generalization of the year-end tax accrual entry assuming that the year's full tax liability is paid early the following year.

Income Tax Expense	a "plug" figure
Deferred Tax Asset	* see below
Deferred Tax Liability	** see below
Income Tax Payable	taxable income x current tax rate

* The amount to increase the deferred tax asset to its required ending balance, which is the total future deductible temporary difference multiplied by the future enacted tax rate. Estimated tax rates are not used, only enacted tax rates. If the required change is a decrease, the asset would be credited.

** The amount to increase the deferred tax liability to its required ending balance which is the total future taxable temporary difference multiplied by the future enacted tax rate. If the required change is a decrease, the liability would be debited. Future tax rates are used to measure the deferred tax accounts because the future tax consequences will be settled or recovered at the future tax rate.

Note: The future and current tax rates are the same if Congress has not enacted a new rate for future years by the end of the current year.

II. Illustrative Example (No beginning deferred tax balances)

A. A firm in its first year has $100,000 of operating income composed of items that are recognized in the same amounts for both financial reporting and tax purposes. **In addition**, the firm has:

1. $10,000 of municipal bond interest;

2. Rent expense of $20,000 for book purposes; and

3. Rent expense of $25,000 for tax purposes.

B. The $5,000 difference in rent expense is the ending prepaid rent. This amount is deductible in Year 1 but is not recognized as rent expense until Year 2. The tax rate for year 1 is 30% but the Year 2 rate, enacted at the close of Year 1, was increased to 35%.

C. Tax accrual entry for Year 1:

Income Tax Expense	24,250	
Deferred Tax Liability ($5,000 × .35)		1,750
Income Tax Payable($75,000 × .30)		22,500*

*Taxable income = $100,000 − $25,000 = $75,000. The municipal bond interest is not taxable. It is not included in the $100,000 amount common to the two reporting systems. Taxable income applies the current (Year 1) tax rate, while the computation of the deferred tax liability uses the future enacted tax rate.

D. The future temporary difference of $5,000 is a taxable temporary difference because taxable income in Year 2 will increase relative to pretax accounting income by this amount when the prepaid rent is recognized as expense for book purposes only. The resulting deferred tax liability is measured using the future enacted tax rate at which the tax will be paid.

E. Income tax expense is the sum of the increase in the deferred tax liability and income taxes payable. This is the only way to compute income tax expense. It is not the product of the current tax rate and pretax accounting income. The $24,250 income tax expense is the total amount of tax expected to be paid on transactions occurring in Year 1. This total amount is allocated via interperiod tax allocation to the current provision of $22,500 (the income tax liability for Year 1) and $1,750 (the amount deferred to Year 2). The $1,750 is the amount of tax payable in the future based on transactions that occurred by the end of Year 1.

Abbreviated income statement for year 1:	
Operating Income Before Rent Expense	$100,000
Rent Expense	(20,000)
Municipal Bond Interest	10,000
Pretax Accounting Income	90,000
Income Tax Expense (from tax accrual entry)	(24,250)
Net income	$ 65,750

F. The **total income tax expense** is classified into two parts, which must be reported either on the face of the income statement or in the footnotes:

Current Provision of Income Tax	$22,500
Plus Deferred Provision of Income Tax	1,750
Total Income Tax Expense	$24,250

G. **Notice** that the income tax expense recognized is not equal to the current tax rate times pretax accounting income (.30 × $90,000 = $27,000). In other words, the current tax rate of 30% is not the effective tax rate for this firm. The effective tax rate is the ratio of income tax expense to pretax accounting income. For this firm, that rate is 26.95% ($24,250/$90,000)

H. **Two factors** explain the difference: (1) the municipal bond interest is included in pretax accounting income but is not taxed (this lowers the effective tax rate), and (2) the higher rate of 35% is applied to the future temporary difference and is reflected in income tax expense (this raises the effective rate). Because of these types of differences, a tax reconciliation footnote is a required disclosure. That footnote would show:

Statutory Tax Rate:	.3000	
Effect of Nontaxable Municipal Bond Interest	(.0333)	$10,000(.3)/$90,000
Effect of Future Rate Increase on Future Temporary Differences	.0028	$5,000(.35 − 30)/$90,000
Effective Tax Rate	.2695	$24,250/$90,000

III. **Practice Example (Permanent and temporary difference)** -- Gem has no beginning deferred tax balances and uses the equity method to account for its 25% investment in Gold. During 20x2, Gem received dividends of $30,000 from Gold and recorded $180,000 as its equity in the earnings of Gold. Additional information follows:

A. All the undistributed earnings of Gold will be distributed as dividends in future periods.

B. The dividends received from Gold are eligible for the 80% dividends received deduction.

C. There are no other temporary differences.

D. Enacted income tax rates are 30% for 20x2 and thereafter.

E. In its December 31, 20x2 balance sheet, what amount should Gem report for deferred income tax liability?

F. **Solution:** With no beginning deferred tax balances, the ending balance in the deferred tax liability equals the change in the deferred tax liability for the period. The change in the deferred tax liability is the future tax effect of the amount of income from the investment that is expected to be taxable in the future, using enacted tax rates. That amount is $9,000 = .30(.20)($180,000 − $30,000). The ($180,000 − $30,000) factor is the total future earnings difference between tax and book accounting. The .20 is the amount taxable after considering the dividends received deduction. The tax rate is 30%. The final result, $9,000, is the anticipated future tax liability, based on current transactions.

G. This problem has both permanent and temporary differences. The permanent difference is the 80% dividends received deduction. Of the $180,000 earnings, 80% or $144,000 will never be taxed. Therefore, 20% or $36,000 will be taxed. By the end of 20x2, .20($30,000 dividends received) or $6,000 has been taxed leaving $30,000 as the future temporary difference. The $30,000 is the amount recognized in 20x2 earnings but will not be taxed until later years. The tax effect of this difference, $9,000 (.30 × $30,000) is the ending deferred tax liability.

IV. **Depreciation, an Example of a Difference Reversing Over More than One Period**

A. Depreciable plant assets often require more than one year for the full temporary difference to originate. In early years, future temporary differences appear to be deductible but should not be treated as such. The entire net future temporary difference for a depreciable asset is treated as a taxable temporary difference.

See the following example.

Example:
A plant asset is purchased at the beginning of Year 1 and will be depreciated as indicated:

Year	Tax Depreciation	Book Depreciation
1	$400	$200
2	300	200
3	200	200
4	100	200
5	0	200
Totals	$1,000	$1,000

At the end of Year 1, the total future temporary difference is $200, the difference between Years 2-5 depreciation for the two systems ($200 + $200 + $200 + $200) − ($300 + $200 + $100). More depreciation ($200 more) in the future (after Year 1) will be recognized for book purposes than for tax purposes. Thus, future taxable income will exceed pretax accounting in the future in total causing the difference to be classified as taxable at the end of Year 1.

Although the difference for Year 2 (only) appears to be a deductible difference (because Year 2 taxable income will be less than pretax accounting income by $100), that difference is an originating difference, not a reversing difference. Thus, the correct approach is to treat the entire future difference at the end of Year 1 as a taxable difference.

B. Other examples include prepaids and warranties covering more than one year. In each case, the full future difference at the end of each year is treated the same—either as a future taxable difference (prepaid) or deductible difference (warranty).

Interperiod Tax Allocation Process

This lesson provides a summary of the interperiod tax allocation process by including beginning balances of deferred tax accounts, temporary differences reversing in the current period, and new temporary differences originating in the current period.

After studying this lesson, you should be able to:

1. *List the steps leading to the tax accrual entry in the most general case.*

2. *Compute the ending balance in the deferred tax asset and liability accounts.*

3. *Determine the change in the deferred tax asset and liability accounts.*

4. *Complete the tax accrual entry.*

5. *Identify the treatment of temporary differences that do not originate in only one period.*

6. *Modify the tax accrual entry for changes in tax rate and tax law.*

I. **General Steps for Interperiod Tax Allocation: Adjusting the Deferred Tax Accounts**

A. In the previous examples, only one temporary difference was used, and there were no beginning deferred tax account balances. This section completes the discussion by including more than one temporary difference and beginning deferred tax account balances. A general process leading to the tax accrual entry is used.

B. Steps Leading to the Tax Accrual Entry:

---

1. Compute taxable income and multiply by current tax rate.

   Result = income tax payable --------- to tax accrual entry ------------------------> XX

2. Analyze all future individual temporary differences, separating them into taxable and deductible categories.

3. Apply the future enacted rate(s) to the taxable differences and aggregate.

   Result = required ending deferred tax liability balance =   XX

   Subtract beginning deferred tax liability balance   (XX)

   Equals required increase or decrease in deferred tax liability ------------------> XX

4. Apply the future enacted rate(s) to the deductible differences and aggregate.

   Result = required ending deferred tax asset balance =   XX

   Subtract beginning deferred tax asset balance   (XX)

   Equals required increase or decrease in deferred tax asset --------------------> XX

5. Net sum equals income tax expense   XX

C. Caution -- Occasionally the CPA exam has asked questions requiring the candidate to determine the income tax payable ending balance after the payment of estimated tax payments. Assume the current tax liability is $50,000 (taxable income x current tax rate). If the firm has made a total of $35,000 of estimated tax payments, then the income tax liability to be reported in the balance sheet is $15,000 ($50,000 − $35,000). This aspect has little effect on the main issue at hand: completing the tax accrual entry.

II. Example - Beginning Deferred Tax Account Balances, Multiple Differences

Example:

Year 1 Pretax accounting income:	$60,000
Ending prepaid insurance balance (coverage for Year 2)	10,000
Recognized lawsuit contingent liability (recognized loss) (to be resolved in Year 2)	15,000

Tax rates: current (30%), enacted for Year 2 and later (35%)

Steps:

		To tax accrual entry
1.	Taxable income = $60,000 − $10,000 + $15,000 = $65,000	
	The prepaid insurance is subtracted because it is an amount paid in Year 1, but not recognized as expense for the books. The contingent loss is added because it is a recognized loss for the books but is not deductible for taxes until paid. Income tax payable = $65,000(.30)	= $19,500
2.	Future taxable difference: $10,000 prepaid insurance. (Future pretax accounting income will decrease relative to taxable income when the insurance expense is recognized for the books.) Future deductible difference: $15,000 contingent liability. (Future taxable income will recognize the loss as a deduction when paid reducing taxable income relative to pretax accounting income.)	
3.	Required ending deferred tax liability = $10,000(.35) = $3,500	
	Beginning deferred tax liability	(0)
	Increase in deferred tax liability	3,500
4.	Required ending deferred tax asset = $15,000(.35) = $5,250	
	Beginning deferred tax asset	(0)
	Increase in deferred tax asset	(5,250)
5.	Income Tax Expense	$17,750

Year 1 Tax Accrual Entry:		
Income Tax Expense	17,750	
Deferred Tax Asset	5,250	
Deferred Tax Liability		3,500
Income Tax Payable		19,500
Current Provision of Income Tax Expense		$ 19,500
Less Deferred Provision ($5,250 − $3,000)		(1,750)
Equals Total Income Tax Expense		$17,750

See the following example.

Example:
Year 2 Pretax Accounting Income $80,000
Depreciation for financial reporting and tax purposes on a plant asset purchased Year 2 will be:

Year	Book Depreciation	Tax Depreciation
2	$10,000	$16,000
3	10,000	9,000
4	10,000	5,000
Totals	$30,000	$30,000

$5,000 of municipal bond interest was received.
$8,000 worth of goods were sold on the installment basis. The entire amount is recognized in revenue for book purposes. No cash is collected in Year 2.
$11,000 of estimated warranty expense is recognized; $4,000 was spent to service claims.
Tax rates have not changed. Current and future years are taxed at 35%.

Steps:

		To tax accrual entry
1.	Taxable Income:	
	Pretax Accounting Income	$80,000
	Municipal Bond Interest	(5,000)
	Expiration of Prepaid Insurance from Year 1	10,000
	Lawsuit Loss from Year 1, Paid in Year 2	(15,000)
	Excess of Tax Depreciation over Book Depreciation	(6,000)
	Installment Sales Revenue Recognized for Books	(8,000)
	Excess of Warranty Expense over Warranty Deduction	7,000
	Taxable Income	$63,000

Income Tax Payable = $63,000 × (.35) =	22,050

The expiration of the prepaid insurance from Year 1 reduced pretax accounting income but does not reduce taxable income in Year 2 because the entire prepayment was deducted in Year 1. The lawsuit loss was not recognized in pretax accounting income because it was recognized in Year 1. It is paid in Year 2 and therefore deducted in Year 2.

2.	Future taxable differences:	To tax accrual entry
	Excess of book depreciation over tax depreciation	$ 6,000
	Installment sales revenue to be recognized for tax	8,000
	Total future taxable differences	$14,000
	Future deductible difference:	
	Excess of warranty expense over warranty deduction	7,000

(Note that the temporary differences from Year 1 have reversed and no longer are "future" differences with respect to the end of Year 2.)

		To tax accrual entry	
3.	Required Ending Deferred Tax Liability = $14,000(.35) =	$4,900	
	Beginning Deferred Tax Liability	(3,500)	
	Increase in Deferred Tax Liability		1,400
4.	Required ending deferred tax asset = $7,000(.35) =	$2,450.00	
	Beginning deferred tax asset	(5,250)	
	Decrease in deferred tax asset		2,800
5.	Income tax expense		$26,250

Year 2 Tax Accrual Entry

Income Tax Expense	26,250	
Deferred Tax Asset		2,80
Deferred Tax Liability		1,400
Income Tax Payable		22,050

Current provision of income tax expense	$22,050
Plus deferred provision ($1,400 + $2,800)	4,200
Equals total income tax expense	$26,250

III. Tax Rate Considerations

A. As already discussed, the future enacted tax rate is used to measure the change in the deferred tax accounts for the year-end tax accrual entry.

B. When the tax rate is changed **during** the year, the new rate is applied as of the beginning of the year (estimate change) to recompute the deferred tax balances. This results in an immediate change to income tax expense. For annual reporting, the normal year-end tax accrual entry automatically accomplishes this effect.

C. Corporations are taxed at an increasing rate as taxable income increases. The average tax rate is used for computing the changes in the deferred tax accounts.

D. When a future temporary difference is expected to reverse at a different rate than the regular tax rate (for example, a capital gains rate), then the specific rate applying to the difference is used when measuring that portion of the change in the deferred tax account.

Classification of Deferred Tax Accounts

The subject matter of this lesson is the presentation of deferred tax accounts in the balance sheet.

After studying this lesson, you should be able to:

1. *Classify the resulting deferred tax asset or liability stemming from a given future temporary difference.*

2. *Identify exceptions to the general rule for classification.*

3. *Determine the final classification of deferred tax accounts for balance sheet purpose.*

I. Internal Classification - Deferred Tax Accounts

A. The classification of the deferred tax account is based on the classification of the item giving rise to it.

1. If a temporary difference is related to a current liability or asset, then the associated deferred tax account is also classified as current.

2. If a temporary difference is related to a noncurrent liability or asset, then the associated deferred tax account is also classified as noncurrent.

B. **Examples**

1. The taxable temporary difference arising from depreciable plant assets is related to a non-current asset. Therefore, the associated deferred tax liability is classified as a non-current liability.

2. The deductible temporary difference arising from a warranty liability (1-year warranty) is related to a current liability. Therefore the associated deferred tax asset is classified as a current asset.

3. If the warranty were a two-year warranty, the portion of the temporary difference relating to the current warranty liability would result in a current deferred tax asset, and the portion relating to the noncurrent warranty liability would result in a noncurrent deferred tax asset.

4. The taxable temporary difference arising from prepaid rent (1-year coverage) is related to a current asset. Therefore, the associated deferred tax liability is classified as a current liability. However, for prepaids covering more than one year, the deferred tax liability pertaining to the noncurrent prepaid is classified as a noncurrent liability.

C. For some items, the future temporary difference is not associated with a specific balance sheet account. For these items, the classification of the deferred tax account is based on the expected period of reversal. For the portion expected to reverse in the year following the current year, the deferred tax account is classified as current. Otherwise the classification is noncurrent.

1. **Organization costs --** This cost is related to the entire firm's early activities and is expensed immediately for financial reporting purposes. The cost is deducted for tax purposes over a relatively short period. In the period of incurrence, a future deductible difference is generated for the portion deductible in future periods. The amount of the deduction for the next year is included in the future deductible differences leading to current deferred tax asset. The remainder leads to the noncurrent deferred tax asset.

    See the following example.

> **Example:**
> Assume in year 1 that $50,000 of organization costs are incurred. They are deductible over years 1-5 at even amount per year. The future deductible difference is $40,000 at the end of year 1 (the first $10,000 is deductible in year 1). Of that amount, $10,000 will reverse in year 2. This $10,000 amount is included in the determination of the firm's ending current deferred tax asset for year 1. With a tax rate of 30%, the current deferred tax asset is increased $3,000. The noncurrent deferred tax asset is increased $9,000 ($30,000 × .30).

2. **Net operating losses** -- This topic is covered in a later lesson. It is a loss for tax purposes that can be carried forward to future years. The loss is not associated with any particular asset or liability. The related deferred tax asset is classified according to the period of expected reversal.

II. Four Deferred Accounts

A. Internal deferred tax accounts are kept separate. It is therefore possible to have four deferred tax accounts internally:

	Current	Noncurrent
Deferred Tax Asset	x	x
Deferred Tax Liability	x	x

B. Each of the four balances is the sum of the relevant future differences as defined above, multiplied by the future enacted tax rate. For example, the current deferred tax liability balance is the sum of future taxable differences across all items giving rise to a taxable difference expected to reverse the following year, multiplied by the enacted tax rate.

III. Classification for Balance Sheet Reporting

A. For external reporting, the current deferred tax accounts are netted together to form one current deferred tax asset or liability, and the noncurrent deferred tax accounts are likewise netted to form one noncurrent deferred tax asset or liability.

B. The rationale for this offsetting is that a future deductible difference reversing next year naturally cancels a future taxable difference reversing next year. For example, a future taxable difference of $10,000 reversing next year cancels a $7,000 deductible difference reversing next year leaving future taxable income exceeding book income by $3,000. The net current deferred tax liability is $900 assuming a tax rate of 30%.

C. Therefore, a firm will report at most two net deferred tax accounts in the balance sheet. The current and non-current deferred tax assets are not added together, nor are the current and non-current deferred tax liabilities.

> **Example:** After recording the year's tax accrual entry, the firm's ending deferred tax balances are:
>
> | | Current | Noncurrent |
> |---|---|---|
> | Deferred Tax Asset | $300 | $600 |
> | Deferred Tax Liability | 900 | 400 |
>
> On the balance sheet, this firm would report:
>
> | | |
> |---|---|
> | Current Deferred Tax Liability | $600 |
> | Noncurrent Deferred Tax Asset | 200 |

Example:
The following future temporary differences have been identified in the process of preparing the tax accrual entry for the current year (future enacted tax rate is 30%):

Amount of (Deductible) or Taxable Temporary Difference	Associated with	Resulting Deferred Tax Account (*)
$4,000	Noncurrent Asset	NDTL $1,200
(3,000)	Noncurrent Liability	NDTA 900
12,000	Current Asset	CDTL 3,600
(8,000)	Current Liability	CDTA 2,400
(12,000)	Noncurrent Liability	NDTA 3,600
7,000	Noncurrent Asset	NDTL 2,100

* Key:

C = Current
N = Noncurrent
DTA = Deferred Tax Asset DTL = Deferred Tax Liability

The deferred tax account balance is the tax rate times the temporary difference.

Aggregating by type, the totals are:

Current Deferred Tax Liability (CDTL)	($3,600)
Current Deferred Tax Asset (CDTA)	2,400
Net current deferred tax liability reported in balance sheet	($1,200)
Noncurrent Deferred Tax Asset (NDTA)	$4,500
Noncurrent Deferred Tax Liability (NDTL)	(3,300)
Net noncurrent deferred tax asset reported in balance sheet	$1,200

Valuation Allowance for Deferred Tax Assets

The subject matter of this lesson is the reported amount of net deferred tax assets.

After studying this lesson, you should be able to:

1. *Determine when a valuation allowance is required for a deferred tax asset.*

2. *Describe the evidence used to determine whether a valuation allowance is required.*

3. *Explain the sources of support for the realization of a deferred tax asset.*

4. *Record the appropriate amount of a valuation allowance from given information.*

I. Limitation on Deferred Tax Assets

A. A deferred tax asset, like any other asset, is an asset only if it has future benefit. A deferred tax asset will reduce income tax payments in the future, if there is taxable income in the future to reduce. (A few other sources of benefit exist as well but future taxable income is the main one).

B. When there is not a sufficient probability of realizing the deferred tax asset, a valuation allowance (contra account) is recorded to reduce the deferred tax asset to the amount expected to be realized.

II. Net Amount of Deferred Tax Asset Reported

A. Definition: **Realization** of a deferred tax asset means that the asset will provide its expected benefits.

B. When there is **better than a 50% chance of realizing** the deferred tax asset, it is reported free of any valuation account.

C. When there is a **50% or less** chance of the deferred tax asset being fully realized, it is reported but also is reduced by a valuation allowance (contra to deferred tax asset) to the amount that has a better than 50% chance of being realized.

D. Another way to say this is: If based on available evidence it is more likely than not that some portion of the deferred tax asset will not be realized, the deferred tax asset is reduced by a valuation allowance to the amount more likely than not to be realized.

E. The valuation allowance account, if needed, is treated as a negative deferred tax asset account. The ending balance is the amount needed at the end of a period, and the change in the valuation account is the required increase or decrease from the previous period. Thus, the same process for updating deferred tax accounts applies to the valuation allowance account.

III. Assessing Whether a Valuation Allowance Valuation Account is Needed

A. A valuation account is suggested if any of the following are present:

1. A history of unused net operating losses;

2. A history of operating losses;

3. Losses expected in future years;

4. Very unfavorable contingencies.

5. A very brief carryback or carryforward period should raise serious doubts about the realization of the deferred tax asset. For example, a significant deductible temporary difference may be expected to reverse in a single year. Alternatively, the enterprise might

operate in a traditionally cyclical business that would limit the length of the carryback or carryforward time period.

B. Evidence suggesting that a valuation account is not needed must also be considered, as exemplified by the following:

1. Existing contracts or sales backlog will produce more than enough taxable income to realize the deferred tax asset;

2. An excess of appreciated asset value over the tax basis of the entity's net assets will produce more than enough taxable income to realize the deferred tax asset;

3. A strong earnings history that suggests that taxable income in the future will be enough to realize the deferred tax asset.

C. Both positive and negative evidence is used when making the decision about whether to recognize a valuation allowance.

IV. Sources for Realizing the Deferred Tax Asset

A. If any one of the following sources is present in sufficient amount (to achieve the 50% threshold), then no valuation allowance is required. More than one source can be used to support a deferred tax asset.

1. Expectation of future taxable income

2. Taxable income in prior years within the two-year carryback period for net operating losses;

3. Future taxable differences;

4. Tax planning strategies.

B. First Source -- The *first* source is the one most popularly used. If sufficient future taxable income is expected, then the deferred tax asset most likely will be realized. The deferred tax asset is credited upon realization, rather than crediting additional income taxes payable. No valuation account is necessary.

C. Second Source -- The *second* source involves carrybacks of net operating losses. If a future deductible amount (giving rise to the deferred tax asset) were the only item to appear in the future tax return, a net operating loss would occur. A net operating loss may be carried back 2 years for a refund of taxes paid earlier. Thus, if a firm has a deferred tax asset at 12/31/x7 and the associated future deductible difference is scheduled to reverse in 20x8, that deductible difference could be carried back first to 20x6 and reduce taxable income in that year causing a refund of taxes.

1. If large enough, the remainder then could be carried back to 20x7 for additional refund. Thus, prior year taxable income within the carry-back period is a source of realizing the deferred tax asset, and, if present, alleviates the need for a valuation allowance.

2. **Example of source 2 and journal entry** -- A firm has a $20,000 future deductible difference at the end of 20x8. The difference is expected to reverse in 20x9. The future tax rate is 30%. Thus, a $6,000 deferred tax asset is recorded. However, the firm has little prospect for future taxable income, has no available tax strategies, and has no future taxable temporary differences (i.e. no other sources of realization). But assume the firm earned $6,000 taxable income in both 20x7 and 20x8.

   a. Therefore, $12,000 of prior years' taxable income can be used to support the deferred tax asset. If the only item on the tax return in 20x9 is the reversing deductible difference, then 20x9 will report a net operating loss of $20,000 which can be carried back to the previous two years to obtain a refund of the tax paid on the $12,000 of taxable income. The tax accrual entry for 20x8 assuming no beginning deferred tax balances for 20x8:

Deferred Tax Asset ($20,000 × .3)	6,000	
Valuation Allowance ($8,000 × .3)		2,400
Income Tax Payable ($6,000 × .30)		1,800
Income Tax Benefit		1,800

      b. Of the $20,000 deductible difference, $12,000 is supported by prior taxable income within the carryback period. The remaining $8,000 is unsupported. The valuation allowance reduces the net reported deferred tax asset to $3,600 ($12,000 × .30). The income tax expense is negative in this year and is labeled Income Tax Benefit. This amount increases net income for 20x8.

D. Third Source -- The *third* source involves the ability of future taxable differences and the future deductible differences (giving rise to the deferred tax asset) to cancel within the carryback or carryforward period. Assume a firm has a future $4,000 deductible temporary difference (giving rise to a $1,200 deferred tax asset assuming a 30% tax rate), and it also has a $6,000 future taxable difference. The deductible difference can be carried back 2 years or forward 20 years. If the taxable difference is within that total carryback or carryforward period, then the deductible difference will cancel $4,000 of the taxable difference, which realizes the deferred tax asset.

E. Fourth Source -- The *fourth* source, tax planning strategies, are actions that (1) must result in the realization of deferred tax assets, (2) might not be taken otherwise, and (3) are prudent and feasible. An example of such a strategy is to accelerate the timing of a future deductible difference so that it falls within the carryback period to enable a tax refund of prior year taxes. Another is the ability to sell a building at a taxable gain (and leasing it back to avoid the disruption of moving the business) to avoid the expiration of a deductible difference in the current year. The resulting increase in taxable income will help to cancel (use) the deductible difference before it expires.

V. Reporting the Deferred Tax Asset and Valuation Allowance

A. The full deferred tax asset and valuation allowance are reported in the balance sheet. Alternatively, the deferred tax asset is reported net in the balance sheet with the footnotes reporting the full asset and the valuation allowance.

B. The classification of the valuation allowance follows the classification of the related deferred tax asset. For example, if 70% of the relevant deferred tax asset is noncurrent, then 70% of the valuation allowance is so classified.

C. The tax rate used to measure the deferred tax asset is based on the source of realization. For example, if the only source of realization of the deferred tax asset is the carryback of the relevant deductible difference, the tax rate in the years available for carryback is used to measure the deferred tax asset.

Uncertain Tax Positions

This lesson considers the accounting for beneficial tax positions that are uncertain.

After studying this lesson, you should be able to:

1. *Determine the appropriate reporting when the chance of the position being sustained is less than or equal to 50%.*

2. *Record the journal entry when the uncertainty is resolved.*

3. *Prepare the journal entry when it is more likely than not that the position will be sustained.*

4. *Record the resolution of the uncertainty.*

I. Uncertainty in Income Tax - The Issue

A. The preparation of a firm's tax return is affected by many estimates and uncertainties. Uncertain tax positions are those that may not be sustainable on audit by the IRS. Examples include uncertain deductions, tax credits, and revenue exemptions. The firm includes the uncertain position in its tax return thus reducing its income tax liability but there remains uncertainty as to the actual benefit of that deduction. If there is at least a 1/3 probability that the tax position will be sustained, there is no legal or professional censure for taking that position.

B. This section explains how the financial benefit of such uncertain tax positions is reported. Income tax expense is reduced (benefit recognized) for an uncertain tax position only if it is "more likely than not" (> 50%) that the position will be sustained upon audit by the IRS.

C. A two-step approach is applied: (1) Is the uncertain position more likely than not to be sustained?, (2) If yes, then a probabilistic approach is applied to determine the amount of benefit recognized in the current year.

II. Probability Less Than or Equal To 50%

A. If it is NOT "more likely than not" that the position will be sustained upon audit by the IRS, then income tax expense is not reduced and an additional tax liability is recognized. No benefit is recognized in the current year.

 Example: Taxable income is $20,000 and the tax rate is 30%. Taxable income reflects an uncertain deduction of $2,000. The firm believes there is less than a 50% chance of the $2,000 deduction being allowed.

Income tax expense	6,600
Income tax payable ($20,000 × .30)	6,000
Liability for unrecognized tax benefit ($2,000 x .30)	600

Income tax expense is not reduced in this case - the deduction is not recognized in the financial statements. Upon resolution however, future income tax expense is reduced if the deduction is upheld.

The liability for unrecognized tax benefits should not be netted against deferred tax accounts. The reason for this second liability is that the firm is proceeding with the uncertain benefit on its tax return; thus the income tax payable reflects the uncertain deduction. The firm will pay only the smaller amount in the current year with resolution of the unrecognized benefit later. The above entry reflects the expectation that the firm will have to pay the additional $600 at a later date.

B. Resolution of the Uncertainty

1. If the deduction is disallowed, the journal entry in the year of resolution is:

Liability for unrecognized tax benefit	600	
Cash		600

Additional amounts may be due for interest and penalties. These amounts are recognized as an expense in the year of payment.

2. If all or a portion of the deduction is allowed, income tax expense is reduced in the year of payment (change in estimate). Assume that $667 of the deduction was allowed (1/3 of the $2,000 deduction taken) yielding a $200 reduction in the amount of tax due, and income tax expense ($667 × .30 = $200).

Liability for unrecognized tax benefit	600	
Cash		400
Income tax expense		200

III. Probability > 50%

A. If it IS "more likely than not" that the position will be sustained upon audit by the IRS, then the firm must estimate specific outcomes of the audit and probabilities associated with each. The amount of benefit recognized is the largest amount for which the cumulative probability of realization exceeds 50%.

Example:
Taxable income is $20,000 and the tax rate is 30%. Taxable income reflects an uncertain deduction of $2,000. The firm believes there is more than a 50% chance of a deduction in some amount being allowed. Estimated amounts of allowable deductions along with their probabilities appear below:

Amount Allowed	Probability	Cumulative Probability
$2,000	.15	.15
1,600	.20	.35
1,400	.30	.65
400	.20	.85
200	.15	1.00

The tax benefit recognized is based on the $1,400 amount, which is the largest amount for which the cumulative probability exceeds 50%. No reduction in income tax expense is recognized for the remaining portion of the deduction ($600).

Income tax expense	6,180	
Income tax payable ($20,000 × .30)		6,000
Liability for unrecognized tax benefit ($600 × .30)		180

Income tax expense is reduced by $420 as a result of the recognition of the current tax benefit associated with the $1,400 amount ($1,400 × .30 = $420).

B. The process of identifying outcomes and estimating probabilities must assume that the taxing authority will have full knowledge of the tax situation.

C. The classification of the liability for unrecognized tax benefit is based on the period of expected settlement. Tax cases often require more than one year for resolution. Therefore, the liability is often classified as noncurrent.

IV. Resolution of the Uncertainty

A. *In a later year, if the expected $1,400 deduction is allowed:*

Liability for unrecognized tax benefit	180	
Cash ($2,000 − $1,400).30		180

B. When the benefit recognized in income tax expense in a prior year is not the same amount as the final actual benefit determined upon resolution, the difference is recognized in income tax expense in the year of resolution (change in estimate).

1. *If no deduction is allowed:*

Income tax expense	420	
Liability for unrecognized tax benefit	180	
Cash ($2,000 × .30)		600

2. *If a $1,600 deduction is allowed:*

Liability for unrecognized tax benefit	180	
Income tax expense ($1,600 − $1,400) × .30		60
Cash ($2,000 − $1,600).30		120

3. *If the entire $2,000 deduction is allowed:*

Liability for unrecognized tax benefit	180	
Income tax expense ($2,000 − $1,400).30		180

V. The Same Approach is Applied to Future Temporary Differences -- For example, if there is uncertainty about the deductibility of a future deductible difference giving rise to a deferred tax asset, the same two step approach is applied. The result is a reduced deferred tax asset, increased deferred tax liability, or both.

Net Operating Losses

The relevant provisions of the tax law and general accounting treatment are discussed in this lesson. It also illustrates the journal entries for both options available when a firm has a net operating loss. The segment on income tax applies the concepts to situations in which the firm has both temporary differences, and a net operating loss carryforward. Other aspects including disclosures for taxes, changes in tax status, and international standards are discussed.

After studying this lesson, you should be able to:

1. *Highlight the important differences in accounting for income tax between U.S. and international standards.*

2. *Briefly explain the effects of a change in tax status on reporting for income taxes.*

3. *Note the important footnote disclosures for income tax.*

4. *Prepare the journal entry for a firm with future deductible differences and a net operating loss carryforward.*

5. *Record the journal entry for the carryback of a net operating loss.*

6. *Accommodate changes in the tax rate for the years after a net operating loss when preparing the tax accrual entry.*

7. *Record the journal entry for the carryforward of a net operating loss under both options available.*

8. *Apply both options for a firm with a net operating loss to determine the tax refund and remaining carryforward.*

9. *Explain the accounting for the carryforward of a net operating loss.*

10. *Describe the accounting for the carryback of a net operating loss.*

11. *Explain how the carryforward reduces future taxes.*

12. *Identify and describe the two options available for a net operating loss.*

I. **Net Operating Losses (NOL**

    A. A net operating loss (NOL) is negative taxable income for a year - a loss for income tax purposes. An NOL occurs when taxable deductions exceed taxable revenues. This provision is solely within the tax code. There is no counterpart in financial accounting. However, financial accounting must report the economic effects of the operating loss.

    B. The tax law allows an NOL to be carried back 2 years, or forward 20 years. Thus, a 23 year period (including the NOL year) is the basis for taxation. This important section of the tax code provides benefits for new firms (which often experience losses early) and also in mergers and acquisitions in which the acquiring firm can obtain the tax benefit from a previous loss of an acquired firm.

    C. Firms with significant NOLs can be attractive merger candidates because the acquirer, in the merger process, may apply those losses to the taxable income of the new taxable entity. Although the IRS may challenge acquisitions done with the sole purpose of obtaining tax benefits, many firms take the chance and challenge the IRS in court by maintaining there were other reasons for the merger.

II. **Two Options** -- When a firm has an NOL, it can choose from two options. The choice is irrevocable for a given NOL year.

    A. **Carryback, Carryforward Option** -- Under this option, the NOL is first carried back to the 2 years before the year of the NOL. The NOL absorbs prior years' taxable income for an immediate refund of taxes paid in those prior years. The refund is based on the tax rate in those years and is limited to the amount of taxes actually paid. The earlier of the two years is used first.

        1. If the NOL exceeds taxable income for the 2 preceding years, the remainder then is carried forward for at most 20 years to absorb future taxable income. Earliest years are used first. No taxes are paid on taxable income absorbed by the NOL in those future years.

    B. **Carryforward Only Option** -- In this option the firm chooses only to carry forward the NOL, rather than carry it back first. The 20 year limitation is in effect in this option. There is no refund of income taxes paid in the past.

III. **Choosing Among the Two Options**

    A. The carryforward aspect is present in both options. The only difference between the options is the carryback feature. The main reason for choosing option B (carryforward only) is to take advantage of significantly higher tax rates in the future. The difference must be large enough to offset the present value benefits of the immediate refund available from the carryback, for option B to make sense.

        1. Some tax credits also have the carryback/carryforward feature and may expire more quickly than the NOL. Tax credits reduce income tax by the amount of the credit and are thus more valuable dollar for dollar. Thus it may be advantageous to use prior year taxable income for these credits. Also there may not be enough prior year taxable income to accommodate both the credits and the NOL.

IV. **Cautions in Applying the Options**

    A. An NOL absorbs taxable income through the carryback and carryforward features, NOT income tax. A $10,000 NOL is worth only $3,000 to the firm if the tax rate is 30%.

    B. The taxable income of the earliest year of the two years before the NOL is absorbed first in a carryback. (FIFO)

    C. The taxable income of the earliest future year is absorbed first, in a carryforward. (FIFO)

    D. NOLs themselves are used on a FIFO basis. An NOL must be completely utilized before a later NOL can be carried back or forward.

    E. The positive taxable income of any year can be absorbed only once in the realization of the tax benefit of an NOL carryback or carryforward.

V. **Example: Two Options**

A firm's history of taxable income follows:

Year	Taxable Income	Tax Rate
A	$1,000	20%
B	2,000	25%
C	3,500	30%
D	4,000	35%
E	(11,000)	38%
F	1,500	40%
G	6,000	40%

A. Carryback, Carryforward Option

1. **Year E** -- The firm pays no income tax because taxable income is negative $11,000. $3,500 of the $11,000 NOL is carried back to year C, and $4,000 is carried back to year D (in that order). The resulting refund generated in year E is $2,450.

$3,500(.30) + $4,000(.35) = $2,450.

Of the original $11,000 NOL, $3,500 remains to carryforward ($11,000 − $3,500 − $4,000).

---

   a. Caution for candidates: remember to go back only 2 years. Often the data includes more than two previous years of taxable income (as in this example) and there is a tendency to use the earliest taxable income provided. Years A and B are unavailable for carryback in this example.

2. **Year F** -- The firm pays no income tax because the taxable income of $1,500 is completely absorbed by the carryforward of $1,500 of the $3,500 NOL remaining. Now only $2,000 of NOL remains to carryforward to year G.

3. **Year G** -- The remaining $2,000 of NOL absorbs a like amount of taxable income, leaving only $4,000 ($6,000 taxable income less the $2,000 NOL carryforward) on which to pay tax. Therefore, the firm pays $1,600 in income tax ($4,000 × .40).

   a. If the sum of the taxable income of years C and D equaled or exceeded $11,000, there would be no NOL to carryforward.

B. Carryforward Only Option

1. The NOL is carried forward to years F and G completely absorbing the taxable income in those years. No tax is paid in those years. The combined taxable income for the two years is $7,500. Thus, $3,500 of the NOL remains to be carried forward to future years. The value to the firm of the remaining NOL at the end of year G is $1,400 ($3,500 × .40) assuming a future tax rate of 40%. The remaining NOL of $3,500 can be carried forward another 18 years beyond year G.

2. If the combined taxable income for years F and G had exceeded $11,000, there would be no remaining carryforward of NOL, and the firm would pay taxes on the amount of taxable income exceeding $11,000.

VI. Accounting for NOLs

A. Carryback

1. A *carryback* generates an immediate refund of tax. The carryback is recorded as follows (in the NOL year):

Refund Receivable	amount of refund
Income Tax Benefit	amount of refund

2. The amount of the refund is limited to the taxes paid in the previous two years. The receivable is a current asset and the income tax benefit is a gain account (or negative income tax expense), reducing the loss for the year.

B. Carryforward

1. The carryforward feature is present in both options. A *carryforward* generates a deferred tax asset. This is the same account that is produced by future deductible differences. Both a carryforward of an NOL and a future deductible difference reduce future taxable income relative to pretax accounting income. The tax benefit of a carryforward is recognized in income in the period of the loss. The carryforward is recorded as follows (in the NOL year):

Deferred Tax Asset	(future enacted rate)(remaining NOL)
Income Tax Benefit	(future enacted rate)(remaining NOL)

2. The "remaining NOL" amount in the above entry depends on the option chosen.

   a. If the carryback/carryforward option is chosen, the remaining NOL amount is the portion of the total NOL remaining after carrying it back to the previous two years to absorb taxable income in those years.

   b. If the carryforward only option is chosen, the remaining NOL amount is the full NOL.

3. The required amount of deferred tax asset from a carryforward contributes to the total required ending deferred tax asset balance, along with the future deductible differences. The deferred tax asset stemming from an NOL is subject to the valuation allowance requirements.

VII. Examples of Accounting for NOLs

A. Recall that a carryback generates a receivable and income tax benefit. A carryforward generates a deferred tax asset, subject to a valuation allowance. The carryforward is present in both options available for the NOL. The benefit recorded for the deferred tax asset is the net of the deferred tax asset increase less any allowance account balance required.

1. A firm has $30,000 of NOL to carryforward. But there is a greater than 50% chance of future taxable income only in the amount of $10,000 (and there are no other available sources to support the deferred tax asset). The tax rate is 30%. In this case, a valuation allowance is required for the portion of the deferred tax asset attributable to $20,000 of the NOL:

Deferred Tax Asset ($30,000 × .30)	9,000
Valuation Allowance ($20,000 × .30)	6,000
Income Tax Benefit	3,000

B. Example—Accounting for Both Options -- The data from the previous example on the two options is repeated below. Assume no temporary or permanent differences (pretax income equals taxable income). The tax rates are enacted in the year before they are effective. For example, the tax rate listed for year F (40%) applies to year F but was enacted in year E. Assume sufficient estimated future taxable income to support a deferred tax asset.

Year	Taxable Income	Tax Rate
A	$1,000	20%
B	2,000	25%
C	3,500	30%
D	4,000	35%
E	(11,000)	38%
F	1,500	40%
G	6,000	40%

1. Example—Carryback, Carryforward Option

Year E accounting:

Refund Receivable	2,450	
Income Tax Benefit		2,450

$3,500(.30) + $4,000(.35) = $2,450

Of the original $11,000 NOL, $3,500 remains to carryforward ($11,000 − $3,500 − $4,000).

Deferred tax asset	1,400	
Income Tax Benefit		1,400

$3,500(.40) = $1,400

The total benefit recorded is $3,850 ($2,450 + $1,400). The 40% tax rate is used because it was enacted in year E. The tax benefit of the remaining $3,500 NOL is $1,400 because in years after year E, the $3,500 NOL will reduce taxable income that would have been taxed at 40%.

Reported net income for year E is negative $7,150 (− $11,000 + $2,450 + $1,400). The bottom of the income statement appears as follows:

Pretax accounting income	($11,000)
Income Tax Benefit	3,850
Net income	($7,150)

Year F Accounting:
The taxable income of $1,500 is completely absorbed by the carryforward of $1,500 of the $3,500 NOL remaining. Now only $2,000 of NOL remains to carryforward to year G. The calculation of the change in deferred tax asset (DTA) is as follows.
Required ending DTA:

$2,000 remaining NOL × .40	$800	(required ending DTA)
Beginning DTA balance	1,400	

Decrease in DTA		$600

Journal Entry:

Income tax expense	600	
Deferred tax asset		600

At the end of year F, the firm can carryforward $2,000 of NOL. The value of that carryforward at a 40% tax rate is $800. The tax journal entry adjusts the DTA to the correct ending balance.

The firm pays no income tax in year F.

Year G accounting:

Income tax expense	2,400	
Deferred tax asset		800
Income tax payable		1,600

$1,600 = .40($6,000 − $2,000 NOL remaining). The NOL carryforward reduces the amount on which tax is levied by $2,000. There is no remaining NOL to carryforward; therefore the DTA balance is closed. The income tax expense amount is a derived amount, as always.

2. Example—Carryforward Only Option

This example uses the same data provided above:

Year E accounting:

Deferred tax asset	4,400	
Income tax benefit		4,400

$4,400 = $11,000(.40). The total income tax benefit of $4,400 exceeds the amount in the carryback, carryforward option ($3,850) because the tax rates in years C and D were lower than in years after year E. This is an example of a situation for which the firm might choose the carryforward-only option.

Reported net income in year E is negative $6,600 (− $11,000 + $4,400).

Year F accounting:
$1,500 of the $11,000 NOL is used to absorb taxable income in year F leaving $9,500 to carryforward.

Required ending DTA:

$9,500 remaining NOL × .40	$3,800
Beginning DTA balance	4,400
Decrease in DTA	$ 600

Journal entry:

Income tax expense	600	
Deferred tax asset		600

The firm pays no tax in year F.

Year G accounting:
$6,000 of the remaining $9,500 NOL is used to absorb taxable income in year G leaving $3,500 to carryforward.

Required ending DTA:

$3,500 remaining NOL × .40	$1,400
Beginning DTA balance	3,800
Decrease in DTA	$2,400

Journal entry:

Income tax expense	2,400	
Deferred tax asset		2,400

The firm pays no tax in year G.

Caution: One of the most important aspects of NOL accounting illustrated by this example is to remember to first compute the ending DTA from the remaining NOL. Computing the amount of NOL "used up" by the current year's taxable income using the current year rate will not always yield the correct answer because the tax rate may have changed, as illustrated in this example.

VIII. NOLs and Temporary Differences; International Standards

A. Temporary Differences and Carryforwards

1. What is the interaction of future deductible differences and NOL carryforwards?

2. Both (1) future deductible temporary differences and (2) NOL carryforwards (which occur in both NOL options) give rise to the required ending deferred tax asset balance. Treat the remaining NOL carryforward amount just like you would a future deductible difference. Always compute the required ending deferred tax asset balance first. Then compare that amount to the beginning balance to determine the change - the amount to enter into the journal entry. The required ending deferred tax asset will reflect the remaining NOL.

   Note:
   The NOL carryforward and the future deductible difference are treated the same way for purposes of computing the deferred tax asset balance.

   See the following example.

Example: A firm has the following beginning deferred tax account balances for the current year (year 3):

Deferred tax liability	$4,000
Deferred tax asset	6,000

The tax rate for year 3 is 40%, and the enacted tax rate for future years is 30%. At the end of year 3, the firm anticipates the following future temporary differences:

Taxable	$5,600
Deductible	3,000

The firm's tax return shows an NOL of $30,000 in year 3 (negative taxable income). The carryforward-only option is chosen.

Required ending deferred tax liability: $5,600(.30) =	$1,680.00
Beginning deferred tax liability	4000
Decrease in deferred tax liability	$2,320
Required ending deferred tax asset = ($3,000 + $30,000)(.30) =	$9,900
Beginning deferred asset	6000
Increase in deferred tax asset	3900

Entry for year 3:

Deferred tax asset	3,900	
Deferred tax liability	2,320	
Income tax benefit		6,220

3. **Disclosures for Income Taxes**

   a. Current and deferred portions of income tax expense;

   b. Any investment tax credits and other credits taken;

   c. Benefits of operating tax loss carryforwards, remaining amounts and expiration dates;

   d. Government grants to the extent they are used to reduce income tax;

   e. Adjustments to deferred tax accounts (and valuation allowance) as a result of a change in enacted tax rates or tax status of the firm.

   f. Total of all deferred tax liabilities;

   g. Total of all deferred tax assets;

   h. Total valuation allowance recognized for deferred tax assets;

   i. Net change in the valuation allowance;

   j. Approximate tax effect of each type of temporary difference (and carryforward);

   k. Reconciliation of reported income tax expense on income from continuing operations, with the tax that would have resulted from applying the statutory tax rate to income from continuing operations;

   l. Any change in the tax status of the firm.

B. U.S. GAAP—IFRS Differences

1. Although the basic procedures and logic of interperiod tax allocation are similar for international and U.S. standards, many of the differences between the two sets of standards unrelated to taxation cause differences in the outcome of applying interperiod tax allocation.

   a. For example, the international-U.S. differences concerning the recognition of contingent liabilities cause differences in when and how much is recorded in the resulting deferred tax asset for the two systems.

   b. In addition, any two firms from different countries using IFRS will have differences in the results of interperiod tax allocation due to differences between their respective tax systems.

2. To measure the change in deferred tax accounts, international standards apply the tax rates that have been enacted or "substantively enacted" by the end of the period. This is an example of substance over form because the time lag between the announcement of the change and enactment may require a few months. For U.S. purposes, the rates must be enacted.

3. International accounting standards allow for an upward revaluation of plant assets and other assets to fair value. The difference between the book value of the revalued asset and its taxable basis is a temporary difference causing a change in the relevant deferred tax account. These changes are reported in equity, rather than income tax expense.

4. For international reporting, deferred tax accounts are always classified as noncurrent. Recall that for U.S. standards, both current and noncurrent classifications are possible. However, for IFRS, if there is a legal right to offset current assets and liabilities and the deferred tax assets and liabilities relate to the same tax jurisdiction, then the deferred tax assets and liabilities may be offset.

5. Deferred tax asset

   a. For international reporting, a deferred tax asset is recognized only when it is probable that it will be realized (the same sources are available as for U.S. standards). Valuation allowance accounts are not used; the deferred tax asset is either recognized or not. Although "probable" is not defined, it is generally understood to be significantly higher than the 50% threshold used in U.S. standards. As a result, all other factors being the same, it is less likely for a deferred tax asset to be reported under international standards, and if they are reported, the amounts may be less, relative to U.S. standards.

   b. For both international and U.S. standards, it is possible for a deferred tax asset not to be recognized in one period (international: not probable; U.S.: 50% or less chance of realization), but for the same future deductible difference, the deferred tax asset could be recognized in a later period, as circumstances change. The opposite is also possible. Both systems, however, use different thresholds and recording procedures as mentioned above.

6. International standards do not specifically address uncertain tax positions. Currently, they are treated as contingencies.

Alphabetical Index

Assets..
    Acquired...249, 329
    Cost of...265, 267
    Current..............................108, 112p., 116, 125p., 204, 260, 267, 338, 379, 394, 400, 451
    Donated...248
    Ending...476pp., 487, 489
    Fair value of..401
    Group of..203, 265
    Held for sale..323, 325p.
    Identifiable...327pp., 331p.
    Impairment of...203
    In Use...323, 325
    Intangible...163, 245, 260, 322, 327, 331p., 334p.
    Liquid..126p., 400
    Long-Term..98
    Manufacturing..260
    Monetary...122p., 387
    PBO and plan..465, 469, 485
    Pension..465p.
    Recognition of...456, 502
    Remaining..400p.
    Return on...476p., 485, 487
    Sale of..108, 456
    Tangible..163, 245, 260, 322, 327, 331p., 334p., 458
    Tax assets...502, 509, 512, 521, 523, 525, 536
    Total...128pp., 266, 395p., 399
    Transferred..195
Assets and Liabilities..
    Current...126
    Definition of...160
    Financial..368, 370
    Monetary...123
    Recognition of...502
    Tax...502, 512
    Terms of..159p.
Assets, Financial..
    And financial liabilities..163
Assets, Net..
    Acquiree's...329
    Change in...85, 268
    Entity's...524
    Identifiable..325, 327, 332
    Statement of..471
    Value of..323
Balance Sheet..
    Classification...413
    Presentation..220, 417p., 442
    Reported in the..........................178, 223, 337, 343, 465, 484p., 487, 516, 525
    Valuation...182, 185p., 188, 219, 226
Disclosure..
    Additional..101, 109p., 115, 117, 319
    And presentation...137
    Balance sheet..190, 441
    Direct Method..103, 108
    Full..12, 118
    Liability...118

Note..118pp., 159, 201, 404
Principle..118
Qualitative..68
Quantitative..59
Required...279, 404, 514
Requirements..58, 63, 163, 316
Specific...58, 319
Financial Accounting Standards Board...17
Generally Accepted Accounting Principles...17, 22, 162, 164
Liability...
Asset or...56p., 457, 465, 520p.
Bond...337p., 361
Book value of the..388
Classification of..465
Contingent...196p., 241, 337, 399, 517
Current...............................118, 125, 175, 336p., 344, 357, 361, 378pp., 392, 450, 465, 520, 522
Disclosures...118
Liability is...343, 421p., 472, 483, 526
Limited..398p.
Long-term..176, 378
Net..356, 361, 369, 381, 384
Pension..463, 465, 469pp., 476pp.
Postemployment..482
Postretirement benefit..484pp.
Recorded...427
Short-term...176
Tax............................221, 457, 502pp., 507, 510, 512pp., 516p., 519pp., 526, 528, 536
Warranty...508, 510p., 520
Recognition...
And measurement..13
Criteria..159p., 184, 351, 439
Delayed..465, 471p., 485
Expense..358, 457, 499
For Long-Term Contracts..449
Full...454, 485
Initial...58, 317
Journal entry for..454
Loss..226, 456
Of contingent liabilities..537
Of postretirement benefit...485, 489
Of profit...440, 454
Principle...343
Separate...324
Revenue Recognition.......................................12, 64, 118, 349pp., 439pp., 445p., 448p., 510
Securities and Exchange Commission..17, 62, 149p.